The Cambridge Companion to
Legal Positivism

Legal positivism is one of the fundamental theories of jurisprudence studied in law and related fields around the world. This volume addresses how legal positivism is perceived and makes the case for why it is relevant for contemporary legal theory. *The Cambridge Companion to Legal Positivism* offers thirty-three chapters from leading scholars that provide a comprehensive commentary on the fundamental ideas of legal positivism, its history and major theorists, its connection to normativity and values, its current development and influence, as well as on the criticisms moved against it.

Torben Spaak is Professor of Jurisprudence, Department of Law, Stockholm University.

Patricia Mindus is Professor in Practical Philosophy, Department of Philosophy, Uppsala University.

Cambridge Companions to Law

Cambridge Companions to Law offers thought-provoking introductions to different legal disciplines, invaluable to both the student and the scholar. Edited by world-leading academics, each offers a collection of essays which both map out the subject and allow the reader to delve deeper. Critical and enlightening, the Companions library represents legal scholarship at its best.

The Cambridge Companion to European Private Law
Edited by Christian Twigg-Flesner

The Cambridge Companion to International Law
Edited by James Crawford and Martti Koskenniemi

The Cambridge Companion to Comparative Law
Edited by Mauro Bussani and Ugo Mattei

The Cambridge Companion to Human Rights Law
Edited by Conor Gearty and Costas Douzinas

The Cambridge Companion to Public Law
Edited by Mark Elliott and David Feldman

The Cambridge Companion to International Criminal Law
Edited by William A. Schabas

The Cambridge Companion to Natural Law Jurisprudence
Edited by George Duke and Robert P. George

The Cambridge Companion to Comparative Family Law
Edited by Shazia Choudhry and Jonathan Herring

The Cambridge Companion to Comparative Constitutional Law
Edited by Roger Masterman and Robert Schütze

The Cambridge Companion to the First Amendment and Religious Liberty
Edited by Michael D. Breidenbach and Owen Anderson

The Cambridge Companion to the Philosophy of Law
Edited by John Tasioulas

The Cambridge Companion to Legal Positivism
Edited by Torben Spaak and Patricia Mindus

The Cambridge Companion to

Legal Positivism

Edited by

Torben Spaak
Stockholm University

Patricia Mindus
Uppsala University

CAMBRIDGE
UNIVERSITY PRESS

CAMBRIDGE
UNIVERSITY PRESS

University Printing House, Cambridge CB2 8BS, United Kingdom

One Liberty Plaza, 20th Floor, New York, NY 10006, USA

477 Williamstown Road, Port Melbourne, VIC 3207, Australia

314–321, 3rd Floor, Plot 3, Splendor Forum, Jasola District Centre,
New Delhi – 110025, India

79 Anson Road, #06–04/06, Singapore 079906

Cambridge University Press is part of the University of Cambridge.

It furthers the University's mission by disseminating knowledge in the pursuit of education, learning, and research at the highest international levels of excellence.

www.cambridge.org
Information on this title: www.cambridge.org/9781108427678
DOI: 10.1017/9781108636377

First published 2021

A catalogue record for this publication is available from the British Library.

Library of Congress Cataloging-in-Publication Data
Names: Spaak, Torben, editor. | Mindus, Patricia, editor.
Title: The Cambridge companion to legal positivism / edited by Torben Spaak, Stockholm University; Patricia Mindus, Uppsala University.
Description: Cambridge, United Kingdom ; New York, NY : Cambridge University Press, 2021. | Series: Cambridge companions to law | Includes bibliographical references and index.
Identifiers: LCCN 2020035123 | ISBN 9781108427678 (hardback) | ISBN 9781108447010 (paperback | ISBN 9781108636377 (ebook)
Subjects: LCSH: Legal positivism. | Jurisprudence. | Law – Philosophy.
Classification: LCC K331 .C353 2021 | DDC 340/.112–dc23
LC record available at https://lccn.loc.gov/2020035123

ISBN 978-1-108-42767-8 Hardback
ISBN 978-1-108-44701-0 Paperback

Contents

Figures

Contributors

Stefano Bertea is an associate professor at the University of Leicester. In his academic career he has been a Marie Curie research fellow at the University of Edinburgh and at the Goethe University of Frankfurt am Main, a visiting research fellow at the University of Amsterdam and at the Planck Institute for Comparative Public Law and International Law in Heidelberg, an Alexander von Humboldt research fellow at the University of Kiel, a senior research fellow at the University of Antwerp and a visiting professor at the University of Catanzaro, at the University of Verona and at the University of Modena and Reggio Emilia.

Brian H. Bix is the Frederick W. Thomas Professor of Law and Philosophy at the University of Minnesota. Previously he taught at King's College London and Quinnipiac University, and held visiting positions at the Georgetown University Law Center and George Washington University Law School. He is a member of the Bar of the States of Minnesota, Massachusetts and Connecticut, and a member of the American Law Institute. He is the author of 17 books and 150 articles in the areas of jurisprudence, contract law and family law.

Martin Borowski is a professor at the Faculty of Law at the Ruprecht-Karls University of Heidelberg where he teaches public law, constitutional theory and legal philosophy. Previously he held a research fellowship of the Humboldt Foundation, based in the United States at the School of Law of Washington University in St. Louis, Missouri, and in the UK at the University of Westminster School of Law, London, and at the Law School of the University of Birmingham.

Pierluigi Chiassoni is a professor of philosophy of law at the University of Genoa and he teaches legal reasoning and legal interpretation for the international Master's programme on global rule of law and constitutional argumentation. He works on general theory of law, history of legal culture, history of analytical jurisprudence, theory of legal interpretation and argumentation, theory of case-law analysis, theory of the constitutional state and constitutional interpretation, logical forms of judicial reasoning, and theory of human rights. He is co-editor of *Materiali per una storia della cultura giuridica* [*Materials for a History of Legal Culture*] and *Analisi del pensiero giuridico* [*Analysis of Legal Thought*].

David Dyzenhaus is the Albert Abel Chair and a professor of law and philosophy at the University of Toronto. He has taught in South Africa, England, Canada, Singapore, New Zealand, Hungary, Mexico and the United States. He has been the Law Foundation visiting fellow in the Faculty of Law, University of Auckland, the Herbert Smith visiting professor in the Cambridge Law Faculty, the Arthur Goodhart visiting professor in legal science in Cambridge, and he has been a fellow of the Institute for Advanced Study, Berlin. He has been a senior scholar of Pembroke College (Cambridge) and he is a fellow of the Royal Society of Canada.

Tomasz Gizbert-Studnicki is a professor of legal sciences specialising in legal theory and head of the Department of Legal Theory at the Faculty of Law and Administration of the Jagiellonian University. Gizbert-Studnicki is also legal counsel, a co-founder and a senior partner in the SPCG law firm. He is a member of the Legal Commission of the Polish Academy of Learning and he has been a member of the Executive Committee of the International Association of Legal and Social Philosophy. He is the curator of the Association of Law Students' Library of the Jagiellonian University and the supervisor of the Science Club of the Philosophy of Law of TBSP.

Leslie Green has been a fellow at Lincoln and at Balliol Colleges (Oxford) and at Osgoode Hall Law School (Toronto), a visiting fellow at Columbia University, a visiting professor at Berkeley and at the University of Chicago, a regular visiting professor at the University of Texas, a member of the Hauser Global Faculty at NY University School of Law and a professor at the University of Oxford. He is a professor and a distinguished university fellow at Queen's University at Kingston (Canada). He is co-editor of Oxford Studies in the philosophy of law and of the monograph series the *Oxford Library of Legal Philosophy.*

Michael S. Green is the Woodbridge Professor of Law at William and Mary Law School. Previously he taught law at George Mason Law School. He clerked for Judge Richard A. Posner on the US Court of Appeals for the Seventh Circuit and practised law at Paul, Weiss, Rifkind, Wharton &

Garrison in New York City. He has been an assistant professor of philosophy at Tufts University and a visiting lecturer in philosophy at the University of Alabama (Huntsville), Wesleyan University and Yale University. He works on civil procedure, conflict of laws, constitutional law, continental philosophy, federal courts, jurisprudence, philosophy of law, and professional responsibility.

Riccardo Guastini is an emeritus professor of philosophy of law at the University of Genoa and director of the Tarello Institute for the Philosophy of Law in the Department of Jurisprudence of the same university. He is co-director of the journals *Analisi e diritto* [*Analysis and Law*], *Ragion pratica* [*Practical Reason*] and *Materiali per la storia della cultura giuridica* [*Materials for the History of Legal Culture*]. His field of research includes the analysis of normative language, fundamental legal concepts, the structure of legal systems and techniques of argumentation and legal interpretation.

Stefan Kirste is a professor at the University of Salzburg and president of the German section of the International Association of Philosophy of Law and Social Philosophy. He is co-founder and president of the History of Ideas working group in the German section of this association. Among other things he has been a lecturer at the Federal University of Minas Gerais, the Federal University of Rio de Janeiro, the Federal University of Pernambuco, the Federal University of Alagoas, the Pontifical Catholic University of Rio Grande do Sul, the University of Santa Cruz do Sul and the Autonomous University Center of Brazil-UNIBRASIL.

Brian Leiter is the Karl N. Llewellyn Professor of Jurisprudence at the University of Chicago Law School and founder and director of Chicago's Center for Law, Philosophy & Human Values. He taught from 1995 to 2008 at the University of Texas School of Law, where he has been founder and director of the Law and Philosophy Program. He joined the University of Chicago in 2008. He has been a visiting professor at universities in the United States and Europe, including Yale University and Oxford University. He works primarily on legal philosophy and continental philosophy, especially Nietzsche and Marx.

Barbara Baum Levenbook is a professor at North Carolina State University where she teaches philosophy of law, ethics, and social and political philosophy. With a background in philosophy from the University of Arizona, she is the author of a number of articles and book chapters on philosophy of law, ethics and more. Levenbook has published her work in journals such as *Philosophy Compass, Legal Theory, Archiv für Rechts- und Sozialphilosophie* [*Archive for Legal and Social Philosophy*], *Law and Contemporary Problems* and *Ethics*. Among her contribution to the field of philosophy of law, her work on Dworkin deserves particular mention as does her research on the social fact thesis.

Michael Lobban is a professor of legal history at the London School of Economics and Political Science, as of 2013, having previously been a professor of legal history at Queen Mary University (London), since 2003. He works on the concept and practice of the rule of law in the long nineteenth century. He is one of the editors of the American Society for Legal History's book series and he was appointed secretary of the Selden Society at the end of 2015.

Jens Kersten is a professor of public law and administrative science at the Ludwig Maximilians University in Munich. A pupil of Ulrich Battis, he studied law at the Universities of Heidelberg, Leeds in the UK and Bonn in Germany. He has been a member of the Ethics Committee of the Charité in Berlin. He works on building law, spatial planning law, administrative, constitutional and European law, as well as legal sociology and constitutional history.

Matthew Kramer is a professor of legal and political philosophy at the University of Cambridge and a fellow of Churchill College (Cambridge) where he has taught since 1994. He has been the director of the Cambridge Forum for Legal and Political Philosophy since 2000. He has authored many works, mainly in the area of meta-ethics, deontological ethics, legal philosophy, political philosophy and moral philosophy, on questions such as legal positivism, legal objectivity, rights and freedom. Kramer is a fellow of the British Academy.

Andrei Marmor is the Jacob Gould Schurman Professor of Philosophy and Law at Cornell Law School. He has been a professor of philosophy and the Maurice Jones Jr Professor of Law at the University of Southern California. Having obtained his first law and philosophy degrees at the Tel Aviv University in Israel, and a doctorate at Oxford University (UK), he returned to Tel Aviv University, where he taught as a professor of law for ten years, before moving to the United States. His research interests are philosophy of law, moral and social philosophy, political philosophy and philosophy of language.

Patricia Mindus is a professor of practical philosophy at Uppsala University and director of the Uppsala Forum for Democracy, Peace and Justice. She has authored four monographs, including an award-winning book on Axel Hägerström, *A Real Mind* (2009), and a bestseller on *European Citizenship After Brexit* (2017). Some of her work is inspired by Scandinavian legal realism and has been translated into Spanish, Portuguese, Slovenian, Chinese and Russian. Mindus is the president of the Swedish IVR association and editor of the Legal Schools of Thought section for the *IVR Encyclopedia of Philosophy of Law*.

J. J. Moreso is a professor of philosophy of law and the former rector of the University Pompeu Fabra in Barcelona. He has taught as a professor of philosophy of law at the Autonomous University of Barcelona, the University of Girona and Pompeu Fabra University in Barcelona. He has been vice-rector of teaching staff and the European Space for Higher Education at Pompeu Fabra University. In October 2010 he was awarded an honorary doctorate from the University of Valparaíso, in Chile, for his career as an academic and jurist. Since 2013, he is the president of AQU Catalunya.

Dennis M. Patterson is the Board of Governors Professor of Law at Rutgers Law School. He has been awarded senior research grants from the Fulbright Commission, Humboldt Stiftung and the American Council of Learned Societies. He has been holder of the Fulbright Distinguished Chair in Law at Trento University. He has been a visiting professor at the universities of Berlin, Vienna, Texas, Georgetown and at the European University Institute in Florence where he has held the chair in legal theory and legal philosophy. He works in the fields of commercial law, trade law and legal philosophy.

Gerald Postema is the Cary C. Boshamer Distinguished Professor of Philosophy at the University of North Carolina at Chapel Hill. Earlier he served as the Arthur L. Goodhart Distinguished Visiting Professor of Legal Science (Cambridge) and was a fellow of Corpus Christi College (Cambridge). He is a former Guggenheim fellow, Rockefeller fellow (Bellagio), Medlin fellow (National Humanities Center), fellow of the Netherlands Institute for Advanced Studies and visiting fellow at the European University Institute (Florence). He works on legal and political philosophy, and ethics.

Cristina Redondo is a professor at the University of Genoa, where she teaches philosophy of law, general theory of law, theories of justice, and techniques of interpretation and argumentation and was previously affiliated with Spanish and Latin American universities. Her research interests include legal and moral theory, argumentation theory and interpretation theory. She is a committee member of the following journals: *Revista de Teoría del Derecho de la Universidad de Palermo* [*Journal of Theory and Law of the University of Palermo*] (Argentina), *Revista Latinoamericana de Filosofía Política* [*Latin American Journal of Political Philosophy*], *Diritto e questioni pubbliche* [*Law and Public Affairs*], *Analisi e diritto* [*Analysis and Law*] and *Discusiones* [*Discussions*]. She is also a member of the editorial board of the Studies of Analytical Philosophy of Law series.

Veronica Rodriguez-Blanco is the inaugural holder of the chair of moral and political philosophy (jurisprudence) in the School of Law, University of Surrey and a member of the Surrey Centre for Law and Philosophy. Her research is located at the intersection of practical reason, philosophy of action, and law. She draws insights from ancient, medieval and contemporary moral psychology, action theory, private law, legal authority, and normativity. She is co-editor of the journal *Jurisprudence: An International Journal of Legal and Political Thought.*

Frederick Schauer is the David and Mary Harrison Distinguished Professor of Law at the University of Virginia and Frank Stanton Professor (Emeritus) of the First Amendment at the Kennedy School of Government, Harvard University. He was previously a professor at the University of Michigan and has been a visiting professor at the Columbia Law School, Fischel-Neil Distinguished Visiting Professor at the University of Chicago, Morton Distinguished Visiting Professor at Dartmouth College, a distinguished visiting professor at the University of Toronto, a visiting fellow at the Australian National University, a distinguished visitor at NY University, and the Eastman Professor and a fellow of Balliol College (Oxford).

Philip Schofield is a professor of the history of legal and political thought at the Faculty of Laws of University College London. Director of the Bentham Project and general editor of the *Collected Works of Jeremy Bentham*, he is the chair of the Bentham Seminar, where scholars present new research on Bentham studies. He is the secretary of the International Society for Utilitarian Studies, which organises major international conferences. Published by Oxford University Press, his *Utility and Democracy: The Political Thought of Jeremy Bentham* has been awarded the Mackenzie Book Prize by the Political Studies Association.

Jan-Reinard Sieckmann is a professor at the Friedrich-Alexander-University Erlangen-Nürnberg. He was previously a research assistant for Robert Alexy at the University of Kiel and has been long-term lecturer at the University of Buenos Aires and a professor at the universities of Cologne, Freiburg and Bamberg. His main research interests are in the field of legal philosophy, legal theory, argumentation theory, constitutional theory, as well as fundamental and human rights. He has a particular research interest in autonomy.

Torben Spaak is a professor of jurisprudence at the Department of Law, Stockholm University where he is also the vice-dean for education. He has co-edited two *Festschrifts* and is the author of three monographs in jurisprudence, including *A Critical Appraisal of Karl Olivecrona's Legal Philosophy* (Springer, 2014). Spaak has also authored contributions to several collections of essays in legal philosophy and has written a number of articles in journals such as *Analisi e diritto* [*Analysis and Law*], *Archiv für Rechts- und Sozialphilosophie* [*Archive for Legal and Social Philosophy*], *Buffalo Law Review*, *Ethics*, *Jurisprudence*, *Law and Philosophy*, *Revus*, *Ratio Juris*, *Theoria* and *The Theory and Practice of Legislation*. He is also series co-editor of Springer's Law and Philosophy Library and has twice been a visiting professor at the University of Minnesota Law School.

Brian Z. Tamanaha is the John S. Lehmann University Professor at the Washington University School of Law in St. Louis. He has delivered the Kobe Memorial Lecture in Tokyo, the Julius Stone Address in Sydney, the Cotterrell Lecture in London and the Montesquieu Lecture at Tilburg University. He spent a year as a member of the Institute for Advanced Study in Princeton. He has been a visiting professor at University of Amsterdam, the European University Institute (Florence), Queen Mary University (London) and Columbia Law School. Four of his books have received awards, including *A General Jurisprudence of Law and Society* (2001), which was awarded the Law and Society prize and another legal theory prize.

Kevin Toh is a senior lecturer in the Faculty of Laws at University College London. Previously an associate professor in the Department of Philosophy at San Francisco State University and an assistant professor in the Department of Philosophy at Indiana University in Bloomington, he is a prolific author in the field of philosophy of law and has also made forays into moral philosophy and constitutional theory. His work in philosophy of law addresses the nature of legal thought, discourse and practice, by exploiting certain theoretical resources from contemporary meta-ethics, aesthetics and philosophy of action.

Michel Troper is an emeritus professor in public law at Paris Nanterre University and also teaches philosophy of law at Sciences Po. He was previously a professor at the University of Rouen. He has been a member of the Institut Universitaire de France, and president and founder of the Société Française de Philosophie Politique et Juridique. He is director of the Centre de théorie et analyse du droit. His field of expertise includes French constitutional law.

W. J. Waluchow is a professor in the McMaster University Department of Philosophy, the Senator William McMaster Chair in Constitutional Studies and an adjunct member of the Graduate Faculty of Osgoode Hall Law School at the University of Toronto. After study at the University of Western Ontario, he joined Oxford University to study philosophy of law under the supervision of Hart. He works on general jurisprudence, philosophy of constitutional law and especially on inclusive legal positivism.

Kenneth Winston is an emeritus lecturer in ethics at the Kennedy School of Government, Harvard University. His work built the school's capacity in comparative international ethics, developing new cases for classroom use and teaching in overseas venues, especially in Asia. He has written extensively on case teaching, professional ethics and legal theory. He has been a fellow of the American Council of Learned Societies, a senior research fellow of the National Endowment for the Humanities and a John Dewey senior fellow. He was selected by the KSG class of 2005 for the Manuel Carballo Award for Excellence in teaching.

Acknowledgements

The editors would like to thank the Bank of Sweden Tercentenary Foundation, the Justice Edvard Cassel Foundation and the Wenner-Gren Foundation for their generous support, which allowed us to hold conferences at Stockholm University in November 2018 and April 2019, at which the contributors to the present volume presented draft chapters. The editors would also like to thank Astrid Söderbergh Widding, President of Stockholm University, for allowing us to host conference dinners at the Scheffler Palace, also referred to as the Haunted Mansion; and Astrid Söderbergh Widding and Astri Muren, Deputy Vice President of Stockholm University, for giving the welcome addresses. In addition, the editors would like to thank Jessika van der Sluijs, Dean of the Faculty of Law at Stockholm University, and the Knut & Alice Wallenberg Foundation, for financing individual visits to Stockholm and Uppsala, respectively, for contributors who were unable to attend the conferences. The visits to Uppsala were financed by the Wallenberg Foundation within the framework of the CIVIS SUM project, directed by Patricia Mindus as a Wallenberg Academy Fellow (2015–21). Special thanks also to those contributors who stepped in to do an additional chapter when the original authors had to withdraw, to Stanley Paulson for his invaluable help and encouragement in the development of the current project and to Jackie Grant at Cambridge University Press for her patience and support. Finally, the editors would like to thank Cyril Holm for his creativity and hard work in the organisation and running of the conferences and for much else besides, Staffan Westerlund for creating the conference posters and for taking photos during the conferences, and Mahendra Kunhody for creating the index.

Introduction 1

Torben Spaak and Patricia Mindus

1.1 What Is Law?

Although the subject-matter of jurisprudence (sometimes called 'legal theory') is not understood in precisely the same way everywhere, everyone agrees that the question of the nature of law falls within the purview of jurisprudence. The central question is 'What is law?', or 'What is the nature of law?', and it is usually here that one encounters legal positivism and its main challenger, natural law theory, for the first time. The central question in the debate between legal positivists and natural law thinkers – the perennial finalists in the world cup of legal theory[1] – is often said to concern the relation between law and (true) morality: Whereas natural law thinkers maintain that law is necessarily moral, that there is a necessary connection between law and morality, legal positivists hold instead that the relation between law and morality is contingent, that law is sometimes moral, sometimes immoral, and argue that the question of whether we have an obligation to obey the law can be answered only after we have considered the content and the administration of the law in the relevant jurisdiction.[2] However, in this introduction we shall focus on legal positivism, not the legal positivism/natural law debate, and we shall attempt to provide a fuller and more adequate characterisation of legal positivism than just saying that legal positivists reject the view that there is a necessary connection between law and morality, as well as to identify certain important types of legal positivism.

However, given the energy expended throughout history by legal philosophers and jurists on the legal positivism/natural law debate and on

[1] See Honoré 1987: 32.

[2] See, e.g., Hart 1958; Coleman 1982: 140–1; Kramer 1999: 1–17. As we shall see, some influential contemporary legal positivists actually reject the separation thesis taken at face value, arguing that there are indeed necessary connections between law and morality.

natural law theory and legal positivism considered separately,[3] one may wonder if yet another volume on legal positivism is needed. But although much has already been said about legal positivism, we believe that there is more to say, not only about what legal positivism is, or might be, and about different types of legal positivism but also about different geographical traditions of legal positivism, about the central figures of legal positivism, about the fundamental tenets of legal positivism, about the problem of legal normativity considered within the framework of legal positivism, about the meta-ethical underpinnings of legal positivism, if any, about the value or disvalue of law positivistically conceived and of positivistic legal arrangements and, of course, about the perceived problems of legal positivism, such as its alleged totalitarian implications. If we add to these questions the circumstance that there is in many quarters a considerable lack of clarity as to what, exactly, the term 'legal positivism' stands for, or should stand for, we believe that there is ample justification for bringing together a number of chapters on legal positivism in a volume such as this.

What we offer in this volume, then, is a rather comprehensive and systematic discussion by experts in the field of these and similar questions. Although some authors find fault with legal positivism, or even doubt its continued significance in the legal-philosophical landscape, we believe that legal positivism will continue to attract considerable interest in the future, not only among legal philosophers and legal scholars in general but also among other students of the humanities and the social sciences, such as philosophers, historians, political scientists, sociologists or economists. For what is interesting about legal positivism is not, of course, the taxonomic question of whether a given theory or approach is or is not positivistic, although this question may sometimes be considered important, for example by writers of textbooks, but rather a variety of general and foundational questions that tend to be raised in almost any discussion of legal positivism. For example, there are questions about what law is, and what its purpose or function, if any, is, about its action-guiding capacity and its capacity to live up to the ideals of the *Rechtsstaat* or the Rule of Law, and about the existence and content of an obligation to obey the law. In addition, there are questions about the relation of law to the state, to coercion, to morality, to norms and human behaviour, to legislation, to

[3] For an illuminating account of the historical development of natural law theory and legal positivism, see Olivecrona 1971: 7–64.

judicial decision-making and to custom, and about how to analyse legal statements and interpret legal norms; and there is the general question of whether and, if so, how we can know the answers to these and similar questions; and more. Questions like these have for a long time attracted, and will surely continue to attract, the interest of almost anyone wishing to understand human affairs.

1.1.1 Legal Positivism as an Intellectual Tradition

As we shall see, this volume assumes that we can speak meaningfully of some central tenets of legal positivism, and that legal positivists are thinkers who accept these tenets. Nevertheless, not everything that is said about legal positivism in the volume immediately concerns these tenets. To see the relevance of matters that do not immediately concern the tenets, one may choose to think of legal positivism along the lines of (what we shall refer to as) normative, theoretical, ideological or methodological positivism (to be introduced in Section 1.1.6) or, alternatively, to think of it not as a theory (or a set of tenets) at all but rather as an intellectual tradition that includes a number of writers in different countries over a long stretch of time, dealing with rather different topics, whose connections to one another are at least partly to be found in an attitude to legal scholarship or an interest in certain themes or questions and, perhaps, ultimately in terms of family resemblance in Wittgenstein's sense.[4] This way of conceiving of legal positivism is in keeping with our claim that there is in many quarters a considerable lack of clarity as to what the term 'legal positivism' stands for, and also with our related claim that in three of the main geographical traditions of legal positivism, the German, the Italian and the French, the equivalents to the English term 'legal positivism' have had no very clear meaning.

1.1.2 Geographical Traditions

Compared to natural law theory, legal positivism is a newcomer on the scene. In Europe, it developed in the nineteenth century along somewhat different lines in England, France, Germany and Italy – in the case of Italy due to

[4] This question has been briefly discussed by Raz 2007: 18–22 and Gardner 2012: 19, among others. On family resemblance, see Wittgenstein 1960: 17–20; 1968: s. 66.

autochthonous re-elaborations of ideas from the French codification-centred tradition, the German tradition and Auguste Comte's positivistic philosophy.[5] Thus, Jeremy Bentham, who wrote on legal positivism already in the late eighteenth century, appears to have been the first legal positivist in England, though it has been said that his predecessor, Thomas Hobbes, too, was a legal positivist, or at least an ancestor of Benthamite legal positivism.[6] In Germany, Gustav Hugo, Friedrich Carl von Savigny and Georg Friedrich Puchta, all writing in the first half of the nineteenth century, can be said to have been the first legal positivists;[7] and in France, the members of the exegetical school, including Jean-Charles Florent Demolombe and Raymond-Théodore Troplong, writing in the nineteenth century, are said to have been the first legal positivists.[8] In Italy, finally, legal positivism in the shape of ideological or methodological (or scientific) positivism was the ruling view until the 1960s; and since then these forms of legal positivism together with theoretical positivism have been the subject of sophisticated meta-philosophical reflections by Norberto Bobbio and Uberto Scarpelli, in particular.[9]

Although the different geographical traditions of legal positivism are similar, being traditions of *legal positivism*, they are also different. For example, Karl Olivecrona points out that nineteenth-century legal positivism in England and Germany differed in that the former type of theory aimed at providing a factual, naturalistic explanation of the nature of law and did not purport to account for the binding (or obligatory) force of law, whereas the latter type of theory did aim to account precisely for the binding force of law, which it conceived in non-naturalistic terms.[10] Moreover, the French tradition of legal positivism appears to differ from the other traditions in that even though some scholars and judges have

[5] See Olivecrona 1971: 7–64.

[6] See Chapter 9. As that chapter explains, one can also view Bentham's legal philosophy in a different light.

[7] See Chapter 5; Olivecrona 1971: 35–41. Interestingly, Kelsen maintains that the doctrine of the *Volksgeist* embraced by von Savigny, according to which both legislation and custom are nothing more than *evidence* of pre-existing law, is a typical variant of natural law theory. Kelsen 1999: 127.

[8] On this, see Chapter 6.

[9] On this, see Chapters 7 and 14.

[10] See Olivecrona 1971: 27–33, 35–41. If Olivecrona is right, this might explain Hart's claim in the Hart–Fuller debate, namely that Gustav Radbruch had misunderstood legal positivism by failing to see that what is legally obligatory is not necessarily morally obligatory. See Hart 1958: 615–21. Hart might not have realised that Radbruch understood legal positivism differently from the way it was (and is) understood in the English-speaking world.

indeed called themselves positivists, or have been called positivists by others, there has been almost no legal-philosophical discussion of legal positivism conceived as a theory of law, though things have begun to change in the past twenty years or so. Indeed, it appears that the equivalents to the English term 'legal positivism' in German, Italian and French – *Rechtspositivismus*, *positivismo giuridico* and *positivisme juridique*, respectively – have for a long time had no very clear meaning and that the debates on legal positivism in these jurisdictions have only in the second half of the twentieth century come to touch on the central tenets of legal positivism, as we understand them today, and as they will be presented in this introduction. The various geographical traditions of legal positivism will be treated in Part II of the volume.

1.1.3 Central Figures

We have said that there is in many quarters a lack of clarity as to what 'legal positivism' stands for, or should stand for. There can, however, be no doubt that, through the years in the respective traditions, some writers have been considered central figures of legal positivism. Thus, central figures in the German tradition, in addition to von Savigny and Puchta, include Rudolf von Ihering, Georg Jellinek, Hans Kelsen and Ota Weinberger; central figures in the Italian tradition, in addition to Bobbio, include Icilio Vanni, Biagio Brugi, Alessandro Levi and, in more recent times, Uberto Scarpelli, Giovanni Tarello and Luigi Ferrajoli; central figures of the French tradition, in addition to the mentioned members of the exegetical school, include Raymond Carré de Malberg and Léon Duguit;[11] and central figures in the British tradition, in addition to Bentham, include John Austin, T. E. Holland, H. L. A. Hart and Joseph Raz. Finally, a central figure in the history of legal positivism is the contemporary Argentinian legal philosopher Eugenio Bulygin. The versions of legal positivism defended by some of these central figures will be treated in Part III of the volume. As the reader will see, however, it is not clear that they are always talking about the same thing, and it may in some cases be a challenge to determine the precise sense in which they were thought to be legal positivists, or

[11] It is worth noting that Kelsen maintains that the doctrine of social solidarity embraced by Duguit, according to which both legislation and custom are nothing more than *evidence* of pre-existing law, is a typical variant of natural law theory. See Kelsen 1999: 127.

precisely how this sense relates to our understanding today of what legal positivism is.

1.1.4 Descriptive Legal Positivism: A Framework Theory

As we have said, we may distinguish between different types of legal positivism, such as descriptive positivism, as we might refer to it, theoretical positivism, normative positivism, ideological positivism and methodological (or scientific) positivism. Our focus in this volume, however, is going to be on descriptive legal positivism, which is considered by most of its defenders to be the central form of legal positivism;[12] and in what follows, we have this version in mind when we speak of 'legal positivism', unless we indicate otherwise.

Accordingly, we might say that what legal positivism does, at least as legal positivists see it, is to lay down conditions that have to be satisfied by anything that purports to be a correct theory of law: If *X* does not satisfy the relevant conditions, *X* will not be, and cannot be, a correct theory of law. Speaking about a central tenet of legal positivism, the social thesis, Joseph Raz puts it thus: the social thesis 'is best viewed not as a "first-order" thesis but as a constraint on what kind of theory of law is an acceptable theory'.[13] On this analysis, Kelsen's, Hart's and Raz's theories are first-order theories of law in the sense that they are theories precisely of *law*, and they are positivistic in the sense that they conform to the fundamental tenets of legal positivism (to be discussed in Section 1.1.5); and we might therefore refer to legal positivism as a second-order theory of law in the sense that it is primarily a theory about *theories* of law, *not* a theory of law.

Alternatively, we might think of legal positivism not as a second-order theory but as a first-order theory that differs from other first-order theories of law, like the ones defended by Kelsen, Hart, Raz and others, by being more general, in much the same way that consequentialism differs from utilitarianism or ethical egoism by being more general. Thus, whereas consequentialism ascribes moral value to actions, events and states of affairs solely because of their consequences, utilitarianism ascribes value

[12] See, e.g., Coleman 1982: 147. For a discussion of this question, see also Chapter 3 and Waldron 2001: 413–14.

[13] Raz 2009: 39.

to such things solely because of their consequences for human happiness (or perhaps welfare).[14] On this analysis, too, legal positivism lays down adequacy conditions for theories of law. Some might prefer this latter way of characterising legal positivism on the grounds that they find the distinction between specificity and generality to be less problematic than the distinction between first- and second-order theories.

If we think of legal positivism as a framework theory in one of the ways suggested, that is, as a theory laying down adequacy conditions for theories of law, we see that it is not much of an objection to legal positivism to point out that in itself it does not say much about what law is, how it should be interpreted and applied, or whether it should be obeyed or disobeyed, and so forth. For, on this analysis, to be a legal positivist is not to have a complete theory of what law is, how it should be interpreted and applied, or about law obedience, and so forth.[15]

1.1.5 Descriptive Legal Positivism: Central Tenets

Even though legal positivists differ on a number of issues, most of them accept three central tenets, namely, the social thesis, the separation thesis and the thesis of social efficacy.[16] In addition, some legal positivists accept a fourth thesis, called the semantic thesis.[17] Crudely put, the social thesis has it that what is law and what is not is a matter of social fact; the separation thesis says that there is no necessary connection between law and morality;[18] the thesis of social efficacy says that the validity (or existence) of law presupposes that the law is socially efficacious; and the semantic thesis has it, in one version, that legal normative or evaluative terms such as 'right', 'duty' and 'authority' have different meanings (senses) from the corresponding moral terms and, in another version, that (first-order) legal statements are statements solely about social facts.

[14] On consequentialism, see Williams 1973: 82–93.

[15] On this, see, e.g., Gardner 2012: 51; Green 2018: 29.

[16] Raz is an exception. He accepts the social thesis but rejects the separation thesis (and the semantic thesis). See Raz 2009: 38–9. Note also that different writers may refer to the same, or very similar, tenets in slightly different ways. For example, Jules Coleman calls the social thesis the 'social fact thesis' and the separation thesis the 'separability thesis'. See Coleman 2001: 75, 104.

[17] See, e.g., Kelsen 1999: 60; Hart 1982: 159–60. See also Holmes 1896–7: 461.

[18] As we saw in footnote 2, this is not quite right. We shall have to qualify this thesis.

Some legal positivists maintain that the backbone of legal positivism is to be found in the social thesis.[19] The precise meaning of the social thesis has been debated by legal positivists for the past forty years or so, however.[20] For example, while exclusive legal positivists argue that, properly understood, the social thesis requires (in a conceptual sense) the use of *exclusively* factual criteria of legal validity, and hold that any reference to moral values (primarily in the rule of recognition but also in, say, constitutional provisions) is best understood as granting the judge power and discretion to create new law,[21] inclusive legal positivists maintain instead that the criteria of validity can, but need not, be of a moral nature, provided they are grounded in (social) facts.[22] That is to say, whereas exclusive legal positivists insist that both the basis and the content of the criteria of validity be factual, inclusive legal positivists hold instead that while the basis of such criteria must be factual, their content need not be factual but can be normative or evaluative. One may, however, also think of this debate as concerning the correct interpretation of the *separation* thesis. On that analysis, whereas exclusive positivists defend the 'separation thesis', inclusive positivists defend the 'separability thesis'.[23]

In more recent years, the jurisprudential debate about the social thesis has also concerned the question of whether the social foundation of law, often taken to be something like a rule of recognition, is to be understood along the lines of legal conventionalism or along the lines of a more recent view called law as a shared activity.[24] Whereas H. L. A. Hart,[25] Gerald J. Postema[26] and Andrei Marmor,[27] to mention only a few, have defended a conventionalist account of the rule of recognition, Jules Coleman and Scott Shapiro have both defended a law-as-a-shared-activity account of this foundational rule.[28] The main difference between these two types of account is that whereas the former takes the social practice underlying, or constituting, the rule of recognition to be necessarily conventional, the latter defends instead an account of said practice according to which a conventional element may, but need not, be part of the practice.

[19] See, e.g., Raz 2009: 38; Coleman 2001: 75; 2009: 383; Simmonds 2002: 127–31.
[20] See, e.g., Soper 1977; Lyons 1977; Dworkin 1978: 345–50. [21] See Raz 1986: 1110.
[22] See Coleman 2001: ch. 7; Hart 1994: 247–8, 250–1; Waluchow 1994.
[23] On this, see Chapter 21. [24] On this, see Chapter 17.
[25] See Hart 1961: 112 and 1994: 255–6. [26] See Postema 1982. [27] See Marmor 2011.
[28] See Coleman 2001: 74–102; Shapiro 2011.

Some legal positivists choose, however, to focus their discussions of legal positivism on the separation thesis instead of the social thesis. For example, although Hart emphasizes the idea of the rule of recognition in the *Concept of Law*, he explicitly identifies legal positivism with the separation thesis;[29] and Matthew Kramer in his *In Defense of Legal Positivism* concentrates on the legal positivist claim that law and morality are 'strictly separable', that legality and morality are 'disjoinable'.[30] Robert Alexy, too, in his critique of legal positivism, chooses to focus not on the social thesis but precisely on the separation thesis because he believes that the social thesis is not unique to legal positivism but is accepted by all serious non-positivists.[31]

The separation thesis, we have said, has it that there is no necessary connection between law and morality, where the relevant morality is understood to be true morality, not the morality or moralities actually accepted by the subjects of the relevant law. But, as we have pointed out, some contemporary legal positivists, including Joseph Raz, Leslie Green and John Gardner, reject the separation thesis, arguing that there are indeed necessary connections between law and morality.[32] Gardner, for example, points out that law and morality 'are necessarily alike in both necessarily comprising some valid norms'.[33] How, then, are we to understand the separation thesis if we wish to think of it as a tenet of legal positivism? The proper way to qualify this thesis, we believe, is to think of the necessary connection in question as a connection between morality and the *content* of law.[34] We may then usefully distinguish between the separation thesis conceived as a thesis about the *content of* (first-order) *legal statements*, namely, a thesis according to which such legal statements do not entail (first-order) moral statements,[35] and the separation thesis conceived as a thesis about *legal status*, according to which even (grossly)

[29] See Hart 1961: 181–2. See also Hart 1958. [30] Kramer 1999: 1. See also Green 2018.

[31] See Alexy 2002: 3, 20–3. Alexy takes the separation thesis to say that 'the concept of law is to be defined such that no moral elements are included'. Thus conceived, he points out, it *presupposes* that there is no necessary connection between law and morality, that is, what we call the 'separation thesis' in this introduction.

[32] See, e.g., Raz 2007: 18–22; Gardner 2012: 48–51; Green 2008. [33] Gardner 2012: 48.

[34] It is worth noting that this appears to be in keeping with what Kelsen and Hart have said on the issue. See, e.g., Kelsen 1992: 56; Hart 1961: 181–2.

[35] To be clear about whether legal statements entail moral statements or not, we should distinguish between a *de dicto* and a *de re* interpretation of the statement content version of the separation thesis. If we do, we also see that, on a *de dicto*, but not on a *de re* interpretation, the status version of the thesis entails the statement content version.

immoral norms can be (part of) law. It seems, however, that the majority of those who consider the separation thesis take it to be primarily a thesis about legal status and only secondarily, if at all, a thesis about the content of legal statements,[36] often with no explicit view of the logical relation between the two versions of the thesis. Kelsen, for example, appears to have in mind the status question when he maintains that '[a]ny content whatever can be law; there is no human behavior that would be excluded simply by virtue of its substance from becoming the content of a legal norm'[37] and the question of statement content when he claims that '[a] statement about the law must not imply any judgment about the moral value of the law, about its justice or injustice'.[38]

To see that there really is a difference between the separation thesis about statement content and the separation thesis about legal status, it may be helpful to consider the position of a moral error theorist, such as John Mackie,[39] as regards the separation thesis. If you are an error theorist, you believe that all moral statements are false, and this means that you will have to accept the separation thesis about legal status, though you may choose to reject the separation thesis about statement content. For if you do not accept the status version of the thesis, you will not be able to recognize the existence of legal systems, and this would be decidedly odd; if, on the other hand, you do not accept the statement-content version of the thesis, you may without much oddity hold that legal statements entail (false) moral statements.

One reason to focus one's attention on the social thesis rather than the separation thesis, conceived as a thesis about legal status, is that the latter thesis follows from the former, assuming that the laws of logic do not allow that a normative (or evaluative) conclusion can follow from a (consistent) set of factual premises.[40] That is to say, if, in keeping with the social thesis,

[36] See, e.g., Hart 1958 and Andrei Marmor's discussion of the separation thesis in Chapter 19.

[37] Kelsen 1992: 56.

[38] Kelsen 1959–60: 273. See also Hart 1982: 159–61, 266–7. To be sure, Kelsen might have intended *both* claims to be about the status question. It is difficult to say what, exactly, he means.

[39] Mackie 1977a: ch. 1. We are here considering – for purposes of illustration – what an error theorist might, or would have to, say about this thesis. We do not attribute any view on this to Mackie himself.

[40] This is one way of understanding Hume's law. The idea is that the entailment relation is such that the conclusion in a valid inference (or argument) only makes explicit what is already implicit in the premises, so that proving a theorem in logic or mathematics is to make explicit the content of one or more axioms.

we determine what the law is using factual criteria, and if we cannot deduce a normative (or an evaluative) conclusion from a (consistent) set of factual premises, the separation thesis about legal status follows. We thus assume here that a factual criterion is necessarily a non-normative, and therefore a non-moral, criterion. If ethical naturalism is true, however, this is not so. For, according to ethical naturalism, moral properties are (necessarily) natural, that is, factual, properties.[41] It does not, however, follow that natural (factual) properties are moral properties; this means that even if it follows from the social thesis that legal properties are natural properties, it does *not* follow from this thesis that they are also moral properties.

The thesis of social efficacy, which has it that the validity of law (in the sense of membership in the system) presupposes that the law is socially efficacious, that, on the whole, the citizens obey and the legal officials enforce the law, is also an important part of the legal positivist package. As Kelsen puts it, '[a] legal order as a whole and the particular legal norms which form this legal order are to be considered valid [in the sense of being binding and, indirectly, in the sense of being members of the system] only if they are, by and large, obeyed and applied, only if they are effective'.[42] This important thesis has not received much attention from either legal positivists or non-positivists, however,[43] and, as a result, its import is not absolutely clear.[44] One may, for example, wonder what counts as obedience, how much obedience or law enforcement is necessary and sufficient for a legal order to be efficacious, or how one is to weigh citizen obedience against the enforcement of the law by officials. For example, should we say that a legal order (a legal system) is socially efficacious, if the citizens disobey its norms but the officials enforce them?

The semantic thesis, too, can be understood in more than one way.[45] As we have seen, it may say that legal normative (or evaluative) terms such as 'right', 'duty' and 'authority' do not have the same meaning (sense) as the corresponding moral terms, or it may instead say that (first-order) legal statements are statements solely about social facts.[46] One may accept the

[41] On ethical naturalism, see, e.g., van Roojen 2015: chs. 11–12. [42] Kelsen 1959–60: 272.

[43] For a brief discussion of this thesis, see Raz 1980: 203–8.

[44] On the import of this thesis, see Chapter 22. See also Burazin 2017.

[45] On this, see Raz 2009: 37–8.

[46] Chapter 23, which treats the semantic thesis, concentrates on the more demanding version of the thesis.

former while rejecting the latter version of the thesis; but if one rejects the former, one will also have to reject the latter, unless one accepts ethical naturalism. In any case, most scholars who have considered the semantic thesis in print have focused on the former version;[47] whereas some prominent legal positivists accept this version of the thesis,[48] others, equally prominent, reject it.[49]

It is worth noting here that one reason to accept the version of the semantic thesis according to which normative or evaluative terms have a special, legal sense is that in this way one can uphold the separation thesis conceived as a thesis about the content of legal statements. For if 'right' and 'duty', say, have special, legal senses, which differ from their moral senses (and do not in any way include the latter), then to maintain that Smith has a legal duty to pay his taxes is not necessarily to maintain that Smith has a moral duty to pay his taxes. If instead one rejects the semantic thesis but wishes to uphold the separation thesis conceived as a thesis about the content of legal statements, one could perhaps follow Raz and maintain that law-appliers and others make detached, instead of committed, legal statements.[50] The fundamental tenets of legal positivism will be treated in Part IV of the volume.

1.1.6 Other Types of Legal Positivism

Legal positivism conceived along these lines – descriptive legal positivism, as we have called it – should be distinguished from *normative* positivism.[51] Whereas the former is an analytical theory that concerns the concept of law, or the nature of law, or both, the latter has it that there are good normative (typically, moral) reasons for accepting one or more of the mentioned main tenets of (descriptive) legal positivism, for example, that the administration of justice becomes more stable and predictable if law-appliers and citizens do not

[47] For a recent discussion of the semantic thesis, see Duarte D'Almeda 2011.

[48] See Hart 1982: 159–60; Kelsen 1999: 59–60.

[49] See Raz 1983: 129–31; MacCormick 1987: 108.

[50] See Raz 1990: 170–7. Note that, on this analysis, the separation thesis would not concern the relation between the contents of legal and moral statements; it would rather concern the relation between detached and committed speech acts. This is because the difference between detached and committed legal statements is to be found not in the contents of the statements but in the propositional attitudes of the speaker. Hence, such a Razian separation thesis would be a slightly different separation thesis.

[51] On normative positivism, see Chapter 3.

have to exercise moral judgement in order to find out what the law is.[52] Thus, as normative positivists see it, the question of which theory of law to embrace is a normative, not an analytical one. To be able to take a stand on whether the basic tenets of (descriptive) legal positivism are correct, they reason, one has to consider questions about the value and function(s) of law and legal arrangements.[53]

Descriptive positivism is also different from both theoretical positivism and ideological positivism, which have been discussed especially, but by no means exclusively, in the Latin world. Whereas *theoretical* positivism (in the narrow sense) is a substantive theory of law, according to which law is a set of commands issued by the sovereign, legal interpretation is a cognitive and the application of law is a deductive enterprise, *ideological* positivism has it that one ought to obey the law because it is the law, or at least that one ought to obey the law if it promotes or realises good values, like peace, order, formal justice, legal certainty and so forth.[54] Finally, descriptive positivism is different from *methodological* positivism, which is a theory not of law but of legal science, and which has it that legal science, properly understood, is descriptive and value-neutral.[55] We might say with Stephen Perry that methodological positivism has it that there is no necessary connection between morality and legal science.[56]

The difference between normative and methodological positivism, then, is that whereas normative positivists maintain that there are good normative (and, in most cases, no non-normative) reasons to espouse the mentioned tenets of (descriptive) legal positivism, methodological positivists are concerned not with law but with legal science, and maintain that legal science, properly understood, is value-neutral. That is to say, whereas both descriptive and normative positivism are concerned with law (or theories of law), methodological positivism is concerned with legal science; and whereas both descriptive and methodological positivism are (or purport to be) descriptive (or analytical), normative positivism is explicitly normative.[57] As Figure 1.1 illustrates,[58] we can thus think of legal positivism as a theory of law (or

[52] See, e.g., Waldron 2001: 421. [53] See, e.g., Waldron 2001: 421.

[54] On theoretical and ideological positivism, see Chapters 7 and 14.

[55] On methodological positivism, see Chapters 7 and 14. See also Perry 2001.

[56] See Perry 2001: 311. Perry speaks not of 'legal science' but of 'legal theory'.

[57] Note that Guastini takes methodological positivism to be a *normative* theory. On this, see Chapter 7.

[58] Here, DP stands for 'descriptive positivism', TP for 'theoretical positivism', NP for 'normative positivism' and MP for 'methodological positivism'. If one wishes to think of legal positivism as a second-order theory in the way explained, one should, strictly speaking,

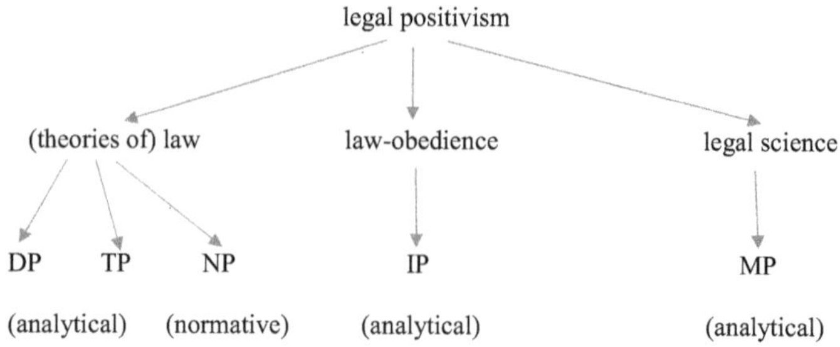

Figure 1.1 Types of legal positivism

a theory of theories of law), as a theory of law-obedience, or as a theory of legal science.

1.1.7 Objections to Legal Positivism

Although legal positivism is, and has been, a fairly widely accepted theory of law, it has not been without its critics. One recurring objection has been that one cannot account for the normativity of law within the framework of legal positivism. Not only have non-positivists, such as Lon Fuller and Ronald Dworkin, objected to Hart's theory of law, that it cannot account for the normativity of law,[59] but also both Kelsen and Hart have objected to John Austin's theory of law, that it cannot distinguish between legal norms and the orders of a highwayman. As Hart once put it, 'Law surely is not the gunman situation writ large, and legal order is surely not to be thus simply identified with compulsion.'[60] This general objection is a bit difficult to assess, however, because it is not obvious how we are to understand the relevant type of normativity.[61] For example, it appears that whereas Fuller and Dworkin, and even Kelsen, had in mind some type of moral normativity, Hart had in mind a specifically legal, non-moral normativity.[62] And whereas it seems clear that one cannot account for the normativity of law

say that whereas descriptive and normative positivism are second-order theories, theoretical positivism is a first-order theory.

59 See Fuller 1958: 648–57.

60 Hart 1958: 603. See also Kelsen 1999: 30–2, 35–7; Hart 1961: 79–88.

61 On this, see, e.g., Bratman 2011.

62 On Hart's conception of normativity, see Chapter 25. On Kelsen's conception of normativity, see the discussion of the difference between the subjective and the objective meaning of the act of command in Kelsen 1960: 3–9; 1959–60: 270. For a different take on Kelsen's conception of normativity, see Paulson 2012.

conceived as a type of moral normativity while insisting on the separation thesis, one could likely account for Hart's specifically legal normativity, while defending this thesis.

A related question is whether legal positivists have to be moral nihilists or sceptics, or at least expressivists (or non-cognitivists) or relativists.[63] The idea would be that if morality is in some sense subjective, then any infusion of moral considerations into the process of determining what the law is would contribute to making the law indeterminate,[64] and this in turn would explain why legal positivists insist on the separation of law and morality. One could, however, also reason that if expressivism, or error theory, is true, the question of whether law is necessarily normative does not make much sense, as there will then be no such property as normativity that the law could have, either contingently or necessarily. Consequently, legal positivists who find the question of the normativity of law to be interesting have good reason to espouse some version of moral cognitivism. As one might expect, a brief survey of the writings of leading legal positivists makes it clear that they have differed quite a bit on meta-ethical questions: Whereas some have espoused versions of non-cognitivism or (meta-ethical) relativism,[65] others have defended moral cognitivism.[66] The questions of the normativity of law and meta-ethics will be discussed in Part V of the volume.

Let us note, finally, that some authors have raised quite different objections either to legal positivism, or to positivist theories of law, such as Hart's theory. For example, Gustav Radbruch has argued that legal positivism facilitated the spread of Nazism in Germany,[67] and Ronald Dworkin has objected that Hart's theory of law cannot account either for the existence of legal principles or for so-called theoretical disagreement.[68] These objections,

[63] On this, see Hart 1958: 624–9.

[64] On this, see Mackie 1977b: 9–10. See also Dworkin's early discussion of 'inclusive', or 'soft', positivism (Dworkin 1978: 345–50), where he suggests that this type of positivism cannot be squared with the ambition (as he understands it) of legal positivists to make the truth of propositions of law 'independent of any controversial theory either of meta-ethics or of moral ontology' (Dworkin 1978: 349).

[65] See, e.g., Kelsen 1948; 1959–60: 273; Ross 1959: 6–11, 274; Olivecrona 1971: 112; Hart 1982: 159–60.

[66] Bentham [1776]1988; Austin [1832]1998, 184–6; Raz 1999; 2001; Coleman 2001; Kramer 2009.

[67] See Radbruch 2006. On this topic, see also Chapters 26 and 33.

[68] See Dworkin 1978: 14–45; 1986: ch. 1. See also Chapter 29 in this volume.

especially Radbruch's objection, conceived as a general claim about totalitarian tendencies of legal positivism, have been rather popular among critics of legal positivism and so deserve close scrutiny.[69] As for the Radbruchian objection, we might say that the idea is that descriptive legal positivism, in at least some of its versions, really amounts to ideological positivism. These objections will be considered in Part VI of the volume.

1.2 Contributions

The volume is divided into six parts. Part I deals with fundamentals of legal positivism, Part II considers the main traditions of legal positivism, and Part III treats central figures of legal positivism. Part IV treats the main tenets of legal positivism, Part V deals with questions of normativity and values, and Part VI, finally, considers various critiques of legal positivism.

Taking the essential thesis of legal positivism to be that all law is positive law or, if you will, that all law has sources, Leslie Green considers in Chapter 2 the relationships between legal positivism and 'its closest cousin', legal realism, focusing mainly on American legal realism. He aims, in particular, to explain why legal realists disagree with legal positivists about the role that legal rules play in the explanation of judicial decision-making. Noting that positivists and realists agree that law is constituted by social facts, that judges sometimes make law, and that law is morally fallible and should be studied in a realistic spirit, Green locates the point of disagreement in their different understandings of the boundary-lines between law and non-law, a boundary-line that is important to legal realists, too. His idea is that, unlike positivists, realists believe that a significant number of sources of law are only permissive sources – that is, sources such as foreign law, international treaties or academic writings, which judges are permitted but not required to use, and which can sometimes, perhaps rather often, be outweighed by considerations of policy, or justice, or the equities of the case and so forth – and that this fact explains why realists can hold that law is so indeterminate as to undermine the causal efficacy of legal rules, while sharing the positivist view that all law has sources. Green also maintains that the dispute between realists and positivists, thus conceived, is partly conceptual and partly empirical because it involves a failure on the part of

[69] On this, see Chapter 33.

the realists to grasp what rule-following involves as well as a failure to look at the given empirical material, that is, instances of rule-following in and out of court.

In Chapter 3, Fred Schauer discusses normative positivism, explaining that this type of positivism comes in two main versions, namely, in the shape of a prescription to legal actors and in the shape of a prescription to legal institutional designers. He begins by distinguishing the position of normative positivists from the position of those who claim that (descriptive) legal positivism is more normative than its proponents have been willing to acknowledge, and he proceeds to consider Jeremy Bentham's normative positivism as well as H. L. A. Hart's thoughts, as expressed in several different writings, about why, normatively and not merely descriptively, a positivistic understanding of the concept of law should be preferred to a non-positivistic one. Having done that, Schauer argues that a full appreciation of the artefactual nature of law leads to the conclusion that a culture can modify its concept of law in order to make it as useful a concept as possible, and that if normative positivism is a plausible position, it follows not only that choosing a concept of law on moral grounds is a moral position but also that choosing to see the enterprise of legal theory in a normative way itself amounts to a normative position.

Brian Leiter continues in Chapter 4 with a consideration of the relation between legal positivism and legal realism. He argues that H. L. A. Hart's theory of law is really a species of legal realism in a general sense that covers both American and Scandinavian realism, and that there are four ways in which this is so, namely, that the law operates primarily outside the courts; that the law is sometimes rationally indeterminate; that the law is explicable in wholly naturalistic terms; and that the law is not necessarily morally good. He points out, however, that American and Scandinavian realism are nevertheless quite different, and argues that H. L. A. Hart's well-known critiques of these two types of legal realism are misguided. Focusing on American legal realism, he explains that Hart fails to distinguish clearly between conceptual rule-scepticism, which is a theory about the nature of law, according to which law consists in court decisions and predictions about them, and empirical rule-scepticism, which says that there are some cases (especially appellate ones) where judges are not bound by legal rules. As Leiter sees it, while conceptual rule-scepticism is indeed mistaken, the Americans do not embrace it, and while they do embrace empirical rule-scepticism, this type of rule-scepticism is justified. Leiter also maintains that Joseph Raz's view that law necessarily claims legitimate authority involves a highly moralised and unrealistic view of what it is for law to claim authority – namely, the so-called service conception of authority – and actually amounts to a repudiation of realism in legal theory, including Hart's realism.

In Part II, our contributors turn to consider the history of legal positivism. Stephan Kirste begins in Chapter 5 with an account of the German tradition. Discussing in chronological order legal scholars who were active in the nineteenth and twentieth centuries, he identifies four main types of German legal positivism, namely, jurisprudential, sociological, naturalistic, and statutory positivism, as well as a fifth type of legal positivism that he calls the general theory of law. His idea is that these theories were legal positivist theories because they shared an epistemological aim, namely, that of establishing legal science as a science in its own right, independent of both the natural and the social sciences, and because they held that only positive law in the sense of enacted norms or customary norms is law. He then considers in more detail the theories of Hans Kelsen and Gustav Radbruch as examples of legal positivist theories, pointing out – contrary to what Radbruch and others have claimed – that the National Socialists were not legal positivists but were actually critical of legal positivism. He also points out that although legal positivism lost its dominance in the wake of the post–World War II revival of natural law theory, it was soon able to reassert its influence, and he considers the theories of Ota Weinberger, Niklas Luhmann and Norbert Hoerster as examples of post–World War II versions of legal positivism. Finally, Kirste points out that since the late sixties, several authors, including Peter Koller and Ottfrid Höffe, have been aiming to overcome the gulf between natural law theory and legal positivism, and that, in contemporary German legal scholarship, the debate between legal positivism and non-positivism continues, although it is now less intense than it used to be, partly because the Basic Law of 1949 has solved many contentious issues by including principles like human dignity, individual freedom, equality and more.

Michel Troper continues in Chapter 6 with an account of the French tradition of legal positivism. Although he points out that there is hardly a single French legal scholar who subscribes to any of the three versions (or aspects) of legal positivism distinguished by Norberto Bobbio,[70] namely,

[70] On Bobbio's versions (or aspects) of legal positivism, see Chapters 7 and 14.

theoretical, methodological and ideological positivism, Troper identifies five groups of French legal scholars who have called themselves legal positivists or have been called legal positivists by others, namely, the exegetical school, the sociological school and Leon Duguit, Raymond Carré de Malberg, the Vichy scholars, and the analytical legal positivists; and he proceeds to consider them in turn. He explains, inter alia, that Carré de Malberg put forward a theory of positive law that aims to be descriptive, according to which positive law is a product of the will of the state and the state possesses an inherent capacity to obligate the citizens by means of its laws. He points out, however, that while Carré de Malberg's description of French positive law aims to reveal an essence of the state, in reality the description proceeds from a set of abstractions that reflect his own normative theory of the state; and that this means that Carré de Malberg, while professing to espouse methodological positivism, is actually closer to defending ideological positivism.

In Chapter 7, Riccardo Guastini considers the Italian tradition of legal positivism and argues that the idea of legal positivism conceived as a type of legal philosophy appeared for the first time in a 1950 essay by Norberto Bobbio, and that Bobbio proceeded in a later essay to make distinctions among methodological positivism, theoretical positivism and ideological positivism. Guastini explains that Bobbio argued that methodological positivism is a (normative) view about legal scholarship, namely, that it should be descriptive; that theoretical positivism is a substantive theory of law, according to which law is a set of commands issued by the sovereign, legal interpretation is a cognitive enterprise and the application of law is a matter of deduction; that ideological positivism is the view that one ought to obey the law regardless of its content; and that all three types of legal positivism share the view that there is no such thing as natural law. Guastini also explains that contemporary Italian legal philosophers reject theoretical positivism and mostly conceive of legal positivism along methodological lines, holding that there is no natural law, that it is important to distinguish between expository and censorial jurisprudence (in Bentham's terminology) and that there is no (objective) obligation to obey the law.

In Chapter 8, Gerald J. Postema considers the British tradition of legal positivism, arguing – contrary to the received opinion – that we may view contemporary, post-Hartian British legal positivism or, more broadly, post-Hartian British jurisprudence as having developed naturally from the legal philosophies put forward by Matthew Hale and Thomas Hobbes in the seventeenth century, which in turn were part of an earlier and philosophically more ambitious, non-positivistic tradition, the thetic tradition, dating back to Marsilius of Padua, Jean Bodin and, ultimately, to Thomas Aquinas. And if we do, Postema continues, we will see that instead of being a quirky ancestor of the British positivist tradition, Jeremy Bentham appears as the high point of the thetic tradition, which came to an end when John Austin disengaged British jurisprudence from Bentham's legal philosophy. We see, then, Postema notes, that Austin's jurisprudence changed the direction of British jurisprudence from the thetic tradition to a positivist approach to the study of jurisprudence, one that continues to this day and sees jurisprudence as isolated not only from moral philosophy and metaphysics but also from history, social theory and comparative studies. He notes in conclusion that one need not embrace Bentham's or Hobbes's substantive doctrines to sense that something may have been lost with the change of direction initiated by Austin.

Part III is devoted to central figures of legal positivism. In Chapter 9, Philip Schofield considers Jeremy Bentham's legal positivism. He explains that Bentham made a fundamental distinction between expository jurisprudence, which concerns the law as it is, and censorial jurisprudence, which concerns the law as it ought to be, and between local and universal expository jurisprudence, and that he took the subject-matter of universal expository jurisprudence to be terms (or concepts), such as 'obligation', 'right' and 'validity', that are common to all legal systems. He proceeds to point out that Bentham introduced a method for analysing or clarifying such terms, namely, the method of *paraphrasis*, according to which the analyst is to focus not on a term in isolation but on a sentence that features the term, and to attempt to find another sentence that is equivalent to the first and is such that its terms correspond to simple ideas that are derived from physical objects that we can perceive with our senses. Finally, Schofield argues, contrary to H. L. A. Hart, that Bentham was neither a substantive nor a methodological legal positivist. For, he explains, Bentham's utilitarianism, characterised by its naturalistic basis and its claim to govern every aspect of human action, led him to conceive of value judgements as a type of empirical statements and hence the idea of a conceptual separation of fact and value, as required by substantive legal positivism, would have made no sense to him. Moreover, he points out, Bentham would not have accepted the methodological view that expository jurisprudence is a value-neutral enterprise, since this enterprise, like every other, was undertaken just because of its value in terms of promoting utility.

Michael Lobban continues in Chapter 10 with a consideration of John Austin's legal positivism. Having explained that Austin thought of jurisprudence as the study of concepts, principles and distinctions that are common to various, possibly only mature, legal systems, he proceeds to consider Austin's command theory and concept of a sovereign as well as Austin's thoughts on the relation between law and morality and on legal reasoning and judge-made law. He explains that, on Austin's analysis, laws properly so-called, as distinguished from rules of positive morality, are commands issued by the sovereign to the subjects, and that something is a command only if there is a sanction behind it. He also explains that a sovereign is a person (or a body of persons) to which the bulk of the population is in a habit of obedience, and who is not themselves in a habit of obedience to another determinate human superior, and considers the objection that the idea of a habit of obedience cannot account for the legal authority of the lawmaker, for the idea of a succession of lawmakers or for the idea of a legally limited lawmaker. Lobban also observes that Austin argued that there is no necessary connection between law and morality, defended a version of rule-utilitarianism and held that the principle of utility was a good index to divine law. Finally, he points out that Austin advocated a textual approach to the interpretation of statutes, that he held that the law in a precedent is to be found in the *ratio decidendi* of the precedent and that customary rules do not become legal rules until they are recognised by courts.

Starting out from the presupposition that legal positivism is premised on the assumption of a strict separation among the world of law, the world of morality and the social world, Jens Kersten explains in Chapter 11 that George Jellinek's phenomenological theory of reflective legal positivism aims to answer the question of how the world of law is connected to, and can respond to, changes in the social world. The general idea of Jellinek's legal positivism, he explains, is that a state has two sides, a legal side and a social side, and three elements, people, territory and political power, and that these elements have to be structured and defined with the help of the concept of legal auto-limitation of political power, that is, the concept of the state's capacity to limit its own power by incurring legally binding obligations. On this analysis, Kersten points out, the central element in Jellinek's legal positivism is that of political power, which structures and defines the territory and the people (the citizens) and also structures and defines the state by binding it to legal rules, especially constitutional rules.

In Chapter 12, Michael Green defends a 'Kelsenian' non-naturalist and non-reductive version of legal positivism that, he argues, is similar to the pure theory of law expressed in Hans Kelsen's works. Kelsen is a peculiar legal positivist by Anglophone standards because he rejects the social thesis. As Kelsen sees it, law does not ultimately depend upon social facts about a community's legal practices. The legal order is normative and so stands outside the spatiotemporal and causal world of nature. Nevertheless, Kelsen can be described as a positivist for two reasons. First, he accepts the separation thesis: law does not ultimately depend upon moral facts. Second, he accepts what Green calls the 'positivity thesis'. When a world without social facts is interpreted in the light of the legal order, there are no legal obligations. All that is interpreted as existing, legally, is an authorisation: human beings are empowered to generate legal obligations by creating communities with legal practices. In this sense, all legal obligations are *posited* – only worlds with certain social facts are interpreted as having legal obligations, and the content of the obligations is drawn from those social facts.

Green argues that the heart of the Kelsenian argument against the social thesis is a form of legal anti-psychologism that is similar to the logical anti-psychologism offered by Gottlob Frege. Inferences from premises about social facts to legal conclusions cannot be based in psychological, social or any other contingent facts because the relationship between the truth of the premises and the truth of the conclusion will not be necessary. These inferences must instead be based in facts about a non-natural legal order. This is similar to Frege's argument that the necessity involved in logical inferences can be explained only by reference to a non-natural 'third realm'. It is also similar to the moral non-naturalist's argument that the necessity involved in moral inferences can be explained only by reference to a non-natural moral order.

A challenge to this Kelsenian position is the view that the non-natural facts upon which legal inferences are based concern the concept of law, not a legal order. According to these concept-of-law facts, each community has an independent legal system, and the way that one should make inferences in that system depends solely upon social facts about the relevant community's legal practices. Green argues that this approach can be successfully resisted by invoking Kelsen's doctrine of the unity of law. He concludes that the question of the viability of the doctrine is therefore a question of the utmost importance in philosophy of law.

Matthew Kramer argues in Chapter 13 that H. L. A. Hart was able to reinvigorate the tradition of legal positivism by disconnecting legal positivism from the command theory of law defended by his predecessors Bentham and Austin; by introducing through his own theory of law some new and fruitful concepts into legal thinking, such as the internal point of view, the distinction between primary and secondary rules, and the idea of a rule of recognition; by clarifying the meaning of and the reasons behind the separability of law and morality through a consideration of the many different ways in which law and morality are, or could be, connected; and by introducing the idea of the minimum content of natural law and clarifying the relation between this idea and the separability of law and morality. Kramer also explains that, even though a legal system can fulfil its basic function of securing the conditions of civilisation only if it includes rules prohibiting murder, assault, fraud and other types of very serious misconduct, the relevant protection provided by the legal system against those types of misconduct need not be extended to all groups of citizens. Consequently, because no true moral principles would permit such a difference in treatment between groups of citizens, Hart's account does not reveal any necessary connections between those principles and legal norms.

In Chapter 14, Pierluigi Chiassoni explains that, in the early 1960s, Norberto Bobbio put forward a descriptive theory of legal positivism consisting of two main parts, namely, a definition of legal positivism as the view that there is no law but positive law (the exclusivity thesis) and an analysis of such a view as one that would encompass 'three aspects', namely, legal positivism as an approach to the study of law (scientific or methodological positivism), legal positivism as a theory of positive law (theoretical positivism) and legal positivism as a doctrine of obedience to positive law qua law (ideological positivism). He proceeds to explain that legal positivism as an approach to the study of law involves a commitment to a value-neutral study of positive law; that theoretical positivism encompasses both a narrow and a broad theory; and that we may distinguish among three versions of legal positivism as a doctrine of obedience to positive law qua law, namely, (i) an unconditional version, (ii) a moderate, conditional, relative version and (iii) a very moderate, conditional, relative version, and that these versions differ in important ways. As a second dimension of Bobbio's discussion of legal positivism, Chiassoni considers Bobbio's theory of legal science, distinguishing three stages of its development and characterising them as amounting, in turn, to an anti-positivist, a positivist and a post-positivist conception of legal science, respectively.

In Chapter 15, Brian Bix considers Joseph Raz's approach to legal positivism. Bix's focus is on Raz's version of the social thesis, the so-called sources thesis, according to which all law is source-based, in the sense that the existence and content of law is determined using exclusively factual (social) considerations. He considers Raz's two main arguments in support of the sources thesis, namely, the argument from authority and the argument from different functions, as well as certain objections to these arguments put forward by other legal philosophers, including Jules Coleman, Ronald Dworkin and John Finnis. The argument from authority, he explains, is that law necessarily claims legitimate authority, that the function of a practical authority is to mediate between reasons for an action and the action, that the authority would not be able to perform this function if the subjects of the authority had to consider the reasons for the action in order to figure out what the authority's decision was, and that the subjects must be able to see the decision as the authority's pronouncement. The argument from different functions is that deliberation and execution are two different functions, that moral considerations are appropriate on the level of deliberation but not on the level of execution, that determining what the law is is a matter of discerning the products of other institutions' prior deliberation, and that while judges applying statutes and deciding cases may be involved both in executing the products of prior legislative and judicial decisions, and in deliberating anew (in modifying existing law or filling in gaps), the distinction between the two remains important.

In Chapter 16, María Cristina Redondo considers Eugenio Bulygin's legal positivism. Having explained that Bulygin is an analytical philosopher who espouses an anti-realist meta-ethics and who conceives of legal philosophy as analytical philosophy applied to the legal domain, she proceeds to explain that Bulygin's legal positivism embraces the separation thesis, a version of the social thesis (which Bulygin calls the 'social sources thesis') and an indeterminacy thesis according to which law is sometimes indeterminate and that in such a case the judge has discretion to decide the case before him; and, she adds, Bulygin holds that it follows from his version of the social thesis that law can be necessarily normative only in a weak, relative sense. Redondo explains that Bulygin espouses two methodological theses that are positivistic, namely, that the task of legal philosophers is to explicate legal concepts, and that we need to maintain in our legal thinking a distinction between norms and normative propositions; and that he espouses three substantive theses that are also positivistic, namely, that legal positivists must adopt a concept of relative normative validity in order to account for the existence of legal rights and duties, that legal interpretation must proceed on the assumption of linguistic conventionalism and that there is a fundamental and unbridgeable distinction between prescriptive and power-conferring norms. She points out that the reason why these theses can be said to be positivistic is that they all, in one way or another, make a value-neutral study of law possible, that is, they make methodological positivism possible.

Part IV is devoted to the main tenets of legal positivism, namely, the social thesis, the separation thesis, the thesis of social efficacy and the (optional) semantic thesis. The first three chapters are devoted to the social thesis. Conceiving of legal positivism as a conceptual theory about the nature, as distinguished from the validity, of law, and focusing on an important version of legal positivism thus conceived, namely social-practice legal positivism, Stefano Bertea considers in Chapter 17 two ways of understanding the social thesis, namely, along the lines of legal conventionalism and law as a shared activity, respectively. He argues that on neither interpretation of the social thesis can social-practice legal positivism account for the necessary normativity of law, that is, for the necessary capacity of law to impose (genuine) obligations and confer (genuine) rights on both officials and citizens. Bertea points out that there are fundamentally two ways in which legal positivists conceptualise legal obligation, namely, as a genuine requirement set forth in the law or else as a perspectival requirement, and that on the former conceptualisation, legal obligations will bind only those who are committed to the legal enterprise, and that on the latter, they will bind only those who adopt the standpoint of the legal system; and he objects that on the former conceptualisation, legal positivism fails to account for legal obligations that apply to the citizens, and that on the latter interpretation, it turns out that law is not really necessarily obligation-imposing at all.

In Chapter 18, Tomasz Gizbert-Studnicki considers the question of how we are to understand the social thesis and whether the social thesis, properly understood, can handle Hume's guillotine, that is, the thesis that one cannot deduce a normative (or an evaluative) conclusion from a (consistent) set of factual premises. Having distinguished three interpretations of the social thesis, he proceeds to focus on one of these, the social fact thesis, according to which the existence and the content of legal facts are ultimately fully determined by brute social facts, and which is stronger than the other two theses. Gizbert-Studnicki then considers three different ways of understanding the relation between social facts and legal facts along the lines of the social fact thesis, namely, reduction, supervenience and grounding. He maintains that, while all three relations are more or less problematic, the grounding relation is to be preferred, and that adopting the idea of grounding helps us avoid Hume's guillotine. For, he points out, grounding is not a matter of entailment, which is a relation between propositions, but is a metaphysical relation that holds between facts.

Torben Spaak argues in Chapter 19 that legal positivists need to consider the social thesis in light of an important distinction between two levels of legal thinking, namely, the level of the sources of law (validity or existence) and the level of the interpretation and application of law (content), and that they have good reason to restrict the scope of the social thesis to the former level. He argues that, by restricting the scope of the social thesis in this way, inclusive legal positivists can avoid having to assume that moral judgements can be true in a non-relative way, that exclusive legal positivists can avoid having to say that judges are creating new law instead of applying pre-existing law, if and insofar as they invoke moral considerations in their interpretation and application of the law, and that both inclusive and exclusive legal positivists can avoid Dworkin's theoretical disagreement objection. He argues in conclusion that legal positivism conceived as a theory about the validity or existence of law will still be a significant theory. For, he points out, since judges and other law-appliers rarely deviate from the plain meaning of statutory provisions, even 'uninterpreted' legal norms can guide human behaviour; and this means that legal positivism thus conceived retains a feature valued by all legal positivists, namely, that it makes it possible to present the law of the land in a morally neutral way.

Andrei Marmor continues in Chapter 20 with a consideration of the separation thesis, which he understands as saying that whether a given norm is legally valid (in the sense of being a member of the relevant legal system) depends on its sources, not its merits. Observing that the distinction between sources and merits is very close to the distinction between *is* and *ought*, he considers the objection – raised by Ronald Dworkin, in particular – that the separation thesis cannot be upheld because it is impossible to distinguish between sources and merits, between is and ought. Responding to this objection, Marmor considers not only the case of what grounds the validity of legal norms but also the parallel case of what makes an object a piece of art, and argues that the separation thesis can indeed be upheld, provided we see it as an answer not to the question 'What is law?' but to the question 'What *counts* as law?'. He concludes by pointing out that his response is in keeping with a central concern on the part of legal positivists, namely, that of providing a reductive explanation of legal validity, that is, a complete explanation of legal validity in terms of social facts, and that it also offers support for exclusive over inclusive legal positivism.

In Chapter 21, Wil Waluchow considers the theories known as inclusive and exclusive legal positivism. He begins by explaining that the idea behind the separation thesis is that there is nothing in the bare notion of law that guarantees that law has any degree of moral merit, and proceeds to present Ronald Dworkin's challenge to the separation thesis, namely, that since law necessarily consists not only of the so-called settled law (statutes, precedents and so forth) but also of the principles of political morality that are part of the best constructive interpretation of the settled law, the connection between what the law is and what the law ought to be is much stronger than the separation thesis allows for. He then considers the responses to Dworkin's challenge by the adherents to exclusive and inclusive positivism, respectively: Whereas exclusive positivists insist that the separation thesis, properly understood, has it that, as a conceptual matter, legal validity cannot depend on morality, inclusive positivists maintain instead that the thesis has it that legal validity can, but need not, depend on morality. Finally, Waluchow considers and rejects Joseph Raz's argument from authority, which supports the exclusivist interpretation of the separation thesis, while accepting Jules Coleman's argument from convention, which supports the inclusivist interpretation of said thesis, adding that inclusive legal positivism can more easily account for the ways in which moral and legal validity appear to interact with each other in modern constitutional democracies.

In Chapter 22, Brian Tamanaha discusses the thesis of social efficacy, that for law to exist it must be generally obeyed by the populace. He begins by arguing that not only are many legal systems not socially efficacious, because in many situations significant parts of the population do not obey the law but follow other sets of norms, but it is also true that two (or more) legal orders may be efficacious in the same society, sometimes in different parts of a country. He concludes from this that what he refers to as the monopoly view of law, that there is in each society one and only one legal order that is supreme, on which much legal theorising is premised, is clearly false. Turning to the idea of law-obedience, which is required by the social efficacy thesis and which he takes to involve as a conceptual matter a conscious attempt on the part of the citizens to follow the law, Tamanaha argues that the notion that the citizens obey the law cannot be squared with the fact that many, perhaps most, people do not really know what the law requires of them, and that this in turn means that we need a different conception of social efficacy, namely, one according to which the social efficacy of law is to be found in the presence of a background legal fabric that people rely on without having any specific knowledge of the content of the law. He then explains the import of this idea of social efficacy in terms of five factors, including the growth and proliferation in the past 200 years of law-utilising public and private organisations as the predominant vehicles of social action, and the frequent use of fixed form contracts.

Michael S. Green concludes this part of the volume, in Chapter 23, with a consideration of a strong version of the semantic thesis, according to which legal statements are descriptive statements solely about social facts. He starts out from the foundational thesis of positivism, the social thesis, which has it that the existence and content of the law are ultimately based solely in social facts about a community. But Green notes that there are two versions of this thesis. Under the reduction version, a legal system and its laws consist of social facts. Under the assignment version, by contrast, they are not social entities at all. They are norms, understood as abstract objects. But the grounds for assigning these abstract objects to a community are ultimately solely social facts. Focusing on the assignment version of the social thesis, Green asks, first, 'Does the semantic thesis follow from the social thesis?' His answer to this question is no. Even if the social thesis is true, legal statements need not be solely about social facts. Indeed, they could be about moral facts. He then asks, 'Even if the semantic thesis does not follow from the social thesis, to what extent do legal statements actually conform to the semantic thesis?' He argues that, for assignment positivists, there is an easy reason to conclude that the answer to the second question is negative in the sense that legal statements describe abstract objects. Green argues that this simple account of the semantics of legal statements is superior to expressivist accounts because it avoids the Frege-Geach problem. It is also superior to Raz's account, in which legal statements describe moral facts, because it can explain why those who make legal statements need not be committed to conformity with the law. He also argues that the simple account, not expressivism, is the one adopted by H. L. A. Hart.

Part V concerns questions about normativity and values in relation to legal positivism. Kevin Toh begins in Chapter 24 by arguing that legal philosophers inquiring into the nature of law should follow meta-ethicists and abandon (what Toh calls) the double-duty presumption – that is, the presumption that the facts that amount to the existence of a legal system must also constitute the ultimate grounds of first-order legal judgments. Still, Toh explores the possibility of there being some sort of non-contingent connection between first-order legal thinking and second-order theorising about the nature of law, or, more specifically, the possibility of the facts that amount to the existence of a legal system imposing some modal constraints on the composition of ultimate legal grounds, so that only norms that satisfy certain moral or all-things-considered normative tests qualify as legally valid norms. He considers, in particular, Peter Railton's recent attempt to strengthen Hart's account of acceptance of norms by arguing that, in genuine normative guidance, acceptances must be accompanied by positive evaluations of the goals or purposes that would be achieved by following the norms. Toh concludes, however, that, in the end, Railton's account of legal systems, based on his account of normative guidance, does not quite implicate a significant modal constraint on the composition of the ultimate legal grounds. And this result counsels against conceiving both legal positivism and anti-positivism as anything more than strictly first-order legal theses about the law of particular jurisdictions.

In Chapter 25, Brian Bix considers the question of the normativity of law within the framework of legal positivism. He begins by pointing out that the very idea of the normativity of law has been understood in different ways by different authors, and while writers on the normativity of law often purport to be 'explaining the normativity of law', it is often left unclear precisely what is meant by that. He goes on to propose that we analyse the concept of normativity in terms of reasons for action, arguing that such reasons must be something more than prudential reasons and pointing out that the proper question is whether law gives us reasons for actions of the relevant type that we would not have without law. He also considers the difficulty that Hume's law creates for legal positivists who wish to account for the normativity of law, and the possibility of legal normativity as *sui generis*. Bix proceeds to consider consequentialist justifications for the normativity of law proposed by Hobbes and Hume, Kelsen's theory of the basic norm, Gerald Postema's claim that the rule of recognition is a coordination convention, Scott Shapiro's planning theory of law, and David Enoch's triggering account, according to which law gives rise to reasons for action by triggering non-legal reasons that already apply to us. Given the problems with these approaches, Bix concludes that it is difficult to establish from within the legal positivist tradition that law creates entirely new moral obligations.

In Chapter 26, José Juan Moreso considers Luigi Ferrajoli's 'Garantismo', a theory of law related to legal positivism that has been quite influential in the Italian- and Spanish-speaking world. He explains that the word 'Garantismo' suggests a conception of law as a system of constitutional guarantees of human rights, and distinguishes two main ideas in Ferrajoli's theory, namely, the separability (separation) thesis and a distinction between valid law and law in force. Ferrajoli's idea, Moreso explains, is that the introduction into a legal system of constitutional rights gives rise to a distinction between validity and social efficacy, since even if a statute enacted by the legislature violates a constitutional right, it might become socially effective. He points out, however, that the distinction between legal validity and legal existence is not new and can actually be traced back to the *Federalist Papers* and the American case *Marbury* v. *Madison* of 1803, and that Ferrajoli's conception of constitutional democracy is very similar to Dworkin's conception. Having done that, Moreso introduces Ferrajoli's distinction between a constitutionalism of guarantees and a constitutionalism of rights, where the former, positivistic conception of constitutionalism accepts the separability thesis and conceives of legal norms as rules, and the latter, anti-positivistic conception rejects the separability thesis and conceives of legal norms as rules or principles. He criticises this distinction and Ferrajoli's preference for the former conception, however, arguing that – contrary to what Ferrajoli thinks – accepting a distinction between rules and principles does not have to lead to lack of legal certainty. Finally, Moreso points out that Ferrajoli is best thought of as an inclusive legal positivist.

Part VI, finally, is devoted to critiques of legal positivism. Martin Borowski argues in Chapter 27 that Radbruch's most important critique of legal positivism is to be found not in his explicit writings on legal positivism but in his own legal philosophy, especially the so-called Radbruch formula of 1946, and that the Radbruch formula entails a rejection of the separation thesis with an eye to the criteria for the identification of valid legal norms. What is more, he argues that Radbruch's basal criterion, according to which 'law is the reality whose meaning is to serve justice' – the basal criterion Radbruch supported even before World War II – implies a necessary connection between law and morality. Radbruch's explicit claim, Borowski goes on, that legal positivism was to blame for the situation in Germany is unconvincing because the Nazis did not, as a matter of fact, hold that law is law and should be applied according to its plain meaning in all circumstances but were actually willing to apply a statute contrary to its wording if this suited their purposes.

In Chapter 28, Kenneth Winston argues that Lon Fuller's critique of legal positivism was rather special in focusing on issues that lay beneath the surface of the usual intramural disputes, and thus related only indirectly to what positivists such as Kelsen and Hart said explicitly when expounding their views. Winston explains that, as a pragmatist, Fuller largely eschewed conceptual or semantic questions, focusing instead on questions of methodology and governance, in particular the adequacy of a scientific approach to understanding human society and the role played by agency and purpose in ordering civic life. In a phrase, Fuller faulted legal positivists for encouraging the kind of social engineering perspective reflected in bureaucratic/regulatory states. As he saw it, the importance of a pragmatic jurisprudence – and its superiority over other social sciences – lies precisely in the practical experience and concerns that lawyers possess (and other social scientists lack) and that they bring to bear in fashioning the participatory social architecture that is better at protecting human freedom.

Dennis Patterson argues in Chapter 29 that Dworkin's critique of legal positivism, specifically Dworkin's critique of Hart's positivistic theory of law, went through two stages, first the critique put forward in Dworkin's 1967 article 'The Model of Rules', which focused on the alleged inability of the rule of recognition to account for the existence of legal principles, and then the critique that found expression in *Law's Empire* and concerned the theory's alleged inability to account for the existence of theoretical disagreement in law. Patterson's conclusion, however, is that, although Dworkin, in his mature critique, made a number of valid points, such as identifying the lack of a thought-out view on legal interpretation in Hart's legal philosophy, he ultimately failed to undermine Hart's theory. As Patterson sees it, although legal positivists lack a thought-out view of legal interpretation, there is nothing in the theory of legal positivism that stops them from developing such a theory, and he suggests three crucial criteria that a positivistic theory of legal interpretation must satisfy, namely, minimal mutilation of existing law, coherence and generality.

In Chapter 30, Veronica Rodriguez-Blanco clarifies and develops John Finnis's objection to legal positivism in the shape of Hart's theory, namely, that it is unstable because it utilises the notion of an internal point of view, which does not have sufficient discriminatory power to distinguish, as participants in the legal practice wish to do, between good and not so good legal norms, between rational and non-rational court decisions, and so forth. She explains that Finnis's account of human action is superior to Hart's because Finnis realises that understanding human action in law involves understanding the *point* of the action, and that such understanding requires the use of the Aristotelian focal meaning (or central case) methodology, which does have sufficient discriminatory power to distinguish between good and not so good norms, and so forth. The reason why theories of Hart's general type are unstable, and theories of Finnis's general type are not, she explains, is that the former, but not the latter, are unable to account for the causal link between mental state and action. Rodriguez-Blanco also argues that, as a result of the concentration in the past fifty years or so on the part of Anglophone legal philosophers on Dworkin's critique of Hart's legal positivism, legal philosophers have missed an opportunity to learn, through studying and debating Finnis's critique of Hart's theory, about the philosophy of practical reason and the theory of action; and that this in turn means that now they are not in as good a position as they might have been to contribute significantly to debates about normative questions and learn about the nature of law and its relation to agency, reasons for action and goodness.

Jan Sieckmann argues in Chapter 31 that the central claim of Robert Alexy's critique of legal positivism is that there is a necessary connection between morality and the content of law, and that therefore the separation thesis is false; and he explains that whereas, in his earlier writings, Alexy adduced three distinct arguments in support of the connection thesis, namely, the argument from injustice, the argument from principles and the argument from the necessary claim of law to correctness, he has substituted in his later writings a more general argument from the dual nature of law for the three mentioned, more specific arguments. Having explained that Alexy situates his critique within the perspective of a participant, as distinguished from the perspective of an observer, Sieckmann goes on to maintain that Alexy has changed the focus of the debate about legal positivism from a primary concern with questions of legal validity to a more general concern with questions of the nature of law by emphasising that in addition to the usual classifying connections between morality, on the one hand, and legal systems, legal acts and legal norms, on the other, there are also qualifying connections. For, he explains, Alexy holds that whereas a (purported) legal system that does not raise a claim to correctness lacks legal character (the idea of a classifying connection), a legal system that raises but does not satisfy a claim to correctness, and individual legal acts and legal norms that do not raise a claim to correctness, or raise one that they do not satisfy, are legally defective (the idea of a qualifying connection). Sieckmann concludes that Alexy has shown that, for those who choose to adopt the perspective of a participant, legal positivism is not an adequate theory of law.

Barbara Baum Levenbook considers in Chapter 32 Mark Greenberg's critique of legal positivism. She explains that Greenberg objects to legal positivism, first, that it is a mistake to hold that legal facts are determined solely by social facts, since this means that one cannot account for the normativity of legal obligations, and, second, that legal positivists are committed to a flawed theory of legal content, according to which the content of authoritative pronouncements, such as statutes, is determined by their linguistic contents. She objects to Greenberg's reasoning, however, that the first objection is premised on the mistaken assumption that it is in the nature of law that the connection between legal facts and the metaphysical determinants of legal facts is, as Greenberg puts it, 'rationally intelligible' in a certain way, and that the second objection is based on the equally mistaken assumption – the bindingness hypothesis – that it is part of the nature of law that it is to reliably ensure that legal obligations are genuinely binding. Levenbook concludes by considering and rejecting Greenberg's own theory of law, the moral impact theory, which has it that legal obligations are moral obligations arising in a certain way from the actions of legal institutions and which, in doing so, offers an alternative account of the (alleged) bindingness of legal obligations.

In the final chapter of the volume, Chapter 33, David Dyzenhaus argues that Hart's defence of legal positivism fails because Hart cannot without contradiction espouse both the claim that there is no necessary connection between law and morality and the claim that law has authority, that law, as Hart once put it, is not the gunman situation writ large. Moreover, a theory that satisfies the two claims in combination would be a theory of the type that scholars in the Latin world refer to as ideological positivism. Dyzenhaus maintains, more specifically, that although Hart argued that legal positivism in the shape of the separation thesis is conducive to clear thinking and facilitates moral critique of the law, his failure to follow through on his insights about the authority of law leads to a theory of law that has the totalitarian implications alleged by several critics of positivism. Dyzenhaus concludes by saying that his plea in this chapter is for legal philosophy to return to the task set out by Radbruch and others of trying to understand how a legal order can vindicate its claim to be an order of legitimate authority, a task that can hardly be accomplished as long as legal scholars adhere to the separation thesis of legal positivism.

References

Alexy, R. 2002. *The Argument from Injustice: A Reply to Legal Positivism.* Oxford University Press.

Austin, J. [1832]1998. *The Province of Jurisprudence Determined* and *The Uses of the Study of Jurisprudence. With an Introduction by H.L.A. Hart.* Hackett.

Bentham, J. [1776]1988. *A Fragment on Government: The New Authoritative Edition by J.H. Burns and H.L.A Hart. With an Introduction by R. Harrison.* Cambridge University Press.

Bratman, M. E. 2011. 'Reflections on Law, Normativity and Plans'. In S. Bertea and G. Pavlakos (eds.). *New Essays on the Normativity of Law.* Hart Publishing: 73–85.

Burazin, L. 2017. 'The Concept of Law and Efficacy'. In M. Sellers and S. Kirste (eds.). *Encyclopedia of the Philosophy of Law and Social Philosophy.* Springer: 1–7.

Coleman, J. L. 1982. 'Negative and Positive Positivism'. *Journal of Legal Studies* 11: 139–64.

Coleman, J. L. 2001. *The Practice of Principle.* Oxford University Press.

Coleman, J. L. 2009. 'Beyond Inclusive Legal Positivism'. *Ratio Juris* 22: 359–94.

Duarte D'Almeida, L. 2011. 'Legal Statements and Normative Language'. *Law and Philosophy* 30: 167–99.

Dworkin, R. 1978. *Taking Rights Seriously.* 2nd ed. Duckworth.

Dworkin, R. 1986. *Law's Empire.* Belknap Press.

Fuller, L. 1958. 'Positivism and Fidelity to Law: A Reply to Professor Hart'. *Harvard Law Review* 71: 630–72.

Gardner, J. 2012. 'Legal Positivism: 5½Myths'. In J. Gardner. *Law as a Leap of Faith.* Oxford University Press: 19–53.

Green, L. 2008. 'The Inseparability of Law and Morality'. *New York University Law Review* 83: 1035–58.

Green, L. 2018. 'Legal Positivism'. In E. N. Zalta (ed.). *The Stanford Encyclopedia of Philosophy.* https://plato.stanford.edu/archives/spr2018/entries/legal-positivism/.

Hart, H. L. A. 1958. 'Positivism and the Separation of Law and Morals'. *Harvard Law Review* 71: 593–629.

Hart, H. L. A. 1961. *The Concept of Law.* Clarendon Press.

Hart, H. L. A. 1982. *Essays on Bentham.* Oxford University Press.

Hart, H. L. A. 1994. *The Concept of Law with a Postscript.* Eds. P. A. Bulloch and J. Raz. 2nd ed. Oxford University Press.

Holmes, O. W. 1896–7. 'The Path of the Law'. *Harvard Law Review* 10: 457–78.

Honoré, T. 1987. *Making Law Bind.* Clarendon Press.

Kelsen, H. 1948. 'Absolutism and Relativism in Philosophy and Politics'. *The American Political Science Review* 42: 906–14.

Kelsen, H. 1959–60. 'What Is the Pure Theory of Law?'. *Tulane Law Review* 34: 269–76.

Kelsen, H. 1960. *Reine Rechtslehre.* 2nd ed. Österreichische Staatsdruckerei.

Kelsen, H. 1992. *Introduction to the Problems of Legal Theory.* Trans. B. Litschewski Paulson and S. L. Paulson. Oxford University Press.

Kelsen, H. 1999. *General Theory of Law and State.* Trans. A. Wedberg. The Lawbook Exchange.

Kramer, M. H. 1999. *In Defense of Legal Positivism: Law without Trimmings.* Oxford University Press.

Kramer, M. H. 2009. *Moral Realism as a Moral Doctrine.* Blackwell Publishing.

Lyons, D. 1977. 'Principles, Positivism and Legal Theory: Dworkin "Taking Rights Seriously"'. *Yale Law Journal* 87: 415–35.

MacCormick, N. 1987. 'Comments'. In R. Gavison (ed.). *Issues in Contemporary Legal Philosophy: The Influence of H.L.A. Hart.* Oxford University Press: 105–13.

Mackie, J. 1977a. *Ethics: Inventing Right and Wrong.* Penguin.

Mackie, J. 1977b. 'The Third Theory of Law'. *Philosophy and Phenomenological Affairs* 7: 3–16.

Marmor, A. 2011. 'The Conventional Foundations of Law'. In S. Bertea and G. Pavlakos (eds.). *New Essays on the Normativity of Law*. Hart Publishing: 143–57.

Olivecrona, K. 1971. *Law as Fact*. 2nd ed. Stevens & Sons.

Paulson, S. L. 2012. 'A "Justified Normativity" Thesis in Hans Kelsen's Pure Theory of Law?' In M. Klatt (ed.). *Institutionalized Reason: The Jurisprudence of Robert Alexy*. Oxford University Press: 61–111.

Perry, S. R. 2001. 'Hart's Methodological Positivism'. In J. L. Coleman (ed.). *Hart's Postscript: Essays on the Postscript to the Concept of Law*. Oxford University Press: 311–54.

Postema, G. 1982. 'Coordination and Convention at the Foundation of Law'. *Journal of Legal Studies* 11: 165–203.

Radbruch, G. 2006. 'Statutory Lawlessness and Supra-Statutory Law'. *Oxford Journal of Legal Studies* 26: 1–11.

Raz, J. 1980. *The Concept of a Legal System*. 2nd ed. Clarendon Press.

Raz, J. 1983. 'Hart on Moral Rights and Legal Duties'. *Oxford Journal of Legal Studies* 4: 123–31.

Raz, J. 1986. 'Dworkin: A New Link in the Chain'. *California Law Review* 74: 1103–19.

Raz, J. 1990. *Practical Reason and Norms*. 2nd ed. Princeton University Press.

Raz, J. 1999. 'Moral Change and Social Relativism'. In J. Raz. *Engaging Reason: On the Theory of Value and Action*. Oxford University Press: 161–81.

Raz, J. 2001. 'Universality and Difference'. In J. Raz. *Value, Respect, and Attachment*. Cambridge University Press: 41–76.

Raz, J. 2007. 'The Argument from Justice, or How Not to Reply to Legal Positivism'. In G. Pavlakos (ed.). *Law, Rights and Discourse*. Hart Publishing: 17–35.

Raz, J. 2009. 'Legal Positivism and the Sources of Law'. In J. Raz. *The Authority of Law*. 2nd ed. Oxford University Press: 37–52.

Ross, A. 1959. *On Law and Justice*. University of California Press.

Shapiro, S. 2011. 'Planning Agency and the Law'. In S. Bertea and G. Pavlakos (eds.). *New Essays on the Normativity of Law*. Hart Publishing: 17–72.

Simmonds, N. 2002. *Central Issues in Jurisprudence*. 2nd ed. Sweet & Maxwell.

Soper, P. 1977. 'Legal Theory and the Obligation of a Judge: The Hart/Dworkin Dispute'. *Michigan Law Review* 75: 473–519.

Van Roojen, M. 2015. *Metaethics: A Contemporary Introduction*. Routledge.

Waldron, J. 2001. 'Normative (or Ethical) Positivism'. In J. L. Coleman (ed.). *Essays on the Postscript to the Concept of Law*. Oxford University Press: 411–33.

Waluchow, W. J. 1994. *Inclusive Legal Positivism*. Oxford University Press.

Williams, B. 1973. *A Critique of Utilitarianism*. In J. C. C. Smart and B. Williams (eds.). *Utilitarianism: For and Against*. Cambridge University Press: 75–150.

Wittgenstein, L. 1960. *The Blue and Brown Books*. 2nd ed. Harper and Row.

Wittgenstein, L. 1968. *Philosophical Investigations*. 3rd ed. Eds. G. E. M. Anscombes and R. Rhees. Trans. G. E. M. Anscombe. Macmillan.

Part I

Fundamentals

Positivism, Realism and Sources of Law 2

Leslie Green[1]

2.1 The Essentials of Legal Positivism

We should not make too much of party labels in philosophy, including 'legal positivism'. Jeremy Bentham and John Austin were energetic partisans, but the party that energised them was philosophical radicalism, not legal positivism.[2] Nor did H. L. A. Hart write *The Concept of Law* to show loyalty to the positivist tradition in English legal thought; he sought to explain the nature of law and, along the way, appropriated ideas from others, including natural lawyers and legal realists. Perhaps Hans Kelsen wrote *in order to* produce a positivist philosophy, that is, with the aim of disciplining theoretical reflection on law by strictures he considered methodologically positivist or, as he put it, 'scientific' – but even Kelsen modified those as his thought developed. And today, influential advocates of legal positivism often adopt that label somewhat diffidently and with qualifications: Jules Coleman, Julie Dickson, John Gardner, Matthew Kramer, Brian Leiter, Andrei Marmor, Joseph Raz, Frederick Schauer, Wil Waluchow and others would probably describe their own theories as 'positivist, but . . .'. Their hesitations reflect a natural reluctance to associate a sound theory of law with the distracting, misleading and even mistaken doctrines that have adhered to it over the years. Thus, it is hard to find contemporary positivists who still hold that law is the command of a sovereign, that law is the product of explicit or tacit legislation, that there is a sharp distinction between applying and creating law or that there are no necessary connections between law and morality – all claims once associated with legal positivism.[3] But one doctrine remains essential: any

[1] I thank Denise Réaume, the late John Gardner and, especially, Brian Leiter for many discussions of these issues and for criticism of earlier versions of this chapter.

[2] See Halevy 1934. Austin grew more conservative in later years.

[3] See Gardner 2001; Green 2008.

theory of law that *a positivist* would be willing to call 'positivist' endorses a version of the following claim: *All law is positive law.*[4]

Of course, nearly everyone agrees that *some* law is positive, meaning that its existence and content are fixed by considerations of social fact, including facts about what people actually believe, want, intend and decide, whether individually or in concert.[5] What is distinctive of legal positivism is the claim that this is true *of all law*. Law is positive if and only if it is created by human thought and action: By actual, datable events such as people deliberating, deciding, ordering, accepting, tolerating, conforming or obeying. As this (incomplete) list shows, not all positive law is created by acts performed with the intention of creating law, so positive law need not be legislated. And, if an artefact is something that is made intentionally, law need not be an artefact either. It can be an *objet trouvé* that someone puts to a fresh, legal use. Law can also be made unintentionally: a custom may emerge by invisible hand mechanisms yet satisfy the prevailing criteria for legal validity in that legal system; a ruling can be made solely to settle a particular dispute, but have the upshot of changing the law for many future cases; a piece of judicial reasoning can silently introduce, en route to its conclusion, a presupposition that is later treated as legally binding. And so on.

Such positive events produce the 'sources' of law in a legal system: the constitutions, treaties, statutes, decisions and customary practices on which lawyers rely in argument and by which judges are bound in their rulings. Another familiar way of epitomising legal positivism is thus to say that it is the view that *all law has sources*, where a source can be identified in a content-independent way, apart from its merits.[6] Moreover, many sources involve

[4] I ignore the pejorative use of 'positivist' once current in American law schools: a mélange of doctrines that no serious philosopher ever endorsed, including the idea that law is always clear, that 'plain meaning' is the only proper approach to interpretation, that judges never make law and that, however foolish or unjust, the law is to be obeyed and applied. For discussion, see Schauer 1999.

[5] The most prominent exception is Ronald Dworkin, who comes close to suggesting that there is *no* fully positive law and that anything worth counting as a legal system and anything worth acknowledging as a law must satisfy a demanding moral condition: Dworkin 1986. Similarly, Greenberg 2014. In contrast, neo-Thomist natural lawyers typically affirm the existence of ordinary positive law: Finnis 2011; Murphy 2006.

[6] Some hold that all law is *ultimately* source based (but may include non-ultimate, non-source-based materials); others hold that all law is *wholly* source based. This is the distinction between 'inclusive' and 'exclusive' legal positivism: Waluchow 1994. I do not examine that debate here. My own view conforms to an exclusive interpretation of the idea that all law is positive. For discussion, see Green and Adams 2019 and Raz 1979: ch. 3.

norms of a general character, rules created under the authority of, or using, other rules. Hence, a third familiar way of characterising positivism is to say that *law is a system of social rules.*

These three characterisations differ in nuance, but I will use them interchangeably. My interest here is not in defending a particular version of legal positivism but in exploring the relationships between positivism (in its essentials) and its closest cousin in the evolution of jurisprudential thought: legal realism. Brian Leiter says that legal realists also believe that all law is positive law, and, at one point, Hart riskily describes his own theory as a kind of 'descriptive sociology' of law.[7] Yet some realists have thought, or said, that they disagree with legal positivism, and textbooks in jurisprudence still include set-piece debates between positivism and realism. How can this be, if realists accept the essentials of legal positivism? I will try to answer that question. Like Leiter's, my conclusion is conciliatory, for I, too, think that the differences have been exaggerated. But I offer a different explanation of how the misunderstandings arose.

2.2 Upshots of the Essentials

Legal positivism has been doubted on many grounds, often rooted in what are taken to be inevitable but unacceptable upshots of the essential positivist thesis. Here are four such claims, each accompanied by a brief remark suggesting how positivists address it. There then follows a fifth upshot of the positivist thesis. I will explain why that one is no mistake, then turn to consider its bearing on the relationship between positivism and realism. Mainly, I have in mind American legal realism – not only the historical variety but also the casual, untheorised 'realism' or 'functionalism' that circulates in many substantive subjects in law schools. Where I need a specific version of legal positivism, I will enlist work by H. L. A. Hart, somewhat inflected by my own views.

First are four familiar objections (to be read in a *reductio* tone of voice):

(1) 'If law were wholly positive, law could have no real value, since mere facts cannot entail values.' *But*: It is wrong to suppose that whatever value law has must follow – and follow as an entailment – solely from true propositions about law's nature.

[7] See Chapter 4 (this volume); Hart 2012: v; Leiter 2007.

(2) 'Law is a purposive activity, so law cannot solely be a matter of fact.' *But*: It is wrong to suppose that a historical, factual activity cannot be identified partly by the purposes for which it is undertaken. An election, for example, is a purposive activity.
(3) 'If law were positive, legal systems could not be identified by their contribution to human goods.' *But*: Institutions and artefacts may have constitutive aims to promote well-being. Nothing is a sewage system that is not oriented to promoting public health, yet the existence (and content!) of a sewage system is a matter of plain empirical fact.
(4) 'If law were positive, there would be no guarantee that there is always a prima facie moral duty to obey it.' *But*: There is no reason to believe in such a duty, as opposed to, say, a duty to give due weight to the requirements of an effective and potentially beneficial institution.

The quoted propositions in (1) to (4) reflect familiar errors about the essential thesis of positivism. The telegraphic replies could be, and have been, endorsed by both legal positivists and legal realists. But now consider this upshot:

(5) 'If law were positive, then the law would be incomplete and, on some matters, there would be no conclusive law.' No *buts* about it: This does indeed follow and is true.

There are three related reasons why the consequent in (5) follows from the essential positivist thesis, together with some other true propositions:

(A) The sources of law are finite. The UK constitution contains all the powers needed to create an infinite number of statutes. But most of those have not *been* created, including many for which there is an overwhelming moral need. Law provides for, and regulates, the creation of law 'dynamically', as Kelsen put it: by being used. Hence, if an existing set of legal norms would justify, or even logically entail, further norms, those further norms would not be law unless someone were to endorse or presuppose or otherwise use that justification.
(B) All legal sources are somewhat indeterminate, owing to the related phenomena of ambiguity, vagueness and the fact that there is always more than one permissible way of applying a legal norm, even a mandatory norm.[8]

[8] 'The higher norm cannot bind in every direction the act by which it is applied. There must always be more or less room for discretion, so that the higher norm in relation to the lower one can only have the character of a frame to be filled by this act'. Kelsen 1967: 349.

(C) There are unresolved conflicts among laws. An action that is permissible according to one rule may be impermissible according to another. Legal systems do have positive, conflict-resolving rules, but the list of conflict-resolving rules is finite (see A), those rules are themselves indeterminate (see B) and they may, in any case, never get applied, since a conflict may go unnoticed or not be worth resolving.

Hence, positive law is incomplete, and some legal disputes lack a single right answer in law. Some writers think that is a powerful objection to legal positivism.[9] But legal realists do not think so, at least not if they have mastered the distinction between legal positivism and so-called formalism. Like positivists, legal realists understand that the rule of law cannot be fully realised, not least because it has multiple desiderata that may conflict *inter se*. The law should be stable, but it should also be clear, such that intolerably vague provisions can be cured only by introducing instability into the law, that is, by changing it. In any event, a society completely ruled by law is not an attractive ideal. It is better to leave judges some discretion to accommodate the equities in a particular case and as a prophylactic against formalistic fantasies of fixing the law for the future, in ignorance of what sorts of law we shall need. Here, positivism and realism are at one.

2.3 Indeterminacy and Realism

Positivism, as I understand it, contributes to a conceptual explanation of law. By that I mean that it aims to deepen our understanding of law by examining *what counts as what*; it has only a secondary interest in counting up instances of the various *whats*. How then could there be any conflict between positivism and a theory that acknowledges that all law is source-based but adds that courts' decisions cannot generally be explained by positive law, though they can be explained by extralegal considerations, including the court's sense of what would be fair in a case, what common sense or efficiency requires, or what suits their judicial style or temperament? The essential positivist thesis is a claim about *how law is determined*, not a claim about *how much of a judicial decision is determined by law*. On the latter issue, Kelsen says that '[t]here *must always be* more or less room

[9] Most insistently, Dworkin 1977. See, in reply, Raz 1979: ch. 4.

for discretion',[10] and Hart insists that, in every legal system, 'a *large and important field* is left open for the discretion of courts and other officials'.[11] Positivists are not indeterminacy-minimisers. Indeed, as the discussion of upshot (5) shows, the incompleteness of law is intimately connected with its nature as a social institution.

One source of friction, if not disagreement, between realists and positivists arises this way: Positivists hold that law is wholly constituted by social facts, but a realist might ask *what use is it* to know fact-constituted law if it gets little traction in court? However, there is such a thing as useless knowledge. Perhaps some realists share Dworkin's view that the only sensible career ambition for jurisprudence is to become a kind of highbrow *amicus curiae*. Felix Cohen wrote:

> Fundamentally there are only two significant questions in the field of law. One is, 'How do courts actually decide cases of a given kind?' The other is, 'How ought they to decide cases of a given kind?' Unless a legal 'problem' can be subsumed under one of these forms, it is not a meaningful question and any answer to it must be nonsense.[12]

Yet Cohen misses something. Whenever we have two meaningful questions, we perforce have a third: What is the relationship between the first two questions?

According to one view, Cohen's questions are independent. There are psychological and sociological questions about the causes of judicial decisions and there are normative questions – moral or legal – about how such decisions ought to be made. These enquiries do not compete and may not converse. This tolerant view takes no sides in general jurisprudence; it is held by H. L. A. Hart[13] but also by Ronald Dworkin, who not only acknowledges the legitimacy of legal sociology but says that it is entitled to its very own concept of law – the 'sociological concept of law'.[14]

Competing with the independence view are two imperialistic ones: for Kelsen, normative questions take conceptual priority over factual ones; for realists, the reverse is true. Kelsen holds that intelligible enquiry into the causes of judicial decisions *presupposes* a normative (but not moral) theory of adjudication. Legal and political entities are norm-constituted, and,

[10] Kelsen 1967: 349 (emphasis added). [11] Hart 2012: 136 (emphasis added).
[12] Cohen 1935: 824. [13] See Hart 1983: 'Problems of the Philosophy of Law'.
[14] Dworkin 2008: 2–3; but contrast his more Kelsenian view in Dworkin 1986: 12–13, relying on the idea that law is *necessarily* an argumentative (normative) practice.

while we can and should aim for a descriptive theory of a normative object, the theory must preserve the character of the object it explains. A legal system is a system of norms directing judges how they *ought* to decide cases, not a set of predictions about how they *will in fact* decide, so the former is the proper object of jurisprudence. Admittedly, Kelsen thinks that sociological jurisprudence and legal positivism cannot come entirely unstuck. He holds that a legal system exists only if it is broadly effective – only if most of its rules are obeyed or applied, most of the time. He also holds that a particular legal rule, if never applied, is liable to be extinguished by the doctrine of desuetude or by the customary practices of the courts. So, he concludes, '[t]he norms which normative jurisprudence regards as valid are norms that are ordinarily obeyed or applied' and 'the results of a sociology of positive law cannot essentially differ from those of normative jurisprudence'.[15] That is over-optimistic, however. System-wide efficacy does not guarantee the efficacy of individual norms, and desuetude is merely a possible rule in positive law. There are valid laws 'on the books' that have long been ignored or gone unused or even been honoured in the breach. (In fact, this weak link between current conformity and continuing validity is one of the things that gives legal systems an edge over many kinds of customary social order.)

A second imperialistic view, attributable to some realists, among others, is that social science should *replace* normative jurisprudence because the norms found in legal doctrine either do not exist or are causally inefficacious in court. We understand the nature of law – to the extent that law has a determinate nature – the same way we study the nature of political parties, electoral systems or markets: only by empirical analysis. When the data do not match the norms held out as valid law, the norms that are efficacious in court are the ones that determine the province of jurisprudence.

Brian Leiter once defended a related view, both on its merits and as an interpretation of the leading ideas of the American legal realists, whom he regarded as presaging a kind of 'naturalized jurisprudence', a jurisprudence fit to keep company with the successful empirical sciences.[16]

[15] Kelsen 1945: 170, 174.

[16] Leiter 2007: especially the essays 'Rethinking Legal Realism: Toward a Naturalized Jurisprudence'; 'Legal Realism, Hard Positivism, and the Limits of Conceptual Analysis'; and 'Legal Realism and Legal Positivism Reconsidered'. Leiter's view changed as he lost confidence in the (current) sciences of judicial decision-making; see especially Leiter 2007: 188–93.

The positivists may have been substantively correct about the nature of law, but they were wrong methodologically: it was just a lucky guess. No armchair analysis of the concept of law can show that law is wholly based on sources. An empirical study of judicial decision-making may reveal that *something like* positive sources figure in the working assumptions about, or operational definition of, law as used by lawyers and sociologists. But that definition is revisable. If doctrinal rules have a place in a theory of law, it must be in virtue of their predictive efficacy somewhere in legal systems.

2.4 Legal Realism and Positivism

Thus, on any account, positivists and realists agree about much: that law is constituted by social facts, that judges have and exercise significant powers to make law and that law is morally fallible and so is to be approached in a realistic spirit in the everyday sense of that term, that is, with attention to facts and without romanticism or mystification. So, what is there left to disagree about? It proves surprisingly hard to say.

For H. L. A. Hart, the Scandinavian realists advocate reductivist theories of rules and the American realists lack an adequate account of the rule-constituted institutions of courts and judges that preoccupy them. (He lays the same charge at the door of the imperativalists, especially Austin.) In both cases, there is a failure to pay attention to the nature and variety of rules in law. These objections are second nature to contemporary positivists, many of whom first met the realists not *in habitat* but in chapter VII of *The Concept of Law*. Returning to the sources, Leiter argues that we have been misled: the most important realists hold views that are either compatible with Hart's positivism or, to the extent of any incompatibility, superior. In particular, the realists are not the 'rule sceptics' that Hart made notorious. They do not deny the *possibility* of legal rules and they do not offer a predictive *analysis* of the concept of a rule – those are both forms of conceptual rule scepticism, and the realists eschew conceptual analysis altogether. They are committed only to empirical rule scepticism, that is, that, owing to indeterminacy, the decisions of appellate courts cannot be predicted on the basis of (positive) law but they *can* be predicted by extralegal considerations, for instance, by 'judges' responses to the underlying facts of the cases', including their beliefs about what would be fair, given those facts.[17] While philosophers like Hart or Kelsen were cogitating, Leiter thinks they should have been counting.

Unfortunately, Hart uses the term 'rule scepticism' in several ways. It covers those who deny that practical rules even exist and instead hold that they are theoretical 'prophecies of what the courts will do in fact'.[18] He also uses it to cover writers who think that those who have final authority to decide also have unfettered authority to decide. And, most generally, he uses it for all who deny 'that for the most part decisions ... are reached either by genuine effort to conform to rules consciously taken as guiding standards of decision or, if intuitively reached, are justified by rules which the judge was antecedently disposed to observe and whose relevance to the case in hand would generally be acknowledged'.[19] These sceptics are different, but Hart thinks that they are all befuddled by a failure to understand *what it would be* for conduct to be rule-guided. Rules can be loose or crisp, they can have exceptions or be defeasible, they can appear *ex ante* in decision-making or appealed to *ex post actu*, when conduct is challenged, but so long as they are shared standards of belief or conduct effectively 'accepted' as appropriate from the 'internal point of view', they are rules, they have practical functions and they constitute both laws and legal institutions.

In his reading of the American legal realists, Leiter argues that they have no stake in any of this. 'Conceptual' claims about the nature of law or rules just leave them cold. Could all the loose talk, in Holmes, in Cohen or in Llewellyn, about 'definitions' or 'ideas' of law or rules merely be jurisprudential *obiter dicta*? Leiter writes:

> [Theirs] is not a claim about the concept of law but, rather, a claim about how it is useful to think about law for attorneys who must advise clients what to do. ... [F]rom the practical perspective of the franchisee, what one wants to know about the law is what, in fact, the courts will do when confronted with the franchisee's grievance. That is all the law that matters to the client. And that is all, I take it, the Realists wanted to emphasize.[20]

Well, some of them *seem* to emphasize more. Beginning with Holmes, it becomes almost an article of realist faith that there are 'really' no primary obligations in tort or in contract; there are only remedial obligations to pay

[17] See Leiter 2007: 61–5. [18] Holmes 1920: 173. [19] Hart 2012: 137.
[20] Leiter 2007: 292.

damages if so ordered by a court. Yet a client – even Holmes's 'bad man' – may think that he has a stake in his reputation for fidelity. He may even care more about what people outside courtrooms think than he cares about the likelihood of being ordered to pay damages. Cohen writes that legal realism is 'a theory of the nature of legal roles, legal concepts, and legal questions. Its essence is the definition of law as a function of judicial decisions.'[21] Yet Cohen insists that '[j]udges are human, but they are a peculiar breed of humans, selected to a type and held to service under a potent system of governmental controls. Their acts are "judicial" only within a system which provides for appeals, rehearings, impeachments, and legislation.'[22] To say that judges' acts are judicial only within a system of effective norms is to say no more than Kelsen says in section II of *Pure Theory*. If these sorts of comment do not actually assert conceptual claims, they do presuppose them.

Of course, the realists are not coming to any of their theoretical conclusions through analysing ordinary language (any more, in truth, than is Hart).[23] And sorting through the realists' opinions – bearing in mind that most of them had no philosophical interests or insight – is a task that calls for an intellectual historian, and a patient one at that. Here, I hazard only two claims.

First, as Leiter agrees, insofar as the realists assert no claims about the concept of law or the concept of a rule, they have no dispute with the essential thesis of positivism. And, as I have stressed, positivists are not indeterminacy-minimisers, certainly not with respect to decisions of appellate courts: the indeterminacy of law follows from positivism's essential thesis.

Second, if realists are nonetheless committed to claims about the concepts of rules and law, then the fact that they do not assert them as such does not immunise them from conceptual mistakes. Conceptual error is a strict liability offence – though it may be an offence of small consequence. If someone complains to his doctor that 'my arthritis has moved into my thigh', what he says is not, as Cohen might have put it, 'nonsense'. It is grammatical and intelligible English. It may even be diagnostically

[21] Cohen 1935: 842. On whom, see Leiter 2007: 291. [22] Cohen 1935: 843.

[23] 'The idea that what demands understanding about law is the concept of law as manifest in ordinary language would have struck [the realists] as ridiculous' (Leiter 2007: 291). On Hart and ordinary language, see my introduction to Hart 2012.

useful. ('He's feeling the sort of pain in his thigh that his arthritis causes in his knee, therefore . . ..') All the same, it *is* a mistake, and a mistake about the concept of arthritis. Of course, the patient has some command of 'arthritis' ('it causes an ache and not an itch', 'it is felt in the limbs but not the ears' and so forth). He is getting by, as we all do, with a partial grasp of concepts prevalent in his society. In a similar way, if lawyers say that there are no such things as legal rules but only decisions of courts made by people called judges, they, too, demonstrate a partial grasp of a concept: they see that law stands in internal relation to the positive activities of courts. Moreover, just as the patient's mistake about arthritis may not matter for clinical purposes, conceptual mistakes about law may not matter for advocacy.

I do not think that Hart considers the typical rule sceptic to be committed to absurd denials that any rules exist. He takes the realists' most extravagant statements to be 'great exaggerations of some truths about law unduly neglected'.[24] The neglected truth is that source-based law is always somewhat indeterminate and, in the most complex and most studied cases, often quite indeterminate. The exaggeration lies in thinking that this is the *ordinary* run of things in an operational legal system, where people use legal rules to find their way through a roundabout, to enter tenancies, to buy cars, to make wills or to get married, often going nowhere near a lawyer, never mind a courtroom.[25] Even in the appellate courts, Llewellyn's idea that 'there is *always* more than one available correct answer, [from which] the court *always* has to select'[26] neglects the fact that, on some points (for example, whether the court has jurisdiction), the law may be as determinate as law ever is. And Llewellyn's claim that 'there are two opposing canons [of interpretation] on almost every point' does not show them to be in equipoise.[27] It is a reminder that advocates have lots of tools to work with, but it is not grounds for a sceptical conclusion. Among our contemporary, garden-variety, 'law-school' realists – especially those teaching American constitutional law – the idea that there is no rule of recognition because courts disagree about the sources of law to an extent inconsistent with the *correct* criteria for the existence of a rule still gets

[24] Hart 2012: 2.

[25] Leiter denies that any realist except Jerome Frank made this error (see Chapter 4 in this volume).

[26] Llewellyn 1935: 396 (emphases added). [27] See Llewellyn 1935: 401.

traction.[28] That, too, rests on a notion of what those criteria are. Unless we are happy with bare stipulations in these disputes, when we wrestle with questions of the form 'What counts as X?' or 'What are the criteria for Y?', we engage with conceptual problems.

Like Kelsen, Hart considers law to be a norm-constituted object, but one that is tractable to descriptive analysis.[29] His arguments against the various characters he labels 'rule sceptics' are cogent but compact. His influential points about the role of legal reasons in legal arguments, about finality versus the infallibility of decisions and about how we detect social rules require expansion and, at points, correction.[30] They do not reach a hard-bitten sceptic who thinks that our entrenched notions of rules, reasons and judicial mistakes involve explicable errors. Nor are they alert to Goodman-type or Kripke-type anxieties about rules in general. But perhaps Hart does not need more for his purposes, since he mainly wants to show that the errors on which predictivism (and so forth) rests are so gross that we should not treat them as literal proposals for a new jurisprudence but as vivid reminders of important, though modest, truths about positive law.

Any realist who is any kind of rule sceptic faces the challenge of keeping his scepticism under control. A dose is needed in respect of the reasoning of appellate courts; but not so much that it makes it dissolve the existence of those institutions, and not so much that it makes ordinary law – law-in-action, law-on-the-ground – unintelligible. Legal institutions, courts, officers and decisions are rule-constituted things. Holmes argued that it might be of value if every word of moral significance were purged from jurisprudence, but he was never tempted by the thought that we should also eliminate all reference to institutional facts about courts, judges or decisions. That is no doubt why Hart says that the only serious form of scepticism *acknowledges* that social rules exist, that they are *indispensable* to understanding law, including both courts and their decisions, and maybe even accepts that statements of rules have non-assertoric, dynamic functions.[31] The sceptic that Hart criticises *accepts* all that but goes on to deny that such rules ever *bind* judges to a unique decision. His main target is the idea that, whatever psychological states judges find themselves in,

[28] See Dworkin 1986: 10.
[29] As my granny put it, 'It disnae take a fat cowherd tae drive fat kine.'
[30] For one correction, see Green 1999. [31] See Hart 2012: 138.

whatever their pretence, *however* predictable their decisions, it is always false to suppose that they are bound by their own practices to decide cases as they do: 'There is nothing which courts treat as standards of correct judicial behaviour, and so nothing in that behaviour which manifests the internal point of view characteristic of the acceptance of rules.'[32] Did American realists of the early generation think this, or is Hart projecting backwards his own concerns? I am not sure; but some such view became sufficiently influential, not only among untheoretical 'law-school realists' but also among the short-lived critical legal studies 'movement', that it is still worth considering how it should be addressed.

2.5 Permissive Sources of Law

How could someone understand the boundary between law and non-law (such as custom, convention or instinct) if they were to deny that the law controls decisions in the higher courts, where these boundaries are produced, usually indirectly, by the application of law?

Leiter notices the resonance between the realist argument from indeterminacy and the positivist view about the boundaries of law. Herman Oliphant's idea that the American promise-not-to-compete cases were decided by accepted norms of business practice *rather than by legal norms* and Holmes's idea that broad policy considerations *rather than legal norms* determine outcomes both depend on a distinction between such norms on the one hand and American law on the other.[33] So they accept that law has boundaries and that its boundaries are determined – to the extent that they are – by social rather than moral or metaphysical considerations. Holmes calls law a 'business with well understood limits, a body of dogma enclosed within definite lines'.[34] Max Radin calms the anxious by reminding them of the common culture of legal thought: 'We need not fear arbitrariness. Our Cokes and Mansfields and Eldons derive their physical and spiritual nourishment from the same sources that we do.'[35] What should we make of this?

Possibly, the realists *presupposed* something like a positivist view of law without working out whether that could be made consistent with sceptical views about rules and appellate decisions. Or maybe the realists were

[32] Ibid. [33] See Leiter 2011: 292–3. [34] Holmes 1920: 171. [35] Radin 1925: 362.

happy to compartmentalise, to be casual positivists in their court pleadings and hard-bitten sceptics in their graduation addresses. But I think that there is another possibility.

I have stressed that the essential doctrine of legal positivism is that all law is positive. On Hart's version, the sources of law are ultimately determined by customary social rules that identify them as valid grounds for judicial decision. But there is a complication here:

> [W]hen it is said that a statute is a source of law, the word 'source' refers not to mere historical or causal influences but to one of the criteria of legal validity accepted in the legal system in question. Enactment as a statute by a competent legislature is the *reason* why a given statutory rule is a valid law and not merely the *cause* of its existence.[36]

The claim is that enactment is both part of the causal history of a statutory rule *and also something else*, namely, one of the criteria identified as a source of law in that system. Since the ultimate recognition rules in every legal system, even ones with a 'written' constitution, are but customary practices of (at least) the courts and other officials, there can be no clear demarcation between an event playing a causal role in the creation of a statute and it being accepted as a criterion of statutory validity. What starts off just *being done* can end up becoming '*the done thing*'. Customary norms emerge higgledy-piggledy out of common practice, not as products of prescription or planning. *Ex post facto* – when a customary norm is well entrenched – courts and others may look back on earlier bits of history as precursors to or even aspects of its contemporary acceptance, but that is as much of a fiction as when we say *Donoghue* v. *Stevenson* was the 'beginning' of our negligence standard. (It became its beginning only later, after other courts reacted to it.) That means there will be grey areas in which something may, or may not, be a source; or a source-to-be; or, I will now suggest, a source of a permissive kind.

In explaining the idea of a source of law, Hart remarks that, in addition to the familiar binding sources of enactments, decisions and customs, a court may also draw on the decision of a foreign court, institutional writers, Roman jurists and even, in some jurisdictions, academics. 'The legal system does not *require* him to use these sources, but it is accepted as perfectly proper that he should do so. They are therefore more than merely

[36] Hart 2012: 294.

historical or causal influences since such writings are recognized as "good reasons" for decisions.'[37] Yet the very same courts might never think it appropriate to cite Rawls's *Theory of Justice* or (thank God) *Leviticus*. Common practice makes the difference.

How then should we characterise 'good reasons' for decisions whose normative force turns on practice but that have not crystallised into binding law? Judges sometimes cite treatises or law dictionaries just for a pithy statement of the law, believing that the statement is, on independent grounds, correct. They also sometimes cite academic arguments they find convincing on their merits, taking them not as authoritative but as persuasive only. Sometimes, however, the very fact that things are generally 'recognized as good reasons' sets them apart. For example, it is a matter of positive practice that Scots courts may cite the seventeenth- and eighteenth-century writers Stair and Erskine. Unlike the way an English lawyer might cite Blackstone, however, the Scots allow their institutional writers some actual, if weak, authority. The very fact that *Erskine declares N* is some reason for holding that *N* is part of Scots law – though it is a subordinate reason and one that cannot resist the contrary authority of, say, statute or case law. Still, Erskine can be used to resist common sense or certain customs or a persuasive argument from a law journal. It may be no legal error to omit Erskine where he could be relevant, yet it may strengthen a case to cite him. (Scots lawyers are canny; they never waste sources.) Something similar holds, in many legal systems, for the judgments of foreign courts.

On Hart's account, whether a norm is mandatory or binding is a matter of degree.[38] Hence, the distinction between what is binding on the courts and what is not is also a matter of degree – just as we would expect in an area of customary obligations. In addition to sources that they are strictly bound to apply, there are sources that courts are by their own customs expressly permitted to apply: practice-based 'good reasons' for decision that are given greater force than they would have had just on their merits and in the absence of the practice.

A 'permissive source' of law is not, of course, a bare permission. Being permitted to φ is not normally any sort of reason to φ (though it may be a reason for others not to interfere). Moreover, absent a source, courts are permitted to act on any sound reasons relevant to a dispute. It is not as if we

[37] Hart 2012: 294, note to 101. [38] See Hart 2012: 82–91.

live in a world in which judges have no grounds to decide anything until law steps in and provides some. The function of sources in law is often to block appeals to what would otherwise be good reasons for decision.[39] We should normally transfer wealth from the rich to the poor – though not when the law of negligence steps in to require a poor negligent driver to compensate a rich one he has injured, thereby blocking reasons of beneficence or charity. So, a permissive source of law differs both from a mere permission and from something that is just on its merits a good reason for decision, for example, a consideration of justice, utility or humanity. Permissive sources get their merit-independent force from the fact that they are recognised and applied as reasons for decision in the practice of the courts, even though they fall short of binding authority.

I therefore conjecture that part of the realists' objection to positivism is that they consider many sources to be permissive – not only Llewellyn's canons of interpretation that hunt in contrasting pairs but also case law and even some statutes, 'judicially considered'. They acknowledge the core of rules that constitute legal institutions and elementary procedures; that is, how they can freely speak of the boundaries of law and legal institutions all the while thinking that the law does little to constrain judges in hard cases. But, in addition to the familiar positivist claims about the finitude, indeterminacy and conflicting character of sources, the realist also supposes that many sources have little more than the weak authority of something like a doctrine of foreign law, or the views of a writer like Erskine or Stair.

On this sort of view, legal doctrine is a limited menu of socially based considerations that courts are entitled to apply, that are recognised as appropriate to apply, that are distinct from things like ordinary commercial customs and social conventions but that have weak authority that is often overborne by considerations of policy, justice, the equities of the case and so forth. Legal reasoning is, just as the positivists hold, source-based, but the control of those sources over judicial decisions is more limited than most people think. Luckily, law can contribute to social life outside the drama of the court-room, and thus outside those cases in which any judicial intervention is called for. That sounds, to me, like the position that realists defend.

[39] See Raz 2009: 195–9.

If this is correct, then there is an empirical and a conceptual dispute between positivists and realists. Hart addresses the empirical point the only way one can: with a plea to look. He does not think that the realists mean to restrict their claim to the American appeals courts only – that would drain a lot of blood from their theory. For a realist should think it an open question to what extent the trial courts follow the high court: The output, not just the input, of appellate cases is legal rules. Hart thinks that, free of the a priori blinders of reductionism, anyone can see the uncontroversial application of rules at some points in the appeal courts, at many points in the trial courts, but, most important, in the myriad ways that law guides daily conduct without the supervision of courts at all. '[B]oth the framework within which ... [judicial decisions] take place and their chief end-product is one of general rules. These are rules the application of which individuals can see for themselves in case after case, without further recourse to official direction or discretion.'[40] This plea is not, I admit, an argument. But neither is it *ipse dixit.* If someone fails to spot the pigeons and then boldly declares that there are none about, it may be enough to say, 'Just look; over there! Pigeons everywhere!' People sometimes miss fairly determinate legal rules because they are looking in the wrong places, and sometimes because they are wrong about what a fairly determinate legal rule looks like.

To this, Hart adds two arguments for believing that there are mandatory legal norms that bind the courts. First, even if judges do not *experience* any special psychological states like 'feelings of compulsion', they may nonetheless *have* an obligation to decide in a certain way.[41] This point may be addressed to the crude behaviourism of Alf Ross or Axel Hägerström's reductionism, or maybe eliminativism, about legal entities.

The second argument is that most judicial decisions are either (a) 'reached by genuine effort to conform to rules consciously taken as guiding standards' or (b) reached 'intuitively' – without conscious effort to conform – but nonetheless 'justified by rules that judges are disposed to observe and whose relevance to the case at hand would be generally acknowledged'.[42] Point (a) reiterates the plea to look. Point (b) is a claim

[40] Hart 2012: 136.

[41] 'What is necessary is that there should be a critical reflective attitude to certain patterns of behaviour as a common standard, and that this should display itself in criticism (including self-criticism), demands for conformity, and in acknowledgements that such criticism and demands are justified' (Hart 2012: 57).

[42] Hart 2012: 141.

about the criteria for the existence of social rules. It is a mistake to think that one uses a rule only if there is a *very high* degree of consensus about what the rule requires over a *wide* range of possible applications, if one is *conscious* of it as a rule, and if one uses it in making an *effort* to conform. This overemphasises the degree to which rule-following is articulate and conscious *ex ante*. It leaves too little room for our familiar experience of the inarticulate, unconscious and instinctive following of rules that are mostly internalised, for example, when we know how to speak our native language, or how to dress for an occasion, or when we know that a certain legal argument 'just won't fly'. Rule-following is also often displayed *ex post actu*, when rules are produced in justifications, used in communicating past decisions to others, or used to explain what was decided or to defend it against criticism, actual or anticipated. To downplay all this is to make a mistake about the concept of a rule, a mistake that can infect one's theory of law.

2.6 The Displacement of Jurisprudence?

Law is an anthropocentric, mind-constituted thing, and one way to understand such things is to get clearer about their conceptual structure. Realists (and their descendants) sometimes use ordinary doctrinal argumentation to show a case for one position, then pile on more of the same to show that there is also a decent case for a contrary position. This is what we expect: If there were no case *at all* on one side, what would the parties be doing in court? Just for a moment, however, think of this as two arguments – each perhaps assigned to a different clerk. Before we get to adjudicating between *P* and *not-P*, we can inspect each limb of the argument – the case for *P*, and the case for *not-P*, temporarily isolated from each other. Before we get to the weighing of arguments and authorities, we want to be sure that each line follows within its artificially constrained limits. It may be policy, personality or preference that tilts the final choice *as between P* and *not-P*; but why doubt that ordinary legal reasoning takes us part of the way *to P*? How should that (partial) argument be understood, if not as positivism explains it: Reasoning with and from positive rules? And, when finally pushed to decide – to 'draw the line' – why doubt that some sort of (non-legal) considerations may be rationally adequate to give a preference for *P* over *not-P*? Llewellyn seems content with that. He contends only for a 'temporary divorce of Is and Ought for the purposes of study'.[43] And Cohen writes: 'When we recognize that legal rules are simply formulae describing uniformities of judicial decision ... then we are ready for the serious business of appraising law and legal institutions in terms of some standard of human values.'[44] Neither of them thinks that the 'serious business' of judicial decision is insulated from reasoned (if sometimes non-legal) argument.

How far could Cohen's 'formulae describing uniformities of judicial decision' replace the doctrinal aspects of legal argument? It depends, I suppose, on what we expect from a replacement. Compare proposals for a naturalised account of knowledge. Reflecting on the failure of foundationalist epistemologies, Quine writes: 'If all we can hope for is a reconstruction that links science to experience in explicit ways short of translation, then it would seem more sensible to settle for psychology.'[45] 'Seeming sensible' is not an entailment relation or even a very compelling reason. That *E* fails is no reason for thinking that *P* will succeed, and certainly no reason for thinking that *P* will succeed *at what E was aiming for*. Perhaps Quine's observation shows that knowledge defies reasoned inquiry of any kind, and that if you want to study *something* naturalistically, you will have to settle for the sociology or psychology of belief. In a Quinean spirit, Leiter writes: '[I]f no normative account of the relation [between legal reasons and judicial decision] is possible, then the only theoretically fruitful account is the descriptive/explanatory account given by the relevant science of that domain.'[46] This sounds more like a reason for studying a *different* domain, one tractable to the methods that 'naturalism' approves. And Kelsen makes the same sort of move: He decides he wants to study law 'positivistically', drafts desiderata for such a programme, then gives no further thought to aspects of legal life that are not tractable given his methods.

In any event, why should the psychology of judicial decisions be worth pursuing only on the condition of the *failure* of doctrinal argument to shed light on questions that psychology is not asking? If Carnap's foundationalism had succeeded, we could still have pursued an independent science studying the extent to which people endorse or follow the principles it constructed. If Bayesianism is the best foundation for decision theory, we

[43] Llewellyn 1931: 1236. [44] Cohen 1935: 487. [45] Quine 1969: 78.
[46] Leiter 2007: 293.

can still study how far, and why, people deviate from its prescriptions. Likewise, where law yields determinate answers, we can still ask why some judges and not others are willing to rule as the law requires. Maybe we will discover that some judges misunderstand the law, or misapply it, or even break it? That would hardly come as a surprise. There are judges and courts who make little effort to apply settled law when it is at variance with the wishes of their patrons; there are many more whose wishful thinking makes the variance invisible to them. Kelsen writes:

> To replace this [normative legal] science by legal sociology is impossible, because the latter is concerned with an entirely different problem. As long as religion exists, there must be a dogmatic theology that cannot be replaced by religious psychology or religious sociology; in precisely the same manner there will be a normative science of law as long as there is law.[47]

This analogy is strained. Some religions did not evolve hand-in-glove with European rationalism, and so were not shaped by its characteristic modes of rationalisation through doctrine. Still, Kelsen is on the mark in thinking that a psychology or sociology of those religions would not deepen our understanding of their meaning for their adherents and would involve changing the subject of inquiry. Are we then tempted to object: But don't some people study astrology with great sophistication and energy, and doesn't that give meaning to their lives? Yes: But in that case, there is no evidence that astrology can do *what it purports to do*, that is predict the future, determine human compatibilities and so on. Astrology fails at the very thing it promises, and its promises are part of its meaning for its practitioners. In contrast, a normative theory of adjudication does not *purport* to predict how judges will decide cases; it purports to explain how they *ought* to decide cases. To the extent that 'ought implies can', it will be interested in the sciences of human decision-making. But none of that undermines the relative autonomy of jurisprudence as a subject.

2.7 Conclusion

The essential thesis of positivism is that all law is positive law – all law has sources; all legal systems are systems of source-based rules. Other legal

[47] Kelsen 1967: 89.

philosophers doubt that, on various (incompatible) grounds. But, as far as I can tell, most legal realists do not doubt it and, in any case, should not doubt it. Their distinctions between traditional legal materials and considerations of policy or judicial psychology suggest that they presuppose that law rests on sources. They may doubt that the sources generally determine judicial decisions, at least in the appellate courts, but more exaggerated assertions of the indeterminacy risk sawing off the branches they sit on – their comfortable, and mostly unexplained, ontology of courts and decisions. Maybe, as Hart holds, they are exaggerating to foreground a phenomenon they consider under-appreciated. Maybe, as Leiter holds, the realists are suggesting that we replace, within limits, an unsuccessful method with a more useful one. (There is no denying that if one really could predict judicial decisions, there would be good money in it.) Maybe – and this is the conjecture I have been exploring here – they think that important cases often turn on sources that are not binding but are instead permissive. Or maybe there is something in all three explanations: They are partly compatible and, as elsewhere in jurisprudence, the truth may be shared among them. But there is no doubt that legal positivism and legal realism have much in common, and not only in temperament. Let us not make them seem more foreign to each other than they really are.

References

Cohen, F. 1935. 'Transcendental Nonsense and the Functional Approach'. *Columbia Law Review* 35: 809–49.

Dworkin, R. 1977. 'No Right Answer?' In P. M. S. Hacker and J. Raz (eds.). *Law, Morality, and Society: Essays in Honour of H.L.A. Hart.* Oxford University Press.

Dworkin, R. 1986. *Law's* Empire. Harvard University Press.

Dworkin, R. 2008. *Justice in Robes*. Harvard University Press.

Finnis, J. 2011. *Natural Law and Natural Rights.* 2nd ed. Oxford University Press.

Gardner, J. 2001. 'Legal Positivism: 5½ Myths'. *American Journal of Jurisprudence* 46: 199–227.

Green, L. 1999. 'Positivism and Conventionalism'. *Canadian Journal of Law and Jurisprudence* 12: 35–52.

Green, L. 2008. 'Positivism and the Inseparability of Law and Morals'. *New York University Law Review* 83: 1035–58.

Green, L. and Adams, T. 2019. 'Legal Positivism'. In E. N. Zalta (ed.). *The Stanford Encyclopedia of Philosophy*. https://plato.stanford.edu/archives/win2019/spr2018/entries/legal-positivism.

Greenberg, M. 2014. 'The Moral Impact Theory of Law'. *Yale Law Journal* 123: 1288–1342.

Halevy, E. 1934. *The Growth of Philosophical Radicalism*. Faber.

Hart, H. L. A. 1983 *Essays in Jurisprudence and Philosophy*. Oxford University Press.

Hart, H. L. A. 2012. *The Concept of Law*. 3rd ed. Introduction by L. Green, eds. P. A. Bulloch and J. Raz. Oxford University Press.

Holmes, O. W. 1920. 'The Path of the Law'. In O. W. Holmes. *Collected Legal Papers*. Harcourt, Brace & Howe.

Kelsen, H. 1967. *Pure Theory of Law*. 2nd ed. Trans. M. Knight. University of California Press.

Kelsen, H. 1945. *General Theory of Law and State*. Trans. A. Wedberg. Russell and Russell.

Leiter, B. 2007. *Naturalizing Jurisprudence: Essays on Legal Realism and Naturalism in Legal Philosophy*. Oxford University Press.

Llewellyn, K. N. 1931. 'Some Realism about Realism: Responding to Dean Pound'. *Harvard Law Review* 44: 1222–1264.

Llewellyn, K. N. 1935. 'Remarks on the Theory of Appellate Decision and the Rules or Canons about How Statutes Are to Be Construed'. *Vanderbilt Law Review* 3: 395–406.

Murphy, M. C. 2006. *Natural Law in Jurisprudence and Politics*. Cambridge University Press.

Quine, W. V. O. 1969. *Ontological Relativity and Other Essays*. Columbia University Press.

Radin, M. 1925. 'A Theory of Judicial Decision, or How Judges Think'. *American Bar Association Journal* 11: 357–62.

Raz, J. 1979. *The Authority of Law: Essays on Law and Morality*. Oxford University Press.

Raz, J. 2009. *Between Authority and Interpretation: On the Theory of Law and Practical Reason*. Oxford University Press.

Schauer, F. 1999 'Positivism as Pariah'. In R. P. George (ed.). *The Autonomy of Law: Essays on Legal Positivism*. Oxford University Press: 31–47.

Waluchow, W. J. 1994. *Inclusive Legal Positivism*. Oxford University Press.

Normative Legal Positivism 3

Frederick Schauer

3.1 The Varieties of Legal Positivism

For most contemporary legal positivists, legal positivism is a descriptive and not a normative position.[1] A theorist working from a positivist perspective, most of these contemporary positivists would insist, is attempting to describe and understand a culture's concept of law, but that concept is external to the theorist's descriptive efforts. And whether the concept so described is desirable or undesirable, useful or useless, beneficial or dangerous, is not the theorist's principal concern.[2]

But it was not always so. In the history of legal positivism, various theorists, originally Jeremy Bentham[3] and, more recently, Tom Campbell,[4] Bruno Celano,[5] Jeremy Waldron[6] and others,[7] have argued that the legal positivist tradition, and perhaps the core of legal positivism itself, contains an important normative or prescriptive dimension. Some of the just-mentioned theorists have maintained that legal positivism is, inter alia, a prescription to legal actors, especially judges, about what they should and should not take into account in making their decisions. Relatedly, others have urged a conception of legal positivism such that legal positivism is a prescription to legal institutional designers about how legal institutions should be structured and regulated. And it has also been argued, under one interpretation of H. L. A. Hart's earlier writings,[8] and also under an understanding of the implications of recognising the artefactual nature of the concept of law,[9] that an entire culture's concept of law is something that the

[1] See Coleman 2001a: 175–217; Dickson 2004; Green 2008; Marmor 2006; Raz 2005.
[2] See Dickson 2004; Hart 2012: 240–1.
[3] See Bentham 1988, 2010; Postema 1986; Steintrager 1977. [4] Campbell 1996, 2004.
[5] Celano 2013. [6] Waldron 2001.
[7] Including the author of this chapter. See Schauer 1993, 2011, 2015a, 2017.
[8] See Hart 1958; Hart 2012: 200–12. [9] See Burazin, Himma and Roversi 2018.

culture that has created the concept can re-create and revise, perhaps better to serve political, pragmatic or moral goals.

Both of these varieties of legal positivism are normative and not simply descriptive. They prescribe as much as they describe. And although it would be inaccurate to assert that either of these normative forms of legal positivism is now dominant among the cohort of contemporary positivist legal philosophers, it would also be inaccurate to assert that normative legal positivism is absent from the contemporary landscape of legal philosophy, or that it has been absent from the history of thinking about law from a positivist perspective. Moreover, the fact that several versions of normative legal positivism have persisted throughout the history of legal positivism suggests not only that we can still learn from one or more of these versions but also that there might be reason to resurrect or accentuate their contemporary importance. The goal of this chapter, therefore, is to explain these two chief varieties of normative legal positivism, and to suggest how and why their value might be recognised and appreciated even today.

3.2 The Evaluative Dimensions of Descriptive Analyses

Before turning to those forms of legal positivism that are truly and self-consciously normative, it is worthwhile discussing, albeit more briefly, the claim that even descriptive legal positivism is more normative (or more evaluative)[10] than its proponents and practitioners have been willing to

[10] It will be important at the outset to emphasise that 'normative' need not refer to *moral* normativity, and that there are forms of evaluation that are not moral evaluation. Norms – and thus 'normativity' in one sense – are oughts, and not all oughts are moral oughts. Some oughts are purely instrumental, and thus their ought-ness is contingent on or relative to some goal, where that goal may well not be a moral one. Thus, the claims that one ought to dress in a certain way in order to be accepted in some social environment, or that one ought to hold a tennis racket in a particular way in order to impart maximum spin, are normative prescriptions with no moral content. In much of the literature on legal normativity, it is assumed that moral normativity – one ought to φ because φ'ing is morally obligatory in itself, or because φ'ing will bring about a morally desirable state of affairs – is what is at issue. But in the context of presenting and discussing the various forms of normative legal positivism, it is important to bear in mind that not all normativity is moral normativity.

It is also important to note that the word 'normative' might be understood to refer to the science of or the analysis of norms, as is most prominent in Kelsenian (Kelsen 1967) legal philosophy. But that sense of 'normative' will be no part of this chapter.

acknowledge.[11] This claim has been advanced most prominently by Stephen Perry,[12] and the essence of his argument is that attempting to describe the concept of law, and especially attempting to describe it from the internal point of view, as Perry understands Hart, in part, to be doing, involves selecting those features of law that are relevant in understanding the phenomenon of law, in understanding the concept by which a culture understands the phenomenon, and in understanding the capacity of law to provide reasons for action. In engaging in that selection process, however, Perry argues, the theorist presupposes a purpose that law is expected to serve.[13] But determining law's purpose necessarily involves an evaluative judgement, Perry maintains, thus making what seems initially to be entirely a descriptive project in reality a project with normative dimensions, normative dimensions that in turn have moral aspects.

Perry's argument, as Perry acknowledges, has its comparatively recent foundations in Ronald Dworkin's arguments, especially in *Law's Empire*,[14] about the interpretive character of law. For Dworkin, both describing law and engaging in legal judgment (whether by a lawyer, by a judge, by a citizen or even by a theorist) are interpretive processes, and such interpretation, which for Dworkin necessarily involves determinations of both fit with the existing data of legal acts and justification of those acts and of the enterprise within which they exist, is thus necessarily a moral determination, at least in part.[15] For Dworkin, description without interpretation is impossible, and purely descriptive interpretation is a contradiction in terms.

Defending the positivist descriptive project, especially in the version advanced by Joseph Raz,[16] against the charges of Dworkin and Perry, Julie Dickson acknowledges that the descriptive enterprise of describing the concept of law involves selecting the relevant and important features from all of the features – some of which are irrelevant and some of which are unimportant – that law and legal systems exhibit.[17] But that selection

[11] For overviews of the issues, see Priel 2007; Rodriguez-Blanco 2006; Walton 2013.

[12] See Perry 1995, 2001. See also Tasioulas 2013.

[13] Among the forebears of Perry's position is Lon Fuller, who, although perhaps less clearly, maintained that it is impossible either to identify or to apply the law without taking into account the moral purpose that law is designed to serve. See Fuller 1958, 1969. See also Powers 1985: 236; Rundle 2012; Summers 1985; Tinturé 2013.

[14] Dworkin 1986. See also Dworkin 2002, 2006. [15] See Dworkin 2006.

[16] Raz 1979. For a selection of valuable and original commentaries on Raz's work in general and his descriptive conceptual project in particular, see Symposium 1989.

[17] See Dickson 2001.

process, she insists, although unavoidably evaluative in some non-moral sense,[18] need not involve moral determinations or moral evaluations.[19] And thus, for Dickson, and also for Kevin Walton,[20] the project of describing the nature of law and the process of describing and interpreting legal institutions can remain faithful to the basic positivist idea of identifying and describing law without necessary recourse to moral criteria.

This prologue is not the place to assess the soundness of Perry's, Dworkin's, Dickson's or Walton's arguments.[21] These arguments are noted and described here, however briefly, principally for the purpose of distinguishing those arguments about the normative aspects of allegedly neutral description, and the debates about those arguments, from the two more thoroughly normative versions of legal positivism, the two versions whose description and evaluation will occupy the remainder of this chapter.

3.3 Normative Legal Positivism

Although it is often claimed, with considerable justification, that the true origins of modern legal positivism can be found in the writings of Thomas Hobbes,[22] and that traces can be located in Kant and Rousseau, among others,[23] the creator of more-or-less modern legal positivism is generally understood to be Jeremy Bentham. Bentham was the first to give us a crisp articulation of the importance of distinguishing between what the law is and what the law ought to be, the first to argue that identifying law requires no necessary recourse to moral criteria, and the first, relatedly, to argue that law is intrinsically and necessarily a social creation with no natural or essential moral foundations.[24]

But although identifying law was thus for Bentham entirely a descriptive project, his legal theory nevertheless contained two different normative dimensions. One of these dimensions, perhaps less important for contemporary

[18] As in note 10. [19] See also Coleman 2001a. [20] See Walton 2013.

[21] Valuable comprehensive treatments of the claims about the normative dimensions of allegedly descriptive analyses include Priel 2007 and Rodriguez-Blanco 2006.

[22] See Coyle 2003; Dyzenhaus and Poole 2012; Ladenson 1980; Murphy 1995; Riley 2009.

[23] See Christie 1973: 292–6.

[24] See Bentham 1988, 2010; Hart 1982; Lyons 1984; Postema 1986, 2002, 2012; Schauer 2015b: 11–22; Steintrager 1977.

academic legal theorists than it was for Bentham the social reformer, was the view that the very purpose of describing law has a normative aspect insofar as the description of law is the necessary precursor for reforming it.[25] Bentham, and to a lesser extent his follower John Austin,[26] was pervasively a social reformer, and his reformist views plainly extended to the legal system he found egregiously defective in countless ways.[27] In purporting to define law in such a way that it could be inspected, rejected and reformed, Bentham gave us a conception of legal positivism that was at one level entirely descriptive and non-normative but that, at a more foundational level, was motivated by Bentham's plainly normative desire to use that description as the vehicle for the necessarily normative project of legal reform. When, more than a century and a half later, Neil MacCormick described the 'Moralistic Case for A-Moralistic Law',[28] he could have been describing Bentham's project, and describing it in a way that emphasised the normative goals that lurked in the background of the seemingly descriptive and non-normative project.

Even more importantly, and apart from the question of Bentham's normative motivations, Bentham's legal theory itself had a more overtly normative focus. Bentham, as is well known, distrusted – perhaps 'despised' would be a better word – judges (as well as most of the lawyers who practised before them), and thus, for him, designing a legal system that would disempower judges – and relegate courts and lawyers to decidedly secondary roles in the operation of a legal system – was a substantial part of his law reform programme.[29] In pursuing this project of designing legal institutions so as to minimise the roles of lawyers and judges, Bentham sought an extensively codified legal environment,[30] one that would enable ordinary citizens to know what the law expected of them without recourse

[25] As Stephen Perry 2001: 311 puts it, 'Hobbes and Bentham employed normative methodologies to defend versions of substantive positivism'.

[26] That Bentham was a social reformer, at least as a matter of intent (whether he was successful in his reform endeavours is a complex question with no easy answer), is pretty much without question. But for Austin, the evidence and the opinions are mixed. See the various conflicting interpretations of Austin, his work and his goals on just this question, in Freeman and Mindus 2013; Morison 1982; Rumble 2005; Schauer 2015a: 167.

[27] See Dyzenhaus 2010: 3–10, describing Bentham's concern with the 'excess veneration' (Raz 1985) of law.

[28] MacCormick 1985. The title notwithstanding, most of MacCormick's article is not about the moral case for why it would be desirable to understand law in a non-moral way; instead, it is primarily about the moral case for law's non-enforcement of social norms of moral behaviour.

[29] See Harrison 1988. [30] See Alfange 1969; DiFilippo 1972; Schofield 2013.

to lawyers or to adjudication.[31] And if by chance a dispute did wind up in the courts, Bentham, at least according to the conventional interpretation,[32] advocated a judicial function limited to interpreting, applying and enforcing the positive law as written (and as positivistically understood), leaving moral considerations, whether moral considerations of utility or of anything else, completely out of the judicial picture.

Even apart from their historical provenance, Bentham's normative prescriptions about judicial (and, by extension, lawyer) behaviour appear to qualify as one version or one aspect of legal positivism because they presuppose the fundamental positivist distinction between law and not-law,[33] that distinction in turn being basic to Bentham's proposed limitation of the behaviour of legal actors to the law side of that divide. In this sense, Bentham's positivism is compatible with the basic insight behind (or motivation for) H. L. A. Hart's idea of the rule of recognition, insofar as the point of a rule of recognition derives from the very existence of non-recognised and thus not legally valid sources.[34] But for Bentham, not just any rule of recognition would do, and thus, for Bentham, the inclusive positivist idea that the rule of recognition could be anything that a society (contingently and not necessarily) decided it would be[35] is only part of the

[31] In order to create the proper incentives for Parliament or any other legislature to write clear and publicly accessible laws devoid of the self-interested corrupting influence of lawyers and judges urging greater and unnecessary complexity, Bentham at least once suggested (Bentham 1843), more or less seriously, that it ought to be unlawful to give legal advice for money. Perhaps ironically, therefore, Jeremy Bentham, despite being born, bred, trained (as a lawyer) and living in a common law jurisdiction, comes down to us as perhaps the most extreme proponent of the purest version (some would say caricature) of the civil law, a title that Bentham might share with the Napoleon of the Napoleonic Code, but with few others.

[32] An important interpretation of Bentham that varies somewhat from the interpretation here, and an interpretation that has Bentham giving a larger role to judges and to adjudication, can be found in Postema 1986.

[33] See Schauer 2004.

[34] The claim in the text is not one about the idea or concept of a rule of recognition, but rather about what might have motivated Hart to come up with the idea of a rule of recognition in the first place and then to give it the label he did. And on that question, it seems plausible to speculate that he would not have done so had he not both acknowledged and observed socially acceptable sources of decision-making guidance that were nevertheless not recognised as acceptable legal sources and, conversely, legally accepted sources of decision that might lack moral, political or social acceptance.

[35] See Coleman 2001a; Himma 2002; Waluchow 1994. Coleman refers to the idea as 'incorporationism' (Coleman 2001b) and, in his Postscript, Hart (2012) gives it the label 'soft positivism'.

story. Even if Bentham might have agreed with the inclusive positivist idea as a matter of the minimal conditions – here, a contingent social and not a natural rule – for the very existence of law properly so-called, he also had normative views about the content of the rule of recognition, and here his ideas more likely overlap with the exclusive positivist idea[36] of rule-of-recognition-recognised law as itself not necessarily incorporating moral considerations. Accordingly, Bentham's legal positivism combined the normative view that law should be understood as excluding direct recourse by law's subjects (and enforcers) to moral considerations with the further normative view that legal systems ought to be designed so that judges, whether by compulsion through the use of coercive sanctions or by the development and enforcement of social and judicial norms, would make their decisions solely on the basis of positive law properly and narrowly defined.

In the contemporary jurisprudential literature, Bentham's brand of normative legal positivism has occasionally been criticised for not being positivism at all. Or, to put the matter more precisely, those contemporary theorists who seek to attach Bentham's views about judicial empowerment – or, more accurately, judicial disempowerment – to the positivist picture of law are accused of mistakenly confusing Bentham's views about what judges ought to do with the positions and commitments that genuinely lie at the core of legal positivism. Most clearly, for example, Jules Coleman criticises those who would confuse legal positivism with the not-necessarily-positivist positions (Coleman calls such positions 'political' rather than, say, 'jurisprudential') that theorists such as Bentham 'happened to hold'.[37]

The view that Bentham's normative prescriptions are not 'really' legal positivism suffers from the flaw that most debates about whether something is really a this or a that suffer from – the unwillingness to recognise that whether something is really or truly or genuinely something depends almost entirely on why we want to know and what turns on the inclusion or exclusion of some item from some larger category or from some definition. Moreover, the view that Bentham's prescriptions are nor part of legal positivism seems to impose on Bentham only (some of) the views about Bentham that are in circulation two centuries (or more) later but would not

[36] See Leiter 2007: 121–35; Marmor 2002; Raz 1979; Shapiro 2011: 269–73.

[37] Coleman 1982:145–7.

have been, even under different names, in Bentham's time. There is nothing necessarily wrong with trying to situate an earlier theorist within contemporary categories, but it is important to recognise that under Bentham's own conception of legal positivism (even if he did not exactly use that term), his views about the relationship between law and morality and his views about what judges ought to be doing were either definitional of legal positivism or followed naturally from it. The argument to the contrary may well be correct (or not) if the point of reference is late-twentieth-century understandings of legal positivism, but it is important not to fall into the trap that historians label 'presentism' – the interpretation of past acts according to the goals and categories of the present. And if we understand legal positivism to designate a tradition and a broad perspective and not simply a late-twentieth-century definition,[38] it is difficult to exclude Bentham's plainly normative views about what the relationship between rule-of-recognition-recognised positive law and the tasks of judges and lawyers ought to be.

If we can forgive the presentism for the time being, however, the argument that Bentham's normative views about the roles of lawyers and judges are not properly considered a part of legal positivism is nevertheless worth taking seriously. And the argument is that Bentham's focus on how legal systems ought to be designed, his concern with restricting judges to decision according to clearly identified positive law, his insistence on distinguishing what the law is from what the law ought to be,[39] and his view of the importance of distinguishing positive law from morality all presuppose a certain kind of descriptive (and definitional) legal positivism and not normative legal positivism.[40] That is, these concerns presuppose a positivist definition of law and a conceptual positivism that looks very much like the enterprise (and the conclusions) of contemporary conceptual positivists such as Coleman and Raz, among others,[41] and that this foundational legal positivism is what legal positivism really is. As a result, the judicial and lawyer decision-making prescriptive programme of Bentham and his more recent followers turns out to be, so it is said, at best peripheral and possibly irrelevant to the core commitments of what we now and

[38] See Schauer 2015a.

[39] In Bentham's terminology, distinguishing *expository* jurisprudence from *censorial* jurisprudence (Bentham 1988).

[40] See Green 2016; Spaak 2016.

[41] See, e.g., Dickson 2001; Marmor 2006; Waluchow 1994.

properly understand legal positivism to be, and equally peripheral and possibly irrelevant to the (general) jurisprudential task of identifying the essential properties of the concept of law in all possible legal systems in all possible worlds.[42]

There are, however, (at least) three responses to this view – the view that Bentham's form of normative prescription for judicial behaviour and legal institutional design is not part of legal positivism at all. First, it is not at all clear that the basic positivist distinction between what the law is and what the law ought to be, a distinction we do owe to Bentham, requires an elaborate conceptual specification of the concept of law at all. As long as we accept a basic, even if fuzzy-edged, understanding of the idea of positive law, then the project of distinguishing what law is from what law ought to be can still be pursued, with no further conceptual analysis of the concept of law being necessary. In other words, a careful and precise specification of the essential properties of law and of the features that demarcate law from other social phenomena is not necessary for distinguishing most instances of law from most instances of non-law, and is thus not necessary to the positivist project, and in particular the normative positivist project, of distinguishing law as it is from law as it ought to be.[43]

Second, even if is true that Bentham's normative views about judicial decision-making presuppose a certain kind of conceptual positivism, it does not follow that that which is presupposed is in some way more important than that which the presupposition supports, and thus that everything that is a necessary condition for Bentham's normative positivism is for that reason more important or more fundamental or more interesting in understanding the positivist perspective and its importance. Bentham's normative prescriptions do, it might be conceded, presuppose a certain concept of law, but they also presuppose a host of views about language, about government, about the political state, about the psychology of decision-making, and much else. That all of these are presupposed by Bentham's normative positivism does not make Bentham's normative positivism any less positivistic or any less important for the broader positivist tradition and perspective. Or, to put it differently, even if

[42] See also Green 2016; Spaak 2016.

[43] See Leiter 2011; Schauer 2015b; Shiner 1992. Indeed, this anti-essentialist view of the category of law, and thus of the category of non-law, might receive some support from the earlier (but not the later) pages of Hart's *The Concept of Law* ([1961] 1994). See Schauer 2013.

normative positivism presupposes conceptual positivism, normative positivism is no less positivism and no less (and probably) important as a component of the broader idea of, and motivation for, legal positivism. Indeed, the mistake might be in supposing that conceptual legal positivism in its modern clothing and normative legal positivism as attributed to Bentham are in some significant way mutually exclusive. Both might have something to say, and to suppose that modern legal conceptual positivism renders Bentham's normative positivism less interesting or even less correct or even less positivistic is fallaciously to assume that the truth of one must necessarily exclude the truth of the other.

Third, and relatedly, 'positivism' is a label, and then the question is what 'positivism' is a label for. If we think of it as a label for a definition, then it is true that normative positivism presupposes a non-normative definition of law, and there is no reason to suppose that Bentham would have denied this. But if we think of positivism as a label for a tradition and a perspective and not simply as a label for a definition or for the conclusion of a conceptual analysis, then the grounds for excluding Bentham's normative views from the positive tradition and the positivist perspective seem even more attenuated.

Historical analysis notwithstanding, the importance of Bentham's brand of normative positivism lies in part in the fact that he appears to have a number of contemporary allies. Perhaps most prominently, Tom Campbell's 'ethical legal positivism'[44] is similar in significant ways to the views that I have just attributed to Bentham.[45] Although Bentham's views about the power of judges were premised on Bentham's belief that judicial disempowerment would maximise utility, Campbell's are based on maximising not utility but democracy. For Campbell, fundamental moral questions, as well as the political decisions that emanate from them and are based on them, should be made by a democratically responsible and responsive body, prototypically a legislature. By keeping such decisions away from judges to the extent possible, Campbell maintains, democratic control, itself for him a first-order (and not merely instrumental) moral value, is maximised. But although Campbell's building blocks differ somewhat from Bentham's, their conclusions are more or less the same – positive legal norms should be formulated with considerable specificity, and judges should, by sanctions or otherwise, be precluded from straying

[44] Campbell 1996, 1998, 2000. [45] See Schauer 2017.

beyond the narrow and precisely drafted rules of positive law. And for Campbell, even more explicitly than for Bentham, the label to be applied to this thoroughly normative position is 'legal positivism'.

Although the Bentham and Campbell positions differ in their justifications, their conclusions are similar. And so too, although less directly, are those of Bruno Celano,[46] who has advocated what he explicitly calls 'normative legal positivism' in part because of the rule of law advantages of providing for citizens a clear way of knowing what the law is. For Celano, this clear way comes from separating 'the grounds of legal judgment [from] the grounds of moral judgment'.[47] Thus, citizens, without having to make recourse to moral evaluations, can discover what the law requires, and the consequent citizen knowledge of the law and its requirements is central to, he believes, the very idea of law. And although Celano appears more focused than Bentham on citizen empowerment and less focused than Bentham on judicial disempowerment,[48] both of them see codification and an accessible rule of recognition as normative desirable. Because the separation of the legal from the moral for purposes of knowing what the law is characterises legal positivists Bentham and Celano, both, along with Campbell, can be considered central figures in the normative legal positivist tradition.

3.4 The Normative Case for Legal Positivism

In his 1958 debate with Lon Fuller[49] on the pages of the *Harvard Law Review*, H. L. A. Hart[50] appeared to argue that legal positivism should be preferred to Fuller's (or anyone else's) version of a natural law position because legal positivism – in particular its insistence on distinguishing what the law is from what the law should be – would best facilitate citizens' and officials' separating what the law requires from what they as citizens or officials ought, morally, to do, and that this separation would, in turn, facilitate citizen and official disobedience to morally iniquitous laws, of which, and especially in 1958, the laws of Nazi Germany were exemplary. And although Fuller vehemently disagreed with Hart on exactly this point, it is noteworthy that Fuller implicitly agreed with Hart that a concept of law

[46] See Celano 2013. [47] Celano 2013: 176–7. [48] Alfange 1969; Celano 2013.
[49] See Fuller 1958. [50] See Hart 1958.

is not something that just exists – or not – but is something that can be chosen by a culture to serve moral (or other) normative goals.[51]

Three years later, in the original 1961 version of *The Concept of Law*, Hart reiterated more or less the same position.[52] He talked about the moral, political and other normative advantages of legal positivism, and used language strongly suggesting that these were not simply incidental advantages but reasons for a society to choose legal positivism as the concept of law that would produce for that society the greatest moral advantages. Hart says, for example, that we might 'adopt' one or the other of two 'rival concepts of law', and urges adoption of the positivist one.[53] Even more explicitly, he talks about a society 'mak[ing] a reasoned choice between [different] concepts of law' on the basis of 'one being superior to the other' in terms of 'advanc[ing' or 'clarify[ing]' our moral deliberations.[54] And with this and other language, Hart makes clear that 'preferring'[55] a narrower concept of law, one that would exclude from the category of law that which failed to meet minimal substantive moral requirements, would foster 'in too crude a way'[56] the avoidance of confrontation with difficult issues of morality and justice that are both 'delicate' and 'complex'.

There is a considerable amount of language in Hart's 1994 Postscript to *The Concept of Law* that supports the view that by the time he wrote the notes that eventually became the Postscript,[57] Hart believed that legal positivism was simply a descriptive position.[58] But although the contrast between Hart's 1958 and 1961 positions, on the one hand, and his 1994 position, on the other, is, at the very least, as Julie Dickson puts it, 'awkward',[59] nevertheless, for the purposes of this chapter, the question of Hartian exegesis is peripheral to the central idea. For whether Hart later backed away from it or not, there is an important position, arguably supported by the 1958 and the 1961 Hart, that is worth recognising on its own.

Thus, the position, undeniably a normative one, is that positivism is not only a descriptive position that should be chosen insofar as its description is accurate; it is also a normative prescription to a society with respect to how that society should understand law and how that society should create

[51] See Waldron 2001. [52] See Hart 2012: 200–12. [53] Hart 2012: 209. [54] Ibid.
[55] Hart 2012: 210. [56] Hart 2012: 211.
[57] See Lacey 2004: 347–53 for a description and analysis of the circumstances that produced the posthumous Postscript.
[58] See Hart 2012: 240–1. [59] Dickson 2009: 164.

the concept of law that embodies this understanding.[60] This form of normative positivism takes as its premise that law is not a natural kind, and thus that law, as a human artefact,[61] not only is created by human beings but also can be modified or re-created by human beings. The appropriate language, occasionally found in the literature, is that of 'conceptual revision'.[62] To ask what our concept of law *should* be is, once we have recognised the artefactual nature of law and concepts of it, hardly a pointless exercise. It is true, of course, that the ability of any individual theorist, or even the collectivity of theorists, to influence how a society understands the idea of law might be minimal, but much the same could be said about the ability of Immanuel Kant and John Rawls to influence how members of a society behave, treat each other and create their political institutions. And so too with the normative project of advocating conceptual revision. Such conceptual revision will, at best, be a gradual and incremental process, a process in which the contribution of academic theorists will rarely be more than minimal. But the basic idea is that a concept of law is how a society perceives and categorises various social phenomena, including the phenomena of moral sensibility, including the institutions and rules for the guidance of behaviour, including the institutions and rules for the settlement of disputes, including the organisation of state power, including the organisation of state decision-making, and including much more. This being the case, different concepts of law in different societies, or at different times, will thus include or exclude these phenomena from the concept of law that those societies adopt and employ.

With the foregoing abstract notion of *a* concept of law (not *the* concept of law in some society) in hand, we can then see that the activity of conceptual prescription, or conceptual revision, as it was practised by Hart and Fuller in 1958, and as seemingly advocated by Hart in 1961, is an entirely sensible enterprise.[63] But it is an activity that is sensible only if there is some criterion of what makes one concept of law superior to another. Various criteria for this assessment might be imagined, including the psychological, the pragmatic, the economic and even the aesthetic, but for Hart and Fuller, and for the position represented in the title of Neil MacCormick's essay[64] even if not by the contents of that essay itself, the most important criterion is moral, and from this there emerges the view

[60] See Waldron 2002. [61] See Burazin, Himma and Roversi 2018. [62] Green 2008.
[63] See Schauer 2005, 2018. [64] MacCormick 1985.

that concepts of law *ought* to be chosen, even if slowly and incrementally, on moral grounds. And if one concept of law sees the criteria of legality either as not including criteria of morality, as the exclusive positivists would have it, or as not necessarily including criteria of morality, as it would be put by the inclusive legal positivists, then what we have is the normative moral case for legal positivism or, more briefly, one form of normative legal positivism.[65]

3.5 Conclusion

To repeat a point from the introductory portions of this chapter, none of the versions of normative legal positivism discussed here can now or yet be considered the dominant form of legal positivism. But each of these versions of normative legal positivism has now and has had in the past prominent proponents. A thorough knowledge of legal positivism and of the legal positivist tradition, therefore, would need to include knowledge of these various forms of normative legal positivism.

Knowledge for its own sake is important, including knowledge of the history of an idea. But also important is the way in which a full appreciation of the artefactual nature of law leads to the conclusion that a concept of law is not only something that is made by a society; it can also be remade by that society. Whether to do so, and on what grounds, is itself a normative position, and, in that sense, normative legal positivism can be understood as simply one branch of normative general jurisprudence, just as normative natural law, or normative Dworkinian interpretivism, or normative anything else, represents other branches. Each of these branches, versions or understandings of some perspective may have its descriptive side, but insofar as there is an argument, other than descriptive accuracy, for selecting one of these approaches over any of the alternatives, we can understand, as elaborated in Section 3.4, how any argument for conceptual revision[66] has normative underpinnings.

If normative legal positivism is itself a plausible position, however, and a position that can be chosen by a theorist or by society, it follows not only

[65] See Murphy 2001.

[66] Or, for that matter, for refraining from revision and maintaining the concept now in operation.

that choosing a concept or theory of law on moral grounds is a moral position but also that, at one remove, so too is choosing to see the enterprise of legal theory in this normative way. Normative legal positivism thus emerges as the product both of seeing concepts of law as having normative advantages and disadvantages (possibly but not necessarily moral) and of seeing a normative approach to legal theory as something that itself can be assessed on normative grounds. Exploring the normative dimensions of a theory of law, therefore, leads into an exploration of the normative dimensions of legal theory as an enterprise. Normative legal positivism, therefore, is best seen as one consequence of normative legal theory. The relationship between the two is not a logical or a necessary one. Descriptive legal theory might describe various normative positions, including but not limited to normative legal positivism. In the final analysis, descriptive and normative versions of legal positivism are both possible, as are descriptive and normative versions of the enterprise of legal philosophy.

References

Alfange, D., Jr. 1969. 'Jeremy Bentham and the Codification of Law'. *Cornell Law Review* 55: 58–77.

Bentham, J. 1843. 'Scotch Reform'. In J. Bowring (ed.). *The Works of Jeremy Bentham* vol. 5. Tait: 1–54.

Bentham, J. 1988. *A Fragment on Government.* Ed. J. H. Burns and H. L. A. Hart. Cambridge University Press.

Bentham, J. 2010. *Of the Limits of the Penal Branch of Jurisprudence.* Ed. P. Schofield. Clarendon Press.

Burazin, L., Himma, K. E. and Roversi, C. (eds.). 2018. *Law as an Artifact.* Oxford University Press.

Campbell, T. 1996. *The Legal Theory of Ethical Positivism.* Dartmouth.

Campbell, T. 1998. 'The Point of Legal Positivism'. *King's College Law Journal* 9: 61–78.

Campbell, T. 2000. 'Democratic Aspects of Ethical Positivism'. In T. Campbell and J. Goldsworthy (eds.). *Judicial Power, Democracy and Legal Positivism.* Dartmouth: 3–24.

Campbell, T. 2004. *Prescriptive Legal Positivism: Law, Rights and Democracy.* UCL Press.

Celano, B. 2013. 'Normative Legal Positivism, Neutrality, and the Rule of Law'. In J. F. Beltran, J. J. Moreso and D. M. Papayannis (eds.). *Neutrality and Theory of Law.* Springer: 175–202.

Christie, G. 1973. *Jurisprudence: Text and Readings on the Philosophy of Law.* West.

Coleman, J. 1982. 'Negative and Positive Positivism'. *Journal of Legal Studies* 11: 139–64.

Coleman, J. 2001a. *The Practice of Principle: In Defence of a Pragmatist Approach to Legal Theory*. Oxford University Press.

Coleman, J. 2001b. Incorporationism, Conventionality, and the Practical Difference Thesis'. In ed. J. Coleman. *Hart's Postscript: Essays on the Postscript to the* Concept of Law. Oxford University Press: 99–148.

Coyle, S. 2003. 'Thomas Hobbes and the Intellectual Origins of Legal Positivism'. *Canadian Journal of Law and Jurisprudence* 16: 243–70.

Dickson, J. 2001. *Evaluation and Legal Theory*. Hart.

Dickson, J. 2004. 'Methodology in Jurisprudence: A Critical Survey'. *Legal Theory* 10: 117–56.

Dickson, J. 2009. 'Is Bad Law Still Law? Is Bad Law Really Law?'. In M. del Mar and Z. Bankowski (eds.). *Law as Institutional Normative Order*. Ashgate.

DiFilippo, T. 1972. 'Jeremy Bentham's Codification Proposals and Their Place in His Theory'. *Buffalo Law Review* 22: 239–51.

Dworkin, R. 1986. *Law's Empire*. Harvard University Press.

Dworkin, R. 2002. 'Thirty Years On'. *Harvard Law Review* 115: 1655–87.

Dworkin, R. 2006. *Justice in Robes*. Harvard University Press.

Dyzenhaus, D. 2010. *Hard Cases in Wicked Legal Systems: Pathologies of Legality*. Oxford University Press.

Dyzenhaus, D. and Poole, T. (eds.). 2012. *Hobbes and the Law*. Cambridge University Press.

Freeman, M. and Mindus, P. 2013. *The Legacy of John Austin's Jurisprudence*. Springer.

Fuller, L. L. 1958. 'Positivism and Fidelity to Law: A Reply to Professor Hart'. *Harvard Law Review* 71: 630–72.

Fuller, L. L. 1969. *The Morality of Law*. Yale University Press.

Green, L. 2008. 'Positivism and the Inseparability of Law and Morals'. *New York University Law Review* 83: 1035–58.

Green, L. 2016. 'Duty, Coercion, and Power'. *Ratio Juris* 29: 164–81.

Harrison, R. 1988. 'Introduction'. In R. Harrison and J. Bentham (eds.). *A Fragment on Government*. Cambridge: vi–xxiii.

Hart, H. L. A. 1958. 'Positivism and the Separation of Law and Morals'. *Harvard Law Review* 71: 593–629.

Hart, H. L. A. 1982. *Essays on Bentham: Jurisprudence and Political Theory*. Clarendon Press.

Hart, H. L. A. 2012. *The Concept of* Law. With an introduction by L. Green. Eds. P. A. Bulloch and J. Raz. Oxford University Press.

Himma, K. E. 2002. 'Inclusive Legal Positivism'. In J. Coleman and S. Shapiro (eds.). *The Oxford Handbook of Jurisprudence and Philosophy of Law*. Oxford University Press: 125–65.

Kelsen, H. 1967. *Pure Theory of Law*. Trans. M. Knight. University of California Press.

Lacey, N. 2004. *A Life of H.L.A. Hart: The Nightmare and the Noble Dream.* Oxford University Press.

Ladenson, R. 1980. 'In Defense of a Hobbesian Conception of Law'. *Philosophy and Public Affairs* 9: 134–59.

Leiter, B. 2007. *Naturalizing Jurisprudence: Essays on American Legal Realism and Naturalism in Legal Philosophy.* Oxford University Press.

Leiter, B. 2011. 'The Demarcation Problem in Jurisprudence: A New Case for Scepticism'. *Oxford Journal of Legal Studies* 31: 663–77.

Lyons, F. 1984. 'Founders and Foundations of Legal Positivism'. *Michigan Law Review* 82: 722–39.

MacCormick, N. 1985. 'A Moralistic Case for A-Moralistic Law'. *Valparaiso University Law Review* 20: 1–37.

Marmor, A. 2002. 'Exclusive Legal Positivism'. In J. Coleman and S. Shapiro (eds.). *The Oxford Handbook of Jurisprudence and Philosophy of Law.* Oxford University Press: 104–24.

Marmor, A. 2006. 'Legal Positivism: Still Descriptive and Morally Neutral'. *Oxford Journal of Legal Studies* 26: 683–704.

Morison, W. L. 1982. *John Austin.* Stanford University Press.

Murphy, M. 1995. 'Was Hobbes a Legal Positivist?'. *Ethics.* 105: 846–73.

Murphy, L. 2001. 'The Political Question of the Concept of Law'. In J. Coleman (ed.). *Hart's Postscript: Essays on the Postscript to the Concept of Law.* Oxford University Press: 371–409.

Perry, S. 1995. 'Interpretation and Methodology in Legal Theory'. In A. Marmor (ed.). *Law and Interpretation: Essays in Legal Philosophy.* Clarendon Press: 97–136.

Perry, S. 2001. 'Hart's Methodological Positivism'. In J. Coleman (ed.). *Hart's Postscript: Essays on the Postscript to the Concept of Law.* Oxford University Press: 311–354.

Postema, G. J. 1986. *Bentham and the Common Law Tradition.* Clarendon Press.

Postema, G. J. (ed.). 2002. *Bentham: Moral, Political and Legal Philosophy.* Dartmouth.

Postema, G. J. 2012. 'Legal Positivism: Early Foundations'. In A. Marmor (ed.). *The Routledge Companion to Philosophy of Law.* Routledge: 31–47.

Powers, W. Jr. 1985. 'Book Review'. *Duke Law Journal*: 221–36.

Priel, D. 2007. 'Evaluating Descriptive Jurisprudence'. *American Journal of Jurisprudence* 52: 139–58.

Raz, J. 1979. *The Authority of Law: Essays on Law and Morality.* Clarendon Press.

Raz, J. 1985. 'Authority, Law and Morality'. *The Monist* 68: 295–324.

Raz, J. 2005. 'Can There Be a Theory of Law?'. In M. P. Golding and W. A. Edmundson (eds.). *The Blackwell Guide to the Philosophy of Law and Legal Theory.* Blackwell: 324–42.

Riley, P. 2009. 'The Legal Philosophy of Thomas Hobbes'. In E. Pattaro, D. Canale, P. Grossi, H. Hofmann and P. Riley (ed.). *A Treatise of Legal Philosophy and General Jurisprudence* vol. 9. Springer: 379–401.

Rodriguez-Blanco, V. 2006. 'The Methodological Problem in Legal Theory: Normative and Descriptive Jurisprudence Revisited'. *Ratio Juris* 19: 26–54.

Rumble, W. E. 2005. *Doing Austin Justice: The Reception of John Austin's Philosophy of Law in Nineteenth-Century England.* Continuum.

Rundle, K. 2012. *Forms Liberate: Reclaiming the Jurisprudence of Lon L. Fuller.* Hart.

Schauer, F. 1993. 'Constitutional Positivism'. *Connecticut Law Review* 25: 797–828.

Schauer, F. 2004. 'The Limited Domain of the Law'. *Virginia Law Review* 90: 1909–56.

Schauer, F. 2005. 'The Social Construction of the Concept of Law: A Reply to Julie Dickson'. *Oxford Journal of Legal Studies* 25: 493–501.

Schauer, F. 2011. 'Positivism before Hart'. *Canadian Journal of Law and Jurisprudence* 24: 455–71.

Schauer, F. 2013. 'Hart's Anti-Essentialism'. In L. Duarte d'Almeida, J. Edwards and A. Dolcetti (eds.). *Reading H.L.A. Hart's 'The Concept of Law'.* Hart: 237–46.

Schauer, F. 2015a. 'The Path-Dependence of Legal Positivism'. *Virginia Law Review* 101: 957–81.

Schauer, F. 2015b. *The Force of Law.* Harvard University Press.

Schauer, F. 2017. 'Jeremy Bentham, Tom Campbell, and the Normative Positivist Tradition'. *Australian Journal of Legal Philosophy.* 42: 204–13.

Schauer, F. 2018. 'Law as a Malleable Artifact'. In L. Burazin, K. E. Himma and C. Roversi (eds.). *Law as an Artifact.* Oxford University Press: 29–43.

Schofield, P. 2013. 'The Legal and Political Legacy of Jeremy Bentham'. *Annual Review of Law and Social Science* 9: 51–70.

Shapiro, S. 2011. *Legality.* Harvard University Press.

Shiner, R. A. 1992. *Norm and Nature: The Movements of Legal Thought.* Clarendon Press.

Spaak, T. 2016. 'Schauer's Anti-Essentialism'. *Ratio Juris* 29: 182–214.

Steintrager, J. 1977. *Bentham.* Cornell University Press.

Summers, R. 1985. *Lon L. Fuller.* Stanford University Press.

Symposium. 1989. 'The Works of Joseph Raz'. *Southern California Law Review* 62: 731–1235.

Tasioulas, J. 2013. 'Hart on Justice and Morality'. In L. Duarte d'Almeida, J. Edwards and A. Dolcetti (eds.). *Reading H.L.A. Hart's The Concept of Law.* Hart: 155–76.

Tinturé, M. K. 2013. 'Concept and Purpose in Legal Theory: How to "Reclaim" Fuller'. *American Journal of Jurisprudence* 58: 75–96.

Waldron, J. 2001. 'Normative or Ethical Positivism'. In J. Coleman (ed.). *Hart's Postscript: Essays on the Postscript to the* Concept of Law. Oxford University Press: 410–34.

Walton, K. 2013. 'Jurisprudential Methodology: Is Pure Interpretation Possible?'. In J. F. Beltran, J. J. Moreso and D. M. Papayannis (eds.). *Neutrality and Theory of Law.* Springer: 255–73.

Waluchow, W. J. 1994. *Inclusive Legal Positivism.* Clarendon Press.

Legal Positivism as a Realist Theory of Law 4

Brian Leiter*

4.1 Introduction

By 'legal positivism', I mean the view about the nature of law that H. L. A. Hart articulated most powerfully in 1961 (while learning from and modifying the work of Hans Kelsen), and that Joseph Raz developed further in the 1970s and 1980s, according to which (1) where a legal system exists, there exists a 'Rule of Recognition' specifying the criteria in virtue of which norms are valid law; and (2) a rule of recognition is nothing more than a complex psycho-social artefact constituted by the practice of officials, in particular the criteria of legal validity they converge upon and which they treat as obligatory or something like that (in Hartian lingo, that they accept from 'an internal point of view').[1] That means that laws and legal systems rest at bottom on the conventional practices of officials.

By realist theories of law, I mean theories that: (1) describe without sentimental or moralising illusions what law is and how it actually operates in human societies (descriptive adequacy takes priority over moralising sermons); (2) recognise that law is never adequate to explain how courts adjudicate all cases that come before them; and (3) account for law and adjudication within the constraints of a naturalistic theory of the world, that is, one that eschews appeal to any entities or properties that do not find a place in successful empirical scientific accounts of natural and social phenomena. Both the American and the Scandinavian (self-identified)

* Thanks to participants in the conference in Stockholm in November 2018 for useful discussion and comments – especially Patricia Mindus, Torben Spaak and Kevin Toh. Thanks also to Michael Sevel for helpful discussion of Raz's views and to Joshua Fox for research assistance.

[1] I take Hart's view to be an improvement on Kelsen's kind of positivism in several crucial respects, most importantly in naturalising the notion of validity via appeal to certain kinds of social practice (Hart, in this regard, has more in common with the Scandinavian Realist Alf Ross than he acknowledges, a point to which I will return). I do not view other self-proclaimed positivist views as serious contenders.

'legal realists' were proponents of realist theories of law in this sense, albeit in very different ways, a point to which I return. Hart was a critic of both American and Scandinavian legal realisms, though in both cases he missed his mark. The irony is that Hart's legal positivism is also a realist theory of law (more in the American than the Scandinavian sense), and once we sort out the misunderstandings and confusions, it will be clear that legal positivists and realists form a unified theoretical front against the moralising and ideological obfuscators about law, from Lon Fuller to Ronald Dworkin.[2] It will also turn out that one of Raz's additions to Hart's theory, namely the idea that law necessarily claims authority in Raz's 'Service Conception' sense, betrays the realist ambitions of Hart's theory.

4.2 The Realism of Hart's Legal Positivism

Hart's theory of law as developed in *The Concept of Law*[3] is a realist theory in four important respects.

First, Hart recognises that law in modern societies operates primarily outside the courts, namely, as a way of guiding ordinary people (sometimes with the help of lawyers) as to what they can and cannot do and, in particular, how they can acquire various legally created powers, such as the power to get married (and accrue the associated legal and tax benefits) or the power to dispose of their property after their death. Any general *theory of law* that focuses primarily on courts is not realistic. It is not simply that courts decide only a minuscule fraction of all legal disputes (massive agreement about what the law requires, after all, is the norm in functioning legal systems);[4] it is that the primary function of law in modern societies is to help people organise their affairs to avoid disputes, either with other citizens or with the state: in other words, *to avoid* adjudication. Law tells people what they need to do to buy a house, to get divorced, to avoid tax penalties, to enter into business relationships, and it also sets conditions under which their freedom can be restricted or their property seized.

Second, adjudication of some legal disputes inevitably involves judgements that are not constrained by law but instead require the exercise of

[2] This is not true of every view that self-identifies as either legal positivism or legal realism, but it is true for the core cases discussed in the text.

[3] Hart 2012. [4] See Leiter 2009: 1226–8.

discretionary judgement, informed by non-legal considerations: the law is sometimes *rationally indeterminate* (that is, the class of legitimate legal reasons underdetermines the decision that the adjudicator must reach).[5] Any theory that presents adjudication as a matter of discovering pre-existing answers in a legal heaven is not realistic. Rules determinate in their application in most instances can never be without uncertainty, unless we adopt patently absurd approaches, such as 'when the rule is unclear, the plaintiff wins'. Hart saw, correctly, that indeterminacy in law was inevitable – though he was wrong in thinking that the 'open texture' of language was its primary cause (a point to which I return) – and he also saw correctly that this was not a feature of law that anyone should try to remedy:[6] We are far better off with officials who can produce authoritative resolution of disputes that no one anticipated than we would be with a system that tried to settle every matter well in advance.

Third, the social phenomenon of law is explicable in wholly naturalistic terms, without recourse to objective moral values or Kantian transcendental conditions on judgement: law and legal systems exist entirely because of psychological and sociological facts about persons. On one reading, the claim that law is part of the natural order is bound to seem trivial (theists and others in the grips of religious illusions to one side): Is not everything part of the 'natural order' of the world? But positivists and realists understand this claim in a more demanding way: Everything real is part of the causal account of nature developed by successful empirical sciences, whether physics or biology or psychology. There are no facts outside the causal order of nature as described by the various sciences. Legal systems have important normative dimensions – officials and sometimes subjects take the system's demands to be obligation-imposing, for example – but this is a complicated psychological and sociological fact about persons, not a fact about the world apart from those psycho-social facts about persons. Any theory that posits transcendental conditions on legal judgment (for example, Kelsen) or mind-independent moral values (for example, Dworkin) is not realistic.

Fourth, Hart recognises that law is not necessarily a good thing, that governance by law has costs, and as a result we should never presuppose that law is morally good or obligatory. This has been the central idea of the positivist tradition in legal theory: We can say what the normative system

[5] See Leiter 2007: 9–12. [6] See Hart 2012: 128–30.

called 'law' requires while recognising that what the law demands may not be what we should do. Talk of law not being 'morally binding' must of course be given a non-cognitivist gloss, consistent with Hart's actual way of marking normative practices.[7] Any theory, like Dworkin's, that builds the justification of coercive power into the nature of law is not realistic.

4.3 Legal Realisms, American and Scandinavian

Hart contributed to the perception that legal positivism was not a realist theory of law by his famous, but ultimately misguided, criticisms of the American and Scandinavian legal realists. The fault is not entirely his, to be sure: The American legal realists were rhetorically exuberant, rather than analytically precise, and an unfortunate translation of Alf Ross's *Of Law and Justice* probably exacerbated the misunderstandings of the Scandinavian position.[8]

Hart also solidified the unfortunate assimilation of the two realisms, American and Scandinavian, when, in reality, they have almost nothing in common: Calling them both instances of 'realism' is mainly an accident of intellectual history and a confusion about words. While the Scandinavians adopted the label 'realism' to signal their opposition to metaphysical idealists, who thought that the nature of reality was dependent on the human mind and its categories,[9] the Americans invoked a different sense of 'realism' – partly colloquial and partly corresponding to an intellectual tradition stretching from Thucydides to Machiavelli and beyond – as being candid about *what really happens* (especially when courts decide cases), without sentimental or moralistic illusions.[10] The latter is the sense of realism I am mainly concerned with here.

The difference should hardly be surprising given the very different professional and intellectual backgrounds of the two groups. The major

[7] Recall that, for Hart, the ascription of the 'internal point of view' to agents is based entirely on behavioural criteria, i.e., what actors do and say. This no doubt betrays the influence of Gilbert Ryle's behaviourism in philosophy of mind.

[8] See the discussion in Leiter and Etchemendy 2017: s. 5.1, drawing on the work of Jakob Holtermann.

[9] Hägerstrom is a case in point: see Mindus 2009: 48. Mindus (2009: 137 n. 2) also notes other writers sceptical about the lumping together of Scandinavian and American Realism.

[10] See Leiter 2012.

American Realists – Karl Llewellyn, Jerome Frank, Herman Oliphant, Max Radin, Underhill Moore, William O. Douglas, among others – were law professors, lawyers and jurists with no philosophical training and, rather obviously, no aptitude for or interest in philosophical questions.[11] What they were all interested in was how courts actually decide cases, and what lawyers and law students needed to know if they were to reliably advise their clients about how they would fare in the courts. They advanced no theses about the nature of law apart from these practical litigation-oriented concerns, though it is striking that their tacit assumptions about the nature of law were all positivist ones, a point to which we will return.[12]

The Scandinavians were different: They were either primarily philosophers or had some formal training in philosophy, and all were primarily academics and scholars who conceived of their jurisprudential questions in philosophical terms. In contemporary terminology,[13] they were occupied with variations on what philosophers call the 'location problem', that is, the problem of how to locate some phenomenon – for example, consciousness or moral value – in a world naturalistically conceived, that is, conceived in the causal terms described by the empirical sciences. So, for example, philosophers interested in the location problem might ask how we make sense of subjective conscious experience, or of the idea that something is morally wrong, in a world that is exhaustively explained by physics, chemistry and biology? Or, how can we locate the experience of Beethoven's *Ninth Symphony* as beautiful, or the sense that genocide is a moral abomination, in a world thought to be composed of nothing other than physical, chemical, biological and/or psychological facts?

For the Scandinavian Realists, the precise issue was how to locate a legal system of norms in a world so conceived. The Scandinavians were philosophically diverse on some issues, so generalising about them will no doubt run roughshod over some individual differences. Yet there are two basic issues at stake: metaphysical (do these norms really exist?) and semantic (what is the *meaning* of legal statements mentioning such norms?). On the metaphysical question, there are elements of eliminativism in the views of Olivecrona and Ross.[14] Just as the eliminativist about religious discourse

[11] Felix Cohen was the exception – although his philosophy PhD served him badly. See, e.g., Cohen 1935, which arguably adopts an indefensible version of rule-scepticism. For discussion, see Leiter 2007: 68–73.

[12] See Leiter 2001. [13] See Jackson 1998. [14] See Olivecrona 1971; Ross 1959.

thinks that the entities that religious discourse refers to (gods, souls, spirits) do not exist, and so should be eliminated from any realistic picture of what the world is like, the legal eliminativist thinks that legal obligations, legal rights and legal duties do not really exist either, since such concepts play no role in a scientific explanation of the world. Because the Scandinavians sometimes seem to be eliminativists at the metaphysical level, they (generally) opt for 'non-cognitivist' views about the semantics, that is, views according to which *statements* about legal obligations, rights and duties do not really try to refer to anything but are simply the expression of the 'attitudes' of legal actors.[15] So, for example, judgments about legal obligations and duties are interpreted as expressing certain non-cognitive attitudes or feelings: A court's judgment of the form 'Mr. Smith has a contractual obligation to pay Mr. Jones $5,000 for those widgets' really means something like 'I, the judge, feel the force of the legal demand that Mr. Smith pay under these circumstances, and if he doesn't, I will sanction him!' The psychologism of some of the Scandinavians held that legal norms, both their existence and their effects on behaviour, were to be explained in terms of the psychological states of persons who accepted these norms, rather than the reality of the norms: That X *believes* or *feels* he has a duty or obligation is what is explanatory of behaviour, not the existence of the duty.[16] A similar kind of psychologism is, I think, implicit in Hart, though he sometimes cannot quite acknowledge it, perhaps because of the influence of J. L. Austin's ordinary language philosophy on his thinking. This requires further explication.

Hart was a metaphysical anti-realist about moral norms: Such norms do not really exist, since the best explanation of the world would not include facts about what is morally right and wrong. This might suggest that the *normativity* of morals – the ability of what is morally right and wrong to give people efficacious reasons to act – should be understood in exclusively psychological terms, that is, as a psychological fact about what particular people believe and feel when they are told that 'it is morally wrong to do X' or 'it is morally right to Y'. The most charitable reading of Hart should understand him as accepting something like this view, since,

[15] See the more detailed discussion in Leiter and Etchemendy 2017: s. 5.1. See also Spaak 2011: 163–5; Spaak 2009: 493–4. As Patricia Mindus reminds me, Hägerstrom is an unusual case, opting for an error theory about 'rights' but a kind of emotivism about judgements of moral value.

[16] See Mindus 2009: 142 n. 31.

unlike Hans Kelsen, his was an 'impure' theory of law in which anti-realism about norms was conjoined with non-cognitivism about the semantics of normative judgement: to judge that doing X is morally (or legally) wrong is just to express a certain kind of attitude or feeling, presumably one tied – psychologically – to motivation and action.[17] Hart did, of course, reject the view he attributed to Alf Ross, namely, that legal *validity* consists in 'a verifiable hypothesis about future judicial behavior and its special motivational feeling'.[18] (Hart failed to realise that this was a stipulative account in Ross, not an ordinary language account: Ross wanted to show how we could 'locate' doctrinal or 'external' statements about what the law is in a world naturalistically conceived, a point to which I return.) For Hart, to say that a legal rule is *valid* is just to say that it satisfies the criteria of legal validity in the Rule of Recognition. But neither I nor Ross is denying Hart's conceptual point about judgments by legal actors about legal validity, namely, that its meaning is not reducible to predictions about behaviour: Even Ross's treatment of such judgments was non-cognitive, like Hart's.[19] Rather, the point at issue here concerns what an anti-realism about *norms*, which Hart accepts, entails about motivation and action. On the realist/naturalist view, to the extent that an agent's judgement that X is *morally right* (or *legally obligatory*) has normative force for the agent, that normative force is explicable in terms of certain psychological facts about the agent. Hart sometimes seems to deny this, for example when he says that 'the internal character of [normative legal judgments, like "you must stop at the red light"] is not a mere matter of the speaker having certain "feelings of compulsion"; for though these may indeed often accompany the making of such statements they are neither necessary nor sufficient conditions of their normative use in criticizing conduct, making claims and justifying hostile reactions by reference to the accepted standard'.[20] But Hart is best understood here as simply revealing his commitment to a kind of Rylean behaviourism about attitude ascriptions: agents manifest the 'internal point of view' simply in virtue of using the right kind of normative language and making the right kinds of justificatory or critical comment about, respectively, conforming or deviant behaviour vis-à-vis some rule. Contemporary naturalists have no reason to accept the behaviourism, given the explanatory fruitfulness of psychological explanations in so many domains.

[17] See Toh 2005. [18] Hart 1983: 165. [19] See Ross 1959: 6–9. [20] Hart 2012: 167.

In sum, the Scandinavians have deeper affinities with the great Austrian legal positivist Hans Kelsen and the great English legal positivist H. L. A. Hart than they do with the American Realists: the latter want to figure out why courts decide as they do, and then let lawyers in on the *real* causes accordingly; while all the former – that is, Kelsen, Hart and the Scandinavians – are interested in traditional philosophical questions about the metaphysical nature of law[21] and (in the case of Hart and the Scandinavians) how it can be located within a naturalistic worldview, that is, one that takes for granted that the world is, more or less, as the sciences describe it. Hart and the Scandinavians differ from Kelsen in their willingness to think that the answer can involve 'naturalising' certain normative concepts in law, that is, understanding them as complicated psychological and sociological artefacts, and thus as part of what Kelsen would have understood to be an 'impure' theory of law.[22]

4.4 Hart's Mistaken Critique of Legal Realism

Hart attributes to legal realism a view he calls 'rule-skepticism', a view he deems correct in certain instances (consistent with his own realism about adjudication). Hart considers two different kinds of rule-scepticism. One, which I will call 'Conceptual Rule-Skepticism', holds that 'talk of rules is a myth, cloaking the truth that law consists simply of the decisions of courts and the predictions of them'.[23] The second, which I will call 'Empirical Rule-Scepticism', is the only important kind for his putative dispute with legal realism. According to this view, 'Rule-scepticism has a serious claim on our attention, but only as a theory of the function of rules in judicial decision';[24] more precisely, this realist/sceptic claims 'that it is false, if not senseless, to regard judges as themselves subject to rules or "bound" to decide cases as they do'.[25]

Conceptual Rule-Scepticism grows out of Hart's conflation of the American and Scandinavian Realists. Conceptual Rule-Scepticism is a claim about the nature of law, namely that it consists only in what courts

[21] None of these philosophers were interested in metaphysical questions about 'grounding', the current fad in Anglophone philosophy.

[22] I have explored that possibility as well: see the essays in Leiter 2007 part II.

[23] Hart 2012: 133. [24] Hart 2012: 135. [25] Ibid.

say or in predictions of what courts will do. Hart's critique of this as an account of the nature of law as reflected in ordinary language is wholly persuasive, in my view:[26] Such a theory of the ordinary concept of law cannot account for how judges think about what the law 'obligates' them to do, or about the way in which lawyers and citizens criticise judicial conduct by reference to the law. But did either the Scandinavians or the Americans endorse Conceptual Rule-Scepticism?

Alf Ross, as we have seen, did proffer something like this, but not because he thought it was adequate to the 'ordinary' usage of the concept of law, or because he was insensitive to the points that Hart raised. He proffered such an analysis as part of a philosophical reconstruction of statements about what the law is by scholars and observers, one that would make sense of its normative concepts in a world naturalistically conceived: by reinterpreting normative claims about 'duties' and 'obligations' as empirical predictive claims, Ross aimed to show that law was not polluted with metaphysical nonsense. Ross was not doing ordinary language philosophy about how things looked to legal insiders; Hart was. Hart criticised Ross as offering an implausible analysis of the 'ordinary' concept; Ross would have agreed. Hart offered no direct response to the actual 'location problem' Ross was concerned with.

In the case of the American Realists, Hart was also guilty of misreading, although, in fairness to him, at least one Realist, Felix Cohen, was, arguably, a Conceptual Rule-Sceptic, although Cohen is nowhere cited by Hart: Hart's American Legal Realism relies on an amalgamation mainly of Frank, Holmes and Llewellyn. Plainly, these writers do talk about the importance of 'predicting' what courts will do. The question is whether, in so talking, they are fairly read as offering an analysis of the concept of law. Only Hart's grossly anachronistic reading suggests an affirmative answer.

The idea that philosophy involves 'conceptual analysis' via the analysis of language (or appeals to intuitions about how concepts or terms apply) is an artefact of Anglo-American analytic philosophy of the twentieth century; indeed, as practised by Hart, it really reflects the influence of fashionable views in philosophy of language current at Oxford in the 1940s and 1950s. The American Realists were not philosophers, let alone analytic philosophers, let alone students of G. E. Moore, Russell and Wittgenstein, let alone colleagues of J. L. Austin. The idea that what demands

[26] See Leiter 2007: 69–73.

understanding about law is the 'concept' of law as manifest in ordinary language and ordinary intuitions would have struck them as bizarre. While the Realists had much to say about adjudication and how legal rules work in practice, they had nothing explicit to say about the 'ordinary' concept of law or our intuitions about it.[27]

So, what did the American Realists mean in talking about 'prediction'? In *Law and the Modern Mind*, Jerome Frank cautions the reader early on that he 'is primarily concerned with "law" as it affects the work of the practicing lawyer and the needs of the clients who retain him'.[28] Holmes begins 'The Path of the Law' by emphasising that he is talking about the meaning of law to lawyers who will 'appear before judges, or . . . advise people in such a way as to keep them out of court'.[29] Against this background, infamous statements like Llewellyn's – 'What these officials do about disputes is, to my mind, the law itself'[30] – make perfect sense. Theirs is a claim not about the 'concept' of law but, rather, about a practical heuristic, how it is helpful to think about law for attorneys who must advise clients what to do. For your client the franchisee in Connecticut does not simply want to know what the rule on the books in Connecticut says; he wants to know what will happen when he takes the franchisor to court. So, from the practical perspective of the franchisee, what one wants to know about the 'law' is what, in fact, the courts will do when confronted with the franchisee's grievance. That is all the law that matters to the client, all the law that matters to the lawyer advising that client. And that is all the American Realists wanted to emphasise.

Ironically, it turns out the American Realists could not have been Conceptual Rule-Sceptics because their arguments for the indeterminacy of law actually presuppose the positivist's concept of law. The central claim of legal indeterminacy is the claim of rational indeterminacy: the claim that the 'class of legal reasons' fails to justify a unique outcome in some or all cases. The

[27] Raz and his followers often obscure this point. Raz, for example, claims that the argument for his 'hard' or 'exclusive' positivism 'is not an argument from the ordinary sense of "law" or any other term. It relies on fundamental features of our understanding of a certain social institution, the primary examples of which are contemporary municipal legal systems' (Raz 1979: 50). But all his examples are examples of ordinary or familiar distinctions people draw between law and other normative systems, between legal and other kinds of normative competence. The giveaway is the appeal to 'our understanding of a certain social institution': what could that possibly be other than an armchair report of what Raz takes people to say and believe about law?

[28] Frank 1930: 47 n. [29] Holmes 1897: 457. [30] Llewellyn 1930a: 3.

'class of legal reasons' is the class of reasons that are taken to properly justify a legal conclusion (and thus 'compel' it insofar as legal actors are responsive to valid legal reasons). So, for example, appeal to a statutory provision or a valid precedent is part of the class of legal reasons in the United States, while appeal to the authority of Plato's *Republic* is not: a judge is not obliged to decide one way rather than another because Plato says so. Any argument for indeterminacy, then, presupposes some view about the boundaries of the class of legal reasons. When Herman Oliphant[31] argues, for example, that the promise-not-to-compete cases are decided not by reference to law but by reference to uncodified norms prevalent in the commercial culture in which the disputes arose, this shows only that the law is indeterminate on the assumption that the normative reasons the courts are actually relying upon are not themselves legal reasons.[32] So, too, when Holmes chalks up judicial decisions not to legal reasoning but to 'a concealed, half-conscious battle on the [background] question of legislative policy',[33] he is plainly presupposing that these policy concerns are not themselves legal reasons. The famous American Realist arguments for indeterminacy that focus on the conflicting but equally legitimate ways that lawyers have of interpreting statutes and precedents[34] show only that the law is indeterminate on the assumption either that statutes and precedents largely exhaust the authoritative sources of law or that any additional authoritative norms not derived from these sources conflict. It is the former assumption that seems to motivate the Realist arguments. Thus, Llewellyn says that judges take rules 'in the main from authoritative sources (which in the case of law are largely statutes and the decisions of the courts)'.[35] In short, the American Realists presuppose something like the positivist idea of a rule of recognition whose criteria of legality are exclusively ones of pedigree: A rule (or canon of construction) is part of the law in virtue of having a source in a legislative enactment or a prior court decision.[36]

31 See Oliphant 1928.

32 According to Oliphant, the courts found ways to enforce sellers' promises not to compete with purchasers because this made good economic sense: there would be no point to the transaction otherwise. By contrast, courts found ways to invalidate employees' promises not to compete with their former employers since such arrangements were disfavoured by trade guilds and took unfair advantage of the bargaining position of employees.

33 Holmes 1897: 467.

34 The classic discussions are Llewellyn 1930a: 72–6; Llewellyn 1950: 395–406; Radin 1930.

35 Llewellyn 1931: 13.

36 One difference is that most positivists recognise customary practices as sources of valid law, whereas it is not clear what the Realists think about this.

Matters are more interesting with respect to what I am calling Empirical Rule-Scepticism. Here is Hart's characterisation of the view in question:

> [I]t amounts to the contention that, so far as the courts are concerned, there is nothing to circumscribe the open texture [of language in which rules are framed]: so that it is false, if not senseless, to regard judges as themselves subject to rules or 'bound' to decide cases as they do. They may act with sufficient predictable regularity and uniformity to enable others, over long periods, to live by courts' decisions as rules. Judges may even experience feelings of compulsion when they decide as they do, and these feelings may be predictable too; but beyond this there is nothing which can be characterized as a rule which they observe.[37]

Empirical Rule-Scepticism on this rendering, then, involves two claims: (1) legal rules are indeterminate; and, as a result, (2) legal rules do not determine or constrain decisions.

Obviously (1) is not an empirical claim but a philosophical or jurisprudential one. But (2) could be true even if (1) were false (that would be pure Empirical Rule-Scepticism, we might say). Yet Hart is surely correct that most American Realists endorse both (1) and (2). Unfortunately, Hart is mistaken about the Realist argument for (1), and thus underestimates the amount of indeterminacy in law. And the real dispute, if there is one, between the American Realists and Hart turns in the end on (2).

Remember that Hart acknowledges that legal rules are indeterminate but claims that that is a phenomenon at 'the margin of rules';[38] the realist sceptic, on Hart's rendering, is simply 'a disappointed absolutist',[39] someone who set the bar for legal determinacy too high. But the American Realists, with some exceptions (notably Jerome Frank), recognised that law was mostly rationally determinate; they pointed out that it tended to be indeterminate, however, in those cases that reached the stage of appellate review. And they argued for that proposition based on the empirical evidence of lines of appellate cases that could not be rationalised in terms of the official doctrine. Their argument for indeterminacy was different from Hart's, which may help explain the *apparent* disagreement.

According to Hart, legal rules are indeterminate because 'there is a limit, inherent in the nature of language, to the guidance which general language can provide'.[40] Language is, in Hart's famous phrase, 'open-textured':

[37] Hart 2012: 135. [38] Ibid. [39] Ibid. [40] Hart 2012: 123.

> There will indeed be plain cases constantly recurring in similar contexts to which general expressions are clearly applicable ('If anything is a vehicle a motor-car is one') but there will also be cases where it is not clear whether they apply or not. ('Does "vehicle" used here include bicycles, airplanes, roller skates?'). The latter are fact-situations, continually thrown up by nature or human invention, which possess only some of the features of the plain cases but others which they lack.[41]

Language is 'open-textured' in that while words have 'core' instances – aspects of the world that clearly fall within the extension of the word's meaning – they also have 'penumbras', cases where it is unclear whether the extension includes the aspect of the world at issue. In cases in which the facts fall within the penumbra of the key words in the applicable legal rule, a court 'must exercise a discretion, [since] there is no possibility of treating the question raised . . . as if there were one uniquely correct answer to be found, as distinct from an answer which is a reasonable compromise between many conflicting interests'.[42]

While some writers have challenged the implicit semantics that inform this argument for the indeterminacy of language (a fortiori of law),[43] I think we should agree with Hart that legal rules must necessarily be indeterminate in some measure given the indeterminacy of language itself, and that this type of indeterminacy resides 'at the margin of rules'.[44] What bears noting here is that the American Realist arguments for indeterminacy did not rely on these claims about language.

The American Realists located the indeterminacy of law not in general features of language itself but in the existence of equally legitimate, but conflicting, canons of interpretation that courts could employ to extract differing rules from the same statutory text or the same precedent.[45] Indeterminacy resides not in the rules themselves but in the ways we have of characterising what rules statutes and precedents contain. Llewellyn argues, for example, that any precedent can be read 'strictly' or 'loosely', and that either reading is 'recognized, legitimate, honorable'.[46] The strict interpretation characterises the rule of the case as specific to the facts of the case; the loose interpretation abstracts (in varying degrees) from the specific facts in order to treat the case as standing for some

[41] Hart 2012: 128. [42] Ibid.
[43] For criticism of such approaches, see Leiter and Etchemendy 2017: s. 5.3.
[44] Hart 2012: 132.
[45] I take it that something similar is true of the Italian Legal Realists of the Genoa School.
[46] Llewellyn 1930a: 74.

general norm. But if 'each precedent has not one value [that is, stands for not just one rule], but two, and . . . the two are wide apart, and . . . whichever value a later court assigns to it, such assignment will be respectable, traditionally sound, dogmatically correct',[47] then precedent, as a source of law, cannot provide reasons for a unique outcome because more than one rule can be extracted from the same precedent.

Llewellyn thinks that the same is true of statutory interpretation, where one can find 'correct', unchallengeable rules of 'how to read' that lead in happily variant directions.[48] By mining the cases, Llewellyn shows that courts have endorsed contradictory canons of construction, like '[A] statute cannot go beyond its text', but also '[To effect its purpose[,] a statute must be implemented beyond its text.'[49] But if a statute can properly be construed in contradictory ways to stand for different rules, then reasoning from the statute will not justify a unique outcome in the case at hand.

One difficulty with these Realist arguments is that they rely on a tacit conception of legitimate legal argument. The assumption is that if lawyers and courts employ some form of argument – a 'strict' construal of precedent, a particular canon of statutory construction – then that form of argument is legitimate in any and all cases. Put in this strong form, the assumption cannot be right: not every strict construal of precedent will be legally proper in every case. Even Llewellyn must recognise this, as suggested by his famous – but clearly facetious – example of the strict reading that yields '[T]his rule holds only of redheaded Walpoles in pale magenta Buick cars.'[50] But that would never be a legitimate construal of a precedent (barring some bizarre scenario in which all these facts turned out to be legally relevant), and Llewellyn surely knows as much. The claim cannot be, then, that any strict or loose construal of precedent is always valid. It must be only that lawyers and judges have this interpretive latitude often enough to inject a considerable degree of indeterminacy into law.[51]

[47] Llewellyn 1930a: 76. [48] Llewellyn 1950: 399. [49] Llewellyn 1930a: 90.

[50] Llewellyn 1930a: 72.

[51] In Chapter 2 of this volume, Leslie Green objects that there appears to be no principled explanation for why the indeterminacy should not go 'all the way down', as it were. But the key is that the argument depends on a 'sociological' notion of which interpretations of sources are 'legitimate', meaning accepted by most lawyers and judges. Lawyers and judges may, of course, treat interpretive moves as acceptable even without a principled basis for doing so.

Notice that the Realist argument for Empirical Rule-Scepticism is actually conceptually severable from the claim that the law is indeterminate. For, centrally, it is based on the observation that the decisions that courts reach do not fall into patterns that correlate with the rules they invoke; rather, the decisions reflect judges' response to the underlying facts of the cases. This was the point of Oliphant's example of the promise-not-to-compete cases mentioned earlier; it is Llewellyn's point, too, in his discussion of the New York sales cases.[52] What causes judges to decide as they do, according to the Realist, is not legal rules[53] but a sense of what would be fair on the facts of the case at hand. All American Realists agreed on this point. Judge Hutcheson claimed that 'the vital, motivating impulse for the decision is an intuitive sense of what is right or wrong for that cause'.[54] Frank invoked the example of 'a great American judge', Chancellor Kent, who had confessed that 'he first made himself "master of the facts". Then (he wrote) "I saw where justice lay, and the moral sense decided the court half the time; I then sat down to search the authorities ... but I almost always found principles suited to my view of the case".'[55] Llewellyn noted that, to understand what appellate courts are really doing, one must appreciate 'how far the proposition which seems so abstract has roots in what seems to be the due thing on the facts [before the court]'.[56] As a result, Llewellyn's advice for the lawyer was 'on the facts ... [to] persuade the court your case is sound', even if the lawyer must also provide a 'technical

[52] Llewellyn 1960: 122–4. According to Llewellyn, a series of New York cases applied the rule that a buyer who rejects the seller's shipment by formally stating his objections thereby waives all other objections. Llewellyn observed that the rule seemed to have been harshly applied in some cases where the buyers simply may not have known at the time of rejection of other defects or where the seller could not have cured in any case. Upon looking at the underlying facts of those cases, however, Llewellyn discovered that what had really happened was that the market had gone sour, and the buyer was looking to escape the contract. The court, being 'sensitive to commerce or to decency', Llewellyn (1960: 124) applied the unrelated rule about rejection to frustrate the buyer's attempted violation of a basic norm of commercial conduct: namely, parties should honour their commitments even under changed market conditions. It is, in short, the 'background facts, those of mercantile practice, those of the situation-type' (Llewellyn 1960: 126) that determine the court's decision.

[53] Some legal rules, of course, structure the presentation of facts to the court, and thus 'the facts of the case at hand' are unintelligible without legal rules. Conceding this point does not change the fact, however, that there still may be a disjunction (as the realists claim) between the substantive rules of law that judges invoke in their decisions and the real bases for their decisions.

[54] Hutcheson 1929: 285. [55] Frank 1930: 104 n. [56] Llewellyn 1930a: 29.

ladder' to the 'sound' result.[57] Frank pointed out that the very same advice had been given by a former president of the American Bar Association.[58] In short, the core of the Realist defence of Empirical Rule-Scepticism is, in fact, empirical: They looked at what the courts (primarily the appellate courts) really did, and found that legal rules were clearly not the determining factors in a large number of cases.

At the same time, the Realists – unlike many of the later Critical Legal Studies writers – did not overstate the irrelevance of rules. For one thing, the American Realists were (generally) clear that their focus was indeterminacy at the stage of appellate review, where one ought to expect a higher degree of uncertainty in the law. Cases that have determinate legal answers are, after all, less likely to be litigated to the stage of appellate review. Most of the time, the Realists seemed to understand this point. Thus, Llewellyn explicitly qualified his indeterminacy claim by saying that 'in any case doubtful enough to make litigation respectable the available authoritative premises . . . are at least two, and . . . the two are mutually contradictory as applied to the case at hand'.[59] And Max Radin noted that judicial 'decisions will consequently be called for chiefly in what may be called marginal cases, in which prognosis is difficult and uncertain. It is this fact that makes the entire body of legal judgments seem less stable than it really is.'[60] Empirical Rule-Scepticism is surely more plausible when it is not advanced as a global claim about adjudication and the law.

Notice now that even if we agreed with Hart that the open texture of language affects rules only 'at the margins' (whatever that means, a point to which we return), the Realists have now given us an additional reason (beyond Hart's) to expect indeterminacy in law. If the Realists are right, then not only do legal rules suffer from the open texture that Hart describes but statutes and precedents will frequently admit of 'manipulatio' – legally legitimate manipulation, of course – and thus be indeterminate in this additional respect as well. The combination of sources of indeterminacy (the open texture of language and the conflicting canons of interpretation) seems sufficient to move indeterminacy from the margins to the centre of cases actually litigated through the stage of appellate review.

Hart is not wholly insensitive to the Realist arguments, though he treats them cursorily. In response to Llewellyn's point, for example, that a court

[57] Llewellyn 1930a: 76. [58] See Frank 1930: 102 n. [59] Llewellyn 1931: 1239.
[60] Radin 1942: 1271.

can interpret a precedent both 'loosely' and 'strictly' and thus extract two different rules from the same prior decision, Hart says simply this: '[I]n the vast majority of decided cases there is very little doubt [as to the rule of the case]. The head-note is usually correct enough.'[61] Alas, a first-year litigation associate knows that this approach to precedent would be a recipe for disaster. To extract 'holdings' without regard to the facts of the case – which is all a head-note typically provides – is mediocre lawyering. Skilful lawyers know exactly what Llewellyn describes: that the 'rule' of a prior case can be stated at differing degrees of specificity and so made to do very different argumentative work depending on the needs of the case at hand.

So, both Hart and the American Realists acknowledge indeterminacy in law, and both acknowledge, accordingly, that rules do not determine decisions in some range of cases. Hart seems to think that they disagree over the range of cases about which these claims hold true, but that is not entirely clear. Consider Hart's ultimate rejoinder to Realist scepticism about the influence of legal rules on court decisions:

> [I]t is surely evident that for the most part decisions ... are reached either by genuine effort to conform to rules consciously taken as guiding standards of decision or, if intuitively reached, are justified by rules which the judge was antecedently disposed to observe and whose relevance to the case in hand would generally be acknowledged.[62]

There is, alas, no argument here: 'it is surely evident' is simply a denial of what the Realist affirms, yet Hart offers no evidence for the denial other than his armchair confidence in the correctness of his own view.

But perhaps Hart and the American Realists are not really disagreeing? That may seem surprising, but I now think it the most plausible interpretation, given the clear Realist elements in Hart's own views, and the clear positivist elements in the views of the American Realists. After all, when Hart limits indeterminacy to the 'margin of rules', this is against the backdrop of one of his central insights, namely, that law exists mainly *outside* the courts as a way for individuals to plan their affairs and guide their conduct. The American Realists sometimes make the 'American mistake' (think of Dworkin) of focusing far too much on courts, but, if we put that parochial prejudice aside, they have no theoretical reason to deny Hart's insight. And that insight is compatible with recognition that cases that

[61] Hart 2012: 131. [62] Hart 2012: 137.

reach the stage of appellate review are especially likely to be ones where the law is indeterminate, precisely for 'selection effect' reasons: parties have more incentive to pursue further litigation when the law is unclear and the result could go either way. Hart has no theoretical reason to deny this latter point.

Remember also that the American Realists explicitly did not discount the role of rules in adjudication. Llewellyn is representative when he asks, 'Do I suggest that ... the "accepted rules", the rules the judges say that they apply, are without influence upon their actual behavior?' and answers, 'I do not.'[63] The Realist approach, says Llewellyn, 'admits ... some relation between any accepted rule and judicial behavior' but then demands that what that relation is requires empirical investigation, since it is not always the relation suggested by the 'logic' (or content) of the rule.[64] As he puts the point elsewhere: Realists deny that 'traditional ... rule-formulations are the heavily operative factor in producing court decisions'.[65] But to deny only this claim is to admit that rules play some causal role in decisions.

We thus arrive at a possible *rapprochement* between two schools of Anglophone realist jurisprudence, that of Hart's positivism and the American Legal Realists. Both Hart and the American Realists agree that valid legal rules (that is, those with the relevant pedigree) matter, that they are often determinate in their application, and that, at the higher levels of adjudication, indeterminacy obtains and judges must exercise discretion. In addition, the Scandinavian Realists can agree that Hart has a satisfactory account of the 'ordinary' concept of law, while disagreeing on whether the best attempt to solve the location problem for law in a world conceived naturalistically requires the theoretical artifice of recasting normative talk in law in predictive terms or whether a non-cognitivist approach, which arguably Hart favours, will suffice for statements about the law by both legal actors and observers. And all the realists and the positivists agree that law does not always suffice to explain what happens in adjudication and all reject the objectivity of moral values. Even if there can be reasonable doubts about whether the muddle-headed American Realists understood all these points, or whether the Scandinavian Realists, in the grips (generally) of logical positivism, did, we can affirm that sensible realist jurisprudence can and must affirm them.

[63] Llewellyn 1930b: 444. [64] Ibid. [65] Llewellyn 1931: 1237.

4.5 Realism, Positivism and Raz's Authority Argument

In the recent positivist tradition, the most influential contribution to the theory comes from Hart's student Raz, who argued, against Hart, that no rule of recognition at the foundation of a legal system could incorporate moral, or content-based, criteria of legal validity.[66] Although a rule of recognition is constituted by the practice of officials – those criteria of legal validity that they converge upon and treat as obligatory – it cannot, on Raz's view, rely on criteria of legal validity that require judges to assess the content of the norms to determine their legal validity. According to Raz, law necessarily claims authority, even if it ultimately lacks a justification for that claim, and only source-based criteria of legal validity are compatible with the possibility of law claiming authority. A legal system can claim authority only if it is possible to identify its directives without reference to the underlying ('dependent') reasons for that directive. This is a 'prerequisite' for claiming authority because what distinguishes a (practical) authority in the first place is that its directives pre-empt consideration of the underlying reasons (including, for example, moral reasons) for what we ought to do, and in so doing actually makes it more likely that we will do what we really ought to do. But Hart's 'soft positivism', as well as Dworkin's view, makes the identification of law depend on the very reasons that authoritative directives are supposed to pre-empt, and thus makes it impossible for law to fulfil its function of providing authoritative guidance. Thus, to the extent that judges purport to treat norms as legally binding based on their appealing moral or other normative content, they are simply exercising discretion under the mask of doing what the law requires.

Soft positivists, defenders of Hart's own official view in his Postscript, have lodged various objections to Raz's argument, but from a realist point of view, the real worry about Raz's argument is that it presupposes a highly moralised and unrealistic conception of what it is for law to claim 'authority'. Raz understands authority in terms of what he calls 'the Service Conception', in which a claim to authority is a claim to provide a subject of authority better 'reasons' for acting in accordance with what Raz calls 'right reason' than the subject would arrive at without the intermediation of the authority.[67] (We can gloss, for purposes here, 'right reason' as *what*

[66] See Raz 1985. [67] See Raz 1985.

one really ought to do). We can bracket for a moment the extravagant metaphysics of reasons that such a view requires – though it is hard to see how to make sense of the objective existence of such reasons from a naturalistic point of view[68] – and make a more modest objection: Why think that when law claims authority it is claiming to help its subjects do *what they really ought to do*? Of course law always *claims authority* in the sense of claiming the right to tell those subject to its jurisdiction what they must do, but the idea that this claim to authority is a claim to Raz's Service Conception looks like ideological obfuscation. Legal systems, after all, claim authority to direct their subjects' behaviour for all kinds of reasons, but they rarely, if ever, do so on the basis that they are thereby performing a 'service' for their subjects.

Raz's account of authority exposes his repudiation of realism in legal theory: for, against Hart's realist aim of a 'descriptive jurisprudence', Raz asserts that 'there is an interdependence between conceptual and normative argument'[69] such that the account 'does not necessarily conform to everyone's notion of authority in every detail. It does claim to be an explanatory account in singling out important features of people's conception of authority.'[70] Of course, no theorist thinks that their descriptive account conforms 'to everyone's notion ... in every detail', so this is just a distraction. But where is the evidence that Raz's account even captures some 'important features of people's [which people?] conception of authority'? Raz, I fear, has simply smuggled in a moralised conception of authority[71] – as providing a service for its subjects – without even the pretence that it satisfies even lax evidential demands of a 'descriptive sociology' as Hart, the realist, proposed.

Does that mean that Hart was correct in the Postscript that rules of recognition can incorporate content-based criteria of legal validity?[72]

[68] See Leiter 2015. [69] Raz 1986: 63. [70] Raz 1986: 65.

[71] Moralised in the sense that its main aim is to explain why deference to authority by rational subjects can be justified.

[72] Shapiro 1998 offers a slightly different argument against soft positivism, one that relies not on a claim about authority but on a claim about what it is to be 'guided' by a rule; 'Hart ... has always claimed that the essence of law is the guidance of conduct' (Shapiro 1998: 487). According to Shapiro, one is 'motivationally' guided by a legal rule when one's 'conformity is motivated by the fact that the rule regulates the conduct in question' (Shapiro 1998: 490). Shapiro argues that, on Hart's view, the rule of recognition must provide motivational guidance to officials (Shapiro 1998: 492) but that a rule of recognition incorporating content-based criteria cannot make a 'practical difference' to the

Not quite, though not for the reasons I have given previously. Hart himself, recall, agrees that a satisfactory account of law must explain how the law fulfils an *epistemic* function, that is, enabling *at least* officials to recognise what the law is in many if not all cases. (Hart himself, in the Postscript, thought that soft positivism was compatible with such an epistemic function.) But I now reject the argument I defended,[73] about what I called the 'Extreme Scenario'. In this scenario, it would be part of the conventional practice of officials to treat 'Natural Law' as the obligatory criterion of legal validity. Of course, the whole history of the world shows that the requirements of the putative 'natural law' are a subject of massive controversy (because there is no such thing), which might appear to mean that if a rule of recognition treated 'Natural Law' as the sole criterion of legal validity, it could not discharge any epistemic function. The problem with this kind of objection – apart from its trading on conceptual possibilities, not nomic actualities – is that, under concrete historical circumstances, agents often do converge on parts of what they take to be 'natural law', and thus appeals to natural law can serve an epistemic function. Hart's own view of meaning – in terms of what competent speakers of a language would take to be extensions of particular terms – should have led him to realise as much: 'due process' and 'equal protection' may have bigger penumbras than 'vehicle', but they still also have a core set of applications that speakers of the same language – and thus adherents to the same moral ideology manifest in that language – will agree upon. And that means that putative content-based tests of legal validity are not all the same: Some are really ideological covers for exercises of discretion (as hard positivists have always correctly emphasised), but others may simply require appeal to a competent speaker's understanding of the content-based terms in the applicable rule (except, of course, where other pedigreed rules of

judges: '[T]he rule makes a practical difference to one's practical reasoning [reasoning about what one ought to do] only if, in this counterfactual circumstance, the agent might not conform to the rule' (Shapiro 1998: 495). But, argues Shapiro, a rule of recognition incorporating moral criteria could provide no motivational guidance, since judges are already motivated to do what morality requires. It should be obvious why this argument fails, even if its conceptual claim about 'providing guidance' is correct: first, it is unrealistic, indeed preposterous, to think that judges are already motivated to do what morality requires; and second, even if individual judges were motivated to act morally, there is no evidence that their understanding of morality coincides with what the rule of recognition might demand of them.

[73] See Leiter 2007: 126–7.

interpretation dictate otherwise). We may still, from a positivist/realist point of view, reject the idea of *genuine* content-based criteria of legal validity, but that would be on the grounds of the explanatory fruitfulness of that way of demarcating the legal from the non-legal[74] and not from claims about the concept of authority. Law claims authority, but not in Raz's sense; judges sometimes treat moral considerations as criteria of legal validity, but in the same way they treat the ordinary understanding of 'vehicle' as a criterion of applied legal validity in a particular case; and the best explanation of law does not need to countenance as 'law' those cases where judges treat moral considerations as criteria of legal validity where that judgment depends entirely on substantive moral judgement and argument.

References

Cohen, F. 1935. 'Transcendental Nonsense and the Functional Approach'. *Columbia Law Review* 35: 809–49.

Frank, J. 1930. *Law and the Modern Mind.* Brentano's.

Hart, H. L. A. 1983. 'Scandinavian Realism'. In *Essays in Jurisprudence and Philosophy.* Oxford University Press: 161–9.

Hart, H. L. A. 2012. *The Concept of Law.* 3rd ed. Oxford University Press.

Holmes, O. W. 1897. 'The Path of the Law'. *Harvard Law Review* 10: 457–78.

Hutcheson, J. C. 1929. 'The Judgment Intuitive: The Function of the "Hunch" in Judicial Decisions'. *Cornell Law Quarterly* 14: 274–88.

Jackson, F. 1998. *From Metaphysics to Ethics.* Oxford University Press.

Leiter, B. 2001. 'Legal Realism and Legal Positivism Reconsidered'. *Ethics* 111: 278–301.

Leiter, B. 2007. *Naturalizing Jurisprudence.* Oxford University Press.

Leiter, B. 2009. 'Explaining Theoretical Disagreement'. *University of Chicago Law Review* 76: 1215–50.

Leiter, B. 2012. 'In Praise of Realism (and Against "Nonsense" Jurisprudence)'. *Georgetown Law Journal* 100: 865–93.

Leiter, B. 2015. 'Normativity for Naturalists'. *Philosophical Issues: A Supplement to Nous* 25: 64–79.

Leiter, B. and Etchemendy, M. 2017. 'Naturalism in Legal Philosophy'. In E. N. Zalta (ed.). *Stanford Encyclopedia of Philosophy.* https://plato.stanford.edu/archives/sum2017/entries/lawphil-naturalism/.

Llewellyn, K. 1930a. *The Bramble Bush.* Oceana Publications.

[74] See Leiter 2007: 175–180.

Llewellyn, K. 1930b. 'A Realistic Jurisprudence: The Next Step'. *Columbia Law Review* 30: 431–65.
Llewellyn, K. 1931. 'Some Realism about Realism: Responding to Dean Pound'. *Harvard Law Review* 44: 1222–64.
Llewellyn, K. 1950. 'Remarks on the Theory of Appellate Decision and the Rules or Canons about How Statutes Are to Be Construed'. *Vanderbilt Law Review* 3: 395–406.
Llewellyn, K. 1960. *The Common Law Tradition*. Little, Brown & Co.
Mindus, P. 2009. *A Real Mind: The Life and Work of Axel Hägerström*. Springer.
Oliphant, H. 1928. 'A Return to Stare Decisis'. *American Bar Association Journal* 14: 71–6.
Olivecrona, K. 1971. *Law as Fact*. 2nd ed. Stevens & Sons.
Radin, M. 1930. 'Statutory Interpretation'. *Harvard Law Review* 43: 863–85.
Radin, M. 1942. 'In Defense of Unsystematic Science of Law'. *The Yale Law Journal* 51: 1269–79.
Raz, J. 1985. 'Authority, Law, and Morality'. *The Monist* 68: 295–324.
Raz, J. 1986. *The Morality of Freedom*. Oxford University Press.
Ross, A. 1959. *On Law and Justice*. University of California Press.
Shapiro, S. 1998. 'On Hart's Way Out'. *Legal Theory* 4: 469–507.
Spaak, T. 2009. 'Karl Olivecrona on Judicial Lawmaking'. *Ratio Juris* 22: 483–98.
Spaak, T. 2011. 'Karl Olivecrona's Legal Philosophy: A Critical Appraisal'. *Ratio Juris* 24: 156–93.
Toh, K. 2005. 'Hart's Expressivism and His Benthamite Project'. *Legal Theory* 11: 75–123.

Part II

History

The German Tradition of Legal Positivism 5

Stephan Kirste

5.1 Introduction: Two Theses about German Legal Positivism

Whether or not the developing jurisprudence of the nineteenth century was positivist is an increasingly contentious issue in contemporary German legal theory.[1] Whereas legal historians refer to influences from Kant and Schelling on both Savigny's Historical and the later Pandectist schools of law, non-positivists point to a catalogue of criteria for legal positivism containing notions such as the separation thesis as well as numerous moral principles, even in the doctrines of the most outspoken positivists.[2]

This chapter supplies a defence of the thesis that one can distinguish different forms of jurisprudential, statutory, sociological positivism and General Theory of Law in the nineteenth- and twentieth-century legal theory. This defence proceeds from two assumptions: firstly, that the classification of legal theorists as legal positivists stems from their epistemological approach, which concerned establishing jurisprudence as a discipline independent of the natural and social sciences and therefore focused on positive law; secondly, that the strongest line of argument in the development of jurisprudential positivism mostly followed the transcendental approach of Immanuel Kant's Critiques, with little weight being given to his *Metaphysics of Ethics*. Such positivistic theories accept only customary or enacted law and not natural law as the object of jurisprudence. Only in the post-1945 era, after a 'Renaissance of Natural Law Theory'[3] and following a series of political crises,[4] did the influence of analytical and utilitarian philosophy become manifest and German legal positivism capable of being identified by a catalogue of more substantive criteria such as the separation thesis of a dualism of law and morality.[5]

[1] See Haferkamp 2010: 181–211. [2] See Alexy 2002: 14–20. [3] Kirste 2015: 100–8.
[4] For post-1945, see Höffe 1983: 313; for criticism of this dualism, Auer 2007: 948–9.
[5] Compare also Paulson 2008: 107.

Franz Wieacker (1908–94) distinguishes two main branches of legal positivism: jurisprudential positivism (*rechtswissenschaftlicher Positivismus*) and statutory positivism (*Gesetzespositivismus*).[6] The first would deduce legal arguments only from concepts and the system of jurisprudence without reference to extralegal values or purposes. Statutory positivism would claim that law consists only of state-enacted and state-enforced norms.[7] This dichotomy neglects, however, the heterogenous use of the term 'positivism' in the nineteenth century among proponents and critics while simultaneously ignoring positivistic authors who refer not to either of those two but to the tradition of philosophical positivism founded by Auguste Comte.[8]

5.2 The Nineteenth Century

The foundation of legal positivism in Germany around the turn of the nineteenth century went hand in hand with a titular change for the discipline of jurisprudence, which went from 'Natural Law' to the 'Philosophy of Law'.[9] This is not to say that rationalistic natural law theory was quickly brushed aside by legal positivism; to the contrary, it continued well into the second half of the nineteenth century.[10] However, as time went on, positivistic approaches came to dominate legal discussions, although the term 'legal positivism' was then rarely applied to an independent group of theories; this title was assigned primarily by later research.[11]

5.2.1 Jurisprudential Positivism

Jurisprudential positivism was based on the Kantian distinction between the matter and the form of knowledge.[12] With this underlying

[6] Wieacker 1967: 431. He defines jurisprudential positivism as a theory 'that deduces legal sentences and their application merely from systems, concepts and tenets of jurisprudence, without admitting extralegal, e.g. religious, social or scientific evaluations or purposes a law generating force'.

[7] See Wieacker 1967: 431–68. [8] See, e.g., Auer 2007: 935–6.

[9] See Hegel and Wood 1991; Welzel 1973: 1–7. [10] See Klippel 1995: 270–92.

[11] But consider Feuerbach 1839–46: 1; Ott 1992: 17–31; Haferkamp 2010: 207–11.

[12] See Wieacker 1967: 431.

epistemological model, legal positivism tried to establish jurisprudence as an independent scientific discipline.[13] Its positivism is based on the combined facticity of the perception of norms with a strong epistemological basis – although today we may refer to meta-ethical assumptions about the non-cognitive quality of value judgements. Important to keep in mind here is that, while these traditional legal norms contained moral principles, the new approach did not lead to a separation of law and morality. The emergence of this Kantian-based positivism achieved the closure of the constructed legal system against social, psychological and other influences by the logical coherence of independent legal concepts and legal institutes such as property, contract and so forth. Initially critical of legislation, early-nineteenth-century legal positivists included customary, judge-made and statutory law into their analysis.

The fact that the Historical School and constructivist jurisprudence intended to form a logically coherent system of legal concepts and dogmatic institutes without gaps does not make it idealistic.[14] The starting point of these systems was not philosophical ideas of justice, freedom, equality, human dignity and so forth, as was the case with enlightened natural law theory, but the historically given concepts of Roman law.

Gustav Hugo (1764–1844),[15] a highly controversial scholar,[16] marks the beginning of this tradition. He followed Kant in adopting a formal conception of jurisprudence,[17] which would have left room for the recognition of merely external legislation.[18] Accordingly, Hugo deemed 'positive law', rather than social or natural facts, to be the material for metaphysical analysis.[19] By this conception, he isolated positive law both from philosophy in general and from natural law theory in particular, as well as from purely natural-science type approaches to law. He thereby confined jurisprudence to positive law. However, because he had no means for

[13] See Wieacker 1967: 348–56; Baratta 1968: 337–8.

[14] Rückert (1984) emphasises the idealism in the historical school; see also Schröder 2012: 327.

[15] See Baratta 1968: 336; Wieacker 1967: 348–81.

[16] Hegel and Wood 1991: 851: annotation blames him for stopping his analysis at the 'positivity' of law without showing any philosophical skills; Marx called him a 'mere Positivist'. Rückert 1990: 96.

[17] See Hugo 1799: 37. [18] See Hugo 1799: 52; Rückert 1990: 113.

[19] See Hugo 1799: 51: 'The Philosophy of positive law then is the reasonable understanding out of concepts of what can be juridically legal.'

a substantial critique, Hugo readily accepted slavery as legal.[20] Despite this and the cloud of controversy that has dogged his reasoning, Hugo set the path for the Historical School in his anti-speculative, decidedly fact-related and therefore positivist approach to law.

Friedrich Carl von Savigny (1779–1861) followed Hugo in combining formal philosophy and substantive history in jurisprudence in founding the Historical School of Law. Whether he was a legal positivist was and still is debated,[21] partially because elements of Kantian philosophy of the critique of understanding persisted in his reasoning. As did Hugo, he began his analysis of law with positive legal norms. However, Savigny conceptualised jurisprudence as a science of norms but without removing the norms from their social reality context.[22] In adopting this approach, he hoped to achieve a scientific ideal that supposedly Roman lawyers had attained using precision methods that allowed accurate calculations to be made from legal concepts.[23] Initially, legal positivism focused on private law, leaving political law to the philosophies of the state.[24] Consequently, Savigny's positivism saw him take a path leading to his rejection of the enlightened idea of codification in the famous 'Controversy about Codification' with Kantian natural lawyer Anton Friedrich Julius Thibaut (1772–1840). Oddly enough, though, it does not fit Savigny's positivist picture that he used the term 'law' in two senses: first as arbitrary,[25] singular and historically given, very much in line with Hugo's views, although, when he speaks of the 'essence of law', the sense projected is that of the nature of law, the law itself in its generality and necessity;[26] and second, not in a moral sense, as in the natural law theory of Kant and the Kantians,[27] but as something with immanent principles such as the spirit of the people, the inner system, life, the nature of things and even freedom.[28] He certainly did not make moral demands on the law: 'Law serves morality, . . . not by fulfilling its commandment, but by ensuring the free expression of its power inherent in each individual will. But its existence is an independent one . . ..'[29] For Savigny, the separation of law

[20] See Hugo 1799: 137–60.
[21] See Kaufmann 1994: 65, 82 for his positivism; Rückert 1984 against.
[22] See Dilcher 1975: 508. [23] See Rückert 1984: 374–5. [24] See Dilcher 1975: 501.
[25] See Rückert 1984: 309–12.
[26] See Savigny 1840: XX. German text translations are mine; otherwise an English translation is mentioned in the references.
[27] See Kirste 2018: 97–136. [28] See Rückert 1984: 411. [29] Savigny 1840: 332.

and morality was patently evident and needed no further philosophical justification.[30]

Friedrich Puchta (1798–1846) not only followed Hugo's and Savigny's distinction of philosophically necessary and substantially arbitrary law but also inspired the later work of the head of the school by referring to Kant and others. Contingent human freedom to choose between right and wrong is the ultimate source of law; reason is the formal quality of the products of human action.[31] This 'free' law, not the necessary natural law, would be the ultimate goal of legal philosophy's task to integrate law into the 'world organism'.[32] Contrary to this holistic philosophical perspective, jurisprudence isolates a particular legal order and analyses it. Because of this difference, Puchta claimed that 'an elaborated system of philosophy is by no means a precondition of jurisprudence'.[33] He neither deduces positive law from natural law, because this would violate the freedom of the legal actors, nor simply describes its historical emergence. Noticeable here also, as it was with Savigny, is that Puchta's positivism resulted from an epistemic decision. As a civil lawyer, he proceeded from Roman law but emphasised the law's 'logical' element of the construction over its historical one. From this, he developed a system based upon the mathematical exactness of legal terms that ultimately produced ever more abstract concepts. Since the acts of the legislator would have to fit into his system to be justified, Puchta is clearly not a statutory positivist.

The resulting 'Pandectists' became the major school in German nineteenth-century private law jurisprudence. Scholars such as Rudolf von Jhering and, most prominently, Bernhard Windscheid (1817–92) were among its advocates.[34] Together with the social foundation of law, Pandectists' moral foundation was separated from jurisprudence, as evidenced by Windscheid's declaration that '[e]thical, political or economic considerations are not matters that lawyers should consider as such'.[35] Accordingly, this strand of German legal positivism became increasingly immune to the social responsibility aspects of law. The German Civil Code of 1900, which emphasised private autonomy and disregarded consumer and employer protection, is an expression of this doctrinal isolation.[36] In the very late nineteenth century, this

[30] See Letter to Fries on 3 February 1802: 295. [31] See Puchta 1841: 6, 9, 96.

[32] Puchta 1841: 97. [33] Puchta 1841: 99.

[34] Critical towards the classification of Windscheid as a member of the conceptual jurisprudence, Falk 1989: VI.

[35] Windscheid 1904: 112. [36] See Dilcher 1975: 525.

jurisprudential legal positivism to some appeared as 'the most backward of all disciplines'.[37]

From the foregoing, we can perceive that the Historical School was indeed positivist because, based on epistemological assumptions, it considered only positive law an appropriate matter of scientific knowledge, and the school's compliance with the substantive criteria of legal positivism, such as the separation thesis, was a consequence of these assumptions.

5.2.2 The Sociological and Naturalistic Legal Positivism

Compared to jurisprudential positivism, other forms of positivism gained little influence and only in the second half of the nineteenth century did sociological and naturalistic forms of legal positivism[38] accompany jurisprudential positivism. Rather than consider traditional, judge-made jurisprudential and statutory norms as positive facts, these later forms of positivism focused on social or natural facts.

Rudolf von Jhering (1818–92) pioneered the change from jurisprudential legal positivism to sociological positivism. Even in his earlier period, when he embraced conceptual jurisprudence and subscribed to a separation thesis,[39] he preferred a more scientific ideal, following Linnaeus and others over the mathematical construction of the jurisprudential system. In *Jest and Severity in Jurisprudence*, he addressed his grievances with the rationale of the Historical School, reserving his strongest sarcasm for its 'heaven of concepts'.[40] His later volume entitled *The Struggle for Law* clearly demonstrated a move towards a more realistic theory, and from this point in time, purpose and force would be central to his theory, where purpose relates to the content and force to the form of law.[41] Jhering argued that legal norms could not pacify conflicting interests if the form of law was not its force: 'Law is the epitome of enforceable norms valid in a state.'[42] As such, he proposed that positive legal provisions are purely the

[37] Menger 1908: 30. [38] See Ott 1992: 76–88.

[39] Law 'is independent of morals, customs, and religion'; Jhering 1852: 30–3.

[40] Jhering 1904: 245–317.

[41] Jhering 1913a: LIV: 'The fundamental idea of the present work consists in the thought that purpose is the creator of the entire law; that there is no legal rule which does not owe its origin to a purpose, i.e., to a practical motive.'

[42] Jhering 1893: 176.

result of this struggle, and not of natural law.[43] Touched by *Darwin's disease* (Wilhelm Dilthey), his empirical positivism[44] led him to evolutionary ideas.[45] Together with Eugen Ehrlich, he was the first to apply the positive methods of Auguste Comte,[46] taking both social and psychological facts into account, the consequence being that the sense of justice gained central importance for the development of law.[47] This, together with the idea that law is an expression of social interests and has to be useful for them, modifies the jurisprudential positivist position.[48] He separated law and morality, not because morality was irrelevant for law or because law would not contain morality but because there is no automatic transformation of morals into law. Jhering had a major influence on sociological jurisprudence in Germany as well as on American legal realism, as evidenced by Roscoe Pound, who highly regarded him,[49] claiming that 'our new realism will be built on Jhering'.[50]

Eugen Ehrlich (1862–1922), also emerging from these sociological approaches to legal positivism, wanted to analyse law as a fact, a perspective that the natural sciences had long taken.[51] Instead of calling his approach theoretical or positive with an explicit reference to Comte, he rather understood it as 'sociological' in character.[52] His realistic perspective on the 'living law' opened the canon of norms that would count as positive law to forms of behaviour in weak state societies with only partially enacted and/or enforced laws. He looked at the elementary legal facts (*Rechtstatsachen*) such as usage, custom, dominion and property as the objects of legal theory,[53] and from these he drew the norms of organisation. Ehrlich, and later Hermann Kantorowicz (1877–1940), rejected jurisprudential positivism as speculative, statutory positivism as reductionist, and Kelsen's 'unrealistic' Pure Theory of Law, all without falling back to natural law theory by placing paramount importance on the free finding of law by judges (*Freirechtsschule*). Ehrlich and Kantorowicz

[43] See Jhering 1913b: 12. [44] See Kaufmann 1994: 65.

[45] See Jhering 1893: XIII; some interpreters consider this an influence of Karl Christian Krause and his school, making it a late idealist concept of evolution rather than Darwinist.

[46] See Comte 1830–42. [47] See Hofmann 2009: 314–15.

[48] See Hofmann 2009: 310–14. [49] See Hofmann 2009: 318–19.

[50] Pound 1930–1: 710. [51] See Ehrlich 1913: 1.

[52] Ehrlich 1913: 19: 'The sociology of law is the scientific theory of law.'

[53] Ehrlich 1913: 82, 169.

established a form of sociological positivism that clearly distinguishes law in the broadest sense (including 'free law') from morality.[54]

Finally, yet another group of legal scholars contended that laws should be perceived as similar to natural laws in a modern scientific sense (naturalistic legal positivism), meaning that human law operates comparably to them and refers to natural needs. For Julius von Kirchmann (1802–84), law was a field of study akin to study in the physical sciences, requiring the same methodological treatment: observation.[55] Since natural law and morals are unobservable, they cannot be assigned scientific certainty.[56] Accordingly, jurisprudence could become a real science only if it exchanged its dogmatic methodology for a truly empirical one. Later, Albert Hermann Post (1839–95) developed his anthropological approach according to which only norms accepted by legal consciousness would count as law.[57] The positivity of law would be achieved by an evolutionary process leading to the differentiation and rationalisation of society,[58] one consisting of the enforceability of norms.[59] With critical voices such as Radbruch and Kelsen calling naturalistic legal positivism the 'euthanasia of legal philosophy' as early as 1914, it remained relatively uninfluential in Germany compared to other positivistic rationales.[60]

5.2.3 Statutory Legal Positivism

With the formalisation of positive law, jurisprudential positivism increasingly yielded to statutory positivism – first in private, then in public law.[61] This decisionistic positivism[62] would differ from its forebears in its focus on statutory law, excluding customary law and judge-made law as positive law.[63]

Hans-Magnus Bergbohm (1849–1927) radically championed this approach. His vision of positivism can be identified by three theses: (1) the non-cognitivist assumption that no objective knowledge of ethical norms exists; (2) the idea that only historically enacted law can properly be called law; and (3) the separation thesis of law and morality. He viewed the legitimate targets of his scientific endeavours to be the poisonous 'ineradicable metaphysics in natural law',[64] which he wanted cured using 'positivist medicine'.[65]

[54] Kantorowicz 1906: 11. [55] See Kirchmann 1966: 9.
[56] See Kirchmann 1873: 173–80. [57] See Post 1884: 20–30, 51. [58] See Post 1867: 48.
[59] See Post 1867: 50–4. [60] Further references in Paulson 2008: 109 n. 40.
[61] See Stolleis 1992: 281–2. [62] See Höffe 1983: 317–20.
[63] See Ott 1992: 25 and 39–44; critical: Schröder 2012: 328. [64] Bergbohm 1892: 34.
[65] Bergbohm 1892: 231.

He diverged from Comte's approach and jurisprudential positivism because they knew neither jurisprudence nor a science of the state but mixed everything into the 'mash of sociology'.[66] Bergbohm assumed that 'only that which functions as law is law, and nothing else; and all of this is law without exception',[67] 'even the vilest statutory law, as long as it has been created in a formally correct way'.[68] Clearly then, positivity for him referred to the enactment of norms rather than the findings of jurisprudence or social facts.

Whereas jurisprudential legal positivism developed in the nineteenth century within private law theory, statutory positivism became an important foundation in the emerging public law theory. Using the results of conceptual positivism in private law[69] reduced positive law to statutes promulgated by the state. The early manifestation of public law positivism was centred on Carl Friedrich Wilhelm von Gerber (1823–91) and Paul Laband (1838–1918), both of whom were intent on clearing public law from all non-legal matters, which naturally included all elements of an ethical or political nature.[70] Laband sought to confine legal doctrine to the construction of legal institutes, tracing back legal concepts to their formal legal principles and from these deducing other possible consequences.[71]

As was the case with private law, sociological and philosophical general theories of the state by Ludwig Gumplowitz (1838–1909), Anton Menger (1848–1906) and especially Georg Jellinek (1851–1911) began emerging in reaction to jurisprudential positivism. Repeatedly heavily criticised by Hans Kelsen, Jellinek was probably the most original public law legal positivist due to his openness towards the social sciences, which clearly distinguished him from the constructivist period of public law positivism.[72] Accordingly, he criticised Laband for trying to logically construct the content of legal norms[73] and strongly opposed the concept of the completeness and closedness of the legal order.[74] Jellinek's theory of the three elements of the state, his theory of the four dimensions ('status') of fundamental rights and his concept of the normative force of the factual are even today influential conceptions.[75] He saw the separation of legal and sociological perspectives of the state as causing fundamental errors about its nature; he considered both perspectives

[66] Bergbohm 1892: 51. [67] Bergbohm 1892: 80. [68] Bergbohm 1892: 144.
[69] See von Oertzen and Dieter 1974.
[70] See Heun 1989: 380, referring to Gerber 1865: 237. [71] See Laband 1911: IX.
[72] See Friedrich 1997: 277. [73] See G. Jellinek 1914: 16–17.
[74] See G. Jellinek 1914: 356–60. [75] See G. Jellinek 1914: 144–8.

necessary.[76] The mediation of the facticity of the state and pure (moral) normativity by the law explains this 'normative force of the factual': People have a tendency to elevate the factual to the normal and the normal to the norm.[77] Therefore, what is expected and recognised as normal by 'socio-psychological powers'[78] is the assurance of the stability of legal norms, meaning that Jellinek subscribed to the social thesis that law is a social practice but not to the separation thesis.

During the Weimar Republic, Gerhard Anschütz (1867–1948) and Richard Thoma (1874–1957) advocated a moderate form of positivism. They felt that early forms of public law positivism had been significantly impoverished, especially by criticism of the completeness of law thesis.[79] However, they shared statutory positivism's inherent focus on statutes and legislature, rejecting forms of constitutional judicial review. Until objections by Jellinek and especially the Weimar era disputes in public law, the historical constructive method gave this form of positivism an identity.[80] This dispute among Hans Kelsen, Rudolf Smend (1882–1975), Hermann Heller (1891–1933), Erich Kaufmann, Carl Schmitt (1888–1985) and others drove nails into the coffin of the juridical method of public law positivism,[81] although without providing a clear-cut result and consigning it to the pages of history. The blossoming of nineteenth-century constitutionalism, and especially the German Reich's establishment in 1871, brought statutory laws into the focus of this form of positivism; the later crisis of the Weimar Republic, however, proved to be insurmountably problematic for it.

The now clear pattern of separating positive law – namely statutory law – from morality was the result of epistemic interest. As with private law, but now following the formalisation of administrative and constitutional law, the science of public law owed its differentiation to the reduction of focus on state-enacted laws.

5.2.4 The General Theory of Law

Another anti-metaphysical group developed a *General Theory of Law*[82] based on their epistemological approach and concept of legal theory.[83] It is

[76] See G. Jellinek 1914: 139 but also 12. [77] G. Jellinek 1914: 314–16.
[78] G. Jellinek 1914: 90. [79] See Anschütz 1906: 323. Stolleis 1999: 159–60.
[80] See Friedrich 1997: 224; Paulson 2005: 530.
[81] See Friedrich 1997: 328; Stolleis 1999: 159. [82] See Funke 2004: 42–50.
[83] See Funke 2004: 116, 122.

not the subject matter of this general theory of law that makes it positivistic but its non-cognitivism. Authors such as Ernst Rudolf Bierling (1841–1919) and Adolf Merkel (1836–96) explain but do not justify positive law. Their goal was not to philosophise about optimal laws but to take laws as they are and abstract general structures from them,[84] the object being to identify positive norms or, as Fritz Somló (1873–1923) called them, 'empirical norms'.[85] Not all members of this group advocated a strict separation of law and morality; Merkel, for example, acknowledged some influence of morality on law.[86]

In its anti-dualistic orientation, Merkel's theory is empirical in nature and presented as an alternative to the supposedly discredited philosophy of law.[87] He envisaged a 'positivistic Philosophy of Law' that had the same task as other sciences and would be 'a science of the principles of law and the laws of its historical development'.[88]

Merkel and Bergbohm's legal positivism was later criticised by neo-Kantian positivists for its naturalism and for failing to apply a dualistic method when analysing the law. Because it lacked a transcendental perspective, Merkel and Bergbohm were incapable of elaborating a general concept of law and stuck only to empirical observations; in short, it lacked the critical dimension that Kelsen's neo-Kantian positivism would provide.[89]

5.3 Legal Positivism in the First Half of the Twentieth Century

5.3.1 Hans Kelsen (1881–1973)

Kelsen considered his *Pure Theory of Law* a 'further development of approaches ... that have been introducing themselves by the positivistic jurisprudence in the nineteenth century'.[90] Developed primarily in the early twentieth century, his effort towards a rational legal theory continued for decades. Similar to the general theories of law, Kelsen's theory aims to describe law as it is and not as an ideal – and therefore tends to be critical

[84] See Bierling 1894: 13; Somló 1917: 5.
[85] See Somló 1917: 58–64 – without confounding norms and facts.
[86] See Funke 2004: 61–2. [87] See Brockmöller 1997: 238–49.
[88] Merkel 1909, s. 363: 157. [89] Kaufmann 1922: 50.
[90] Kelsen [1934]2008: 4; see also Kelsen 1960: III.

of both ideology and natural law.[91] The progress that Kelsen made lay in a neo-Kantian dualistic approach that allowed for a critical attitude to law in general: For science, the value of knowledge trumps all other goals; in law, this would include justice.[92] Kelsen's dualism also distinguishes him from the Viennese empirical positivism of Moritz Schlick and others, being based on an epistemological concern to establish a pure legal theory unencumbered by empirical and political elements.[93] 'Juridical positivism must be distinguished from philosophical positivism' by the is/ought distinction.[94] According to this distinction, juridical positivism cannot be directed at facts, only at the normative meaning of certain facts, namely acts of will.[95] Only this will can be observed and interpreted with respect to its meaning. In Kelsen's eyes, this would harmonise with the positivisms of W. Friedmann, John Austin and legal realists in the United States. However, based on the is/ought distinction, he clearly distances himself from the Austinian theory of law as a command by stating that the mere existence of a command can never be the reason to consider this command as valid and binding.[96]

The principal consequence of his juridical positivism is the separation of law and morality, including natural law. According to his moral relativism,[97] morals are not subject to scientific knowledge, a conviction that yields two consequences. The first of these consequences arises because, although not objecting to a legal philosophy altogether, Kelsen did not consider it a scientific discipline but rather viewed it as being on a par with legal politics.[98] Second, non-cognitivism and moral relativism call for democracy.[99] Both the Weimar Constitution of 1919 and the Austrian Federal Constitution of 1920 followed this relativist concept and included no strong substantive assumptions, leaving them to the political process itself.

'Natural law' is part of a substantive and static order with the ultimate principle of justice on top, whereas positive law is a formal and dynamic

[91] See Kelsen 1960: 112; Kelsen 1965: 465. [92] See Kelsen 1928: 70.

[93] See Kelsen 1960: III, 17, 60. Nevertheless, Kaufmann (1994: 72) sees influences from Carnap.

[94] Kelsen 1965: 465 against Moritz Schlick's logical positivism. [95] See Kelsen 1960: 80.

[96] See Kelsen 1960: 197.

[97] Kelsen 1960: 67, 104; sometimes he uses 'relativism' for his non-cognitivism because we have no absolute knowledge with which to decide between different relative concepts of morality; Kelsen 1948: 906.

[98] See Kelsen 1965: 468. [99] See Kelsen 1929: 100–4.

hierarchical order ('Stufenbau') of legal norms, which ultimately makes the Basic Norm a transcendental condition allowing an explanation of law.[100] Whereas legal norms are the meaning of an act of will, this Basic Norm is a presupposed pure norm. This hypothetical norm's purity provides a circuit-breaker with which to interrupt the infinite recourse that would alternatively be available to seek the recognition of law out of ever-higher legal norms.[101]

In elucidating this highly elaborated form of legal positivism based on a Kantian epistemology, Kelsen has proved to be the most influential German legal positivist down to the present day.

At the beginning of the twentieth century and increasingly after 1918, legal positivism lost its dominance gained in the late nineteenth century, being replaced by new-Hegelian, phenomenological, natural, non-positivist and other developments in legal philosophy. With the establishment of jurisprudence, epistemological questions receded even further in favour of substantive questions. This rapid remoulding of the legal philosophy landscape in the inter-bellum period casts considerable doubt on whether waning positivism can be blamed for facilitating National Socialist legal ideology.

5.3.2 Was Gustav Radbruch a Legal Positivist?

At first glance, Radbruch should be mentioned in the list of positivists before 1945 but not afterwards.[102] Someone who states that 'value-judgements are open not for knowledge, but only for confession' and therefore regards it as necessary 'to *decide* questions of justice if we cannot *assess* justice' and calls for the submission of judges to the law regardless of a possibly deviating decision of conscience[103] must be a legal positivist.[104] Indeed, H. L. A. Hart considered him one.[105] However, upon closer examination, his substantially Kantian approach prevents him from joining the positivists' ranks. Even in his earliest writings, Radbruch was critical of the naturalist legal positivism and statutory legal positivism being put forward around the turn of the twentieth century.[106]

[100] See Kelsen 1928: 10–11; 1960: 198–200. [101] Kelsen 1960: 209.

[102] See Neumann 2007: 12–17 and 27–8, who is critical about this distinction of periods.

[103] See Radbruch 1999: 208.

[104] Accordingly, Adomeit (2003: 162) holds that he is 'a classic modern legal positivist'.

[105] See Hart 1958: 616. [106] See Paulson 2008: 109, 112; Neumann 2007: 17.

Although both Radbruch and Kelsen were influenced by the neo-Kantian movement – Kelsen more by the northwestern/Marburg, epistemological neo-Kantianism and Radbruch by the southwestern/Heidelberg School of Emil Lask (1875–1915) – the kind of transcendental condition for understanding law that each favoured highlights a stark difference between the two. For Radbruch, the idea of law – that is, justice – is the *substantive* condition for understanding law. Accordingly, he saw at least a weak connection between law and morality, a value orientation from which Kelsen abstracted. For Kelsen, however, the Basic Norm ('Grundnorm') had to be *formal* and in this alone rests the transcendental condition for understanding the meaning of legal acts of will as norms of a dynamic hierarchical legal order. This methodological difference makes Kelsen a positivist and Radbruch not.[107]

5.3.3 Positivism during National Socialism

Understanding the difficult position of legal positivism after 1945 requires understanding that, at the time, it was seen as the key factor facilitating National Socialism's crop of acquiescent lawyers. However, with the benefit of hindsight, one can now confidently claim that the opposite is more likely to be true: 'The rejection of legal positivism was quasi an axiom' for legal theory in the Third Reich.[108] Legal positivism was blamed for its anti-moralism, its formalism and its individualism, and as Georg Dahm (1904–63) wrote in 1934:

> We know now the gaining of independence, the neutralization of law, the separation and contraposition of law and state, law and politics, law and people's world view, law and ethics as the core of the evil. Overcoming these dichotomies and the realisation of the unity within the law is quasi the precondition for a real renewal of our legal life.[109]

Carl Schmitt adopted the term 'law' to refer to the 'plan and will of the Führer' as the supreme enforcer of the 'right to life of the German People' as the natural source of law.[110] Karl Larenz (1903–93) and others blamed empirical positivism and subjective idealism for the individualistic social and moral foundations of law.[111]

[107] See Funke 2004: 163. [108] Pauer-Studer and Fink 2014: 20. [109] Dahm 1934: 826.
[110] Schmitt: Rechtsstaat. In Frank 1935: 32. [111] See Larenz 1935: 158, 160–1.

Legal ideologues such as Hans Frank (1900–46) replaced liberal legal principles with a trivialised utilitarianism and the 'consciousness of the people' as the fundaments of law: 'Everything that serves the people, is law; everything that harms it, is injustice.'[112] The 'leader principle' ('Führerprinzip') swept away the separation of powers.[113] Karl Larenz called for a 'fight against positivism, especially against the Pure Theory of Law', and found Kelsen guilty of 'unhinging law from its natural cohesion with the national ethos and morality'.[114]

Radbruch saw the ambivalent relationship between National Socialism and legal positivism, and this deeply impacted his own view over time as evidenced by the fact that in 1939 he had considered positivism 'as an ideal that would be desperately necessary for us',[115] but by 1946 he blamed positivism for having facilitated National Socialist legal ideology.[116] Ironically, Radbruch appears to have been correct on both accounts as National Socialism seemingly instrumentalised both natural law, which it perverted into a blood and soil ideology, and a primitive understanding of legal positivism, which it twisted into a law and order ideology.[117]

5.4 Positivism after World War II

5.4.1 Fall and Rise of Legal Positivism

After 1945, natural law enjoyed a 'renaissance' and again began dominating German legal philosophy as well as jurisprudence.[118] In contrast, legal positivism was so strongly disdained that, in 1951, Georg Jellinek's son Walter asked, 'Is the denotation "positivist" an offence?'[119] Soon, however, the great hopes placed in natural law and its application by the German Courts were dashed, opening the door again for legal positivism, which had not only survived its own 'darkest hour' but begun to reassert its influence.[120] Carl Schmitt[121] in 1967 and Ernst-Wolfgang Böckenförde

[112] Frank 1935: 4. [113] Schmitt 1934: 946; critical: Rottleuthner 1987: 29.
[114] Larenz 1934: 15, 12. [115] Radbruch 1968: 129, quoted after Rottleuthner 1987: 389.
[116] 'Positivism, with its principle that "a law is a law", has in fact rendered the German legal profession defenseless against statutes that are arbitrary and criminal' (Radbruch 1946/2006: 6); critical: Dreier 2007: 137–9; Walther 1989: 263–80; Rottleuthner 1987: 383–6.
[117] See Kaufmann 1994: 65–6.
[118] See Wieacker 1956; Heun 1989: 378–9; Kirste 2015: 100–9. [119] W. Jellinek 1952: 73.
[120] Hilgendorf 2005: 26–9. [121] See Schmitt 1967: 53–5.

in 1988[122] objected to the justification of law based on a hierarchy of values. They perceived that the subjectivity of the knowledge of values, the historicity of a precarious value consensus in a society being used as the foundation of law, put the stability of law itself at risk.

This critique aside, both natural law theory and public law positivism could coexist with the new constitution's fundamental rights containing many substantive principles that were expansively interpreted by the Federal Constitutional Court. Most importantly, principles involving the legal state *(Rechtsstaat)*, democracy and human dignity, while unalterable constitutionally, could be criticised by positivists.[123] A notion developed that Bernhard Schlink has critically called 'Federal Constitutional Court Positivism', meaning an increasingly uncritical and apologetic justification of the rulings of the Federal Constitutional Court.[124]

The situation of legal theory in the German Democratic Republic (GDR) was perhaps unsurprisingly somewhat different. Gerhard Haney discovered a strong positivist thinking influence in Stalin's and Wyschinski's theories.[125] Because of its exclusivity, even Marxism became a positivist doctrine as the voluntarist aspect of applying Marxism ousted its critical aspects and humanism. In his view, positivism united with the Marxist holistic worldview produced the unsurmountable totalitarianism that had dominated the GDR since it came into being.[126] In Austria, public law positivism, which had originally found an adequate formal constitution without many substantive provisions, could coexist with the constitutional substantivisation occurring through European integration and the incorporation of the European Convention on Human Rights (ECHR).

Given jurisprudence's establishment as a science and the many natural law principles being transformed into the constitution's positive law and statutes based on it, discussions in legal positivism shifted from epistemological questions of the foundation of jurisprudence to more substantive ones. The separation thesis, the 'proprium of jurisprudence' against social sciences, politics and natural law, along with genuine hermeneutics or argumentation,[127] became the cornerstones upon which contemporary positivism is built. However, time brings change, and the East German

[122] See Böckenförde 1990: 33–46; see also Gusy 1989: 509–10. [123] Kriele 1969: 154.
[124] Schlink 1989: 161–73. [125] See Haney 1991: 115. [126] See Haney 1991: 121.
[127] 'Legal arguments are such, which intend to develop the meaning of a norm out of itself or from other legal norms', Gusy 1989: 515.

regime's demise led to renewed debate between positivism and non-positivist theories of law.

5.4.2 Critical Rationalism

Critical rationalism was a legal positivism that, even after 1945, proceeded most strongly from epistemological questions. As was the case with Ludwig Wittgenstein, Karl Raimund Popper (1902–94), at the beginning of his career, kept in loose contact with the Vienna Circle of logical positivism, although later breaking away and being especially critical of Moritz Schlick's inductive method, which Popper replaced with his sceptical theory of falsification.[128] In Popper's view, biological and psychological naturalisms and certain forms of (legal and decisionist) positivism would overlook the fundamental dualism of (ethical, legal) norms and natural laws.[129] However, in his anti-metaphysical furore and rejection of essentialist ethics, Popper shares at least some positivist positions. Based on his dualistic view ('observation and reasoning'), jurisprudence has to begin its analysis with empirical facts – which can be normative convictions – but must analyse them and elaborate a technology for the concrete solution of social problems.[130] As Hans Albert later (b. 1921) put it: '[J]urisprudence is social control using norms.'[131]

For Albert himself, natural law theories, as all attempts to find firmly grounded knowledge, succumb to the Münchhausen trilemma, because they lead to (1) an infinite regress in the search for normative grounds and the grounds of these grounds and so forth, or (2) to a logical circle of deduction relying on principles already determined to be precarious and needing justification, or (3) to the aborting of such a search altogether, leading to an arbitrary suspension of the principle of sufficient reason.[132] This trilemma then requires piecemeal social engineering[133] and a form of jurisprudence that functions as 'social technology'.[134] Clearly then, given his rejection of natural law theories in all their guises, Albert is a legal positivist.[135]

Also inspired by the Vienna Circle of logical empiricism but simultaneously following Hans Kelsen, Ernst Topitsch (1919–2003) criticised the ideological

[128] See Popper 2002: 316. [129] See Popper 1947 I: 57, 210.
[130] See Popper 1947 I: 142, 245–6 at 8. [131] Albert 1991: 29. [132] See Albert 1991: 15.
[133] See Popper 1947: 18, 138–9. [134] Albert 1994: 185. [135] See Engländer 2007: 115.

character and the inner contradictions of natural law.[136] He explicitly understands his positivism not as a legal positivism but as an 'empirical-rational conception of science in the sense of the Anglo-Saxon "philosophy of science"'.[137] Attempts for an ultimate justification by natural law theory would, from a logical and mathematical standpoint, lead to aporias or 'as-if justifications' or the understanding that all values are human decisions.[138]

Although it is a highly sophisticated theory, critical rationalism in legal theory has never attained the significance of nineteenth-century epistemological justifications of legal positivism, perhaps due to its non-cognitivist emphasis on interpreting the value-influenced German legal system while having few instruments with which to accurately do so.

5.4.3 Parallel Invention: Weinberger's Institutional Positivism

At approximately the same time in the early seventies, Neil MacCormick and Ota Weinberger[139] developed the idea of a form of institutional legal positivism. Whereas Weinberger started with a critique of Hans Kelsen's Pure Theory of Law,[140] the respective reference for MacCormick is H. L. A. Hart,[141] although he also incorporated 'speech acts' and 'institutional facts' by Anscombe and Searle. Institutional legal positivism analyses the structures in which law can rationally be expressed, and the logical operators are the basis of the legal system and its processes.[142] In this value-sceptical structural analysis, legal systems are categorised as social institutional facts[143] where the meaning of law is produced by the institutions and reconstructed by hermeneutics.

Although Weinberger advocates a non-cognitivist approach where reasonable arguments *de lege ferenda* would be possible, he, going further than Kelsen, advocated a reconstructive theory of justice with certain criteria independent of justice.[144]

[136] Topitsch 1950: 121–40. [137] Topitsch 1963: 1. [138] See Topitsch 1963: 2.
[139] See Ott 1992: 97–103.
[140] See Weinberger 2000: 305. On him, see also Herget 1996: 93–103.
[141] See MacCormick and Weinberger 1985. [142] See Weinberger 2000: 306.
[143] Weinberger in MacCormick and Weinberger 1985: 143; 49–50: 'Why I consider myself a legal positivist'.
[144] See Weinberger 2000: 318–22.

5.4.4 The Dreier/Alexy–Hoerster Debate in the Mid-Eighties

From the late eighties and persisting until after the fall of the Berlin Wall, a renewed debate over natural law and legal positivism unfolded between Ralf Dreier (1931–2018) and Robert Alexy (b. 1945) on one side and Norbert Hoerster (b. 1937) and others on the positivistic side, with both arguing based on analytic philosophy.[145] Positivism for Dreier excludes the claim to correctness and defines law only by authoritative regulation and/or social effectiveness.[146] Alexy also identifies positivism with the separation thesis and calls other theories not subscribing to it 'non-positivist'.[147] Both introduced Dworkin's argument from principle to the German legal discourse[148] and complemented it with a claim to correctness. Their arguments were fruitfully used in the 'border guard trials' in the nineties when the German Courts also applied the Radbruch Formula.[149]

Positivists criticised this attempt to overcome the separation of law and morality by assuming that moral principles, in order to become legal ones, must be transformed into law by the respective authorities.[150] Against the non-positivist critique of legal positivism, Norbert Hoerster in particular has freely admitted that some positivist arguments may be flawed; however, not all are mutually connected, meaning that some may still be valid.[151] Independently from this, legal positivism would indeed claim that positive law is neutral towards a normative-moral evaluation. Therefore, if they are enacted in a constitutional way, all norms can be law, even those of an immoral regime. Furthermore, one could reject non-cognitivism but still assume that law is neutral towards morality. At the core of Hoerster's positivism, then, is the neutrality thesis and, accordingly, he distinguishes between the law's form and its content, where form is expressed in the concept of law but reveals nothing about the law's morality because it is dependent upon the concrete legal order.[152] Norms that do not meet the criteria of the concept of law are non-law; legal norms in this sense that do not meet the substantive criteria of morals may appear as illegal from a moral point of view but are still law.

[145] See Dreier 1986: 370–1. [146] See Dreier 1986: 376. [147] Alexy 2002: 3, 14–20.
[148] See Dreier 1991: 56. [149] See Alexy 1993: 3–40.
[150] See Hoerster 1986: 2481; Luhmann 1993: 85; Kirste 2010: 86, 108.
[151] See Hoerster 1989: 7–8. [152] See Hoerster 1989: 21.

5.4.5 Niklas Luhmann (1927–1998)

Niklas Luhmann's legal positivism is not founded on a substantive premise such as the separation thesis or on a non-cognitivist approach to the norms of action, but it is the result of his historically informed sociological approach. He draws his premises primarily from phenomenology, Parsons and biological systems theory.

Social systems are communicative and functionally differentiated, producing their own premises: Only legal systems can produce law; others may provide outputs that belong to the systems of morality, politics or economy. Kelsen's formal system of a hierarchy of norms is replaced by the legal system's operative closure. Law is autonomous because only legal communications can reproduce it,[153] but only if all of these communications are directed by the binary code 'legal–illegal' and if its concretising programmes contribute to this auto-poetical law.[154] Positivity of law solves the problem of the stasis of normative expectations. It institutionalises the possibility to learn even in a system of normative expectations such as law. Justice is merely a 'contingency formula' that is used in legal communications precisely *because* it does not have any content. Validity is only a symbol of legal communications and nothing else, signifying that the current operation fits the legal system,[155] thereby expressing its continuity in the discontinuity of legal operations.[156]

Although cognitively open, all noise from other functionally differentiated systems (morals, economy, science) has to be reorganised within the system to provide it with meaningful information. Finally, even the theoretical observer can be observed and does not have an independent position as the natural lawyer presupposes. Therefore, legal theory cannot observe law from a point of view outside of society because it is intrinsically embedded.[157]

Luhmann's sociological theory of law has been strongly criticised by the discourse theory of Jürgen Habermas, legal positivists and others for its functionalism. Apart from Hans Kelsen's Pure Theory of Law, however,

[153] Luhmann 1993: 174–9: 'self-referentiality'.

[154] See Luhmann 1993: 57. Here, it is a historical machine where all acts refer to previous legal acts and become possible starting points for future communications.

[155] See Luhmann 1993: 98–110.

[156] Luhmann 1981–6: 122: 'As positive we denominate law that has been enacted and is valid because of decision.'

[157] See Luhmann 1988: 16.

Luhmann's conception of law is certainly the most advanced German positivist approach put forward in the late twentieth century.[158]

5.4.6 The Search for a Middle Ground between Natural Law and Positivism

The sixties saw many scholars try to overcome the natural law theory-legal positivism dichotomy.[159] In 1968, Alessandro Baratta (1933–2002) opined that the times of ideological confrontation between natural law and legal positivism were over and an objective evaluation of the achievements of both sides would be possible.[160] In an attempt to mediate the strict dualism of agreement or disagreement on the separation thesis, Peter Koller (b. 1947) analysed the achievements of both theory groups and drew two conclusions: first, that sociological legal positivism clarified the factual conditions for the validity of law; and second, that legal positivism has properly analysed the inner system of law.[161] This appears to be a significant progressive step because, in justifying the positive results of both theory groups with less demanding and perhaps more satisfying methods and assumptions, a mediation between these positions seems possible. This could be achieved by distinguishing, first, between the concept and the validity of law and, second, between legal validity and moral validity.[162]

Others such as Otfried Höffe (b. 1943) and Arthur Kaufmann (1923–2001) found that the debate between natural law theory and legal positivism had become fruitless,[163] deeming that each should include essential insights of the other.[164] Höffe accepted the conceptual distinction between law and morality but not the normative one.[165] Kaufmann held that 'Legal Philosophy has to be located beyond natural law and legal positivism.'[166] Indeed, given his perspective on the matter, he could have advocated many post-World War II legal positivism approaches in Germany.[167] More recently, Joachim Lege (b. 1957) does not primarily distinguish between positivity and the morality of law in the sense of the separation thesis but instead makes a division between reason and will as the human capacities necessary to realise law. If we typically identify nature with reason and

[158] See Bolsinger 2001: 3–4. [159] See Auer 2007: 947–54.
[160] See Baratta 1968: 325–49. [161] See Koller 1983: 349. [162] See Koller 1983: 356.
[163] See Höffe 1983: 303–10. [164] See Höffe 1983: 305. [165] See Höffe 1983: 313.
[166] Kaufmann 1991: 148. [167] See, e.g., Kriele 1969: 156.

positivity with will, real law is neither but actually a cultural product born of their interaction.[168]

5.5 What Remains

Given the death of legal positivism being more vociferously proclaimed in recent years and the re-emergence of positivist influence, it may be premature to postulate the end of both legal positivism and the non-positivist era approaches,[169] especially given the heterogeneity of the terms in the German tradition.[170]

As we have seen, Kantianism and neo-Kantianism did play, and continue to play, an important role in the debate. Kantian formalism and other later epistemologies have given legal positivism a methodical foundation. Only when the Kantian approaches lost their impact after 1945 did positive law in both Germany and Austria transform demands from the natural law tradition into their constitutions.[171] Furthermore, at the end of the Cold War, at the time of the GDR's collapse and as a reaction to natural law's renaissance, legal positivism could be identified by more substantive claims, namely the separation thesis.[172] Although general philosophical debates continue worldwide, the struggle between positivism and natural law theory has lost much of its earlier intensity. Certainly, in the German sphere, without another great historical crisis such as was created by National Socialism and the Marxist-Socialist regime, debate seems likely to continue to simmer rather than boil.

Currently, one can put legal philosophers on the subject of legal positivism broadly into four different categories according to attitude: (1) those sceptical of the concept as a whole;[173] (2) users of the broad term 'non-positivism' seeking to demonstrate that seemingly positivistic theories contain at least some elements of natural law;[174] (3) those embracing mediation theories in an attempt to find common ground between the two legal theory groups;[175] and (4) advocates of mostly Kelsenian and

[168] See Lege 2007: 28; also Hollerbach 1988: 757. [169] Critical Rüthers 2006: 958–60.

[170] Critical Auer 2007: 931–8: if the terms 'legal positivism' and 'natural law theory' are indeed as useless as some deem them, their resurfacing is inexplicable.

[171] See Adomeit 2003: 162; Dreier 1986: 894. [172] See Paulson 2008: 107.

[173] See Haferkamp 2010. [174] See Alexy 2002: 3–4, 10, 42, 45, 47, 50–2, 61, 68–83, 87.

[175] An argument could be the historical insight that the struggle between the two is aporetic; Dreier 2007: 126.

system-theoretical legal positivism. Given the difficulties of the vagueness of the term 'legal positivism' in the German tradition, it may be helpful to reconstruct the concept of law not from its opposition to 'natural law theory' but in order to analyse the elements of law – namely norms, their origin, their effects and their content – and then to consider its positivity and validity as attributes of these norms.[176] Based on this, legal positivism is more helpful for analysing the legal form, whereas natural law theory can help to analyse its (moral) content. In this regard, Germany's legal landscape is well placed for such an undertaking given the achievements of both legal theory groups, which are present in contemporary German legal theory.

References

Adomeit, K. 2003. 'Der Rechtspositivismus im Denken von Hans Kelsen und von Gustav Radbruch'. *Juristenzeitung* 58(4): 161–6.

Albert, H. 1991. 'Erkenntnis, Recht und soziale Ordnung'. In R. Alexy, R. Dreier and U. Neumann (eds.). *Rechts- und Sozialphilosophie in Deutschland heute: Beiträge zur Standortbestimmung*. Steiner: 16–29.

Albert, H. 1994. *Kritik der reinen Hermeneutik*. Mohr.

Alexy, R. 1993. *Mauerschützen*. Vandenhoeck&Ruprecht.

Alexy, R. 2002. *The Argument from Injustice: A Reply to Legal Positivism*. Oxford University Press.

Anschütz, G. 1906. 'Lücken in den Verfassungs- und Verwaltungsgesetzen'. *Verwaltungsarchiv* 14: 315–40.

Auer, M. 2007. Normativer Positivismus – Positivistisches Naturrecht. In A. Heldrich, I. Koller and J. Prölss (eds.). *Festschr. f. Claus-Wilhelm Canaris zum 70*. Beck: 931–62.

Baratta, A. 1968. 'Rechtspositivismus und Gesetzespositivismus'. *ARSP* 54(3): 325–50.

Bergbohm, K. 1892. *Jurisprudenz und Rechtsphilosophie*. Duncker & Humblot.

Bierling, E. R. 1894. *Juristische Prinzipienlehre*. Mohr.

Böckenförde, E.-W. 1990. 'Zur Kritik der Wertbegründung des Rechts'. In R. von Dreier (ed.). *Rechtspositivismus und Wertbezug des Rechts*. Steiner: 33–46.

Bolsinger, E. 2001. 'Autonomie des Rechts?'. *Politische Vierteljahresschrift* 42(1): 3–29.

Brockmöller, A. 1997. *Die Entstehung der Rechtstheorie im 19. Jahrhundert in Deutschland*. Nomos.

[176] See Kirste 2020: 79–114.

Comte, A. 1830–42. *Cours de philosophie positive*, vols. 1–6. Alfred Costes.
Dahm, G. 1934. 'Die Erneuerung der Ehrenstrafe'. *Deutsche Juristenzeitung* 39: 821–32.
Dilcher, G. 1975. 'Der rechtswissenschaftliche Positivismus'. *Archiv für Rechts und Sozialphilosophie* 61: 497–528.
Dreier, R. 1986. 'Der Begriff des Rechts'. *Neue juristische Wochenschrift* 39(14): 890–6.
Dreier, R. 1991. 'Zur gegenwärtigen Diskussion des Verhältnisses von Recht und Moral in der Bundesrepublik Deutschland'. In R. Alexy, R. Dreier and U. Neumann (eds.). *Rechts- und Sozialphilosophie in Deutschland heute: Beiträge zur Standortbestimmung.* Steiner: 55–67.
Dreier, H. 2007. 'Naturrecht und Rechtspositivismus'. In W. Härle, B. Vogel *Vom Rechte das mit uns geboren ist.* Herder: 125–37.
Ehrlich, E. 1913. *Grundlegung der Soziologie des Rechts.* Duncker & Humblot.
Engländer, A. 2007. 'Grundzüge des modernen Rechtspositivismus'. *Juristische Arbeitsblätter*: 113–18.
Falk, U. 1989. *Ein Gelehrter wie Windscheid.* Klostermann.
Feuerbach, L. 1839–46. 'Über das Wunder'. In *Ludwig Feuerbachs sämtliche Werke* vol. 1. Wigand: 1–41.
Frank, H. 1935. 'Grundsätze des nationalsozialistischen Rechtsdenkens und Rechtswollens'. In H. Frank (ed.). Nationalsozialistisches Handbuch für Recht und Gesetzgebung. Zentralverlag der NSDAP.
Friedrich, M. 1997. *Geschichte der deutschen Staatsrechtswissenschaft.* Duncker & Humblot.
Funke, A. 2004. *Allgemeine Rechtslehre als juristische Strukturtheorie.* Mohr.
von Gerber, C. F. 1865. *Grundzüge eines Systems des Deutschen Staatsrechts.* Verlag von Bernhard Tauchnitz.
Gusy, C. 1989. 'Staatsrechtlicher Positivismus'. *Juristenzeitung* 44(11): 505–16.
Haferkamp, H.-P. 2010. 'Positivismen als Ordnungsbegriffe einer Privatrechtsgeschichte des 19. Jahrhunderts'. In F. Wieacker (ed.). *Historiker des modernen Privatrechts.* Wallstein: 181–211.
Haney, G. 1991. 'Das Widerspruchsvolle des Rechtsbegriffs'. In R. Alexy, R. Dreier and U. Neumann (eds.). *Rechts- und Sozialphilosophie in Deutschland heute: Beiträge zur Standortbestimmung.* Steiner: 110–29.
Hart, H. L. A. 1958. 'Positivism and the Separation of Law and Morals'. *Harvard Law Review* 71: 593–629.
Hegel, G. W. F. and Wood, A. W. 1991. *Elements of the Philosophy of Right.* Cambridge University Press.
Herget, J. 1996. *Contemporary German Legal Philosophy.* University of Philadelphia Press.
Heun, W. 1989. 'Der Staatsrechtliche Positivismus in der Weimarer Republik'. *Der Staat* 28: 377–403.
Hilgendorf, E. 2005. *Die Renaissance der Rechtstheorie zwischen 1965 und 1985.* Ergon.

Hoerster, N. 1986. 'Zur Verteidigung des Rechtspositivismus'. *Neue Juristische Wochenschrift*: S. 2480–2.

Hoerster, N. 1989. *Verteidigung des Rechtspositivismus.* Metzner.

Höffe, O. 1983. 'Das Naturrecht angesichts der Herausforderung durch den Rechtspositivismus'. In D. Mayer-Maly and P. M. Simons (eds.). *Das Naturrechtsdenken heute und morgen.* Duncker & Humblot: 303–35.

Hofmann, H. 2009. 'From Jhering to Radbruch: On the Logic of Traditional Legal Concepts to the Social Theories of Law to the Renewal of Legal Idealism'. In E. Pattaro and C. Roversi (eds.). *A Treatise of Legal Philosophy and General Jurisprudence.* Springer: 301–54.

Hollerbach, A. 1988. 'Rechtswissenschaft'. In *Görres-Gesellschaft Staatslexikon* vol. 4. 7th ed. Herder: 757.

Hugo, G. 1799. *Lehrbuch eines civilistischen Cursus. Naturrecht als einer Philosophie des positiven Rechts. Zweyter, ganz von neuem ausgearbeiteter Versuch.* Mylius.

Jellinek, G. 1914. *Allgemeine Staatslehre.* O. Häring.

Jellinek, W. 1952. 'Contribution to the Discussion'. *VVdStRL* 10: 73.

von Jhering, R. 1852. *Geist des römischen Rechts auf den verschiedenen Stufen seiner Entwicklung. Bd. 1.* Breitkopf und Härtel.

von Jhering, R. 1893. *Der Zweck im Recht* vol. 1. Breitkopf und Härtel.

von Jhering, R. 1904. *Scherz und Ernst in der Jurisprudenz.* 9th ed. Breitkopf und Härtel.

von Jhering, R. 1913a. *Law as a Means to an End.* Trans. I. Husik. Editorial Preface by J. H. Drake. Introductions by H. Lamm and W. M. Geldart. The Boston Book Company.

von Jhering, R. 1913b. *Die Entwicklungsgeschichte des römischen Rechts* vol. 2. J.F. Lehmanns.

Kantorowicz, H. (=Gnaeus Flavius). 1906. Der Kampf um die Rechtswissenschaft. Heidelberg (Carl Winter's Universitätsbuchhandlung).

Kaufmann, F. 1922. *Logik und Rechtswissenschaft.* Mohr.

Kaufmann, A. 1991. 'Fünfundvierzig Jahre erlebte Rechtsphilosophie'. In R. Alexy, R. Dreier and U. Neumann (eds.). *Rechts- und Sozialphilosophie in Deutschland heute: Beiträge zur Standortbestimmung.* Steiner: 144–62.

Kaufmann, A. 1994. 'Rechtsbegriff und Rechtsdenken'. *Archiv für Begriffsgeschichte* 37: 21–100.

Kelsen, H. 1928. *Die philosophischen Grundlagen der Naturrechtslehre und des Rechtspositivismus.* Rolf Heise.

Kelsen, H. 1929. *Vom Wesen und Wert der Demokratie.* 2nd ed. Mohr.

Kelsen, H. [1934]2008. *Die Reine Rechtslehre.* Mohr Siebeck.

Kelsen, H. 1948. 'Absolutism and Relativism in Philosophy and Politics'. *American Political Science Review* 42(5): 906–14.

Kelsen, H. 1960. *Die Reine Rechtslehre.* Manz.

Kelsen, H. 1965. 'Was ist juristischer Positivismus?'. *Juristenzeitung*: 465–9.

von Kirchmann, J. H. 1873. *Die Grundbegriffe des Rechts und der Moral als Einleitung in das Studium rechtsphilosophischer Werke.* 2nd ed. Heimanns.
von Kirchmann, J. H. 1966. *Die Wertlosigkeit der Jurisprudenz als Wissenschaft.* WBG.
Kirste, S. 2020. *Einführung in die Rechtsphilosophie.* 2nd Ed. NOMOS.
Kirste, S. 2015. 'Natural Law in Germany in the Twentieth Century'. In E. Pattaro and C. Roversi (eds.). *Legal Philosophy in the Twentieth Century in Civil Law Countries.* Springer: 91–109.
Kirste, S. 2018. 'Das Urrecht der Menschenwürde in der vernunftrechtlichen Debatte der Wende zum 19. Jahrhundert'. In C. Enders et al. (eds.). *Europa nach Napoleon.* Mentis: 97–136.
Klippel, D. 1995. 'Naturrecht und Rechtsphilosophie in der ersten Hälfte des 19. Jahrhunderts'. In D. Klippel and O. Damm (eds.). *Naturrecht – Spätaufklärung – Revolution.* Meiner: 270–292.
Koller, P. 1983. 'Zur Verträglichkeit von Rechtspositivismus und Naturrecht'. In D. Mayer-Maly and P. M. Simons (eds.). *Das Naturrechtsdenken heute und morgen.* Duncker & Humblot: 337–58.
Kriele, M. 1969. 'Rechtspositivismus und Naturrecht – politisch betrachtet'. *Juristische Schulung*: 149–156.
Laband, P. 1911. *Das Staatsrecht des Deutschen Reiches.* 5th ed. Mohr.
Larenz, K. 1934. *Deutsche Rechtserneuerung und Rechtsphilosophie.* Mohr.
Larenz, K. 1935. *Rechts- und Staatsphilosophie der Gegenwart.* 2nd ed. Junker und Dünnhaupt.
Lege, J. 2007. 'Recht als Kulturgut'. *ARSP*: 21–38.
Luhmann, N. 1981–6. 'Positivität des Rechts als Voraussetzung einer modernen Gesellschaft'. In N. Luhmann (ed.). *Ausdifferenzierung des Rechts.* Suhrkamp: 113–53.
Luhmann, N. 1988. 'Positivität als Selbstbestimmtheit des Rechts'. *Rechtstheorie* 19: 11–27.
Luhmann, N. 1993. *Das Recht der Gesellschaft.* Suhrkamp.
MacCormick, N. and Weinberger, O. 1985. *Grundlagen des institutionalistischen Rechtspositivismus.* Duncker & Humblot.
Menger, A. 1908. *Das Bürgerliche Recht und die besitzlosen Volksklassen.* 4th ed. Laupp.
Merkel, A. 1909. *Juristische Enzyklopädie.* 4th ed. Guttentag.
Neumann, U. 2007. 'Naturrecht und Positivismus im Denken Gustav Radbruchs'. In W. Härle, B. Vogel *Vom Rechte, das mit uns geboren ist.* Herder: 11ff.
von Oertzen, P. and Dieter, S. (eds.). 1974. *Die soziale Funktion des staatsrechtlichen Positivismus.* Suhrkamp.
Ott, W. 1992. *Der Rechtspositivismus.* 2nd ed. Duncker & Humblot.
Pauer-Studer, H. and Fink, J. 2014. *Rechtfertigungen des Unrechts.* Suhrkamp.
Paulson, S. 2005. 'The Theory of Public Law in Germany 1914–1945'. *Oxford Journal of Legal Studies* 25: 527–45.

Paulson, S. 2008. 'Ein ewiger Mythos: Gustav Radbruch als Rechtspositivist – Teil I'. *Juristenzeitung*: 105–15.

Popper, K. R. 1947. *The Open Society and Its Enemies* I/II. Routledge.

Popper, K. R. 2002. *The Logic of Scientific Discovery*. Routledge.

Post, A. H. 1867. *Das Naturgesetz des Rechts. Einleitung in eine Philosophie des Rechts auf Grundlage der modernen empirischen Wissenschaft*. Bremen Verlag von Hermann Gesenius.

Post, A. H. 1884. *Die Grundlagen des Rechts und die Grundzüge seiner Entwicklungsgeschichte. Leitgedanken für den Aufbau einer allgemeinen Rechtswissenschaft auf soziologischer Basis*. Schulzesche Hofbuchhandlung.

Pound, R. 1930–1. 'The Call for a Realistic Jurisprudence'. *Harvard Law Review* XLIV: 697–711.

Puchta, G. F. 1841. *Cursus der Institutionen*. Breitkopf & Härtel.

Radbruch, G. 1946/2006. 'Statutory Lawlessness and Supra-Statutory Law'. *Oxford Journal of Legal Studies* 26: 1–11.

Radbruch, G. 1968. *Breife*. Ed. E. Wolf. Göttingen.

Radbruch, G. 1999. *Rechtsphilosophie 1932*. Müller.

Rottleuthner, H. 1987. 'Rechtspositivismus und Nationalsozialismus'. *DuR Vierteljahresschrift*: 373–94.

Rückert, J. 1984. *Idealismus, Jurisprudenz und Politik bei Friedrich Carl von Savigny*. Gremer.

Rückert, J. 1990. '. . . daß dies nicht das Feld war, auf dem er seine Rosen pflücken konnte . . .?'. In R. von Dreier (ed.). *Rechtspositivismus und Wertbezug des Rechts*. Steiner: 94–128.

Rüthers, B. 2006. 'Zwischenruf aus der methodischen Wüste: "Der Richter wird's schon richten"(?)'. *Juristenzeitung* 61: 958–60.

von Savigny, F. C. 1840. *System des heutigen römischen Rechts Bd. 1*. Berlin.

Schlink, B. 1989. 'Die Entthronung der Staatsrechtswissenschaft durch die Verfassungsgerichtsbarkeit'. In B. Schlink. *Der Staat*. Duncker & Humblot: 161–73.

Schmitt, C. 1934. 'Der Führer schützt das Recht'. *Deutsche Juristenzeitung* 39(15): S. 946–50.

Schmitt, C. 1967. 'Die Tyrannei der Werte'. In E. Forsthoff (ed.). *Säkularisation und Utopie*. Ebracher Studien. Kohlhammer Verlag: 37–62.

Schröder, J. 2012. *Recht als Wissenschaft. Geschichte der juristischen Methodenlehre in der Neuzeit (1500–1933)*. 2nd ed. Beck.

Somló, F. 1917. *Juristische Grundlehre*. Meiner.

Stolleis, M. 1992. *Geschichte des öffentlichen Rechts in Deutschland II*. Beck.

Stolleis, M. 1999. *Geschichte des öffentlichen Rechts in Deutschland III*. Beck.

Topitsch, E. 1950. 'Das Problem des Naturrechts'. *Wiener Zeitschrift für Philosophie, Psychologie, Pädagogik* 3: 121–40.

Topitsch, E. 1963. 'Die Menschenrechte. Ein Beitrag zur Ideologiekritik'. *Juristenzeitung*: 1–7.

Walther, M. 1989. 'Hat der juristische Positivismus die deutschen Juristen im 'Dritten Reich' wehrlos gemacht?' *Kritische Justiz* 21(3): S. 263–80.

Weinberger, O. 2000. 'Der Neo-Institutionalismus als Basis der inhaltlichen Rechtsbetrachtung'. In M. Fischer, P. Koller, W. Krawietz (eds.). *Aus intellektuellem Gewissen. Aufsätze von Ota Weinberger über Grundlagenprobleme der Rechtswissenschaft und Demokratietheorie*. Duncker & Humblot: 305–22.

Welzel, H. 1973. Gedanken zur Begriffsgeschichte der Rechtsphilosophie. In K. Lackner et al. (eds.). *Festschr. f. Wilhelm Gallas zum 70. Geburtstag*. De Gruyter: 1–7.

Wieacker, F. 1956. 'Rudolf von Jhering'. *Zeitschrift für Rechtsgeschichte, Rom. Abt.* LXXXVI: 1–36.

Wieacker, F. 1967. *Privatrechtsgeschichte der Neuzeit*. 2nd ed. Vandenhoeck u. Ruprecht.

Windscheid, B. 1904. Die Aufgaben der Rechtswissenschaft (Leipziger Rektoratsrede). In B. Windscheid. *Gesammelte Reden und Abhandlungen*. Ed. P. Oertmann. Duncker & Humblot: 100–16.

6 The French Tradition of Legal Positivism

Michel Troper

6.1 A Heterogenous Tradition

The French term 'positivisme juridique' is hardly an accurate translation of 'legal positivism'. If there is such a thing as a 'French tradition', it is certainly not homogeneous and the term is being used in a great variety of ways, either by those who claim to be positivists or by those who depict others as positivists.

It is usually safe to start from Bobbio's distinction among what he calls 'three aspects of legal positivism', or three manners in which legal positivism presented itself historically and corresponds to three concepts of legal positivism.[1] The first aspect can be characterised as a scientific approach to the law. The positivists are those who distinguish between the law that is and the law that ought to be, abstain from moral judgements and remain ethically neutral in order to describe the law as an objective phenomenon. Thus, legal science is sharply separate from its object, the law.

The second aspect is that of legal positivism as a theory closely connected to the emergence of the modern state: it is the idea that law is a system of rules posited by the state, that court decisions are mere applications of pre-existing rules, that interpretation is a description of the true meaning of a legal text. However, Bobbio stresses that there are among positivists very different and in some cases conflicting views on the nature of these rules, whether they are produced by the will, whether they are objectively binding or what it means to apply a rule and whether courts can use some discretion. Similarly, Hart identifies five theories but stresses that not all positivists accept every one of them.[2]

[1] See Bobbio 1972: 103–5.

[2] Hart 1983: 57 n. 54:

> It may help to identify five meanings of 'positivism' bandied about in contemporary jurisprudence: (i) the contention that laws are commands of human beings . . ., (ii) the contention that there is no necessary connection between law and morals or law as it is and ought to be . . ., (iii) the contention that the analysis (or study of the meaning) of legal concepts is (a) worth

Finally, legal positivism, according to Bobbio, is an ideology, the view that positive law is just, by the mere fact of being positive, that is, of having being posited by the will of a political authority, and therefore that it ought to be obeyed, whatever its content.

Bobbio is very careful to stress that there is no necessary connection among the three aspects of legal positivism and that they may even be incompatible. For example, legal positivism as a scientific approach is characterised by a commitment to neutrality and a refusal to prescribe, while legal positivism as an ideology is precisely a set of prescriptions, namely to obey the law.

This distinction is extremely precious from a conceptual point of view, in particular for those who wish to argue in favour of some aspect of positivism and discuss arguments by anti-positivists. Naturally, using these concepts would lead us to label 'positivists' authors who do not think of themselves as positivists, in particular those living at a time when the word did not exist. But there is nothing wrong with that approach. Concepts are anachronic. The great historian Marc Bloch stressed that, although men living in Western Europe in the Middle Ages were not aware that they lived in a feudal society, we can perfectly use that concept to describe that society and examine whether it is also adequate to refer to other societies in Russia or Japan.[3] In the same way, we sometimes label ancient authors positivists.

However, this method cannot easily be used to describe legal positivism 'in the French tradition', for several reasons. First, unlike 'feudal society' that can be the object of a simple and practical definition, we may be forced to use different concepts of legal positivism, with the consequence that one and the same lawyer or legal scholar could easily be identified either as positivist or as non-positivist depending on the 'aspect' that one has chosen. For example, there are very few positivists in the first sense defined

pursuing and (b) to be distinguished from historical inquiries into the causes or origins of laws, from sociological inquiries into the relation of law and other social phenomena, and from the criticism or appraisal of law …, (4) the contention that a legal system is a 'closed logical system' in which correct legal decisions can be deduced by logical means from predetermined legal rules without reference to social aims, policies, moral standards, (5) the contention that moral judgments cannot be established or defended … by rational argument, evidence or proof….

Bobbio quotes this passage (Bobbio 1972: 103).

[3] See Bloch 2014: 463.

by Bobbio, and even in that case, some who claimed to be positivists may be denied that quality by others, just as Kelsen was called a quasi-positivist by Alf Ross.[4] On the other hand, with some of the most extensive definitions, such as that of Leslie Green, namely 'the thesis that the existence and content of law depends on social facts and not on its merits',[5] we would probably find in modern times very few lawyers or scholars who could not qualify as positivists.

There is another reason that is more specific to the French case: Bobbio discusses positivism from a meta-theoretical point of view, which has not been shared by French scholars. We do not find a French tradition of legal philosophy focusing on epistemological issues. There never was a systematic reflection *on* legal positivism, and no French scholar has produced a theory that would come close to the views professed by authors such as Kelsen, Ross, Bobbio or Hart on the nature or merits of legal positivism. There were, of course, many authors who claimed to give a 'scientific' description of the law, although what they meant by that expression was very far from the empiricist conception defined by Bobbio; there were also authors who accepted some of the theories usually labelled as positivist, such as the view that rules are an expression of human wills or that adjudication is a rational process, and authors who believed that positive law, because it emanates from the state, is good or ought to be obeyed, but such theories have been shared by non-positivists; moreover, almost none would argue that one ought to construct a legal science distinct from its object, or that men have a duty to obey the state.

We might thus be tempted to conclude that there are no positivists in the French legal tradition. However, such a conclusion would be misleading. While there may be no positivists in any of Bobbio's senses, it is a fact that a number of authors or movements who certainly do not explicitly profess a coherent and self-conscious positivist view of the law are nevertheless called positivists for one reason or another. This should be our point of departure.

Instead of starting from some definition of legal positivism and looking for authors whose work could fall under the category, we shall start from those authors who have been called – or have called themselves – positivists and ask if they have some common characteristic and, in the affirmative, what that common characteristic may be. In other words what is the

[4] See Ross 1998: 147–64. [5] Green 2018.

meaning of 'positivist' for those who use that word in the French tradition and why do they use it?

Unfortunately, we cannot rely on an accepted lexical definition, which would be hard to find in a French legal dictionary. Most do not mention the term, except very recent ones, influenced by foreign writings. For example, the foremost legal dictionary, the *Vocabulaire juridique de la langue française*, does not even have an entry either for 'positivisme juridique' or for 'droit positif'.[6]

There are several explanations. The first is the lack of interest for legal philosophy or legal theory, which, until very recently, was not part of the curriculum of law schools and was not the object of research. Indeed, legal philosophy in general has often been viewed in France either as a useless and obscure metaphysics or, on the contrary, in the case of positivism, as dry and sterile reductionism, precisely because it refuses metaphysics. Such broad judgements obviously do not require precise definitions.

Another reason is the prevailing distinction in the French legal culture between public law and private law. The distinction that corresponded to a division between the two court systems, with two supreme courts, was justified by law professors and presented as two different systems, one regulating the organisation of the state and its relations with private individuals – however, criminal law was and still is not considered part of public law – and the other regulating the relations between private individuals, the former being created by unilateral or heteronymous rules and the latter by way of contracts between individuals endowed with subjective rights. In this, *summa divisio* priority is given to private law and professors of private law because, as one very influential professor put it, 'it is the calling of civil law that it should serve as a model for other branches of the law'.[7] Therefore, the course *General Introduction to the Law*, mandatory for all first-year students, is almost always taught by a professor of civil law and the introduction is only general by name; it definitely contributes to the formation and perpetuation of the legal culture of French lawyers.

Such introductions may include a simple definition of positivism, for example the idea that 'there exists a positive law made of all legal rules that are in force in a given State at a given time . . . and the law as a whole is identified with these rules and it is pointless to search for anything beyond'.[8] This does not tell us what attitude, according to Carbonnier, positivists

[6] See Cornu et al. 1987. [7] Carbonnier 1969: 9. [8] Carbonnier 1969: 60.

believe they should adopt, or effectively adopt, towards these rules, nor the nature of their relation to the state, but when civil law professors later enumerate the sources of law, they name but two: statutes and custom, which implies that only general rules are legal rules and *jurisprudence* (judge made law) is not, since courts may not issue general rules but only decide on concrete cases. And such simple definitions cannot help to distinguish positivism from non-positivism.

The most important reason goes back to the French revolution, which blurred the distinction between natural law and positive law. The revolution made statutory law the only source of law; statutory law was defined by article 6 of the Declaration of the Rights of Man and the Citizen as the expression of the general will. This document itself, as the title tells, is not an act of will but a declaration of the natural rights of men in society. This does not mean that statutes *ought* to be the expression of the general will but that they are presumed to express that will and those who express the will are presumed to be representatives of the sovereign. Thus, when a statute has been adopted, its transformation into positive law is based on natural law. But the substance of the law is also both positive and natural. The legislative process is viewed not as a confrontation of opinions but as a search for the general will, and it is a search for truth. Sieyès compared it to a logical deduction, similar to what a court does. Instead of applying a statutory rule to a case, the legislature deduces a statute from natural law after having heard arguments pro and contra. Thus, when a court applies a statute, it applies positive law directly but, indirectly, also natural law. This explains the later style of comments and interpretation that is common in French legal dogmatics.

Since statutes are the expression of the general will, they are not the supreme but the only source of law. This means not only that there can be no such thing as judge-made law – Robespierre famously said that 'the word *jurisprudence* ought to be eliminated from the language of a free people' – but also that courts may not interpret statutes because to interpret is to recreate the law, which would amount to a usurpation of the legislative power or to an act of rebellion. The national assembly therefore issued in 1790 a general prohibition to interpret the law under very severe penalties and the prohibition was later repeated in the civil code. With courts whose powers were so narrowly limited, the practice later called positivist of applying the law was the only possibility and could not even be discussed.

Naturally, it was obvious from the beginning that there would always be difficulties in applying general rules to concrete situations and that the general prohibition was untenable because it could lead to situations where judges would refuse to rule. The revolutionaries therefore not only allowed what they called 'interpretation *in concreto*' but also made it mandatory. However, this was not called 'interpretation' but 'application' of the law and one could appeal a court decision not because it was based on a wrong interpretation but because it was a wrong application of the law. Of course, this was not just playing with words because the fiction had very important consequences: Since the courts could not acknowledge that they interpreted, they could not provide any justification for the interpretation they could not avoid making. Thus, the extreme brevity characteristic of French court decisions. The end result was just the opposite of what the revolutionaries had expected: An interpretation by the court of cassation in a concrete case was easily generalised to similar cases and the court was able to produce general rules while maintaining the fiction that it was merely applying pre-existing statutes. One then could use the argument that positivism had vanquished and that courts had no discretion, while, on the contrary, their margin of discretion was greatly increased by the fiction.

Obviously, courts, when they did create law, used standards taken from political or moral preferences, but, since they were prohibited from mentioning them, they kept the appearance of applying the law. In other contexts, one of the functions of the distinction between positivism and natural law from the point of view of courts is to justify a refusal to apply positive law or a broad interpretation of the law, but French courts did not need such justification because they could always impose their moral or political preferences and present them as mere application of the law.

Another reason is the importance of *la doctrine*. The term should not be translated with *legal doctrine* if in the English language it refers to a set of principles or a policy that will help deciding cases. In French, from the mid-nineteenth century, it is first the opinions of legal scholars, the *comunis opînio doctorum*, but the word also refers not to an opinion but to the community of legal scholars taken as a group.[9] Their work is at the same time descriptive and normative and, since it is influential, scholars discuss whether *la doctrine* can be considered a source of law. The answer is usually in the negative, as for *la jurisprudence*, mainly because this

[9] See Chevallier 2002; Jestaz and Jamin 2004.

would go against the dogma of the monopoly of statutory law. Thus, most authors, *la doctrine dominante*, settle for the idea that, like *jurisprudence*, they are not a source but an *authority*. They are all the more persuasive when they present their own opinions as a description of positive law, even when their views result from an interpretation or from their political or moral views. Moreover, most authors reject the distinction between the language of the law and the metalanguage of scholarly writings. Thus, while positivists would frequently label these opinions as natural law, some of these authors would still call themselves positivists because they insist that they are dealing with positive law only.

Thus, not only can we not proceed by confronting different authors with Bobbio's distinctions and trying to identify them as positivists when they correspond to one or the other aspect, but we cannot rely on a definition of legal positivism commonly accepted in the French tradition, either, because there is none. Nevertheless, we can start by looking at those authors who are usually identified or who identify themselves as positivists and then say what is or what are the meanings of the label.

Yet, the reason for choosing this method is not only the absence of a definition of legal positivism that would work well in the French tradition; we also have a positive reason: Because we want to speak of a *French tradition*, we must look at an important dimension that Bobbio himself repeatedly stressed: While there is no logical or conceptual connection between the three aspects of legal positivism, there is a factual or historical relation and the same could be said of resistance to legal positivism. If we are looking for a specific French tradition, the historical connection between the different aspects of positivism is precisely what we need to identify. But we must not overlook another aspect of the French legal tradition: that some authors who would not be labelled positivists may nevertheless, for some historical reasons, be considered positivists in France.

To understand this fact, we must start from the use of the word 'positivist' in the language of lawyers, which can refer to a number of authors and is being used in a variety of situations. In addition to some lawyers who refuse any theoretical discussion, because they view it as vain metaphysics, and take pride in being 'mere positivists', who limit themselves to the knowledge of the technicality of the law, the real law,[10] we may identify five groups of authors, mostly law professors, who call themselves or are

[10] See Sueur 2012.

called positivists by others and describe the use of the word. The list is mainly chronological.

6.2 The Exegetical School

This group of lawyers, almost exclusively from private law, is often mentioned even as advocating strict positivism.[11] After the publication of the civil code, lawyers in a quasi-religious awe before the *code Napoléon* considered that the only appropriate method, as for the Bible, was the exegesis, that is, explaining the provisions of the code, interpreting them literally and following the order of the sacred text. The books they wrote were entitled not *Droit civil* but *Cours de code civil* and one of these authors once famously said, 'I do not teach civil law, but the *code Napoléon*.' Their commitment to the code, that is, to statutory law, is the main reason why they were called positivists by later scholars, but it would be difficult to find other characters that could be linked to positivism.

Some of them do not distinguish between law and morality, but others blame them for not making the distinction. Their relation to natural law is complex. Bobbio famously argued that natural law theories assume that there are two systems of law, natural law and positive law, while positivism maintains that only positive law exists. Yet, the exegetical school also admits two. They insist that the law that is really binding is positive law, but also that positive law is merely a translation of natural law. Therefore, natural law ought to play an important role in the process of interpretation,[12] but the main method ought to be an analysis of the language of the law because its perfection expresses the intention and the wisdom of the lawmaker.

Some go much further than simply exposing the code. They write huge treatises, accepting having to use what they start to call legal dogmatics, after the Germans. Others still do not hesitate to include *jurisprudence* in their exposition of the law, at least to illustrate the way the code is being applied. Indeed, it would have been difficult to omit case law, especially in the late nineteenth century, after the court of cassation had produced a considerable body of law in the field of torts, expanding on three articles of the code.

[11] See Chevallier 2009. [12] See Demolombe 1845: 2s.

In fact, if they are positivists, it is only in a very broad sense and mostly because they describe or pretend just to be describing positive law and define positive law as the law set out in the code. However, they do not share the ideal of value neutrality, when they view their approach as scientific; this is not because they accept a distinction between the subject and the object of knowledge but only because they wish to extract from the code a number of principles that would help to present the code as a rational system. They do accept the idea that adjudication is – or ought to be – a rational process or that there is no room for interpretation, but this is mostly because the code is so perfect that any other operation would ruin it. Even their religion of the code is different from what Bobbio called positivism as an ideology, because the reason why they praised the code was not so much that it had been issued by the state and was a product of the will but, rather, that the code had captured the true principles of natural laws.[13]

The exegetical school was severely criticised at the beginning of the twentieth century, particularly by Gény.[14] Gény attacked the cult of statutory law, which the exegetical school wrongly believed to be coherent and complete and to provide solutions for every possible problem. He also condemned the school's lexical and grammatical method of interpretation. He believed, on the contrary, that lawyers should not limit themselves to the formal sources of law. They should also look at 'real' sources, which can be found in society and also in natural law by means of 'free scientific research'. Gény thus acknowledged the role of *la doctrine* and exerted a great influence on private law, but he also found some common ground with certain professors of public law, particularly Léon Duguit.

6.3 Sociological Positivism and Duguit

This is the second group of authors usually identified as positivists at the end of the nineteenth century, mainly because they held that the law could be the object of positive science, meaning that it consists in social facts.[15] Another reason is a weak connection with sociology among whose first

[13] See Xifaras 2001. [14] See Geny 1914–21, 2016. [15] See Carbonnier 1969: 9.

exponents was Auguste Comte, also the founder of philosophical positivism. Auguste Comte had indeed authored a *Cours de philosophie positive*.[16] There has been a discussion on the relation between philosophical positivism and legal positivism. However, Comte's version of positivism was closer to natural law, since he pretended that science can and should produce a total reorganisation of society and submit the individual to society or that, although positive philosophy repudiates theology and metaphysics in favour of science, it could still produce a religion based on science. As for Duguit, he greatly admired Comte, but he did not do more than stress the need for legal thought to go beyond the theological and the metaphysical stages, get rid of a priori principles and abstract beliefs, and reach the 'positive' or scientific stage.[17]

Léon Duguit became famous for his work in public law and legal philosophy. He was a colleague and friend of the sociologist Émile Durkheim at the University of Bordeaux and was influenced by his work, but only to some extent.[18] He was definitely far from sharing the positivist ideology, claiming that positive law is good because it has been produced by the state and, unlike the exegetic school and classical positivism, refusing to define law as a product of the state.

One reason why he is sometimes called a positivist was that he claimed to be a realist. He dismissed metaphysical conceptions of entities like the state, sovereignty, subjective rights or legal person and even denied that the state could be a legal person, because only facts exist and legal persons are not facts. As one of his followers, Jèze, famously said, 'I have never lunched with a legal person.' The law, which he calls 'objective law', is a social norm, produced by a group. It becomes a legal norm after the group has decided that it is necessary that it be sanctioned. However, only those norms that the group deems necessary for society ought to be enforced. Power should thus be limited and judges ought to refuse applying a statute that would go against a social norm.

This shows the limits of his positivism. Not only does he step over the limit between description and prescription, but, as Pierre Brunet rightly stresses, he is also forced to contradict himself by justifying the state: If the state is a fiction and only individuals exist, and the state is only that group of people exercising power over others, then how can one tell that the

[16] Comte 1966. [17] See Pinon 2011/12. [18] See Duguit 2003.

norms they produce qualify as 'objective law'?[19] Duguit's answer is that 'no contradiction is possible between the interest of the individual and the collective interest, between the individual and the State, because of the solidarity between them . . . since there is between collective and individual aims a permanent and absolute coincidence'. This coincidence he sees as a social fact. And from this statement of fact – whose truth-value we may still doubt – he draws a normative conclusion: That the exercise of power is law, which is exactly the normative fallacy and also a circular definition.[20]

6.4 Carré de Malberg

Carré de Malberg is one of the rare self-proclaimed positivists who came out with a theory of positivism. At first sight, his version of positivism seems to encompass all of Bobbio's three aspects of positivism. He proclaims an ambition to describe positive law and distinguish the point of view of the legal scholar from that of the law itself. This is apparent in the subtitle of his major work, *Contribution à la Théorie générale de l'État, spécialement d'après les données fournies par le droit constitutionnel français*.[21] Unlike previous French writers in constitutional law, he will not base his work on moral premises or on abstractions but on positive law. Thus, while he grants in the foreword that 'modern positive law is based on the power of the state', he criticises the German theory of the Herrschaft because 'it implies that not only law in the positive and practical sense, but moral law itself, are only based on the power of the state'.[22] The positivist approach is characterised not only by an attention to positive law and the promise to be strictly descriptive but also by the analysis of language, a method that Carré de Malberg uses very efficiently. For example, when he discusses the problem of whether sovereignty is indivisible, he stresses that the German language has three words for sovereignty, while the French has only one, and he then distinguishes three different meanings of the French term. This allows him to show that, in some sense of the word, sovereignty is perfectly divisible, but indivisible in another sense.

Then, he views law as a product of the will of the state. He accepts the traditional definition of the state, by three elements, territory, population

[19] Brunet 2014: 187–208. [20] Ibid. [21] Carré de Malberg 2004.
[22] Carré de Malberg 2004: XX.

and public power (*puissance d'Etat*, a term he uses to translate the German *Staatsgewalt*), adding that the state is a legal person, distinct from its members.

Finally, he also shares the positivist ideology, consisting in a glorification of the state, characterised by the fact that 'it possesses the capacity to impose the general will even to opposing members, and thus bring together all citizens so that they form a unity, such that none of them could prevent or break it'.[23] True, the state is not a real person, but it is not a pure fiction. It is a *legal* person. By this, he means that the legal order makes it that some of the actions of some individuals are attributed to the state – Kelsen would say 'imputed' – and thus, the state becomes a being, with a capacity to form and express a will. And then he adds that 'to attack this idea would amount to an attempt to overthrow the legal order as a whole and, thus, the State that is based on that order'.[24]

While we understand, after this very brief summary, why Carré de Malberg considered himself and is considered by others a positivist, we may also note that it is quite specific. And this is not only because it mixes aspects of legal positivism that Bobbio thought logically independent (the wish to approach the law scientifically, by describing positive law as a separate object on one hand and glorification of the state on the other) but also because actually, and contrary to what he says, he proceeds not from 'facts' or positive law but from abstractions.

Let us take the strange relation between the title, *Contribution to A General Theory of The State*, and the subtitle, *Spécialement d'après les données fournies par le droit constitutionnel français*. What is strange is not the commitment in the subtitle to start from positive law but the idea that it could be possible to build on that base a General Theory of the State, one that would be valid for all states, by way of induction from one specific positive legal system, namely the French. Yet Carré de Malberg thinks that this is possible because French positive constitutional law is made of principles that correspond to the essence of the state and are therefore valid for all states.

This is the reason why, for him, the French Revolution is so important. The revolutionaries have not willed and posited those principles. They have discovered them. Carré de Malberg was an Alsatian, influenced by the

[23] Carré de Malberg 2004: XIV. [24] Carré de Malberg 2004: I. 28.

German legal scholars, especially Romanists, on one hand and the school of public law of Laband and Jellinek on the other. The former had claimed that the Romans had developed a science of law, which was a system of law valid not only for Rome but also for other times. Thus, there was no need in Germany for the French civil code, since roman Law was almost readily available. But Carré de Malberg was also a French patriot and wanted to do with public law what the German Romanists had done for civil law, that is, claiming that the French Revolution had similarly created a science of valid constitutional law, which he called 'General Theory of the State'. To take just one example, he tried to show that the concept of a state organ had not been invented or discovered by the Germans, or by Jellinek, but by the Revolution. The French Constitution of 1791 does not use the word 'organ'; it uses the word 'representative'. Yet, says Carré de Malberg, both words refer to the same concept.

Carré de Malberg may have been wrong on this point, but the reasoning nevertheless has three characteristics, one that we can today accept as positivist, the others that would lead in the opposite direction. The first is that the reasoning is held from a metalinguistic point of view. Carré de Malberg does not stop at the words in the text but uses a meta-concept, that of 'organ', to describe their meaning. The other characteristic, which, on the contrary, would be considered anti-positivist and which runs against Carré de Malberg's own commitment, is, of course, that he starts from statements about the nature or essence of the law, the state or sovereignty. Thus, in his definition of the state, he supplements the traditional view that the state is composed of three elements of fact, population, territory and some sort of power over the members of a society, with the idea that '*the essence of every state* community is that it forms a unity, because of its organization'. That community is a nation and the state is a personification of a nation.[25] Then, he analyses the work of the French revolutionaries, trying to show that they, too, reasoned in that way and deduced their concept of organ from what, according to him, they had recognised as the essence of national sovereignty.[26] The third character that would induce us to refuse the qualification of positivist is his view of legal science as one that discovers concepts inherent in the law. This is the reason why he claimed that the

[25] Carré de Malberg 2004: 9. [26] See Maulin 2002; Troper 2018.

Revolution, having discovered such concepts, had set the basic principles of a general theory of the state.

6.5 The Vichy Scholars

The term positivist is applied in yet another, derogatory, sense, to refer to the attitude of those scholars who pose as positivists but at the same time give a (positive) evaluation of the law. This was a particularly sensitive matter in the nineteen eighties, as a new generation of legal scholars started to review the attitude of lawyers during the Vichy period. They mainly directed their attention not to judges who had obediently applied the law, sometimes with some zeal, but to law professors who had commented on legislation, specifically anti-Semitic legislation. In an article called 'The Waywardness of Positivism', Daniele Lochak wrote 'c'est au nom des principes positivistes que les juristes ont participé à la banalisation du droit antisémite, contribuant ainsi à légitimer la politique antisémite de Vichy'.[27] These professors, she argued, did not write from a natural law point of view and had claimed to adopt a purely scientific attitude, to remain neutral and to describe the law objectively. But by treating that specific legislation as they would have treated any kind of legislation on other subjects, they made it appear as 'normal' and 'respectable' law, thus facilitating its acceptance and application. In other words, neutrality is impossible and the very fact of describing a law amounts to a contribution to the policy that served as a motive for that law.

Lochak is right when she says that these law professors did not merely describe its provisions but also reconstructed the reasons behind that kind of legislation and that those reasons were clearly anti-Semitic. The reconstruction implied some preferences and value judgements and was thus, clearly, far from a plain description. Explaining, for example, a law that barred Jews from the civil service by the fact that they could not be assimilated or that they had no sense of the national interest was clearly a justification, but one that was obviously not implied by a commitment to neutrality. What was striking was that some of the authors who had been the subjects of this attack also called themselves positivists and claimed

[27] Lochak 1989: 265; see also Troper 1989: 286.

that they had been neutral because they had correctly described the law, not only its substance but also the intentions of the lawmaker.

A third position was still available: Claiming that positivism does imply neutrality and that it is possible for a positivist to describe the law and even the intentions of the lawmaker without making a value judgement on these intentions. Thus, the Vichy lawyers wrote the way they did, making favourable value judgements on the intentions of the lawmaker, not because they were positivists (in Bobbio's first sense) but because they were not.

However, because of the French conception, already mentioned, of *la doctrine*, scholars do not clearly distinguish between description and prescription. What they claim to describe is not only a text but also all the values on which the text is based. These values cannot be perceived empirically. They must necessarily be reconstructed, and such reconstruction is itself value-laden, so that scholars posing as positivists are inevitably normative.

Thus, from the point of view of a positivist epistemology, such as Bobbio's, the lawyers criticised by Lochak were the opposite of positivists. Yet, from a lexical point of view, we must notice that Lochak and others call them positivists and that they also call themselves by that name.

6.6 Analytical Positivism

Finally, the term 'positivist' is normally applied to a group of scholars related either to the normativists, to the English school after H. L. A. Hart, or to the realists. Positivism in this sense has been introduced in France very late and very slowly.

This has notably been the case for Kelsen's ideas. The great scholars of public law of the beginning of the century had some knowledge of Kelsen. Duguit, already mentioned, was a co-founder with Kelsen of the *Revue international de théorie du droit* and they co-signed the editorial for the first issue. They may have agreed on the importance of a general theory of law, but, short of that, there were very few points of contact. Carré de Malberg was closer and he even published, in 1933, a short book to compare his views to those of Kelsen.[28] At that time, few of Kelsen's

[28] See Carré de Malberg 2008.

works had been published. Nevertheless, one of Carré de Malberg's students, Charles Eisenmann, wrote his doctoral dissertation on the Constitutional Court of Austria, established under the influence of Hans Kelsen, who wrote a preface, justifying the institution and claiming an ambition to contribute to the solution of practical problems.[29]

Eisenmann later translated some other works, particularly the second edition of the *Pure Theory*.[30] Nevertheless, its influence was extremely limited for a number of reasons (little interest for legal theory or legal philosophy, the prevailing concept of *la doctrine*, the prevalence of Catholicism . . .). It was only in the seventies, because judicial review was suddenly developing, after having been considered from the time of the Revolution as incompatible with the theory that the law is the expression of the general will, that scholars, searching for some justification, turned to Kelsen. Paradoxically, the aspect of Kelsen's work that is best known in France is precisely that which, in Bobbio's typology of positivism, would be farthest from positivism as a scientific approach to the law.

There is little to say about Hart's influence. His works were not translated until very late and this happened in Belgium, where the tradition and culture are different.[31] The French context was not favourable because of a lasting lack of interest in Anglo-American analytical philosophy. The same can be said of the Italian analytical school. It was not until 1995 that the first translations of Bobbio or Scarpelli were published.[32]

Since then, the climate has changed considerably. Among scholars of the young generation, there is a growing interest in legal theory, particularly analytical theory, also among scholars primarily concerned with dogmatics, and there are more translations from the English and Italian authors. However, they are far from forming a school or even having some common characteristic, and although some relate to Kelsen or, less frequently, to Hart, these are very loose relations.[33]

The same can be said of the realists until the very end of the twentieth century. There were almost no translations from the American, the Scandinavian or the Italian realists, and we have witnessed the development of a French version, mostly derived from the Italian. The French version can be characterised by three features. Unsurprisingly, the first is a focus on legal interpretation, with a radically sceptical view; perhaps

[29] See Eisenmann 1986. [30] See Kelsen 1962. [31] See Hart 2005. [32] See Bobbio 1998.
[33] See Hochmann, Magnon and Ponsard 2019.

more original is the idea that positive law is made not only of legal texts but also of reasoning in a historical context, so that attention ought to be given to the substance of the law and the discourse used to justify it;[34] and third is an attempt to introduce causal reasoning into legal theory.[35]

Thus, it seems that, if we insisted in using Bobbio's definitions of legal positivism, we would find very few French authors who accept the view of a legal science on the model of empirical sciences, and those are only part of a very recent tradition.

On the contrary, as far as the second aspect of legal positivism in Bobbio's sense is concerned, we could certainly find some French authors who accept one or the other of the characteristic theories of positivism, for example, that the law is only the expression of a human will, or some sort of separation between law and morals, or that judicial decisions are the conclusion of a syllogism. However, this would hardly be conclusive, first, because they would not form a homogeneous group since, as Hart pointed out, all positivists do not accept all of these theories, and, second, because these authors would share these theories with other authors who are not positivists in another sense of the word and even with some who claim to be anti-positivists.

Finally, few authors, if any, would correspond to Bobbio's third aspect, profess the positivist ideology that positive law is always good for the sole reason that it is the law of the state, but many authors, including anti-positivists, would accept a soft version, namely that positive law ought to be obeyed.

We should also add that all the discussions that have been going on among legal theorists in other countries on new versions of legal positivism, post-positivism or inclusive versus exclusive positivism, institutionalism and so forth have had almost no echo in France.

Bobbio's analysis then does not help us to identify positivists. On the other hand, if we stick to those authors who have been called positivists, we find that all of them qualify in some sense of the word. Could we say at least that they have some family resemblance? Certainly, but we would then have to include in the family other authors who are usually not called positivists. Do all of them share some characteristic that escapes Bobbio's analysis? The answer is definitely in the negative.

[34] See, e.g., Troper 2001. [35] See Troper, Champeil-Desplats and Grzegorczyk 2005.

If the meaning of a term is its use in the language, then legal positivism has no precise meaning in the French legal language. All the authors who are called positivists are so different and some of them resemble non-positivists so closely that they cannot even be said to have a family resemblance, or, otherwise, we should include these non-positivists in the family. The label is being assigned, mostly without an explicit justification, to a great variety of authors who have very little in common but the label itself. But, precisely, if what we are looking for is some specific feature, not of legal positivism but of the French legal tradition, we may have found at least one: It is the absence, because of structural and historical reasons, of a common conception of, or even a discussion on, legal positivism.

References

Bloch, M. 2014. *Feudal Society*. Routledge.

Bobbio, N. 1972. *Giusnaturalismo e positivismo giuridico*. Edizioni di Comunità.

Bobbio, N. 1998. *Essais de théorie du droit*. LGDJ.

Brunet, P. 2014. 'Le "positivisme" français dans la lumière du Nord'. *Revus* 24: 187–208.

Carbonnier, J. 1969. *Droit civil. 1: Introduction*. Presses Universitaires de France.

Carré de Malberg, R. 2004. *Contribution à la Théorie générale de l'État*. Dalloz.

Carré de Malberg, R. 2008. *Confrontation de la théorie de la formation du droit par degrés avec les idées et les institutions consacrées par le droit positif français relativement à sa formation*. Dalloz.

Chevallier, J. 2002. 'Doctrine juridique et science juridique'. *Droit et Société*: 103–19.

Chevallier, J. 2009. 'L'enseignement du droit en question'. In J.-C. Froment (ed.). *Administration et politique: une pensée critique et sans frontières*. Presses Universitaires de Grenoble: 111–20.

Comte, A. 1966. *Cours de philosophie positive*. 6 vols. Anthropos.

Cornu, G. et al. 1987. *Vocabulaire juridique*. Presses Universitaires de France.

Demolombe, C. 1845. *Cours de code Napoléon*. Durand et Hachette.

Duguit, L. 2003. *L'état, le droit objectif et la loi positive*. Dalloz.

Eisenmann, C. 1986. *La justice constitutionnelle et la Haute Cour Constitutionnelle d'Autriche: édition de 1928*. Paris Economica.

Geny, F. 1914–21. *Science et technique en droit privé positif: nouvelle contribution à la critique de la méthode juridique*. Soc. du Recueil Sirey.

Geny, F. 2016. *Méthode d'interprétation et sources en droit privé positif: essai critique*. LGDJ.

Green, L. 2018. 'Legal Positivism'. In E. N. Zalta (ed.). *Stanford Encyclopedia of Philosophy*. https://plato.stanford.edu/archives/spr2018/entries/legal-positivism/.

Hart, H. L. A. 1983. *Essays in jurisprudence and philosophy*. Oxford University Press.

Hart, H. L. A. 2005. *Le concept de droit*. Fac. Univ. Saint-Louis.

Hochmann, T., Magnon, X. and Ponsard, R. 2019. *Un classique méconnu: Hans Kelsen*. LGDJ.

Jestaz, P. and Jamin, C. 2004. *La doctrine*. Dalloz.

Kelsen, H. 1962. *Théorie pure du droit*. Dalloz.

Lochak, D. 1989. 'La doctrine sous Vichy ou les mésaventures du positivisme'. In D. Lochak (ed.). *Les usages sociaux du droit*. Presses Universitaires de France: 252–85. www.u-picardie.fr/curapp-revues/root/23/lochak2.pdf.

Maulin, É. 2002. 'Carré de Malberg et le droit constitutionnel de la Révolution française'. *Annales historiques de la Révolution française* 328. http://journals.openedition.org/ahrf/583.

Ross, A. 1998. 'Validity and the Conflict between Legal Positivism and Natural Law'. In S. Paulson and B. Litschewski Paulson (eds.). *Normativity and Norms: Critical Perspectives on Kelsenian Themes*. Clarendon Press.

Pinon, S. 2011/12. 'Le positivisme sociologique: l'itinéraire de Léon Duguit'. *Revue interdisciplinaire d'études juridiques* 67: 69–93. www.cairn.info/revue-interdisciplinaire-d-etudes-juridiques-2011-2-page-69.htm.

Sueur, J.-J. 2012. 'Variations sur un thème (trop) connu [Je ne suis qu'un affreux positiviste]'. In P. Charlot and M. Doat (eds.). *Liber amicorum Darcy. Détours juridiques: le praticien, le théoricien et le rêveur*. Bruylant: 765–95.

Troper, M. 1989. 'La doctrine et le positivisme (à propos d'un article de Danièle Lochak)'. In D. Lochak (ed.). *Les usages sociaux du droit*. Presses Universitaires de France: 286–92.

Troper, M. 2001. *Le droit, la théorie du droit, l'État*. Presses Universitaires de France.

Troper, M. 2018. 'Souveraineté et représentation'. In M. Albertone and D. Castiglione (eds.). *Les défis de la représentation: langages, pratiques et figuration du gouvernement*. Classiques Garnier: 75–89.

Troper, M., Champeil-Desplats, V. and Grzegorczyk, C. (eds.). 2005. *Les contraintes juridiques*. LGDJ.

Xifaras, M. 2001. 'L'École de l'Exégèse était-elle historique? Le cas de Raymond-Théodore Troplong (1796–1869), lecteur de Friedrich Carl von Savigny'. In H. Mohnhaupt and J.-F. Kervégan (eds.). *Influences et réceptions mutuelles du droit et de la philosophie en France et en Allemagne*. Klostermann: 177–209.

7 The Italian Tradition of Legal Positivism

Riccardo Guastini

7.1 A Common Attitude

In a sense, legal positivism is but the common attitude of modern 'positive' legal scholars (civil lawyers, criminal lawyers, constitutional lawyers and so on) as distinguished from professional legal philosophers.[1]

In this sense, almost all Italian legal scholars were legal positivists since at least the second half of the nineteenth century. They studied and commented on the 1848 Constitution, the 1865 Civil Code and so forth. Some of them discussed legal-theoretical issues, such as legal gaps, in a clearly positivistic mood.[2] Sure, natural law was still alive most of all within legal-philosophical literature, but, as far as I can see, natural law had no serious weight in juristic and judicial reasoning.[3]

However, legal positivism as a specific legal philosophy (or theory) makes its very first appearance in 1950 with a seminal essay written by the most distinguished Italian legal philosopher of the twentieth century – Norberto Bobbio.[4] It is worth noting that, in this essay, legal positivism looks strictly connected with analytical philosophy and logical empiricism.

1 'Positive jurists', in Italian legal parlance, are usually distinguished from legal philosophers, legal historians and legal sociologists.

2 See, e.g., Donati 1910/1966 and Romano 1925 on legal gaps. An important positivistic (although not analytical) general theory of law was formulated by Carnelutti 1940. See the commentary in Bobbio 1955: 1ff., 27ff.

3 Nonetheless, there is a natural-law flavour in the rhetoric argument of 'the nature of things', frequently used by jurists and judges to solve linguistic indeterminacy of legal texts and/or fill up legal gaps.

4 A comprehensive view on Bobbio's legal philosophy can be found in Ruiz Miguel 1980, 1983; Borsellino 1991; Portinaro 2008; Losano 2018.

7.2 Law as Discourse

In his essay, devoted to legal science and linguistic analysis, Bobbio assumes law to be a discourse, and nothing else, namely the discourse of – the set of normative sentences issued by – the law-giving authorities.[5] Hence, law is an artificial object not 'discovered' by human reason but 'created' by human acts of will.

From this point of view, legal rules are nothing but linguistic entities.[6] Jurisprudence in turn – understood as 'prudentia juris' – is but the (metalinguistic) analysis of legislative discourse. A short quotation is in order:

> The subject matter of jurisprudence is a set of rules of behaviour. . . . Such rules are expressed by . . . normative sentences. . . . Jurists do not observe phenomena as empirical scientists. . . . Jurisprudence is no empirical science . . .. Its subject . . . is the specific content of a given language (the language of the lawgiver, the language of laws). . . . The common critical and necessary part of any science is the so-called *analysis of language*. Well, now jurisprudence is essentially analysis of language, namely of that peculiar language which consists in the normative sentences formulated by the lawgiver. . . . Interpreting the law is but analysing the lawgiver's language, that is, the language in which legal rules are expressed.[7]

This view looks like an analytical-*philosophical* 'translation' of a couple of Bentham's and Austin's analytical-*jurisprudential* theses (at the very beginning of legal positivism): (i) law is but the set of commands issued by the sovereign,[8] and (ii) jurisprudence – namely, local, particular, 'expository', as opposed to 'censorial', jurisprudence – is the description of the normative contents of such commands.[9] This way, Bobbio builds up a bridge between analytical jurisprudence and analytical philosophy – such a bridge will never be broken within the Italian tradition of legal positivism.

[5] The same views are developed in Bobbio 1950b and shared by Scarpelli 1953.

[6] See Bobbio 1950a: 13, 15ff. [7] Bobbio 1950a: 13–15ff.

[8] An analytical view on legal norms, however, was already present in Bentham: see Chiassoni 2016a: ch. 1.

[9] See Bentham 1789/1996, Austin 1879. On the origins of legal positivism in England, see Agnelli 1959 and Cattaneo 1962. Cattaneo's book includes an analysis of 'legal positivism', discussed by Bobbio 1965: 147ff.

7.3 Contributions to Analytical Legal Positivism

During the fifties and the beginning of the sixties, Bobbio offers a great deal of contributions to analytical legal positivism: among them, at least the following are worth mentioning.

(i) One of the main concerns of Bobbio, in this period, is the double distinction between (a) particular jurisprudence or legal dogmatics and general legal theory, on the one hand, and (b) legal theory and legal philosophy properly understood, on the other.

The first distinction is construed by means of the opposition between 'form' and 'content'.[10] The subject matter of jurisprudence is the content of legal norms – its task is ascertaining, by means of interpretation, what is commanded (prohibited, permitted) to whom in which circumstances. The subject matter of legal theory, on the contrary, is the form of legal norms and systems. In this context, 'form' refers: on the one hand, to the properties (as revealed by logical analysis) of normative language and fundamental legal concepts, the classification of norms and so forth; on the other hand, to the structure of legal systems, their hierarchical frame, the ways in which norms are produced, modified and repealed.

The second distinction is grounded on the is-ought or facts-values dichotomy.[11] Legal theory, according to Bobbio, is a scientific, value-free enterprise –[12] the conceptual part of 'expository jurisprudence'. Legal philosophy, according to his stipulation, is nothing but normative moral philosophy, the philosophy of justice: not science but 'ideology' – an evaluative political enterprise, in short (in a Benthamite mood), 'censorial jurisprudence'.[13]

[10] Bobbio 1955, 34ff. Bobbio 1955 collects a number of essays already published in various journals and books between 1949 and 1955. One of them is devoted to a strong defence of Kelsen's pure theory against the criticisms of both natural law philosophy and sociological jurisprudence. Besides, in 1954 Bobbio publishes an essay – the very beginning of logical-deontic studies in Italy – where he introduces a couple of crucial distinctions: first, between the norms issued by law-giving authorities and the metalinguistic descriptive statements about norms formulated by legal scholars; second between the 'logic of law' (the logical relations among norms) and the 'logic of jurisprudence' (the logical relations among normative propositions). See Bobbio 1954.

[11] See Bobbio 1955: 49ff., 79.

[12] 'No science without objectivity', says Bobbio 1955: 77, meaning, by 'objectivity', axiological neutrality – the same attitude as Weber's *Wertfreiheit.*

[13] In another essay, however, Bobbio will sketch a different, non-normative picture of legal philosophy (as distinguished from legal theory), namely, the analysis of the various

Notice, however, that, in Bobbio's view, each legal theory is the theory of a particular positive legal system, not necessarily applicable to others:[14] a legal theory is 'general' only in the sense of 'formal', since it leaves aside the contingent content of the law in force in different systems but not in the sense that it could be applied to any legal system whatsoever.

(ii) In 1958 and 1960 respectively, Bobbio published two remarkable courses of lessons: the first devoted to the theory of legal norms,[15] the second to the theory of legal orders.[16] Bobbio's 'general theory of law',[17] strictly positivistic, is by and large inspired by Kelsen's pure theory.

However, most Kelsenian theses are 'transcribed' into analytical terms: for example, norms are conceived of as prescriptive sentences and classified, accordingly, along distinctions such as the different deontic modalities, the different legal positions (right, power and so on), the relative 'force' (for example, commands distinguished from recommendations, demands and advices).[18]

Bobbio agrees with Kelsen's theory of the basic norm grounding the unity of the legal order. Some years later, however, he will reject such a theory, arguing that the ultimate foundation of the legal order is not a norm but a de facto power – the power that gives rise to the (first) constitution of the legal order at hand.[19]

At any rate, Bobbio does not share Kelsen's theses about the necessary completeness and consistency of legal orders. In his view, completeness and consistency are contingent and, as a matter of fact, they do not obtain, since in most legal orders there are both gaps and normative conflicts.

theories of justice and the logical analysis of value-judgements and their relations with fact-statements; Bobbio 1965: 47ff.

[14] See Bobbio 1955: 40. [15] See Bobbio 1958. [16] See Bobbio 1960.

[17] Both courses were later collected under the heading *General Theory of Law*; Bobbio 1993.

[18] An original classification of legal norms was proposed by Carcaterra 1974. He distinguishes between 'prescriptive' and 'constitutive' norms. Prescriptive norms are commands. Constitutive norms, in turn, are those norms that do not command anyone to do anything (in such a way that they have no addressees, they cannot be either obeyed or violated) but directly produce their effect: e.g., derogatory norms ('Norm N is hereby derogated') that neither describe nor prescribe but simply perform a derogation. To be sure, such norms are 'constitutive' in a sense different from the one stipulated by Searle 1969.

[19] See Bobbio 1970a/2012: 72ff. Various features of the general theory of legal orders were developed by some Bobbio's disciples, such as Gavazzi 1959, 1967; Conte 1962; Lazzaro 1965; Losano 1968. See Barrere Unzueta 1990.

7.4 Some Important Distinctions

The sixties is the decade, in Italy, of the great flourishing of legal positivism as a subject of analysis, definition and debate.[20] Once more, Bobbio's works are at the front of the scene. Bobbio issues a new course of lessons devoted to legal positivism in 1961 and, in 1965, a collection of essays on legal positivism and natural law.[21] His new contributions include both a criticism of natural law and an analysis of legal positivism.

(1) As to natural law doctrines, Bobbio makes three moves. First, he assumes that so-called natural law is no law at all – law being, by definition, a set of positive, artificial, man-made norms regulating the use of force (a strictly Kelsenian view). Natural law, properly speaking, is but critical morality.[22] Second, he observes that, in the natural law tradition, many different versions of natural law, a lot of competing critical moralities, in fact exist – for example, one claiming natural equality among men, another maintaining inequality; one claiming private property to be a natural state of affairs, another maintaining common property to be the natural condition of mankind; one requiring obedience to political power, another justifying the right to resistance; and so forth.[23] Third, he wonders: what is the common element that keeps together all such different views about nature (the nature of human beings, the nature of social relationships)? His answer is that the only common element is neither a shared view about nature nor a substantive ethical thesis but a meta-ethical one – at a logical level higher than ethics – concerning the justification of such different normative theses. All natural law doctrines, indeed, claim to ground their normative theses on facts (or statements about facts).[24]

This amounts to an evident violation of Hume's principle: no norms can (logically) flow from knowledge of facts, no normative sentence may be

[20] Since the sixties, the Italian positivistic-analytical scholars have arranged a great deal of conferences. Among them, at least the following are worth mentioning: (i) the conference on legal positivism held in Bellagio in 1960 (the proceedings were never published; for a short account, however, see Falk and Shuman 1961); (ii) the conference on the concept of obligation ('Studi sull'obbligo giuridico', *Rivista di filosofia*, LXII, 2, 1966); (iii) the conference on 'Is and Ought in Legal Science' (*Rivista internazionale di filosofia del diritto*, XLIV, 3, 1967); and (iv) the conference on the is/ought question ('La logica e il dover essere', *Rivista di filosofia*, LXVI, 4, 1976).

[21] See Bobbio 1961, 1965. [22] See Bobbio 1965: 163ff.

[23] See Bobbio 1965: 169ff., 172, 182ff. [24] See Bobbio 1965: 138ff., 190ff.

logically derived from a set of purely cognitive premises, such as propositions describing nature (or any other kinds of fact whatsoever).[25] Norms can stem only from those human acts that enact – 'posit' – them by uttering normative sentences.

Thus, after all, natural law is no specific critical morality or normative ethics. Rather, Bobbio represents it as a peculiar 'meta-ethics' – a second-order discourse about ethics, namely a cognitivist, objectivist, meta-ethics.[26] Natural law is not a set of substantive ethical theses but a 'formal' meta-ethics concerning the proper way of justifying normative ethical theses (whatever ethical thesis indeed), assuming 'nature' – a completely indeterminate concept – as a source of norms.[27]

(2) As to legal positivism, Bobbio introduces an unsurpassed distinction.[28] In his view, the phrase 'legal positivism' is actually used in juristic literature with different meanings, referring to three different and logically independent doctrines.[29]

(i) *Methodological positivism.* In the first place, legal positivism is a methodological attitude, namely a value-free approach to law, that presupposes the separation of law and morals (Hart) or facts and values (Kelsen). The philosophy of the (legal) science of legal positivism circumscribes the object of (legal) science to the law as it actually is, excluding any inquiry about the law as it ought to be. Legal cognition is *expository*, not *censorial*, jurisprudence.[30]

[25] The main Italian contributions on this topic are Carcaterra 1969; Celano 1994.

[26] See Bobbio 1963a: 67. In this context, 'meta-ethics' clearly has not the same sense in which such a phrase is usually understood within the analytical philosophy tradition (roughly speaking, the logical analysis of moral language: see, e.g., Hare 1952).

[27] See Gavazzi 1961.

[28] Conceptually unsurpassed, in my view, although disputable from the historical point of view, Bobbio's distinction is used by Grzegorczyk, Michaut and Troper 1992: part 2.

[29] See Bobbio 1961: part II; Bobbio 1965: 101ff.

[30] Bentham 1789/1996: 293ff.; Austin 1879: I, 33, 176ff., 220. The same attitude is shared by Kelsen: his 'pure theory' purportedly responds to 'the required separation of legal science from politics' (Kelsen 1934/1992: 3). The pure theory 'is being kept free from all the elements foreign to the specific method of a science whose only purpose is the cognition of law . . .. A science has to describe its object as it actually is, not to prescribe as it should be or should not be from the point of view of some specific value judgments. The latter is a problem of politics, and, as such, concerns the art of government, an activity directed at values, not an object of science, directed at reality' (Kelsen 1945: xiv).

It should be stressed that, according to Bobbio, this methodological attitude is actually shared by modern legal scholars, who are used to distinguish between *jus conditum* and *jus condendum* and consider only *jus conditum* as the appropriate subject of their inquiry – in other words, in his view, the actual work of legal scholars is a purely descriptive enterprise.[31] At any rate, the positivistic value-free approach to law presupposes a criterion of identification of positive law itself – such a criterion is provided by a theory of law, and this is the second face of legal positivism (or legal positivism *par excellence*).

(ii) *Theoretical positivism.* In the second place, legal positivism is a theory of law, namely the theory generally shared by nineteenth-century jurists,[32] which includes a number of substantive theses, such as the following:
   (a) law is the set of commands enacted by a sovereign authority;
   (b) the binding force of such commands is guaranteed by the threat of sanctions;
   (c) law is a complete and consistent system, in such a way that no gaps and no normative conflicts exist;
   (d) legal interpretation is a cognitive enterprise consisting in ascertaining the will of the legislative authority;
   (e) the application of law is an eminently logical activity consisting in (ascertaining facts and) inferring individual prescriptions from general rules ('All thieves ought to be punished. X is a thief. Hence X is to be punished.').

(iii) *Ideological positivism.* In the third place, legal positivism is an ideology, that is, a normative stance according to which positive law ought to be obeyed – there is a (moral or political) obligation to obey the law. In the footsteps of Hobbes, justice is identified with positive law.

Remark that ideological positivism, understood this way, is no specified substantive (normative) ethics – rather, it is a 'formal' meta-ethics in the sense that it does not command any definite behaviour but simply commands compliance with the rules issued by legal authorities (whatever their content may be). Such an attitude – equal and contrary, so to say, to natural

[31] Bobbio 1966: 79. But, as we shall see (Section 7.8), Bobbio will change his opinion on the matter.

[32] This is, Bobbio says, legal positivism *stricto sensu*, and this is what is usually meant by 'legal positivism' in jurists' common language.

law doctrine, as characterised by Bobbio – is labelled 'ethical legalism' or 'ethical formalism'.

To be sure, these three positivistic doctrines, although logically independent, share the 'no natural law' thesis – that is, that no natural law exists, the only existing 'law' (properly understood) being positive law, that is, law 'posited' by human norm-creating acts. Laws are not 'given' to men but 'made' by them.[33]

As to Bobbio's own ideas on the matter:[34] first, 'facing the clash of ideologies', he declares himself a natural lawyer (*giusnaturalista*), meaning (as far as I can see) that he is an enemy of ideological positivism (no obligation to obey positive law exists) and an advocate of human rights; second, as to the method of legal science, he declares himself definitely positivist; third, as to legal theory, he declares himself neutral, in the sense that he does not share all the tenets of classical positivistic theory (such as the necessary completeness and consistency of legal systems, as noted).[35]

7.5 Another Distinction

Recently, Bobbio's distinction among three forms or features of legal positivism was criticised by Pierluigi Chiassoni, who proposes, in turn, to distinguish simply between ideological and epistemic positivism.[36]

The first is the attitude of a great deal of nineteenth-century legal scholars (the *École de l'exégèse* in France, the Historical School and the *Allgemeine Staatslehre* in Germany, and so on) whose positivism – the 'no natural law' thesis – is meant to recommend obedience (by citizens) and

[33] See Scarpelli 1984 and 1989: 461. The legal character of any entity (a fact, a subject, etc.) depends entirely on its being the object of a legal norm that refers to it: Carcaterra 1984: 5.

[34] See Bobbio 1965: 146.

[35] Bobbio's methodological attitude was criticised by Matteucci 1963, who endorsed a normative (viz., liberal) concept of constitution, rejecting the descriptive one. Bobbio's reply to Matteucci is contained in an only recently published private letter to him (Bobbio 1963b). Besides, the normative concept of constitution is shared by a lot of constitutional lawyers: among them, Sartori 1987: 11ff.

[36] Chiassoni 2013a: 20ff.; Chiassoni 2016b: 92ff. Among other things, Chiassoni rightly criticises the ascription of the no natural law thesis to legal positivism in general, since one of the most prominent representatives of legal positivism in the nineteenth century – Austin – admitted the existence of natural, side by side with positive, law.

faithful application (by judges) to the laws enacted by the sovereign. In other words, according to Chiassoni, there is no genuine positivistic descriptive 'theory' distinct from positivistic normative 'ideology'.[37]

The second, on the contrary, is the attitude of a great deal of legal philosophers – Austin and Bentham, of course, as well as Kelsen, Hart, the legal realists, both American and Scandinavian, and so forth – who advocate for the axiologically neutral (*wertfrei*) knowledge of the law in force. The 'no natural law' thesis, accordingly, has no prescriptive import – it is simply meant to circumscribe the proper subject of any scientific (empirical) investigation in the legal domain.

Both Bobbio's and Chiassoni's distinctions can be fruitfully compared to the one introduced by Olivecrona between two views about legal science: on the one hand, the idea according to which the only subject matter appropriate for legal science is positive law (there is no room for the supposed 'law of nature'); on the other hand, 'the general view that science has to do with observable phenomena only', refraining from any valuations.[38]

7.6 Scarpelli's Legal Positivism

In 1965, the very same year of the release of Bobbio's book on legal positivism and natural law, Uberto Scarpelli – a distinguished scholar of the Italian analytical school – publishes his own work devoted to legal positivism.[39]

While Bobbio defends the methodological version of legal positivism,[40] Scarpelli, in turn, defends a form of 'political' positivism in the following sense.

By 'legal positivism', Scarpelli understands nothing other than the actual practice of 'positive' jurists, that is, the set of attitudes, methods and

[37] This is so, among other things, since some of the theses (correctly) ascribed by Bobbio to legal positivistic theory (the necessary completeness and consistency of legal systems, the cognitive character of interpretation, etc.) are secretly prescriptive, and in this sense 'ideological'.

[38] Olivecrona 1971: 51, 54. The second view, as Olivecrona remarks, was already held by Hägerström.

[39] See Scarpelli 1965. Scarpelli's main contributions to legal philosophy are devoted to the semantics of normative language: Scarpelli 1955, 1959.

[40] See Bobbio 1966.

doctrines held by judges, public officials at large, legal scholars and lawyers.[41] Juristic operations – such as ascertaining the validity of norms, interpreting legal materials, qualifying behaviours according to norms, as well as filling gaps, solving normative inconsistencies, and so forth – do not amount to 'expository jurisprudence', the value-free knowledge of the law in force. Rather, they are practical operations using and applying, not simply describing, the law.[42] Legal cognition is a committed enterprise – committed, namely, to the acceptance of the existing legal system. Juristic operations presuppose the 'internal point of view' (in Hart's sense).[43]

Thus, juristic sentences – in particular, validity-judgments, where validity is conceived of as binding force –[44] are 'internal' statements that presuppose the acceptance of the 'fundamental principle' (Kelsen's basic norm, Hart's rule of recognition) of the legal system at hand, understood at the same time as a conceptual criterion of identification[45] (that refers to the set of rules of change) and a duty-imposing norm.[46] Besides, according to Scarpelli, the acceptance of a legal system and/or its fundamental principle cannot be justified by the principle of effectiveness (whatever effective legal system is valid). This is so since no norm or normative attitude can be derived from facts (Hume's guillotine) – acceptance depends on a political decision. In this sense, Scarpelli's positivism is 'political' in nature.[47]

In a sense, this is a form of ideological positivism: law deserves obedience. In Scarpelli's view, however, law deserves obedience only under given circumstances: in particular, constitutional democracy and the rule of law. Thus, not the law as such ought to be obeyed but only a legal order that is politically just. According to Bobbio,[48] this results in a natural law thesis.

[41] See Scarpelli 1966.

[42] Contrary to Bobbio, Scarpelli has a quite realistic view about actual jurisprudence.

[43] Hart 1961. This is perhaps the only significant influence of Hart on Italian legal positivism, which is by and large influenced by Kelsen. See, however, Jori 1985: 109–202.

[44] See the well-known criticism by Ross 1961, addressed to Kelsen but equally applicable to Scarpelli (and Hart, for sure).

[45] As maintained, e.g., by Bulygin 1991; Bulygin 2015: 117ff.; Guastini 2013.

[46] As maintained, e.g., by Raz 1971: 93, and Ruiz Manero 1990: ch. 2 (among many others).

[47] Scarpelli's version of legal positivism has been defended in many circumstances by Jori: see, e.g., Jori 1976, 1987.

[48] See Bobbio 1966: 73.

7.7 The Following Debates

The release, in the same year, of two such very different books on legal positivism (Bobbio's and Scarpelli's) gave rise to debates – in particular within a roundtable where a great deal of outstanding Italian legal philosophers discussed both books. Among the several interventions, at least two are worth mentioning for their theoretical significance.

(a) In Scarpelli's book, validity-judgements are understood as (internal) assertions: for example, 'The norm N is valid.' Amedeo Conte argues, against Scarpelli, that juristic validity-judgements should be understood not as assertions but as conditional statements – '*If* such and such are the criteria of validity of the legal system, *then* the norm N is valid' – where the criteria of recognition are not used but just mentioned (conditionals do not affirm either the antecedent or the consequent but only the material implication between them).[49]

(b) In Bobbio's book, three forms or features of legal positivism are distinguished. Those who accept this or other similar distinctions,[50] whenever they talk about legal positivism, are forced to specify: 'legal positivism in such or such a sense'. Giovanni Tarello argues that, if there is no generally accepted and shared meaning of the phrase, there is no reason to go on talking about 'legal positivism'. Instead of specifying, for example, 'legal positivism understood as the thesis of the separation of law and morals', 'legal positivism understood as the thesis according to which there is a moral obligation to obey the law', and so forth, would not it be simpler talking about the separation of law and morals, the obligation to obey the law, and so forth, omitting legal positivism? The phrase 'legal positivism' could (or maybe should) be definitely removed from the language of legal philosophy and historiography.[51]

7.8 The 'Crisis' of Legal Positivism

In 1967, Bobbio releases a new essay devoted to legal science.[52] Such an essay will by and large be considered a sign of the 'crisis' of legal

[49] See Conte 1966. [50] E.g., those proposed by Hart 1958 or Cattaneo 1962.

[51] See Tarello 1966.

[52] See Bobbio 1967, which includes a sharp analysis of the different senses in which legal science can be labelled 'normative', namely, (a) dealing with norms, (b) creating norms, (c) formulating normative, i.e., deontic sentences (*Sollsätze*). See also Bobbio 1968, 1970b.

positivism – namely a disavowal, by Bobbio, of methodological legal positivism.[53]

First, Bobbio distinguishes between descriptive and prescriptive language. Second, he distinguishes between language and metalanguage, namely between (a) the language of legal science, or 'jurisprudence', understood as the actual practice of legal scholars and judges, and (b) the language of the theory of legal science, labelled as 'meta-jurisprudence'. Third, by an exercise of *ars combinatoria*, he crosses such distinctions, singling out (i) a descriptive meta-jurisprudence describing a de facto prescriptive jurisprudence[54] and (ii) a prescriptive meta-jurisprudence recommending (prescribing) a descriptive jurisprudence.[55] Switching from the conceptual apparatus to the empirical observation, he ascertains the following.

As a matter of fact, actual jurisprudence is not a purely descriptive discourse, as it claims to be (as Bobbio himself claimed till 1966). On the contrary, it is by and large drenched with value-judgements. Most of all, jurisprudence, legal dogmatics in particular, contributes to shape and change the law. Notwithstanding the models of a neutral legal science proposed by legal philosophers, jurisprudence, in every legal system, de facto played and plays the role of an informal source of law.

On the other hand, positivistic meta-jurisprudence, recommending a purely descriptive jurisprudence, is prescriptive in nature, hence somehow 'ideological' – at least, politically oriented. The practical function of the ideal of *Wertfreiheit* in jurisprudence is safeguarding the authority of legislators.

To be sure, ascertaining the prescriptive character of the positivistic ideal of legal science does not amount to discrediting it. In Bobbio's essay, there is no rejection of methodological positivism.

[53] See, e.g., Pattaro 1972; Jori 1987.

[54] This concept applies, e.g., to American legal realism. See Tarello 1962.

[55] This is the case of Kelsen. See, e.g., Kelsen 1928: 7:

> La science du droit ne peut ni ne doit – ni directement ni indirectement – créer le droit; elle doit se limiter à connaître le droit que créent les législateurs, les administrateurs et les juges. Cette renonciation, incontestablement douloureuse pour le jurisconsulte, parce que contraire à l'intérêt compréhensible de son état, est un postulat essentiel du positivisme juridique, qui, en opposition consciente avec toute doctrine de droit naturel, avouée ou secrète, rejette résolument le dogme que la doctrine soit une source de droit.

Rather, in his essay, there is an important criticism of a Kelsenian thesis concerning the language of legal science. According to Kelsen, the only proper way of describing (the content of) a norm – 'murderers ought to be punished' – is repeating (more or less) the norm itself as an echo: 'murderers ought to be punished'.[56] In other words, both the norm (*Rechtsnorm*) and the juristic sentence (*Rechtssatz*) that describes it are deontic sentences (*Sollsätze*). But, Kelsen maintains, while, in the language of legal sources, the German verb *sollen* (ought) has a prescriptive meaning; in juristic sentences, on the contrary, the same word has a descriptive sense. According to Bobbio, it is the context (prescriptive or descriptive, respectively), not the meaning of the word, that changes.[57] This amounts to say that the distinction between describing and prescribing lies not in words, and not even in sentences, but in utterances – one and the same sentence can be used either to describe or to prescribe.[58]

7.9 Ferrajoli's Positivism

Within the Italian legal-positivistic school, a peculiar position is held by Luigi Ferrajoli, whose whole theory is ruled by the (Hobbesian) principle 'auctoritas non veritas facit legem'.[59] His contribution to legal theory – although claiming to be 'formal'[60] and therefore 'general' – is focused, in particular, on contemporary constitutional states and results in an overall criticism of both the legal positivism of the nineteenth century and the pure theory of law.[61]

In his view, constitutional legal systems[62] are crowded with antinomies. The validity of a norm – he says – must be carefully distinguished from its existence (or being in force). This is so since a lot of statutory norms exist – since they were actually promulgated and possibly applied – that are,

[56] According to Scarpelli 1967, juristic sentences are 'iterated prescriptions' (*precetti reiterati*). See also Hart 1963.

[57] Bobbio suggests (although does not explicitly state) that juristic *Rechtssätze* are metalinguistic sentences that do not use, but just mention, the deontic expressions.

[58] In such a way that the distinction between descriptive and prescriptive language is pragmatic, not semantic, in nature.

[59] Ferrajoli 1989 and 2007.

[60] In the sense stipulated by Bobbio, as noted.

[61] Ferrajoli 2016.

[62] 'Constitutional', i.e., governed by a rigid constitution protected by the judicial review of legislation.

however, invalid, being at variance with the constitution. The task of legal science is to denounce such conflicts between statutory and constitutional ('higher') law and soliciting, in this way, the annulment of such invalid norms by the constitutional court.

Moreover, the same legal systems are also crowded with legal gaps. This is so since most constitutional rights – especially social rights (right to work, education and so on) – are not actually implemented by ordinary legislation. Conceptually, any right requires a 'corresponding' obligation but, where the legislation is silent, nobody has the legal obligation to satisfy the right at hand. The task of legal science is denouncing such gaps in legislation and promoting, in this way, the appropriate legislative concretisation of constitutional principles.

Such theses give rise to a meta-jurisprudence – not envisaged by Bobbio – which, contrary to the ordinary positivistic (namely, Benthamite, Austinian, Kelsenian) view, assigns legal science not a descriptive but a prescriptive task. Legal scholars should not simply describe the law in force – rather, they should recommend the legislature and the constitutional court to put into effect the constitution.[63]

On this basis, Ferrajoli criticises both normativism and realism.[64] Both, he says, do not distinguish between valid norms and norms in force. So, normativism is unable to recognise the existence of norms in force although invalid. Realism, in turn, is unable to recognise the existence of invalid, although in force (or effective), norms.[65]

7.10 On Giovanni Tarello

Another peculiar, worth mentioning standpoint within the Italian legal-positivistic school is held by Giovanni Tarello, a legal scholar of manifold intelligence and scientific interests, whose works include (inter alia) the

[63] There is a flavour of ideological positivism (or, better, ideological constitutionalism) in Ferrajoli's theses. See Comanducci 2010: 154ff.

[64] As well as the doctrine of natural law and ideological positivism, for sure. Natural lawyers, not distinguishing between validity and justice, are unable to admit the existence of valid, although unjust, norms. Ideological positivists, in turn, not distinguishing between justice and validity, are unable to admit the existence of unjust, although valid, norms.

[65] Ferrajoli treats the realistic description of actually applied norms as a sort of apology of the law in force, as if neutral description were the same as approval.

first Italian study on American legal realism, a study in empirical meta-jurisprudence on the doctrines of labour law scholars in the post-war era, a great deal of studies on normative language and the language of jurisprudence, a history of modern legal thought (with a special look to the processes of codification on the Continent) and a general theory of legal interpretation and reasoning.[66]

A few contributions of his are worth mentioning in this context: the first is about legal philosophy as such; the second is a piece of analysis of language (as applied to legal discourse); the third is about legal interpretation.[67]

(a) Tarello has a neo-positivistic attitude towards philosophy: philosophy is, basically, philosophy of science. The proper object of any philosophical work is some kind of scientific discourse (physics, mathematics, the social sciences and so forth) – there is no place for a philosophy without adjectives, a *Weltanschauung* deprived of any specific object.

Therefore, he conceives of legal philosophy as the philosophy of legal science, namely, as a descriptive meta-jurisprudential enterprise – the logical, pragmatic, political and historical analysis of legal scholars' (and judges') discourse and practice.[68]

(b) Tarello carefully distinguishes between sentences (both types and tokens) and meaning. As a matter of course, such a distinction has no originality. Nonetheless, it was quite unusual within legal philosophy before Tarello.[69] Most of all, this obvious distinction, when applied to legal discourse and practice, results in the sharp (not at all obvious)

[66] See Tarello 1962, 1967, 1974, 1976, 1980. See Castignone 1989; Chiassoni 2016b: ch. V.

[67] Tarello initiated a school of thought, established (mainly) in Genoa, characterised by the defence of an analytical style in philosophy, a non-cognitivist meta-ethics (and the connected thesis of the separation between law and morals), a realistic theory of interpretation (and a realistic view, in particular, as to the 'law-creating' practice of legal scholarship). Tarello's disciples, however, are also by and large influenced by the Argentinian analytical legal philosophy, too, especially by Alchourrón and Bulygin (1971, 1991; Bulygin 2015). On Genoese realism, see Ferrer and Ratti 2011; *Revista brasileira de filosofia*, LVII (240) 2013 (monographic issue devoted to the 'Genoese Realistic School'); Comanducci 2016: 217ff.; Barberis 2017.

[68] The same view is held by Ross 1958: 19–28.

[69] A similar distinction, between legal provisions and norms, was introduced in constitutional jurisprudence by Crisafulli 1964 (with a look to the so-called 'interpretive' decisions of the Italian Constitutional Court, where the Court declares the unconstitutionality not of a given legal provision but of one of its possible meanings).

distinction between normative sentences (the legal provisions enacted by normative authorities) and norms.

Interpretation, that is, meaning-ascription, is the link between normative sentences and norms, in the sense that it is interpretation that draws norms from normative sentences. Therefore, norms are not the object but the product of interpretation. And legislators enact not norms but just normative sentences – no norm exists before interpretation. One should not talk about the 'meaning of norms', as jurists usually do: Norms have no meaning since they *are* meanings.[70]

(c) Tarello has a realistic attitude towards interpretation – interpretation is a volitional, not cognitive, enterprise. This is so since, usually, any normative sentence (any legal provision) admits a plurality of competing interpretations, that is, it incorporates not just one, univocal meaning but as many meanings as plausible or admissible interpretations – admissible, according to the interpretive methods (or arguments) and the juristic doctrines by and large accepted in the existing legal culture.

However, there is no criterion for deciding the truth or falsity of interpretive sentences: in fact, they are neither true nor false. Legal interpretation is no scientific operation, as jurists usually claim – it is a form of legal politics. By means of interpretation, legal scholars do not describe but contribute to shape the law.

[70] Tarello echoes J. C. Gray (1948: 124ff):

> After all, it is only words that the legislature utters; it is for the courts to say what these words mean; that is it is for them to interpret legislative acts. [. . .] And this is the reason why legislative acts, statutes, are to be dealt with as sources of Law, and not as a part of the Law itself. [. . .] The courts put life into the dead words of the statute.

Gray (1948: 102) quoted Benjamin Hoadley, Bishop of Bangor: 'Whoever hath an *absolute authority* to *interpret* any written or spoken laws, it is *he* who is truly the *Law-giver* to all intents and purposes, and not the person who first wrote or spoke them.' Gray (1948: 170) further stated:

> It may be urged that if the Law of a society be the body of rules applied by its courts, then statutes should be considered as being part of the Law itself, and not merely as being a source of the Law; that they are rules to be applied by the courts directly, and should not be regarded as fountains from which the courts derive their own rules. . . . And if statutes interpreted themselves, this would be true; but statutes do not interpret themselves; their meaning is declared by the courts, and *it is with the meaning declared by the courts, and with no other meaning, that they are imposed upon the community as Law.*

Most meta-jurisprudential (both analytical and empirical) studies by Tarello are meant precisely to show the ways – doctrines, methods, arguments – in which legal scholars (and judges, for sure) do shape the law in particular circumstances. His historical studies, in turn, are meant to reconstruct the political and ideological process that gave rise, in modern times, to the positivistic illusion[71] of the merely technical and non-political nature of the social role of jurists and judges.

7.11 On the Opposition between Legal Positivism and Legal Realism

In Italian legal-philosophical literature, legal positivism is often (or even usually) opposed to legal realism.[72] One has to wonder, however: what kind of legal positivism and what kind of legal realism are we talking about?

(i) As to legal realism, those scholars who oppose realism and positivism have in mind most of all Scandinavian realism, especially Olivecrona and Ross,[73] disregarding American (as well as Italian or French) realism. This is doubly surprising.

It is true that Olivecrona is a severe critic of legal positivism, but the kind of legal positivism he criticises is essentially the voluntaristic view about legal norms held by nineteenth-century jurists, such a view being a component of legal positivism understood as a theory of law (in Bobbio's sense).[74] However, Olivecrona, on the tracks of Hägerström,[75] definitely shares the methodological side of legal positivism – the view according to which science (in general, including legal science) is a *wertfrei* empirical enterprise that has to do only with observable phenomena.[76]

Ross, in turn, is a strong defender of methodological legal positivism – against Kelsen's concept of validity understood as binding force, that he pictures as a sort of disguised natural law thesis ('quasi-positivism'),[77] as well as against Hartian 'internal point of view'.[78] Legal science, according to him, is a set of purely descriptive 'external' sentences identifying the law in force.

[71] One of the characteristic features of the nineteenth-century positivistic theory of law.
[72] See, e.g., Pattaro 1966, 1971, 1972; Jori 1987. [73] See Olivecrona 1971; Ross 1958.
[74] Olivecrona 1971: chs. 1, 2. [75] See Hägerström 1953. [76] See Olivecrona 1971: 56.
[77] See Ross 1961. [78] See Ross 1962.

(ii) As to legal positivism, those scholars who oppose realism and positivism have in mind either the nineteenth-century prevailing theory of law or Kelsen's pure theory.[79]

To be sure, the opposition between legal realism and the pure theory is sound. Nonetheless, such an opposition does not arise from a supposed anti-positivistic stance of legal realists. It depends on two non-positivistic theses endorsed by Kelsen: the concept of validity as binding force[80] and the normative theory of legal science, conceived of as a set of deontic (non-factual) sentences echoing valid (that is, binding) norms.[81]

The opposition between legal realism and nineteenth-century legal positivism is equally sound, but it does not hold when referred to contemporary legal positivism.

7.12 On Contemporary Legal Positivism

Nowadays, in the legal philosophy of the twentieth and twenty-first centuries – since Hart in 1958 and Bobbio in 1961 – legal positivism is mainly conceived as a methodological attitude towards the law.[82] All 'classical' positivistic views – as to the very nature of law (viewed as a set of commands backed by the threat of sanctions), the structure of legal systems (assumedly gapless and consistent), and legal interpretation (conceived of as a merely cognitive enterprise) – are by now mostly dismissed.[83]

The main theses, strictly methodological, of contemporary legal positivism (shared by Kelsen) are the following.[84]

[79] See, e.g., Pattaro 1982. [80] See Ross 1961. [81] See Ross 1958: 38ff.

[82] See Bulygin 2006.

[83] Kelsen maintains the classical positivistic views about completeness and consistency of legal systems, but he does not share at all the other mentioned positivistic tenets. In his view, legal norms are not 'backed' by sanctions; rather, the use of force is their very content (see Bobbio 1970a/2012: 101ff.). Moreover, in his view, interpretation (namely, 'authentic' interpretation) is a volitional, not a cognitive, act. See Troper 1994: chs. 4, 5; Troper 2001: 69ff.; Chiassoni 2012, 2013b.

[84] A perfect characterisation of contemporary legal positivism can be read in von Wright 1998: 380:

> The term 'legal positivism' embraces a variety of positions among which there is a family resemblance. A common feature of many members of the family is the idea of a sharp separation of Is and Ought. Another is the non-cognitivist view that norms are

(i) First, contemporary positivism denies the existence of so-called natural law (however conceived), assuming law to be a human artefact. There are no norms in the very nature of 'things' or human relationships – no norm exists without a human act of normative creation. As Kelsen (echoing W. Dubislav) rightly says: 'Kein Imperativ ohne Imperator', that is, no command without anyone commanding.[85] So-called 'natural law' is not law properly understood but a critical morality (in fact, a set of competing critical moralities). Natural law arises from an evident violation of Hume's principle – no norms can be (logically) derived from factual statements.[86]

(ii) Second, legal positivism is a scientific attitude towards the law, grounded on the separation of law and morals and the distinction between expository and censorial jurisprudence – between the law as it actually is and the law as it ought to be. Describing the existing law and evaluating it are two different and independent intellectual enterprises. Besides, it is precisely this feature of legal positivism that is currently refused by non-positivist (as well as 'soft positivist') legal scholars – they claim that law cannot even be identified without some kind of moral evaluation.[87]

(iii) Third, as a consequence of Hume's principle, no 'objective' (moral or political) obligation to obey the law exists – the knowledge of legal norms does not involve any obligation to obey them. To be sure, obedience is what lawmakers demand, but no binding force, no obligation to obey, is conceptually entailed by the very existence or legal validity of a norm. Obedience presupposes not only cognition, or 'recognition' (in Hart's sense), but also axiological acceptance by the addressees.[88]

prescriptions and therefore neither true nor false. As a third we may count the view that norms are 'posited'.

85 See Kelsen 1965.

86 This does not imply that a norm cannot be logically entailed by other norms. This is simply meant to underline that deducing is not deciding; thus, an entailed norm comes to 'legal existence', that is, acquires membership in a legal system, only when it is actually 'posited' by a law-creating agency.

87 In contemporary Italian literature, this tenet of legal positivism is under attack, in particular by several constitutional lawyers. See, e.g., Zagrebelsky 1992, 2008; Baldassarre 2005; Modugno 2008. On the relationships between legal positivism and 'new-constitutionalism', see Comanducci 2009 and 2010: 115ff., 251ff.

88 'According to the non-cognitive view, acceptance is constitutive' of binding force (Ross 1968: 61).

All three features of contemporary legal positivism are shared by legal realism,[89] which combines an empiricist conception of legal cognition with a sceptical view on interpretation. Legal realism is an openly positivistic view about the law. To be sure, not all positivist legal scholars are realist, but all realists are ('hard') positivists.

References

Agnelli, A. 1959. *John Austin alle origini del positivismo giuridico.* Giappichelli.

Alchourrón, C. E. and Bulygin, E. 1971. *Normative Systems.* Springer.

Alchourrón, C. E. and Bulygin, E. 1991. *Análisis lógico y derecho.* Centro de Estudios Constitucionales.

Austin, J., 1879. *Lectures on Jurisprudence or The Philosophy of Positive Law.* 4th ed. John Murray.

Baldassarre, A. 2005 'Miseria del positivismo giuridico'. In AA.VV. *Studi in onore di Gianni Ferrara* vol. I. Giappichelli: 201–16.

Barberis, M. 2017. 'Genoese Legal Realism'. In M. Sellers and S. Kirste (eds.). *Encyclopedia of the Philosophy of Law and Social Philosophy.* Springer. http://link-springer-com-443.webvpn.jxutcm.edu.cn/referenceworkentry/10.1007/978-94-007-6730-0_69-2.

Barrere Unzueta, M. A. 1990. *La escuela de Bobbio.* Tecnos.

Bentham, J. 1789/1996. *An Introduction to the Principles of Morals and Legislation.* Eds. J. H. Burns and H. L. A. Hart. Clarendon Press.

Bobbio, N. 1950a. 'Scienza del diritto e analisi del linguaggio'. Reprinted in N. Bobbio. 2011. *Saggi sulla scienza giuridica.* Giappichelli: 1–31.

Bobbio, N. 1950b. *Teoria della scienza giuridica.* Giappichelli.

Bobbio, N. 1954. 'La logica giuridica di Eduardo García Máynez'. Reprinted in N. Bobbio. 1994. *Contributi ad un dizionario giuridico.* Giappichelli: 133–55.

Bobbio, N. 1955. *Studi sulla teoria generale del diritto.* Giappichelli.

Bobbio, N. 1958. *Teoria della norma giuridica.* Giappichelli.

Bobbio, N. 1960. *Teoria dell'ordinamento giuridico.* Giappichelli.

Bobbio, N. 1961. *Il positivismo giuridico.* Giappichelli.

Bobbio, N. 1963a. *Locke e il diritto naturale.* Giappichelli.

Bobbio, N. 1963b. 'Lettera di Norberto Bobbio a Nicola Matteucci'. *Materiali per una storia della cultura giuridica* XXX. 2000: 416–25.

Bobbio, N. 1965. *Giusnaturalismo e positivismo giuridico.* Comunità.

Bobbio, N. 1966. 'Intervento'. In L. Bagolini, A. Baratta, B. Leoni and M. Losano (eds.). 1966. *Tavola rotonda sul positivismo giuridico. Quaderni della rivista Il politico.* Giuffré: 69–73.

[89] See Bobbio 1965: 156.

Bobbio, N. 1967. 'Essere e dover essere nella scienza giuridica'. Reprinted in N. Bobbio. 1970a/2012. *Studi per una teoria generale del diritto*. Giappichelli: 119–48.

Bobbio, N. 1968. 'Scienza giuridica tra essere e dover essere'. *Rivista internazionale di filosofia del diritto* XLV: 475–86.

Bobbio, N. 1970a/2012. *Studi per una teoria generale del diritto*. Giappichelli.

Bobbio, N. 1970b. 'Sein and Sollen in Legal Science'. *Archiv für Rechts – und Sozialphilosophie* LVI: 7–29.

Bobbio, N. 1993. *Teoria generale del diritto*. Giappichelli.

Borsellino, P. 1991. *Norberto Bobbio metateorico del diritto*. Giuffré.

Bulygin, E. 1991. 'Algunas consideraciones sobre los sistemas jurídicos'. *Doxa. Cuadernos de Filosofía del Derecho* 9: 257–79.

Bulygin, E. 2006. *El positivismo jurídico*. Cátedra Ernesto Garzón Valdés Fontamara.

Bulygin, E. 2015. *Essays in Legal Philosophy*. Oxford University Press.

Carcaterra, G. 1969. *Il problema della fallacia naturalistica*. Giuffré.

Carcaterra, G. 1974. *Le norme costitutive*. Giappichelli.

Carcaterra, G. 1984. *Il principio di normatività*. Bulzoni.

Carnelutti, F. 1940. *Teoria generale del diritto*. Il Foro Italiano.

Castignone, S. (ed.). 1989. *L'opera di Giovanni Tarello nella cultura giuridica contemporanea*. Il Mulino.

Cattaneo, M. A. 1962. *Il positivismo giuridico inglese*. Giuffré.

Celano, B. 1994. *Dialettica della giustificazione pratica*. Giappichelli.

Chiassoni, P. 2012. 'Il realismo radicale della teoria pura del diritto'. *Materiali per una storia della cultura giuridica* XLII: 237–61.

Chiassoni, P. 2013a. *Positivismo giuridico. Una investigazione analitica*. Mucchi.

Chiassoni, P. 2013b. 'Wiener Realism'. In L. Duarte d'Almeida, J. Gardner and L. Green (eds.). 2013. *Kelsen Revisited: New Essays on the Pure Theory of Law*. Hart: 131–62.

Chiassoni, P. 2016a. *Da Bentham a Kelsen*. Giappichelli.

Chiassoni, P. 2016b. *El discreto placer del positivismo jurídico*. Universidad Externado de Colombia.

Comanducci, P. 2009. 'Constitucionalización y neoconstitucionalismo'. In P. Comanducci, M. A. Ahumada and D. González Lagier. *Positivismo jurídico y neoconstitucionalismo*. Fundación Coloquio Jurídico Europeo.

Comanducci, P. 2010. *Hacia una teoría analítica del Derecho. Ensayos escogidos*. Centro de Estudios Políticos y Constitucionales.

Comanducci, P. 2016. *A proposito di . . . Note sparse sulla teoria del diritto del secondo Novecento*. Marcial Pons.

Conte, A. G. 1962. *Saggio sulla completezza degli ordinamenti giuridici*. Giappichelli.

Conte, A. G. 1966. 'Intervento'. In L. Bagolini, A. Baratta, B. Leoni and M. Losano (eds.). 1966. *Tavola rotonda sul positivismo giuridico. Quaderni della rivista Il politico*. Giuffré: 67–8.

Crisafulli, V. 1964. 'Disposizione (e norma)'. In *Enciclopedia del diritto* vol. XII. Giuffré.

Donati, D. 1910/1966. *Il problema delle lacune dell'ordinamento giuridico*. In D. Donati. *Scritti di diritto pubblico* vol. I. Cedam.

Falk, R. A. and Shuman, S. I. 1961. 'Un colloquio sul positivismo giuridico'. *Rivista di diritto civile* VII: 542–57.

Ferrajoli, L. 1989. *Diritto e ragione. Teoria del garantismo penale*. Laterza.

Ferrajoli, L. 2007. *Principia Juris. Teoria del diritto e della democrazia* vol. I *Teoria del diritto*. Laterza.

Ferrajoli, L. 2016. *La logica del diritto*. Laterza.

Ferrer, J. and Ratti, G. B. (eds.). 2011. *El realismo jurídico genovés*. Marcial Pons.

Gavazzi, G. 1959. *Delle antinomie*. Giappichelli.

Gavazzi, G. 1961. 'Le buone ragioni del positivismo giuridico'. In *Studia ghisleriana* vol. III. Tipografia del libro: 166–78.

Gavazzi, G. 1967. *Norme primarie e norme secondarie*. Giappichelli.

Gray, J. C. 1948. *The Nature and Sources of the Law*. Macmillan.

Grzegorczyk, C., Michaut, F. and Troper, M. (eds.). 1992. *Le positivisme juridique*. LGDJ.

Guastini, R. 2013. 'The Basic Norm Revisited'. In L. Duarte d'Almeida, J. Gardner and L. Green (eds.). 2013. *Kelsen Revisited: New Essays on the Pure Theory of Law*. Hart: 63–74.

Hägerström, A. 1953. *Inquiries into the Nature of Law and Morals*. Ed. K. Olivecrona. Almqvist and Wiksell.

Hare, R. M. 1952. *The Language of Morals*. Clarendon Press.

Hart, H. L. A. 1958. 'Positivism and the Separation of Law and Morals'. Reprinted in H. L. A. Hart. 1983. *Essays in Jurisprudence and Philosophy*. Clarendon Press: 49–87.

Hart, H. L. A. 1961. *The Concept of Law*. Clarendon Press.

Hart, H. L. A. 1963. 'Kelsen Visited'. Reprinted in H. L. A. Hart, 1983. *Essays in Jurisprudence and Philosophy*. Clarendon Press: 286–308.

Jori, M. 1976. *Il metodo giuridico tra scienza e politica*. Giuffré.

Jori, M. 1985. *Saggi di metagiurisprudenza*. Giuffré.

Jori, M. 1987. *Il giuspositivismo analitico italiano prima e dopo la crisi*. Giuffré.

Kelsen, H. 1928. 'Préface'. In C. Eisenmann. (ed.). *La justice constitutionelle et la Haute Cour constitutionnelle d'Autriche*. LGDJ. Reprinted Économica-Presses Universitaires d'Aix-Marseille. 1986.

Kelsen, H. 1934/1992. *Introduction to the Problems of Legal Theory*. Eds. B. Litschewski Paulson and S. L. Paulson. Clarendon Press.

Kelsen, H. 1945. *General Theory of Law and State*. Harvard University Press.

Kelsen, H. 1965. 'Law and Logic'. Trans. P. Heath. In H. Kelsen. 1973. *Essays in Legal and Moral Philosophy*. Reidel: 228–53.

Lazzaro, G. 1965. *L'interpretazione sistematica della legge*. Giappichelli.

Losano, M. G. 1968. *Sistema e struttura nel diritto. I. Dalle origini alla Scuola storica*. Giappichelli.

Losano, M. G. 2018. *Norberto Bobbio. Una biografia culturale*. Carocci.
Matteucci, N. 1963. 'Positivismo giuridico e costituzionalismo'. *Rivista trimestrale di diritto e procedura civile* XVII: 985–1100.
Modugno, F. 2008. *Scritti sull'interpretazione costituzionale*. ESI.
Olivecrona, K. 1971. *Law as Fact*. Stevens & Sons.
Pattaro, E. 1966. 'Validità o verificabilità del diritto?'. *Rivista trimestrale di diritto e procedura civile*: 1005–56.
Pattaro, E. 1971. 'Il realismo giuridico come alternativa al positivismo giuridico'. *Rivista internazionale di filosofia del diritto* 48: 61–126.
Pattaro, E. 1972. *Il positivismo giuridico italiano dalla rinascita alla crisi*. Il Mulino.
Pattaro, E. 1982. 'Per una critica della dottrina pura'. In E. Pattaro (ed.). *Contributi al realismo giuridico*. Giuffré: 451–87.
Portinaro, P. P. 2008. *Introduzione a Bobbio*. Laterza.
Raz, J. 1971. 'The Identity of Legal Systems'. Reprinted in J. Raz. 1979. *The Authority of Law*. Clarendon Press: 78–102.
Romano, S. 1925. 'Osservazioni sulla completezza dell'ordinamento statale'. Reprinted in S. Romano, 1969. *Lo Stato moderno e la sua crisi. saggi di diritto costituzionale*. Giuffré.
Ross, A. 1958. *On Law and Justice*, Stevens & Sons.
Ross, A. 1961. 'Validity and the Conflict between Legal Positivism and Natural Law'. Reprinted in S. L. Paulson and B. Litschewski Paulson (eds.). 1998. *Normativity and Norms: Critical Perspectives on Kelsenian Themes*. Clarendon Press: 147–63.
Ross, A. 1962. 'Review of H.L.A. Hart's *The Concept of Law*'. *Yale Law Journal* LXXI: 1185–90.
Ross, A. 1968. *Directives and Norms*. Routledge.
Ruiz Manero, J. 1990. *Jurisdicción y normas*. Centro de Estudios Constitucionales.
Ruiz Miguel, A. 1980. 'Bobbio y el positivismo jurídico italiano'. In N. Bobbio. 1980. *Contribución a la teoría del derecho*. Fernando Torres: Prólogo.
Ruiz Miguel, A. 1983. *Filosofía y derecho en Norberto Bobbio*. Centro de Estudios Constitucionales.
Sartori, G. 1987. *Elementi di teoria politica*. Il Mulino.
Scarpelli, U. 1953. Filosofia analitica e giurisprudenza. Reprinted in U. Scarpelli. 2014. *Filosofia analitica del diritto*. Ed. A. Pintore. ETS: 35–127.
Scarpelli, U. 1955. Il problema della definizione e il concetto di diritto. Reprinted in U. Scarpelli. 2014. *Filosofia analitica del diritto*. Ed. A. Pintore. ETS.
Scarpelli, U. 1959. *Contributo alla semantica del linguaggio normativo*. Giuffré.
Scarpelli, U. 1965. *Cos'è il positivismo giuridico*. Comunità.
Scarpelli, U. 1966. 'Intervento'. In L. Bagolini, A. Baratta, B. Leoni and M. Losano (eds.). 1966. *Tavola rotonda sul positivismo giuridico. Quaderni della rivista Il politico*. Giuffré: 77–86.
Scarpelli, U. 1967. 'Le proposizioni giuridiche come precetti reiterati'. *Rivista internazionale di filosofia del diritto* XLIV: 465–82.

Scarpelli, U. 1984. 'Auctoritas non veritas facit legem'. *Rivista di filosofia* LXXV: 29–44.

Scarpelli, U. 1989. 'Il positivismo giuridico rivisitato'. *Rivista di filosofia* 80: 461–76.

Searle, J. R. 1969. *Speech Acts: An Essay in the Philosophy of Language*. Cambridge University Press.

Tarello, G. 1962. *Il realismo giuridico americano*. Giuffré.

Tarello, G. 1966. 'Intervento'. In L. Bagolini, A. Baratta, B. Leoni and M. Losano (eds.). 1966. *Tavola rotonda sul positivismo giuridico. Quaderni della rivista Il politico*. Giuffré: 62–5.

Tarello, G. 1967. *Teorie e ideologie nel diritto sindacale*. Comunità.

Tarello, G. 1974. *Diritto, enunciati, usi. Studi di teoria e metateoria del diritto*. Il Mulino.

Tarello, G. 1976. *Storia della cultura giuridica moderna. I. Assolutismo e codificazione del diritto*. Il Mulino.

Tarello, G. 1980. *L'interpretazione della legge*. Giuffré.

Troper, M. 1994. *Pour une théorie juridique de l'État*. Presses Universitaires de France.

Troper, M. 2001. *La théorie du droit, le droit, l'État*. Presses Universitaires de France.

von Wright, G. H. 1998. 'Is and Ought'. In S. L. Paulson and B. Litschewski Paulson (eds.). 1998. *Normativity and Norms: Critical Perspectives on Kelsenian Themes*. Clarendon Press: 365–82.

Zagrebelsky, G. 1992. *Il diritto mite*. Einaudi.

Zagrebelsky, G. 2008. *La legge e la sua giustizia*. Il Mulino.

8 The British Tradition of Legal Positivism

Gerald J. Postema

8.1 Introduction

The task of this chapter is to sketch a profile of the British tradition of legal positivism. It traces a thematic thread through English, and broadly Anglophone, legal philosophy since the seventeenth century. Ownership of the title 'positivism' is contested in contemporary Anglophone jurisprudence. If we were to take the core theses embraced by contemporary legal positivists to identify the key figures in their tradition, the story would be very brief, starting, perhaps, with Hart.[1] They usually include Bentham and Austin in their hall of fame, and often Hobbes; yet, by their own admission, none of these predecessors has clear title to membership. Hence, rather than tracing a line of development of a coherent jurisprudential tradition, I will sketch in broad outlines the transformation of Anglophone legal philosophy since Hobbes. For this task, however, we cannot begin with Bentham and Austin, or even Hobbes, because their approaches to questions about the nature of positive law were decisively shaped by the project and doctrines of what we might call the 'thetic' tradition of legal theory[2] with origins in late medieval jurisprudence and by the practice and theory of English common law, which their theories were meant fundamentally to challenge.

8.2 Contemporary Positivism

I begin this story at the end with a brief characterisation of post-Hartian positivism. Positivism is based on two observations: that law as it is must

[1] As Frederick Schauer (2009) has argued.

[2] From the Greek *tithenai*, meaning to lay down or posit. On this conception, law is seen to be explicitly made and imposed on law-subjects.

not be confused with law as it ought to be and that law is a social phenomenon. Of course, there is nothing distinctively positivist about these thoughts; few writers in the history of legal philosophy would deny them. They merely pick out positive law as the object for philosophical investigation. The distinctive post-Hartian positivist thesis is the *sources thesis*:[3] what counts as a valid legal norm in a jurisdiction is determined solely by its sources in non-moral social facts. That is, the existence and content of laws depend exclusively on their sources rather than their merits.

The sources thesis is a multi-layered doctrine. At the methodological level, it holds that a proper *theory* of law must be purely descriptive ('methodological positivism'). Positivist theory seeks an account of what makes something *a law*, what determines its existence and content, and it insists that the account must be reductive: all that claims to be *law* must be reduced to *non-moral facts* about *laws*. As a substantive thesis, it holds that the non-moral facts must be social facts. The metaphysically ultimate determinants of laws are facts about the conduct, beliefs and attitudes of legal officials. Facts of official practice determine the conditions of validity of legal norms.

Post-Hartian positivism is distinctive in that it limits positivism to the sources thesis. No legal philosopher can be only a positivist, they concede;[4] yet positivism takes no stand on any more general theory about the nature of law. Positivism is not a view about the value of law or the rule of law, or about whether legal facts entail moral facts; it is not a view about how laws identified by sources should figure in legal reasoning; neither is it a view about the relative merits of legislation or common law determination of laws.[5] Post-Hartian positivism embraces only a thesis about legal validity and about the proper methodology of jurisprudence.

8.3 Headwaters

John Austin subtitled his *Lectures on Jurisprudence* 'The Philosophy of Positive Law'.[6] His work was a contribution to an enterprise that can be traced back at least to the groundbreaking work of Thomas Aquinas.[7] Yet,

[3] See Dickson 2012; Gardner 2001; Marmor 2006; Raz 1979: ch. 3. [4] See Green 2019.
[5] See Gardner 2001. [6] Austin 1890. [7] See Murphy 2005.

as we shall see, Austin decisively disengaged Anglophone jurisprudence from this enterprise and the effects of this disengagement are evident in post-Hartian positivism. To appreciate the significance of this break, we must trace the evolution of this enterprise from its headwaters in the late Middle Ages to the innovative work of Bentham. Although theorists who were engaged in this enterprise employed different philosophical assumptions and modes of explanation, they worked within a common theoretical frame.

8.3.1 A Common Theoretical Frame

The common frame had three components: (1) a set of presuppositions about the salient features of law; (2) a view about the project or the mode of explanation to be used; and (3) a basic concept or set of concepts deployed in the explanation. Within this frame, three features of positive law, taken together, required explanation. First, law was seen to be *directive* of the behaviour of human agents; law operates in the domain of obligation. It was recognised that laws not only indicate what is good or right to do but also make demands on, and claim the allegiance of, human agents. To be subject to law, theorists observed, is to be addressed by the law with a demand meant to be taken as authoritative. Second, laws were seen as *positive*, the product of human activity, contrived or instituted by human beings. Hence, laws were seen as artefacts, contingent and changeable, and situated, or 'practised', we might say, in the ordinary life of the community. Finally, law was typically seen as the expression of power of one agent over another. Hence, theorists recognised that law could, and often did, go wrong.

Theorists who were engaged in this enterprise sought to explain these features of law. How can the legal directive be obligatory, they wondered, if it is artificial, contingent and fallible? They sought a practically oriented, rather than metaphysical, explanation. They sought to understand law not as a stand-alone social phenomenon but rather as a vital part of the structure of social and political life. Law was depicted as the best, or the only available second-best, solution to a range of problems faced by human beings living in close proximity and dependent on each other in a variety of ways.

It was natural for theorists engaged in this enterprise to think of law in thetic terms. Law, they surmised, was not merely instituted but *posited*, the product of the will of someone empowered to direct human conduct. Resort to the concept or metaphor of command was common because it enabled theorists to represent laws as *addressed* to agents capable of grasping and applying directives, providing them binding reasons to act. But, they realised, laws could genuinely direct action only if they issued from an authority. So it was critical to give an account of the practical ground of the law-giver's authority. Despite the attractions of the concept of command, many found the need to stretch it to cover legal norms that were not explicitly enacted, most notably binding custom. The concept proved a supple, yet constraining model for law.

8.3.2 Aquinas

To understand Aquinas's theory of law, we must relate his familiar definition of law to his notion of *ius*.[8] Aquinas linked *ius* directly to *iustitia*: justice is what *ius* is about.[9] *Ius*, as it pertains to human beings, is an ordered state of affairs, a rational arrangement that instantiates a pattern of external actions and relations among people in a community characterised by a kind of equality.[10] This pattern is normative, offering a measure or model of how people ought to relate to each other. The pattern is either the natural ordering of creation and creatures (*ius naturale*) or the order practised in some community (*ius positivum*). *Ius* is positive by virtue of being the product of human activity or invention. Provided it is consistent with *ius naturale*, it is normative for members of the community by virtue of its mode of institution, either because it has settled into the lives and practices of the community (a matter of 'mutual agreement') or because it has been deliberately imposed by political authority.[11] Aquinas's notion of *lex* articulates and explains the phenomena of *ius positivum*. The notions of *lex* and *ius* refer not to two kinds of law but to two ways of regarding law. *Ius* views the ordering of external actions in a community 'objectively', while *lex* views law 'agentively', as it were, that is, as it pertains to and is taken up by rational agents.

[8] See Aquinas [1485] ST I-II 90–7. All references to Aquinas's *Summa Theologica* can be found in Dyson 2002.

[9] See ST II-II 57.1. [10] See ST II-II 79.1 ad 1. [11] See ST II-II 57.1; ST II-II 60.5.

Aquinas defines *lex* as a rule or measure directing action to the common good that is promulgated by one who has care of the community[12] and is authorised to enforce the rule with coercion.[13] Several features of this definition are noteworthy. First, the model of *lex* is deliberately enacted law; *lex* is not *ius* but rather the *expression* of *ius*.[14] The rule or measure is a pattern for action that takes the form of a prescription, a determination of *ius*. Second, *lex* represents law in its *agentive* mode in two ways: (a) laws begin their lives in the mind of the maker[15] and are *addressed* to law-subjects; and (b) law involves a kind of *moving* of the subjects' actions. This *directive* dimension is important because it explains how law *obligates* ('induces') action.[16] The agent is moved by 'necessity of justice'[17] – that is, by reasons grasped by the agent's intellect.

Lex has the intrinsically obligating force of law only if three conditions are met. First, its commands must be in accord with reason, otherwise they distort law.[18] Second, it must be made (a) by one with authority to do so (b) within the scope of that authority, and (c) it must have the required 'form' (it must fairly distribute its burdens).[19] Third, it must be promulgated.[20] This requirement lies at the heart of law, marking its essential communicative aspect.

Human communities need authoritatively instituted law even though natural law is accessible to human reason, according to Aquinas. This is so for three reasons: (1) it is difficult to work out the implications of the moral law for particular situations; (2) natural law is silent on some matters and leaves other matters for creative, reason-guided determination; and (3) human rationality is prone to error and human motivation is weak. Thus, even individuals exercising their own best judgement cannot be assured that they will settle on common modes of orderly interaction. Publicly accessible laws, issuing from a recognised authority, and promising external incentives for the recalcitrant make coordination of necessary social interaction possible. Law compensates for the cognitive, perspectival and motivational deficiencies of human beings.

Thus, positivity of law is essential if it is to provide rational guidance for orderly conduct in political communities; just content of norms alone is

[12] See ST I-II 90.4. [13] See ST I-II 95.1 ad 1; ST I-II 96.5. [14] See ST II-II 57.2 ad 2.
[15] See ST I-II 91.1. In ST II-II 57.1 ad 2, Aquinas draws an analogy with a craftsman or artist who begins his project with an image in his mind of the object he seeks to make.
[16] See ST I-II 90.1. [17] ST II-II 104.4. [18] See ST I-II 90.1 ad 4. [19] See ST I-II 96.4.
[20] See ST I-II 90.4.

not sufficient. On the other hand, law's intrinsic obligating force does not depend solely on law's formal properties; unjust laws may lose this force. Nevertheless, the practical importance of the publicly recognised standing of law in the community is not erased by this injustice, and subjects may still be bound to comply with it for reasons deriving from the practical need for positive law.

8.3.3 Marsilius of Padua

Marsilio focused his attention exclusively on civil law. He was no moral sceptic, but he insisted that all normative ordering of human communities depends on human institution.[21] Marsilio viewed positive law as a hybrid, combining a judgment of just ordering and an imperative for action. The former alone is not sufficient for law, he argued, because it indicates only what is good, right or just to do; it lacks a moving principle. The latter is also insufficient because it may fail properly to direct agents to just actions or ends, or fail to be sufficiently 'universal' or public.[22] A law is a command of someone in authority over another, explicitly laying down and making public a rule for conduct based on prudential judgement concerning justice and the common good and backed by coercive power.

Like Aquinas, Marsilio offered this definition of law in explanation of salient features of positive law. He sought to uncover the nature of law by asking what life would be like in a society without law and what problems arising there law is well-equipped to solve. He built his explanation on assumptions about general features of human nature and typical conditions of social interaction. Human beings, he argued, are rational but passionate creatures, driven together by natural necessity and mutual dependency. If human beings are to live and live well,[23] human passions must be 'tempered' by subjecting them to social order. Untempered, human beings inevitably conflict, and conflict undermines 'tranquility', the essential condition of living and living well.

In domestic arrangements, an elder naturally rules as *dominus* without explicit rules, and punishes or pardons at pleasure. In this mini-society, 'what is just in civic terms does not properly speaking exist';[24] this domain is beyond the circumstances of justice, in Hume's sense. The village, in

[21] See Marsilius 2005: 253. [22] See Marsilius 2005: 57. [23] See Marsilius 2005: 18–19.
[24] Marsilius 2005: I.3.4.

contrast, is properly communal and falls within the circumstances of justice, but it lacks functional differentiation and law. Members have a nascent sense of justice and equity. One who exercises ruling power in the village is expected to judge impartially according to what is advantageous for the village as a whole, but he faces a serious problem of credibility. He finds it difficult to convince all members of his community that his decisions are fair because he has no public, impartial standards to appeal to. When he fails to convince them, they tend to resort to violence, to vindicate their private assessment of justice. Without law, Marsilio argued, the legitimate expectation of justice being done cannot be met.

Thus, law must provide a *guide* – an articulated standard of justice and right conduct – that is public and impartial, not beholden to any party or faction of the community, and a *guardian* or *executor* of that standard, who can command and coerce, and thereby motivate compliance with its judgments according to law. Moreover, Marsilio added that ruling must always be done *with* and *according to* law, and that all who exercise ruling power are subject to the law. Law, he insisted, 'should be prince over all'.[25]

8.3.4 Bodin

One further stream in the headwaters of British legal theory flowed from the pen of Jean Bodin. Bodin embedded his understanding of law in a broad exploration of the necessary features and constitution of ruling power. The defining feature of a unified political community, for Bodin, was the common subjection of its members to supreme political power.[26] His concept of sovereignty articulated and gave structure to this essential condition. Chief among the powers of the sovereign ruler, encompassing all the others, was the right to make and repeal laws. Law, in Bodin's view, is the product of the exercise of will of a superior over the wills of inferiors.[27] In making and enforcing laws, the sovereign not only makes people behave as it wishes; it also substitutes its will for the wills of inferiors, and does so with right. Making, unmaking and derogating from law at its pleasure, he thought, is the greatest manifestation of the sovereign's power.

According to Bodin, sovereignty is defined by four necessary properties: the sovereign is supreme, undivided, perpetual and absolute.[28] Necessarily,

[25] Marsilius 2005: 61. [26] See Lee 2016: 172. [27] See Bodin 1992: 38, 51.
[28] See Bodin 1992: 1–45.

sovereign power is above all other powers and concentrated in one person or body; it must be neither shared nor divided. The sovereign is subject to no one's command and legitimately commands all others; it is subject to no limit of time or law. The absolute power of the sovereign is limited by divine and natural law and by political realities, of course, but the sovereign is above all civil law and all forms of human accountability. Ruling power, he argued, must be located ultimately in a single, undisputed and indisputable source.

Bodin clearly distinguished between the sovereign in a polity and its government. The sovereign constitutes by law the institutions and offices of government and installs officials in them. It may remove itself from the daily exercise of governmental power, although it reserves the right to intervene in governmental matters at any point and is always available to settle disputed matters when needed. The sovereign may also constitute institutions to hold government officials accountable to the law. Thus, government officials, exercising delegated powers, may be made subject to the law and to institutions of accountability, even though the sovereign source of their power is absolute. Likewise, remaining behind the scenes, the sovereign may not be the actual author of laws, although it is, necessarily, their ultimate source of authorisation.

Bodin meant his definition of sovereignty to descriptively characterise existing political phenomena, but his methodology is not plausibly characterised as positivist. Bodin sought a 'universal' and in that sense 'scientific' theory of political authority, and criticised Aristotle for valorising local political arrangements,[29] but his defence of sovereignty appeals to the political necessity of sovereign ruling power. Dismayed by the disorder within and between European states in the mid-sixteenth century, Bodin argued that only a single, undisputed, absolute source of ruling power could maintain order. Finality, guaranteeing that all disagreements over rights and religion have a clear, determinate and indisputable resolution, was the key to internal peace and external independence. To secure finality, all exercises of power, including law making, must be located manifestly in the hands of a single, unitary, supreme and absolute power. Like medieval legal and political theorists before him, his argument for political authority was normative; unlike them, the conclusions he drew from similar normative premises were strikingly radical.

[29] See Lee 2016: 165–71.

8.4 English Jurisprudence in the Seventeenth Century

To tell the story of the British contribution to positivist jurisprudence, we must begin with English jurisprudence in the seventeenth century. The language of classical common-law jurisprudence owed much to natural-law theory but was distinctively inflected by the practice and modes of thought of common-law judges.[30] The core idea was that common-law rules, whether originating in acts of Parliament or in decisions of common-law courts, were valid by virtue not of being laid down by law-making authorities but of being taken up in the reasoning of judges exercising their distinctive mode of 'artificial reason', reflecting immemorial usage in the community at large. Common law was sovereign, and even royal prerogatives were defined and limited by law.

Against this stream, John Selden[31] argued in the early seventeenth century that, viewed through the lens of history, common law was the product not of expert reasoning but of the exercise of royal, parliamentary or judicial power. Far from immemorial, he argued, rules of common law could be traced to origins in determinable legislative acts. His strongly voluntarist notion of morality influenced his understanding of positive law. Law, in his view, makes right and wrong; and authority, not reason, makes law. Moreover, coercion was an essential component of law in Selden's view. Law without the likelihood of punishment, he argued, is as unintelligible as the idea of a father without a child.[32]

8.4.1 Matthew Hale

Matthew Hale, although mentored by Selden, adopted a more nuanced view of positive law that blended thetic and common-law elements.[33] Hale, following earlier theorists, located his account of positive law in a theory of practical reasoning and political authority. We speak of 'reason' in three different ways, Hale observed.[34] First, we speak of reason *in things*, referring to their ordering according to rational principles. Second, we speak of reason *in us*, referring to the faculty by which we come to know the reason

[30] See Postema 2002, 2003. [31] See Lobban 2007: 61–3.
[32] Quoted in Lobban 2007: 62.
[33] See Hale 2017; the discussion here follows my introduction to the volume.
[34] See Hale 2017: 187–9.

in things. This natural faculty, common to all human beings, is discursive and deliberative; with it, we discern what is right and good to do. Third, we speak of reason that is in some human beings by virtue of their training: the reason of doctors, watchmakers, statesmen and the like. Ordinary practical reason is trained to deal with the distinctive features and problems of a particular domain of life.

According to Hale, human law is positive; it exists *ex instituto*. Its distinctive features arise from its role in supplementing natural law's practical guidance. Natural law fixes broad principles to govern social interaction and determines what we owe to each other, but only some of its principles are available to unaided human reason. Like Aquinas, Hale thought that natural law is silent on some matters and needs determination on others. Natural law is also indeterminate by virtue of the limitations of human reason. In some cases, the implications of natural law, while rationally determinate, are difficult for many to grasp with confidence (or confidence that others have grasped them). So, it is possible for disagreements to arise. Yet, for peaceful and fruitful social interaction, human beings need common rules on which they can depend; moreover, fairness and impartiality require consistency of application of such rules over time. Natural law's *lex permissiva* comprises these areas of indeterminacy.

Instituted law operates in the domain of *lex permissiva*. Law designed for this task, in Hale's view, takes a familiar thetic shape. Hale defined law as rules of moral (voluntary) action given to beings capable of understanding and will by one with authority to give law and exact obedience.[35] His definition of law rests on the following now familiar thoughts. First, law is addressed to 'intelligent creatures' concerning their voluntary actions, directing them towards that which is good or against that which is evil. Law guides by engaging the understanding and the will of free agents. The *vis indicativa* of the law 'discovers' to human understanding the moral quality of actions and law's *vis preceptiva* makes them obligatory. Like Marsilio, Hale argued that law's indicative power is insufficient because it only marks actions as good or choice worthy; law makes actions *binding*, *owed to* another party who is in a position to hold the agent accountable for his compliance.

Because law is obligatory, and obligation is a special kind of normative relationship between two parties, the one who 'gives' or underwrites the

[35] See Hale 2017: 3–16.

law must have 'just right' or standing to do so. Thus, on Hale's view, law presupposes a *nomothetes* (law-giver) who stands in a particular kind of normative relationship to those addressed by law. The *nomothetes* need not author every law, but it authorises and underwrites all law. The binding character of law rests on the relationship between the *nomothetes* and those addressed by law. That relationship, in Hale's view, is broadly speaking consensual, a matter of 'mutual interposition of faith between the governed and the governor',[36] twisted like a rope into one *fides publica*.

Despite his adoption of the thetic model, Hale remained faithful to classical common-law jurisprudence. Instituted law, he insisted, defines a domain of practical life and establishes a discipline of practical reasoning. Law is not *reason* but *reasoned*, the product of an 'artificial reason', disciplined through practice in a public forum by a community of lawyers and judges answerable directly to its members and indirectly to the community at large. Law's discipline of practical reasoning is a shared practice, continually drawing on and contributing to the common stock of rules and principles, developing measures and methods for dealing with practical situations that daily call for resolution.[37] Thus, on Hale's view, reason itself is given institutional shape in the domain of *lex permissiva*. Instituted law is needed to supply common public standards, but it does so not merely by defining a set of authoritative rules but also by instituting a disciplined practice of public practical reasoning.

8.4.2 Hobbes

Hobbes sought to explain positive law in much the same way as philosophers from Aquinas to Hale did. Like them, he was drawn to the thetic model to capture the salient features of civil law, and he sought an explanation of these defining features of law in a problem of social ordering to which law offered a compelling solution. The uniqueness of his theory lies in the depth of his analysis of this problem and the subtlety of the doctrine of law he offered as a solution.

Law, Hobbes argued, is the command of one to whom one is antecedently obligated to obey, declaring publicly what one may do or must do or forbear to do.[38] He contrasted law with counsel or advice.[39] An advisor

[36] Hale 2017: 209. [37] See Hale 2017: 159–60. [38] See Hobbes 1996: ch. 26.2.
[39] See Hobbes 1996: chs. 25.2–25.4, 26.2.

offers reasons to the advisee, but these reasons are conditioned on the advisee's aims; they are not obligating. In contrast, law is the public expression of will of a person[40] that is meant to be taken by another as sufficient reason to act as directed. This reason is categorical and unconditional;[41] it replaces the addressee's practical reasoning with the commander's.[42]

On this definition, law is addressed to rational agents capable of directing their own behaviour *by appeal to reasons*. The will, on Hobbes's view, is merely the last appetite in deliberation; it *executes* the agent's reason. Thus, Hobbes's definition of law *conceptually* links law with practical reason. (The commander's ability to attach sanctions to the commands is important in Hobbes's account, but it is important for practical, not conceptual, reasons.) Moreover, law puts in place a fundamental contrast not between will and reason but between the *private* reason of each law subject and the *public* reason of the sovereign. Law is 'right reason' – not transcendent reason, nor each person's natural reason, nor the 'artificial reason' of a judicial elite, but rather the natural reason of the sovereign that law-subjects deem as reason for them.[43]

Hobbes's account of law presupposes an account of sovereign authority. Law is the command of one 'to whom we have given sovereign authority, to make rules for the direction of our actions'.[44] Law's authority is rooted proximately in consent but more deeply in political necessity. In the absence of authority, Hobbes argued, there are no common standards by which right and wrong can be judged; individuals can rely only on private judgement. In the state of nature, laws of nature speak to individuals, but, because each claims his or her judgement as the proper expression of reason, individuals are pitted against each other. Enmeshed in networks of interdependency, disagreements regarding the right lead to disorder and disorder leads inevitably to the war of all against all. The fundamental problem of the state of nature lies not in conflicts of interests but in the privacy of judgement. The consequences of this problem can be escaped, Hobbes argued, only by instituting an authority authorised to define and effectively enforce public norms. The only solution to the radically disordering plurality of judgements is to replace them with one authoritative voice, one source of judgement. Each individual takes the reason and

[40] See Hobbes 1996: ch. 25.2–25.3. [41] See Hobbes 1996: ch. 42.100.
[42] See Hobbes 1998: ch. 14.1. [43] See Hobbes 1998: ch. 14.17.
[44] Hobbes 1996: ch. 42.42.

judgement of the sovereign as their own. Political necessity forces them to treat the natural reason of the sovereign as public reason. Law, Hobbes wrote, 'is all the Right Reason we have'.[45] Because the root of the problem of the privacy of judgement lies in the absence of common standards, authority must speak the language of public law, and it is essential that all laws have their source solely in sovereign law-making and law-deciding activities.

Although the power of the sovereign must be absolute, the sovereign's power is bound by natural law and the terms of the covenant to rule in the public interest. Moreover, since sovereign power must be exercised through law, necessary formal features of law limit that power. Because law must serve as public reason,[46] it must be publicly declared (promulgated)[47] and manifestly authentic;[48] its meaning must be 'perspicacious';[49] and it must be general and prospective.[50] Moreover, adjudication must conform to standards of procedural justice, that is, equality before the law[51] and impartiality,[52] and it must give each party a fair hearing and be responsive to the evidence presented.[53] Common law failed as law, Hobbes argued, because it was endlessly disputable and a smoke-screen for judicial usurpation of law-making power; it failed to meet the conditions of publicity that political necessity demanded of law.

In addition to the formal and procedural conditions on law, Hobbes also acknowledged a role for appeals to substantive moral considerations in determining the content of law. All laws need interpretation,[54] he recognised, and the power of interpreting law, like law-making power, must rest ultimately and manifestly in sovereign hands. But, since the sovereign is not able to exercise adjudicative power unaided, it must delegate this power to subordinate judges, empowering them to interpret the law in accord with the sovereign's intention. However, the 'intention of the sovereign' was to be determined in accordance with equity and natural law. Hobbes's argument required that the sovereign articulate his will in law, and both natural law and the covenant required that the sovereign make laws consistent with equity and the *salus populi*. So, he concluded, the proper standard for determining that which the sovereign's law leaves

45 Hobbes 1839–45: 192. 46 See Hobbes 1998: ch. 14.11–14.13.
47 See Hobbes 1996: chs. 26.12, 26.15, 31.3. 48 See Hobbes 1996: ch. 26.16.
49 Hobbes 1998: ch. 14.13. 50 See Hobbes 1996: ch. 28.11.
51 See Hobbes 1996: chs. 15.23, 30.15–30.16. 52 See Hobbes 1996: ch. 15.31–15.32.
53 See Hobbes 1996: ch. 15.33. 54 See Hobbes 1996: ch. 26.21.

indeterminate is the judges' best understanding of equity and natural law. After all, Hobbes argued, it would be a great offence to attribute to the sovereign the aim of subverting natural law.[55] Thus, judges must take the meaning of any particular law to be that which most clearly complies with natural law even when another would seem more obvious from the language of the law.[56] Of course, the sovereign is empowered to overturn any judicial interpretation; the sovereign's absolute power is not limited by this standard of interpretation. Thus, it is true that the sovereign's intention ultimately determines the existence and content of the law, but that 'intention' is a complex mix of moral argument and social fact. The content of law is not solely determined by non-evaluative, merely formal, source-based considerations. Hobbes's solution to the problem of the privacy of judgement was finality, reducing the plurality of voices to one voice, not disengaging the determination of legal validity from considerations of equity or morality.

8.5 Transformations of English Jurisprudence

8.5.1 Bentham

Despite his scathing critique of Blackstone's confusion of 'expository' and 'censorial' jurisprudence, Bentham located his 'universal jurisprudence' firmly in his normative social and political philosophy, following the lead of Hobbes and the medieval theorists before him.[57] On the principle of utility, he built a general public philosophy, at the heart of which he placed his principle of publicity.[58] He argued that, in the domain of social life, to which the principle of utility was primarily addressed, practical principles can guide actions effectively only if they are publicly accessible and intelligible. Law's primary task, Bentham argued, is to secure the expectations of rational individuals engaged in complex networks of social interaction. In his view, English common law failed miserably to meet the demands of utility-serving publicity. Alleged 'rules' of common law, derived from patterns of judicial decisions over time, were merely 'inferential entities', products of private conjecture. A strict doctrine of *stare*

[55] See Hobbes 1996: ch. 26.26. [56] See Dyzenhaus 2012: 201. [57] See Postema 2019a.
[58] See Postema 2019b: ch. 13.

decisis only exacerbated the problem by making law simultaneously rigid and indefinitely elastic.[59] To meet the demands of publicity and solve the conundrum of stability versus flexibility, Bentham devised a three-part strategy for his jurisprudential theory. He articulated a general conception of law drawn from the thetic tradition; he fixed the content of law in a code articulated according to principles of 'natural', utility-manifesting arrangement; and he designed a complex set of institutions for the application, interpretation and adjustment of this code.

Like Hobbes, Bentham held that law offered the best answer to the problem of the privacy of judgement. Law secures expectations, in his view, by articulating accessible, intelligible public norms. Law is 'authentic' just when it can be seen by all as the expression of the will of the accustomed law-giver expressed according to accustomed formalities,[60] that is, as commands of a sovereign. However, Bentham's sovereign did not look much like Hobbes's or Bodin's sovereign. Although it was the source of all valid laws, it could be, and often is, divided or shared, and may be legally limited. Moreover, the habit of obedience on which sovereign authority rests, according to Bentham, congeals around a set of broadly based conventions that identify and authorise the law-maker, determine the formalities by which laws are validly to be made, and keep the exercise of ruling power within something like constitutional limits.[61]

Although he never officially abandoned this thetic conception of law, Bentham introduced qualifications, the cumulative effect of which was significantly to efface the model. Expanding the simple concept of command, Bentham developed a sophisticated 'logic of imperations' (deontic logic), and, unlike Hobbes, he denied law's imperations *peremptory* practical force. Law demands submission of conduct, he argued, but not submission of judgement.[62] It seeks to engage the understanding of those it addresses, rather than to dominate their wills. Bentham also shifted the focus of his jurisprudence from the immediate directive function of law to its larger and more pervasive constitutive function. To secure expectations, he argued, law not only mandates or prohibits conduct; it also defines

[59] See Postema 2019a: 273–9.

[60] See Bentham MSS, University College London, box 69, folio 87.

[61] See Postema 2019a: 227–31 (Bentham's 'interactional' conception of sovereignty); Postema 2019a: 244–50 (laws in principem limit the sovereign); Postema 2019b: 244–50; see also Postema 2019b: 198, 279–81.

[62] See Bentham 1977: 346.

relationships, forms of social interaction and institutions within which citizens give meaningful shape to their lives.

Most fundamentally, Bentham came to recognise the essential systemic character of law. The meaning of any given rule of law is determined by its place in the body of law. He insisted that law is a command only when it is 'entire', that is, when it brings together all the elements that are necessary to give determinate rational guidance to law subjects. This is possible, he argued, only when the rule is fitted into the body of law, making clear its substantive and procedural connections to other parts of the law. He concluded that the only adequate model of law is not the statute but a code. Thus, on Bentham's view, the content of any legal norm is not discoverable simply by looking to empirically determinable social facts; rather, it requires locating the norm in the code, keeping in mind the substantive, internal relations among its norms. The code, of course, must meet canonical standards of formal validity, but particular legal norms owe their existence and content not to social facts of their making but rather to their place in the code. Determining the content of a legal norm, on this view, involves actively engaged practical reasoning.

For the code to meet the demands of publicity, it must not only satisfy the formal conditions of validity but also be rationally accessible. For this purpose, its arrangement, and principles of interpretation, must accord with the public's sense of moral relevance. Moreover, the reasons for a given law must be placed alongside the rules; the code must include 'a perpetual commentary of reasons'.[63] This commentary of reasons serves four key functions.[64] First, it enhances the intelligibility ('cognoscibility') of the laws. Second, it aids interpretation, providing judges, officials and ordinary citizens with a common basis and touchstone for determining the implications of law for specific cases. Third, it offers an important constraint on the arbitrary exercise of ruling power. Finally, it offers a common focus for public debate and criticism of the law.

On Bentham's understanding of law, publicity is not merely a good-making property of law; it is essential to its functioning as law. Like Hobbes, Bentham thought that the exercise of public reason must not be limited to the judicial elite; however, Bentham's understanding of the role of law in public reason contrasts sharply with Hobbes's. Hobbes thought of law as a surrogate for the ordinary practical reasoning of citizens; their

[63] Bentham 1838–43: vol. 1, 163. [64] See Postema 2019b: 295–7.

practical reasoning was disengaged, replaced by that of the sovereign's will. Bentham insisted upon a partnership between law and utilitarian practical reasoning. He looked to law to focus, facilitate and enhance the practical reasoning of ordinary citizens. He regarded law as a joint venture between authority and reason. Law is a set of formally valid, publicly articulated norms, drawn together into a rationally intelligible systematic structure.

8.5.2 Austin

John Austin published *The Province of Jurisprudence Determined*[65] in 1830, two years before Bentham's death, but it had little impact at the time of its publication. His *Lectures on Jurisprudence*, published four years after his own death in 1859, established his reputation. Austin drew heavily on the thetic tradition, especially Hobbes (and, through him, Bodin) without appreciating the transformation of that tradition wrought by Bentham. Although there is little that is original in Austin's understanding of law, he (and his nineteenth-century followers) engineered a dramatic shift in English jurisprudence, the effects of which are still evident in post-Hartian positivism.

Law, 'properly so-called',[66] is posited; it is the command of the sovereign in a state, Austin wrote. Law is explicitly made, the signification of a wish regarding the behaviour of a class of persons and an intention to inflict some form of evil on those who fail to comply, of one who has the capacity to command and is subject to no one else's command.[67] Austin offered this as a definition of law rather than an explanation of positive law. The boundary stone of the province of jurisprudence, it marked out what Austin took to be the only appropriate subject for students of English law.[68]

Several features of this definition are noteworthy. First, Austin followed Bodin holding that positive laws are imposed by a superior on persons in subjection to the superior. Moreover, every 'rule of positive law exists as such by the pleasure (*ad placitum*) of the sovereign'.[69] Second, departing from the thetic tradition from Aquinas to Bentham, Austin played down the role of publicity in law. He maintained that promulgation is not a necessary feature of positive law. Law need not be known by those

[65] Austin 1955. [66] Austin 1955: 124. [67] See Austin 1955: 14, 132.
[68] See Austin 1955: 365, 379. [69] Austin 1890: 36.

bound by it;[70] strictly speaking, it need not even be expressed, since the sovereign may 'command' merely by silence, declining or merely failing to overturn judicial or community custom.[71] Third, Austin imported into his definition of law core elements of Bodin's account of sovereignty: commands count as laws only if the commander is unique, supreme and illimitable.[72] However, unlike Bodin, Austin assumed that these are logically necessary features of the concept of sovereignty, not requirements of peace and security in otherwise conflict-ridden political societies. Finally, echoing Bentham, Austin identified the sovereign as the one person or body of persons who enjoys the habit of obedience of the bulk of the community and who habitually obeys no one.[73] Although he did not embrace Bentham's interactional understanding of the habit of obedience, he did not simply reduce it to the behavioural response of members of a community to a particular kind of environmental cue, as Hart may have assumed. For Austin, the relevant behaviour was a matter of *obedience* to commands *for reasons*, including the utility of government and a preference of government over anarchy.[74] Like Bodin, Austin found this account of sovereignty useful because it marked the boundaries of a unified and independent state[75] and a unified system of law. Law exists as a coherent system, on his view, just when it has a single ultimate source in the commands of a unique, supreme and illimitable commander.

Despite the strongly thetic character of his definition, Austin did not follow the lead of Hobbes and Bentham in his treatment of common law. Hobbes and Bentham, observing major differences between the common law and its distinctive mode of reasoning and their preferred models of law, offered strong reasons for rejecting common law, as 'a thing imaginary', as Bentham put it. In contrast, Austin sought to regiment common law to his model of law. He understood judicial decisions as law-making events, issuing commands and intimating sanctions for non-compliance that are adopted explicitly or tacitly by the sovereign.

Contemporary commentators often notice that Austin's understanding of the jurisprudential enterprise departed in significant ways from the earlier English (and medieval) approach. Yet, the nature of this departure is frequently misunderstood. Austin is best known for his slogan '[T]he existence of law is one thing, its merit or demerit is

[70] See Austin 1890: 36. [71] See Austin 1955: 32. [72] See Austin 1955: lecture VI.
[73] See Austin 1955: 195. [74] See Austin 1890: 302–3. [75] See Austin 1955: 193–4.

another.'[76] Taken just on its terms, this slogan merely highlights a salient feature of positive law, a datum to be explained. The explanation offered by many in the thetic tradition from Aquinas to Bentham turned on the ability of publicly accessible and authorised norms to resolve conflicts endemic to political society. Austin, in contrast, took his slogan as a call for a distinctive method of analysis of law, one that required the jurist to suspend evaluation.

Austin's 'separation thesis' has been taken by many philosophers of law as the core of a distinctively positivist methodology. However, Austin's aim in proposing this shift in the focus of the jurisprudential enterprise was not metaphysical. He did not have in mind a naturalistic reduction of law's normative elements to strictly empirical elements. Several considerations compel this conclusion. First, while Austin sharply distinguished law from other conventions working at the periphery of law, he never denied their normative force; he only denied their status as laws and, for that reason, thought them improper subjects of jurisprudential investigation. He was drawn to the command model, not for meta-ethical reasons but for strictly jurisprudential reasons. Second, while he sought a 'science' of law (and of 'positive morality'),[77] his idea of science was that of a systematic exposition and arrangement of 'principles, notions, and distinctions common to various systems'.[78] His project was analytical, not metaphysical. His aims were entirely and explicitly *pedagogical*. He meant his definition to isolate 'the appropriate subject of jurisprudence'[79] for the student of English law. This student, presumably, had no need for inquiring into the moral merits of laws or their ontological status; such inquiries were, in Austin's view, distracting. Austin's, or perhaps subsequent Austinian, analytic jurisprudence was detached from moral inquiry and from philosophy in general. Modularity, not naturalistic reduction, was the aim.

8.6 Austinians and Their Critics

Austin inaugurated a mode of jurisprudential inquiry that was further developed by his late-nineteenth-century followers. In their hands, jurisprudence was increasingly isolated from other disciplinary approaches to

[76] Austin 1955: 184. [77] See Austin 1955: 124–6. [78] Austin 1955: 365.
[79] Austin 1890: 148; Austin 1955: 365, 379.

the study of law, not only moral philosophy and metaphysics but also history, social theory and comparative studies.[80] T. E. Holland's *Elements of Jurisprudence* (thirteen editions from 1880 to 1924) epitomised this trend. In his view, the jurisprudential task was strictly expository without any normative or practical dimensions. His model was grammar. He argued that because jurisprudence is a science, its method must be formal and analytical, focusing on concepts basic to legal practice. He assumed, without investigation, that these concepts were common to all legal systems.

Holland's notion of law echoed Austin's. Law depends on the state, he argued; thus, before the state is constituted, there cannot be law. Law is to be understood as a set of laws, mandates of the authority paramount in the state. Unlike Austin, he focused more attention on the state's exercise of coercive power, and hence on the state's institutions of enforcement, than on the making or promulgation of laws. In this respect, he resembled his American contemporary Oliver Wendell Holmes, Jr.

Always impressed by power, Holmes took coercive power as the most salient feature of law; yet, his understanding of law was complex.[81] Law, he held, is the ultimate expression of power, yet it moves by the distinctive kind of practical reasoning deployed by the courts. He developed two accounts of law, one static, the other dynamic, both focused on the activity of courts and their role in the exercise of power. On the one hand, he argued that the defining feature of law is not its sovereign source but its coercive enforcement. Against Austin, he insisted that commands are not necessary features of law but that certainty of enforcement is. 'The will of the sovereign is law', he maintained, 'because he has the power to compel obedience and for no other reason'.[82] 'Lawyers' law', the proper object of jurisprudence, is a matter of court-enforced rules. However, he also maintained that legal rules are the 'motives' or grounds that figure in a court's reasoning. Lawyers' predictions of what the court will do are not empirical or probabilistic but normative and rule-based. Viewed dynamically, the law is the product of the interaction of two kinds of practical rational force: considerations of form (demands of consistency, local coherence and analogy) and reasons of substance (considerations of 'good sense' and good public policy). Rather than accept Austin's regimentation of judicial

[80] Postema 2011: 26–9; for a discussion of Holland's jurisprudences, see Postema 2011: 5–6.
[81] See Postema 2011: ch. 2. [82] Holmes 1995: vol. 1, 294.

decision-making to a form of legislation, Holmes offered a subtle, if incomplete, analysis of the process of common-law reasoning.

8.7 Positivism Recast

Austinians dominated British jurisprudence from the late nineteenth century through the first several decades of the twentieth century. However, their core positivist doctrines, both substantive and methodological, were subjected to penetrating criticism. Two of the most perceptive critics were Frederick Pollock and John Salmond.[83]

Both challenged what they regarded as the Austinians' blinkered view of jurisprudential method. Pollock argued that the features of law that Austinians regarded as universal were merely familiar and ready to hand. Their narrow view of familiar legal practice could not yield significant insights into the nature of law.[84] Salmond distinguished three key branches of jurisprudence – historical, ethical and analytical – and he rejected the Austinians' sharp separation of jurisprudence from philosophical reflection on the nature of right and wrong and the meaning and grounds of obligation. 'It is a defect of English jurists', Salmond wrote, 'that they have attempted to deprive the idea of law of that ethical significance which is one of its most essential elements'.[85] He regarded jurisprudence as a form of applied practical philosophy, closely linked to moral philosophy, although separated for purely pragmatic disciplinary reasons. Jurisprudence, in his view, depends on philosophical reflection on concepts and principles of political morality. Like the Austinians and Holmes, he took the activity of courts as a key to understanding the nature of law, but, unlike them, he thought that the defining feature of the courts was their commitment to administering justice, rather than to coercively enforcing rules. Law, he argued, 'is the body of rules and principles recognized, applied and acted upon by courts acting as agents of the state, fulfilling its primary task, the administration of justice'.[86]

[83] Born in England but raised in New Zealand, Salmond studied law in London but returned to New Zealand for a distinguished career as lawyer, professor of law and judge. For a discussion of Salmond's contribution to Anglophone jurisprudence, see Postema 2011: 6–13, 18–25.

[84] See Pollock 1872: 190–1. [85] Salmond 1893: 10. [86] Salmond 1924: 39–40.

Salmond and Pollock also challenged key elements of Austin's definition of law. Salmond argued that laws cannot all be reduced to commands. Laws take many forms and their nature and typical functions are distorted by forcing them into the mould of a command. Laws that set out conditions for valid acts-in-law, for example, cannot be seen as commands without distortion.[87] Similarly, Pollock criticised Austin's treatment of custom. Austin got the matter backward, he argued. Courts discover that this or that custom is valid law, but their decision does not make it so.[88] Both challenged the Austinian doctrine of sovereignty. In familiar legal systems, such as English common law, the (legislative) sovereign cannot be the sole source of law because its law-making capacity is created and allocated by laws that cannot be the product of sovereign law-making. Moreover, they argued, parliamentary sovereignty itself is a *legal* status; the existence and powers of the sovereign presuppose law. The root problem with the doctrine of the legal illimitability of the sovereign, Salmond argued, is that it treats a local principle of English law as a conceptual necessity.[89] Pollock added that, far from accounting for the systemic character of law, the combination doctrine of sovereignty left the law utterly unsystematic, a mere jumble of disparate, unconnected rules.[90]

Salmond's positive conception of law is his most significant contribution to modern Anglophone legal theory. The law of a given society, Salmond maintained, is the systematic arrangement of principles that are implicit in the various sources of law and recognised by the courts. Judicial recognition of principles, he argued, is manifested in the courts' use of them. Principles are principles of law of a state by virtue of being received and operative in its courts.[91] Although they are meant to establish and maintain justice, their status as principles of law depends strictly on judicial recognition. Judges are bound to apply and comply with these principles because they are recognised by the courts, not because they are just or right. Professional obligation, underwritten by the opinion of the bar and the public, holds judges to this practice. This obligation is professional (and moral), not legal. A principle is a principle of law not because judges are bound to observe it but because judges *do* observe it.[92]

On Salmond's view, the legal validity of legal norms is not due to sovereign law-making or to judicial enforcement but rather to the courts'

[87] See Salmond 1893: 103–4. [88] See Pollock 1872: 193–5. [89] See Salmond 1893: 140.
[90] See Salmond 1893: 203. [91] See Salmond 1924: 57. [92] See Salmond 1924: 57.

consistent practice of identifying and applying principles derived from sources, and the practice is rule-governed. 'A rule of law does not mean a judicial practice, but the reason to the consistent acceptance and application of which such practice is due.'[93] Particular legal rules have their roots in sources of law; a source of law is any fact that determines judicial recognition of a rule as having the force of law. Such facts accord legal validity to rules by virtue of a rule that calls for such recognition, and various source-constituting rules rest in yet more fundamental rules or principles. This chain of validation ends in one or more source-identifying and validating principles that are ultimate and self-existent.[94]

Salmond shifted jurisprudential attention not only from law-making to law-applying institutions but also, more fundamentally, from sovereignty to the recognitional practice of the courts as the ultimate ground of law. This marked a quiet but decisive shift in Anglophone jurisprudence from the thetic model to a judicial practice model of the foundations of law. He thus brought British legal theory to the brink of positivism's social thesis, but his view of the general shape of the jurisprudential enterprise did not incline him to methodological positivism. He also opened the door to further philosophical exploration of the foundations of law closed by Austin and the Austinians, although he left that task to others.

8.8 Conclusion

Viewing its development from Austin, the trajectory of Anglophone jurisprudence into the twentieth century seems smooth, and Hart's emergence in mid-century seems entirely natural. From this vantage point, Bentham provided the raw materials that Austin forged into a coherent jurisprudential enterprise. Austin defined the project of jurisprudence and provided a convenient target for criticism and further refinement. Austin's critics challenged most of his key theses but stayed within the province of his project. They offered ideas, sometimes in embryonic form, that Hart fashioned into a powerful articulation of modern-day positivism. Post-Hartian positivists, on this trajectory, have carried that refinement to a higher pitch of philosophical sophistication.

[93] Salmond 1893: 88. [94] See Salmond 1924: 169.

However, viewing the evolution of British jurisprudence from Hale and Hobbes (and their predecessors), a different trajectory emerges. Bentham, on this view, appears not as the quirky ancestor of the modern British positivist tradition but as the apotheosis of a different and philosophically more ambitious jurisprudential enterprise, an enterprise in which contemporary positivists seem to have lost interest. One need not embrace Bentham's substantive doctrines, or those of Hobbes, to sense that something may have been lost with the Austinian turn.

References

Austin, J. 1890. *Lectures on Jurisprudence.* J. Murray.

Austin, J. 1955. *The Province of Jurisprudence Determined.* Ed. H. L. A. Hart. Wiley & Nicolson.

Bentham, J. 1838–43. *Works of Jeremy Bentham.* Ed. J. Bowring. William Tait.

Bentham, J. 1977. *Comment on the Commentaries and Fragment on Government.* Eds. H. L. A. Hart and J. H. Burns. Athlone Press.

Bodin, J. 1992. *On Sovereignty.* Ed. J. H. Franklin. Cambridge University Press.

Dickson, J. 2012. 'Legal Positivism: Contemporary Debates'. In A. Marmor (ed.). *The Routledge Companion to Philosophy of Law.* Routledge: 48–64.

Dyson, R. W. 2002. *Aquinas: Political Writings.* Cambridge University Press.

Dyzenhaus, D. 2012. 'Hobbes on the Authority of Law'. In D. Dyzenhaus and T. Poole (eds.). *Hobbes and the Law.* Cambridge University Press.

Gardner, J. 2001. 'Legal Positivism: 5½ Myths'. *American Journal of Jurisprudence* 46: 199–227.

Green, L. 2019. 'Legal Positivism'. In E. N. Zalta (ed.). *Stanford Encyclopedia of Philosophy.* https://plato.stanford.edu/entries/legal-positivism/.

Hale, M. 2017. *On the Law of Nature, Reason, and Common Law.* Ed. G. J. Postema. Oxford University Press.

Hobbes, T. 1839–45. 'Questions Concerning Liberty, Necessity, and Chance'. In W. Molesworth (ed.). *The English Works of Thomas Hobbes*, vol. V. The British Library.

Hobbes, T. 1996. *Leviathan.* Ed. R. Tuck. Cambridge University Press.

Hobbes, T. 1998. *On the Citizen.* Eds. R. Tuck and M. Silverthorne. Cambridge University Press.

Holmes, O. W. Jr. 1995. *Collected Works of Oliver Wendell Holmes.* Ed. S. M. Novick. University of Chicago Press.

Lee, D. 2016. *Popular Sovereignty in Early Modern Constitutional Thought.* Oxford University Press.

Lobban, M. 2007. *A History of the Philosophy of Law in the Common Law World, 1600–1900.* Springer.

Marmor, A. 2006. 'Legal Positivism: Still Descriptive and Mortally Neutral'. *Oxford Journal of Legal Studies* 4: 683–704.

Marsilius of Padua. 2005. *The Defender of the Peace*. Trans. A. Brett. Cambridge University Press.

Murphy, J. B. 2005. *The Philosophy of Positive Law*. Yale University Press.

Pollock, F. 1872. 'Law and Command'. *Law Magazine and Review* NS 1: 189–205.

Postema, G. J. 2002. 'Classical Common Law Jurisprudence: Part I'. *Oxford University Commonwealth Law Journal* 2: 155–80.

Postema, G. J. 2003. 'Classical Common Law Jurisprudence: Part II'. *Oxford University Commonwealth Law Journal* 3: 1–28.

Postema, G. J. 2011. *Legal Philosophy in the Twentieth Century: The Common Law World*. Springer.

Postema, G. J. 2019a. *Bentham and the Common Law Tradition*. 2nd ed. Oxford University Press.

Postema, G. J. 2019b. *Utility, Publicity, and Law: Essays on Bentham's Legal and Moral Philosophy*. Oxford University Press.

Raz, J. 1979. *The Authority of Law*. Oxford University Press.

Salmond, J. 1893. *The First Principles of Jurisprudence*. Stevens & Haynes.

Salmond, J. 1924. *Jurisprudence*. 7th ed. Sweet & Maxwell.

Schauer, F. 2009. 'Positivism Before Hart'. *Canadian Journal of Law and Jurisprudence* 24: 455–71.

Part III

Central Figures

Jeremy Bentham and the Origins of Legal Positivism 9

Philip Schofield

9.1 Hart and Bentham

H. L. A. Hart is generally recognised as the most influential twentieth-century exponent of the doctrine of legal positivism. According to Hart, Jeremy Bentham (1748–1832), the philosopher and reformer, 'opened the long positivist tradition in English jurisprudence'.[1] Stephen Perry points out that Hart's legal positivism contains two doctrines, namely substantive and methodological legal positivism, though Hart himself did not explicitly distinguish them. The former consists in the claim that there is no necessary connection between morality and the content of law and the latter in the claim that there is no necessary connection between morality and legal theory.[2] Hart in effect attributed both doctrines to Bentham when referring to 'Bentham's sharp severance ... between law as it is and law as it ought to be and his insistence that the foundations of a legal system are properly described in the morally neutral terms of a general habit of obedience'.[3] Bentham's view that there was no necessary connection between law and morality (his 'sharp severance ... between law as it is and law as it ought to be') and his description of a legal system in 'morally neutral terms' were equivalent to Hart's substantive and methodological doctrines respectively. Hart, moreover, indicated that Bentham's methodological legal positivism had been subservient to his substantive legal positivism: '[Bentham] insisted on a precise, morally neutral vocabulary for use in the discussion of law and politics as part of a larger concern to sharpen men's awareness ... of the distinction between what is and what ought to be.'[4]

[1] Hart 1982: 53. [2] See Perry 2001: 311–54. [3] Hart 1982: 53.

[4] Hart 1996: lxxxv. See also Hart 1982: 28: '[A]mong Bentham's many claims to be an innovator none is better founded nor, I think, more important than his insistence on a precise and so far as possible a morally neutral vocabulary for use in the discussion of

According to Hart, therefore, Bentham's substantive legal positivism divided the subject of jurisprudence into two branches, law as it is and law as it ought to be, while his methodological legal positivism was concerned with the elucidation of key terms when describing law as it is – in other words, Bentham began by distinguishing between what is (fact) and what ought to be (value), and then, within the field of fact, the explanatory task was undertaken in morally neutral terms. As we shall see, the distinction between law as it is and law as it ought to be – between what he termed expository and censorial jurisprudence respectively – and, within expository jurisprudence, the elucidation of such leading terms as were found in all legal systems were prominent features of Bentham's legal theory. To this extent, Hart's identification of Bentham as the founder of legal positivism appears plausible. Yet it is doubtful that the historical Bentham is properly described as either a substantive or a methodological legal positivist, since the principle of utility permeated his thought in such a way that the separation of fact and value and the notion of moral neutrality would have made little sense to him.[5] In what follows, the focus will be on Bentham's early writings on jurisprudence dating from between 1775 and 1782, on which Hart himself mainly drew and which has formed the basis for much of the relevant scholarship.[6] Such a focus seems reasonable given the fact that, throughout his long career, Bentham remained committed to the basic positions that he had established in these formative years.

9.2 Expository and Censorial Jurisprudence

Bentham distinguished between 'law as it is' and 'law as it ought to be' in *A Fragment on Government* (1776), his first major published work. This work emerged from a more ambitious enterprise entitled 'A Comment on the Commentaries', which was intended as a detailed examination of the 'Introduction' to William Blackstone's *Commentaries on the Laws of England* (1765–9), which had quickly established itself as the standard account of English law and, therefore, presented a suitable target for

law and politics . . . The terms that Bentham uses to define law are all flatly descriptive and normatively neutral'.

5 See further Schofield 2010.

6 For an account of the development of Bentham's legal theory in the 1770s and early 1780s, see Lieberman 1989; for a wide-ranging reconstruction, see Postema 1986.

someone trying to establish his reputation as a legal author. Bentham eventually abandoned 'A Comment on the Commentaries' without publishing it,[7] but he detached a critique of a short passage of Blackstone's on government and published it on its own account as *A Fragment on Government*.[8] In explaining the reasons for 'that war which, for the interests of true science, and of liberal improvement, I think myself bound to wage against' Blackstone's *Commentaries*, Bentham pointed to the 'two characters, one or other of which every man who finds any thing to say on the subject of Law, may be said to take upon him; – that of the *Expositor*, and that of the *Censor*'. The role of the former, in explaining what the law is, was to discover facts, while the role of the latter, in observing what the law ought to be, was to discuss reasons. 'That which *is* Law', noted Bentham, 'is, in different countries, widely different: while that which *ought to be*, is in all countries to a great degree the same. The *Expositor*, therefore, is always the citizen of this or that particular country: the *Censor* is, or ought to be the citizen of the world.'[9]

Bentham noted that Blackstone's task, given that his 'professed object was to explain to us what the Laws of England *were*', was that of the expositor, and had he restricted himself to that task, there would have been no reason to criticise him. Not satisfied, however, with this 'humbler function', he had gone on 'to give *reasons* in behalf of' the institutions and practices of English law. Bentham lamented that more praise was given to someone who defended old established institutions than to someone who censured them when wrong. Unless a system was censured, it would never be improved, while a determination to approve of everything that existed and disapprove of nothing would 'stand as an effectual bar to all the *additional* happiness we can ever hope for; pursued hitherto would have robbed us of that share of happiness which we enjoy already'. Bentham asked, 'Under a government of Laws, what is the motto of a good citizen?' and answered, '*To obey punctually; to censure freely.*'[10]

[7] For the provenance of the work, see Bentham 1977: Editorial Introduction xxiv–xxviii.

[8] Bentham 1977: Editorial Introduction xxix–xxx.

[9] Bentham 1977: 397–8. In his mature writings on codification, Bentham argued that 'universally applying circumstances' were far more important and far more common than 'exclusively applying circumstances', and that the laws that were best for one country would, therefore, very often be best for every other: see Bentham 1998: 291–3.

[10] Bentham 1977: 399–400.

Commenting on a passage in which Blackstone had stated that the supreme power in a state had a duty to make laws,[11] Bentham complained:

He sets out with the word '*duty*' in his mouth; and, in the character of a *Censor*, with all due gravity begins talking to us of what *ought* to be. 'Tis in the midst of this lecture that our *Proteus* slips aside; puts on the *historian*; gives an insensible turn to the discourse; and, without any warning of the change, finishes with telling us what *is*. Between these two points, indeed, the *is*, and the *ought to be*, so opposite as they frequently are in the eyes of other men, that spirit of obsequious *quietism* that seems constitutional in our Author, will scarce ever let him recognize a difference.[12]

This passage echoes and at the same time reverses David Hume's complaint about authors who moved from propositions containing 'is' and 'is not' to propositions containing 'ought' and 'ought not', but without explaining how they had derived the latter from the former.[13] For Bentham, Blackstone had moved from propositions concerning what ought to be to propositions concerning what is. He took Blackstone's statement, made in the context of the English law of heresy, that 'every thing is now as it should be'[14] as typifying the conservative mentality.

While Blackstone's general purpose was 'to inculcate unreserved submission' to authority, noted Bentham, he had been led into an 'inconsistency' through his adoption of the natural law formula *lex iniusta non est lex*, which again confounded the two roles of expositor and censor but with a very different outcome. In his *Commentaries*, Blackstone had asserted the primacy of natural law over positive law:

This law of nature, being co-eval with mankind and dictated by God himself, is of course superior in obligation to any other. It is binding over all the globe, in all countries, and at all times: no human laws are of any validity, if contrary to this; and such of them as are valid derive all their force, and all their authority, mediately or immediately, from this original.

While there were many areas of conduct where the natural law was 'indifferent' and the human legislator could pass such laws as were found to be convenient, continued Blackstone, no human legislator could make right what God had willed to be wrong or make wrong what God had willed to be right. If a human law required or allowed us to disobey the divine law,

[11] See Blackstone 1765–9: i. 52–3. [12] Bentham 1977: 498. [13] See Hume 2007: i. 302.
[14] Blackstone 1765–9: iv. 49.

we were 'bound to transgress' the human law.[15] In Bentham's view, this was a 'dangerous maxim' in that the 'law of nature' was 'nothing but a phrase' and any appeal to it merely represented an appeal to the likes and dislikes – founded on the interests – of the person making the appeal. No government could exist under such conditions. In deciding whether to resist or to obey government (Bentham was writing at the onset of the American War of Independence when this was a practical question), the proper course was to appeal to the principle of utility.[16] The confounding of the roles of the expositor and the censor, as Blackstone had done, would, therefore, lead either to ultra-conservatism or to anarchy: if you liked a law, you claimed that it accorded with the natural law and should be obeyed; if you disliked it, you claimed that it did not accord and should be disobeyed.

Having said that, for Bentham, the whole purpose of the utilitarian legislator was to align law as it is with law as it ought to be. He divided the role of the expositor 'into two branches: that of *history*, and that of simple *demonstration*'. Hence, the expositor might deal with the state of the law at some point in the past or with the state it was in at the time of writing. The latter included 'the several businesses of *arrangement*, *narration* and *conjecture*'. Narration was the description of the law where it was 'explicit, clear, and settled', while conjecture or interpretation was where it was 'obscure, silent, or unsteady'. Bentham's main interest in *A Fragment on Government*, however, was with the question of arrangement, which was concerned with general denomination – that is, with the distribution of legal terms under general headings. There were two sorts of arrangement: the technical and the natural. Blackstone had provided 'an arrangement of the elements of Jurisprudence, as wants little, perhaps, of being the best that a technical nomenclature will admit of', but a technical arrangement would always be '*confused* and *contradictory*'. The point became clear when a technical was compared with a natural arrangement. The latter took the property in actions that 'men in general are, by the common constitution of man's nature, disposed to attend to', namely 'the *tendency* ... *to*, or *divergency* ... *from*' the promotion of happiness, in other words from their tendency to promote utility. Hence the principle of utility would

[15] Blackstone 1765–9: i. 39–43. [16] Bentham 1977: 482–3.

preside over and govern, as it were, such arrangement as shall be made of the several institutions or combinations of institutions that compose the matter of this science . . . . Governed in this manner by a principle that is recognized by all men, the same arrangement that would serve for the jurisprudence of any one country, would serve with little variation for any other.

The leading terms in a natural arrangement of jurisprudence would be offences, which were actions that were prohibited because of their mischievousness. A bad law was one that prohibited an action that was not mischievous, but, within a natural arrangement, it would be 'impracticable' to designate the action in question as an offence without making an assertion that would be 'contradicted by experience'. While it would be difficult to find a place for a bad law in a natural arrangement, a technical arrangement was 'a sink that with equal facility will swallow any garbage that is thrown into it'. A natural arrangement would align the law as it is with law as it ought to be: it would 'at once be a compendium of *expository* and of *censorial* Jurisprudence'. The terms that stood at the head of a synopsis of natural jurisprudence, given their relationship to happiness and hence in turn to pain and pleasure, would 'belong rather to Ethics than to Jurisprudence'. In contrast, names of classes that were 'purely technical', such as 'offences ... against prerogative, with misprisions, contempts, felonies, præmunires', which Blackstone had incorporated into his *Analysis of the Laws of England*,[17] but which bore no relation to the 'common end' of happiness, would either be 'banished' from a natural arrangement or placed in 'the corners and bye-places' where, instead of appearing to give, they might receive, elucidation.[18]

9.3 Universal Expository Jurisprudence

In 1780–2, Bentham devoted much of his time to composing an introduction to a proposed major work that he described as 'a plan of a penal code *in terminis*'.[19] The first sixteen chapters and the first two sections of the seventeenth chapter of this introduction, though written and printed in 1780, were eventually published as *An Introduction to the Principles of Morals and Legislation* in 1789. The seventeenth chapter, entitled 'Of the Limits of the Penal Branch of Jurisprudence', had grown into a book-length

[17] Blackstone 1771: [xii]. [18] Bentham 1977: 414–18. [19] Bentham 1970a: 1.

study in its own right, and, apart from these first two sections, was never published by Bentham himself.[20] In the second section, entitled 'Jurisprudence, its branches', Bentham further developed his distinction between law as it is and law as it ought to be. He presented the distinction as one within jurisprudence, that is, within the study of law, and one that was grounded in his theory of logic and language. Having stated that 'Jurisprudence is a fictitious entity', he went on to say that, in order to understand what the word jurisprudence meant, it was necessary to accompany it 'with some word that shall be significative of a real entity'. The way to do this, Bentham explained, was to talk about 'a book of jurisprudence', with the 'book' being the real entity through which the fictitious entity 'jurisprudence' could be understood. As we will see, the name of a fictitious entity represented an abstraction, while the name of a real entity represented a body with physical substance. Bentham reiterated the distinction between the expositor and the censor that he had made in *A Fragment on Government*:

> A book of jurisprudence can have but one or the other of two objects: 1. To ascertain what the *law* is: 2. To ascertain what it ought to be. In the former case it may be stiled a book of *expository* jurisprudence; in the latter, a book of *censorial* jurisprudence; or, in other words, a book on the *art of legislation*.[21]

He thereupon made several further distinctions within books of expository jurisprudence. The first distinction was between books of authoritative and unauthoritative jurisprudence, depending respectively upon whether it was the work of the legislator himself or the work of any other person. The second distinction was between books of local and universal jurisprudence, depending respectively upon whether it dealt with the laws of a particular nation or group of nations or those of 'all nations whatsoever'. The latter would have a very particular focus. No two nations had laws that were throughout exactly the same in substance, and even where the laws of the two nations agreed to some extent in substance, they would certainly not be expressed in exactly the same words and often would not 'have so much as a single *word* in common'. Yet, remarked Bentham, 'among the words that are appropriated to the subject of law, there are some that in all

[20] The text was first published in Bentham 1945, then in Bentham 1970b, and most recently in Bentham 2010.

[21] Bentham 2010: 16.

languages are pretty correspondent to one another: which comes to the same thing nearly as if they were the same. Of this stamp, for example, are those which correspond to the words *power, right, obligation, liberty,* and many others.'

Hence, a book of universal expository jurisprudence could not be authoritative, since there was no legislator with the power to enact laws that were valid throughout the world; nor could it be unauthoritative as far as the substance of the law was concerned, since there existed no universal laws for the legal commentator to describe. The only possible subject-matter for universal expository jurisprudence, therefore, was the form of the law – in other words, it could deal only with 'the import of words: to be, strictly speaking, universal, it must confine itself to terminology'.[22] In contrast, as Bentham had explained in *A Fragment on Government*, there was much greater scope for universality in relation to censorial jurisprudence, since there were 'some leading points ... in respect of which the laws of all civilized nations might, without inconvenience, be the same'.[23]

For the publication of *An Introduction to the Principles of Morals and Legislation* in 1789, Bentham composed a 'Preface', in which he explained the provenance of the text and the factors that had delayed its publication. He went on to give an account of the scope of the proposed introduction to his penal code. It would contain ten parts, the first nine of which would deal with the principles of legislation in various branches of law. The tenth part would consist of the following:

> Plan of a body of law, complete in all its branches, considered in respect of its *form*; in other words, in respect of its method and terminology; including a view of the origination and connexion of the ideas expressed by the short list of terms, the exposition of which contains all that can be said with propriety to belong to the head of universal jurisprudence.

In a note, he added: 'Such as obligation, right, power, possession, title, exemption, immunity, franchise, privilege, nullity, validity, and the like.'[24] Bentham's point was that each legal system had its own terms for entities that could be found in every other legal system, and that a sensible exposition could be offered for each of those terms. This was the task of universal expository jurisprudence. Bentham's notion of universal expository jurisprudence appears to equate to the morally neutral description of

[22] Bentham 2010: 16–17. [23] Bentham 2010: 17–18. [24] Bentham 1970a: 6 and n.

a legal system that characterised Hart's methodological legal positivism. Bentham, moreover, located universal jurisprudence as a branch of the study of law as it is, which appears to confirm Hart's view of the structure of Bentham's legal theory. A closer examination of Bentham's universal expository jurisprudence, however, shows him to have been engaged in a very different exercise from that which Hart ascribed to him.

9.4 The Key to Universal Expository Jurisprudence

Bentham had worked out a method of exposition for abstract terms in general, and hence for legal abstract terms in particular, and thereby to accomplish the task of universal expository jurisprudence, in manuscripts written in the mid-1770s and headed 'Preparatory Principles'.[25] This material, which was related both to Bentham's critique of Blackstone and to his attempt to draft a complete penal code, constituted, as it were, a storehouse of ideas on which he drew when composing his more systematic texts in the mid-to-late 1770s and early 1780s. At various points in this material, Bentham suggested titles for a book or perhaps a series of books dealing with jurisprudence in general. One such title was 'A Key to Universal Jurisprudence',[26] reflecting the fact that many passages in 'Preparatory Principles' are concerned with the exposition of abstract legal terms, the subject-matter of universal expository jurisprudence. The 'key' to unlocking the mystery of legal terminology consisted in demonstrating the relationship between legal discourse and the physical world. Bentham adopted the word 'metaphysics' to represent 'that science which teacheth the signification of words, and [the] origination of the ideas which they signify'. The task of exposition was accomplished when 'the idea annext to any one word' was distinguished from 'the idea annext to any other' and when it had been shown 'how all the ideas we have that are complex, arise from, and are made up of, simple ones'.[27] Every science had its 'leading terms', which were used in order to make other terms understood. The metaphysics of the science of law consisted 'in ascertaining the meaning, in fixing [the] ideas, belonging to the several terms of universal

[25] See Bentham 2016. The text consists of a series of passages, ranging from one or two lines in length through to several pages, on various aspects of jurisprudence.

[26] Bentham 2016: 365. [27] Bentham 2016: 265.

Jurisprudence, through the medium of which the technical terms of the particular Jurisprudence of any country are endeavoured to be explained'.[28]

The method of exposition traditionally adopted by lawyers was 'the old method *per genus et differentiam*', but, argued Bentham, attempts to define abstract terms, such as 'Power, Possession, Property, etc. in Morals: Ratio, Part, Multiple, etc. in Mathematics', by such means were doomed to failure because the terms in question had no superior genus to which they could be referred. The best that could be done was to provide a synonym, but often that only made matters worse. The terms characteristic of universal jurisprudence, such as power and right, had no superior genus by which they could be made known. If you heard the word cacalianthemum, and wanted to know the meaning of it, you would be told that a cacalianthemum was a sort of plant, and that would give you some idea of the import of the word. A right or power, however, was not a sort of anything. The expositors who used 'the old method', nevertheless, pursued their '*routine*' and attempted to find a higher genus: 'The consequence is they either take up such a definition as is useless, or give up altogether the task of finding one, as being either unnecessary or impracticable. 'Tis by this means that so many words, of a sort that want it most, have either no definition at all, or such an one as is worse than none.'[29] The failure to explain the meaning of words by definition *per genus et differentiam* did not mean that the attempt was hopeless. The problem lay not with 'the science itself' but in the method that had hitherto been employed. There was 'but one way' that could be successful, though it was a method that 'never has been attempted yet'.[30]

Bentham's new approach was based on the view that abstract terms could only be understood by reference to simple ideas and that simple ideas were derived from physical objects that were perceived by the senses. He credited John Locke with the insight that '[a] discourse containing words in it meant to convey complex ideas is never made intelligible, till the simple ideas involved in those complex ones are made assignable',[31] but he went beyond Locke in his account of the role of language in this process. The clarification of the import of an abstract term, stated Bentham, required more than a single definition, but rather 'a chain of Definitions' in

[28] Bentham 2016: 196–7. [29] Bentham 2016: 97–8, 111–12. [30] Bentham 2016: 157.
[31] Bentham 2016: 75. See Locke 1975: 292.

which the first consisted of 'words expressive of simple ideas'.[32] Again he stated, 'No Definition can be a good one, unless it either come home to simple ideas, or fit into an uninterrupted chain of other Definitions of which the first link *does*.'[33] Simple ideas were those by which 'sensible images' were impressed on the mind and consisted of events and situations: events were bodies in motion, while situations were bodies at rest.[34] Everything that was perceived by 'our exterior senses' was constituted by matter and motion, but motion was itself a quality of matter, and not something distinct: hence, '[w]hether there be motion in any case or whether there be none, it is still matter and matter only that exists'.[35] In short, the sole source of simple ideas was matter, which was distributed into different bodies. The distinction between one single body and another – between one individual and another – was not an objective feature of the physical world but a construct of the perceiving mind. Matter could be divided almost without limit, and there was no objective way of determining what should be deemed a single body and what several bodies. The same was true of the distinction between one act and another. There was no objective way of determining what should be deemed a single act and what several. 'There is no body that can for any purposes be spoken of as a whole', stated Bentham, 'but what may to other purposes, with equal propriety, be spoken of as distinguished into parts. There is no quantity of motion, therefore, that can be spoken of as one act, but may with equal propriety be spoken of as several acts.' The individual body and the individual act were a product of language: 'What determines a portion of matter to be spoken of as one is unity of name. What determines a quantity of motion to be spoken of as one is, in like manner, unity of name.'[36] Bentham summarised his position as follows: 'The existences that fall within the cognizance of our senses are comprizable in a single appellative,

[32] Bentham 2016: 104.

[33] Bentham 2016: 141. See also Bentham 2016: 119: 'Simple ideas are the *ne plus ultra* of expository investigation: the mind neither can go deeper in its researches, nor has occasion. He who cannot understand a word when the explanation of it is rightly conducted upon that plan, can never.'

[34] Bentham 2016: 169.

[35] Bentham 2016: 369. Bentham distinguished the object and the perception. In strictness, we did not see an object itself but the rays of light that issued from it. Similarly, we did not smell an object itself but its 'odorous particles'. See Bentham 2016: 126. For motion as a property of matter, see Bentham 2016: 169–70.

[36] Bentham 2016: 395.

Bodies. What is common to all these Bodies is that they are either in a state of rest, or in a state of Motion.' The only things that were perceptible to our senses, in other words the only things that could be said to have existence, were bodies.[37] In other words, names were invented to demarcate these bodies and such names represented simple ideas.

Bentham went on to point out that such entities as golden mountains, diamond billiard balls and sphinxes, which did not exist in reality and yet constituted ideas in the mind, were very different in nature from the fictitious entities that formed the subject-matter of universal jurisprudence. We could take any figure or shape that we had seen and associate it with any colour that we had seen, even though we had never seen that figure and colour associated in nature,

> and thus form ideas of imaginary substances at pleasure .... A Diamond Billiard Ball is what I have never seen: but I have seen a Diamond, and I have seen a Billiard Ball. A Diamond Billiard Ball is, therefore, what I can imagine. Though I never have had the substance of a Diamond Billiard Ball before my eyes, I can have, I now have, the idea of it in my mind.[38]

Such a combination of simple ideas produced what Bentham termed a fabulous entity. Hence, in the course of composing 'Preparatory Principles', Bentham settled on the terminology that he would apply throughout the remainder of his career – noun substantives might signify entities that were real, fictitious or fabulous. The names of real entities represented bodies existing in the physical world: 'The only objects that really exist are *substances*: they are the only real entities.' The names of fictitious entities represented entities that did not actually exist in the physical world but were spoken of as if they did exist: 'To convey any notion by words which are the names of any objects [other] than substances, we are obliged to attribute to such objects what in truth is attributable only to substances: in a word, we are obliged to feign them to be substances. Those others, in short, are only fictitious entities.'[39] Fictitious entities, though given names that 'in strictness' were 'proper only for real beings, viz: substantives', were not to be considered as 'being represented seriously as existing', but were rather 'feigned' to exist 'merely for the

[37] Bentham 2016: 397. See also Bentham 2016: 395, where Bentham suggested that mental processes were reducible to matter: 'Even in an act of the mental kind, some distinguishable, assignable portion of matter is necessarily concerned.'
[38] Bentham 2016: 169–71. [39] Bentham 2016: 424.

purposes of discourse'. The names of fictitious entities included 'Liberty, Right, Condition, Quality, disposition, etc.'. The names of fabulous entities were combinations of real entities assembled by the imagination but which did not exist in such combinations in the physical world.[40]

Given that any chain of definitions had to begin with simple ideas, that is, those images in the mind created by bodies that were immediately perceptible, and were not themselves definable, it followed that '*[t]he origin of our ideas relative to Law can, therefore*, be sought for in no other source'.[41] The problem with the leading terms found in law was that, as noted, they were 'nothing'. Legal powers, for instance, were 'not to be defined. They belong to no genus. Take them by themselves, no notion is to be formed of them at all. The words are Substantives: but they are not names of substances ... they are not names of any thing[s] that exist.' To define power, like right and wrong, as a single word was 'impossible'. Rather, a term such as 'power' had to be placed in a sentence, or more precisely in a proposition.

This proposition may be translated into another proposition that is equivalent: and that is composed of words which, taken separately, shall either be capable of a definition, or what is still better, need none. To create a power in a person over a thing, or what is shorter and more familiar, to give a person a power over a thing, is to restrain another person from meddling with that thing, the first person being left unrestrained.[42]

Referring to the names of real entities as proper noun substantives and the names of fictitious entities as improper, Bentham stated:

A proper substantive, the name of a real entity, is understood immediately and of itself it offers a certain image to the conception. An improper substantive offers no such image. Of itself it has no meaning. It means nothing till, with other words, it be compounded into some sentence. It then is seen to have a meaning, which is the clearer, the more clearly it is seen to be equivalent to some sentence the terms of which are names of real entities.[43]

As well as external bodies in motion and at rest, simple ideas included pain, pleasure and volition:

These [words] nobody defines, or if any one defines, nobody makes clearer by defining. They need not be defined, they can not. For to define a word is to point

[40] Bentham 2016: 387. [41] Bentham 2016: 200. [42] Bentham 2016: 380.
[43] Bentham 2016: 401.

out, in some way or other the simple ideas that go to the composing of the more complex idea of which usage has made that word the sign. But of these, each is the sign of one simple idea, and no more.

The meaning of terms signifying simple ideas was grasped directly from perception, and this was where the attempt to expound the terms that belonged to universal jurisprudence would begin. It was by relating the terms of universal jurisprudence to terms that signified simple ideas that the former terms would be understood. 'These [simple ideas] are the Capital we have to trade with. These, to speak with the Algebraists, are our known quantities, our *a*'s, *b*'s and *c*'s. 'Tis by reference to these that we are to elicit the import of the *x*'s, *y*'s and *z*'s, whose import there is occasion to make known.'[44]

Bentham referred to this technique of translating propositions as paraphrasis and claimed that it was the only means by which the names of fictitious entities could be expounded: 'To expound an improper substantive by Paraphrasis is to compleat it into a sentence, and for that sentence to find an equivalent sentence consisting of words significative of real entities.'[45] In order to understand what was meant by the word right, for instance, it had to be included in a sentence, and that sentence expounded 'by such another sentence as contains in it words that *are* capable of being defined'.[46] The word right was a noun substantive, but it did not signify a substance, neither a 'real concrete' nor a 'fictitious abstract' substance (that is a fabulous entity), and hence was no more significant of itself than a preposition such as the word 'for': 'Who is there that ever supposed it possible to define "for"? No man. As little is it possible to define "a right".' In order to understand the word 'for', it was necessary to bring forward a sentence in which the word appeared, and the same was true in relation to the word 'right'.[47] When Bentham gave the following example of paraphrasis in *A Fragment on Government*, he was drawing on the 'metaphysics' that he outlined in 'Preparatory Principles':

A word may be said to be expounded by *paraphrasis*, when not that *word* alone is translated into other *words*, but some whole *sentence* of which it forms a part is translated into another *sentence*; the words of which latter are expressive of such

[44] Bentham 2016: 102–3. [45] Bentham 2016: 386. [46] Bentham 2016: 247.
[47] Bentham 2016: 249.

ideas as are *simple*, or are more immediately resolvable into simple ones than those of the former.

There was no other method that could explain the meaning of 'the words *duty*, *right*, *power*, *title*, and those other words of the same stamp that abound so much in ethics and jurisprudence'. A person had a legal duty to perform an action when another person had a right to have him be made to do it. In other words, the person under the duty was liable to be punished at law for not performing the action, and to be punished in this way meant suffering a pain inflicted by command of the lawmaker. The abstract term duty was, therefore, placed in a proposition, and that proposition was translated into a proposition with the same meaning but which referred to real entities – in this case such real entities as persons, pains and expressions of will.[48]

Once terms had been properly expounded, claimed Bentham, many jurisprudential puzzles would be solved: 'The words defined are all so many given quantities, and possessing which, the Jurist finds himself rich in means for the solution of any problem in his science.'[49] Indeed, once terms were properly expounded, their meaning would be 'fixed for ever'.[50] It might, however, be necessary to invent new words in order to represent any new ideas generated, since 'the words of the current stock are, many of them, stuffed and crammed with three or four ideas stuck in them at once'.[51] In the course of 'Preparatory Principles', Bentham identified several benefits that would result from the creation of a science of universal expository jurisprudence. One benefit was that it would bring an end to disputes of law as opposed to questions of fact: 'All Questions of Law are no more than questions concerning the import of words. Questions the solution of which depends upon skill in Metaphysics. As that master science, therefore, advances to it's [*sic*] perfection, this source of litigation will be contracted.'[52] Unless the words used in law had a clear meaning, they could not fulfil the function of law, which was to guide conduct. 'Words, to be of use, must serve for signs to our ideas, must serve to excite precise ideas in the minds of those that hear them. A text that will not serve

[48] See Bentham 1977: 494–5 n. [49] Bentham 2016: 223. [50] Bentham 2016: 278.

[51] Bentham 2016: 254. See also Bentham 2016: 361: 'No department of science can receive any considerable improvement but the language must receive a new modification. New ideas struck off from the general mass must, like the old ones, have words of their own to dress them in. These words must be, in some sort, new.'

[52] Bentham 2016: 282.

to call up precise and distinct ideas, such a text, in the instances where it fails of doing so, will not serve for any thing.'[53] It was only by 'Metaphysics' – through clear exposition – that 'controverted points in Law can be clearly solved'.[54] Bentham referred to the dispute with the American colonists as evidence of the importance of words: 'A great part of the merits of the American controversy, as far as concerns the matter of right, centers on the signification of the words Give, grant, consent, representation, taxation, legislation, constitution.'[55] Bentham's point was that disputes arose from competing definitions of legal terms – once a settled exposition had been given, there would be no basis for disagreement insofar as legal terminology was concerned.

A second benefit was that sensible communication would be established between jurists of different nations:

> By banishing as many as we can spare of the terms peculiar to our own local Jurisprudence, and giving a clear and steady exposition of such as we are obliged to retain in terms of universal jurisprudence, an easy and profitable intercourse may be kept up between the Jurists of the several nations, and an Englishman might read a comment upon his own laws in the languages of Spain or Sweden.[56]

'[A]n expository treatise on the Laws of England written in terms of universal jurisprudence,' noted Bentham, 'couched in untechnical universal language, at the same time that it is a key to the Laws of England, is a Key to the Laws of any other country.' It would then be a relatively straightforward matter to apply it elsewhere:

> To the Laws of England, it is a key, ready fitted to the lock. To the Laws of France, it is a key ready to be fitted into the lock, by any Artist who can enter, with a tolerable degree of facility, into the views of him that made it. A work written on this plan, even upon the Laws of our Island, would bear translation into the languages of the continent.[57]

A third benefit was that, by giving 'paraphrases' of 'the several sorts of fictitious legal entities – Powers over persons, over things; over persons – Rights to services – Protection etc.', not only would Bentham be able to use these terms in his own work but he would also clarify their meaning when used by other writers.[58]

[53] Bentham 2016: 106. [54] Bentham 2016: 265. [55] Bentham 2016: 266.
[56] Bentham 2016: 260. [57] Bentham 2016: 138–9. [58] Bentham 2016: 344–5.

9.5 Moral Neutrality

Did Bentham separate fact and value and hence commit himself to substantive legal positivism, and did he intend that his universal expository jurisprudence should lead to the production of a vocabulary of morally neutral terms and hence commit himself to methodological legal positivism? In other words, did the conceptual separation of fact and value underpin Bentham's distinction between law as it and law as it ought to be, and did universal expository jurisprudence, therefore, belong to the domain of (morally neutral) fact? The answer to both questions is in the negative and for the same reason – namely, the particular form of Bentham's utilitarianism and its relationship to his psychological theory, both of which were grounded in the naturalistic ontology discussed in Section 9.4.

In later writings, Bentham emphasised the point that logic (the term that he came to use instead of 'metaphysics') was, far from being a morally neutral activity, crucial to well-being or happiness – in other words, to the promotion of utility. In his essay on 'Logic', he explicitly linked the clarification of terminology – which was the task of universal expository jurisprudence – to the promotion of utility. He defined logic as 'the art, which has for its object or end in view, the giving to the best advantage, direction to the human mind and thence to the whole human frame, in its pursuit of any object or purpose, to the attainment of which it is capable of being applied'.[59] He went on to state that, '[o]f the art and science of logic, the prime and that the most immediate use is the establishment of clear and determinate ideas', and that this objective would be achieved through such operations as methodisation, distinction, definition, division and exposition.[60] Given that the pursuit of well-being was 'the end of every action', logic had the same end.[61] Again, in *The Book of Fallacies*, he noted that '[b]y Logic taken at large may be understood the art of applying to best advantage to the purpose of discourse the faculty of discourse', and referred to it as 'this all-comprehensive art and science'.[62] As we have seen, when discussing universal expository jurisprudence in 'Preparatory Principles', Bentham drew attention to the benefits that would accrue from

[59] UCL Bentham Papers, box ci, fo. 92 (3 August 1814).
[60] UCL Bentham Papers, box ci, fo. 103 (5 August 1814).
[61] UCL Bentham Papers, box ci, fo. 107 (25 September 1815). [62] Bentham 2015: 408 n.

an accurate definition of terms. In similar vein, the final section of *Of the Limits of the Penal Branch of Jurisprudence* was entitled 'Uses of this chapter'. Bentham marked each 'use' according to whether it belonged to 'form' or to 'matter', that is, whether it belonged to expository or to censorial jurisprudence. Both enterprises were justified by their utility.[63] Finally, given Bentham's theory of motivation, in which no action was undertaken except with a view to experiencing pleasure or averting pain, no one would be motivated to undertake the task of either censorial or expository jurisprudence unless they expected to gain some benefit, and hence some pleasure, in performing it. There was no such thing as an unmotivated action.[64] The expected pleasure might arise from the satisfactory completion of a difficult intellectual enterprise, from the gaining of knowledge, from the hope of benefiting one's community or humanity in general, or merely because one was paid to do it. As Bentham stated in his essay on 'Logic': 'Desire of pleasure and of exemption from pain, in one word *interest*, [are] in some shape or other the source of every thought as well as the cause of every action, and, in particular, of every action by which names are employed in the designation of persons and of things.'[65] Every action was motivated by a desire for pleasure and an aversion to pain, and every action had consequences in terms of promoting pleasure and avoiding pain – and wherever pleasure and pain was involved, so was morality. There was no space for moral neutrality.

It should be emphasised that Bentham put forward a unified theory: there was only one physical world, and hence only one source of experience and of knowledge. Fact and value did not belong to separate or separable domains.[66] On the one hand, for Bentham, a statement of value was a statement of fact. A statement of value only made sense insofar as it was resolved by paraphrasis into a statement about the existence of the real entities of pain and pleasure – it was a statement about a matter of fact in the physical world. On the other hand, a statement of fact, insofar as it was true, was of positive value because it told us something worth knowing about the state of the physical world, and, conversely, insofar as it was false, of negative value because it misled us about the state of the physical

[63] Bentham 2010: 219–33. [64] Bentham 1983b: 87, 98–9, 112.

[65] UCL Bentham Papers, box cii, fo. 42 (28 September 1814).

[66] See, e.g., 'Encyclopedical Table, or Art and Science Table' in Bentham 1983a: between 178 and 179, where the whole field of knowledge appears under the joint headings of 'being' and 'well-being'.

world. The statement of what the law is, therefore, while a statement of fact, consisted of useful knowledge and hence was valuable, and no one would be motivated to make any investigation into what the law is unless they expected some benefit to arise from doing so. Bentham's ontology did not allow for that carving up of experience into a physical world of morally neutral fact and a transcendent world of value that seems to be required by Hart's notion of the separation of fact and value.

It might be argued in response that Bentham criticised the use, in the description of motives, of what he referred to as 'eulogistic' and 'dyslogistic' terms, which carried associations of praise and blame respectively, and instead suggested the use of 'neutral' terms. In relation to pleasures and pains of the religious sanction, for instance, eulogistic terms for corresponding motives included 'piety' and 'devotion', dyslogistic terms included 'superstition' and 'bigotry', and neutral terms included 'sense of religious duty' and 'fear of God'. He referred to eulogistic and dyslogistic terms as 'censorial' because of their connection with sentiments of approval or disapproval, which presumably meant that he regarded neutral terms as expository. He continued: 'Thus it is that, in addition to the import which, in the character of a *simple term*, properly belongs to it, will be found involved in every such censorial appellation the import of at least one entire *proposition*: viz. a proposition expressive of a *judgement* of *approbation* or *disapprobation*.' The problem with the use of a dyslogistic term was that any beneficial effects, and conversely with a eulogistic term any mischievous effects, tended to be ignored.[67] As Bentham further explained in *The Book of Fallacies*, the use of these terms involved a begging of the question. The approval or disapproval of a particular practice, for instance, would depend on the associations of the term by which it was described, rather than on its substantive utility. Moreover, the very choice of term would be motivated by some interest: for instance, if one wished to disparage a certain person, one would choose a dyslogistic term to describe that person. It was, therefore, conducive to utility to adopt terms that were neutral in relation to the ideas that were associated with them.[68] But neutral terminology did not, for Bentham, imply moral neutrality. While he advocated a vocabulary that did not carry 'censorial' associations, he did so not because such a vocabulary would be morally

[67] See Bentham 1983b: 83, 95. [68] Bentham 2015: 315–18, 322 n.

neutral but because it would promote utility – in other words, it would be valuable.

It is worth drawing attention to two short passages that illustrate the point that Bentham did not subscribe to Hart's conceptual separation of law and morality. First, in *Letters to Count Toreno* (1822), having discussed the principles on which a penal code ought to be grounded, Bentham stated: 'Thus, not only in a direct way, by the application made of it to each particular case, but in an additional way by means of the method to which it gives birth, does the principle of the greatest happiness of the greatest number, cover the whole field of legislation with its salutary influence.' Hence, 'the whole field' – which included both the content of the law and the method by which it was organised, the subject-matters of censorial and universal expository jurisprudence, respectively – was subject to the principle of utility.[69] Second, in notes for 'Table of the Springs of Action' (1817), Bentham wrote: 'Principles of utility two, or if but one, it is understood in two senses – viz. the *censorial* and the *expositive* or *exhibitive*.'[70] Expository jurisprudence – identification of what the law is – and censorial jurisprudence – recommendation of what the law ought to be – were both aspects of the principle of utility. The gloss put upon Bentham's distinction between what the law is and what the law ought to be by Hart was a product of his commitment to the separation of fact and value, but such a separation had no place in Bentham's thought because a statement of value was also a statement of fact, and there was no statement of fact that did not have value, whether positive or negative. For Bentham, the distinction between law as it is and law as it ought to be did not represent the distinction between fact and value that characterised substantive legal positivism, but rather a distinction between an actually existing state of affairs (whether past or present) and a proposed state of affairs, with the latter being deemed more valuable in terms of its utility than the former. For Bentham, universal expository jurisprudence was not the attempt to conduct legal theory in the morally neutral terms that characterised methodological legal positivism; it was an attempt to find stable, sensible and hence useful expositions of abstract legal terms in order to advance legal science and thereby facilitate the construction of

69 Bentham 2012: 208.

70 See Bentham 1983b: 9. The 'notes' in question were copies of summaries of the main text that Bentham wrote in the margin. The relevant text sheet is missing.

a utilitarian code of laws. For Bentham, both enterprises were value-laden. Seen through the lens of Hart's twentieth-century philosophy, Bentham's legal theory may plausibly appear to open the legal positivist tradition, but to ascribe legal positivism to the historical Bentham is an anachronism.

References

Bentham, J. University College London Library. Bentham Papers. Manuscript boxes i–clxxvi.

Bentham, J. 1945. *The Limits of Jurisprudence Defined.* Ed. C. W. Everett. Columbia University Press.

Bentham, J. 1970a. *An Introduction to the Principles of Morals and Legislation.* Eds. J. H. Burns and H. L. A. Hart. Athlone Press.

Bentham, J. 1970b. *Of Laws in General.* Ed. H. L. A. Hart. Athlone Press.

Bentham, J. 1977. *A Comment on the Commentaries* and *A Fragment on Government.* Eds. J. H. Burns and H. L. A. Hart. Athlone Press.

Bentham, J. 1983a. *Chrestomathia.* Eds. M. J. Smith and W. H. Burston. Clarendon Press.

Bentham, J. 1983b. *Deontology together with A Table of the Springs of Action and Article on Utilitarianism.* Ed. A. Goldworth. Clarendon Press.

Bentham, J. 1998. *'Legislator of the World': Writings on Codification, Law, and Education.* Eds. P. Schofield and J. Harris. Clarendon Press.

Bentham, J. 2010. *Of the Limits of the Penal Branch of Jurisprudence.* Ed. P. Schofield. Clarendon Press.

Bentham, J. 2012. *On the Liberty of the Press, and Public Discussion and Other Legal and Political Writings for Spain and Portugal.* Eds. C. Pease-Watkin and P. Schofield. Clarendon Press.

Bentham, J. 2015. *The Book of Fallacies.* Ed. P. Schofield. Clarendon Press.

Bentham, J. 2016. *Preparatory Principles.* Eds. D. G. Long and P. Schofield. Clarendon Press.

Blackstone, W. 1765–9. *Commentaries on the Laws of England.* 4 vols. Clarendon Press.

Blackstone, W. 1771. *An Analysis of the Laws of England.* 6th ed. Clarendon Press.

Hart, H. L. A. 1982. *Essays on Bentham: Studies in Jurisprudence and Political Theory.* Clarendon Press.

Hart, H. L. A. 1996. 'Bentham's Principle of Utility and Theory of Penal Law'. In J. Bentham. *An Introduction to the Principles of Morals and Legislation.* Eds. J. H. Burns and H. L. A. Hart. Introduction by F. Rosen. Clarendon Press: lxxix–cxii.

Hume, D. 2007. *A Treatise of Human Nature: A Critical Edition.* 2 vols. Eds. D. F. Norton and M. J. Norton. Clarendon Press.

Lieberman, D. 1989. *The Province of Legislation Determined: Legal Theory in Eighteenth-Century Britain*. Cambridge University Press.

Locke, J. 1975. *Essay Concerning Human Understanding*. Ed. P. H. Nidditch. Clarendon Press.

Perry, S. R. 2001. 'Hart's Methodological Positivism'. In J. Coleman (ed.). *Hart's Postscript: Essays on the Postscript to the Concept of Law*. Oxford University Press: 311–54.

Postema, G. J. 1986. *Bentham and the Common Law Tradition*. Clarendon Press.

Schofield, P. 2010. 'Jeremy Bentham and HLA Hart's "Utilitarian Tradition in Jurisprudence"'. *Jurisprudence* 1: 147–67.

John Austin 10

Michael Lobban

10.1 Introduction

John Austin's fame derives from his *Province of Jurisprudence Determined*, first published in 1832 out of lectures delivered at the University of London, and from the broader set of lectures which were published after his death in 1859.[1] The lectures were shaped by two influences. The first was the jurisprudence of Jeremy Bentham, as elaborated in the *Introduction to the Principles of Morals and Legislation*, *Fragment on Government* and *Traités de Législation civile et pénale*. The second was the German Pandectist literature which Austin encountered in Bonn, where he went to prepare his lectures after his appointment to his chair.[2] Austin's work became the staple of late-nineteenth-century jurisprudence examinations in the universities, and his method inspired a number of later-nineteenth-century textbook writers.[3] At the same time, given that the second edition of the *Province* was published in the same year as Henry Maine's *Ancient Law*,[4] Austin's work was often seen as only a partial view of jurisprudence, which gave a useful analytical vocabulary of legal science but failed fully to explain the nature and the development of law.

Austin's fame rested on the formal jurisprudence set out in his lectures, where he offered a set of analytical concepts which could be used to explain existing law, in terms intended to be morally neutral. His conceptual apparatus was designed to enable the jurist to identify what counted as a 'law', as distinguished from any other kind of norm (such as a social, moral or religious one), in order to define the parameters of a legal system. His work was

[1] In what follows, all quotations will be taken from the fourth edition of his work: Austin 1873.

[2] See Lobban 2013 and Schwarz 1934–5.

[3] See Holland 1880; Markby 1871.

[4] Maine 1861.

pioneering insofar as it sought to sketch out an area of study – 'jurisprudence' – which was distinct from the study either of substantive law or of moral philosophy. Although numerous later jurists criticised the Austinian vision for being too narrow, his aim to explore the distinct character of law and a legal system was a significant intellectual innovation.

Austin's 'general jurisprudence' was 'concerned directly with principles and distinctions which are common to various systems of particular and positive law'.[5] The 'various systems' which interested him were the 'ampler and maturer' ones: he wanted to examine what was understood to be 'law' in developed systems, rather than what was understood to be law in any society. His aim was to seek out 'necessary principles, notions and distinctions, … [f]or we cannot imagine coherently a system of law (or a system of law as evolved in a refined community), without conceiving of them as constituent parts of it'.[6] These 'pervading' notions included the notions of duty, right, liberty, injury, punishment, and redress. Austin's theory was open to the criticism made by Maine that the legal concepts which he saw as 'essential' had themselves developed over time, as jurists began to rethink the norms which underpinned changing social relations.[7] This has led to some debate over whether Austin was making empirical or conceptual claims in his jurisprudence.[8] His work is perhaps best seen as seeking to elucidate what was generally understood by the notion of law in modern states, rather than in any conceivable society. This entailed identifying the 'independent political societies' which made up modern states, and then defining the kinds of law which were the marking characteristic of those states. It was the task of the jurist to tease out the concepts which followed as a matter of reason or logic from those definitions, in order to provide for clearer juristic thought.

10.2 Austin's Command Theory

Austin began by stipulating what he considered to be the 'matter of jurisprudence': it was the study of 'positive law', the law set by political superiors to political inferiors. Admitting that the term 'law' was used in various senses, he sought to distinguish between them, for the sake of

[5] Austin 1873: 33. [6] Austin 1873: 1108. [7] See Maine 1861; Maine 1871: 4, 67–8, 70.
[8] See Cotterrell 2003: 81–3; Lobban 1991: 224–5.

clarity in identifying different kinds of norm. Taken literally, the term 'law' embraced both rules set by political superiors to inferiors, and 'rules or laws' not established by political superiors. For the sake of distinction, Austin chose to classify the second set under the term 'positive morality', since they were posited by men (unlike divine law) but were distinct from the 'positive law' of the political superior.[9] The various attempts he made to set out what was 'properly' (or sometimes 'strictly speaking') called a law were Austin's own stipulative definitions, designed to distinguish forms, rather than being stronger claims as to their 'essential' nature as 'law'.

For Austin, all law 'properly so called' came from commands: 'parties invested with rights *are* invested with rights because other parties are bound by the command of the sovereign to do or perform acts, or to forbear or abstain from acts'.[10] The notion of command was inextricably linked with that of sanction: a command expressed the will of a party with the 'power and purpose ... to inflict an evil or pain'[11] on the addressee if disobeyed. Furthermore, '*command*, *duty* and *sanction* are inseparably connected terms',[12] each embracing the same ideas as the others. They also connoted the superiority of the commander, who had the power to enforce.[13] When discussing sanctions, Austin stated that William Paley had erred in arguing that the sanction had to offer a sufficiently 'violent motive' to comply for a duty to be generated by a command.[14] For Austin, the violence of the motive to comply said nothing about the existence of a duty; it pertained only to how effective it would be. In real life, commands were often disobeyed, regardless of how strong was the motive to comply; nonetheless, 'where there is the slightest chance of incurring the smallest evil, the expression of a wish amounts to a command, and therefore, imposes a duty'.[15] As he saw it, it was the threat of a sanction which identified the command.[16]

[9] Austin 1873: 88–9.

[10] Austin 1873: 407; see also 816–17: 'I *have* no right, independently of the injunction or prohibition which declares that some given act, forbearance or omission, would be a violation of my right.'

[11] Austin 1873: 91. [12] Austin 1873: 94. [13] See Austin 1873: 100.

[14] Paley 1785: 51.

[15] Austin 1873: 93. This is a passage which has troubled some commentators, who struggle to see how a duty can exist if there is no real chance of a penalty being imposed. See, e.g., Kramer 2013.

[16] As Raz (1980: 11–12) points out, while Austin did not explicitly state that the sovereign expressed his intention to punish, it was implicit from his contrasting definition of an imperfect law.

Austin was far from being the first English jurist to define law in terms of commands backed by sanctions.[17] In contrast to these jurists, H. L. A. Hart – perhaps Austin's foremost critic – argued that sanctions are tangential in most legal systems: people generally obey laws because they recognise their authority, not because they are coerced by the threat of punishment. In Hart's view, law is more concerned with coordination than coercion, informing people about what to do 'to plan life out of court', rather than signalling to the 'bad man' the circumstances in which he might be punished. Consequently, 'there seems no good reason for limiting the normative idea of obligation to rules supported by organized sanctions', even if sanctions might be necessary as a guarantee 'that those who would voluntarily obey shall not be sacrificed to those who would not'.[18] From the Austinian perspective, such a view overlooks the centrality of the idea of enforcement. For Austin, sanctions were not simply external guarantees: it was only by identifying the sanction that the lawyer or citizen could identify which duties the sovereign was prepared to enforce, and which therefore came within the ambit of the laws of the state. This was not simply designed to help the bad man predict the factual question of when he might be punished; it told him whether his conduct constituted a breach of the law.

As numerous commentators later perceived, Austin's definition that all laws properly so-called were commands was open to the objection that this definition was unable to account for all kinds of law. In particular, it seemed to omit consideration of power-conferring rules, such as the rules which determined what constituted a valid contract or will.[19] Austin's sanction-backed theory might promise to explain the fact that the legal system would enforce rights derived from contracts or wills, but it did not appear to explain how those rights came into being. As he explained it, these rights might be known only in the most oblique way: 'The law which gives the remedy, or which determines the punishment, is the only one that is absolutely necessary. For the remedy or punishment implies a foregone injury, and a foregone injury implies that a primary right or duty has been violated.'[20] This omitted discussion of the various rules which stipulated

[17] Austin was particularly influenced by the work of Hobbes and Bentham. See Bentham 1970: 35; Bentham 1977: 496 note b.

[18] Hart 1961: 39, 193, 213.

[19] For earlier versions of this criticism, see Harrison 1878: 688.

[20] Austin 1873: 794.

what kinds or rights would be enforced, and the conditions under which duties would be imposed. Austin was well aware of such rules, including (for instance) those concerning the 'solemnities' to be 'annexed to contracts' before courts would enforce them. They included judge-made doctrines, such as consideration, and legislated ones, such as the Statute of Frauds.[21] Despite his penchant for meticulous distinction-making, Austin did not devote much attention to explaining how laws like the Statute of Frauds fitted his definition of law as commands backed by sanctions. Nonetheless, he seemed to offer two possible ways of understanding such statutes. The first was to argue that sanctions might take the form of 'nullities'. As he explained (in a passage with the marginal heading 'laws [are] sometimes sanctioned by nullities'):

> The legislature annexes rights to certain transactions; for example, to contracts, on condition that these transactions are accompanied by certain circumstances. If the condition be not observed, the transaction is void, that is, no right arises; or the transaction is voidable, that is, a right arises, but the transaction is liable to be rescinded and the right annulled.[22]

The notion that nullity could operate as a sanction has been justly criticised.[23] If it is at best artificial to see the provisions of the Statute of Frauds as a command to a contracting party, who is sanctioned by having his contract regarded as null in case of disobedience, it is even harder to see the nullification of an invalid will as a sanction against the deceased testator. Austin's recognition that some contracts are merely voidable further complicated the question of the role of sanctions here. However, given that Austin was well aware of the law relating to contracts and wills (and sought to explain it in his lectures), and given that he mentioned nullity as a sanction only briefly in a section otherwise devoted to distinguishing tort and crime (as areas where the sanction was imposed at the behest of a civil party or the state), it should not be assumed that he considered power-conferring rules to be the same kind of imperative laws as the laws which enforced breaches of those rights, backed by a sanction of nullity.

Austin's second answer to the problem of power-conferring rules was to see them as 'permissive' rules which were not 'properly speaking' laws but which were nonetheless within the province of jurisprudence.

[21] See Austin 1873: 940. [22] See Austin 1873: 522 and also 523, 923.
[23] See Hart 1961: 33–5.

In fragmentary notes, he wrote that 'Law is imperative or permissive . . . [A]s conferring a right, it is permissive . . . [S]anction is not of the essence of permissible law.'[24] Austin did not develop this line of thought in any detail.[25] However, it is not insignificant that he referred to a footnote in Bentham's *Introduction to the Principles of Morals and Legislation* which discussed the concepts of powers and rights. Bentham stated here that for every right the law conferred on one party, it imposed a duty on another. He added that 'the commands and prohibitions, by which the *powers* and *rights* that compose those several modifications [of property] are created, are of many different forms',[26] which would best be treated under the civil branch of jurisprudence. In his unpublished work, Bentham sketched out more fully the relationship between the penal and the civil branches of the law, and his idea of a complete law, showing that every complete law terminated with the creation of an offence. In his view, for the purposes of clear arrangement, it was useful to separate out the penal and the civil aspects of the law, even though logically they formed part of a unified whole. Thus, Bentham explained, the legal title to a piece of property was defined by the penal prohibition on all save the title-holder from meddling with it; but a law forbidding entry to property by those without title also required the exposition of what 'title' meant.[27] In the Benthamic view, 'power-conferring' rules were part of the legal domain but were themselves part of larger 'complete laws' which were ultimately enforced penally.

Although he did not articulate his own theory of a complete law, it is evident that Bentham's suggestions on the topic informed Austin's distinction between primary and secondary (or sanctioning) rights. His statement that the only absolutely necessary part of any law was that secondary or sanctioning part which determined the punishment[28] was influenced by Bentham's comment that punitory laws contained the import of imperative laws by implication.[29] Austin's notion of primary rights echoed Bentham's

[24] Austin 1873: 366.

[25] He did refer to them as 'merely analogous to laws in the proper acceptation of the term', but still appropriate subjects of jurisprudence, since they were 'closely connected with positive laws': Austin 1873: 220. When he spoke of 'permissive laws', he generally had in mind laws which repealed earlier laws, and thereby permitted what had previously been forbidden (ibid.: 101, 366). In thinking of 'permissive' laws in terms of repealing laws, Austin may have been influenced by Bentham's definition of 'discoercive' laws as ones revoking a coercive law; Bentham 1970: 302, 307.

[26] Bentham 1970: 206. [27] See Bentham 2010: 309–11. [28] See Austin 1873: 794.

[29] See Bentham 1970: 303.

'civil' aspect of law.[30] Furthermore, he devoted lectures to the topic of titles to property, which engendered or extinguished primary rights. For Austin, the rules of law pertaining to titles were clearly part of the province of jurisprudence, even though they could themselves not be directly formulated as kinds of command. Furthermore, he spoke of 'laws properly so called' which were set by men 'as private persons, in pursuance of legal rights'.[31] This had strong echoes of Bentham's notion (found in his unpublished work) that contractual rights were the product of the imperative power of the sovereign and the 'accensitive' power of the subject.[32] Although he did not do this, it may be inferred that Austin might have developed a Benthamic solution to the problem of power-conferring rules.

If all law was ultimately imperative, what commands underpinned the common law? For Austin, the relevant commands were not those issued by a court at the point of decision, whether to the defendant to pay a sum in damages or to a gaoler to imprison the accused. For he made it clear that where commands were individual or particular, they could not be 'denominated a law or rule': such a denomination could be given only to commands which obliged generally to acts or forbearances of a class.[33] Consequently, a 'law (or rule of law) made by judicial decisions exists nowhere in a general or abstract form'. However, it could be extracted from particular decisions by looking at the '*general reasons* alleged by the Court for its decisions'. These reasons 'will apply universally to cases of a class' and could serve as a rule of conduct in the same way that statutes did.[34] The *ratio decidendi* was 'itself a *law*'.[35] However, the command which underpinned it was very oblique:

> Though not a rule in form, it is tantamount to a general command proceeding from the sovereign or state, or from any of its authorised subordinates. For, since it is its known will that the general reason of a decision on a particular or specific case shall govern decisions on future resembling cases, the subjects receive from the state (on

[30] Austin (1873: 794) also noted that primary and secondary rights were logically intertwined, though they were separated out for convenience. As he explained, the legal duty *sic utere tuo ut alienum non laedas* could not be understood without knowing the meaning of both '*tuum* and injury'. He also stated that 'a primary right or duty is not of itself a right or duty, without the secondary right or duty by which it is sustained; and *e converso*'.

[31] Austin 1873: 174. [32] Bentham 2010: 104–5. [33] Austin 1873: 95.

[34] See Austin 1873: 642.

[35] Austin 1873: 648. Austin's phrase was: '*Ratio decidendi* is itself a *law*: Or, at least, it is the general ground or principle of a judicial decision or decisions.'

the occasion of such a decision) an expression or intimation of its sovereign will, that they shall shape their conduct to the reason or principle thereof.[36]

This was put too strongly: in many areas of private law, parties were required to shape their conduct to the rules teased out of case law only *if* they wanted the protection of the courts. The *ratio decidendi* of much case law might therefore take the form of power-conferring rules. Although Austin did not articulate it, the commands he may have thought underpinned the system were even more general implied ones which themselves lay behind the *rationes decidendi*, such as *pacta sunt servanda*, the ultimate breach of which was redressed by the state.

The commands issued by the common law were highly imperfect expressions of the sovereign's will. Under his view of the common law, the root of the jurist's knowledge of the 'law' could only be the courts' decisions applying 'sanctioning rights' and thereby recognising an injury. It would then be a matter of inference to figure out the ambit of the primary right which was being protected, which was to be inferred from the *rationes decidendi* of a large number of decisions over a long range of time. This inferential process fell foul of all Bentham's objections to the common law. However, Austin himself acknowledged the imperfections of the common law method, and also recommended a codification of law, which would identify the rules much more clearly. At the same time, he was prepared to argue that the rules of the common law could be identified, and defined as law. Even if it might not always be clear exactly what they were, since they might be uncertain or unclear, the jurist could as a practical matter identify the common law as that body of rules enforced by the courts.[37]

10.3 The Sovereign and the Habit of Obedience

Austin's prime concern was to identify the law in independent political societies. In his view, the defining feature of such societies was that they had sovereigns, who were in a position to oblige the members of the society to comply with their wishes.[38] Sovereignty was defined by two features: first, there was a determinate and common superior to which the '*bulk* of

[36] Austin 1873: 648; see also 663, where he attributes this view to Bentham.
[37] Indeed, its rules were sometimes clearer than statutes. Austin 1873: 684.
[38] See Austin 1873: 99.

the given society are in a *habit* of obedience'; and second, that common superior was not in a habit of obedience to another determinate human superior.[39] Unlike the earlier contractarian theorists, Austin (like Bentham) identified sovereignty by reference to the social fact of a habit of obedience, rather than to a moral principle. The test was not perfect: the line between a natural society and a political society was a matter of degree, depending on how large the society was. It was also a matter of debate when a state, which followed the commands of another state, did it so regularly as no longer to be considered an independent political community.[40] Similarly, it was a matter of judgment to decide when a state which had fallen into civil war ceased to be a state, or had broken into separate states.

Austin's concept of the sovereign has attracted much criticism, particularly from Hart. Hart argued that the notion of the habit of obedience could not account for the authority of the law-maker. In his view, Austin's sovereign had only the authority of a gunman, who was obeyed out of fear rather than out of a sense of obligation which did not derive from coercion alone. Nor could the idea of a mere 'habit' account for the persistence of law and sovereign power, when one ruler died and was replaced by another. Explaining sovereign power in terms of a 'habit' of obedience seemed to suggest that one would only know whether the new incumbent was a sovereign, and whether the old laws persisted, once it had become clear that the people had developed a habit to obey him. More importantly still, it could not explain how a sovereign could be limited in his powers. In Hart's view, these problems could only be overcome by rethinking the foundations of the theory and replacing the notion of the habit of obedience with a new concept, the 'rule of recognition'. This (in its first aspect) is a social rule, which imposes an obligation from an 'internal point of view' to obey laws which derive from a certain source, which is regarded as authoritative. At the same time (in its second aspect), it operates as a power-conferring rule, conferring power on those exercising legal powers, while also being able to place limits on those powers.

Some of Hart's criticisms of the concept of the habit of obedience may be misplaced. There is no reason to assume that Austin's concept of a 'habit' simply connoted regularities of behaviour, rather than rule-following, or that they were motivated by fear alone. According to his definitions, if

[39] See Austin 1873: 226. [40] See Austin 1873: 229.

people obeyed a sovereign because they felt that there was a general social rule which bound them to do so, this rule would itself be a customary rule. It could not be seen as part of the realm of law, imposing 'legal' obligations, but had to be seen as a rule of positive morality. Nonetheless, such a social rule could explain the authority of the sovereign in the community: rather than deriving his authority from a legal norm, the sovereign's authority came from a norm of positive morality, which made people feel under an obligation to obey him. Since this was for Austin a pre-legal matter, it was not something for detailed exploration in a work on jurisprudence. From the point of view of the jurist, it was a matter of social fact: it was not necessary to explore *why* people obeyed a ruler; it was enough *that* they did so.

Furthermore, Austin did consider the question of the succession of sovereigns and the persistence of laws. In societies where the sovereign was made up of a composite group, the rules of succession were clearly determined by a law which persisted, and so the problem did not arise.[41] The problem arose only in simple monarchies where the king or emperor was sovereign. Discussing such monarchies, Austin argued that where rulers occupied the throne 'by a given generic title', there would be greater stability than in societies lacking them, and the office would be 'styled legitimate . . . or constitutional'.[42] However, the rules which determined the generic title – such as the pre-Revolutionary French Salic laws of succession – were part of the province of positive morality, rather than positive law.[43] If an eighteenth-century absolutist French king had legislated to change the rules of succession, his act would have been regarded as unconstitutional by the people (Austin argued), but it could not be seen as illegal.[44] In such a case, where customary rules found in the Salic laws came into conflict with the (valid) law laid down by a king before his death, it would only be apparent who was the rightful heir when it was clear whose orders were obeyed.

[41] See Austin 1873: 192.

[42] Austin 1873: 197. Austin noted that the Roman empire was itself subject to this instability, as a result of the lack of generic rules.

[43] Austin 1873: 73n: 'In a country governed by a monarch, constitutional law is extremely simple: for it merely determines the person who shall bear the sovereignty . . . In a country governed by a monarch, constitutional law is positive morality merely.'

[44] See Austin 1873: 275.

That the ultimate source of political power rested on an indeterminate social rule or 'habit' of accepting the authority of the ruler was as true in composite states as in absolute monarchies. According to his theory, sovereigns were by definition legally illimitable. Where sovereignty lay in a 'composite' body, its individual component parts were legally limited to their defined powers.[45] However, where sovereignty lay in a unitary body, or where the composite body acted under its plenary powers, it could only be limited by positive morality. Under this theory, the sovereign body would be deterred from passing 'unconstitutional' laws only by the fear that the people would cease to obey. Thus, the Parliament of the United Kingdom, or the bodies with the power to amend the United States Constitution might have the full *legal* power to transfer all political power to a despot; but whether the despot would then be obeyed was a matter of social fact.[46] It was for that reason that Austin argued that 'constitutional law' was different in nature from positive law, being 'a compound of positive morality and positive law, which fixes the constitution or structure of the given supreme government'. What differentiated it from positive law was the nature of the sanction: whether constitutional law took the form of express promises by the sovereign 'or simply consists of principles current in the political community',[47] it was enforced by the indeterminate sanction of public opinion.

At the same time, Hart was surely correct to point out that Austin's theory of the nature of sovereign power was at best incomplete. Even if his concept of the habit of obedience was able to explain how the community conferred authority on the sovereign power, it said nothing about how that sovereign power was itself legally constituted or how it might be legally limited. While a habit of obedience might account for the sovereignty of a simple monarch, it was not able properly to account for sovereignty in states in which the authority of particular power-holders itself derived from law. Austin's difficulty derived from the fact that he conceived of the sovereign in terms of humans holding power over others. '[T]he one or the number which is sovereign' had to be a determinate individual or body of persons, for if it were not so determinate 'it could not command expressly or tacitly, and could not be an object of obedience'.[48] He ran into considerable difficulties when trying to identify the actual people who

[45] See Austin 1873: 279. [46] See Austin 1873: 275. [47] Austin 1873: 274.
[48] Austin 1873: 196 and also 174, 181, 225–6, 229.

held such power in complex constitutional systems. In the United Kingdom, he located it in the Crown, the Lords and those people who elected the members of the House of Commons.[49] This was clearly a flawed definition: electors were not a determinate body whose commands were obeyed by their representatives.[50] Austin also ran into difficulties when seeking to locate the actual people who held unlimited sovereign power in the United States. In a footnote, he appeared to locate sovereignty in the 'aggregate body' which had to approve changes to the constitution, according to the mechanisms set out in the constitution itself.[51]

Austin expanded on his understanding of the American constitution in an article on 'Centralization' published in 1847. Austin may by now have realised the artificiality of describing a process which had not occurred in his adult lifetime as the sovereign power whose commands were obeyed by the bulk of the people.[52] For he now drew a distinction between 'constituent or latent' sovereigns and 'active or ostensible' ones. In the United States, the body which framed the constitution – the original constitutional convention and the succeeding aggregated bodies with power to amend it – was 'merely constituent': 'It defines the constitution and attributes of the federal government, and thus modifies (by implication) the powers of the states' governments. It leaves, however, the ordinary business of a government to those respective authorities.'[53] Austin saw that, in some states, the sovereign body might itself exercise political power (though, even here, much was delegated to functionaries), while, in others, those who enacted and administered the ordinary positive law which was obeyed by the people were not themselves sovereign but derived their power from another source.

Austin did not develop this theory in any detail, to acknowledge that the source of the power exercised by those who made laws and issued commands to officials might itself derive from a power-conferring law, such as

[49] See Austin 1873: 253.

[50] In the end, Austin had to admit that the only way in which the electors could themselves impose legal constraints on their representatives was if they were themselves part of a superior legislating body, such as a constitutional convention; Austin 1873: 254–5.

[51] Austin 1873: 268.

[52] The twelfth amendment to the American constitution came in 1804, when Austin was fourteen, and the thirteenth amendment passed in 1865, just over five years after his death.

[53] Austin 1847: 228.

a constitution. He did not explain how a *constitution* might be regarded as authoritative, and be enforced in the courts. Even in his late work, he still clung to the notion that the source of all legal powers in a state was a sovereign made up of determinate persons who were obeyed by the bulk of the population. It was at best highly artificial to describe the American people as being in a habit of obeying the will of that complex aggregate body which had the power to meet and change the constitution but chose not to do so, and thereby by implication reaffirmed the existing provisions and commanded people to follow the rules derived from it. But it was impossible under his theory to account for constitutions which lacked amendment provisions, as where a constitution might have been framed by a particular body of people meeting in a convention which later disbanded, and consequently no longer existed to be obeyed. Such a constitutional document was itself a legal instrument created by a set of people whose authority to have done so was accepted by the people, which then conferred legal powers on other people – such as the officials within the system who were given power to issue the commands that Austin expected people to obey. It could not itself be explained in terms of a habit of obeying a set of political superiors.

Austin perceived that the rules which constituted the state were different in nature from the rules which emanated from the state, and that the latter were tools of power-holders exercising them for particular purposes in a way that the former were not. His analysis of the rules which constituted the state was in the end flawed and undeveloped, and he failed to recognise that there was – at least in states with distinct constitutional law – another layer to be explained, which lay between the social rule or habit which underpinned the legal system and the laws generated by the law-makers in the state. However, this may have been so because his main interest was to identify and explain how law worked within the unitary British state, where the Crown in Parliament had full plenary powers.

His concern to define positive law in terms of the commands of determinate persons reflected his conception of the state as a political entity defined by its use of coercion to enforce its rules. This contrasts strongly with Hart's theory, in which the state itself is marginalised. Not resting on the coercive apparatus of the state, Hart's theory can also envisage a perfectly law-obedient society operating without having to apply any sanctions, where all citizens simply accept the authority of the ruler to guide them. Austin associated this kind of society with an anarchist vision which envisaged a society without any government, 'without a commanding head and without law which properly commands'.[54] He could not himself imagine a modern political society holding together without a ruler: and, in his view, any rules which merely coordinated social interaction, without any sanction expressed, were not properly *laws*. In Austin's vision, what ultimately defined the state and its laws was official enforcement by coercive means. Thus far, he appears to have shared Weber's conception of the state as the body which claimed the monopoly of the legitimate use of physical violence in a territory: and it was this aspect which his definition of law sought to account for. Austin's theory of law thus sought to identify the law of the state and to explain its nature; but, by focusing on the determinate individuals who exercised the state's powers, he omitted to explain fully the legal nature of these powers.

10.4 Law and Morality

One of the main reasons Austin had for defining law in terms of imperative rules set by a sovereign was to distinguish the law of the state from moral rules. This entailed two different ambitions: to distinguish the rules of law from rules of morality which were followed in society; and to distinguish the rules which actually applied in society from the rules which moral philosophers or theologians argued ought to govern human conduct.

The first of these aims was an entirely practical one: the student seeking to identify what was law needed to know how to distinguish it from other social norms. The feature which defined positive law as opposed to positive morality was that it was enforced at the behest of an identifiable superior sovereign. What distinguished rules of positive morality – which might embrace both the rules of fashion and the rules of international law[55] – was that they were not derived from sovereign commands, and were not 'clothed with legal sanctions'.[56] Both their source and their method of enforcement were indeterminate. They were set by the general opinion of a class of people, and did not express a single wish, in the form of a command armed with a determinate 'legal' sanction.[57] If the community's rule were breached, it would generate displeasure, and 'in

[54] Austin 1873: 790. [55] See Austin 1873: 89–90. [56] Austin 1873: 184.
[57] See Austin 1873: 189.

consequence of that displeasure, it is likely that *some* party (*what* party being undetermined) will visit the party provoking it with some evil or another'.[58] While the norms of positive morality might be enforced, it would never be certain exactly who the enforcer would be. However, such rules were 'closely analogous' to such 'proper' laws and were a proper object of study. Like the rules of positive law, the rules of positive morality could be identified without regard to their goodness or badness: the jurist could study what moral rules *were* acted on without asking the deontological question of what moral rules *should be* acted on.[59] Austin was also aware that the rules of positive law and the norms of positive morality might conflict (as in the case of whether duelling was permissible); and so a well-informed legislator needed to be aware of the moral or religious sentiments of a community, to avoid passing superfluous or impotent laws.[60]

Although Austin's description of international law as an aspect of 'positive morality' was widely criticised, he did consider it as a body of rules which were applied in practice by human actors who considered them to be binding and who acted on them.[61] Indeed, he even described 'international law' as 'the law obtaining between nations, [which] regards the conduct of sovereigns as related to one another'.[62] The point of his seeking to classify it jurisprudentially as something different from 'positive law' was to indicate that it was a different kind of norm from those found within the state. The key difference was that the sanctions imposed for breach were not by his definition 'legal' (deriving from a determinate sovereign); they were 'moral', since they rested on 'fear on the part of ... sovereigns, of provoking general hostility, and incurring probable evils, in case they shall violate maxims generally received and respected'.[63] Critics objected to his classification of international law as 'positive morality' on the grounds that it seemed to downgrade the normative force of its rules, but Austin's point that international law was different in nature, and needed to be distinguished from municipal law, was sound.

Austin's view that customary rules acquire legal force only when they have been given the character of law by the legislator, either directly or through a judicial decision,[64] was also challenged by jurists who argued

[58] Austin 1873: 188. [59] See Austin 1873: 176. [60] See Austin 1873: 203.
[61] See Austin 1873: 189–90. [62] Austin 1873: 231. [63] Austin 1873: 232.
[64] Austin 1873: 37. See also his rejection of the German view that the sovereign enforced only the customary laws which were already legally obligatory; Austin 1873: 103.

that customs are enforced by the courts because they are already regarded as binding legal norms.[65] However, if it is borne in mind that Austin was writing about the law in the modern political societies of his day, rather than for any historical society, then his point may seem less contentious. According to his argument, it could not be known whether a custom was part of the legal system until it had been enforced by a court, or incorporated by legislation, even though such customs might be followed in the community. As a statement of English law in his era, this was perhaps not far off the mark: 'general custom' was in effect nothing other than the common law, whose origins might have been admitted to be customary but whose rules were entirely fashioned by the courts; while particular local customs were only (retrospectively) admitted as law if they passed certain tests regarding their age, continued use and reasonableness. Austin's desire was to distinguish the rules which were part of the legal system from other norms. In his view, the simple fact that certain norms were customarily observed in the community did not *ipso facto* make them laws.

Austin's second aim was to show that there was no necessary connection between law (or morality) as it was and law (or morality) as it ought to be. The study of positive law or positive morality was in essence a study of the facts of human conduct, whereas the study of legislation or deontology was the study of matters of ethics. As he put it, '[t]he existence of law is one thing; its merit or demerit is another . . . A law, which actually exists, is a law, though we happen to dislike it.'[66] Austin ridiculed the familiar trope of natural law jurisprudence that God's laws were superior in obligation to all other laws, and that no human law could be allowed to contradict them: '[T]o say that human laws which conflict with the divine law are not binding, that is to say, are not laws, is to talk stark nonsense.'[67] Pernicious laws were routinely enforced as laws by judicial tribunals.

Austin's aim, like Bentham's, was to show that those seeking to identify which laws would be enforced by the sovereign authority could not find their answer by looking directly to the content of natural law. In his view, there was no certain way for humans to know what the law of nature was, assuming (as he did) that 'natural law' was that part of divine law not to be known from revelation.[68] Austin rejected the theory that it could be known through a moral sense, or instinct.[69] His scepticism led him to conclude (in

[65] See Maine 1871: 65–102; see also Holland 1880: 47. [66] Austin 1873: 220n.
[67] Austin 1873: 221n. [68] See Austin 1873: 106. [69] See Austin 1873: 152–6.

Benthamic vein) that notions such as the 'moral sense, innate practical principles [and] conscience' were 'merely convenient cloaks for ignorance or sinister interest: they mean either that I hate the law to which I object and cannot tell why, or that I hate the law, and that the cause of my hatred is one which I find it incommodious to avow'.[70] Those who claimed that the law in a state was not to be obeyed because it violated the law of nature were simply inviting anarchy without attempting to explain why the law was pernicious.

Austin argued that the principle of utility was a much better index to divine law, and he spent considerable time in discussing this principle. This has sometimes been a cause of puzzlement for Austin's critics, since his jurisprudence – premised as it was on the strict separation of law and morality – seemed to be compatible with any moral theory.[71] There was, however, good reason for its inclusion, since it was part of his armoury both for explaining why the theory of moral sense had to be rejected and for showing why citizens had to look to the positive law of the state for guidance. Unlike Bentham, Austin believed that there was a divine law, which was both a proper form of law and the test of all human law and morality. However, since they had not been revealed directly to man, most of God's laws were 'signified obscurely to those upon whom they are binding, and ... [were] subject to inevitable and involuntary misconstruction'.[72] The closest approximation which could be had was to use the principle of utility as an index or guide to the unrevealed law of God.[73] Although utility was not an infallible guide to the divine will,[74] it was a more reliable guide than the moral sense. It encouraged people to give reasons why they disliked a particular law, by questioning its utility instead of denouncing it in vague terms.

Austin famously set out a rule-utilitarian theory. To uncover God's law via the application of the principle of utility, it was necessary to consider the tendency of the class of actions involved. While it might be harmless for a poor man to steal from a rich neighbour, theft in general would be harmful: and hence one needed a rule against it, in order to guide action. Austin argued that it had to be assumed that God forbade actions such as theft '*without exception*', so that fear of his punishment would induce people to obey (else 'we should frequently *stretch* the exception to cases

[70] Austin 1873: 221n. [71] See Maine 1875: 344. [72] Austin 1873: 142.
[73] See Austin 1873: 109. [74] See Austin 1873: 221n.

embraced by the rule').[75] Setting out his theory of utility, Austin expected people to follow rules which had become settled in their memory, and to which particular sentiments had become attached from 'previous habits of thought' and education.[76] His belief that individuals should follow rules rather than make direct-utility calculations themselves seems to have rested on two foundations. The first was the assumption that individuals would always give themselves the benefit of any doubt, and might err if they assumed that their case fell in the class of exceptions that God would forgive. The second was the belief that the science of ethics (like the science of political economy) was a complicated matter which the masses could not understand, at least without further education. In the meantime, it was safer for the public to follow settled rules. '[I]f a system of law or morality were exactly fashioned to utility, its constituent *rules* might be known by all or most', he noted, but the reasons on which it was based would need to be taken 'on *authority*, *testimony*, or *trust*'.[77]

Although Austin counselled individuals in general to be rule-utilitarians, he qualified this in one important way: individuals would always make their own ultimate judgment on the utility of obeying the rule. On occasion, he noted, 'the evil of observing the rule might surpass the evil of breaking it'.[78] In such cases, individuals should shape their conduct by a direct appeal to utility. The example he gave was of the citizen's decision to break the divine command to give obedience to established governments, in cases when the mischiefs generated by a bad government exceeded the mischiefs of anarchy. The ultimate decision of whether or not to obey governments would be a direct-utility decision. Nor was it only in such cases that the individual might weigh the utility of particular rules. In one of his later lectures, Austin criticised the distinction traditionally made by jurists between *mala in se* – violations of natural law rules – and *mala prohibita* – violations of rules introduced in particular societies for reasons of utility. Austin retorted that both kinds were equally useful in their contexts, and so might equally be inferred to be the divine will: what jurists described as *mala in se* were simply positive rules which were universally followed since their utility was universally perceived. This raised the question of how to respond if the law set by a particular country were pernicious? In answering this, Austin adapted the traditional

[75] Austin 1873: 112. [76] Austin 1873: 120. [77] Austin 1873: 127.
[78] Austin 1873: 121.

terminology to his own uses. Where the law was a good one, he argued, its breach would constitute *malum in se*; where the law was a mischievous one, but to break it would have mischievous consequences (such as encouraging violations of beneficent obligations), its breach would be *malum prohibitum*; and where no mischievous consequences followed the breach, it would be an 'innocuous offence' which would not violate the law of God or Nature.[79] Putting together Austin's discussion of disobedience in these two places, it can be seen that he felt that the citizen would be justified in disobeying any pernicious laws, if in doing so he did not undermine the entire system of laws; and he would be justified in disobeying pernicious laws and undermining the entire legal system if the evils of continued obedience outweighed the benefits of revolution. All this seemed to suggest that, from the individual's point of view, the default rule-utilitarianism might always be overridden by direct-utility decisions.

The importance of rule-utilitarianism for Austin becomes more evident if we consider utility as a guide for legislators. Austin conceded that the laws made by human sovereigns would never 'accord completely and correctly' with divine laws, since they could only be imperfectly known by induction and observation from the tendencies of human actions.[80] Under these circumstances, legislators were best placed to fashion rules for the guidance of society: while one might not be certain that the legislated rule accorded with the divine will, it was the best approximation which could be hoped for. Those who challenged whether a law really did accord with the divine will were invited by Austin to set forth clear reasons grounded on 'determinate views of *utility*', which might lead to its abrogation,[81] but were expected save *in extremis* to continue to obey the law. In some respects, this reflects a Hobbesian view that humans can never have certain knowledge of what the law of nature dictates, and so need to be guided by the sovereign. Unlike Hobbes, however, the utilitarian Austin always permitted the individual to rest his ultimate obedience to the sovereign on his own utilitarian calculation.

10.5 Legal Reasoning and Judge-Made Law

One criticism which has been made of Austin's definition of jurisprudence is that it took an excessively narrow analytical approach, excluding from

[79] Austin 1873: 591. [80] Austin 1873: 144. [81] Austin 1873: 221n.

its province the question of how judges were to reason.[82] Although Austin did not set out a theory of adjudication, he did give some indications as to how judges were to identify and apply the law. When it came to statutes, he felt that the literal meaning of the words was generally to be followed by the judges.[83] Austin disapproved of the kind of 'equitable' interpretation whereby judges looked for the underlying reason of a statute and inferred a legislative will to apply it to a case not covered by it.[84] Such an approach, he thought, rendered the law uncertain[85] and tempted judges to legislate against the will of the law-maker.[86] However, he did acknowledge that where the meaning of the legislator was ambiguous, the court had to look to the *ratio legis*, using 'the reason of the law as its index or guide'.[87]

If judges were to look to the *ratio legis* only rarely when engaged in statutory interpretation, Austin expected them routinely to seek out the *ratio decidendi* of decided cases when identifying the rules of 'judiciary law'. Since the language used by a judge in a case gave only 'faint traces from which the principle may be conjectured',[88] it was not possible to use the kind of literal approach used in interpreting statutes. Regarding the *ratio decidendi* as the law, and not simply the reason underpinning a distinct law, he spoke of the process of uncovering it as one of 'induction' rather than 'interpretation' (though he regarded it as 'analogous' in nature).[89] The process of uncovering the *ratio decidendi* required the jurist to seek resemblances among cases and to extract a rule. Austin admitted that this was an imperfect way to identify what was the law, for there was no certain 'test by which the validity of a rule made judicially can be ascertained'.[90] It could never be absolutely certain that the rule would be followed in the future by other judges. This concession not only admitted the artificiality of describing the rules and principles to be teased out of case law as implicit commands of the legislator; it also seemed to raise questions about Austin's separation of law and morality. For this process of inducing the rule from the case appeared to be to some degree an

[82] See Halpin 2013. [83] See Austin 1873: 644. [84] See Austin 1873: 597.
[85] See Austin 1873: 599.
[86] He admitted that there were times when judges extended or restricted the wording used in a statute, by seeking to make it fit the end or purpose for which it was originally intended: but he suggested that when judges did this, they were in fact engaged in an act of legislation, and not of interpretation. Austin 1873: 650.
[87] Austin 1873: 597. [88] Austin 1873: 561. [89] Austin 1873: 650.
[90] Austin 1873: 677.

evaluative exercise. When the judge looked to the 'general reasons' given by a previous court, abstracted from the 'peculiarities of the case' in order to tease out the principle of the decision,[91] he had to make a judgment on the purpose which the court had in mind: what the decision, and the principle underlying it, was seeking to achieve. In seeking resemblances and differences among sets of different cases, the judge was equally required to decide which rule should apply in the case before him, which also required an evaluation of purposes. This might suggest that, at least in cases which were not squarely covered by precedent, judges seeking to know what the law to be applied *was* would invariably also be faced with the question of what the law *should be*, potentially undermining his distinction between law and morality. Indeed, Austin's very notion of 'judiciary law' appeared to mingle adjudication and legislation. Although, at some points, he argued that judges applied an existing set of rules to be found in the case law,[92] he also described judiciary law as a whole as 'law made by judicial or improper legislation'.[93] Austin's view seems to have been that, in some cases, the judge could infer a rule from past cases without legislating: as where there was a single case on which a rule was founded, or a series of resembling cases applying the same rule.[94] In other cases, however, laws were made 'judicially' on the occasion of a decision.[95] Here, Austin argued, the judge 'legislates *as properly judging*, and not *as properly legislating'*.[96] This was at least to concede the overlap between legislation and adjudication.

If they overlapped in the process of adjudication, however, they were still in Austin's mind distinct concepts: moral norms were not of themselves part of law until they had been applied by a judge. He specifically rejected the notion that there were multiple sources of law which were binding, independently of the exercise of the sovereign will. He therefore argued that it was an error to regard customary law, the opinions and practices of lawyers or the law of nature as 'sources' of law: they were rather 'various causes' which 'suggested' judiciary law. Judges might adopt

91 Austin 1873: 643.

92 Thus, Austin (1873: 149) spoke of 'the process of induction, by which a rule made judicially is collected from decided cases'.

93 Austin 1873: 641.

94 See Austin 1873: 654.

95 'Where there is no rule in the system applicable to the case, the judge virtually makes one, if he decides at all, or decides on any general ground' (Austin 1873: 659–60).

96 Austin 1873: 642.

a custom, or follow the opinion of jurists or natural lawyers, or they might incorporate rules from the law of nations; but, until they had done so, this was not positive law.[97] When Austin turned in his (extremely brief) discussion to the question of how judges developed the law, he focused on only two methods (which he suggested were historically sequential). Firstly, having adopted customary rules, judges extended them by consequence or analogy. Secondly, they established rules '*ex proprio arbitrio*: *i.e.* according to their own notions of what *ought* to be the law, whether the standard be utility or any other'.[98] This was, in fact, a well-established common lawyer's view, which saw judges as simply elaborating the already accepted principles of the common law, and resorting to abstract 'reason' only when the precedents ran out.[99] Insofar as they were developing the common law, they were legislating as they went along: they were not simply applying an already obliging set of norms. Unlike some of his successors, Austin did not think that the judges were guided by an underlying purpose, such as the pursuit of justice.[100] For him, the very notion of 'justice' would have fallen foul of the same objections that he put to the moral sense: it was too subjective and indeterminate. Judges were to follow the rules to be found in the legal system: where they ran out, he expected them to resort to utility, as he expected the legislator also to do.

References

Austin, J. 1847. 'Centralization'. *Edinburgh Review* 85: 221–58.

Austin, J. 1873. *Lectures on Jurisprudence.* 4th ed. Ed. R. Campbell. John Murray.

Bentham, J. 1970. *An Introduction to the Principles of Morals and Legislation.* Eds. J. H. Burns and H. L. A. Hart. Athlone Press.

Bentham, J. 1977. *A Comment on the Commentaries and a Fragment on Government.* Eds. J. H. Burns and H. L. A. Hart. Athlone Press.

Bentham, J. 2010. *Of the Limits of the Penal Branch of Jurisprudence.* Ed. P. Schofield. Oxford University Press.

Cotterrell, R. 2003. *The Politics of Jurisprudence.* Oxford University Press.

Hale, M. 1713. *The History and Analysis of the Common Law of England.* J. Walthoe.

[97] Austin 1873: 551 and see also 560. [98] Austin 1873: 655.

[99] Hale 1713: 69–70, referred to in Austin 1873: 660. [100] See Salmond 1902: 16–17.

Halpin, A. 2013. 'Austin's Methodology? His Bequest to Jurisprudence'. In M. Freeman and P. Mindus (eds.). *The Legacy of John Austin's Jurisprudence*. Springer: 15–40.

Harrison, F. 1878. 'The English School of Jurisprudence'. *Fortnightly Review* 24: 682–703.

Hart, H. L. A. 1961. *The Concept of Law*. Clarendon Press.

Holland, T. E. 1880. *Elements of Jurisprudence*. Clarendon Press.

Kramer, M. H. 2013. 'John Austin on Punishment'. In L. Green and B. Leiter (eds.). *Oxford Studies in Philosophy of Law* vol. 2. Oxford University Press: 103–21.

Lobban, M. 1991. *The Common Law and English Jurisprudence*. Clarendon Press.

Lobban, M. 2013. 'Austin and the Germans'. In M. Freeman and P. Mindus (eds.). *The Legacy of John Austin's Jurisprudence*. Springer: 255–70.

Maine, H. S. 1861. *Ancient Law: Its Connection with the Early History of Society and Its Relation to Modern Ideas*. John Murray.

Maine, H. S. 1871. *Village Communities in the East and West*. John Murray.

Maine, H. S. 1875. *Lectures on the Early History of Institutions*. John Murray.

Markby, W. 1871. *Elements of Law, Considered with Reference to Principles of General Jurisprudence*. Clarendon Press.

Paley, W. 1785. *The Principles of Moral and Political Philosophy*. R. Faulder.

Raz, J. 1980. *The Concept of a Legal System: An Introduction to the Theory of a Legal System*. 2nd ed. Clarendon Press.

Salmond, J. W. 1902. *Jurisprudence, or the Theory of the Law*. 2nd ed. Stevens and Haynes.

Schwarz, A. B. 1934–5. 'John Austin and the German Jurisprudence of His Time'. *Politica* 1: 178–99.

11 The Normative Power of the Factual: Georg Jellinek's Phenomenological Theory of Reflective Legal Positivism

Jens Kersten

11.1 Introduction

When contemporary jurisprudence discusses legal positivism, the focus lies on the ambivalent relationship between legal and moral standards. In a more traditional understanding, however, legal positivism concentrates not only on the dualism of legality versus morality but also on an epistemological triangle that distinguishes between three worlds: the world of facts, the world of morality and the world of law. In this triangle, we are used to the suspenseful 'relationship' of law and morality, whereas the 'relationship' of facts and law sounds unfamiliar because we are inclined to understand law and legal rules as a 'social practice' today. Even if we do so, we still have to make a difference between a simple individual habit or social custom and a social behaviour that follows a legal rule. For this reason, legal positivists always have to concentrate on all three elements of the triangle: facts, morality and law. Positivists must not conclude, for example, that a factual habit is automatically legal; and the identification of moral values does not instantly turn them into legal rules. There is no bypass from the factual world to the world of morality, and there are no 'shortcuts' from the factual and moral worlds to the world of law. If we want to create a legal rule, we need a normative act of recognition. An individual habit or social custom itself does not create a legal rule. However, a common practice that is accompanied by the normative conviction that it should be legally binding may result in customary law. Moreover, additional ways to recognise legal norms and decisions have been institutionalised by the modern state: Parliament passes laws, government makes decisions, courts pronounce judgments. Thomas Hobbes phrased this in a nutshell: *Auctoritas non veritas facit legem*. The authority, not the truth, makes the law – and we might add that facts and morality do not make law either.

Since legal positivism insists on this difference between facts, morality and law, this distinction has been challenged. The legal history of the twentieth century, for example, cannot be understood without the knowledge of the controversy between legal positivism and natural law. In Germany, this dispute culminates in the question of the legitimacy and legality of the legal system of National Socialism with all its violence and crimes, with World War II and the Shoah. In 1946, Gustav Radbruch tried to 'solve' this controversy with his well-known formula: 'The positive law, secured by legislation and power, takes precedence even when its content is unjust and fails to benefit the people, unless the conflict between statute and justice reaches such an intolerable degree that the statute, as "flawed law", must yield to justice.'[1] But the question of the relationship between facts, morality and law is not only evident in the extreme and existentialistic context of totalitarian dictatorship. Legal positivism is confronted with these questions in the everyday practice of law as well: What happens if a legal rule is not applied as intended by the legislator in the social, political and economic world? How can we explain the 'legal fact' that statutes change their regulatory impact under changing social, political and economic circumstances? And, with respect to the relationship of morality and law, legal positivists have to cope, for example, with the problem that sweeping clauses in civil and administrative law refer to moral standards of individuals and society. How is this possible? Is the law – in these cases – moralised; or – the other way around – are morals legalised? Some legal positivists might think that they enjoy the methodological privilege to ignore these questions and simply apply legal rules without asking how they relate to factual situations and moral ideas. If legal positivists, however, want to answer these questions, they might turn to Georg Jellinek (1851–1911), who developed a phenomenological theory of reflective legal positivism.

This chapter offers an introduction into Jellinek's phenomenological theory of reflective legal positivism. It starts, in Section 11.2, with a short survey of Jellinek's life, work and teaching in Vienna and Heidelberg in the second half of the nineteenth and the beginning of the twentieth century: Why did legal positivism suddenly become a too tight paradigm

[1] Radbruch 2006: 7.

of legal thinking in public law? Section 11.3 focuses on Jellinek's epistemological reaction to this crisis of legal positivism: Why was and is a critique of legal judgment so important? In Section 11.4, we look at Jellinek's social and legal definition of the state: How does his central methodological paradigm of a social and a legal 'side' of the state work? Section 11.5 discusses – last but not least – the bridges that Jellinek builds to cross the uncanny valley between social analysis and legal construction of constitutional institutions: Are these bridges (still) methodologically solid? Section 11.6 concludes.

11.2 Vienna and Heidelberg

Georg Jellinek was born on 16 June 1851 in Leipzig.[2] His father, Adolf Jellinek (1821–93), was a renowned Jewish scholar and liberal preacher in Leipzig and Vienna, where the Jellineks lived from 1856. Georg Jellinek's liberal uncle Hermann Jellinek (1823–48) was executed because of his political and journalistic commitment against the reactionary system of Metternich in the revolution of 1848. This arbitrary act of the reactionary ancien regime shaped Georg Jellinek's liberal convictions. The sympathy for the liberal German Constitution of 1849, written and enacted by the national assembly in Frankfurt and overthrown by German monarchs and their military, influenced his scientific work and political engagement. Jellinek studied philosophy and law in Vienna, Heidelberg and Leipzig. In 1872, he received his doctorate in philosophy from the University of Leipzig with a thesis on optimism and pessimism in the philosophies of Leibniz and Schopenhauer.[3] After his legal dissertation in Vienna, Jellinek began an academic career that was overshadowed from the very beginning by anti-Semitic discrimination. In 1878, Jellinek's work on *The Socio-Ethical Meaning of Law, Injustice and Punishment*[4] was rejected by the Vienna Faculty of Law as a habilitation thesis. In this monograph, Jellinek tried to build his first bridges between social analysis and legal construction: He describes law as the 'ethical minimum' of a society; and his attempt to develop a social-psychological approach to social ethics and

[2] See Kersten 2000: 17–30; Kersten 2018; Anter 2004. Also see Kempter 1998 for a comprehensive family biography of the Jellineks from 1820 to 1955.

[3] Jellinek 1872. [4] Jellinek 1878.

criminal law had a wide and sustainable impact on criminology, social science and legal philosophy, influencing, for example, Émile Durkheim.[5] With respect to further publications on criminal law and criminology, the Vienna Faculty granted Jellinek in 1879 the *venia legendi* – the right to lecture – for legal philosophy and in 1880 for international law.

In the following years, Jellinek expanded his research in international law. Here again, he was confronted with the profound breach between the political world of the states and the legal understanding of sovereignty: Whereas an international community with various types of treaty and other forms of bilateral and multilateral cooperation had developed in the social world, lawyers and legal scholars still understood the sovereignty of states as the legal capacity of a perfectly free and arbitrary political power acting without any legal restrictions. So Jellinek challenged the traditional legal understanding of sovereignty. In two monographs on *The Legal Nature of State-Treaties*[6] and *The Theory of the Associations of States*,[7] he developed his legal concept of sovereignty as a legal self- or auto-limitation of political power: Sovereignty does not give states the right to do what they want. Quite contrarily, sovereignty rather – according to Jellinek – needs to be understood as the capacity of states to enter into legally binding obligations. We will discuss this widely disputed theory of the legal auto-limitation in more detail in Sections 11.4 and 11.5, as it is one of Jellinek's central concepts linking the social and legal worlds. This concept exemplifies Jellinek's work: As a legal positivist, he asks whether the concepts of positive law can cope with new social phenomena. If the positive law is not capable of handling these new social developments, Jellinek suggests new legal constructions aiming to bridge the gap between the social and the legal world. In the case of sovereignty and international law, this bridge is the concept of legal auto-limitation of political power: The factual, free political will of the state binds itself normatively by entering into legal obligations and has no capacity (anymore) to free itself from these legal obligations with the simple reference to sovereignty. As such, social analysis of the development of an international community of states leads to a change of the legal construction of positive law by a new understanding of the factual and the normative power of states in a politically changing world. In 1887, Jellinek applied this innovative approach to administrative and constitutional law. He uses his concept of

[5] See Gephart 1993: 326. [6] Jellinek 1880. [7] Jellinek 1882.

legal auto-limitation of the will of the state in his monograph *Statute and Ordinance* to unfold a system of legal forms of regulation in public law.[8]

Despite the fact that Jellinek had already developed an academic reputation that reached far beyond Vienna and Austria, his appointment as an extraordinary and then as a full professor at the Vienna Faculty of Law failed several times between 1883 and 1889. Because of this anti-Semitic discrimination, Jellinek resigned from the University of Vienna in 1889. This academic demission led to a vivid reaction in the German-speaking legal word. In the same year, the Faculty of Law of the University of Berlin announced the habilitation of Georg Jellinek. After a short academic interlude at the University of Basel, Jellinek was appointed as a full professor at the Faculty of Law of the University of Heidelberg and there, from 1891 until his death twenty years later, he taught legal philosophy, politics and state theory, public and international law with a growing international reputation.[9] He became part of the 'academic myth' of Heidelberg on the turn into the twentieth century. Especially his friendship with Max Weber was an inspiration for both scholars. Although this relationship between Jellinek and Weber was not without academic and personal tensions, it encouraged Jellinek to open his phenomenological theory of reflective legal positivism for sociology and political science.[10] In Heidelberg, Jellinek wrote his international bestsellers: in 1892 his favourite book on the *System of Subjective Public Rights*,[11] in which he uses the idea of the legal auto-limitation of political power to unfold four dimensions of civil rights; in 1895 his small but very influential and – again – highly disputed study on *The Declaration of the Rights of Man and of Citizens*, in which he argues that the historical origins of human rights lie not primarily in the French Revolution but in the Anglo-American struggle for the freedom of faith and conscience;[12] and – of course – in 1900 his *General Theory of the State*,[13] which is the intellectual and systematic capstone of his scientific work. In all these monographs, Jellinek uses his 'two-sided doctrine' (*Zwei-Seiten-Lehre*) of legal institutions and especially of the state to develop his phenomenological theory of reflective legal positivism. This approach distinguishes between a social and a legal side of institutions

[8] Jellinek 1887. [9] Jellinek 2016; see Ziemann and Funke 2016.
[10] See Breuer 1999; Anter 2000, 2016a, 2016b: 25–46; Kersten 2000: 123–7.
[11] Jellinek 1892, 1905a. [12] Jellinek 1895, 1901, 1904; Stolleis 2000; Kelly 2004.
[13] Jellinek 1900, 1905b, 1914; Kersten 2000: 266–303.

and looks, at the same time, for connections between these two sides. On this methodological ground, he developed a phenomenological concept to analyse the evolutionary development of constitutions in his monograph *Constitutional Amendment and Constitutional Change* (1906).[14] Importantly, Jellinek did not just reflect on the tensions of social development, political life and legal order protected in the academic ivory tower; he was a public intellectual. He argued, for example, in favour of the establishment of constitutional courts (1885),[15] he intervened in the Badeni Crisis (1897–8)[16] and he pleaded – in the Daily Telegraph Affair (1908–9) – for the establishment of a parliamentary government in the political crisis of the German Empire.[17] Georg Jellinek's wife Camilla Jellinek, *née* Wertheim (1860–1940), was very active in the Women's Movement especially with regard to legal aid for women and the reform of criminal law. Jellinek died on 11 January 1911 in Heidelberg.

11.3 Critique of Legal Judgment

Georg Jellinek was – in Vienna and in Heidelberg – a legal positivist who worked on a 'critique of legal judgment'.[18] With this methodological approach, Jellinek saw himself in a Kantian tradition: What are the epistemic foundations of legal reasoning?

To answer this question, we have to take a short look at the academic and scientific context of legal positivism in German public law in the second half of the nineteenth century. After the failed democratic revolution of 1848, liberal professors of public law – such as Robert von Mohl (1799–1875) and Caspar David Bluntschli (1808–81) – turned to the academic genres of *Staatswissenschaft* (state science) and *Allgemeine Staatslehre* (general theory of the state). In this way, they could avoid writing and lecturing on the positive law of the reactionary regime; instead, they did research on political and legal theory and concentrated on comparative and international law. After the foundation of the German Empire in 1871, a new school of legal positivism focused on the new,

[14] Jellinek 1906; see Wolff 2000; Kirste 2016.
[15] Jellinek 1885; see Kersten 2001: 224–31.
[16] Jellinek 1898, 1912; see Kersten 2001: 231–40.
[17] Jellinek 1909; see Schönberger 1998: 268–82.
[18] Jellinek 1905a: 13.

written constitution. Inspired by the clear-cut dogmatic methodology of civil law, Paul Laband (1838–1918) published *The State Law of the German Empire* (*Das Staatsrecht des Deutschen Reiches*).[19] While this may sound clumsy, it is important to note that Staatsrecht (state law) cannot simply be translated as *constitutional law*. Indeed, not the constitution but the state was the epistemological paradigm of this new school, being named 'legal positivism of the state' (*Staatsrechtlicher Positivismus*). Thus, with his *Staatsrecht*, Laband did not merely write a commentary on Bismarck's constitution but rather published an academic textbook in which he presented a positivistic construction of the state as a legal person whose 'will' is unfolded in a 'dogmatic' reconstruction of the written constitution. In this context, 'legal dogmatic' (*Rechtsdogmatik*) represented a 'system' of terms, concepts and rules of practical legal reasoning; 'legal person', 'state will', 'statute', 'budget' and 'government body' are the keywords. This concept of dogmatic legal reasoning has shaped constitutional and administrative law in Germany for the last 150 years. And, indeed, Laband's constructive power was – and still is today – epistemologically impressive. Of course, Laband and his school of legal positivism were not unpolitical.[20] They were – in general – conservatives, and their construction of the *Staatsrecht* was conservative as well. And it was not – or at least not primarily – the intention of Laband and his school to 'hide' their conservative political opinions 'behind' their legal dogmatics. There was nothing to 'hide' because, in their legal construction, the political affirmation of the authoritarian German Empire was quite obvious. But irrespective of this conservative political imprint, Laband and his school wanted to offer a 'pure' legal method that excluded all social, political and historical reflections from their legal dogmatics and constructions of the state:[21] the academic task of this legal positivism was the dogmatic construction of the law of the state as it was 'given', without any critical social or political reflection. And because Laband was a very good lawyer, he identified at once the social, political and historical 'troublemaker' that would 'contaminate' the 'pureness' of the positivistic and dogmatic approach to public law: the *Zweck im Recht*. Again, there is no straightforward translation of this term. This *Zweck im Recht* refers to the social,

[19] Pauly 1993; Stolleis 1999: 330–78; Kersten 2000: 31–68; Kelly 2004: 512–18.
[20] See Schlink 1992.
[21] See Laband 1876: VII–VIII; Laband 1880: 56–7; Kersten 2000: 58–63.

economic and political means, purpose or interests of legal rules, and to the social, economic and political function of law. According to Laband, any social and political interests and functions should be excluded from the definition of a legal term, right, good or institution.[22] In this social, political and historical abstinence of his legal construction, Laband wanted to guarantee the emancipation of his positivistic and dogmatic *Staatsrecht* from society and politics.

This attempt to immunise legal dogmatics against social, political and historical reflections and critique led into the methodological crisis of legal positivism in German public law, when – in the 1890s – the German Empire fell into its (final) social and political crisis.[23] This had a very simple reason: The legal construction of the *Staatsrecht* had been completed in the 1880s. And because Laband and his school of legal positivism did not allow social, political and historical reasoning and critique within their dogmatic canon of legal methods and positions, they were unable to reflect social, political and historical changes, and especially the political crisis of the German Empire, that began in the 1890s and ended in World War I. The brand new *Staatsrecht* of the 1870s became a political and legal fossil within only a few years. This was exactly the time when Georg Jellinek stepped in with his phenomenological theory of a reflective legal positivism. To put it in a nutshell: Jellinek 'rescued' legal positivism in public law in Germany. His phenomenological theory of reflective legal positivism saved German constitutional and administrative law from dogmatic sclerosis. In 1900, Jellinek reanimated the old liberal genre of the 'common theory of the state', which had been intellectually deserted since the German Empire was founded in 1871 because the majority of legal scholars had followed Laband's methodological postulate of legal positivism in public law. When Jellinek published his *General Theory of the State* in 1900, he brought back social, political, philosophical and historical reflection into legal construction, emphasised the methodological importance of comparative law, and was more than prepared to expand the scope of public law by including supranational and international law.[24]

But how can legal positivism open up to social, political and historical reflection? How was – and still is – interdisciplinary work possible?

[22] See Laband 1887: 317. [23] See Schönberger 2000: 10–13.

[24] For the renaissance of the general theory of the state around 1900, see Kersten 2000: 69–90.

Jellinek was, after all, a legal positivist himself. He was a (distant) member of Laband's school. That was why he wanted to preserve the dogmatic legal construction of the *Staatsrecht* but extend its perspective at the same time. Jellinek found the answer to this challenge in his 'two-sided doctrine' (*Zwei-Seiten-Lehre*): every institution – and especially the state – has two sides, a social and a legal side; and because the social and the legal perspective focus on the same object, the two sides can influence each other in the epistemic understanding of the object under examination. In his works, Jellinek has offered different versions of this two-sided doctrine. The most elaborated upon is found in his monograph on the *System of Subjective Public Rights.*[25] This book was an epistemic beacon in the *Staatsrecht* because Jellinek dedicated his *System* to Rudolf von Jhering (1818–92) – a famous scholar of civil law and intellectual father of a sociological school of law. Jhering argued that law is the legal expression of interests.[26] Therefore the crucial term of this approach was the *Zweck* (that is, purpose, interest, function) of legal institutions. This becomes quite obvious in the title of Jhering's monograph *Der Zweck im Recht* (*Law as Means to an End*),[27] which followed the motto: The *Zweck* is the creator of the whole law.[28] Quite to the contrary, we have just seen that Laband excluded the *Zweck* from the *Staatsrecht*. In contrast, with his reference to Jhering's work, Jellinek brought back the *Zweck* into public law. Accordingly, he defined the subjective public right as the legal ability of a person to set legal norms into legal actions to pursue individual interests.[29] This example of the subjective public right shows quite clearly that Jellinek understood legal institutions as 'teleological' entities that are constituted by social, economic and political interests. For Jellinek, it was evident that a change in social, economic and political interests will result in a change of legal institutions. With this understanding of interests in the law, Jellinek found a way to bring back epistemic flexibility to German public law in the crisis of the sclerotic *Staatsrecht* in the 1890s.

His epistemic tool to do this was the two-sided doctrine of legal institutions. In the *System of Subjective Public Rights*, Jellinek explains the epistemic fundament of this interdisciplinary approach of the two-sided doctrine with a famous example:[30] A symphony can be analysed

[25] Jellinek 1905a: 12–18. [26] See Jhering 1865: 327–9. [27] See Jhering 1913.
[28] See Jhering 1877, 1883. [29] See Jellinek 1905a: 51, 56–7, 79, 106, 112, 127, 196.
[30] See Jellinek 1905a: 14–15.

scientifically from different perspectives. In physiological and psychological considerations, a symphony does not exist as a constant object. For scientists, a symphony is a composition of air vibrations and sound sensations that give rise to tone upon integration of signals via the ears and the brain. For aestheticists, however, the symphony is an object of reality. Despite the fact that Jellinek refers epistemologically to Immanuel Kant when he calls this methodological reasoning a 'critique of legal judgment', he does not present or follow a neo-Kantian approach.[31] In neo-Kantian philosophy, scientific perspectives constitute their objects. This was a major point of critique with respect to Jellinek's methodological programme, put forward mainly by Hans Kelsen (1881–1973).[32] Jellinek was, however, not a neo-Kantian scholar. He argued, quite contrarily to the neo-Kantians, that a given object can be analysed by different scientific perspectives. The different disciplines describe this object according to their own methodological standards. That is why they can enter into an interdisciplinary discourse about this object without simply mixing their scientific methods.[33] In the end, the two-sided doctrine serves three strategic goals: On the legal side, this doctrine secures a save space for legal dogmatics and constructions in the tradition of Laband and his school: The state is a legal person, and public law is the construction of this legal person's will. On the social side, the two-sided doctrine opens up legal dogmatics and constructions to the kind of interdisciplinary dialogues with sociology and political science that began to develop as academic disciplines on the turn into the twentieth century. And third, the two-sided doctrine allows overcoming the crisis of public law in the 1890s, by reflecting the state as a teleological institution in its dynamic interdependence with society, politics and culture.

11.4 A General Theory of the State

In 1900, Jellinek published his *General Theory of the State*, which pulls together all the strings of his phenomenological theory of reflective legal positivism. The table of contents already announces the new epistemology: the first part of the book is dedicated to the methodological approach of the two-sided doctrine, whereas the second part presents the social analysis

[31] See Lepsius 2000. [32] See Kelsen 1922: 116; Kelsen 1928: 11.
[33] See Jellinek 1905a: 13–14; Jellinek 1914: 74.

and the third part the legal construction of the state. The new programme sounds easy: A state has two sides and three elements that have to be constructed by applying the concept of legal auto-limitation of political power.

First step: A state has two sides. According to the two-sided doctrine, the state has a social and a legal dimension. Jellinek does not define the state in itself. Like the example of the symphony (Section 11.3), the state in itself remains a distant object under interdisciplinary observation, taking shape only in the specific disciplinary perspectives of sociology and law.[34] In the social perspective, the state is a social-psychological synthesis of human relationships that are characterised by the exercise of political power. The function of the state develops with the purpose and interest (*Zweck*) that guide the exercise of power. Jellinek describes this development as an evolution from the national to the 'cultural state' (*Kulturstaat*), and from the 'cultural state' to the social and welfare state.[35] In the social perspective, the state is an original political power ruling people that live in a territory. In the legal perspective, Jellinek defines the state as a legal person, exercising sovereign legal power with respect to people on a territorial basis. These two definitions do reflect the three strategic goals of the two-sided doctrine (Section 11.3): the legal definition of the state allows the construction of the state as a legal person whose normative will has to reflect the dynamic development of the social functions of the state.

Second step: A state has two sides and *three elements*: people, territory and power. These three elements are – as we have seen – part of both definitions of the state. In social and legal terms, the state 'consists' of people, territory and power. Jellinek profiles his social and legal definition of the state as a typological term that focuses on elements that all political entities qualifying as states in the political world have in common. This way of typological profiling is well known in legal methodology, where it is used, for example, to establish 'the' contract as a general legal type that is then able to distinguish between different special types, for example purchase, lease, employment and so forth.[36] On first sight, Jellinek's general type of the state is quite different from the ideal type of state used by Max Weber in *Politics as a Vocation* (1919): 'Today, however, we have to

[34] Jellinek 1914: 174–83; see Kersten 2000: 269–78.

[35] Jellinek 1911; see Kersten 2000: 337–9. [36] See Kelly 2004: 519.

say, that the state is a human community that (successfully) claims the monopoly of the legitimate use of physical force within a given territory.'[37] While Jellinek 'counts' the three elements – people, territory and power – that states have generally in common, Weber focuses right away on the most interesting of these three elements: political power in the form of physical force. These differences of epistemological interests explain why Weber turned down the offer to continue Jellinek's *General Theory of the State* after Jellinek died in 1911. On the other hand, we must not underestimate the epistemological, political and legal success of Jellinek's three-elementary definition of the state. Epistemologically, Jellinek used this definition successfully to analyse the political world and identified a variety of specific variations: from federal to centralised states, from sovereign to non-sovereign states, from fragments to associations of states.[38] Politically, the three-elementary definition of the state became a cornerstone of international law.[39] And, legally, Jellinek was able to use the three elements for his normative construction of the state as a legal person integrating the legal positivism of his time, especially with Laband and his school.

Third step: A state has two sides and three elements *that have to be constructed by applying the concept of legal auto-limitation of political power.* Jellinek – like Weber – thought that political power is the key to understanding the modern state. Weber defines the state by its monopoly for the legitimate use of physical force. Quite contrarily, Jellinek characterises power as the central element of the state that structures all three elements politically, defines them legally and thereby transforms the state from a political entity into a legal person:[40] Firstly, the element of political power structures and defines the territory as the location where political government 'takes place' and where the laws of the state apply. Secondly, the element of political power structures and defines the political and legal status of the citizens in four dimensions:[41] the negative status of individual freedom, the positive status of rights to citizenship and public services, the active status of political and legal participation, and the passive status to execute laws and orders of the state. With respect to this theory of the four

[37] Weber 1946: 78. [38] See especially Jellinek 1896.

[39] See Art. 1 of the (Montevideo) Convention on the Rights and Duties of States (inter-American) 26 December 1933.

[40] Jellinek 1914: 394–434; Kelly 2004: 519–21; see Loughlin 2010: 192–4.

[41] Jellinek 1905a: 94–193; Jellinek 1914: 406–27; Pauly 2000; Kersten 2001, 2011.

status of citizens, Jellinek argues – as a liberal in the authoritarian German Empire – that political, cultural and social progress will result in an unfolding of the negative, positive and active status, while the passive status of the tributary subject – the German *Untertan* – will be more and more reduced.[42] Thirdly, political power structures and defines itself legally by binding itself to legal rules, especially to the constitution. With this act of legal auto-limitation, the state as a subject of political power transforms itself into a subject of law.[43] This maxim of legal auto-limitation of political power to become a legal person is one of the concepts that Jellinek offers to bridge the social and the legal side of the state, which shall be discussed in more detail in Section 11.5.

11.5 Social and Legal Perspectives

The two-sided doctrine calls for concepts that distinguish and interconnect the social and the legal dimensions of the state. Three of those concepts are discussed in the following: the concept of law, the legal concept of sovereignty, and the two rules of legal construction.

11.5.1 A Psychological Concept of Positive Law

The first paradigm to distinguish and connect facts and norms is Jellinek's concept of law itself. According to Jellinek, law is – like the state – a function of society. This social function of law is not primarily to protect goods but to structure social relationships and to give normative orientation in the social world. Therefore, Jellinek describes law as a normative concept that rests on a psychological fundament:[44] Laws are normative rules that unfold social effects through the thoughts and actions of humans. Because law shares this psychological mode with social, economic and religious rules, Jellinek defines law as a special type of norms:[45] A legal rule is a norm that (i) organises the 'external', social relationships of people, (ii) is given by an 'external', accepted lawmaker, and (iii) has its adherence guaranteed by 'external' powers. With this 'internal' psychological foundation and this

[42] Jellinek 1905a: 86–7.
[43] Jellinek 1905a: 201: 'Wandlung vom Machtsubjekt zum Rechtssubjekt.'
[44] See Jellinek 1914: 333–4. [45] See Jellinek 1914: 333.

'external' social guarantee of law, Jellinek tries to escape from the dilemma of legal positivism: On the one hand, Jellinek does not want to follow the track of natural law and thus enter directly into legal metaphysics. On the other hand, he is not in favour of reducing the concept of law to the legal rules that are practically in force and thus regulate the social world. That means: Jellinek is unwilling to dismiss the idea of natural law and the realism of law as a social practice either. For that reason, he combines both the idealistic and the realistic dimensions of law in his legal-psychological approach, which unfolds on two levels.

First level: Positive law is leading a 'double life'. Every legal rule – argues Jellinek – leads a 'double life' in the world of norms and in the world of facts.[46] The normative 'life' of a legal rule is the intention to regulate the factual world, whereas its factual 'life' is the effect a legal rule has in society. Both 'lives' can concur if the legal rule is applied as intended by the lawgiver. This is, however, not always the case: a legal rule might deviate in its factual 'life' from the lawgiver's intentions. Its normative content might even change in different social, economic and political contexts. Jellinek further developed this idea into his theory on the evolution of constitutions (Section 11.5.3).

Second level: Positive law has two psychological sources. The 'double life' of legal rules is influenced by two psychological sources of law:[47] on the one hand, the normative power of the factual and, on the other hand, the factual power of the norms. These two psychological sources of law influence primarily the content and hence the normative 'life' of legal rules, but they have – of course – an impact on the practical application and thus the social 'life' of legal rules as well. The first psychological source of law is the normative power of the factual, which rests on habits, rules, customs and conventions that exist, structure and influence the social world. Jellinek explains this with the example of the normative power of fashion. The second psychological rule is the factual power of norms or – maybe better – of normative ideas. The factual power of normative ideas refers to the psychological perception of justice. With this second psychological source of law, Jellinek integrates the idea of natural law into his psychological concept of legal positivism. An example for this factual power of norms is the expansion of the idea of civil rights, which

[46] See Jellinek 1914: 138, 337.

[47] Jellinek 1914: 337–60; see Kersten 2000: 364–75; Kelly 2004: 522–3; Loughlin 2010: 216–21.

started – according to Jellinek – not with the French Revolution but with the fight for the freedom of conscience and religion in the Anglo-American world (Section 11.2).[48] Jellinek identifies the normative power of the factual with the conservative sentiments of humans and societies, whereas the factual power of norms expresses the evolutionary and revolutionary ideas that motivate humans and societies for change. This last generalisation does not seem to be quite consistent because Jellinek describes, for example, the '(r)evolutionary' changes in fashion as an expression of the normative power of the factual and not of the factual power of normative ideas. Furthermore, Jellinek argues in his reflection on the legal consequences of political revolutions not with the factual power of ideas but with the normative power of the factual that might lead to the acceptance of a new revolutionary government.[49] This argument was taken up by courts and scholars to reflect the consequences of the revolution of 1918–19, which abolished monarchy in Germany and led to the Weimar Constitution (1919) and the Republic (1919–33).[50] Maybe the reason for this lies primarily not in the concept but in the suggestive phrase of the normative power of the factual, which resulted in an almost worldwide reception as a common byword. In contrast to this 'success' of the paradigm of the normative power of the factual, the factual power of normative ideas as a psychological reservoir of natural law was doomed to a shadowy existence in legal theory and practice. Also interesting is the very ambivalent history of the reception of the normative power of the factual, especially with respect to the end of the Weimar Republic and the rise of National Socialism in 1933.[51] It is very important to note that, according to Jellinek's concept of positive law, the normative power of the factual as well as the factual power of normative ideas are just psychological sources of law. Neither facts nor ideas are automatically translated into legal rules. There has to be an act of positive legal recognition to turn factual habits, rules, customs and conventions or ideas of natural justice into positive law. In the case of positive law, this act of recognition is the privilege of the accepted lawmaker, who is integrated in Jellinek's definition of legal rules, as we have seen. This means, in practice, that the act of normative recognition of a legal rule shifts from the individual to the politically legitimate lawmaker.

[48] Jellinek 1895, 1901, 1904; see Kelly 2004. [49] Jelinek 1914: 358–60.
[50] See Anschütz 1926: 6–7; Kersten 2000: 376–90.
[51] See Anschütz 1933: VI; Kersten 2000: 390–1.

With this psychological concept of law, Jellinek does not 'solve' the conflict between positive and natural law. But what should be acknowledged is that he saw the problem and tried to integrate it into his legal concept. Jellinek openly addressed this conflict in his controversial footnote on the Spanish Inquisition:[52] The victims of the Spanish Inquisition regarded the legal rules that led to their conviction not as law but as brutal violence. In a social perspective – Jellinek argues evasively – a conflict of the acceptance of a legal rule will affect the legal system as a 'living process'. In the legal perspective, Jellinek takes a somewhat clearer stand: the lawyer cannot help the victims if the conflict is restricted to a few single cases. Only if the conflict has developed 'a certain intensity and extent' does the legal question arise of whether new customary law has replaced the 'unjust' old rule. Today, we might be inclined to read Jellinek's footnote on the Spanish Inquisition as a prefigurement of Radbruch's formula (Section 11.1). For Jellinek, however, the conflict of positive law and the idea of justice is a conflict within a legal system. Quite to the contrary, Radbruch had to argue with his formula from 'outside' the legal system because there was no place for the idea of justice in the perverted legal order of National Socialism, which constituted a totalitarian and racist dictatorship and led directly to World War II, the German War crimes and the Shoah. In other words, Jellinek's footnote on the Spanish Inquisition is written before World War I and Radbruch's formula after World War II with the experience of National Socialistic dictatorship and crimes. Despite the fact that Jellinek himself was a victim of anti-Semitic discrimination (Section 11.2), as a liberal bourgeois of the nineteenth and very early twentieth century, he believed in social and scientific progress (*Fortschritt*) and in the development of political and legal culture, especially with respect to civil and human rights. National Socialism and the Shoah, in which members of his family had been discriminated against, tyrannised and murdered,[53] lay beyond his humanistic imagination.

11.5.2 A Legal Concept of Sovereignty

The question of how the state as a sovereign institution can be bound by law is at the heart of Jellinek's theory of law and state (Sections 11.2 and 11.3). Jellinek was confronted with the problem of how the rule of law can bind

[52] Jellinek 1914: 334 n. 1; see Kersten 2000: 358–62. [53] See Kempter 1998: 476–525.

a political sovereign state, especially to guarantee civil rights, and constitutional and international law. Jellinek's answer was the concept of legal auto-limitation of the state. Today, this concept is widely seen as an outdated approach to establishing the rule of law in the political system. The classical 'instrument' to explain the political creation and legal limitation of the state is the metaphor of the social contract of citizens. Whereas the social contract is regarded as the democratic instrument per se to legitimise and legalise political power, the idea of legal auto-limitation of the sovereign seems to belong to the past times of authoritarian politics in Germany in the nineteenth century: after the reactionary abatement of the democratic revolution of 1848–9, a possible way to foster the rule of law and the constitutional bindings of the authoritarian regimes was their legal and constitutional auto-limitation. Furthermore, Jellinek's legal concept of sovereignty matches only too well with the dogmatic foundations of Laband and his school of legal positivism: the state is a legal person whose 'will' is unfolded in a 'dogmatic' reconstruction of the written constitution of the German Empire from 1871 (Section 11.3). Nevertheless, the significance of Jellinek's doctrine of the legal auto-limitation of the state reaches – at least in German constitutional law – far beyond the nineteenth century. The preamble and Article 146 of the Basic Law use the anthropomorphic metaphor of the democratic people to describe the *pouvoir constitué* as a collective person that gives and binds itself to the constitution. And in 2009, the German Constitutional Court used – in its decision on the Treaty of Lisbon – the three-elementary definition of the state and the concept of legal auto-limitation to reflect the integration of the Federal Republic of Germany into the European Union.[54] Accordingly, Jellinek's concept of legal auto-limitation has not lost its topicality and is still applied to explain the transformations of sovereignty we experience today.

In the course of his academic career, Jellinek offered different explanations for the normative auto-limitation of the state as a legal person.[55] In his early writings on international law, Jellinek claims that the free sovereign will of the state is bound by law because of the social necessity of guaranteeing an international legal system.[56] In his further writings on

[54] Bundesverfassungsgericht 2009: 346, 381–406. Although the Federal Constitutional Court did not quote Jellinek!

[55] See Kersten 2000: 409–44; Loughlin 2010: 216–21, 320.

[56] See Jellinek 1880: 30, 38–43.

administrative and constitutional law and on state theory, Jellinek regards his concept of normative auto-limitation as a legal variation of Kant's categorical imperative: 'I ought never to proceed except in such a way that I could also will that my maxim should become a universal law.'[57] The 'early' Jellinek had been quite critical towards a social generalisation of the Kantian understanding of the relationship of morals, reason and law.[58] That changed, however, especially with respect to Jellinek's legal concept of sovereignty, when he discovered that Kant's categorical imperative included in its structure everything he looked for to transform sovereignty into a legal concept:[59] the categorical imperative is founded in the *free will* that *reflects normatively on itself*, to create a *binding obligation* with respect to the reasonable *standard of a social generalisable law*, and is thereby *bridging the factual and the normative world* by a concept that understands itself as a *proof of autonomy*. This understanding allowed Jellinek to interpret his transformation of sovereignty as a legal variation of the categorical imperative. Of course, Jellinek struggled to make this plausible as a principle of the political and social world. In his *System of Subjective Public Rights*, he argued that the legal auto-limitation of the state is the normative expression of the common interest.[60] The *Common Theory of the State* gives a social-psychological explanation:[61] the legal binding of political power to its constitution and laws as well as to its international obligations is the necessary result of political, legal and cultural evolution. Any legal rule includes the covenant of the state that the rule is binding for the state itself; the citizens can and do expect this rule of law politically and legally. Therefore, Jellinek can conclude, the legal auto-limitation of the state with respect to the rights of the citizens and the international community does transfer sovereignty into a legal concept that helps us to understand the rule of law. Sovereignty is no longer the bright, shining political attribute of statehood that is able to dissolve the state from the rule of law. According to Jellinek, sovereignty is just a legal construction for understanding the rule of law in a changing social world and in the development of an international community.

[57] Kant 2011: BA 17.

[58] Jellinek 1878: 15–16; Jellinek 1880: 17; see Kersten 2000: 322–5, 416–17.

[59] See Jellinek 1882: 30–6, 301; Jellinek 1887: 199; Jellinek 1905a: 200–1; Jellinek 1914: 480–4.

[60] See Jellinek 1905a: 200–1. [61] See Jellinek 1914: 367–75.

The doctrine of legal auto-limitation has been criticised until the present day: illogical play on words and intellectual circularity are the main points of critique.[62] Kelsen rejects the concept as a confusion of social and legal science.[63] We should, however, ask ourselves: Is the concept of legal auto-limitation as an explanation for the inseparable relationship of state and law really less convincing than the metaphorical use of the social contract? In a way, the legal auto-limitation of the state can be interpreted as following from the 'basic norm' (*Grundnorm*) that defines the basis of Jellinek's systematic understanding of law and state by building a bridge between the social and the legal world: 'The last reason of all law lies in the no longer derivable conviction of its validity, its normative motivating power.'[64] For that reason, it is possible to read Jellinek's concept of legal auto-limitation of political power as an attempt to legally relativise the classical concept of sovereignty as an epistemological contribution of legal positivism to the post-metaphysical explanation of the rule of law.

11.5.3 Two Rules of Legal Construction

If legal positivists have to build bridges between the social and the legal worlds, they have to engage in interdisciplinary dialogue with sociology and political science, history and economics. For Jellinek, this was self-evident and reflected the way he worked himself. In his *General Theory of the State*, however, he even goes one step further when he offers two rules of legal construction.[65] The first rule of legal construction reads: The politically impossible should not be the subject of serious legal analysis and construction. This first rule simply transforms Jellinek's understanding of law (Section 11.5.1) into a methodological rule: If law has the function to regulate society and politics, only relevant social or political problems should be legally discussed. It does not make sense for Jellinek to waste time answering, for example, the constitutional question 'What has to happen if no new chancellor is appointed?' The second rule of legal construction is much more ambivalent: There is a presumption for the legality of the actions of the supreme organs of the state. Jellinek concludes from this rule that any violation or breach of law by supreme organs of the

[62] See Kersten 2011: *29–*32; Kelly 2004: 523–5; Loughlin 2010: 216–21, 320.
[63] See Kelsen 1923: XIX; Kelsen 1928: 45–7, 168–74; Kelsen 1934: 116.
[64] Jellinek 1914: 317. [65] Jellinek 2016: 13–19; see Kersten 2000: 196–203.

state does create new law, if it is not corrected by the legal system itself. In this second rule, Jellinek reflects his understanding of political power and the rule of law. Obviously, the doctrine of the legal auto-limitation of the state does not guarantee the rule of law effectively; it has to be legally stabilised by the separation of powers. In the German Empire and the Weimar Republic, the question of how to handle breaches of law, especially by the executive power, provoked the normativity of the constitution because there was no constitutional court or at least no effective constitutional jurisdiction to 'solve' these conflicts between political power and the rule of law. Jellinek was prepared to accept legally undisputed violations of legal rules as new law. This was a consequence of his concept of legal auto-limitation in the case of a constitution with fragmented legal guarantees. The improvement of legal guarantees of the rule of law was in Jellinek's view a question of social, political, cultural and legal evolution and progress: Jellinek was an advocate of constitutional courts and jurisdiction (Section 11.2).

With these two rules of legal construction, Jellinek offers two methodological tools with which to analyse the changes and evolution of public and especially constitutional law. This became quite obvious in the debates on the evolutionary changes of the constitution of the German Empire. At the turn of the twentieth century, the meaning, importance and significance of provisions and institutions of the constitution from 1871 had changed, although the text of the constitution was still the same. Laband was unable to offer an appropriate legal reflection on constitutional change because he had excluded any social and political analysis to secure his epistemological ideal of 'pure' legal construction. For Laband and his school, the only way to cope with the question of constitutional change was legal historiography.[66] Quite contrary to Laband, Jellinek published a fulminant monograph on *Constitutional Amendment and Constitutional Change* in 1906.[67] Already, the subtitle of the study – *A Constitutional-Political Treatise* – shows that Jellinek wanted to combine political and legal analysis to explain constitutional changes on the basis of his two-sided methodological approach. Accordingly, he unfolds an opulent phenomenology of constitutional change through the interpretation of the constitution, constitutional practice, new understanding of constitutional institutions, political necessity, dispositive and customary constitutional law, non-exercise of constitutional

[66] See Laband 1895, 1907. [67] Jellinek 1906.

competences, and – last but not least – breaches of the constitution; and Jellinek used these scenarios of constitutional crisis to develop perspectives on the reform of the political and legal system.

11.6 Conclusion

Georg Jellinek opened legal positivism up to social analysis and political reflection. This methodological approach was already challenged by the opponents of the Weimar dispute on constitutional theory, who radicalised themselves in their self-stylisation as the methodologically lost generation: Carl Schmitt and Rudolf Smend on the factual side, and Hans Kelsen on the normative side. However, it is precisely the reflection on the risks and side-effects of the Weimar 'jurisprudence of crisis'[68] that draws our attention back to the phenomenological theory of reflective legal positivism developed by Georg Jellinek, on whose shoulders we still stand today.[69]

References

Anschütz, G. 1926. *Die Verfassung des Deutschen Reiches vom 11. August 1919. Ein Kommentar für Wissenschaft und Praxis.* 3rd and 4th ed. Stilke.

Anschütz, G. 1933. *Die Verfassung des Deutschen Reiches vom 11. August 1919. Ein Kommentar für Wissenschaft und Praxis.* 14th ed. Stilke.

Anter, A. 2000. 'Max Weber und Georg Jellinek. Wissenschaftliche Beziehung, Affinitäten und Divergenzen'. In S. L. Paulson and M. Schulte (eds.). *Georg Jellinek – Beiträge zu Leben und Werk.* Mohr Siebeck: 67–86.

Anter, A. 2004. 'Modernität und Ambivalenz in Georg Jellineks Staatsdenken'. In A. Anter (ed.). *Die normative Kraft des Faktischen. Das Staatsverständnis Georg Jellineks.* Nomos: 37–59.

Anter, A. 2010. 'Georg Jellinek'. In R. Voigt and U. Weiß (eds.). *Handbuch Staatsdenker.* Franz Steiner: 195–7.

Anter, A. 2016a. 'Max Weber auf den Spuren Georg Jellineks'. In W. Brugger, R. Gröschner and O. W. Lembcke (eds.). *Faktizität und Normativität. Georg Jellineks freiheitliche Verfassungslehre.* Mohr Siebeck: 39–62.

Anter, A. 2016b. *Max Weber und die Staatsrechtslehre.* Mohr Siebeck.

[68] Jacobson and Schlink 2001. [69] See Anter 2010: 197; Kersten 2004.

Breuer, S. 1999. *Georg Jellinek und Max Weber. Von der sozialen zur soziologischen Staatslehre.* Nomos.

Bundesverfassungsgericht (Federal Constitutional Court). 2009. 'Urteil. 30. Juni 2009 – 2 BvE 2, 5/08, 2 BvR 1010, 1022, 1259/08, 182/09'. In Mitglieder des Bundesverfassungsgerichts (eds.). *Entscheidungen des Bundesverfassungsgerichts.* Volume 123. Mohr Siebeck: 267–437.

Gephart, W. 1993. *Gesellschaftstheorie und Recht. Recht im soziologischen Diskurs der Moderne.* Suhrkamp.

Jacobson, A. and Schlink, B. 2001. *Weimar: A Jurisprudence of Crisis.* University of California Press.

Jellinek, G. 1872. *Die Weltanschauungen Leibniz' und Schopenhauer's. Ihre Gründe und ihre Berechtigung. Eine Studie über Optimismus und Pessimismus.* Hölder.

Jellinek, G. 1878. *Die socialethische Bedeutung von Recht, Unrecht und Strafe.* Hölder.

Jellinek. G. 1880. *Die rechtliche Natur der Staatenverträge. Ein Beitrag zur juristischen Construction des Völkerrechts.* Hölder.

Jellinek, G. 1882. *Die Lehre von den Staatenverbindungen.* Hölder.

Jellinek, G. 1885. *Ein Verfassungsgerichtshof für Österreich.* Hölder.

Jellinek, G. 1887. *Gesetz und Verordnung. Staatsrechtliche Untersuchungen auf rechtsgeschichtlicher und rechtsvergleichender Grundlage.* Mohr Siebeck.

Jelinek, G. 1892. *System der subjektiven öffentlichen Rechte.* Mohr Siebeck.

Jellinek. G. 1895. *Die Erklärung der Menschen – und Bürgerrechte. Ein Beitrag zur modernen Verfassungsgeschichte.* Duncker & Humblot.

Jellinek, G. 1896. *Ueber Staatsfragmente.* Koester.

Jellinek, G. 1898. *Das Recht der Minoritäten. Vortrag gehalten in der Juristischen Gesellschaft zu Wien.* Hölder.

Jellinek, G. 1900. *Allgemeine Staatslehre. Das Recht des modernen Staates 1.* Häring.

Jellinek, G. 1901. *The Declaration of the Rights of Man and of Citizens: A Contribution to Modern Constitutional History.* Holt.

Jellinek. G. 1904. *Die Erklärung der Menschen – und Bürgerrechte. Ein Beitrag zur modernen Verfassungsgeschichte.* 2nd ed. Duncker & Humblot.

Jelinek, G. 1905a. *System der subjektiven öffentlichen Rechte.* 2nd ed. Mohr Siebeck.

Jellinek, G. 1905b. *Allgemeine Staatslehre.* 2nd ed. Häring.

Jellinek, G. 1906. *Verfassungsänderung und Verfassungswandlung. Eine staatsrechtlich-politische Abhandlung.* Häring.

Jellinek, G. 1909. *Regierung und Parlament in Deutschland. Geschichtliche Entwicklung ihres Verhältnisses.* Teubner.

Jellinek, G. [1894]1911. 'Die Entstehung der modernen Staatsidee'. In W. Jellinek (ed.). *Ausgewählte Schriften und Reden* vol. 2. Häring: 45–63.

Jellinek, G. 1912. *Rights of Minorities.* King.

Jellinek, G. 1914. *Allgemeine Staatslehre.* 3rd ed. Häring.

Jellinek, G. 2016. *Allgemeine Staatslehre und Politik. Vorlesungsmitschrift von Max Ernst Mayer aus dem Sommersemester 1896*. Eds. S. Ziemann and A. Funke. Mohr Siebeck.

Jhering, R. V. 1865. *Geist des römischen Rechts auf den verschiedenen Stufen seiner Entwicklung* 3rd part, vol. 1. Breitkopf und Härtel.

Jhering, R. V. 1877. *Der Zweck im Recht* vol. 1. Breitkopf und Härtel.

Jhering, R. V. 1883. *Der Zweck im Recht* vol. 2. Breitkopf und Härtel.

Jhering, R. V. 1913. *Law as Means to an End*. Boston Book Company.

Kant, I. [1786]2011. *Groundwork of the Metaphysics of Morals*. Ed. J. Timmermann. 2nd ed. Cambridge University Press.

Kelly, D. 2004. 'Revisiting the Rights of Man: Georg Jellinek on Rights and the State'. *Law and History Review* 22: 493–529.

Kelsen, H. 1922. *Der soziologische und der juristische Staatsbegriff. Eine kritische Untersuchung des Verhältnisses von Staat und Recht*. Mohr Siebeck.

Kelsen, H. 1923. *Hauptprobleme der Staatsrechtslehre entwickelt aus der Lehre vom Rechtssatze*. 2nd ed. Mohr Siebeck.

Kelsen, H. 1928. *Das Problem der Souveränität und die Theorie des Völkerrechts. Beitrag zu einer Reinen Rechtslehre*. 2nd ed. Mohr Siebeck.

Kelsen, H. 1934. *Reine Rechtslehre. Einleitung in die rechtswissenschaftliche Problematik*. Deuticke.

Kempter, K. 1998. *Die Jellineks 1820–1955. Eine familienbiographische Studie zum deutschjüdischen Bürgertum*. Droste.

Kersten, J. 2000. *Georg Jellinek und die klassische Staatslehre*. Mohr Siebeck.

Kersten, J. 2001. 'Mehrheit und Minderheit im Minoritätenstaat. Georg Jellineks rechtspolitische Schriften 1885 bis 1906 als Beitrag zum Verhältnis von Staatsrechtslehre und Politik im Spätkonstitutionalismus und darüber hinaus'. *Der Staat* 40: 221–42.

Kersten, J. 2004. 'Warum Georg Jellinek? Jellinek und die Staats – Staats- und Europarechtslehre der Gegenwart'. In A. Anter (ed.). *Die normative Kraft des Faktischen. Das Staatsverständnis Georg Jellineks*. Nomos: 175–199.

Kersten, J. 2011. 'Georg Jellineks System. Eine Einleitung'. In G. Jellinek. *System der subjektiven öffentlichen Rechte*. 2nd ed. (1905). Ed. J. Kersten. Mohr Siebeck: *7–*52.

Kersten, J. 2018. 'Georg Jellinek (1851–1911)'. In P. Häberle, M. Kilian and H. Wolff (eds.). *Staatsrechtslehrer des 20. Jahrhunderts. Deutschland – Österreich – Schweiz*. 2nd ed. Walter de Gruyter: 77–86.

Kirste, S. 2016. 'Verfassung und Verfassungswandel bei Georg Jellinek'. In W. Brugger, R. Gröschner and O. W. Lembcke (eds.). *Faktizität und Normativität. Georg Jellineks freiheitliche Verfassungslehre*. Mohr Siebeck: 209–35.

Laband, P. 1876. *Das Staatsrecht des Deutschen Reiches* vol. 1. Laupp.

Laband, P. 1880. *Rede über die Bedeutung der Rezeption des Römischen Rechts für das deutsche Staatsrecht*. Heitz.

Laband, P. 1887. 'S. Brie. Theorie der Staatenverbindungen. 1886' (Book Review). *Archiv des öffentlichen Rechts* 2: 311–20.

Laband, P. 1895. *Die Wandlungen der deutschen Reichsverfassung. Vortrag gehalten in der gehe-Stiftung zu Dresden am 16. März 1895.* Zahn & Jaensch.

Laband, P. 1907. 'Die geschichtliche Entwicklung der Reichsverfassung seit der Reichsgründung'. *Jahrbuch des öffentlichen Rechts* 1: 1–46.

Lepsius, O. 2000. 'Georg Jellinek's Methodenlehre im Spiegel der zeitgenössischen Erkenntnistheorie'. In S. L. Paulson and M. Schulte (eds.). *Georg Jellinek – Beiträge zu Leben und Werk.* Mohr Siebeck: 309–43.

Loughlin, M. 2010. *The Foundation of Public Law.* Oxford University Press.

Pauly, W. 1993. *Der Methodenwandel im deutschen Spätkonstitutionalismus. Ein Beitrag zur Entwicklung und Gestalt der Wissenschaft vom Öffentlichen Recht im 19. Jahrhundert.* Mohr Siebeck.

Pauly, W. 2000. 'Jellinek's System der subjektiven öffentlichen Rechte'. In S. L. Paulson and M. Schulte (eds.). *Georg Jellinek – Beiträge zu Leben und Werk.* Mohr Siebeck: 227–44.

Radbruch, G. [1946]2006. 'Lawlessness and Supra-Statutory Law'. *Oxford Journal of Legal Studies* 26: 1–11.

Schlink, B. 1992. 'Laband als Politiker'. *Der Staat* 31: 553–69.

Schönberger, C. 1998. *Das Parlament im Anstaltsstaat. Zur Theorie parlamentarischer Repräsentation in der Staatsrechtslehre des Kaiserreichs (1871–1918).* Klostermann.

Schönberger, C. 2000. 'Ein Liberaler zwischen Staatswille und Volkswille. Georg Jellinek und die Krise des staatsrechtlichen Positivismus um die Jahrhundertwende'. In S. L. Paulson and M. Schulte (eds.). *Georg Jellinek – Beiträge zu Leben und Werk.* Mohr Siebeck: 3–323.

Stolleis, M. 1999. *Geschichte des öffentlichen Rechts in Deutschland* vol 2. C.H. Beck.

Stolleis, M. 2000. 'Georg Jellineks Beitrag zur Entwicklung der Menschen - und Bürgerrechte'. In S. L. Paulson and M. Schulte (eds.). *Georg Jellinek – Beiträge zu Leben und Werk.* Mohr Siebeck: 103–16.

Weber, M. [1919]1946. 'Politics as a Vocation'. In H. H. Gerth and C. Wright Mills (eds.). *From Max Weber: Essays in Sociology.* Oxford University Press: 77–128.

Wolff, H. A. 2000. 'Verfassungswandel und ungeschriebenes Verfassungsrecht im Werke Georg Jellineks'. In S. L. Paulson and M. Schulte (eds.). *Georg Jellinek – Beiträge zu Leben und Werk.* Mohr Siebeck: 133–53.

Ziemann, S. and Funke, A. 2016. 'Einleitung: Zur Archäologie eines juristischen Klassikers'. In G. Jellinek. *Allgemeine Staatslehre und Politik.* Eds. S. Ziemann and A. Funke. Mohr Siebeck. XIII-XXXIV.

12 Hans Kelsen's Non-Reductive Positivism

Michael S. Green *

12.1 Introduction

Hans Kelsen described his pure theory of law as a form of legal positivism.[1] Anglophone philosophers of law might disagree. For them, positivism is defined by *the social thesis*: law ultimately depends solely on social facts about a community's legal practices.[2] Kelsen rejects the social thesis. Social facts occur within the spatiotemporal and causal world of the *is* (the world of *Sein*), not the world of the *ought* (the world of *Sollen*).[3] The two worlds are separated by an unbridgeable gap.[4] Law, as a normative order, is therefore distinct from social facts. Indeed, the legal order is distinct from nature as a whole. It stands outside the spatiotemporal and causal world.[5]

But how can the legal order be outside space and time, when social facts can create law? Assume that Rex (the absolute monarch of Ruritania) makes an announcement and, as a result, people are legally obligated to drive on the left. Their legal obligation did not exist until he made his announcement. Doesn't that mean that the legal order exists in time (if not in space)?

Kelsen makes it clear that talk about social facts creating law is merely a 'figurative expression' for the interpretation of the meaning of social facts in the light of the legal order.[6] The social facts that are interpreted are in space and time, but the legal order in the light of which they are interpreted is not.

Consider, by analogy, someone who holds a non-naturalist theory of morality.[7] She might still speak of Fred's promising to take Felicia to the zoo as creating a moral obligation to take her to the zoo. That does not

* Many thanks to Brian Bix, David Dyzenhaus, Stanley Paulson, George Pavlakos, Alexander Somek and Torben Spaak for helpful comments and corrections.

[1] See Kelsen 1945: xiii; Kelsen 1967: 106. [2] See Raz 1994: 210. [3] Kelsen 1992: 25.

[4] See Kelsen 1911: 8. [5] See Kelsen 1992: 12.

[6] Kelsen 1973: 156. See also Kelsen 1981: 180–1. [7] See, e.g., Enoch 2011a.

mean that she thinks Fred possesses a God-like power to change morality. Fred's act leaves the moral order unchanged. She simply means that when we interpret Fred's promise in the light of the moral order, he has an obligation to take Felicia to the zoo. As the moral non-naturalist sees it, the moral order consists of a set of fundamental moral principles that predetermine the moral consequences of any social fact. It is a timeless moral fact – a fact that obtains in all possible worlds, even those in which humans do not exist – that *if* Fred promises to take Felicia to the zoo (and any other required social facts obtain),[8] he will have an obligation to take her to the zoo. When she says that his promise creates an obligation, she is interpreting his promise in the light of that timeless moral fact.[9]

By the same token, for Kelsen the legal order is unchanged by the social facts that have legal consequences. Talk about social facts creating law is really the interpretation of social facts in the light of the legal order. Although it results in some distortion of Kelsen's views (because it obscures his particular type of neo-Kantianism),[10] we can think of the Kelsenian legal order as similar to the moral order as the non-naturalist understands it. It is a fundamental legal principle (or set of legal principles)[11] that predetermines the legal consequences of any possible set of social facts. It is a timeless legal fact that *if* Rex's announcement occurs (and any other required social facts obtain),[12] people will be legally obligated to drive on the left.

Although Kelsen rejects the social thesis, there are two senses in which he can nevertheless be described as a positivist. Another thesis commonly associated with positivism is *the separation thesis*: law does not ultimately depend upon moral facts.[13] The separation thesis follows from the social thesis: if law ultimately depends solely upon social facts, it does not ultimately depend upon moral facts. But the social thesis does not follow from the separation thesis. One can consistently hold that law ultimately depends upon neither moral nor social facts.

[8] See Section 12.3.2.

[9] One way of putting this point is that Fred's act simply triggers, or makes applicable, a pre-existing moral fact. See Enoch 2011b.

[10] See Section 12.4.3.

[11] For Kelsen, the basic norm, which stands at the basis of the legal order, is singular. But, under the Kelsenian position I offer here, the legal order, like the non-naturalist's moral order, might consist of a plurality of fundamental legal principles.

[12] See Section 12.3.2.

[13] For a criticism of more expansive readings of the separation thesis, see L. Green 2008.

That is Kelsen's position.[14] The foundation of the legal order, the basic norm, is not a moral norm.[15] What is more, the basic norm does not condition law-making power upon whether the laws issued satisfy moral criteria.[16] But Kelsen nevertheless rejects the social thesis. The basic norm and the legal order of which it is the foundation are part of the world of the ought, not the world of the is, including the world of the social.

To repeat, to say that social facts create a legal obligation is, for Kelsen, to interpret those facts in the light of the pre-existing legal order. The second sense in which Kelsen might legitimately be described as a positivist concerns the extent to which social facts 'create' legal obligations in the relevant sense. As we have seen, even the moral non-naturalist can accept that some moral obligations (like Fred's) are 'created' by social facts. Fred is interpreted as having a promissory obligation because a social fact (namely his promise to Felicia) obtained, and the content of his obligation is drawn from that social fact. In that sense, the moral non-naturalist might describe promissory obligations as *posited* – they are created by human acts of will. But many moral obligations (such as the obligation not to cause unnecessary harm) are not posited in this sense: they are binding no matter what social facts obtain and their content is not drawn from social facts. One way of putting this point is that when a world without any human beings (and so without any social facts) is interpreted in the light of the moral order, there are still moral obligations, although there are no human beings around to which these obligations can apply. The same point is true of moral permissions.

As Kelsen sees it, the legal order is different.[17] All legal obligations are 'created' by social facts and their content is drawn from those facts. When a world without any human beings is interpreted in the light of the legal order, there are no legal obligations. Nor are there any legal permissions.[18]

[14] See generally Paulson 1993.

[15] See Kelsen 1967: 5–7, 218; Kelsen 1992: 59–60; Paulson 1975: 770–1.

[16] One way of putting this point is that there are no systemic moral conditions of legal validity. That does not mean that Kelsen didn't accept the possibility of non-systemic moral conditions of legal validity, that is, conditions introduced by authorisations subordinate to the basic norm. See Kelsen 1945: 132.

[17] See, e.g., Kelsen 1967: 4–5. In fact, Kelsen believes that, properly understood, morality is a fully positive order as well. See Section 12.4.3.

[18] This is clearly true concerning what Kelsen calls 'positive permissions', which are 'created' by a human act of will; Kelsen 1967: 16. The matter is less clear concerning negative permissions – which exist by virtue of the absence of a prohibition. But Kelsen argues that

All that is there is an authorisation: human beings are empowered to generate legal obligations and permissions by establishing communities with legal practices. This is, in effect, the content of the basic norm.[19] Let us call Kelsen's view that all legal obligations and permissions are posited the *positivity thesis*.[20] The positivity thesis also applies to all legal authorisations, with the exception of the foundational authorisation in the basic norm.

Although Kelsen's acceptance of the separation and the positivity theses entitles him to be described as a positivist, in rejecting the social thesis he occupies an otherwise empty space in the philosophy of law. If law does not ultimately depend upon social facts (due to the falsity of the social thesis) and does not ultimately depend upon moral facts (due to the truth of the separation thesis), upon what does it ultimately depend? Kelsen believes that this question cannot, and should not, be answered. 'To comprehend something legally', he insists, 'can only be to comprehend it as law.'[21] He offers a *non-reductive* theory of law.[22]

Anglophone philosophers of law take it for granted that law is not metaphysically basic.[23] It is grounded in other facts. At least some of those facts are social. The debate is about whether they also include moral facts. Because he challenges their common assumption, one might think that Anglophone philosophers of law would be curious about Kelsen's works. But he tends to be ignored or summarily dismissed.[24]

My goal is to try to remedy this situation by showing that Kelsen's non-reductivism deserves to be taken seriously. Because I wish to show Kelsen's

negative permissions exist only in the context of a normative order that obligates actions; see Kelsen 1967: 16. And, given that there are no legal obligations in a world without human beings, it would appear that there are no negative permissions in such a world either.

19 For a discussion of some of the differences between the basic norm as Kelsen understands it and the Kelsenian position presented in this chapter, see Section 12.4.3. One important difference is that Kelsen speaks of the basic norm in terms of the empowerment of the creators of a historically first constitution; Kelsen 1945: 115–16; Kelsen 1967: 200. Under the Kelsenian position I present here, by contrast, the fundamental authorisation applies to law-makers in multiple (indeed an infinite number of) possible communities.

20 Kelsen's acceptance of the separation and the positivity theses is arguably why Anglophone philosophers of law commonly describe him as a positivist. See, e.g., Gardner 2001: 200.

21 Kelsen 1992: 11.

22 See Marmor 2011: 17. For Marmor, however, Kelsen fails to offer a consistent form of non-reductivism; Marmor 2011: 20. I disagree.

23 Greenberg 2004: 158–9.

24 See Bix 2016: 18–20.

relevance to Anglophone philosophers of law, I will present his position largely in the context of terminology and themes with which they would be comfortable, rather than in Kelsen's language itself. In addition, my reading will be very limited in scope. It will present only what I believe to be the philosophical heart of Kelsen's non-reductivism, shorn of problematic or idiosyncratic elements.[25] Likewise, I will concentrate on the essence of Kelsen's neo-Kantianism,[26] while marginalising the (sometimes questionable) details.[27] For these reasons, the non-reductivist position I present here can be described as Kelsenian only, not as Kelsen's own. But the plausibility of this neglected Kelsenian position is, I believe, testimony to the power and originality of Kelsen's philosophical views.

12.2 Ontology, Not Practical Reason

Let us start by addressing a fundamental misunderstanding that stands in the way of appreciating Kelsen's theory of law. It is crucial to recognise that, for Kelsen, the existence of law as a normative order distinct from social facts does not mean that it provides justifying reason for action of the sort that would figure in practical reasoning.[28] Kelsen makes it clear that someone can reject conformity with the law and still understand it as a normative order in the relevant sense.[29]

To understand Kelsen's position, it is helpful to consider it in the context of the philosophy of the social sciences. A fundamental problem in that field is making sense of the reality of the social world, including the law.[30] One possibility is individualism, that is, explaining the social in terms of psychological facts about a community's members. But holists, such as Émile Durkheim, believe that it is necessary to draw a distinction between

[25] See notes 11 and 19. Another difference is that I ignore Kelsen's view that law solely concerns the conditions for appropriate sanctions by officials; Kelsen 1945: 61; Kelsen 1967: 55. I assume that a legal obligation can bind private individuals directly.

[26] I also ignore the extent to which his neo-Kantianism changed over his almost seventy years of productive activity and may have been abandoned in the end. For discussion of the periodisation of Kelsen's works, see Heidemann 1997; Paulson 1998; Paulson 1999.

[27] See Section 12.4.3.

[28] See Delacroix 2004, 2006: 43–4; Paulson 2000, 2012; Pavlakos 2018: 6; Wilson 1982.

[29] See Kelsen 1967: 218 n. 82. For examples of this misreading of Kelsen, see Marmor 2011: 27; Raz 1979: 136–7.

[30] See Jackson and Pettit 1992.

social and psychological facts.[31] As Durkheim puts it, 'Social phenomena must therefore be considered in themselves, detached from the conscious beings who form their own mental representations of them. They must be studied from the outside, as external things, because it is in this guise that they present themselves to us.'[32] Durkheim is a holist about the social, not because he thinks that it necessarily entails justified reasons for action but because we conceive of it as distinct from psychological facts.

Anglophone positivists tend to be sociological individualists. Although they describe the social thesis as the view that law ultimately depends solely upon social facts, by 'social facts' they mean psychological facts – facts about the beliefs, attitudes and behaviour of a community's members.[33] The example of sociological holism shows that someone can reject the social thesis as Anglophone positivists understand it without thereby taking law to necessarily provide justified reasons for action.

Of course, holists like Durkheim still understand the social, including the law, as dependent upon natural facts. It is grounded in a community, which exists in space and time. Kelsen, by contrast, insists that the legal order is non-natural. Indeed, he criticises Durkheim for succumbing to an inappropriate methodological syncretism – the attempt to connect the worlds of nature and norm.[34] The law cannot be grounded in a non-psychological, but naturalistic entity like the community or the state.[35]

We shall turn to Kelsen's arguments for non-reductivism. But the example of holism in the philosophy of the social sciences can nevertheless provide us with a model of the question Kelsen seeks to answer: What theory best accounts for the way that we conceive of the law, even if the law does not provide one with justifying reasons for action? Kelsen's concern is, one might say, avoiding *ontological* anarchism (the failure to make a proper place for law within one's theory of what exists), not *practical-reason* anarchism (the denial that law necessarily makes a claim on our practical reasoning).

That Kelsen's goal is avoiding ontological anarchism must always be kept in mind in my discussion of arguments for non-reductivism. Because Anglophone philosophers are generally familiar with moral non-naturalism,

[31] See Cotterrell 1999: 9–16, 215–17. [32] Durkheim 2013: 37. [33] Plunkett 2012: 145.

[34] See Kelsen 1922a: 129–30; Kelsen 1922b: 51–5.

[35] See Kelsen 1945: 191–2. Curiously, Kelsen does not extend this non-naturalism to other social phenomena. Concerning them, he is an individualist: they are reducible to psychological facts; Kelsen 1922a.

I find it helpful to draw analogies between legal non-naturalism and its moral equivalent. But – to repeat – the legal order, unlike the moral order, does not necessarily provide one with justified reasons for action.

12.3 Why Non-reductivism?

We now have an idea of the question that Kelsen was trying to answer. But why does he think that doing justice to the way we conceive of legal phenomena compels one to adopt a pure theory of law, in which it is not reducible to moral or social facts? What are his arguments for accepting the separation thesis and rejecting the social thesis?

12.3.1 Arguments for the Separation Thesis

One of Kelsen's main arguments in favour of the separation thesis – one he shares with Anglophone positivists –[36] is that the content of the law can diverge dramatically from the content of morality.[37] One can be legally obligated to do what is morally prohibited. Because their content can differ, to identify the legal and the moral orders would constitute an 'uncritical justification' of the government's coercive force.[38]

In fact, the observation that the content of morality and law can differ is insufficient on its own to show that the separation thesis is correct. We are all aware of how social facts can generate moral obligations to conform to what is, considered in isolation, a morally incorrect standard. For example, having mistakenly used an incorrect standard for her son, considerations

[36] See Shapiro 2011: 16–17; Hart 1994: 203. [37] See Kelsen 1945: 113; Kelsen 1967: 201.

[38] See Kelsen 1967: 69. Kelsen draws a host of other distinctions between the legal and the moral orders that are tied to positions that are unlikely to be shared by Anglophone positivists. For example, he draws a functional distinction between the two orders, insofar as the legal order is essentially coercive (that is, it essentially concerns appropriate sanctions by officials), while moral norms can bind individuals directly. See Kelsen 1967: 62. Some other distinctions that Kelsen draws between the legal and the moral orders attribute to the latter characteristics that he believes to be philosophically incoherent. The moral order is understood as making a justified claim upon our practical reasoning, and Kelsen (1967: 196) rejects the very idea of practical reason. The content of fundamental moral norms is understood as self-evident (an idea that Kelsen associates with natural law), and Kelsen rejects the idea of norms with self-evident content. See, e.g., Kelsen 1957: 141–2; Section 12.4.3.

of fairness might morally obligate a parent to use the same standard for her daughter – and morally obligate the daughter to conform to the standard.[39]

That said, it is unlikely that such considerations are so pervasive that the separation thesis can be rejected. A legal standard can be so abhorrent that it is not morally justified, even pro tanto justified, for officials to apply – or for the population to conform to – that standard. It is for this reason that so many philosophers of law believe that there is no general moral duty, not even a pro tanto duty, to obey the law.[40] Kelsen agrees.

12.3.2 Argument against the Social Thesis: Legal Anti-psychologism

The more challenging problem is identifying Kelsen's reasons for rejecting the social thesis. Here, the heart of his argument is the inadequacy of 'psychologism' in the philosophy of law.[41]

Psychologism is most commonly understood as a position in the philosophy of logic, according to which logical laws are understood as psychological facts.[42] Logical psychologism was famously rejected by Gottlob Frege, who argued that it cannot account for the nature of logical inferences.

Consider the following inference:

Logical inference 1
(1) Grass is green and crows are black.
Therefore . . . (2) Grass is green.

This is an example of logical entailment: 2 is true in all possible worlds in which 1 is true. In particular, it is an example of the law of conjunctive simplification: If a conjunction is true, then any one of its conjuncts is true. It is by virtue of the law of conjunctive simplification that there is logical entailment.

If logical psychologism is correct, the law of conjunctive simplification is a psychological fact, such as the fact that people are disposed to accept a conjunct having accepted a conjunction. But that fails to explain why 1 logically entails 2: why 2 is true in all possible worlds in which 1 is true,

[39] See Greenberg 2014: 1310–19. [40] See Edmundson 2004.

[41] Ebenstein 1945: 51–59; M. S. Green 2003: 398; Kelsen 1925: vii; Kelsen 1992: 33; Paulson 2005: 282; Paulson 2012: 100–2.

[42] See Brockhaus 1991: 494–506.

even in worlds in which people's inferential dispositions are different (or worlds in which there are no people at all).[43]

In order to explain logical entailment, Frege argued that one must look to the necessary relations between the propositions expressed by statements. It is because the proposition expressed by 1 necessarily contains, or is structured out of, the proposition expressed by 2 that 2 must be true if 1 is. This relationship between propositions can be necessary only if they are independent of people's mental activities.[44] Indeed, they must be part of a 'third realm' independent of *all* natural facts, whether they be psychological, social or physical.[45]

A similar argument can be offered against moral psychologism. Consider the following inference in which a moral conclusion is derived from a non-moral premise:

Moral inference 1
(3) Fred promised to take Felicia to the zoo.
Therefore . . . (4) Fred morally ought to take Felicia to the zoo.

Here, 4 is arguably true in all possible worlds in which 3 is true,[46] even though the relationship is not one of logical entailment (the proposition expressed by 3 does not contain the one expressed by 4). It is a *moral* fact, not a fact concerning the relations between propositions, that takes one from 3 to 4. This moral fact is, say, the moral principle of promissory obligation MP_1: if a person makes a promise, then he morally ought to keep it:

Moral inference 1
(3) Fred promised to take Felicia to the zoo.
Therefore (via MP_1) . . . (4) Fred morally ought to take Felicia to the zoo.

For 3 to morally entail 4, MP_1 cannot be understood as a psychological fact, such as the fact that the speaker, or people generally, has a positive attitude towards keeping promises and so is disposed to accept 4 if they have accepted 3. 4 is true in all possible worlds in which 3 is true, whatever people's psychological states might be in those worlds.

From the necessity of moral principles, the moral non-naturalist concludes that they concern a moral order that is distinct from people's psychological

[43] See Baker and Hacker 1984: 35–7; Frege 1984a: v–vii. [44] See Frege 1979: 127, 134–7.

[45] See Frege 1984b: 363.

[46] We can understand this moral obligation to be pro tanto only, which allows 4 to be true even in possible worlds in which other moral obligations override Fred's promissory obligation.

states. Indeed, the moral order must be independent of *all* natural facts, whether they be psychological, social or physical. It is a timeless fact about the moral order – a moral fact that obtained before there were any human beings – that if Fred promises to take Felicia to the zoo, then he morally ought to take her to the zoo.

Some would argue, however, that 3 does not morally entail 4. Fred's promise would not create a moral obligation if he and Felicia were in a community that lacked the practice of making and keeping promises.[47] If so, we must add a statement about Fred and Felicia's community (call it community A) as an additional premise for there to be moral entailment. Let us call this added premise C_A. The relevant moral principle that allows one to derive 4 from 3 and C_A would now be something like MP_2: One morally ought to comply with just and useful social practices:[48]

Moral inference 2
(C_A) Fred and Felicia are in community A, which has the practice of promise-making.
(3) Fred promised to take Felicia to the zoo.
Therefore (via MP_2) . . . (4) Fred morally ought to take Felicia to the zoo.

MP_2 would also be in play in inferences about promissory obligations in other communities:

Moral inference 3
(C_B) Rob and Rebecca are in community B, which has the practice of promise-making.
(5) Rob promised to take Rebecca to her job interview.
Therefore (via MP_2) . . . (6) Rob morally ought to take Rebecca to her job interview.

But the need to add a premise concerning a community for there to be moral entailment does not change the argument against moral psychologism. For 4 to be true in all possible worlds in which C_A and 3 are true, MP_2 cannot be understood as a psychological, social or physical fact. It must be understood as a timeless fact about a non-natural moral order.

In rejecting *legal* psychologism, the Kelsenian argument is that the character of legal inferences can be explained only by reference to a non-natural legal order. Let us begin by identifying inferences in which there is a necessary relationship between non-legal premises and a legal

[47] Rawls 1971: 344–50. [48] Scanlon 1998: 296.

conclusion.[49] Consider the following possibility (concerning Rex, the King of Ruritania):

Legal inference 1
(7) Rex has announced that one ought to drive on the left.
Therefore … (8) Joe legally ought to drive on the left.

To conclude that 8 is true in all possible worlds in which 7 is true, one would have to believe that an announcement by Rex, in whatever context it might occur, creates a legal obligation on Joe.

That is not how we make legal inferences. A premise concerning social facts about a community (in this case, Ruritania) needs to be added to 7 for 8 to follow necessarily. Let us call this premise $C_{Ruritania}$. The details of $C_{Ruritania}$ are likely to be contested. But, for our purposes, let us assume that it describes the social facts that Anglophone positivists generally think would have to be in place for the Ruritanian legal system to exist.[50] Whether $C_{Ruritania}$ accurately captures the required social facts does not actually matter for the Kelsenian argument against legal psychologism. (Nor does it matter whether $C_{Ruritania}$ accurately captures what Kelsen takes to be the required social facts.)[51] What is important is that some statement about social facts concerning a community is required for there to be entailment.

Let us call a standard that identifies those standards that people ought to obey and that officials ought to enforce a *meta-standard.* A meta-standard (and the standards it identifies) are abstract objects that can guide people's behaviour if they choose to follow them. Meta-standards do not, by their bare existence as abstract objects, have any legal (or moral) consequences.

[49] Kelsen calls the necessary relationship in a legal inference 'imputation' [*Zurechnung*]. See Kelsen 1967: 76–81; Kelsen 1992: 23–5; Paulson 2001; Pavlakos 2018. (In particular, the form of imputation at issue is what Kelsen calls 'peripheral'.) The heart of Kelsen's anti-psychologist argument against the social thesis is this doctrine of imputation. My goal is to present the doctrine free of the more idiosyncratic elements of Kelsen's legal theory. In particular, I change the legal inferences at issue. For Kelsen (1967: 89–91), imputation links content provided by social facts (such as the act creating the first constitution, an act of legislation, an act violating the law, and a sanction) with a normative necessity that is analogous to the way that a causal judgment links experienced events. The inferences I discuss here, by contrast, are between premises about non-legal facts and a legal conclusion. For Kelsen, the legal conclusion would itself be understood as a judgment normatively linking content provided by social facts.

[50] See, in particular, Hart 1994: 79–123. [51] See note 19.

There is, after all, an infinite number of meta-standards telling people that they ought to follow standards of all kinds.

Under the meta-standard M_{Rex}, people ought to obey and officials ought to enforce all standards announced by Rex. Of course, I have left open many essential details about M_{Rex}. To which people and officials does M_{Rex} refer? All people and all officials? Or only Ruritanian officials and Ruritanians (or people currently in Ruritania)? Can Rex delegate his power? What happens when he dies? These details would have to be filled in for a complete account of M_{Rex}'s content.

Under $C_{Ruritania}$, two social facts are the case concerning M_{Rex}. First, Ruritanian officials accept it as a guide for their enforcement of standards.[52] Although M_{Rex} might apply to non-Ruritanian officials, it is not necessary that those officials accept it. All that is required is that Ruritanian officials do. Second, those standards identified by M_{Rex} must, by and large, be conformed to by the Ruritanian population.[53] Again, although M_{Rex} might identify Rex as having the power to create standards for non-Ruritanians outside Ruritania, all that is necessary is that there is compliance in Ruritania or by Ruritanians. Let us say that if these two social facts obtain, M_{Rex} is *efficacious* in Ruritania.

Our inference would now look something like this:

Legal inference 2
($C_{Ruritania}$) M_{Rex} is efficacious in Ruritania.
(7) Rex has announced that one ought to drive on the left.
Therefore . . . (8) Joe legally ought to drive on the left.

We now have entailment: 8 is true in all possible worlds in which $C_{Ruritania}$ and 7 are true.

Once we have entailment, the Kelsenian argument is that it cannot be explained except by reference to a non-natural legal order. A fundamental legal principle (or set of legal principles) must obtain in all possible worlds, in the light of which 8 can be derived from $C_{Ruritania}$ and 7. Let us assume that this fundamental legal principle (LP_1) is the following: One legally ought to conform to the standards identified by a community's efficacious meta-standard. Whether LP_1 accurately captures this fundamental legal principle does not really matter for the Kelsenian argument against legal

[52] Anglophone positivists disagree concerning the type of acceptance required. See, e.g., Shapiro 2011: 154–233, where the relevant acceptance is understood as an act of planning.
[53] See, e.g., Hart 1994: 114.

psychologism. (Nor does it matter whether it accurately captures what Kelsen himself takes to be the content of the basic norm.)[54] What is important is that some fundamental legal principle is necessary for there to be entailment.

If LP_1 is that legal principle, the following inference (concerning Basil, the King of Fredonia) would also be a matter of legal entailment:

Legal inference 3
($C_{Fredonia}$) M_{Basil} is efficacious in Fredonia.
(9) Basil has announced that one ought to drive on the right.
Therefore (via LP_1) . . . (10) Joe legally ought to drive on the right.

For $C_{Ruritania}$ and 7 to legally entail 8 and for $C_{Fredonia}$ and 9 to legally entail 10, LP_1 must obtain in all possible worlds. If so, it cannot be understood as fact about the psychological, social or physical. And that means that the social thesis is false. Law does not ultimately depend upon social facts about a community's legal practices. It ultimately depends upon legal facts, namely LP_1. Social facts about a community's legal practices are simply relevant (like facts about Rex's or Basil's announcements) to LP_1.

12.3.3 An Alternative: Conceptual Anti-psychologism

But there is an alternative position, which the Anglophone positivist would take. This is to understand the entailment not as legal but as conceptual.[55] The fact taking one from $C_{Ruritania}$ and 7 to 8 and from $C_{Fredonia}$ and 9 to 10, although obtaining in all possible worlds, is a fact about the concept of law, not a fact about the law. According to this concept-of-law fact, each community has an independent legal system, and the way that one should make inferences in that system depends solely upon social facts about the relevant community's legal practices (like those described by $C_{Ruritania}$ or $C_{Fredonia}$). The necessity involved in legal inferences 2 and 3 might be reasons to understand concept-of-law facts as concerning a non-natural realm distinct from the psychological, social and physical.[56] But it is not a reason to come to the same conclusion about the law. A community's legal system and the law of that system can still be understood as ultimately

[54] See note 19. [55] See Plunkett 2012.
[56] This would involve distinguishing between the concept of law, understood as an abstract object, and our psychological act of grasping that object.

dependent solely upon social facts about the relevant community's legal practices.

As an analogy, consider the fact, which obtains in all possible worlds, that if there is an unmarried human male, there is a bachelor. That is a conceptual fact – a fact about the concept of a bachelor – not a fact about bachelors. Facts about bachelors (such as the prevalence of empty pizza boxes in their apartments) require actual unmarried human males. Concept-of-bachelor facts do not. In the absence of unmarried human males, there are no bachelor facts, although there still are concept-of-bachelor facts. By the same token, the Anglophone positivist would argue, legal facts require an actual community with legal practices. In the absence of such a community, there are no legal facts, although there still are concept-of-law facts.[57]

If what is at play in these legal inferences is a conceptual fact, then we have no reason to believe that the social thesis is false. To be sure, we still have a fundamental legal principle for each community that determines how to make legal inferences within that community's legal system. But there is no fundamental legal principle that is independent of all communities and that determines how to make legal inferences concerning any possible community.

This is not to say that the fundamental legal principle *for* a community might not allow one to make legal inferences from social facts about *another* community's legal practices. Assume that, under M_{Rex}, everyone (including people in Fredonia) ought to follow the standards in Rex's announcements. If so, one can conclude that Basil's announcements have no legal effect, even in Fredonia. But this remains a legal inference from within the Ruritanian legal system.[58] The appropriate inference within the Fredonian legal system will be different.

[57] The term 'legal fact' is not one used generally by Kelsen himself. But we can think of a legal fact obtaining if and only if a legal proposition (such as the proposition that Joe is legally obligated to drive on the left) is true; Plunkett 2012: 145.

[58] It is important to note, however, that most Anglophone positivists would insist that the fundamental legal principle for Ruritania cannot be the social facts described in $C_{Ruritania}$, or any other social facts. It must instead be an abstract object (like M_{Rex}) that stands outside space and time. See, e.g., Shapiro 2011: 127. Likewise, the standards identified by the abstract object – the legal norms of the Ruritanian legal system – must themselves be abstract objects. Otherwise the necessity of legal inferences within the Ruritanian legal system could not be explained. See Chapter 23 in this volume. In this sense, these positivists accept a (limited) form of legal anti-psychologism. That legal norms are non-natural objects

If the Anglophone positivist is correct, the social thesis remains true – there is no law in the absence of a community with legal practices. It is also the case that Ruritanian law is as separate from Fredonian law as one bachelor is from another. The unity of Ruritanian and Fredonian law under the concept of law no more shows that there is a fundamental legal principle unifying them than the unity of all bachelors under the concept of a bachelor shows that all bachelors are really one.[59]

12.3.4 The Unity of Law

The Kelsenian approach, by contrast, is to argue that it is a legal fact, not a conceptual fact, that takes one from $C_{Ruritania}$ and 7 to 8 – the same legal fact that takes one from $C_{Fredonia}$ and 9 to 10. Consider, by analogy, moral inference 2. The need to add social facts about community A to Fred's promise for him to have a moral obligation to take Felicia to the zoo did not mean that the entailment was conceptual and that community A had a moral system that was independent from community B's. The fact that stood behind the inference, MP_2 (the duty to comply with just and useful social practices), is a moral fact, not a concept-of-morality fact. If God somehow extinguished morality, MP_2 would no longer obtain, although concept-of-morality facts still would. (It would be in the light of concept-of-morality facts that one would conclude that morality has disappeared.)

A similar point, the Kelsenian can argue, is true of LP_1. This principle, which obtains in all possible worlds, is a legal fact, not a concept-of-law fact. This is not to deny that there are concept-of-law facts or that these facts obtain in all possible worlds. But what these concept-of-law facts tell us is precisely that there is a single legal system and that all law ultimately depends upon the fundamental legal principle (or principles) of that system.

Which approach is right? How can one tell whether the fact standing behind legal inferences 2 and 3 is legal or conceptual? Here, it is helpful to consider why we are willing to believe that MP_2 is moral rather than conceptual. One important reason is the non-relativistic character of

has been most clearly emphasised by Scott Shapiro (2011: 103). But similar positions can plausibly be attributed to other Anglophone positivists, including Joseph Raz and H. L. A. Hart.

[59] See Hart 1983: 322.

promissory obligations that occur in different communities. Fred's obligation to Felicia, occurring in community A, and Rob's obligation to Rebecca, occurring in community B, are not relativised to their respective communities. It is not as if Fred had a promissory obligation from A's perspective and Rob had one from B's perspective. Their obligations are co-participants in a single moral order that is independent of any particular community. It is true that community A's existence is required for Fred's moral obligation and that community B's existence is required for Rob's. We might therefore speak of Fred as having a community A promissory obligation and of Rob as having a community B promissory obligation. But that is the case only in the light of a moral order that does not depend upon any community.

Saying that Fred's and Rob's obligations are part of the same moral order does not mean that they cannot conflict. Conflicts of promissory obligations can arise even within the same community or concerning the same person. Fred might have promised to take Felicia to the zoo and promised to take Felix, who is also in community A, to his job interview at the same time. The fact that these two obligations conflict does not mean that they inhabit different moral orders. Indeed, it is only because they are part of the same moral order that they *can* conflict. The same point is true of promissory obligations arising in different communities, such as Fred's and Rob's.

We must therefore consider whether Joe's Ruritanian legal obligation to drive on the left and his Fredonian legal obligation to drive on the right can legally conflict or whether they are relativised to the Ruritanian and Fredonian communities in a way that makes legal conflict between them impossible. For them to legally conflict does not mean (or does not just mean) that they cannot both be satisfied. The conflict must be the legal equivalent of the conflict between moral obligations. There must be normative resistance between the two – even if this resistance cannot be resolved – that is analogous to the normative resistance between two conflicting moral obligations. If so, there is a unity to law that is analogous to the unity of morality.

The Kelsenian approach is to treat the law as unitary.[60] To be sure, Kelsen himself takes the stronger position that the legal norms of different

[60] See, e.g., Kelsen 1967: 333. For Kelsen (1967: 214–15), the unity of law is presented in the context of a particular community's legal system, which assigns to various communities' officials a sphere of law-making authority in space and time. The foundational community

communities must all be legally consistent.[61] Legal conflict is impossible. But, in fact, the existence of legal conflict between the legal norms of two communities would be enough to prove the Kelsenian point that all law is part of a unitary system.

That said, another piece of evidence in favour of the unity of law is the extent to which the social facts in different communities are legally interpreted in a manner that reduces, or eliminates, legal conflict. Assume, for example, that Joe is a Fredonian living in Fredonia. He has never been to Ruritania. The absence of a connection with Ruritania might lead one to interpret Rex's announcement as not creating any legal obligation on Joe. Even though Rex's announcement purports to apply to everyone – and under M_{Rex}, which is accepted by Ruritanian officials, everyone in the world ought to abide by the standards in Rex's announcements – as a legal matter, Rex's command extends only to those with a sufficient connection to Ruritania (such as people driving within its borders). Because this limitation on the validity and scope of Ruritanian legal obligations cannot be derived from social facts about Ruritanian legal practices, the social thesis is false. The limitation must instead follow from a legal fact that does not itself depend upon any community.

Let us add this limitation to LP_1 (and call the result LP_2). A legal inference concerning Rex's and Basil's announcements would look something like this:

Legal inference 4
($C_{Ruritania}$) M_{Rex} is efficacious in Ruritania.
($C_{Fredonia}$) M_{Basil} is efficacious in Fredonia.
(7) Rex has announced that one ought to drive on the left.
(9) Basil has announced that one ought to drive on the right.
Therefore (via LP_2) . . . (11) Joe (who has sufficient connection only to Fredonia) legally ought to drive on the right.

A third, and related, type of evidence that the Kelsenian could offer consists of the legal facts in LP_2 itself – legal facts that obtain in the absence of any social facts about a community's legal practices. If it is

could be a nation (a position Kelsen sometimes calls 'state subjectivism'; Kelsen 1945: 386; Kelsen 1967: 345; Kelsen 1992: 116) or it could be the community of nations (which Kelsen sometimes calls 'objectivism'; Kelsen 1945: 386; 1967: 344). In the Kelsenian position I present here, by contrast, the unity of law follows from a foundational legal authorisation that is not tied to any particular community, not even the community of nations. See note 19.

61 See Kelsen 1967: 74, 205–8; Kelsen 1992: 112.

a legal fact that a community's officials cannot impose a legal obligation on those who have no connection with the community, that fact would pre-exist the communities to which it applies. The existence of this legal fact would mean that the social thesis is false.

In short, the Kelsenian argument against the social thesis is essentially connected to his doctrine of the unity of law.[62] If the doctrine is false and the law of one community exists independently of the law of another community, then the social thesis follows: law ultimately depends upon social facts about a community's legal practices.[63] It is for this reason that Kelsen, having rejected legal psychologism (and so the social thesis), consistently and unequivocally states that the unity of law is inescapable.[64]

The way that Kelsen structures his argument can lead one to conclude otherwise, because he generally saves his discussion of the unity of law towards the end of his major works.[65] Before that point, he tends to talk about the law of a particular nation, assuming that the person cognising the law takes that nation's law to be the only possibility. But he makes it clear that insofar as we consider it possible for there to be multiple nations, each possessing valid laws – which we in fact do – we must be viewing these nations' laws as subsystems of a unitary legal system.

Whether Kelsen is right about the unity of law is, therefore, a question of the utmost importance in the philosophy of law, one that has so far been ignored by Anglophone philosophers of law. They must consider whether the laws of multiple communities fit together legally – whether they legally interact with one another (at a minimum such that they conflict) – or whether they are always relativised to a particular community's perspective.

It is irrelevant whether such universalistic reasoning about the law, which takes one into the realm of international law (both public and private), is a recent phenomenon.[66] The *ordo cognoscendi* does not reveal the *ordo essendi*. After all, it is very likely that moral reasoning originally consisted of members of a community thinking solely about what they ought to do. It was only when they were exposed to different communities that they began to think about how another community's existence might

[62] See Kelsen 1992: 113. [63] See Kelsen 1945: 375–6; Kelsen 1992: 114.

[64] See Kelsen 1945: 363–4, 373; Kelsen 1967: 328–35; Kelsen 1992: 111–14.

[65] See Kelsen 1945: 363–88; Kelsen 1967: 320–47; Kelsen 1992: 111–12.

[66] For this mistake, see Marmor 2011: 23 n. 18, who describes Kelsen's doctrine of the unity of law as 'anachronistic'.

generate different moral obligations for its members – and how the moral obligations of the members of different communities fit together morally. The fact that thought about this overarching moral order came later tells us nothing about moral priority: it is the overarching moral order that is morally foundational. The same point, the Kelsenian can argue, applies to the law.

There is some similarity between the Kelsenian non-reductivist argument, so understood, and a position in the philosophy of law recently advanced by Mark Greenberg.[67] The foundation of Greenberg's argument is that an adequate theory of law must account for what he calls the *rational-relation requirement.*[68] The idea, roughly, is that it must be intelligible how social facts about legal practices in a community determine legal facts. Greenberg argues that positivists, for whom the determination-relation is itself solely based in social facts about a community's legal practices, cannot satisfy the requirement. As Greenberg puts it, law practices themselves cannot determine how they contribute to the content of the law.[69]

Greenberg's position is supported by the Kelsenian non-reductivist's observation that the social facts upon which the positivist seeks to base the determination-relation (like the facts described by $C_{Ruritania}$) are among the facts to which the determination-relation itself applies. An example is legal inference 4. If the determination-relation applies to the facts in $C_{Ruritania}$, it cannot be based on the facts in $C_{Ruritania}$.

Greenberg argues that the best way of making the determination-relation intelligible is by reference to moral facts.[70] The Kelsenian's commitment to the separation thesis takes this off the table. Instead, he appeals to legal facts, like LP_2.

One final note: In my argument, I have drawn analogies between the moral and the legal orders. I did so because Anglophone philosophers of law are familiar with arguments for a non-natural unitary moral order. But there is an essential difference between the two. The legal order does not necessarily give people justifying reasons for action. Our goal is solely to argue for the existence of a non-natural unitary legal order, not to show that it makes a justified claim on our practical reasoning.

[67] On these similarities, see Pavlakos forthcoming. [68] Greenberg 2006: 265.
[69] See Greenberg 2004: 178–84. [70] See Greenberg 2004: 163–4.

12.4 Kelsen's Neo-Kantianism

If the Kelsenian position is correct and the legal order exists independently of social or other natural facts, it follows that we cannot confirm empirically that law exists. We do not experience the law, even though we experience the events that have legal consequences in its light. If so, how can the law be known? How is such knowledge possible given that there is no connection between the law and the human beings who have beliefs about it?

12.4.1 Transcendental Idealism

It is here that Kelsen's neo-Kantianism plays a role. Kelsen was most strongly influenced not by Kant himself but by forms of neo-Kantianism prevalent in the late nineteenth and early twentieth centuries.[71] For our purposes, we can set aside their details and consider, at a very high level of abstraction, three of their most important characteristics.

The first is anti-scepticism. Rather than seeking to convince the sceptic that we have a certain body of knowledge, one takes its existence as an established fact and explores its presuppositions – in particular, elements that cannot be derived from experience.[72] The second is idealism. In rejecting scepticism, these neo-Kantians did not assume that we have some sort of non-sensory contact with these non-experienced elements. Instead, the elements are understood as a condition for representing the objects of our knowledge. These objects are mind-dependent in the sense that they are subject to the conditions for representing them.[73]

The third characteristic is scrupulous anti-psychologism. One might think that adopting idealism would mean accepting that what is known is not objective, that it varies depending upon the characteristics of the person representing it. If we submit the objects of our knowledge to different conditions for representation, we will have different objects. But it is crucial to see that the idealism at issue is transcendental, not empirical. A distinction is drawn between human psychology (including any

[71] On the influence of neo-Kantians (and especially Hermann Cohen) on Kelsen, see Ebenstein 1945: 3–42; Edel 1998; M. S. Green 2003: 389–405; Paulson 1992.

[72] On this aspect of the neo-Kantians, see Poma 1997: 61–3; Edel 1988: 504–5.

[73] This is, of course, Kant's 'Copernican Revolution' in philosophy; Kant 1965: Bxvi.

presuppositions we might make as a psychological fact) and the objects of our knowledge.[74] The latter do not depend upon the former. Thus, although the world that we know is subject to the conditions for representing it, what is represented is an objective world – a world that does not depend upon the people knowing it. Just how the neo-Kantians resolved the tension between idealism and anti-psychologism is not our concern here.[75] What is important is that they, and Kelsen, thought that it could be resolved.

Thus, Kelsen's approach to the legal order was anti-sceptical. He does not try to respond to someone who doubts its existence or our ability to know it. One can, of course, be an ontological anarchist and refuse to see the world in the light of the legal order,[76] although such a stance would render '[t]he thousands of statements in which the law is expressed daily ... senseless'.[77] But Kelsen assumes our knowledge of the legal order and explores its presuppositions.[78] Among these presuppositions is what he calls the basic norm (or what I call fundamental legal principles).

Kelsen does not assume that we have some kind of non-sensory access to the basic norm. Instead, it is understood as a condition for representing the legal order. In this sense, he was an idealist: '[T]he science of law as cognition of the law, like any cognition, has constitutive character – it "creates" its object insofar as it comprehends the object as a meaningful whole.'[79] But that does not mean that the legal order is subjective, in the sense that it is relative to our way of thinking about it. Kelsen distinguished between the law and the people who know it: 'The Pure Theory of Law does not look to mental processes or physical events of any kind in seeking to cognize norms, in seeking to comprehend something legally. To comprehend something legally can only be to comprehend it as law.'[80] What is

[74] For Kant (1965: B131–3), anti-psychologism followed from the fact that the subject representing the world is the transcendental self – a subject of experience that cannot be made an empirically known object. But the neo-Kantians who influenced Kelsen were anti-psychologists while dispensing with talk about the activities of a transcendental self. See Edel 1998: 205–7; M. S. Green 2003: 395–8; Poma 1997: 18–19.

[75] For a discussion, see M. S. Green 2003: 389–98.

[76] Kelsen 1967: 101; Kelsen 1992: 33.

[77] Kelsen 1945: 436; Kelsen 1967: 104.

[78] One way of putting this point is that Kelsen does not seek to provide a progressive but at most a regressive transcendental argument; Paulson 2013. Anglophone positivists tend to assume that Kelsen's neo-Kantianism is viable only if he sought to offer a progressive argument, according to which interpreting experience legally is, in some sense, inescapable. See, e.g., Marmor 2011: 21 (the basic norm must be 'something like a necessary feature or category of human cognition').

[79] Kelsen 1967: 72.

[80] Kelsen 1967: 11.

represented is an objective legal order independent of human beings.[81] His goal was 'the passage from the subjective sphere of psychologism to the field of logical-objective validity'.[82]

The fact that Kelsen's idealism is transcendental is essential to understanding his occasional statements that the law has a validity that is only 'relative' to the adoption of a basic norm.[83] These might appear to mean that the law is not objective – that it depends upon psychological facts about how we, or members of a community, think about the law. But such a reading attributes to Kelsen the very psychologism that he rejected. Instead, to say that the law has a relative validity is to deny metaphysical realism concerning the law (a position that Kelsen associates with a natural law approach),[84] that is, the view that the law has reality independent of the conditions for representing it and that we possess some sort of non-sensory contact with it.

12.4.2 Efficacy

Appreciating the transcendental nature of Kelsen's legal idealism also allows us to make sense of his otherwise puzzling statements about the relationship between law and efficacy, where efficacy is understood, roughly, as the fact that legal norms are generally applied by officials and generally obeyed by the relevant population.[85] These statements are commonly taken to mean that Kelsen ultimately accepted the social thesis.[86]

Sometimes these statements are simply the articulation of the content of a legal norm from which law of various communities follows.[87] As we have seen, the fact that LP_1 refers to a meta-standard that is *efficacious* within a community does not mean that the social thesis is true, since LP_1 does not itself depend upon social facts.

At times, however, it appears that Kelsen is not talking about the content of a legal norm but, instead, about the conditions under which the basic norm standing at the basis of all law is presupposed. A basic norm is not

[81] For an example of a psychologistic reading of Kelsen, see Marmor 2011: 23. For more on Marmor's reading, see M. S. Green 2016: 39–40, 47–9.

[82] Kelsen 1925: vii.

[83] See, e.g., Kelsen 1945: 393–6; Kelsen 1967: 217–18.

[84] Ebenstein 1945: 93; Kelsen 1945: 396; Kelsen 1967: 220.

[85] See Kelsen 1967: 210.

[86] See, e.g., Marmor 2011: 20.

[87] See Kelsen 1945: 121; Kelsen 1967: 211.

presupposed unless it validates an efficacious system of legal norms.[88] But these statements do not mean that he accepted the social thesis either.

In keeping with his transcendental idealism, Kelsen distinguishes between the legal order, which is outside space and time, and people's judgements about the legal order, which are facts about the natural world. Kelsen's claims about efficacy concern the conditions for our judgements about the legal order, not the conditions for the legal order itself.[89] As a psychological matter, a basic norm is not presupposed unless it validates an efficacious system of norms. From such psychological facts, nothing about the conditions for law itself follows.

Consider a moral analogy. A moral non-naturalist can concede that we make moral judgements only if certain psychological facts are in place. We do not judge that X is good unless we have a positive attitude towards X or the members of our community by and large approve of X. But she can still insist that nothing about morality itself follows from these facts about our moral judgements.

That said, there are times when Kelsen's discussion of the role of efficacy in connection with a choice of a basic norm does not appear to be purely psychological. Instead, efficacy plays a role in determining whether a choice of a basic norm is justified.[90] One *should* interpret social facts in the light of a basic norm that validates an efficacious system of norms.[91] But even these statements do not mean that Kelsen accepted the social thesis.

Let us imagine someone who interprets social facts in the light of a basic norm that fails to satisfy the requirement of efficacy. An example is the basic norm that everyone in the world legally ought to obey the standards announced by Rex and all officials ought to enforce those standards. Such a person would conclude that Basil's announcements in Fredonia and the

[88] See Kelsen 1967: 210; Kelsen 1992: 60.

[89] Kelsen commonly speaks of the role of efficacy in explicitly psychological terms: see Kelsen 1967: 11 ('A norm that is not obeyed by anyone anywhere, in other words a norm that is not effective at least to some degree, *is not regarded* as a valid legal norm'); 86 ('[N]ormative order *is considered* valid only if it is by and large effective'); 210 ('As soon as the old constitution loses its effectiveness and a new one has become effective, the acts that appear with the subjective meaning of creating or applying legal norms *are no longer interpreted* by presupposing the old basic norm, but by presupposing the new one') (emphases all mine).

[90] See Kelsen 1920: 94–101; Kelsen 1945: 436–7; Kelsen 1967: 201.

[91] See Kelsen 1992: 59–60.

actions of Fredonian officials that enforce these announcements are without legal consequence (except, perhaps, as treasonous acts). The legal situation in Fredonia becomes very simple. By contrast, once one adopts a basic norm that satisfies the requirement of efficacy (such as LP_1 or LP_2), a wealth of legal meaning in Fredonia emerges. This problem with the choice of a basic norm that violates the requirement of efficacy is *legal* – the impoverishment of the legal consequences of social facts. The problem is not that law is reducible to social facts about efficacy.

Consider the following moral analogy. The moral non-naturalist can accept that something like the requirement of efficacy applies concerning promissory obligations. There should be substantial overlap between what is morally required for a promissory obligation to exist and what people think is required. If one assumes a principle of promissory obligation that violates this requirement (for example, that only promises in writing create moral obligations), promissory obligations become too rare. And that is a *moral* problem: the impoverishment of the moral consequences of social facts. Accepting that there is this moral problem with a non-efficacious principle of promissory obligation does not mean accepting that promissory obligations are reducible to social facts about efficacy.

12.4.3 The Basic Norm

Up to this point, I have assumed that what stand behind our legal inferences are fundamental legal principles to which one might explicitly appeal, just as one might explicitly appeal to fundamental moral principles in one's moral inferences. An example is legal inference 4, in which we concluded that Joe has only a legal obligation to drive on the right by reference to LP_2, according to which a community's officials cannot create legal obligations on those who have an insufficient connection to the community. As a personal matter, I believe that such fundamental legal principles have been articulated, if imperfectly, in the fields of international law (both public and private).[92] This makes the argument in favour of Kelsenian non-reductivism relatively straightforward. Since these fundamental legal principles obtain in all possible worlds, including worlds in which there are no human communities, the social thesis is false.

[92] See M. S. Green 2018.

Kelsen approaches the matter differently. The basic norm cannot be appealed to in legal inferences, although it plays an essential role in them. In this sense, the basic norm is not a legal norm. My goal here is not to spell out the details of Kelsen's views but solely to describe enough to show why his doctrine of the basic norm is nevertheless compatible with non-reductivism.

We have understood a fundamental legal principle like LP_2 as obtaining in all possible worlds. It is, for that reason, unconditioned: it does not depend for its existence on any contingent fact. An analogy in causal reasoning would be a first cause (a prime mover), which brings about an effect without itself being caused. Of course, Kant thought that an appeal to first causes inappropriately takes the category of causality beyond possible experience.[93] Although the category is not derived from experience, it is appropriately applied only when linking experienced content. It should not be applied in the absence of such content.

Kelsen adopted a similar view concerning legal inferences. To explicitly appeal to the unconditioned in legal inferences is as inappropriate as appealing to first causes in science.[94] This is the case even though legal dependence, unlike causal dependence, does not go on forever. There will be a point at which there is experienced content – the creation of what Kelsen calls the historically first constitution –[95] that cannot be legally linked to earlier experienced content.

Kelsen nevertheless insisted that legal and causal inferences are analogous. Appropriate legal inference links content provided by experience – in particular, content provided by social facts.[96] It follows that the positivity thesis applies universally: all legal obligations, permissions *and authorisations* are 'created' by social facts. By contrast, under the Kelsenian non-reductivist position I presented, LP_2 was a non-posited legal authorisation.

Kelsen does not merely think that appropriate *legal* inference must link content derived from social facts; he has the same view about any appropriate normative inference, including moral inference. Most people have no problem with justifying moral inferences by reference to foundational moral principles whose content is not derived from social facts. These fundamental moral principles are considered self-evident. That is how

[93] See Kant 1965: A444–51/B472–9.

[94] See Ebenstein 1945: 85; Kelsen 1921; Kelsen 1945: 396.

[95] Kelsen 1967: 200.

[96] See Kelsen 1950; Kelsen 1967: 71; Kelsen 1992: 24–5; Paulson 2001: 55–9.

I have understood MP_1 and MP_2. Kelsen would treat this as an inappropriate appeal to natural law.[97] In this sense, he believes that a positivity thesis should apply to the moral order too: all moral obligations, permissions and authorisations should be understood as 'created' by social facts.

I think that the analogy that Kelsen draws between normative and causal inference, which generates his peculiar views about the basic norm, is mistaken. But what is important for our purposes is that his doctrine of the basic norm remains compatible with his legal non-reductivism. Because the basic norm is not a legal norm, some read Kelsen as grounding the law in some sort of non-legal facts.[98] That is a mistake. Although his views on the basic norm varied,[99] his goal remained explaining the presuppositions involved in judgements about the irreducibly legal.

References

Baker, G. P. and Hacker, P. M. S. 1984. *Frege: Logical Excavations.* Oxford University Press.

Bix, B. 2016. 'Kelsen in the United States: Still Misunderstood'. In J. Telman (ed.). *Hans Kelsen in America.* Springer Verlag: 17–29.

Brockhaus, R. R. 1991. 'Realism and Psychologism in 19th Century Logic'. *Philosophy and Phenomenological Research* 51: 493–524.

Cotterrell, R. 1999. *Émile Durkheim: Law in a Moral Domain.* Edinburgh University Press.

Delacroix, S. 2004. 'Hart's and Kelsen's Concepts of Normativity Contrasted'. *Ratio Juris* 17: 501–20.

Delacroix, S. 2006. *Legal Norms and Normativity.* Hart.

Durkheim, É. 2013. *The Rules of Sociological Method and Selected Texts on Sociology and Its Method.* 2nd ed. Palgrave Macmillan.

Ebenstein, W. 1945. *Pure Theory of Law.* University of Wisconsin Press.

Edel, G. 1988. *Von der Vernunftkritik zur Erkenntnislogik: Die Entwicklung der theoretischen Philosophie Hermann Cohens.* Alber.

[97] See Kelsen 1967: 220–1. As Kelsen understands them, natural law theorists can accept the separation thesis provided that they appeal to unconditioned self-evident legal facts in legal inferences. Thus, Kelsen would describe the non-reductive Kelsenian approach that I have offered as a 'natural law' approach.

[98] An example is L. Green 2019.

[99] In addition to understanding it as analogous to a Kantian category, he also treats it as a Cohenian hypothesis – see Edel 1998 – and a Vaihingerian necessary fiction – see Paulson 1992: 269–70; Stewart 1980: 207–8.

Edel, G. 1998. 'The Hypothesis of the Basic Norm: Hans Kelsen and Hermann Cohen'. In S. Paulson and B. Paulson (eds.). *Normativity and Norms: Critical Perspectives on Kelsenian Themes.* Clarendon Press: 195–220.

Edmundson, W. 2004. 'State of the Art: The Duty to Obey the Law'. *Legal Theory* 10: 215–59.

Enoch, D. 2011a. *Taking Morality Seriously: A Defense of Robust Realism.* Oxford University Press.

Enoch, D. 2011b. 'Reason-Giving and the Law'. In L. Green and B. Leiter (eds.). *Oxford Studies in Philosophy of Law* vol. 1. Oxford University Press: 1–38.

Frege, G. 1984a. *The Foundations of Arithmetic.* 2nd ed. Trans. J. Austin. Northwestern University Press.

Frege, G. 1984b. 'Thoughts'. In B. McGuinness (ed.). *Collected Papers on Mathematics, Logic, and Philosophy.* Trans M. Black et al. Basil Blackwell: 351–72.

Frege, G. 1979. *Posthumous Writings.* Blackwell.

Gardner, J. 2001. 'Legal Positivism: 5½ Myths'. *American Journal of Jurisprudence* 46: 199–227.

Green, L. 2008. 'Positivism and the Inseparability of Law and Morals'. *New York University Law Review* 83: 1035–58.

Green, L. 2019. 'Legal Positivism'. In E. N. Zalta (ed.). *Stanford Encyclopedia of Philosophy.* https://plato.stanford.edu/entries/legal-positivism/.

Green, M. S. 2003. 'Hans Kelsen and the Logic of Legal Systems'. *Alabama Law Review* 54: 365–413.

Green, M. S. 2016. 'Marmor's Kelsen'. In J. Telman (ed.). *Hans Kelsen in America.* Springer Verlag: 45–84.

Green, M. S. 2018. 'Legal Monism: An American History'. In C. Bezemek, M. Potacs and A. Somek (eds.). *Vienna Lectures on Legal Philosophy.* Hart: 23–48.

Greenberg, M. 2004. 'How Facts Make Law'. *Legal Theory* 10: 157–98.

Greenberg, M. 2006. 'Hartian Positivism and Normative Facts: How Facts Make Law II'. In S. Hershovitz (ed.). *Exploring Law's Empire: The Jurisprudence of Ronald Dworkin.* Oxford University Press: 265–90.

Greenberg, M. 2014. 'The Moral Impact Theory of Law'. *Yale Law Journal* 123: 1288–1342.

Hart, H. L. A. 1983. *Essays in Jurisprudence and Philosophy.* Oxford University Press.

Hart, H. L. A. 1994. *The Concept of Law.* 2nd ed. Oxford University Press.

Heidemann, C. 1997. *Die Norm als Tatsache: Zur Normentheorie Hans Kelsens.* Nomos.

Jackson, F. and Pettit, P. 1992. 'Structural Explanation in Social Theory'. In D. Charles and K. Lennon (eds.). *Reduction, Explanation, and Realism.* Clarendon Press: 97–131.

Kant, I. 1965. *Critique of Pure Reason.* Trans. N. Smith. St. Martin's Press.

Kelsen, H. 1911. *Hauptprobleme der Staatsrechtslehre: Entwickelt aus der Lehre vom Rechtssatz.* Mohr.

Kelsen, H. 1920. *Das Problem der Souveränität und die Theorie des Völkerrechts*. Mohr.

Kelsen, H. 1921. 'Das Verhältnis von Staat und Recht im Lichte der Erkenntniskritik'. *Zeitschrift für öffentliches Recht* 2: 453–510.

Kelsen, H. 1922a. 'Der Begriff des Staates und die Sozialpsychologie'. *Imago* 8: 97–141.

Kelsen, H. 1922b. *Der soziologische und der juristische Staatsbegriff*. Mohr.

Kelsen, H. 1925. *Algemeine Staatslehre*. Julius Springer.

Kelsen, H. 1945. *General Theory of Law and State*. Trans. A. Wedberg. Harvard University Press.

Kelsen, H. 1950. 'Causality and Imputation'. *Ethics* 61: 1–11.

Kelsen, H. 1957. *What Is Justice?* University of California Press.

Kelsen, H. 1967. *Pure Theory of Law*. 2nd ed. Trans. M. Knight. University of California Press.

Kelsen, H. 1973. *Essays in Legal and Moral Philosophy*. Reidel.

Kelsen, H. 1981. 'On the Basis of Legal Validity'. Trans. S. Paulson. *American Journal of Jurisprudence* 26: 178–89.

Kelsen, H. 1992. *Introduction to the Problems of Legal Theory*. Trans. B. Paulson and S. Paulson. Oxford University Press.

Marmor, A. 2011. *Philosophy of Law*. Princeton University Press.

Paulson, S. L. 1975. 'Review: Constraints on Legal Norms: Kelsen's View in the *Essays*'. *University of Chicago Law Review* 42: 768–86.

Paulson, S. L. 1992. 'Kelsen's Legal Theory: The Final Round'. *Oxford Journal of Legal Studies* 12: 265–74.

Paulson, S. L. 1993. 'Continental Normativism and Its British Counterpart: How Different Are They?'. *Ratio Juris* 6: 227–44.

Paulson, S. L. 1998. 'Four Phases in Hans Kelsen's Legal Theory? Reflections on a Periodization'. *Oxford Journal of Legal Studies* 18: 153–66.

Paulson, S. L. 1999. 'Arriving at a Defensible Periodization of Hans Kelsen's Legal Theory'. *Oxford Journal of Legal Studies* 19: 351–65.

Paulson, S. L. 2000. 'The Weak Reading of Authority in Hans Kelsen's *Pure Theory of Law*'. *Law and Philosophy* 19: 131–71.

Paulson, S. L. 2001. 'Hans Kelsen's Doctrine of Imputation'. *Ratio Juris* 14: 47–63.

Paulson, S. L. 2005. 'Some Issues in the Exchange between Kelsen and Kaufmann'. *Scandinavian Studies in Law* 48: 269–90.

Paulson, S. L. 2012. 'A "Justified Normativity" Thesis in Hans Kelsen's Pure Theory of Law? Rejoinders to Robert Alexy and Joseph Raz'. In M. Klatt (ed.). *Institutionalized Reason: The Jurisprudence of Robert Alexy*. Oxford University Press: 61–111.

Paulson, S. L. 2013. 'The Great Puzzle: Kelsen's Basic Norm'. In L. Duarte d'Almeida, J. Gardner and L. Green (eds.). *Kelsen Revisited: New Essays on the Pure Theory of Law*. Hart: 43–62.

Pavlakos, G. 2018. 'Kelsenian Imputation and the Explanation of Legal Norms'. *Revus* 37: 47–56. https://journals.openedition.org/revus/4808.

Pavlakos, G. Forthcoming. 'A Non-naturalist Account of Law's Place in Reality'. In B. Brozek, J. Hage and N. Vincent (eds.). Law and Mind. A Survey of Law and the Cognitive Sciences. Cambridge University Press.

Plunkett, D. 2012. 'A Positivist Route for Explaining How Facts Make Law'. *Legal Theory* 18: 139–207.

Poma, A. 1997. *The Critical Philosophy of Hermann Cohen.* Trans. J. Denton. SUNY Press.

Rawls, J. 1971. *A Theory of Justice.* Harvard University Press.

Raz, J. 1979. *The Authority of Law.* Oxford University Press.

Raz, J. 1994. *Ethics in the Public Domain.* Oxford University Press.

Scanlon, T. M. 1998. *What We Owe to Each Other.* Harvard University Press.

Shapiro, S. J. 2011. *Legality.* Harvard University Press.

Stewart, I. 1980. 'The Basic Norm as Fiction'. *Juridical Review* 25: 199–224.

Wilson, A. 1982. 'Joseph Raz on Kelsen's Basic Norm'. *American Journal of Jurisprudence* 27: 46–63.

The Legal Positivism of H. L. A. Hart 13

Matthew H. Kramer *

13.1 Introduction

H. L. A. Hart was the foremost Anglophone philosopher of law in the twentieth century, and he was rivalled only by Hans Kelsen as the foremost philosopher of law in any language during that century.[1] Among his many sterling accomplishments in the philosophy of law was his reinvigoration of the tradition of legal positivism. His revival of that tradition greatly strengthened it by transforming it in some major respects – not least by severing it from the command theory of law that had been propounded (in distinct versions) by his illustrious predecessors Jeremy Bentham and John Austin. Yet, in spite of the distance that Hart put between himself and those predecessors, he was firmly aligned with them in his emphasis on the distinction between what legal institutions are and what legal institutions morally ought to be. With his general insistence on the separability of law and morality, he established himself as an opponent of natural-law theorists and their efforts to show that law is an inherently moral phenomenon. Indeed, the arguments through which he impugned a multiplicity of natural-law lines of reasoning are one feature of his book *The Concept of Law* that has cemented its place as a classic text with which generations of legal philosophers will perennially grapple.

In the first several chapters of *The Concept of Law*, Hart developed the 'positive' side of legal positivism by elaborating an account of the nature of law without any suggestion that law is an inherently moral

* I am grateful to Torben Spaak for his salutary comments on an earlier draft of this chapter, and I am likewise grateful to the participants in a workshop at the University of Stockholm in April 2019 for their feedback.

[1] Hart touched on Kelsen's work intermittently in *The Concept of Law*, but his main engagements with Kelsen are in Hart 1983: chs. 14–15. There are also some interesting reflections on Kelsen in Hart 2013: 287–92.

phenomenon. In the penultimate chapter of the book, he took up the cudgels on behalf of the 'negative' side of legal positivism by denying forthrightly that law is an inherently moral phenomenon.[2] He did not entirely avoid confusion and misjudgements in his discussions of legal positivism, but those discussions overall have been invaluable in enhancing the rigour and clarity of subsequent treatments of the topic. Both by elaborating some of the principal theses of legal positivism and by assailing many of the misconceptions about it that have been propagated in the writings of its opponents, Hart sharpened the thinking of legal philosophers about the sundry relationships between law and morality. Writing at a time when the horrors of Fascism and Communism had led numerous jurisprudential theorists to denounce legal positivism for what they perceived as its excessively deferential attitude towards the directives of legal-governmental officials, he cogently maintained that such strictures against positivism were based on badly distortive misapprehensions about its orientation. Albeit positivism does not in itself commit its proponents to any particular positions on matters of politics or legal interpretation, its tenets are highly serviceable for theorists who are vigilantly distrustful of the demands issued by governments. Hart himself was such a theorist, whose espousal of legal positivism stemmed partly from his resistance to the idea that legal requirements are always morally binding. By making clear that positivism can fruitfully be drawn upon in furtherance of social justice against the legal mandates that emanate from the institutions of government, he helped to dispel one of the most pernicious jurisprudential misconceptions. In so doing, he performed a service not only for the advocates of legal positivism but also for its detractors.

13.2 The Rejection of the Command Theory of Law

Before defending legal positivism against its opponents, Hart had to save it from its champions. In the early chapters of *The Concept of Law*, he endeavoured to dissociate legal positivism from the command theory of law that had been developed by Austin in the first half of the nineteenth

2 On the distinction between 'positive' and 'negative' legal positivism, see Coleman 1982 (though I understand each side of that distinction more broadly than does Coleman).

century.[3] (In a number of later essays, Hart devoted attention to Bentham far more than to Austin. However, because Hart's objections to the Austinian model of law are more influential and systematic than anything in his later work, I will concentrate on them here.) In Austin's strongly top-down account, every law in any jurisdiction is a mandate issued by a sovereign to members of the citizenry. The sovereign's directives are backed by threats of sanctions that are to be imposed in the event of any non-compliance by citizens with those directives. Whereas the sovereign is habitually obeyed by everyone else in the jurisdiction, the sovereign does not obey anyone.

Hart landed an array of telling blows against the Austinian command model, but every one of his queries was aimed at demonstrating the inadequacy of a theory that is so unattuned to the operativeness of norms in legal systems. By obfuscating rather than illuminating the normativity of law, an Austinian approach distorts virtually every major aspect of law of which it treats. In his critique of Austin and throughout his theorising, Hart took norms to be standards (of varying degrees of generality or specificity) which prescribe how people ought to conduct themselves. Crucial for one's accurate understanding of his critique – and specifically of its location in the tradition of legal positivism – is one's recognition that the norms to which he adverted are not necessarily moral. Normativity, including law's normativity, always involves an orientation towards what ought to be; but, as Hart repeatedly remarked, the 'ought' in question is not perforce a moral 'ought'.

Still, although the norms of a legal system are not necessarily moral in their content or in certain other respects that will be expounded later, they are indeed norms which underlie and guide the operations of such a system. Austin's jurisprudential theory is to be rejected largely because of its thoroughgoing disregard of the roles of those norms. For example, because the Austinian theory presents all laws as mandates that are backed by threats of sanctions for disobedience, it obfuscates the crucial roles of power-conferring norms in any legal system of governance. Hart allowed that there is some resemblance between the mandates of an Austinian sovereign and the statutes of criminal law or tort law that impose legal duties on people. However, he submitted that there is no such resemblance

[3] For a much longer treatment of Hart's rejection of the Austinian command theory of law, see Kramer 2018: 32–59.

between Austinian mandates and the sundry laws of any jurisdiction that confer legal powers on people. Among those latter laws are norms that enable people to carry out private transactions such as the formation of contracts or the conveyance of real estate or the donation of funds to charities. Also among the power-conferring laws are norms that authorise public officials to perform their functions of legislation or administration or adjudication. Such power-conferring laws are integral to the very existence and operativeness of any legal system, yet they find no place in Austin's model of law. As Hart proclaimed, 'there is a radical difference between rules conferring and defining the manner of exercise of legislative powers and the rules of criminal law, which at least resemble orders backed by threats'.[4]

Dissimilarities between duty-imposing norms and power-conferring norms are especially salient in public-law settings. While recounting a host of laws that empower officials to engage in their legislative or administrative or adjudicative activities,[5] Hart drew on a legislative example to accentuate vividly the divergences between such laws and duty-imposing mandates:

> If a measure before a legislative body obtains the required majority of votes and is thus duly passed, the voters in favour of the measure have not 'obeyed' the law requiring a majority decision nor have those who voted against [the measure] either obeyed or disobeyed [that law]: the same is of course true if the measure fails to obtain the required majority and so no law is passed.[6]

As Hart declared: 'The radical difference in function between [a law that prescribes the majoritarian procedures and a law that imposes some duty] prevents the use here of the terminology appropriate to conduct in its relation to rules of the criminal law.'[7]

Hart, in his sundry criticisms of Austin, showed time and again that the Austinian model of law presupposes the operativeness of power-conferring norms even while it fails to supply any account of their operativeness. His general strategy is well exemplified in his complaint about the inability of the command theory to explain how the members of a sovereign legislative body can be bound by their own directives.[8] Though the members of the

[4] Hart 1994: 31. [5] See Hart 1994: 28–32. [6] Hart 1994: 31–2. [7] Hart 1994: 32.
[8] See Hart 1994: 42–4.

supreme legislative body in virtually any society are exempt from some of the legal requirements that apply to most other people, they along with everyone else are subject to most ordinary legal requirements. Like everyone else, those members are not legally at liberty to engage in acts of arson or murder or fraud or rape. Yet, in this respect as in sundry other respects, the actualities of virtually every system of governance do not fit the Austinian model of a gunman writ large. When a gunman issues his behests to his victims, he is solely the addressor of those behests and not an addressee thereof. Austin's top-down model of law, with its portrayal of a sovereign whose mandates are imposed on citizens from a position of dominant ascendance, does not leave room for a sovereign body whose members are bound by those very mandates.

As Hart observed, the most enticing route of escape for a defender of Austin lies in differentiating between the capacity of each legislator as a private individual and the capacity of each legislator as a sovereign official. Legal requirements incumbent on each legislator have been imposed on him or her in his or her private capacity by the legislators collectively, each of whom has acted in his or her public capacity as a member of a sovereign body. So a defender of Austin might be inclined to respond. A private/public distinction of this kind is irreproachable in itself, but, as Hart remarked, it is not available to a supporter of Austin. After all, any such private/public distinction presupposes the operativeness of power-conferring laws that invest some people with public powers as legislators – yet, as we have seen, power-conferring laws have no place in an Austinian command theory. When somebody invokes a private/public distinction to accommodate Hart's observation that ordinary legal requirements in any typical society apply to the members of the topmost legislative body therein, he or she has abandoned the Austinian understanding of law.

Thus, by advancing the observation just mentioned as well as by advancing his volley of other objections, Hart revealed how the insuperable weaknesses of the Austinian command theory flow from that theory's blindness to the normativity of law. Time and again, a defender of Austin will find that the limitations of the command theory can be overcome only through the renunciation of that theory in favour of an approach which recognises that any legal system operates as a matrix of complicatedly interrelated norms. That same basic point emerged in every one of the criticisms which Hart marshalled against Austin.

13.3 The Components of Hart's Jurisprudential Theory

Having distanced himself from the Austinian command theory of law, Hart put together the components of his alternative approach.[9] Though he remained firmly within the tradition of legal positivism to which the command theory in its several versions had also belonged, he set out to dissociate that tradition from the misrepresentations and distortions which he had exposed in the Austinian account of law. Instead of trying to tinker with the command theory to remedy its shortcomings while staying within its confines, he sought to displace that theory and to steer the tradition of positivism along a markedly different path.

Hart assembled most of the constituents of his own jurisprudential model after he had completed his critique of the command theory, but he introduced some of them in the course of that critique. The latter constituents include his distinctions among the several viewpoints or perspectives which people can adopt in relation to any norms. Although he presented his chief discussion of those viewpoints after he had finished his confrontation with Austin, he initially adverted to them while he was still waging that confrontation. Partly for that reason, and partly because the distinctions among the various points of view are of such moment in Hart's legal philosophy, this section will commence with them.

13.3.1 The Different Points of View

Especially important in Hartian jurisprudence is the internal point of view, which is the perspective of a person who participates in some practice or activity or institution. Such a person seeks to uphold the duty-imposing norms of the practice or activity or institution, by adopting a critical reflective attitude in relation to them. Hart explained that that critical reflective attitude manifests itself as a triad of behavioural dispositions: a general disposition to comply with the requirements of some duty-imposing norm(s) insofar as they are applicable to one's conduct; a general disposition to object to contraventions of those requirements by other

[9] For a much longer exposition of Hart's alternative to the Austinian command theory, see Kramer 2018: 60–109. Unfortunately, I will not be able to say anything in this chapter about Hart's account of legal reasoning and interpretation. For an exploration of that account, see Kramer 2018: 110–47.

people; and a general disposition to acknowledge the appropriateness of censure that is directed against one's own contraventions of those requirements. Somebody who has adopted the critical reflective attitude in relation to some duty-imposing norm N is thereby accepting N and displaying a commitment to N. However, the stance of commitment need not be based on any perception of N as morally worthy. A person can adopt the critical reflective attitude towards N for moral reasons, of course, but her embrace of such a stance might alternatively be grounded on self-interested considerations or some other factors. Hart commented more than once that the motivations which impel citizens or officials to uphold legal norms can be quite diverse.[10] Still, whatever may be the considerations that prompt someone to assume a posture of commitment in relation to N, that posture is distinctive of the viewpoint of a participant. Anyone who occupies such a perspective – the internal perspective – maintains that the requirements established by N are binding on himself or herself and on others.

Naturally, the internal standpoint of a participant in a practice is to be contrasted with the external standpoint of an observer. However, there are two varieties of the external perspective that should be taken into account here.[11] Somewhat peculiarly, Hart in *The Concept of Law* devoted most of his attention to an implausibly extreme variety of the external perspective, and he devoted considerably less attention to a far more important variety. An observer who adopts the extreme external viewpoint in relation to some practice or institution will regard that practice or institution as a configuration of regularities in the behaviour of the people who participate therein. Such an observer makes no effort to understand people's actions in the ways in which they are understood by the people themselves. Instead, while charting the patterns of their conduct, he or she proceeds in much the same manner as a meteorologist who monitors the formation of clouds. Though such an observer might not deny that people harbour outlooks and beliefs, he or she ignores such mental states in order to concentrate solely on the surface of their behaviour.

Quite different is the approach of someone who theorises from a moderate external perspective. While such an observer certainly does not ignore the aspects of institutions and practices that are the preoccupation of an extreme external theorist, he or she attributes normative attitudes and beliefs and concerns to the people who participate in those institutions

[10] See Hart 1994: 197, 203, 231–2, 257. [11] See Hart 1994: 89–91.

or practices. Such an observer takes account of the ways in which those people perceive their own conduct, and he or she incorporates their perceptions into his or her overall exposition of their institutions or practices. Although such an observer of course detects the regularities of behaviour in which those institutions or practices consist, he or she also recognises that outlooks of acceptance or commitment or allegiance are operative in those patterns of behaviour, and he or she ascribes such outlooks to the people involved. A moderate external observer, qua external observer, does not harbour those attitudes towards the institutions or practices which he or she studies – but he or she discerns that any adequate analysis of the institutions or practices will have to reveal how they are animated by those attitudes on the part of participants. Moreover, of course, a moderate external observer might be a participant in some of those institutions or practices as well as an observer of them; if so, then he or she too displays the attitudes which he or she imputes to the other participants. (Note that, because the outlooks of acceptance or commitment harboured by participants in institutions and practices do not necessarily derive from moral concerns, a moderate external observer of those institutions and practices should typically leave open the nature of the underlying considerations that prompt people to participate supportively in them. As has been mentioned, Hart himself left open this very matter when he recounted the internal viewpoints of citizens and officials in relation to legal institutions.)

Now, whereas the moderate external viewpoint is the perspective from which Hart presented his theory of law, the internal viewpoint is the perspective of greatest importance within that theory.[12] Only through the adoption of the internal point of view by certain people – especially by legal-governmental officials – can the operations of a legal system of governance ever emerge and persist. In the absence of the adoption and sustainment of the internal viewpoint by those people with regard to the norms of such a system, the system would not exist at all.

13.3.2 The Primary/Secondary Distinction

In addition to differentiating among the standpoints that people can adopt in relation to norms, Hart differentiated among types of norms. Having already noted his distinction between duty-imposing norms and power-conferring

[12] On a further distinct perspective, the simulative perspective, see Kramer 2018: 65–70.

norms, we should now briefly ponder his related distinction between primary norms and secondary norms. That latter distinction is fundamental to his theory of law, for he took the essence of every central instance of a legal system to reside in the complex combination of primary and secondary norms.

Though Hart sometimes appeared to suggest that the distinction between primary norms and secondary norms is equivalent to the distinction between duty-imposing norms and power-conferring norms, we should not credit any such suggestion. Instead, he stated the primary/secondary dichotomy accurately when he submitted that secondary norms are parasitic upon primary norms (whereas there is no similar relationship of dependence in the other direction).[13] Hart was here using the term 'parasitic' in a somewhat technical philosophical sense to mean that the contents of secondary norms presuppose the existence of other norms. He was seeking to make the same point which he articulated in his somewhat later assertion that secondary norms 'may all be said to be on a different level from the primary rules, for they are all *about* such rules'.[14] Now, on the one hand, it is indeed true that the content of every power-conferring norm presupposes the existence of some additional norm(s). On the other hand, however, the contents of some duty-imposing norms and of some liberty-conferring norms also presuppose the existence of additional norms. For example, a judge can be under a legal duty to exercise a legal power of sentencing in specified circumstances; the content of the law that imposes the duty presupposes the existence of a law that confers the power of sentencing. Similarly, the judge is legally at liberty to exercise the power of sentencing in specified circumstances. That legal liberty has been conferred upon the judge by a norm whose content presupposes the existence of a law that confers the power of sentencing. Hence, when the distinction between primary norms and secondary norms is drawn with reference to the property of being parasitic, it does not correspond to the distinction between duty-imposing norms and power-conferring norms. All power-conferring norms are parasitic, but not all parasitic norms are power-conferring. Some parasitic norms are duty-imposing, and some are liberty-conferring.

In the fifth chapter of *The Concept of Law*, Hart encouraged his readers to imagine a society in which there are no secondary norms. He pointed to three main sets of problems that would afflict any such society. First, there

[13] Hart 1994: 81. [14] Hart 1994: 94 (emphasis in original).

would be irresolvable uncertainty concerning the existence and contents of the prevailing primary norms. As Hart wrote, 'if doubts arise as to what the rules are or as to the precise scope of some given rule, there will be no procedure for settling this doubt, either by reference to an authoritative text or to an official whose declarations on this point are authoritative'.[15] Second, a severe problem of stagnancy would obtain, as there would not exist any way in which the prevailing primary norms could be deliberately changed. Even more outlandish is that there would not exist any way in which the rights and duties and liberties bestowed by the prevailing primary norms could be deliberately changed.[16] Third, there would be further irresolvable uncertainty concerning the occurrence or non-occurrence of contraventions of the prevailing primary norms. Even if the members of the fanciful society could all agree about the existence and content of some norm N, they might disagree intractably over the question whether N has been contravened in some particular setting. There would be no means of resolving such a question peacefully and authoritatively.[17] Furthermore, even were there no doubt about the occurrence of some contravention, there would not be any authoritative way of administering a sanction or some other remedy in response to that contravention. Self-help, perhaps with assistance from the members of one's family or clan, would be the only recourse.

Hart delineated three main types of secondary norms, which serve to avert or minimise the incidence of the three grave afflictions that have just been described.[18] First is the Rule of Recognition, which provides for the authoritative ascertainment of the norms that are laws in any given society. Despite the designation attached to it by Hart, which will be explained shortly, the Rule of Recognition is an array of norms. Some of those norms impose duties on legal officials to put into effect certain criteria that specify the fundamental sources of laws in a jurisdiction, and the remaining norms in the Rule of Recognition confer powers on the officials to bind other people and themselves with their law-ascertaining determinations. Through the imposition of those duties and the conferral of those powers, the problem of irresolvable uncertainty about the existence and contents of the regnant laws is addressed. To be sure, the alleviation of that problem is consistent with some disagreements

[15] Hart 1994: 92. [16] See Hart 1994: 92–3. [17] See Hart 1994: 93–4.
[18] See Hart 1994: 94–8.

among the legal officials themselves about the substance of the Rule of Recognition. Officials in a functional legal system converge with one another in their understandings of the key criteria laid down by their Rule of Recognition, but they can and frequently do diverge from one another over the details of the criteria – much as the speakers of English or some other natural language diverge from one another over details of usage and grammar. Still, the wide-rangingness of the convergence among the officials is what largely removes any irresolvable uncertainty about the laws that are applicable to people's conduct.

Next among the secondary norms which Hart enumerated are the norms of change. These are many of the power-conferring laws to which he had adverted in his critique of Austin. For example, included in this category are the laws that enable individuals to form sundry legal arrangements such as contracts, marriages, wills, trusts, and conveyances. Besides the laws that confer those private powers are laws that confer public powers of legislation and administrative rule-making. Laws that confer these public powers enable the creation or modification or rescission of general legal norms, while laws that confer the private powers enable the creation or modification or rescission of the legal positions – such as claim-rights, duties, liberties, powers, and immunities – that have been established under the general norms. Through these power-conferring laws, then, the problem of crippling stagnancy is averted.

Hart designated his final category of secondary norms as 'rules of adjudication',[19] but he thereby exhibited his inordinate preoccupation with the activities of courts and his relative inattention to the activities of administrators. He displayed that inordinate preoccupation throughout his work in legal philosophy, but it is not integral to his analysis of the operations of legal systems or to his arguments in support of legal positivism. Hence, readers are well advised to eschew his excessive focus on adjudicators and to take equal account of the roles of administrators (who range from the directors of large agencies to low-level police officers). Of course, in most legal systems, the determinations of administrators are subject to being overturned by the rulings of adjudicators. However, much the same is true of the determinations reached by adjudicators in the lower tiers of a judicial hierarchy; those determinations are subject to being overturned by the rulings of upper-tier adjudicators. Moreover, unless

[19] Hart 1994: 97.

the decisions of administrators are indeed overturned, they remain binding on everyone to whose conduct they are applicable. Consequently, the laws that bestow public powers on administrators as well as the laws that bestow public powers on adjudicators are the means by which a legal system of governance addresses the problem of irresolvable uncertainty concerning the occurrence and extent of any contraventions of the prevailing laws. Instead of labelling Hart's final category of secondary norms as 'norms of adjudication', then, we should label it as 'norms of adjudication and administration' or more pithily as 'norms of law-application'. In most legal systems, those norms establish arrangements for the centralised administration of sanctions and other remedies – though self-help measures are never completely superseded by such arrangements.

13.3.3 The Rule of Recognition

Crucial though the norms of change and norms of law-application are in the operations of any legal system, the Rule of Recognition is what Hart characterised as 'the foundations of a legal system'.[20] Embedded in the power-conferring standards and duty-imposing standards that constitute a Rule of Recognition are criteria which specify the basic sources of law in the relevant jurisdiction. While the duty-imposing standards obligate legal-governmental officials to abide by the embedded criteria as the officials authoritatively ascertain the existence and contents of the legal norms that prevail in their jurisdiction, the power-conferring standards invest the officials with legal powers that enable them to bind other people and themselves with their law-ascertaining determinations. Were the Rule of Recognition not duty-imposing, the officials in a system of governance would be legally at liberty to identify any norms at all as the laws of their system. Were the Rule of Recognition not power-conferring, the officials would be unable to identify the law in a legally binding fashion and would thus be unable to carry out their adjudicative and administrative responsibilities as officials. They would not be able to undertake authoritatively the processes of law-ascertainment which they are duty-bound to undertake in accordance with the requirements imposed upon them by their Rule of Recognition. In short, only the hybrid composition of a Rule of

[20] Hart 1994: 100.

Recognition provides both the structured constrainingness and the dynamic operability of a legal system.

With its power-conferring norms and duty-imposing norms, a Rule of Recognition underlies and structures the law-ascertaining activities of the officials in any system of law. Those officials rely upon the norms implicitly or explicitly while determining what counts as legally binding and what does not. The standards in the Rule of Recognition are operatively presupposed even if they remain unarticulated by the officials whose determinations are grounded on them. Perhaps the officials would not be able to articulate some of the criteria in their Rule of Recognition even if they attempted to do so, or perhaps they simply do not attempt to do so. Whatever may be the reason for the fact that those criteria remain unexpressed (if they do indeed remain unexpressed), they can guide and undergird the officials' law-ascertaining endeavours all the same. In this respect, the standards that constitute a Rule of Recognition are similar to the rules of a natural language. Competent speakers of a language adhere to any number of semantic and syntactic and pragmatic rules even if those rules are never articulated overtly – and indeed even if the speakers are incapable of articulating most of them. Whether or not such rules ever get stated explicitly by anyone, they inform the speakers' discourses. They exist as norms that are presupposed by the multitudinous utterances and interpretations which the users of the language undertake in their daily activities of communication and understanding. The operativeness of those norms as basic presuppositions and guides is in no way dependent on their being explicitly enunciated by the users.

As I have argued at far greater length elsewhere,[21] there need not be and typically will not be a wholly univocal Rule of Recognition in any particular system of law. Typically, the officials in such a system do not all adhere to exactly the same set of criteria for ascertaining the law. Commonly, there are some variations among the officials' understandings of the regnant criteria – which is why the officials in certain knotty cases disagree with one another at the level of their Rule of Recognition rather than exclusively at the level where the uniformly embraced standards in their Rule of Recognition are brought to bear on problematic matters of classification. Those divergences among the officials are fully compatible with the functionality of a legal system of governance, so long as the points

[21] See Kramer 1999: 142–6; Kramer 2004: 105–6; Kramer 2013: 44–9; Kramer 2018: 84–91.

of contention among them concern only the ancillary layers of their Rule of Recognition. If officials converge with one another on the chief criteria for identifying the norms that count as laws which belong to their system, they can diverge from one another over the remaining criteria without jeopardising the system's regularity and stability.

Especially in a large system of law, any thorough consentaneity among the system's officials on all the minutiae of their law-ascertaining criteria is formidably unlikely. Hence, if the notion of a single overarching Rule of Recognition somehow implied full agreement among all the officials on those minutiae, we would have to conclude that there never has existed any legal system (no central instance of a legal system, at any rate). After all, there never has existed a Rule of Recognition with a content that is undisputed in every detail among the officials who uphold it. In fact, of course, we should instead realise that no such thorough consentaneity among the officials is necessary for the existence of a single overarching Rule of Recognition and thus for the existence of a legal system. We can correctly maintain that a single Rule of Recognition exists in this or that legal system even though the officials therein do not all subscribe to exactly the same set of criteria for legal validity – just as we can correctly maintain that the people in some community speak a single language even though they do not all adhere to precisely the same set of semantic and syntactic rules. Exhaustive uniformity is not prerequisite to the unity that is a hallmark of a legal system. Hart emphasised as much throughout the final section of the seventh chapter in *The Concept of Law*, where he dwelt on the inevitability of disagreements among legal-governmental officials about the peripheral aspects of their Rule of Recognition.[22]

In any credible setting, the potential for conflicts among the law-validating criteria in a Rule of Recognition will have occasioned the prioritisation of some of the criteria over others. Whether explicitly through what the officials of a legal system say or implicitly through what they do, their prioritisation of the sources of law within the system will be discernible by any careful observer. To be sure, the rankings will very likely remain unsettled in some of their details – either because the officials take disparate views of those details or because many questions to be answered by the intricacies of their scheme of prioritisation have not yet been addressed. Nevertheless, the unsettledness of the Rule of Recognition in such matters of

[22] See Hart 1994: 147–54.

detail is something that Hart rightly and readily acknowledged. As has been mentioned, he famously contended that any Rule of Recognition will partake of an open texture on its periphery. He was correct in thinking that the functionality of a legal system as a unified array of institutions does not necessitate the unequivocality of its Rule of Recognition in every jot and tittle. Some involuted questions pertaining to the rankings of the criteria in the Rule of Recognition, as well as some involuted questions pertaining to the contents of those criteria, might lack determinate answers at any given juncture.

On the one hand, as a designation for the whole assortment of power-conferring and duty-imposing standards in which are embedded the ultimate criteria of legal validity in any jurisdiction, the phrase 'Rule of Recognition' is admittedly quite misleading – since it tends to convey the erroneous impression that the foundation of the processes of law-ascertainment in the specified jurisdiction is a single norm. On the other hand, despite the misleadingness of that phrase, Hart adduced a solid reason for using it. Writing about a Rule of Recognition with multiple criteria, he explained that '[t]he reason for still speaking of "a rule" at this point is that, notwithstanding their multiplicity, these distinct criteria are unified by their hierarchical arrangement'.[23] Whether a scheme of prioritisation is internal to the power-conferring and duty-imposing norms that contain the law-validating criteria, or whether it instead ensues from supplementary rules of ranking that are also comprised by the Rule of Recognition, it ties the power-conferring and duty-imposing norms together as a coherently interrelated set of standards. The integratedness which it bestows upon them is what justifies us in affirming that those norms and their rankings are an overarching Rule of Recognition. Although the label 'Rule of Recognition' is misleading in the respect that has already been touched upon, it well captures the unity of a throng of law-ascertaining touchstones that stand in quite clear relationships of superiority and subordination to one another.

As Hart explained at some length,[24] the Rule of Recognition that underpins a legal system is ultimate in that its authoritativeness throughout the system does not derive from any other laws that belong thereto. Whereas every one of the other laws of the system owes its status as a law to its being picked out directly or indirectly by some standard(s) contained in the Rule

[23] Hart 1983: 360. [24] See Hart 1994: 107–10.

of Recognition, the Rule of Recognition does not similarly owe its status to any other norms of the system. As has already been remarked, the Rule of Recognition comprises an array of power-conferring and duty-imposing standards in which are embedded the various criteria that specify the fundamental sources of any laws that belong to the system. In Hart's parlance, a norm is *valid* within a legal system if and only if it belongs to the system as a law that is to be given effect by virtue of its having emanated from one or more of those aforementioned sources.[25] Hence, while all the other laws of the system are valid, the Rule of Recognition itself as the basis of all validity is neither valid nor invalid. As Hart declared, we have to draw on the notion of legal validity

> to answer questions which arise *within* a system of [legal] rules where the status of a rule as a member of the system depends on its satisfying certain criteria provided by the rule of recognition. No such question can arise as to the validity of the very rule of recognition which provides the criteria; it can neither be valid nor invalid but is simply accepted [by the officials of the system] as appropriate for use in this way.[26]

13.4 Separability Theses

Having enriched the tradition of legal positivism with an elaborate alternative to the command theory of law, Hart turned his attention to the debates between legal positivists and their natural-law opponents. One commendable aspect of his ruminations on those debates, which quite a few contemporary philosophers of law have not fully absorbed, is that he recognised the diversity of the points of contention that have pitted the devotees of positivism against the devotees of natural-law theories. Whereas some present-day philosophers of law are inclined to refer to 'the separability thesis' of legal positivism – with the definite article 'the' as a signal that there is one defining point of dispute between legal positivists and their opponents – Hart knew that there is no single such thesis. He countered the notion of a single defining thesis, indeed, in the opening

[25] This formulation takes account of an astute observation in Lamond 2013: 113 n. 85. Note, incidentally, that the domain of correct moral principles can be one of the fundamental sources of laws under this or that Rule of Recognition.

[26] Hart 1994: 109 (emphasis in original).

sentence of his chapter on positivism: 'There are many different types of relation between law and morals and there is nothing which can be profitably singled out for study as *the* relation between them.'[27] Hart was keenly aware that natural-law theorists have postulated numerous connections between law and morality that putatively clinch the character of law as an inherently moral phenomenon, and he rightly held that legal positivism poses a challenge to nearly every one of those connections and to the claim that any unimpugned connection serves to establish the inherently moral character of law. Far from being confined to a solitary separability thesis, legal positivism consists in a wide-ranging affirmation of the separability of law and morality – an affirmation that contests the multifarious endeavours of natural-law theorists to present law as intrinsically moral.

To be sure, Hart himself inadvertently abetted the tendency of later philosophers of law to equate legal positivism with one pithy thesis. In the second paragraph of his chapter on positivism in *The Concept of Law*, he announced that he would 'take Legal Positivism to mean the simple contention that it is in no sense a necessary truth that laws reproduce or satisfy certain demands of morality, though in fact they have often done so'.[28] Although Hart here broached the proposition that was most saliently at issue in the debates between legal positivists and their opponents during past centuries – and although that proposition continues to be quite a prominent focus of controversy in the present day, both among legal positivists and between legal positivists and their adversaries – he went astray in suggesting, even *en passant*, that legal positivism is concerned with only one main way in which law and morality have sometimes been viewed as indisseverable. Later in his ninth chapter, and in some of his subsequent writings, Hart revealed that any such suggestion is unfounded. There he charted and entered some of the other principal tussles between legal positivists and natural-law theorists that have occurred both in recent decades and in bygone eras. Moreover, immediately before the somewhat ill-advised suggestion that has just been quoted, Hart readily accepted that the phrases 'Legal Positivism' and 'Natural Law' have each 'come to be used for a range of different theses about law and morals'.[29]

Thus, we are well advised here to ponder the complex diversity of the debates between legal positivists and their opponents. Those debates concern the relationships between law and morality, but there is no single

[27] Hart 1994: 185 (emphasis in original). [28] Hart 1994: 185–6. [29] Hart 1994: 185.

understanding of morality that runs through all of them. Of course, one reason for the profuseness of the conceptions of morality in those debates is that the participants therein subscribe to varying substantive moral standards. At least as important, however, is that different aspects or dimensions of morality are at issue across the sundry disputes between positivists and natural-law theorists. Each of those aspects or dimensions can illuminatingly be approached through a distinction between morality and something else that serves as a point of contrast.

First, then, is a diremption between morality and immorality. It is a distinction that gets invoked pervasively in everyday life, and is construable in either of two chief ways. On the one hand, it is construable as a division between the permissible and the impermissible or between the legitimate and the illegitimate or between right and wrong (where those three pairings are taken to be interchangeable). On the other hand, it can additionally be construed as a division between the morally commendable and the morally deplorable or between the morally salutary and the morally noxious or between virtue and vice (where, again, those three pairings are taken to be interchangeable).

Second is a distinction between morality and prudence, which pertains to the reasons that might underlie the actions of any person P. A prudential reason for some action by P is focused exclusively or primarily on the interests of P and only derivatively, if at all, on the interests of anyone else. A moral reason for some action by P is focused exclusively or primarily on the interests of other people and only derivatively, if at all, on the interests of P. Although prudential reasons and moral reasons are readily combinable and are often overlapping, they are distinguishable in the manner just indicated.

A third dichotomy to be noted here is the division between moral matters and descriptive matters. Roughly stated, that division lies between what morally *should* be done and what *is* being done or what *has* been done or what *will* be done. This distinction between moral facts and descriptive facts is a feature of everyday life but is also of far-reaching importance in philosophy. When the moral/descriptive distinction is elaborated along epistemic lines, it amounts to a contrast between moral reasoning and purely empirical or logical or mathematical reasoning.

Finally, a fourth distinction is the divide between moral phenomena and non-moral phenomena. In the sense that is relevant here, non-moral phenomena are those things to which moral concepts or categories are not appositely applicable.[30] Virtually all natural processes and states of affairs are non-moral in this sense. By contrast, the doings and decisions and practices undertaken by human beings are always appropriately susceptible to some moral assessments. In precisely that respect, all such doings and decisions and practices are moral rather than non-moral.

Now, as should be apparent, the fourth aspect or dimension of morality – the moral versus the non-moral – is not associated with any genuine disputation between positivists and their opponents. Patently, the operations of legal systems of governance are run by human beings whose attitudes and beliefs and conduct are integrally constitutive of those operations. Hence, given that all the doings and decisions and practices undertaken by human beings are appositely susceptible to moral appraisal, the operations of legal systems are appositely susceptible to moral appraisal. Although particular moral judgements about a legal system or about some laws and decisions within a legal system can of course be mistaken, the sheer fact that moral concepts have been applied to such a system or to such laws and decisions is never itself inapposite. Thus, if we are asking whether law is inherently moral, and if the contrast implicit in the question is between the moral and the non-moral, the answer is that law is indeed inherently moral. No legal positivist in his or her right mind has ever suggested otherwise.

By contrast, each of the other three aspects of morality delineated above is associated with a number of debates between legal positivists and natural-law theorists. Because of constraints of space, we can glance here at only one set of debates associated with each aspect.[31] First, morality as contrasted with immorality is the focus of the debates to which Hart alluded when he offered his one-sentence encapsulation of legal positivism that I have quoted. Those debates are what Bentham and Austin were addressing when they strenuously proclaimed the distinction between what the law is and what the law ought to be. That is, some natural-law theorists over the centuries have declared that the status of any norm N as a law in any legal system is always dependent on the norm's satisfaction of some test of moral legitimacy. Unless the substance of N is at or above a threshold of moral soundness, N is not genuinely a law in any system of governance – even if the officials in some such system treat N as though it

30 Kramer 2017: 189–90.

31 For a much longer treatment of this matter, see Kramer 2018: 149–64.

were a law. So have proclaimed a bevy of natural-law theorists from ancient times through the present day. Legal positivists are unanimous in rejecting the idea that any such test is an essential feature of law.

Second, when morality contrasted with prudence is the orienting concern, the thesis most commonly propounded by natural-law philosophers is that there are no credible prudential reasons for the officials in any system of governance to abide by the rule of law. These philosophers submit that, in every system of governance, the sole credible reasons for officials to uphold the restrictions integral to the rule of law are moral rather than self-interested. Contrariwise, Hart expressly left open the nature of the considerations that would motivate the officials in a system of governance to run it as a legal system. He thereby positioned himself against the conclusions of the natural-law philosophers who rule out prudential factors as credible bases for the self-restraint involved in the operations of a legal system. Their conclusions have been impugned at much greater length by me in my previous books and articles on legal positivism.[32]

Third, with regard to the moral/descriptive distinction, legal positivists submit that the endeavours of officials in ascertaining the existence and contents of laws are not necessarily guided by any moral assumptions. Those endeavours can instead concentrate strictly on matters of empirical fact. In this or that jurisdiction, it can be the case that moral soundness is neither a necessary condition nor a sufficient condition for the status of any norm as a law. In reply to Dworkin and other theorists who insist that moral deliberations and judgements are essential in all processes of law-ascertainment, legal positivists such as Hart have held that the role of moral deliberations and judgements in the processes of law-ascertainment in any particular jurisdiction is a contingent matter that depends on the prevailing Rule of Recognition.

Now, although this laconic discussion has not presented any arguments in support of the positivist insistence on the separability of law and morality, and although it has simply limned a few of the sundry points of contention that have led positivists to develop an array of pertinent arguments, it has provided a glimpse of the rich multifariousness of the disputes between legal positivists and their foes. It has therefore signalled how much is omitted when anybody suggests that the wide-ranging positivist

[32] See especially Kramer 1999: chs. 3–8; Kramer 2004: chs. 5–7.

insistence on the separability of law and morality can be encapsulated in one terse thesis. When we keep in view the several aspects or dimensions of morality that have been disentangled here, we can grasp how expansively variegated the altercations between positivists and their opponents have long been.

13.5 The Minimum Content of Natural Law

In the second main section of the penultimate chapter in *The Concept of Law* – a portion of the book that has elicited vast amounts of commentary ever since its publication – Hart mulled over the indispensability of some basic legal prohibitions in any viable human society.[33] He observed that certain elementary facts of the human predicament combine to render the existence of law necessary for the durability of any credibly possible community that is larger than a few families. If a society on even a moderate scale is to stand any chance of lasting, it must be held together in part by a scheme of legal governance that enforces some general restrictions on people's conduct.

The five familiar features of human beings and their environments to which Hart directed the attention of his readers are as follows: (1) the vulnerability of each human being to harms that might be inflicted by other human beings; (2) the approximate equality of most human adults, in that the physical and mental disparities among them are generally not overwhelming; (3) the mixture of selfishness and solicitous benevolence in the make-up of virtually every human being; (4) the moderate scarcity of most resources, and the fact that many resources have to be subjected to considerable labour before they can satisfy human wants directly; and (5) the limitedness of each person's understanding and strength of will, which leads some people to favour their short-term interests at the expense of their long-term interests. Given these characteristics of human beings and of the world in which they live, no credibly possible community beyond a tiny size can endure without a system of legal governance. Moreover, among the mandates imposed by any such system, there must be certain fundamental prohibitions. As Hart observed, legal norms forbidding murder, assault, arson, serious fraud, and other grave misdeeds are unforgoable

[33] See Hart 1994: 193–200.

in setting the terms for human interaction over any extended period of time. If such norms were absent or wholly unenforced, then – given the facts of the human condition which Hart invoked – the security that distinguishes civilisation from the frenzy of chaotic anarchy would be gone. Every viable scheme of governance must therefore encompass the basic proscriptions mentioned by Hart, if it is to encompass anything at all. Yet, since the contents of those proscriptions are apparently at one with the substance of key moral precepts, Hart's elementary facts of the human condition appear to make unavoidable a convergence between the demands of law and the demands of morality. The area of that inevitable convergence is what Hart labelled as the 'minimum content of natural law'.

As Hart's label indicates, his observations about the nature of human beings bear importantly on the debates between legal positivists and natural-law theorists over the separability of law and morality. If the system of governance in every viable society must include legal mandates that coincide in content with some key principles of morality, then there is a significant necessary connection between legal requirements and moral requirements. However, as Hart himself aptly recognised, any such necessary connection turns out to be illusory. He remarked: 'The protections and benefits provided by the system of mutual forbearances which underlies both law and morals may, in different societies, be extended to very different ranges of persons.'[34] Although the conditions of security that are essential for the sustainment of a society must be extended to quite a few people therein, they might not be extended to everyone. A community can persist as such even if some people residing within it are denied the basic protections that are enjoyed by other people, who belong to relatively privileged groups. '[I]t is plain that neither the law nor the accepted morality of societies need extend their minimal protections and benefits to all within their scope, and often they have not done so. In slave-owning societies[,] the sense that the slaves are human beings, not mere objects to be used, may be lost by the dominant group.'[35] As Hart elaborated: 'These painful facts of human history are enough to show that, though a society to be viable must offer *some* of its members a system of mutual forbearances, it need not, unfortunately, offer them to all.'[36] People excluded from the protective ambit of the elementary legal prohibitions are very likely worse

[34] Hart 1994: 200. [35] Ibid. [36] Ibid. (emphasis in original).

off than they would be in a situation of lawlessness. As far as they are concerned, the coercive mechanisms of legal governance are exerted to

> subdue and maintain, in a position of permanent inferiority, a subject group whose size, relatively to the master group, may be large or small, depending on the means of coercion, solidarity, and discipline available to the latter, and the helplessness or inability to organize of the former. For those thus oppressed there may be nothing in the system to command their loyalty but only things to fear. They are its victims, not its beneficiaries.[37]

Of major jurisprudential significance is this point by Hart about the credible possibility of societies in which some people are deliberately excluded from the protective reach of prohibitions on very serious misconduct. In such societies, those elementary prohibitions do not coincide in content with any veritable principles of morality. After all, no genuine principle of morality forbids the perpetration of very serious misconduct against white people only (or against non-slaves only); any true principle of morality that forbids the perpetration of such misconduct against white people is also a prohibition on the perpetration of such misconduct against other people. Thus, given that the legal norms which proscribe very serious misconduct in any particular jurisdiction can differ from the correct principles of morality on exactly this point, the 'minimum content of natural law' does not constitute any necessary connections between the substance of law and the substance of morality. Hart's meditations on the plight of humanity do not betoken any such connections, despite initial appearances to the contrary.

Elsewhere, I have adduced at length some further considerations in support of the conclusion just reached.[38] Some of those considerations were glimpsed by Hart. Indeed, what makes his reflections on the 'minimum content of natural law' a fitting matter with which to conclude this chapter about his legal positivism is that he there displayed unsurpassedly both his intellectual integrity and his philosophical adroitness. He put together a line of reasoning that appeared to militate powerfully in favour of an anti-positivist understanding of the nature of law, yet he then managed to show that such an understanding is not tenable. In his defence of legal positivism against the onslaughts of natural-law

[37] Hart 1994: 201. [38] Kramer 1999: 264–308; Kramer 2018: 166–72.

philosophers, as in his rescuing of legal positivism from the champions of the command theory, Hart endeavoured to think through the implications of his opponents' positions more incisively than those opponents themselves had done.

References

Coleman, J. 1982. 'Negative and Positive Positivism'. *Journal of Legal Studies* 11: 139–64.

Hart, H. L. A. 1983. *Essays in Jurisprudence and Philosophy*. Oxford University Press.

Hart, H. L. A. 1994. *The Concept of Law*. 2nd ed. Oxford University Press.

Hart, H. L. A. 2013. 'Answers to Eight Questions'. In L. Duarte d'Almeida, J. Edwards and A. Dolcetti (eds.). *Reading HLA Hart's The Concept of Law*. Hart: 279–97.

Kramer, M. 1999. *In Defense of Legal Positivism*. Oxford University Press.

Kramer, M. 2004. *Where Law and Morality Meet*. Oxford University Press.

Kramer, M. 2013. 'In Defense of Hart'. In W. Waluchow and S. Sciaraffa (eds.). *Philosophical Foundations of the Nature of Law*. Oxford University Press: 22–50.

Kramer, M. 2017. 'There's Nothing Quasi about Quasi-Realism'. *Journal of Ethics* 21: 185–212.

Kramer, M. 2018. *H.L.A. Hart: The Nature of Law*. Polity Press.

Lamond, G. 2013. 'The Rule of Recognition and the Foundations of a Legal System'. In L. Duarte d'Almeida, J. Edwards and A. Dolcetti (eds.). *Reading HLA Hart's The Concept of Law*. Hart: 97–122.

From Savigny to Linguistic Analysis: Legal Positivism through Bobbio's Eyes 14

Pierluigi Chiassoni

Besides as a contrast between generations or between conceptions of the law, the opposition between natural law theory and legal positivism takes place, finally, inside each one of us, between our scientific call and our moral conscience, between our profession as scientists and our mission as men ... We are constantly tempted at defending the requirements of legal positivism as scientists, and in so doing we show the same commitment and the same coherence ... we adopt when we defend the ultimate reasons of natural law theory as free men. There is therefore a boundary between positivism and natural law theory that cuts through our very personality, and in force of which we happen to be either positivists or natural lawyers ... according to the role we play in society.[1]

14.1 Bobbio and Legal Positivism: A Complex Posture

During his long academic career, Norberto Bobbio (1909–2004) has been a positivist legal theorist, a historian and a theorist of legal positivism, a critic of legal positivism and also, what may appear surprising, a staunch defender of a secular, de-naturalised, rationalistic variety of natural law theory.[2] My aim in this chapter is to provide two snapshots of Bobbio's complex posture. The first snapshot is about Bobbio's theory of legal

[1] Bobbio 1965: 12–13.

[2] In Bobbio's own words: '[I]n front of the clash between ideologies, where no beating around the bush is possible, well, I am a natural lawyer; concerning method, I am, with as much conviction, a positivist; finally, as regards to legal theory, I am neither the one, nor the other' (Bobbio 1965: 146). See also Bobbio 1993: vii–x. It goes without saying that these are but a few aspects of Norberto Bobbio's immense philosophical interests and gigantic intellectual personality. For an overview, see, e.g., Bobbio 1992, 1994, 1997; Redazione

positivism.[3] The second snapshot concerns Bobbio's theory of legal science.[4]

14.2 The Theorist of Legal Positivism

Any theory of legal positivism either is a discourse purporting to explain what legal positivism in fact is (descriptive theory of legal positivism) or is a discourse that, to sòme avowed purpose (for instance, in view of promoting certain sorts of inquiry concerning the law of a given society, or law in general), purports to establish what legal positivism should be (prescriptive theory of legal positivism). In the former event, it belongs to descriptive meta-philosophy of law; in the second one, to its constructive and prescriptive counterpart.

In a series of essays published between 1961 and 1965, Bobbio sets forth a descriptive theory of legal positivism.[5] The theory turns on two components:

1) a *definition* of legal positivism;
2) an *analysis* of legal positivism presenting it as characterised by three 'aspects'.

Being a scholar with a historicist mind cast, who considered the diachronic dimension of legal ideas paramount, Bobbio draws heavily from a reconstruction of the several distinct trends composing legal positivism from the late eighteenth century to the sixties, and also from a constant eye to natural law theory.[6]

14.2.1 The Definition of Legal Positivism

Bobbio's definition of legal positivism results from a comparison with natural law theory. Natural law theory – the set of theories of natural law

Reset and Ocone 2003; Rossi 2005; Portinaro 2008; Zolo 2008; Agosti and Revelli 2009; Vitale 2010; Losano 2018.

[3] See Section 14.2. [4] See Section 14.3. [5] See Bobbio 1961, 1965, 1993.

[6] See Bobbio 1961: part I where, after a short historical account of natural law and positive law from classical thinking to the XVIII century, he devotes separate chapters to the 'origins' of legal positivism in Germany, France and England, from the end of the eighteenth century to the mid-eighteenth century.

in Western legal and philosophical-political thought from the age of the Sophists to the present[7] – endorses two basic theses about the law: the duality thesis and the superiority thesis.

The *duality thesis* is an ontological claim holding that two different sorts of law exist regulating the behaviours of humans in a society: namely, natural law and positive law. The standards (rules, precepts, principles) of natural law are to be found in nature: that is, in the (evident) essential properties of human beings, of things, of the universe. Contrariwise, the standards of positive law are human-made entities, originating from acts of production by socially authorised human beings.

The *superiority thesis* is an axiological claim holding that natural law is superior in value to positive law and, in case of conflict, it should, at least in principle, prevail.

By contrast, legal positivism, in its several trends, is characterised as endorsing one (ontological) thesis concerning the law: namely, the exclusivity thesis. According to the *exclusivity thesis*, *only one sort of law* (properly so-called) exists regulating the behaviours of humans in a society, and that law is *positive* law. *There exists no other law, but positive law*: this is the motto of legal positivism.[8]

14.2.2 The Analysis of Legal Positivism

In his 1958 essay 'Positivism and the Separation of Law and Morals', Herbert Hart puts to work an analytic-linguistic approach in order to dissolve whatever mystery may surround legal positivism. Assuming a deconstructive, disarticulating attitude, Hart notices that the expression 'legal positivism' occurs in legal-philosophical discourse to refer to five different things, not necessarily related to each other. These are: (1) the imperative conception of legal norms; (2) the separation thesis ('there is no necessary or conceptual connexion between law and morals'); (3) the idea that the analytical study of law – purporting to clarify or elucidate the concept of law and the related concepts of legal right, legal duty, sanction, validity, responsibility and so forth – is a worthwhile undertaking; (4) the idea that 'legal systems are logically closed systems', which preludes to

[7] See, e.g., Duke and George 2017.

[8] Bobbio 1961: 18–19; Bobbio 1965: 107, 127–8, 135. See also Ross 1961/1999: 80–3; Olivecrona 1971: 5–6, 268.

a cognitivist theory of interpretation and adjudication; and (5) ethical non-cognitivism, which denies the possibility of an ultimate rational justification of moral judgements.[9] In a later essay, Hart enriches the list with one further element: the idea that the very existence of positive legal orders implies an unconditional moral duty of obedience on the part of those who happen to be the addressees of their laws.[10]

Bobbio takes a different path. In his view, the definition of legal positivism –suggested, as we have seen, by a comparison with natural law theory (legal positivism is the philosophical view endorsing the exclusivity thesis) – identifies what is to be regarded as a *unitary*, though *complex* and not 'monolithic', phenomenon in the history of Western legal thought. It is precisely in order to bring to the fore the complexity of the unitary 'doctrine of legal positivism' that Bobbio's analysis of legal positivism steps in, as a necessary move towards a deeper understanding.

The analysis, as anticipated, points to 'three aspects'. The first aspect characterises legal positivism as an *epistemological posture* concerning the proper way to make scientific investigations about the law ('a certain way of approaching the study of law'). The second aspect characterises legal positivism as a *theory of positive law* ('a certain theory of law', 'a theory of law and state'). The third, and last, aspect characterises legal positivism as an *ideology* ('a certain ideology of law', 'a political ideology', 'a determinate ideology of justice').[11] The three aspects are ('logically' and 'causally') *independent*: the first one 'does not necessarily produce', 'nor implies', the second one, which in turn 'does not necessarily produce', 'nor implies', the third one.[12]

14.2.2.1 Legal Positivism as an Approach to the Study of Law

As an approach to the study of law, as a 'method' concerning juridical investigations, legal positivism invites jurists to perform genuinely scientific inquiries about the law (positive law) '*as it is*', about the '*real law*', about the law as a complex *social fact*. Genuinely scientific inquiries about law are to be conceived, in turn, as empirical investigations to be carried out by strict adherence to the principle of ethical *Wertfreiheit*. To be sure, jurists should also perform an evaluative, critical task as regards positive law. Such a task, however, should not interfere whenever the pursuit of

[9] See Hart 1958: 57 n. 25; Hart 1961: 185–93, 302. [10] See Hart 1967: 237–40.
[11] Bobbio 1961: 154; Bobbio 1965: 77, 104. [12] Bobbio 1965: 104–5.

objective knowledge about positive legal orders as they are in fact is at stake.[13]

14.2.2.2 Legal Positivism as a Theory of Positive Law

As a theory of positive law, legal positivism is the theory, inside Western legal culture, that purports to provide an account of the basic features of the positive legal orders of the modern state, the centralised political organisation and the monopolist user of coercion within a territory that celebrated its heyday during the nineteenth century.[14]

Casting a historian's glance, Bobbio distinguishes two different positivist theories of positive law: the positivist theory in a narrow sense (*narrow theoretical positivism*) and the positivist theory in a broad sense (*broad theoretical positivism*).

Narrow theoretical positivism is a product of the nineteenth century and the early part of the twentieth century. It consists in a set of theoretical claims concerning law, legal norms, legal sources, legal orders and the judicial interpretation and application of law. Narrow theoretical positivism conceives of law as a coercive normative order, legal norms being *imperatives* (prescriptions making behaviours non-optional but either obligatory or forbidden) backed up by *coercive sanctions* (*coercitive imperativism*). It considers legislation as what is, and should be, the paramount source among legal sources (*legalism*). It claims legal systems (legal orders) to be 'logically' complete (gapless) and coherent (antinomies-proof) normative sets (*logical completeness* and *coherence*). It accounts for the judicial application of law as a 'mechanical task', where judges, having come to know both the law (by means of interpretation as a pure act of cognition) and the facts of the individual case, identify the individual norm (the decision) to be issued by means of a logical inference.

Bobbio considers narrow theoretical positivism a 'naïf' theory of law. It conceives legal norms as (primarily) addressed to people at large. It does not pay attention to the logical form, or logical structure, of legal norms. It makes theoretically unsound claims: in particular, those about the law's intrinsic ('logical') coherence and completeness, and the mechanistic

[13] See Bobbio 1961: 155–69; Bobbio 1965: 105–7; Bobbio 1967b: 69–70. In common-law jurisprudence's terminology, the epistemological aspect of legal positivism corresponds roughly to 'methodological positivism': to the claim that legal theory can and should provide a morally neutral description of positive law in general (see Perry 2001: 311).

[14] See Bobbio 1961: 17–42.

theory of interpretation and adjudication. According to Bobbio, such naïve views explain why, from the mid-twentieth century on, narrow theoretical positivism was superseded by a second positivist theory of positive law: broad theoretical positivism.

Broad theoretical positivism replaces imperativism with a more articulated typology of legal norms, also encompassing permissions, authorisations, interpretation and derogation norms (*norm-pluralism*). It provides a more sophisticated view about the connection between law and coercion (law and coercive sanctions, law and force), where legal rules are no longer 'backed by coercive sanctions' but, rather, are prescriptions that *establish* coercive sanctions (connecting them to unlawful behaviours) and, accordingly, regulate the use of coercion in a society. It adopts a more realistic posture as to the priority of statutory law among the legal sources. It rejects any idea of the 'logical' (intrinsic) completeness and coherence of legal systems, emphasising, contrariwise, that those properties are – and cannot be but – contingent features of ongoing legal systems.[15] It rejects, as plainly wrong, the mechanistic conception of judicial interpretation and application of law, adopting instead a realistic account, according to which interpretation always is an act of will and, to some extent, a law-creating activity.[16]

In Bobbio's approving words, broad theoretical positivism represents a 'critical' theory of positive law. It avoids the major mistakes of narrow theoretical positivism. It presents legal organs (judges and other law-enforcement officials) as the primary addressees of legal norms, and also sets forth claims about the logical form, or logical structure, of legal norms.[17]

14.2.2.3 Legal Positivism as an Ideology of Obedience to Positive Law

In the third, and last, aspect, Bobbio brings to the fore legal positivism characterises as *ideological positivism* (ethical formalism, ethical legalism), that is, as an ideology *about the obedience due* to positive law qua positive law. Bobbio distinguishes three varieties: In the absolute, unconditional, extreme variety, which Bobbio traces back to Hegel and the Hegelian

[15] See Bobbio 1961: 284. [16] See Bobbio 1961: 284–5.

[17] Bobbio 1961: 284–5. In common-law jurisprudence's terminology, the theoretical aspect of legal positivism corresponds roughly to what is sometimes called 'substantive positivism' (see Perry 2001: 311–12).

philosophy of law, ideological positivism claims that every human being has the moral duty to obey the positive laws of the land, whatever their content may be, just because they are positive laws.[18] In the moderate conditional variety, ideological positivism sees every human being as having the moral duty to obey the positive laws of the land, whatever their content may be, insofar as such laws do in fact promote the values of order, peace, formal equality and legal certainty as predictability of the legal consequences of individuals' behaviours. Finally, in the very moderate conditional variety, ideological positivism sees every human being as having the moral duty to obey the positive laws of the land if, and only if, such laws do in fact realise the values of order, peace, formal equality, legal certainty *and*, furthermore, are not at odds with other values – like respect for human life, human liberty and human dignity – that moral conscience may consider paramount.[19]

14.2.3 Bobbio's Theory of Legal Positivism: A Critique

Bobbio's theory of legal positivism is a clear instance of a philosophical success. It is the standard view about legal positivism in contemporary Latin legal cultures. It works as a paradigm of analysis followed to capture the key features of other intellectual movements.[20] The success can be easily explained. Bobbio's theory of legal positivism is nothing but the output of applying to the legal positivism phenomenon the sound meta-philosophical claim according to which a philosophy of law is, quite often, a mixed discourse, consisting in some peculiar combination of epistemological, theoretical and ideological claims.

A few critical remarks are, nonetheless, in order.

1. Bobbio's theory of legal positivism is troublesome. On the one hand, he presents legal positivism as a unitary phenomenon (he talks of 'the

[18] By the way, Samuel Pufendorf, one of the leading seventeenth-century natural law theorists, maintained a position similar to Hegel's and the Hegelians' (see, e.g., Pufendorf 1673: 175).

[19] See Bobbio 1961: 265–77, 282–4; see also Bobbio 1965: 115–16, where, to my knowledge for the first time, he also considers the last variety.

[20] For instance, it has been used in analysing the different strands in contemporary constitutionalism ('neo-constitutionalism' as it is sometimes called). See, e.g., Comanducci 2003; Prieto 1997; Chiassoni 2011.

doctrine of legal positivism').[21] On the other hand, he identifies three *independent* aspects of it.[22] There is a tension afoot (how can a *unitary* phenomenon be made of *independent* epistemological, theoretical and ideological components?), which, apparently, is resolved by the unifying property Bobbio finds in the exclusivity thesis (there exists no other law but positive law).

Now, on closer inspection, the exclusivity thesis appears to be misleading. It is not *one* thesis. It stands, rather, for *three* different theses that must be carefully kept apart. The first thesis is epistemological. It maintains that there exists no other law, *as a suitable object of scientific (empirical) enquiry*, but positive law. The second thesis is ideological. It maintains that there exists no other law, *as a set of norms endowed with superior practical value and commanding obedience (at least prima facie)*, but positive law. The third thesis is of a mixed character. It maintains that there exists no other law but positive law, *both* as a suitable object of scientific (empirical) inquiry *and* as a set of norms endowed with superior practical value and commanding obedience (at least prima facie). The fact that the exclusivity thesis is not, really, one thesis but stands, rather, for three different exclusivity claims suggests that the unity of legal positivism is, all things considered, a *meta-philosophical fiction*: a misleading doing-as-if, disproved by a dispassionate analysis of the phenomenon.[23] So, provided Bobbio's theory of legal positivism appears to be flawed by a misleading fiction, which account of legal positivism, if any, should be adopted in its stead?

If, also profiting from Bobbio's inquiries,[24] we look at 'legal positivism' from a historical perspective, it seems worthwhile distinguishing two basic strands within such a complex cultural phenomenon: namely, scientific (epistemological) positivism and doctrinal (ideological) positivism. *Scientific positivism* is a movement striving for genuine scientific knowledge about positive law. Be it for knowledge's sake, or in view of some further, practical goal (like, for example, rational law reform). *Doctrinal positivism*, contrariwise, is a movement advocating a general

[21] Bobbio 1961: 149. [22] Bobbio 1965: 104–5. See also Section 14.2.2.

[23] For instance, if the exclusivity thesis were *one* thesis, as Bobbio suggests, and were ontological in character, John Austin, the quintessential legal positivist, should be considered a non-positivist, since he endorsed the duality thesis. See Austin 1885: lecture I.

[24] See Bobbio 1961: 5–147.

practical attitude of favour towards positive law qua positive law. Such an attitude of favour requires in turn: on the part of jurists, a disposition to (unconditional or conditioned) cooperation in view of the smooth, efficient functioning of the positive legal order they happen to work in; on the part of people at large, a disposition to (unconditional or conditioned) obedience to the positive laws regulating their behaviours. Scientific positivism is the seal of the legal philosophers belonging to the analytical tradition: from Bentham and Austin, to Kelsen, Ross, Bobbio and Hart. Doctrinal positivism, by contrast, is endorsed, for instance, by the French jurists of the Exegetical School, by Savigny and the representatives of the Historical School, by Rudolf von Jhering, by the German nineteenth-century jurist supporters of 'naked (legalistic) positivism'.[25]

2. The 'methodological aspect' of legal positivism is not, therefore, a feature of the unitary phenomenon legal positivism, which, as I claim, is a meta-philosophical fiction. As soon as we introduce the distinction between scientific positivism and doctrinal positivism, it just refers to (and captures) the basic epistemological principle of scientific positivism. Any positive legal order is a social phenomenon, consisting in a (very) complex set of facts concerning the production, interpretation and application of 'legal norms'. Accordingly, it is, and should be regarded as, a suitable – the only suitable – object of empirical, scientific, objective legal knowledge. And the jurists – when they are really after the empirical knowledge of a positive legal order – must carefully abide by the ethical *Wertfreiheit* principle: they must look for the law as it is in fact at any time, and avoid projecting into it, by wishful thinking, any desired content (the law as it should or ought to be).

3. Concerning the theoretical aspect of legal positivism (theoretical legal positivism), Bobbio, as we have seen, singles out narrow theoretical positivism from broad theoretical positivism. The former is the output of nineteenth-century naïve legal positivism; the latter is the output of twentieth-century critical positivism.

On closer inspection, however, the distinction between a narrow and a broad positivistic theory of law (and the state) is misleading. The two positivistic "theories" are not *theories* in the same way. The positivist

[25] See Chiassoni 2013: 7–31.

theory in a broad sense is a genuine piece of theory. It is a set of genuinely theoretical, true theses about law, legal norms, the properties of legal orders and the nature of judicial interpretation. Contrariwise, the positivist theory in a narrow sense is not, as a whole, a genuine piece of theory. It combines genuinely theoretical claims (the coercion claim, the imperative claim and, to a certain extent, the legalism claim) with claims that are clearly ideological in character. These are the claims providing a value-laden, idealised picture of legal orders as *necessarily* ('logically') complete and coherent systems of norms that (should) come from a legislature and wait to be mechanically interpreted and applied by judges.

From the standpoint of the distinction between doctrinal and scientific legal positivism, the difference between the two 'theories' can be easily explained. The positivist theory in a narrow sense belongs to – is an output of – doctrinal positivism. Contrariwise, the positivist theory of law in a broad sense belongs to – is an output of – scientific positivism.

4. Finally, the idea of an 'ideological aspect' of legal positivism is also troublesome. At least two counts of dissatisfaction must be considered. First, as I mentioned, doctrinal positivism is more than an ideology addressed to ordinary people and preaching the existence for them of a moral duty to obey positive laws qua positive laws, either unconditionally or subject to some more or less stringent set of conditions. Rather, it encompasses, also and primarily, a *juristic ideology*: the ideology, addressed to jurists (and judges), of faithful and active cooperation to the efficient working of existing legal orders – again, unconditionally or, as is often the case with twentieth-century doctrinal positivists, upon condition of the legal orders being liberal, democratic, constitutional legal orders.[26] Second, as Bobbio himself makes clear, the different ideologies of positive law making up 'the ideological aspect' of legal positivism are so diverse as to be at odds. Accordingly, it seems misleading to speak of 'the' ideological aspect of legal positivism. It seems better to talk of different ideologies – extreme (Hegelian) ideological positivism, quasi-extreme (Hobbesian) ideological positivism, moderate ideological positivism and very moderate ideological positivism – historically adopted by different strands of doctrinal positivism.

[26] See e.g. Scarpelli 1965: 97–218; Scarpelli 1967: 77–86. On Scarpelli's interpretation of legal positivism, see Chapter 7 in this volume.

14.3 The Theorist of Legal Science

Since the very beginning of his investigations, Bobbio stands for a *juristic* and *bottom-up* variety of legal philosophy.[27] Such a conception requires legal philosophy to be constantly in touch with, and grounded upon, legal experience. Legal experience, in turn, is to be conceived broadly. It encompasses, to be sure, positive legal orders, as complex normative orders established by legislators and applied by judges and other officials. It also encompasses, however, a further component, which plays a momentous, though indirect, role in the shaping of positive legal orders. This is the component that, on the Continent, is usually captured by expressions like 'legal science', 'doctrinal study of law', or even 'jurisprudence' (meaning by that what was 'local expository jurisprudence' to Bentham and 'particular jurisprudence' to Austin), and consists in the everyday working of jurists and their literary outputs (commentaries, hornbooks, essays, case-law analysis and so forth). According to Bobbio, no (serious) philosopher of positive law should ever overlook the existence and operations of legal science. Bobbio faithfully abided by this requirement. The present section aims at providing a swift account of such a faithful abiding.[28]

It seems worthwhile to distinguish three stages in Bobbio's theory of legal science. In the first two stages – roughly, from 1934 to 1950 – Bobbio approaches legal science from the standpoint of the *scientificity problem*. Assuming a constructive, ideal-model-building posture, he looks for the conditions, if any, at which legal science can be a truly scientific enterprise. In the third and last stage, from the late 1950s to the mid-1960s,[29] Bobbio abandons the constructive posture of earlier stages and takes up an analytic and descriptive perspective instead (coupled, as we shall see, with a normative preoccupation). He believes that there was an urgent need, to begin with, for a truly scientific ('descriptive') theory of legal science, and conceives a theory of legal science as a theory that, aided by symbolic logic and the 'new rhetorics' pioneered by Chaïm Perelman, retrieves the old path of *logica legalis*, explores the recurrent operations that jurists do in fact perform, and casts light on the tools they make use of,

27 See Bobbio 1934a; Bobbio 1938; Bobbio 1965: 43–6.

28 On Bobbio's theory of legal science, see also, e.g., Guastini 2011: ix–xxii; Chiassoni 2017: 129–36; Chapter 7 in this volume.

29 Anticipations can be read in Bobbio 1938 (a 'historical' and 'logical' inquiry about analogical reasoning) and Bobbio 1954 (on juristic reasoning).

when carrying out their job of 'setting up' the norms of a positive legal order, either in view of solving some practical problem or as a starting point for systematisation work.[30]

In the first stage, Bobbio argues for the scientific character of legal science by also resorting to an ingredient taken from the phenomenological philosophy of Edmund Husserl. In the second stage, he advances the same claim – with an important qualification, as we shall see – by appealing to logical positivism's 'modern conception of science'. In the third, and last, stage, adopting an ordinary language philosophy approach, Bobbio finally comes to regard legal science as a thoroughly unscientific, practical enterprise, ultimately standing for a negative answer to the scientificity problem.

Coming to the positivist character of Bobbio's theory of legal science, it is worthwhile emphasising, by way of anticipation, that the account I am going to offer will bring to the fore a changing, mostly antagonistic relationship to Kelsen's theory, assumed as representative of the positivist theory of legal science. Its developments suggest, in fact, the following conclusions. In the first, *phenomenological*, stage, Bobbio advocates an *anti-positivist* conception of legal science, openly criticising Kelsen's for its inchoateness.[31] In the second, *logical-positivist*, stage, Bobbio proposes instead a *positivist* conception of legal science, though very different from Kelsen's.[32] In the third, *ordinary language philosophy*, stage, Bobbio finally turns to a *post-positivist* conception, repudiating the very possibility of a purely descriptive legal science: 'descriptive legal science' being, as Bobbio comes to suggest, a self-contradictory expression.[33]

14.3.1 The Savigny-Husserl Model

In *Scienza e tecnica del diritto*,[34] one of his earliest essays, Bobbio provides a partially positive answer to the scientificity problem. He does so by means of a model of legal science that, for reasons that will appear soon, deserves the name *Savigny-Husserl model.* The core of the Savigny-Husserl model can be recounted as follows.

[30] See Bobbio 1965: 48–9, 73. [31] As noted in Section 14.3.1.
[32] As noted in Section 14.3.2. [33] As noted in Section 14.3.3. [34] Bobbio 1934a.

1. Legal science is commonly characterised as being, *as a whole*, a 'normative science'.
2. The phrase 'normative science' is ambiguous, though. Some legal philosophers use it to mean (a) that legal science is a *nomothetic science*, one that discovers the general laws actually governing legal phenomena, as opposed, for instance, to legal history, which is instead an *idiographic* science. Other legal philosophers (notably, Hans Kelsen among them) use it to mean (b) that legal science looks for, and provides, a normative knowledge of legal norms, that is, one that is *not explanatory-causal* in character, unfortunately without making clear which the positive properties of such a science would be.[35] Still others use it to mean (c) that legal science is a *technical enterprise* providing solutions to practical problems on the basis of some presupposed theoretical inquiry.[36]
3. The previous characterisations of legal science as a normative science, however, are either uninformative (a and b), or misleading (c). The proper way of conceiving legal science is, contrariwise, one that distinguishes two dimensions ('characters', 'directions') inside of it: the purely theoretical dimension and the technical, theoretical-practical or theoretical-normative dimension. These dimensions identify two different but related disciplines coexisting under the expression 'jurisprudence as a normative science'.[37]
4. In its *purely theoretical dimension*, legal science makes inquires on 'legal phenomena', that is, on the subset of social phenomena composing the 'sphere' or 'region of law'. Following Savigny (tacitly, though unmistakably), Bobbio sees in *legal relations* and *legal institutes* (for example, property, will, contract, servitude, and so forth) the grounding materials that make up the deep layers of legal reality and are usually

[35] See Bobbio 1934a: 7–9. By way of conjecture, Bobbio considers that Kelsen understands legal science as a 'normative science', as a formal science of norms. In such a case, however, his conception should be abandoned. No science, claims Bobbio, can be, at the same time formal and normative. Indeed, how can a 'formal' science account for the *content* of legal norms?

[36] See Bobbio 1934a: 5–11.

[37] Bobbio 1934a: 14; 13: '[T]o solve the initial problem, it is necessary to distinguish sharply the theoretical character of jurisprudence from its practical function, keeping in mind that under the generic expression "jurisprudence" is usually included both the *pure science* of law, which, being a theoretical science, is not normative, and the *technical discipline* of law, which, being a normative discipline, is not pure science.' See also Bobbio 1938: 25–7.

incorporated into the norms, laws, statutes and codes of positive legal systems.[38] The task of the theoretical branch of legal science is not limited to ascertaining legal relations and legal institutes, though. It must get to the *essence* of legal institutes, transpose such essence into proper legal concepts (the proper concept of property, will, contract, servitude, and so forth), and, finally, bring to the fore the systematic arrangement holding among the several legal concepts. How to get from the rough data of legal reality to their essence? Here, Husserl's phenomenological philosophy steps in to provide the needed tool for the inquiry. The essence of the legal data must be 'apprehended' by means of an 'essentialist' or 'eidetic' *intuition*: 'legal science, as a science of concepts, is a science of [pure] essences, its task being the task of *Wesenserfassung*, of apprehending the essence of property, of servitude, and so on of every single institute and, therefore, [the essence] of the relations among the singular essences',[39] taking into account, in so doing, both the 'historical forms' of the law – that is, the 'relations among men and institutes of men' – and its 'psychological exigencies' – that is, the 'essential and ineradicable purpose' of each institute.[40]

5. Finally, in its *technical dimension*, legal science is a 'theoretical-normative' activity performed in view of not theoretical ('ontological') but practical ('deontological') purposes.[41] It starts where theoretical, pure, legal science ends. It must take up the (arrangement of essences and) concepts brought to the fore by pure legal science in order to perform two different practical tasks. On the one hand, it must provide suitable formulations of (new) legal norms: that is, such as to be both perfectly tuned to the essence and the concept of the incorporated institute, and capable of realisation (legal science as *normative technique*).[42] On the other hand,

[38] See Bobbio 1934a: 12, 27–8. For a short account of Savigny's conception of law, see Chiassoni 2016: ch. III, s. 2.

[39] Bobbio 1934a: 25–6; 22: 'Legal science, in its theoretical value, means … the formation and ordering of legal concepts.' Following Savigny again, Bobbio emphasises that norms, laws, statutes and codes are not to be regarded as the primary matter of the inquiry of pure legal science. They can play, at most, an auxiliary function. The scientist must discover the essence of legal institutes going *beyond* the norms, laws, statutes and codes, since they may be grounded on wrong representations of the true essences of legal phenomena. See also Bobbio [1934b]2018.

[40] Bobbio 1934a: 29–31, 34. [41] Bobbio 1934a: 37, 47.

[42] Following Jhering, Bobbio (1934a: 38) claims that 'a norm that is conceived in such a way that it cannot be applied, remains an empty formula, has no normative force, does not regulate anything and anybody[;] it is not yet or not anymore a norm'.

it must bring the pure essence and concept of legal institutes to bear on the interpretation of statutory (or codes') provisions, in view of the 'preservation and betterment of the norms that have already been posited' (legal science as *interpretive technique*). This task involves three sorts of activity: 'reconstituting' the texts of the laws, whenever 'obscure'; completing 'missing text[s]' (filling up legal 'gaps'); and reconciling contradictory texts (resolving legal antinomies).[43]

14.3.2 The Logical-Positivist Model

The second stage of Bobbio's theory of legal science is characterised, as I anticipated, by a dramatic change in philosophical background. As a consequence of his involvement in the activities of the *Centro di Studi Metodologici* (Centre for Methodological Studies), founded in Turin immediately after the end of World War II, Bobbio abandons Husserl's phenomenology in favour of logical positivism.[44]

Logical positivism provides Bobbio with a conception of science ('the modern conception of science') he considers adequate for establishing the scientificity of legal science.[45] The core of Bobbio's logical-positivist model consists in the following tenets.

1. According to logical positivism, the scientific character of a discipline does not necessarily depend on the (empirical or formal) *truth* of its propositions. It depends, rather, on the *rigour* of the language by means of which scientific propositions are originally formulated or derived.
2. Every science contains two dimensions ('parts'). The *constitutive dimension* consists in carrying out research the outputs of which are scientific propositions. The *critical dimension* consists, contrariwise, in making the language of science rigorous, by subjecting scientific propositions to linguistic analysis.
3. Legal science can be regarded as a true science according to logical positivism's standards. To be sure, legal science has *no constitutive dimension*. The 'propositions' making up the matter of its inquiries are not the outputs of scientific inquiries; rather, they are the 'normative propositions' ('rules of behaviour') enacted by a legislator and

[43] Bobbio 1934a: 35–45. [44] See Bobbio 1997: 134–6.
[45] Bobbio 1950a: 11–17; Bobbio 1950b: 200–17.

composing a positive legal order (or some part thereof).[46] Legal science, as a true science, has, accordingly, *a critical dimension only.* In its critical dimension, it aims at making the language of normative propositions (legislative language, the language or discourse of the legal order, legislative sentences) rigorous.

4. In order to make the language of normative propositions rigorous, legal science must subject them to linguistic analysis. Linguistic analysis, as performed by legal science, is nothing but the very *interpretation* (in a broad sense of the word) that jurists have always performed in their centuries-old dealing with positive legal orders. It encompasses three related activities: purification, completion and ordering.
5. By means of *purification*, legal science removes the indeterminacies (ambiguity, vagueness) of legislative language. In so doing, it fixes up the *formation rules* of legislative language, whenever they prove indeterminate. This means, in perhaps clearer and more familiar terms, that purification provides legislative terms (for example, 'contract', 'marriage', 'property' and so forth), so far as possible, with precise definitions. Different jurists may propose different definitions for the same indeterminate legislative term, though. In such an event, the only way to adjudicate the dispute is by applying the standards of simplicity (the proposed definition must be simple, not unduly complex), instrumental coherence (the proposed definition must be coherent with the goal that the defined concept is supposed to serve) and substantive coherence (the proposed definition of a concept must be coherent with the extant definitions of other concepts). Contrariwise, any argument for a definition of a legislative term claiming that it would be adequate to the "true", objective legal concept is to be rejected. There are, in fact, no such things as true, objective legal concepts.[47]
6. By means of *completion*, legal science fills up the gaps that the legislator has left by omitting to draw *all* the normative consequences that derive from its expressed normative propositions. In order to fulfil this task, legal science must discover the *transformation rules* of legislative language, which usually encompass, for instance, the rule of analogical extension or analogical reasoning. The filling up of gaps is not an

[46] Bobbio 1950a: 15–16. Bobbio uses 'normative propositions' to refer to legislative sentences: the sentences making up statutes and codes.

[47] See Bobbio 1950a: 17–22.

unbound activity, though. According to Bobbio, legislative legal orders contain a 'closure rule'. According to the closure rule, a normative proposition belongs to the legal order if, and only if, either it has been enacted by the legislator or it is derived from enacted propositions by means of the rules of transformation of the legal order.[48]

7. Finally, by means of *ordering*, legal science copes with normative conflicts (antinomies). Here, according to Bobbio, a problem arises. If by an antinomy we mean a conflict that cannot be resolved by way of some pre-constituted, internal criterion of resolution, legal science must face the situation in which the legal order allows for (true) antinomies, leaving to the judges their resolution on a case-by-case way. Indeed, assuming that the legal order *prohibits* antinomies would involve using criteria of conflict resolution that, by hypothesis, do not belong to the legal order and, therefore, would involve violating the closure rule.[49]

Bobbio considers resorting to the logical positivism's conception of science as a success. To begin with:

> Unlike the conceptions of science worked out up to the present time, the neo-positivistic conception allows including the research of the jurist in the domain of the [real] sciences, and helps the jurist to realize, with an enhanced consciousness, what is the nature of his own job, when he builds up that coherent system of [normative] propositions that is [the output of] the general and particular theory of a determinate positive law, or jurisprudence.[50]

Furthermore, it allows regarding as a truly and thoroughly scientific enterprise what, in the first, phenomenological stage of his theory of legal science, Bobbio considered as legal technique: as a *hybrid* 'theoretical-normative' enterprise.

Finally, it does so in a way that, unlike Kelsen's inchoate theory, provides a clear picture of legal science's dealing with the legal norms that a legislature enacts.[51] And, in so doing, it provides a working legal positivist model of legal science as true science.

Should we accept Bobbio's logical-positivist model of legal science? Is Bobbio right in his logical-positivist account of (traditional) legal science?

As I said, and as we shall see, in the third and final stage of his theory, Bobbio abandons the logical-positivist model, judging it unsatisfactory.

[48] See Bobbio 1950a: 22–6. [49] See Bobbio 1950a: 26–31. [50] Bobbio 1950a: 13.
[51] See Bobbio 1950a: 14–15.

Bobbio justifies his change of posture by invoking the need to finally put down the never-ending, all-things-considered fruitless pursuit of legal science's scientificity, in favour of more fruitful investigations on juristic actual argumentation techniques.[52]

The justification that Bobbio provides appeals, so to speak, to an external reason for changing his view about the purpose of his enquiry on legal science: from looking for the solution to the scientificity problem to providing a realistic and reliable account of the actual tools of juristic reasoning. However, by way of a concluding, critical remark, an internal reason for Bobbio's change can also be offered. This is a reason having to do with the very theoretical soundness of the logical-positivist model that Bobbio proposes.

On closer inspection, Bobbio's legal-positivist model of legal science appears to be the result of a blunder. Recall how Bobbio describes the 'modern conception of science'. His description shows that he presents as *science* what logical positivists regard, rather, as *philosophy*. In their view, the *critical dimension*, the task of making the language of science (and scientific propositions) rigorous, does not belong to science properly conceived but, rather, to philosophy understood as linguistic analysis and rational reconstruction of the language of the several sciences, in view of their unification.[53]

[52] See Bobbio 1965: 48; in this chapter, Section 14.3.3.

[53] See, e.g., Hahn, Neurath, Carnap 1929: 96–7; Carnap 1935: 'The sole proper task of *Philosophy* is *Logical Analysis*' (italics in the text, s. 7); Geymonat 1945: 14–15; Ayer 1946: 25–6, 31–2, 46–59. Guastini presents (what I call here) Bobbio's Logical-Positivist Model as the output of a 'free adaptation to meta-jurisprudence of some meta-scientific thesis of logical positivism, and, in particular, of Otto Neurath (though without quoting him expressly)' (Guastini 2011: xiv). Otto Neurath (Neurath 1931–2: 17–18), however, recognises that the critical task of concept clarification is considered by other members of the Vienna Circle as the proper task of 'philosophy', and motivates his aversion to using that word inside of a scientific conception of the world by claiming that 'the "clarification of the meaning of concepts" cannot be separated from the "scientific method" to which it belongs'. This suggests that the critical task Neurath has in mind, to be truly scientific, must be about *scientific propositions* identified by *scientific method*. It is this internal, methodological connection between the constructive side and the critical side of science that ensures the scientificity of the critical (philosophical) side. Furthermore, Neurath claims that legal science (*Jurisprudenz*) can in fact contain 'elements of a *genuinely scientific character*', but these are propositions that can be 'incorporated in the *structure of sociology*', i.e., proper of an *empirical, causal-explanatory* and *predictive* social science (Neurath 1931–2: 44–5). Bobbio's 'adaptation' to the theory of legal science of Neurath's metascientific ideas, therefore, looks something more than a 'free adaptation'. It looks like

A delusive conclusion follows. By the very logical positivism's standards that Bobbio invokes to support his view, legal science is *not* (true) *science*. It is, rather, a *philosophy of a normative language*: the analytic philosophy of the normative language of legislators. Furthermore, it is a philosophy of a normative language the *Wertfreiheit* of which is, to say the least, dubious. As Bobbio himself comes to acknowledge in the third, and last, stage of his theory.

14.3.3 The Ordinary Language Theory

Considering the never-ending series of models worked out, along the history of legal thought, in order to provide a 'correct' (positive or negative) answer to the scientificity problem, seeing the 'bewildering variety of opinions' that such a pursuit has begotten, Bobbio comes to think it wiser to 'reverse course':

> instead of building a model [of 'true' legal science], drawn from the most diverse fields of learning and then adapted to the work of jurists, start with making an analysis of the different types of argumentations employed by the jurists in their daily working, to the purpose of working out a new *logica legalis*, taking advantages of the services ... of modern logic (symbolic logic and *nouvelle rhétorique*).[54]

The third stage in Bobbio's theory of legal science is the output of such a further dramatic change in his meta-philosophical attitude.

To perform this new task, Bobbio puts to work the toolbox of ordinary language philosophy. The outcome – in *Essere e dover essere nella scienza giuridica*[55] – is a crystal-clear theoretical architecture (something like *La città ideale* at the National Gallery in Urbino) where Bobbio, working as an analytic philosopher of legal science, draws three basic distinctions: first, the distinction between *legal science* and the 'critical reflection upon legal science', for which he coins a new term: *metajurisprudence*;[56] second, the distinction between *metajurisprudence* and *meta-metajurisprudence*, or the critical reflection upon *metajurisprudence*;[57] and third, the distinction between *prescriptive* and *descriptive metajurisprudence*, the former purporting to *prescribe how* legal science *should be* and the latter purporting,

turning them upside-down. Or else, as I suggest in the text, if considered from the standpoint of mainstream logical positivists, it looks like a (fantastic) blunder.

[54] Bobbio 1965: 48. [55] Bobbio 1967a: 117–42. [56] Bobbio 1967a: 121.

[57] Bobbio 1967a: 135.

contrariwise, to *describe how* legal science *is in fact*, that is, what jurists *in fact do* in some legal experience.[58]

On the basis of these distinctions, Bobbio works out the final version of his theory of legal science by way of an analysis of the claim, commonplace among meta-jurisprudes, according to which 'legal science (jurisprudence) is a normative science'. The gist of Bobbio's theory may be recounted as follows.

1. The claim that 'legal science is a normative science' can be understood in three different ways. First, legal science *has to do with norms*. Second, legal science assumes a *normative perspective* in assessing human behaviours and results in *normative propositions* (propositions about norms, *Sollsätze*); these neither *prescribe* what ought to be (*Sollnormen*) nor *describe what in fact is* (*Seinsätze*) but, rather, *describe what ought to be* according to the valid norms of a positive legal order. Third, legal science *contributes*, in a reflexive way, *to the formation and transformation* of positive legal orders (legal science is *a source of law*). The first and third understandings belong to traditional metajurisprudence. The second represents the kernel of Kelsen's metajurisprudence.[59]

2. If we take the first understanding of the claim seriously (legal science *has to do with norms*), we must assume the perspective of descriptive metajurisprudence. What do jurists *do in fact*, here and now? Jurists use legal norms as 'instruments' or 'tools' for solving legal problems about what people can, ought to, or ought not to do. They do not find such instruments ready-made for that task, though. Contrariwise, the instruments – the norms – have to be *set up* by the very jurist who is going to use them: *either* in view of solving some legal problem at hand (direct application of legal norms) *or* in view of the systematic work of defining legal concepts and bringing to the fore the relationships between them, which, in turn, preludes to solving legal problems.

The *setting up* of norms for solving legal problems (or as a basis for systematisation work) is, in turn, a complex operation. It is necessary to distinguish the *detection of norms* from the *revision of norms*. Norms-detection requires that jurists *ascertain* legal norms (identify the legal provisions relevant to the task), *understand* legal norms (interpret the legal provisions previously identified) and, finally and eventually, *find*

[58] Bobbio 1967a: 121–7. [59] See Bobbio 1967a: 117–21.

out legal norms (fill up the gaps). It may happen, however, that the detected norms (which make up the *ius conditum*) prove unsatisfactory. In such a case, the jurist will proceed to *revise* them: that is, to identify the norms that, as a matter of proper law reform (*de iure condendo*), should be applied instead to the problem at hand.[60]

3. If we take seriously the Kelsenian understanding of the claim that 'legal science is a normative science', we are doomed to poor results. First, the idea that legal science assumes a *normative standpoint* is shared also by traditional conceptions of legal science. Second, Kelsen's theory of *normative propositions* rests on confusion. What has a descriptive or a prescriptive sense is not, as Kelsen erroneously claims, the modal verb *Sollen*, which has always the same prescriptive meaning. It is, rather, the *sentence* inside of which the modal verb occurs. Third, Kelsen's theory of legal science is flawed since it adopts a naïf, misleading understanding of the distinction between description and prescription. Kelsen equates prescribing to the issuing of imperative norms. However, there are many different ways of prescribing, for instance the way, typical to legal science, of formulating counsels (or recommendations) about how the law should be properly understood, filled up or revised.[61]

4. Finally, if we take seriously the third understanding of the claim that 'legal science is a normative science' (legal science is a source of law, contributing reflexively to the formation and transformation of legal orders), such a claim turns out to be empirically true. Descriptive metajurisprudence shows that value-judgements and law-shaping operations are a pervasive, necessary component of jurists' everyday dealing with legal norms.[62]

As I said, Bobbio's theory of legal science, in its third and last stage, can be characterised, by comparison to the second stage, as a *post-positivist theory*. It is time to provide some argument.

1. Bobbio associates legal positivism, and Kelsen as its leading representative, with the idea of a prescriptive metajurisprudence committed to showing the path to a genuinely descriptive, truly scientific legal science. It is, in other terms, characteristic of positivism to endorse a *prescriptive* metajurisprudence that *prescribes* to legal science (how) to be *descriptive*.

[60] See Bobbio 1967a: 127–30. [61] See Bobbio 1967a: 130–5, 139–40.
[62] See Bobbio 1967a: 135–42.

2. Descriptive metajurisprudence, however, suggests that we face a dilemma: *either* we approach the law in the way that legal science actually does, and has always done, but then we are not carrying out truly scientific inquiries anymore; *or* we carry out truly scientific inquiries, but then we are not doing what legal science does, and did, anymore.[63]
3. The dilemma drives Bobbio to the following holdings. The positivist, Kelsenian pursuit of the scientificity of legal science is a hopeless venture, to be definitely abandoned.[64] The only theory of legal science that should be considered worthwhile pursuing is, therefore, a post-positivist, post-Kelsenian metajurisprudence, endowed both with *a descriptive* and with *a prescriptive* side.

In its *descriptive side*, post-positivist metajurisprudence should provide analytic descriptions of what the jurists do in fact, going into the details of their operations and bringing to the fore the extent to which they are value-laden and contribute to the formation and transformation of positive legal orders.

In its *prescriptive side*, post-positivist metajurisprudence should prescribe to jurists the ideologically 'correct' way of making value-judgements and performing their law-shaping activities. This requires metajurisprudence to endorse, and argue for, some ideological conception of law and legal science. For instance, it may stand for an innovative and progressive legal science, and against a traditional and conservative one, or vice versa.[65] The positivist metajurisprudence prescribing how to describe must, in the end, be replaced by a post-positivist metajurisprudence prescribing how to prescribe.

[63] 'Jurisprudence *is*, with a greater or lesser success according to times and places, *one of* [the] *forces*' that contribute to '*the development of a legal order*' (Bobbio 1967a: 138 (italics added); see also 142).

[64] Indeed, for the reasons Bobbio makes clear, it would necessarily lead to the 'duplication of legal science', to a legal science that is not the legal science corresponding to the traditional social function of the jurists, which is a value-laden, law-shaping enterprise. Bobbio 1967a: 124–7: 'While prescriptive metajurisprudence, proper to *positivistic metajurisprudence*, had found its call ... in *prescribing to describe*, the present metajurisprudence, carrying out its call to *description*, discovers that jurisprudence *does not describe*, but *prescribes*' (126 (italics added) ndr); Bobbio 1967b: 70–1, 73.

[65] See Bobbio 1967a: 141–2. Bobbio's post-positivist conception of legal science has been taken up by Luigi Ferrajoli, the leading representative of the *garantismo* variety of contemporary constitutionalism. See Carbonell 2003; Chiassoni 2011.

References

Agosti, P. and Revelli, M. (eds.). 2009. *Bobbio e il suo mondo*. Aragno.

Austin, J. 1885. *Lectures on Jurisprudence, or The Philosophy of Positive Law*. 5th ed. Murray & Sons.

Ayer, A. J. 1946. *Language, Truth and Logic*. 2nd ed. Dover Publications.

Bobbio, N. 1934a. *Scienza e tecnica del diritto*. Istituto Giuridico della R. Università.

Bobbio, N. [1934b]2018. *L'indirizzo fenomenologico nella filosofia del diritto*. Ed. P. Di Lucia. Giappichelli.

Bobbio, N. 1938. *L'analogia nella logica del diritto*. Ed. P. Di Lucia. Giuffrè.

Bobbio, N. 1950a. 'Scienza del diritto e analisi del linguaggio'. In N. Bobbio. 2011. *Saggi sulla scienza giuridica*. Giappichelli: 1–31.

Bobbio, N. 1950b. *Teoria della scienza giuridica*. Giappichelli.

Bobbio, N. 1954. 'Sul ragionamento dei giuristi'. In N. Bobbio. 2011. *Saggi sulla scienza giuridica*. Giappichelli: 33–46.

Bobbio, N. 1961. *Il positivismo giuridico*. Giappichelli.

Bobbio, N. 1965. *Giusnaturalismo e positivismo giuridico*. Comunità.

Bobbio, N. 1967a. 'Essere e dover essere nella scienza giuridica'. In N. Bobbio. 2011. *Saggi sulla scienza giuridica*. Giappichelli: 117–42.

Bobbio, N. 1967b. 'Intervento'. In AA.VV. 1967. *Tavola rotonda sul positivismo giuridico*. Giuffrè: 69–73.

Bobbio, N. 1992. 'Autobiografia intellettuale'. In N. Bobbio. 1996. *De senectute e altri scritti autobiografici*. Ed. P. Polito. Einaudi: 121–41.

Bobbio, N. 1993. *Teoria generale del diritto*. Giappichelli.

Bobbio, N. 1994. 'Diritto e potere'. In N. Bobbio. 1996. *De senectute e altri scritti autobiografici*. Ed. P. Polito. Einaudi: 154–62.

Bobbio, N. 1997. *Autobiografia*. Ed. A. Papuzzi. Laterza.

Carbonell, M. (ed.). 2003. *Neoconstitucionalismo(s)*. Trotta.

Carnap, R. 1935. *Philosophy and Logical Syntax*. K. Paul, Trench, Trubner and Co.

Chiassoni, P. 2011. 'Constitutionalism out of a Positivist Mind Cast: The Garantismo Way'. *Res Publica* 17(4): 327–42.

Chiassoni, P. 2013. *Positivismo giuridico. Una investigazione analitica*. Mucchi Editore.

Chiassoni, P. 2016. *Da Bentham a Kelsen. Sei capitoli per una storia della filosofia analitica del diritto*. Giappichelli.

Comanducci, P. 2003. 'Formas de (neo)constitucionalismo: un análisis metateórico'. *Isonomía* 2003: 75–98.

Duke, G. and George, R. P. (eds.) 2017. *The Cambridge Companion to Natural Law Jurisprudence*. Cambridge University Press.

Geymonat, L. 1945. *Studi per un nuovo razionalismo*. Chiantore.

Guastini, R. 2011. 'Bobbio sulla scienza giuridica. Introduzione alla lettura'. In N. Bobbio. 2011. *Saggi sulla scienza giuridica*. Giappichelli: ix–xxii.

Hahn, H., Neurath, O. and Carnap, R. 1929. *Wissenschaftliche Weltauffassung. Die Wiener Kreis.* Trans. *La concezione scientifica del mondo. Il Circolo di Vienna.* Laterza.

Hart, H. L. A. 1958. 'Positivism and the Separation of Law and Morals'. In H. L. A. Hart. 1983. *Essays in Jurisprudence and Philosophy.* Clarendon Press: 49–87.

Hart, H. L. A. 1961. *The Concept of Law.* With a Postscript. 3rd ed. Introduction L. Green. Eds. P. A. Bulloch and J. Raz. Oxford University Press.

Hart, H. L. A. 1967. 'Legal Positivism'. In P. Edwards (ed.). *The Encyclopedia of Philosophy.* Macmillan. Losano, M. G. 2018. *Norberto Bobbio. Una biografia culturale.* Carocci.

Neurath, O. 1931–2. 'Soziologie im Physikalismus'. Trans. *Sociologia e fisicalismo.* In O. Neurath. 1968. *Sociologia e neopositivismo.* Introduction and trans. G. Statera. Ubaldini: 17–53. Olivecrona, K. 1971. *Law as Fact.* 2nd ed. Stevens & Sons.

Perry, S. R. 2001. 'Hart's Methodological Positivism'. In J. Coleman (ed.). *Hart's Postscript: Essays on the Postscript to the Concept of Law.* Oxford University Press: 311–54.

Portinaro, P. P. 2008. *Introduzione a Bobbio.* Laterza.

Prieto, L. 1997. *Constitucionalismo y positivismo.* Fontamara.

Pufendorf, S. 1673. *De officio hominis et civis juxta legem naturalem libri duo* [*On the Duty of Man and Citizen According to Natural Law*]. Cambridge University Press.

Redazione Reset and Ocone, C. (eds.). 2003. *Bobbio ad uso di amici e nemici.* Marsilio.

Ross, A. 1961/1999. 'Validity and the Conflict between Legal Positivism and Natural Law'. In S. Paulson and B. Litschewski Paulson (eds.). *Normativity and Norms. Critical Perspectives on Kelsenian Themes.* Clarendon Oxford: ch. 7.

Scarpelli, U. 1965. *Cos'è il positivismo giuridico.* Eds. and introduction A. Catania and M. Jori. Edizioni Scientifiche Italiane.

Scarpelli, U. 1967. 'Risposta'. In AA.VV. 1967. *Tavola rotonda sul positivismo giuridico.* Giuffrè: 77–86.

Vitale, E. (ed.) 2010. *Norberto Bobbio e Alessandro Passerin d'Entrèves. Profili intellettuali a confronto.* Giappichelli.

Zolo, D. 2008. *L'alito della libertà. Su Bobbio.* Feltrinelli.

Joseph Raz's Approach to Legal Positivism 15

Brian H. Bix

15.1 Introduction

Joseph Raz has been one of the most influential writers on legal positivism, in his earlier works defining key concepts as well as defending legal positivist positions in general and one form of legal positivism ('exclusive legal positivism')[1] in particular. This chapter will give an overview of Raz's positions and supporting arguments, as well as discussing some criticisms that Raz's writings have evoked.

There are reasons to be cautious about this task. First, some commentators have argued that Raz's works across a range of topics – in legal philosophy, moral philosophy and political philosophy – hang together as parts of a general view, such that one can miss the larger point if one focuses too narrowly on particular parts of the theory.[2] However, the brief for this chapter *is* to focus on just one portion of Raz's works, and, while other parts of Raz's writings will be brought in where clearly relevant, there is no effort here (in part because there is insufficient space) to offer an overview of Raz's views as a whole. Second, in his later works, Raz has become less comfortable with – and has at times been dismissive regarding – the division of legal theories into schools of thought like 'legal positivism'.[3] He would

[1] 'Exclusive legal positivism denies, whereas inclusive legal positivism accepts, that there can be instances where determining what the law is, follow from moral considerations about that which it is there to settle . . . [E]xclusive legal positivism maintains that a norm is never rendered legally valid solely in virtue of its moral content' (Marmor 2002: 104, 105). Exclusive legal positivism is also sometimes called 'hard positivism'.

[2] See, e.g., Sevel 2014.

[3] See, e.g., Raz 2003: 253 (describing it as an error to suggest that there is a 'nature' to legal positivism, rather than speaking of legal positivism simply as 'a historical tradition containing writings some of which bear greater similarity in their central tenets to writings outside it . . . than to each other, a tradition which cannot be characterized by adherence to any central tenet or tenets'); Raz 2009a: 317 ('I believe that the classification of legal theories as legal positivist and non-legal positivist . . . is unhelpful and liable to mislead'); Raz 2009b: 9 ('so-called "legal positivist" theories').

likely today resist any inquiry about 'his view of legal positivism'; he would probably prefer a characterisation of 'his views, which tend to fall in the historical tradition known as "legal positivism"'.[4] This chapter will thus focus primarily on the particular claims that Raz has defended (and the particular views he has criticised), with less attention to the boundary lines of 'legal positivism', and which views qualify or fail to qualify for that label.

In what follows, Section 15.2 summarises Raz's 'sources thesis' as well as Raz's views on the separation thesis and detached normative statements. Section 15.3 looks at Raz's major arguments for (his version of) legal positivism – the argument from authority and the argument from different functions. Section 15.4 summarises and evaluates some responses to Raz's arguments, and Section 15.5 concludes.

15.2 The Sources Thesis

15.2.1 Origin and Explanation

Raz has argued at length and in various places for what he at one point characterised as the 'fundamental' view of legal positivism,[5] the claim that 'the content of the law can be established without resort to moral considerations bearing on the desirability or otherwise of any human conduct, or of having any particular legal standards'.[6] He restated the view as the 'social thesis':[7] 'what is law and what is not is a matter of social fact'.[8] Social facts, in this context, are clearly intended to contrast with moral facts (and, of course, with physical facts as well); and they include 'complex facts about what people and institutions believed, wanted, and intended'.[9]

Raz advocated what he viewed as a stronger form of the social thesis, 'the sources thesis': 'All law is source based.'[10] He elaborated: 'A law is source-

[4] See note 3. [5] Raz 2009a: 38.

[6] Raz 2009b: 4 (footnote omitted). Raz (2009a: 37–8) argued that legal positivism often combined this 'social thesis' with a 'moral thesis' (that the moral merit of particular laws or whole legal systems is a contingent matter) and a 'semantic thesis' (that distinguishes the meanings of 'right' and 'duty' in legal and moral contexts). While Raz (2009a: 38–9) observed that '[t]he moral and semantic theses are often thought to be necessitated by the social thesis', he himself did not accept that derivation; see also Raz 1990: 162–70.

[7] Raz 2009a: 45–8. [8] Raz 2009a: 37. [9] Green 2005: 504.

[10] Raz 1994: 194. Raz uses 'source' in a wide sense, to include not only statutes and precedents but also '"interpretive sources", namely all the relevant interpretative materials.

based if its existence and content can be identified by reference to social facts alone, without resort to any evaluative argument.'[11] (A weaker version of the social thesis would be roughly equivalent with 'inclusive legal positivism', allowing moral considerations to determine legal content where (but only where) this has been authorised by posited legal norms.)[12] In a later work, Raz asserted that the social thesis (and, it would follow, the sources thesis as well) is 'not a "first-order" thesis but [rather] a constraint on what kind of theory of law is an acceptable theory'.[13] That is, we are dealing, technically, not with a theory of law but, instead, with something that is one level up: a meta-theory, an analysis of limitations that any theory of law must meet if it is to be successful.

This also touches, indirectly, on the distinction between legal positivism qua analytical or conceptual theory (the usual understanding of legal positivism) and 'normative legal positivism', a *prescriptive* theory for how law *should be*.[14] Normative legal positivism is a view about what factors a legal system *should* use in determining the content of law, in contrast to a position like Raz's, which asserts that there are certain limitations, *grounded in the nature of law*, for determining legal content (in all past, present and possible legal systems).

While both the social thesis and the sources thesis were originally presented as claims central to legal positivism ('theses or groups of theses round which [legal positivism] revolves'),[15] it remains important to try to interpret these claims in ways such that reasonable theorists might disagree with them. This is a general problem with ideas associated with legal positivism: what are presented as its central views too often come across as either obviously true or so vague or general that few would contest them.[16] A theory that is trivially true is not worthy of serious discussion. Relating

The sources of a law thus understood are never a single act (of legislation, etc.) alone, but a whole range of facts of a variety of kinds' (Raz 2009a: 48).

11 Raz 1994: 195.

12 See Raz 2009a: 45–8. On inclusive legal positivism (also known as 'incorporationist' or 'soft' legal positivism), see, e.g., Waluchow 1994; Himma 2002.

13 Raz 2009a: 39. 14 See, e.g., Celano 2013. 15 Raz 2009a: 37.

16 See Finnis 2000: 1611: 'Positivism does no more than repeat (1) what any competent lawyer ... would say are (or are not) intra-systemically valid laws, imposing "legal requirements," and (2) what any street-wise observer would warn are the likely consequences of noncompliance.' A similar objection can be raised against natural law theories, of course. One response to this objection when raised against natural law is given by Murphy 2015: 127–40.

to that point, one might recall that John Finnis, a prominent natural law theorist (a position that is generally treated as the 'opponent' of, or at least the primary alternative to, legal positivism), argued that he (and natural law theory in general) could affirm almost every view or 'dogma' associated with legal positivism, including the sources thesis.[17] He further commented that the 'truths' of legal positivism require supplements: 'Though human law is artefact and artifice, and not a conclusion from moral premises, both its positing and the recognition of its positivity (by judges, professionals, citizens, and then by descriptive and critical scholars) cannot be understood without reference to the moral principles that ground and confirm its authority or challenge its pretention.'[18] Of course, the fact that one's theory about the nature of law is not sufficient to answer all practical questions relating to law (for example, what standards should guide the interpretation of legal texts and the resolution of legal disputes)[19] need hardly render such a theory (legal positivist or not) valueless. However, advocates in this area do need to find a reading of the social thesis, the sources thesis, Raz's theory in particular, or legal positivism in general, with which a natural law theorist, or other legal theorist, might reasonably disagree, or seek an alternative theory that would meet this standard.[20]

15.2.2 The Separation Thesis

In an early summary of the approach now known as 'legal positivism', John Austin wrote: 'The existence of law is one thing; its merit or demerit is

[17] See Finnis 2011: 185. However, Finnis elsewhere endorsed the idea that the moral prohibition of 'crimes against humanity' is a valid norm in a legal system, even if never posited by a legal official or institution, and even if a presumptively valid legal norm purported to negate that prohibition (the Nuremberg Trials issue); Finnis 2020 s. 3.1.1. And it is hard to see *that* claim as being consistent with the sources thesis.

[18] Finnis 2011: 186. Elsewhere, Finnis (2020 s. 5) writes:

> [N]o legal philosopher need, or should, be a legal positivist? For law's dependence upon social facts is fully acknowledged, and also accounted for, in natural law theories of law. And this is not a 'concession' by natural law theorists, for their main positions were clearly articulated by Aquinas, many centuries before legal positivism emerged with its challenge to (what it took to be) natural law theory. Positivist critiques of natural law theory, when they do not rest upon scepticism about the possibility of moral judgment ... rest on misunderstanding of passages from the works of natural law theorists.

[19] Green 2003: s. 4.3: 'No legal philosopher can be only a legal positivist.'

[20] The author is confident that the present volume will show legal positivism to be a sufficiently substantial and sufficiently controversial position to be worthy of scholarly attention.

another.'[21] The idea that legal positivism is essentially about asserting a 'separation' of law and morality was strongly affirmed (for English-language legal theorists) by H. L. A. Hart's article, *Positivism and the Separation of Law and Morals*, which elaborated and defended that separation.[22] While Raz denies conceptual links between law and morality based on defining law in moral terms,[23] he has also rejected the separation thesis when more broadly stated.

In a response to Robert Alexy's characterisation of the separation thesis,[24] Raz observed certain problems in asserting the thesis in general, and in application to Raz's own version of legal positivism. The general problems include the difficulty of demarcating moral and non-moral concepts.[25] And Raz's theory about the nature of law is grounded on the idea that law, necessarily, claims moral authority;[26] that claim, Raz asserts, is a moral claim.[27] Raz notes other possible 'necessary moral properties' of law: e.g., 'that rape cannot be committed by law',[28] and that the formal (non-moral) properties of law (for example, rule of law properties, like those elaborated by Lon Fuller)[29] may have moral *effects*, making arbitrary and immoral state action less likely.[30]

Raz used the occasion of his rejection of Alexy's version of the separation thesis to reassert his discomfort with 'legal positivism' as a clear category, as

[21] Austin [1832]1995: lecture V, at 157. [22] Hart 1958. [23] See, e.g., Raz 1990: 163–5.

[24] Alexy (2002: 3) argued that the 'separation thesis' is what is common to all legal positivist theories, and that this thesis states that 'the concept of law is to be defined such that no moral elements are included. [It] presupposes that there is no conceptually necessary connection between law and morality.' (Raz's part in the debate with Alexy was published in Raz 2007 and Raz 2009a: 313–35. Citations to Raz's response in the present work will give the page numbers from Raz 2009a.)

[25] See Raz 2009a: 315. [26] See Raz 1994: 199–204.

[27] 'It is a moral claim because of its content: it is a claim which includes the assertion of a right to grant rights and impose duties in matters affecting basic aspects of people's life and their interactions with one another' (Raz 2009a: 315–16).

[28] In a similar spirit, Leslie Green lists: 'Necessarily, law regulates objects of morality', '[n]ecessarily, law makes moral claims of its subjects', '[n]ecessarily, law is justice apt', and '[n]ecessarily, law is morally risky' (Green 2008: 1047, 1048, 1050, 1052). For a contrary view, defending the traditional understanding of the separability of law and morality (as central to legal positivism), see Kramer 2004.

[29] See Fuller 1969: 41–91.

[30] See Raz 2009a: 317–19. Relevant to this point, Scott Shapiro (2011: 8–9) helpfully distinguishes 'identity questions' from 'implication questions'. Thus, one might be able to distinguish law from non-law using social sources, but law, so determined, might still have (positive or negative) moral consequences.

opposed to speaking merely of 'theories in the positivist tradition'.[31] What theories of that 'tradition' may have in common, Raz stated, is the view that 'determining what the law is does not necessarily, or conceptually, depend on moral or other evaluative considerations about what the law ought to be in the relevant circumstances'.[32]

15.2.3 Detached Normative Statements

Basic issues arise when discussing propositions in and about law. The law tells us to do certain things, and to avoid doing other things[33] (along with creating constitutive rules and power-conferring rules of various kinds).[34] Talk within and about the law thus involves references to rights and duties, but this invites confusion with our moral (or, if one prefers, our 'all things considered') rights and duties. But no theorist, either legal positivist or natural law, would equate law with morality completely. So the semantics or truth-making aspects of legal talk can become complicated or confused. 'You have an obligation to do X [some task required by law]' seems, on the surface, to communicate a 'real' (moral, all-things-considered) obligation, when it may be only, at best, a legal obligation.

Raz responded to this problem by introducing 'the legal point of view', propositions that state 'what ought to be done if legal norms are valid norms'.[35] The legal point of view is an example, Raz argues, of a category of propositions: statements from a (normative) point of view.[36] For example, one can tell vegans or Orthodox Jews what they ought to do, or avoid doing, given their belief systems, even if one does not adopt or endorse that belief system.[37] Similarly, the legal scholar or advocate can

[31] Raz 2009a: 319.

[32] Ibid., quoting Marmor 2001: 71. He goes on to characterise his own 'sources thesis' as a 'stricter' version of the thesis quoted (Raz 2009a: 319).

[33] In modern legal systems, legal texts rarely say directly 'do this' or 'don't do that', but they get the same message across indirectly, by connecting certain behaviours with sanctions or positive incentives.

[34] Legal power-conferring rules include the rules relating to contracts, wills, trusts, marriage, etc.

[35] Raz 1990: 175. Such 'detached legal statements' also respond to certain criticisms Raz made of H. L. A. Hart's writings. For a summary of those criticisms, and an argument that Hart's views can be defended against them, see Toh 2007. Another critique of Raz's notion of detached normative statements can be found in Duarte d'Almeida 2011.

[36] See Raz 2009a: 153–7.

[37] See, e.g., Raz 2009a: 156–7.

report what ought to be done, and avoided, based on treating the law as creating 'real' (moral, or all-things-considered) rights and duties.

15.3 Supporting Arguments

15.3.1 The Argument from Authority

According to Raz, law necessarily claims to be a practical authority.[38] (It is a *practical* authority, rather than a *theoretical* authority, in that it tells us how to act, not what to believe.)[39] The next step in Raz's argument is that to claim to be an authority, an entity needs to be the kind of thing *that can be* an authority.[40] Here and elsewhere, Raz is careful to note that he is not claiming that law always *succeeds* in being a practical authority.[41] In fact, Raz argues that legal systems generally *fail* to be practical authorities, or at least that their success is sporadic, varying significantly from law to law and from person to person.[42]

In order for something to be a practical authority, it must be possible to determine what to do from the authority's pronouncements, without further reference to the underlying reasons for action that apply to the question.[43] And it must be possible to recognise the pronouncement 'as someone's view of how subjects ought to act'.[44] An authority works as a mediator between the reasons that apply and the action to be taken (based on those reasons). The role of an authority is not served if we are told only 'do what is best' or 'do what morality requires'. Citizens 'can benefit by [an authority's] decisions only if they can establish their [the decisions'] existence and content in ways which do not depend on raising the very same issues which the authority is there to settle'.[45]

[38] See Raz 1994: 199–200, 213; Raz 2009b: 107, 112. It follows almost directly, that if one is or claims to be an authority, one is or claims to be a *legitimate* authority; Marmor 2001: 34–7.

[39] But see Hurd 1990, arguing that law purports to be a *theoretical* authority.

[40] See Raz 1994: 199–202.

[41] There is the complication that 'the law is a structure of authority, as well as . . . the product of that structure of authority, which it itself constitutes' (Raz 2009b: 106–7).

[42] See Raz 1994, 199–200, 325–38. [43] See Raz 1994: 202. [44] Raz 1994: 202–3.

[45] Raz 1994: 203. Raz grounds his argument on a specific conception of authority (the 'service conception' of authority; see Raz 1986: 23–69; Raz 2006). However, Raz (1994: 204) adds that the argument could also go forward on a weaker, alternative understanding of authority.

Again, the argument is not that law always *succeeds* at being an authority for (all) citizens, but rather that, as the sort of thing that *can be an authority*, it can only fail in certain ways. Legal rules can display incompetence or be immoral, but that is still consistent with law being the sort of thing that *could be* a practical authority (in a way that a rock or a bridge generally *cannot* be a practical authority).

In a later work, Raz wrote: 'Since the moral force of the law, its moral claim to our attention derives from the moral authority, if any, of the authorities which made it into law, it follows that the content of the law can be identified without resort to moral argument.'[46] We need to be able to determine what those who have the moral authority to choose on behalf of the community *have in fact chosen*. This is a factual question, not a moral one. This does not guarantee that determining the answer to that question will always be either easy or uncontroversial. For example, if according to the understandings and conventions of our legal system, a constitutional provision means what the drafters of that provision intended it to mean, *and* the provision was written over two hundred years ago, *and* the record of the drafters' intentions is incomplete, the meaning of that constitutional provision may be difficult to ascertain, and reasonable legal commentators will disagree about what it is.

The basic point expressed in the sources thesis is that, given the kind of institution law is – the role it is set to play in our practical reasoning – we must be able to determine the content of the law without recourse to moral evaluation. Though, of course, this is not to say that morality cannot or should not play a role in the creation of new law, or in the resolution of legal disputes.

15.3.2 The Argument from Different Functions

Raz's argument from different functions connects to, but is distinct from, the argument from authority. The different functions in question are deliberation and execution. That is, we all know the difference between the process of deciding what to do – evaluating, comparing and weighing

[46] Raz 2009b: 114. Raz (2009b: 235) recognises a potential problem in grounding legal content and legal legitimacy based on the authority of those who made the law, in circumstances where the laws were made by lawmakers now long dead. He argues that following such laws may still be ethically justified, the justification based in part on the importance of continuity in the guidance of citizens.

reasons for action for different alternatives – deciding, and then, having decided, putting that decision into action.[47] Moral considerations are generally appropriate at the deliberative stage (depending on the nature of the matter being decided), but they are not appropriate at the executive stage. One simply goes ahead with the course of action chosen (one can, of course, reopen a matter previously decided, prior to action, but that is simply a return to the deliberative stage).[48] And so with law: '[L]aw consists of the authoritative positivist considerations binding on the courts and belongs essentially to the executive stage of the political institution . . . of which it is a part.'[49] Determining what the law is is a matter of ascertaining what the legal authorities have decided; morality often has a role in making decisions, but not in determining what decisions have been made.

While courts are bound to apply legal rules, the results of the deliberations by other legal institutions, Raz is not claiming that the courts can (or do) apply *only* such factors in their decisions: '[T]the courts apply . . . both legal (that is, authoritative positivist) and non-legal considerations. They rely both on executive and deliberative reasons, yet the law belongs to the first kind only.'[50] It is part of the nature of judicial decision-making that decisions resolving particular cases often include elements of both enforcement of existing law and the modification of law, and that these aspects are not always clearly distinguished by the court (or easy to distinguish by commentators).[51] This may be especially true in the legal interpretation of statutes and constitutional provisions, as well as the application of precedent.[52] However, the fact that the line is not always precise between declaring and applying existing law, on one hand, and making new law or modifying existing law, on the other hand, is no reason to ignore that distinction or its significance for a theory about the nature of law.[53]

[47] See, e.g., Raz 1994: 190–2. [48] See Raz 1994: 190–1.

[49] Raz 1994: 191. Raz (2009a: 48–50) offers a similar argument based on the difference between settled and unsettled law, and the difference between judges' legal doctrinal skills and their understanding of human nature. Stephen Perry's response was that these distinctions 'are not so much systematized by the sources thesis as they are implied by it' (Perry 1987: 228).

[50] Raz 1994: 191. [51] See Raz 2009b: 9–10, 235–40. [52] See, e.g., Raz 2009b: 223–40.

[53] There is one potential argument for the sources thesis that David Lyons attributes to Raz, but which the latter disowns. The argument is that '[t]he social order is liable to break down if substantive moral arguments used in adjudication are counted as helping to interpret the law, because that would encourage members of the society to break the law in the hope of avoiding the legal consequences by "challenging the justification of the standard"' (Lyons 2003: 92). It is unclear where Lyons finds this argument in Raz's work, as this purported

15.3.3 Issues of Characterisation

It is important to observe that the disagreement between Raz and his critics is generally *not* in terms of what legal officials *should* do or what it would be *legitimate* for them to do, because, as already discussed, Raz, in his works relating to theories of the nature of law, is not prescribing what should be done.[54] Instead, the disagreement is frequently best understood as *competing characterisations* of actions by legal officials that have occurred or could occur. For example, the disagreement between exclusive legal positivism and inclusive legal positivism regarding constitutional judicial review is not about whether judges *should* have the power to invalidate legislation based on moral terms derived from a constitutional text, or when such power should be exercised.[55] The disagreement is, rather, about *the correct way to understand* this process. For inclusive legal positivists (and many non-positivists), judges in these circumstances are declaring that certain enactments are not, and never have been, valid law, because they conflict with constitutional provisions. For exclusive legal positivists, the same action would be understood as judges using delegated powers to invalidate a previously valid legal rule. It is true that judges in such cases sometimes use terminology to describe their actions in ways that seem to be more consistent with the inclusive legal positivists' understanding (for example, that the enactment that was held to conflict with the constitution was 'void ab initio', and so forth). Raz would say that such judicial conventions of presentation should hardly be conclusive, when analysis points clearly to a different understanding.[56] Additionally, the inclusive legal positivist approach creates its own problems and mysteries: should we understand all legislative enactments as then being only

summary of Raz's view contains no citations to Raz's writings. Raz responded to Lyons' characterisation: '[N]othing remotely like this ever crossed my mind or my pen' (Raz 1994: 219 n. 18). Other commentators have also found Lyons's characterisation to be unsupported; e.g., Waluchow 1994: 126.

54 Consider the following comment, which was part of Raz's critique of Ronald Dworkin's legal theory: 'It is important to realize that the disagreement I am pursuing is not about how judges should decide cases . . . [Even if we assume that Dworkin's] advice to judges on how to decide cases is sound[, w]e still have a disagreement regarding what judges do when they follow his advice . . . [Do judges] follow the law or do they make law?' (Raz 1994: 209).

55 Raz (1994: 217) also emphasised that the sources thesis does not entail (and is not entailed by) any particular approach to legal interpretation.

56 See Marmor 2001: 68.

'*prima facie* valid', for any of them could, in principle, be invalidated on constitutional grounds by a later court decision?[57]

Similarly, there is a question of characterisation or proper labelling regarding some applications by courts of moral standards. As Raz points out, legal systems can and do enforce (and judges can have a legal duty to enforce) standards from 'external' or 'foreign' normative systems and sources: corporate charters, laws of other jurisdictions, contracts and so forth.[58] Conflict of law provisions in legal systems and choice of law provisions in transactions are common. A court may have occasion to apply the law of another jurisdiction because that is where a transaction or an accident occurred, or because that was the law chosen by the parties as part of their agreement. Thus, American courts may have a legal duty on some occasions to apply French law, but that does not make the relevant French provisions part of American law. Analogously, the court may, as part of the resolution of a dispute, be required to interpret and apply a corporate charter or the by-laws of an organised club or group. The application of moral norms by courts might be similarly understood.[59] Courts may have occasion to apply moral norms, but that no more makes those moral norms part of that particular legal system than the courts' application of corporate charters or the laws of foreign jurisdictions makes *those* norms part of the legal system.

Also, legislatures often delegate law-making power to courts or to agencies, and direct those decision-makers to focus on particular factors (moral factors like fairness or other factors like health or cost-efficiency). Thus, courts or agency officials may sometimes have a legal duty to apply moral standards in making law, but it would be misleading (or at least unhelpful) to characterise the moral standards in those circumstances as existing legal norms.[60]

[57] See, e.g., Marmor 2001: 64. One might respond that the alternative, that enactments (or contracts) are *defeasibly* valid, subject to the discretion of the courts, raises its own set of problems. See Endicott 2003: 111–14; Green 2005: 504–9.

[58] See Raz 2009b: 193–5. [59] See Green 2003: s. 3.

[60] Raz writes: 'References to morality ... indicate to the courts or to the regulatory agencies or delegated legislature that while the maker of the law has considered moral and other considerations and found that they justify the legislated standards, it did not consider, or did not exhaustively consider, the impact of the so-called incorporated moral considerations, and it is for the court or regulator and so on to do that' (Raz 2009b: 197–8 (footnote omitted)); see also Raz 2009b: 201.

Raz has offered another way to come at the general point he is making. Judges and other legal officials – *like all of us* – are subject to moral reasons. As Raz has written about at length and in many places, law purports to pre-empt or supplant the moral (and other) reasons that otherwise apply to our practical reasoning.[61] In a sense, then, purported examples of the law 'incorporating' moral standards might in fact be better understood as limits to the pre-emption or supplanting of moral reasons that would otherwise apply. 'References to moral considerations in constitutions are typically not cases of the incorporation of morality but blocks to its [morality's] exclusion or modification by ordinary legislation.'[62]

15.3.4 Authority, Agency and Incorporation

One can connect Raz's responses to inclusive legal positivism to his responses to coherence theories of law. The latter is represented by Ronald Dworkin (at least in some stages, or some aspects, of Dworkin's works). For Raz, the problem with coherentist approaches is that, for them, what the law is does not reflect choices or views of those who claim a right to rule.[63] Raz writes that incorporationist approaches similarly are inconsistent with the claim law makes to be an authority, for the 'mediating role of authority implies that the content of an authoritative directive is confined to what the authority which lends the directive its binding force can be said to have held or to have presented itself as holding'.[64] As Gerald Postema points out, Raz's sources thesis, unlike many coherentist approaches, 'assumes . . . that necessary features of *law* are always features of individual *laws* (or discrete relations among them)'.[65]

15.4 Responses

Many theorists who have participated in the debates about legal positivism, or within legal positivism, have responded to Raz's arguments. There is

[61] See, e.g., Raz 1990: 148–99. [62] Raz 2009b: 196.

[63] See Raz 1994: 210. Most of the comments Raz offers about Dworkin's approach would likely apply as well to the more recent work of Mark Greenberg, e.g., Greenberg 2011, 2014, 2017, though Raz has not commented directly on Greenberg's writings.

[64] Raz 1994: 213. Raz adds: 'The mistake of the incorporation thesis is to identify being entailed by the source-based law with being endorsed by the sources of law' (Raz 1994: 213).

[65] Postema 2011: 356 (emphasis in original).

obviously not space enough here to offer a comprehensive survey of those responses, but this section tries to sample some representative criticisms raised by prominent scholars, both coming from supporters of inclusive legal positivism and coming from critics of legal positivism.

15.4.1 Inclusive Legal Positivists

15.4.1.1 Jules Coleman

Jules Coleman offers an understanding of legal authority meant to compete with Raz's understanding, one that, Coleman argues, allows an inclusive legal positivist approach. Coleman asserts that such an inclusive approach is more consistent with the surface grammar of constitutional judicial review and other apparent uses of moral standards in law.[66] More particularly, Coleman rejects the notion that law's status as a purported authority requires that no recourse to moral reasons be necessary to determine what law requires. Raz's argument, recall, had been that authoritative pronouncements, by their nature, displace underlying reasons for action, so needing recourse to the underlying reasons for action is contrary to the nature of law, qua purported authority. Coleman's answer is that in many of the places where law seems to incorporate moral standards – most prominently, in constitutional judicial review – the moral standards being applied are frequently *different from* the moral standards that grounded the law. For example, a murder statute might be challenged on the grounds of the inequality in its application.[67] Equality is a moral standard, but it is not salient among the moral reasons for action for which a rule prohibiting murder is a reasonable summary or substitute. So, to evaluate a murder statute on equality grounds *is not* to return to the reasons for action that the murder statute was meant to replace.

One rejoinder might be that Coleman's objection here does not in fact undermine Raz's analysis. Even if the set of moral grounds for potentially invalidating legislation (as part of constitutional judicial review) are different from the set of (moral) reasons that the initial legislation was

[66] See Coleman 2001: 106–19.

[67] See Coleman 1998b: 271. Wil Waluchow (1994: 138–9) makes a similar point. Brian Leiter's response (to both) is that singular counter-examples do not undermine Raz's argument; the burden of proof works the other way, and singular examples of moral standards overlapping the underlying reasons for the law would be sufficient to prove the point for exclusive legal positivism; Leiter 1998: 541.

intended to replace, the basic structure of analysis remains. Law must be able to make a difference, law must be able to guide behaviour, and the notion of moral tests for legal validity or invalidity would undermine that possibility.[68]

Coleman has a reply, in his argument that legal positivism should reject, or at least alter, what he calls 'the Practical Difference Thesis'.[69] Coleman suggests that one could 'explain the sense in which law is a normative social practice, the sense in which it makes a practical difference, without committing ourselves to the claim that it is part of our concept of legality that nothing can count as law unless it purports to make such a difference'.[70] The point is that law may make a practical difference *most of the time*, but there is no reason to believe that it does so *all the time*, or that rules that fail to make a practical difference, for that reason, lack or lose their legal status.[71] Raz would likely respond that this line of critique misunderstands his basic approach: to say, as Coleman appears to, that it would be sufficient for law *most of the time* not to need recourse to moral standards, and *most of the time* to 'make a practical difference', is to miss the extent to which Raz's view reflects analytical (conceptual) connections among law, authority and practical reasoning.[72]

15.4.1.2 Wil Waluchow

Wil Waluchow offers a number of defenses of inclusive legal positivism against Raz's arguments. In particular, he asserts that inclusive legal positivism would be able to support the distinctions Raz relies on to argue for exclusive legal positivism: between settled and unsettled law, and between the legal and moral evaluation of judicial outcomes.[73] Waluchow offers an example to show how (legal) validity and authority are consistent with the need to have recourse to moral analysis; the example involves legislation requiring that employers give employees fair severance pay.[74] For Raz, this is a grant of discretionary power to

[68] See Marmor 2001: 63–4.

[69] Coleman (1998a: 383) summarises the 'Practical Difference Thesis' as follows: '[I]n order to be law, authoritative pronouncements must in principle be capable of making a practical difference'; see also Shapiro 1998.

[70] Coleman 1998a: 424. [71] See Coleman 1998a: 424–5.

[72] See Marmor 2001: 49–70; Sevel 2014. According to Raz (1990: 149), '[l]egal philosophy is nothing but practical philosophy applied to one social institution'.

[73] Waluchow 1994: 113–17. [74] See Waluchow 1994: 138.

judges, to set what counts as 'fair severance pay', using moral (or other) considerations. Whether one accepts that characterisation or not,[75] it still remains the case, even under Raz's characterisation, that the statute (the law) 'is authoritative, ... even though it fails to pre-empt and replace all dependent reasons'.[76]

Waluchow also challenges Raz's analytical approach at a basic level, questioning whether we must see law's function as being, by nature, the settlement of disputes. Waluchow states: 'Why should we believe that the authoritative settling of disputes about dependent reasons by way of exclusionary directives is law's only defining function, or a function of essential importance?'[77] Here, as elsewhere in the debates between Raz and his critics, there are questions about how to progress – beyond 'yes, it is' / 'no, it isn't' – in evaluating disagreements about law's essential nature. Some critics have argued that we simply have different intuitions on this question and (a) choices among those different intuitions should or must be made on moral grounds;[78] or (b) the idea that there is only one right answer, and what that answer is held to be simply reflects the dominance of a particular group within the sub-discipline.[79]

15.4.1.3 Matthew Kramer

Matthew Kramer argues at length against Raz's view that 'judges' statements of legal obligations ... are perforce statements of moral obligations as well'.[80] Kramer does not think that law by its nature claims to be a practical (moral) authority and make moral claims. He offers as a counter-example a mafia-like entity in control over a country: issuing 'stark imperatives'[81] but never purporting to be making claims of or about morality.[82] Here would be law, Kramer argued, with no claims to moral authority.

Leslie Green responded that such a system would not be a legal system, since it is in the nature of law to tell us 'what we must do, not merely what it would be virtuous or advantageous to do, and it requires us to act without regard to our individual self-interest but in the interests of other individuals, or in the public interest more generally ... That is to say, law

[75] Raz would not, as discussed in Section 15.3.3. [76] Waluchow 1994: 138.
[77] Waluchow 1994: 134. [78] See, e.g., Perry 1995. [79] Leiter 2007: 178–9.
[80] Kramer 1999: 78. In ibid., 78 n. 1, Kramer lists locations in Raz's work where this claim is made.
[81] Kramer 1999: 95. [82] See Kramer 1999: 89–101.

purports to obligate us.'[83] Because of the sort of thing law asks of us – demands of us – law must be understood as making a *moral* claim.

The debate between Kramer and Green touches on a general concern regarding Raz's authority argument. The first step in Raz's analysis was that law, by its nature, necessarily claims to be a practical authority. Kramer's response modifies the assertion about law's nature, about law's claim, arguing that even if that characteristic were absent (a governing system clearly did *not* claim to be a practical authority), one would still have law. This returns us once again to a basic question for jurisprudence: How, if at all, can one ground either claim – indeed, any claim – about law's nature?[84]

15.4.2 Critics of Legal Positivism

15.4.2.1 Ronald Dworkin

Ronald Dworkin and Joseph Raz had a long-running disagreement about the connection between judicial duty, on one hand, and the line between 'law' and 'not law', on the other. In an early exchange, the question was characterised on whether all the standards a court had a (legal) duty to apply were, for that reason, '*legal* standards' (Dworkin said 'yes', Raz 'no').[85] The theme was taken up twenty years later, with Dworkin arguing that it would be 'bizarre' for the distinction between judicial enforcement of the law and 'other judicial acts and decisions that must rely on a different and more controversial kind of justification' to 'turn on an abstract analysis of the concept of authority'.[86] One can understand having concerns about so much of Raz's theory appearing to be grounded on a theory of authority that remains controversial. By contrast, Dworkin's own theory of law purports to be an interpretation of our current practices, and thus, in principle, responsive to common understandings. One reply might be that Raz's argument based on authority[87] need not be seen as dependent on a particular view of authority. It could, instead, be seen as ultimately little more than a more sophisticated restatement of the

[83] Green 2003: s. 4.2. Raz (2009b: 188) makes a similar argument.

[84] A sample of explanatory and critical views regarding references to law's essence or nature can be found in Dickson 2001; Bix 2003; Leiter 2007.

[85] See Raz 1983: 83–6; Dworkin 1983: 260–3.

[86] Dworkin 2006: 199 (a reprint of a review that was originally published in 2002).

[87] See Section 15.3.1.

argument in terms of function:[88] the difference between stating what the existing law is, versus making new law.

Dworkin also raised questions about Raz's idea that the law claims authority. In particular, he thought that this was at best a metaphorical assertion, and the likely ways to unpack the metaphor would lead to positions that were unjustified.[89] The objection based on personification also arose regarding the idea that citizens must be able to determine what guidance the lawmaker(s) intended. With legislation a collective enterprise, often involving compromise and drafting done by others, there was, Dworkin argued, no simple intention to discern. And with the common law, with the law being built up by accretion from judicial decisions over the centuries, the problems were even more severe.[90] Additionally, Dworkin wondered why, under Raz's analysis, being 'capable of being an authority' means meeting all the *non-moral* prerequisites of authority but not the *moral* prerequisites.[91] One could just as easily argue, Dworkin writes, that law must meet the moral prerequisites of authority, such that wicked legal systems would not count as law (and legal positivism would be refuted).[92]

The differences between Dworkin and Raz can seem monumental, not least in the way that Dworkin's theory makes us act as though we are participants in the practice, while Raz leaves us as detached and analytical observers.[93] However, in some ways their projects converge: while Dworkin accuses Raz of personifying law, through speaking of its claim to authority, something quite similar goes on with Dworkin's concept of 'integrity' – that is, legal officials and legal commentators are to interpret

88 See Section 15.3.2.

89 Dworkin 2006: 199–200. On the topic of law's claiming, see, e.g., MacCormick 2007; Gardner 2012: 125–48; Duarte d'Almeida and Edwards 2014.

90 See Dworkin 2006: 203–4.

91 A similar doubt is raised in Postema 2011: 359. Dworkin (2006: 201) additionally argued that if law's claiming to be an authority meant that lawmakers thought that law by its nature is capable of being a legitimate authority, it would be sufficient, by way of response, to note that people can be mistaken in beliefs of this sort.

92 See Dworkin 2006: 200–1. The natural law theorist Mark Murphy in fact makes an argument along these lines: that 'being constitutionally capable of being a rational standard' is an 'essential feature of law', and that merit- or moral-based standards must thus be met for something to be 'law' (Murphy 2013: 19–20).

93 Raz (1994: 186–7) famously said that Dworkin 'developed a theory of adjudication and regards it willy-nilly and without further argument as a theory of law'.

the actions of legal officials to make law speak with a coherent and principled voice.[94]

15.4.2.2 John Finnis

John Finnis suggests that exclusive legal positivists might be the unknowing theoretical descendants of Friedrich Nietzsche and others, in equating moral standards exclusively with the standards posited by human beings.[95] When considering exclusive legal positivism in detail, Finnis's view is that classical natural law theory would accept much of it, but that disagreement would likely come in the details. He asks: 'What does it mean to say that a rule, principle, or other standard "has been posited by a social-fact source"?'[96] Inevitably, courts must use reasoning (analogical reasoning, reasoning based on coherence, and so forth) that goes beyond the mere fact of particular norms having been posited, and Finnis wonders how an exclusive legal positivist like Raz can justify that.[97] Finnis notes that Raz admits that judges can and should use moral standards in resolving disputes; Finnis adds that courts use legal reasoning[98] in ways that use moral standards to develop the law. The new law, so developed, 'was in an important sense already part of the law'; Finnis adds: '[e]xclusive legal positivism's refusal to countenance such a way of speaking is unwarranted and inadequately motivated'.[99]

One response would be that the exclusive legal positivism's refusal *is* sufficiently warranted and explained by the considerations discussed in Section 15.3. Raz's argument would be that there are reasons of analytical clarity for insisting on the distinction between determining the law as it currently is and a judicial decision to add to or alter existing law, however much the line might be difficult to discern or however much the decision to change the law might be predictable or grounded in broadly accepted reasons.[100]

[94] See, e.g., Dworkin 1986: 164–8. [95] See Finnis 2002: 8. [96] Finnis 2002: 10.

[97] See Finnis 2000: 1601.

[98] Finnis (2000: 1601–2) reminds us that this is a distinctive form of reasoning, narrower than the form of reasoning used by legislators.

[99] Finnis 2000: 1602 (footnote omitted).

[100] H. L. A. Hart made a similar point in his famous debate with Lon Fuller; Hart 1958: 612–15; see Raz 1994: 214 ('Authorities can and do direct and guide by implication. It does not follow, however, that they imply all that is entailed by what they say, let alone all that is entailed by it with the addition of true premisses. The limits of the justifiable imputation of directives are no wider . . . than the limits of the imputation of belief').

15.4.2.3 Robert Alexy

In a debate with Joseph Raz,[101] Alexy criticised Raz (and other legal positivists) for not recognising sufficiently the internal connection between law as fact and law as ideal.[102] In particular, Alexy focused on the 'Radbruch Formula', which holds that extremely unjust rules lose their status as valid legal norms.[103] Regarding the Radbruch Formula, Raz's response was that it was entirely consistent with legal positivism: for judges can have *moral* duties not to apply very unjust laws, and this does not go to the intra-systemic validity of the enactments in question.[104]

Alexy also noted how his own 'correctness thesis' – 'that individual legal norms and individual legal decisions as well as legal systems as a whole necessarily lay claim to correctness'[105] – is similar to Raz's assertion that law necessarily claims to be a legitimate authority. Alexy asserted that both the correctness thesis and Raz's legitimate authority claim show a necessary connection between law and morality, and thus disprove legal positivism.[106] However, in a different work, Alexy conceded that a legal positivist 'could endorse the argument from correctness and nevertheless insist on the separation thesis'.[107] A *claim* to correctness, or to legitimate authority, though a connection of sorts between law and morality (and, as earlier discussed, Raz has consistently asserted that there *are* some necessary connections),[108] is not the sort of connection that undermines or is contrary to the sources thesis.

15.5 Conclusion

Raz's approach is associated with a particular variation of legal positivism: exclusive legal positivism. His analysis is constructed around particular views about reasons for action and authority, and the connection between the two. It is central to the view that the law claims to be a practical authority, telling citizens what to do via legal rules. Therefore, citizens must be able to determine what the law is without the application of underlying (moral) reasons, and must be able to see the law as the choice

[101] See Alexy 2007; Raz 2009a: 313–35. [102] See Alexy 2007: 37; see also Alexy 2002.
[103] See Alexy 2007: 39. For the origins of the Radbruch Formula, see Radbruch 2006.
[104] See Raz 2009a: 327. [105] Alexy 2002: 25–6. [106] See Alexy 2007: 44–5.
[107] Alexy 2002: 39; see also Raz 2009a: 327–33.
[108] See Section 15.2.2; see also Raz 2009a: 314–19; Raz 2009b: 166–9.

of those with the power to decide for the community. The approach does not assume or assert any view about whether judges do or should use moral reasons in making their decisions. It entails only that when judges *do* use moral reasoning to resolve cases, they are making new law, not declaring existing law.

References

Alexy, R. 2002. *The Argument from Injustice: A Reply to Legal Positivism*. Trans. S. L. Paulson and B. L. Paulson. Oxford University Press.

Alexy, R. 2007. 'An Answer to Joseph Raz'. In G. Pavlakos (ed.). *Law, Rights, and Discourse*. Hart: 37–55.

Austin, J. [1832]1995. *The Province of Jurisprudence Determined*. Ed. W. E. Rumble. Cambridge University Press.

Bix, B. 2003. 'Raz on Necessity'. *Law and Philosophy* 22: 537–59.

Celano, B. 2013. 'Normative Legal Positivism, Neutrality, and the Rule of Law'. In J. F. Beltrán, J. J. Moreso and D. M. Papayannis (eds.). *Neutrality and Theory of Law*. Springer: 175–202.

Coleman, J. L. 1998a. 'Incorporationism, Conventionality, and the Practical Difference Thesis'. *Legal Theory* 4: 381–425.

Coleman, J. L. 1998b. 'Second Thoughts and Other First Impressions'. In B. Bix (ed.). *Analyzing Law*. Oxford University Press: 257–322.

Coleman, J. L. 2001. *The Practice of Principle*. Oxford University Press.

Duarte d'Almeida, L. 2011. 'Legal Statements and Normative Language'. *Law and Philosophy* 30: 167–99.

Duarte d'Almeida, L. and Edwards, J. 2014. 'Some Claims about Law's Claims'. *Law and Philosophy* 33: 725–46.

Dickson, J. 2001. *Evaluation and Legal Theory*. Hart.

Dworkin, R. 1983. 'A Reply by Ronald Dworkin'. In M. Cohen (ed.). *Ronald Dworkin and Contemporary Jurisprudence*. Rowman & Allanheld: 247–300.

Dworkin, R. 1986. *Law's Empire*. Harvard University Press.

Dworkin, R. 2006. *Justice in Robes*. Harvard University Press.

Endicott, T. 2003. 'Raz on Gaps: The Surprising Part'. In L. H. Meyer, S. L. Paulson and T. W. Pogge (eds.). *Rights, Culture, and the Law*. Oxford University Press: 99–115.

Finnis, J. 2000. 'On the Incoherence of Legal Positivism'. *Notre Dame Law Review* 75: 1597–1611.

Finnis, J. 2002. 'Natural Law: The Classical Tradition'. In J. Coleman and S. Shapiro (eds.). *The Oxford Handbook of Jurisprudence and Philosophy of Law*. Oxford University Press: 1–60.

Finnis, J. 2011. *Philosophy of Law: Collected Essays* vol. IV. Oxford University Press.

Finnis, J. 2020. 'Natural Law Theories'. In E. N. Zalta (ed.). *Stanford Encyclopedia of Philosophy*. https://plato.stanford.edu/entries/natural-law-theories/.

Fuller, L. L. 1969. *The Morality of Law*, rev. ed. Yale University Press.

Gardner, J. 2012. *Law as a Leap of Faith*. Oxford University Press.

Green, L. 2003. 'Legal Positivism'. In E. N. Zalta (ed.). *Stanford Encyclopedia of Philosophy*. https://plato.stanford.edu/entries/legal-positivism/.

Green, L. 2005. 'Three Themes from Raz'. *Oxford Journal of Legal Studies* 25: 503–23.

Green, L. 2008. 'Positivism and the Inseparability of Law and Morals'. *New York University Law Review* 83: 1035–58.

Greenberg, M. 2011. 'The Standard Picture and Its Discontents'. In L. Green and B. Leiter (eds.). *Oxford Studies in Philosophy of Law* vol. I. Oxford University Press: 39–106.

Greenberg, M. 2014. 'The Moral Impact Theory of Law'. *Yale Law Journal* 123: 1288–1342.

Greenberg, M. 2017. 'The Moral Impact Theory, the Dependence View and Natural Law. In G. Duke and R. P. George (eds.). *The Cambridge Companion to Natural Law Jurisprudence*. Cambridge University Press: 275–313.

Hart, H. L. A. 1958. 'Positivism and the Separation of Law and Morals'. *Harvard Law Review* 71: 593–629.

Himma, K. E. 2002. 'Inclusive Legal Positivism'. In J. Coleman and S. Shapiro (eds.) *The Oxford Handbook of Jurisprudence and Philosophy of Law*. Oxford University Press: 125–65.

Hurd, H. 1990. 'Sovereignty in Silence'. *Yale Law Journal* 99: 945–1028.

Kramer, M.H. 1999. *In Defense of Legal Positivism: Law Without Trimmings*. Oxford University Press.

Kramer, M. H. 2004. 'On the Separability of Law and Morality'. *Canadian Journal of Law and Jurisprudence* 17: 315–35.

Leiter, B. 1998. 'Realism, Hard Positivism, and Conceptual Analysis'. *Legal Theory* 4: 533–47.

Leiter, B. 2007. *Naturalizing Jurisprudence*. Oxford University Press.

Lyons, D. 2003. *Moral Aspects of Legal Theory*. Cambridge University Press.

MacCormick, N. 2007. 'Why Law Makes No Claims'. In G. Pavlakos (ed.). *Laws, Rights, and Discourse*. Hart: 59–67.

Marmor, A. 2001. *Positive Law and Objective Values*. Oxford University Press.

Marmor, A. 2002. 'Exclusive Legal Positivism'. In J. Coleman and S. Shapiro (eds.). *The Oxford Handbook of Jurisprudence and Philosophy of Law*. Oxford University Press: 104–24.

Murphy, M. C. 2013. 'The Explanatory Role of the Weak Natural Law Thesis. In W. Waluchow and S. Sciaraffa (eds.) *Philosophical Foundations of the Nature of Law*. Oxford University Press: 3–21.

Murphy, M. C. 2015. 'Two Unhappy Dilemmas for Natural Law Jurisprudence'. *American Journal of Jurisprudence* 60: 121–41.

Perry, S. R. 1987. 'Judicial Obligation, Precedent, and the Common Law'. *Oxford Journal of Legal Studies* 7: 215–57.

Perry, S. R. 1995. 'Interpretation and Methodology in Legal Theory'. In A. Marmor (ed.). *Law and Interpretation.* Oxford University Press: 97–135.

Postema, G. J. 2011. *Legal Philosophy in the Twentieth Century: The Common Law World.* Springer.

Radbruch, G. 2006. 'Statutory Lawlessness and Supra-Statutory Law'. Trans. B. L. Paulson and S. L. Paulson. *Oxford Journal of Legal Studies* 26: 1–11.

Raz, J. 1983. 'Legal Principles and the Limits of Law'. In M. Cohen (ed.). *Ronald Dworkin and Contemporary Jurisprudence.* Rowman & Allanheld: 73–87.

Raz, J. 1986. *The Morality of Freedom.* Clarendon Press.

Raz, J. 1990. *Practical Reason and Norms.* Princeton University Press.

Raz, J. 1994. *Ethics in the Public Domain.* Clarendon Press.

Raz, J. 2003. 'Comments and Responses'. In L. H. Meyer, S. L. Paulson and T. W. Pogge (eds.). *Rights, Culture, and the Law.* Oxford University Press: 253–73.

Raz, J. 2006. 'The Problem of Authority: Revisiting the Service Conception'. *Minnesota Law Review* 90: 1003–44.

Raz, J. 2007. 'The Argument from Justice, or How Not to Reply to Legal Positivism'. In G. Pavlakos (ed.). *Law, Rights and Discourse.* Hart: 17–35.

Raz, J. 2009a. *The Authority of Law.* 2nd ed. Oxford University Press.

Raz, J. 2009b. *Between Authority and Interpretation.* Oxford University Press.

Sevel, M. 2014. 'The Constitution of Authority'. *Jurisprudence* 5: 430–41.

Shapiro, S. J. 1998. 'On Hart's Way Out'. *Legal Theory* 4: 469–507.

Shapiro, S. J. 2011. *Legality.* Harvard University Press.

Toh, K. 2007. 'Raz on Detachment, Acceptance and Describability'. *Oxford Journal of Legal Studies* 27: 403–27.

Waluchow, W. J. 1994. *Inclusive Legal Positivism.* Clarendon Press.

16 Bulygin's Analytical Legal Positivism

María Cristina Redondo *

16.1 Introduction

Eugenio Bulygin is a prominent example of a positivist legal theorist. His intellectual contribution to this field is a rich and sophisticated corpus of ideas that shows the strength of the positivist methodology among legal scholars in the Latin world. The specific way Bulygin understands legal positivism has been highly influential among Spanish, Italian and Latin American researchers and gave rise to a research programme that still has a strong vitality. In many aspects, his approach is at odds with the current dominant tendency within legal positivism. Part of the objective of this chapter is to show some of these differences.

In this chapter, I shall limit myself to presenting a restricted set of theses that, in my view, outline the main traits of Bulygin's conception of legal positivism. Before doing so, it must be stressed that a relevant part of Bulygin's ideas was conceived of along with Carlos Alchourrón. As Bulygin has emphasised, in their joint works, their thoughts are so intertwined that it is difficult to distinguish the individual contribution of each one of them.[1] For this reason, it should not be surprising that quite often the quotations or the references taken into account are books or articles signed by both authors.

16.2 Bulygin's Position in the Context of Contemporary Philosophy

There is no doubt that Bulygin's work must be read within the frame of analytical philosophy. According to Bulygin, the analytical conception of

* The discussion held at the conference on legal positivism in April 2019 at the University of Stockholm has been of great benefit for the final version of this chapter. I would especially like to thank Patricia Mindus and Torben Spaak for their fine comments.

[1] See Alchourrón and Bulygin 1991: XVII. Also, Bulygin 2015: 355–6.

philosophy does not imply adherence either to a corpus of substantive ideas or to a specific philosophical method.[2] It is a style of philosophical thought, a way of understanding philosophy compatible with different and even contradictory substantive theories regarding specific subjects. Without the intention of offering an exhaustive explanation, Bulygin mentions what he considers to be the most typical features of this philosophical conception. First, and most importantly, philosophy is conceptual analysis. This implies the acknowledgement of a qualitative difference, on the one hand, between philosophy and science and, on the other hand, between philosophy and classical metaphysical speculations. Therefore, philosophy is not a kind of scientific research; it does not refer directly to the world; it is instead focused on the conceptual components of experience, that is, on the conceptual apparatus that enables human beings to have scientific knowledge as well as to cope with reality. Such conceptual components are displayed in the logical structure of language, and this explains why analytical philosophers are highly interested in studying language and logic. According to Bulygin, even though not all analytical philosophers devote themselves to the study of logic, there is a clear tendency among them to take advantage of logical techniques in conceptual analysis. This also explains the characteristic conceptual and expository accuracy that is displayed by analytical philosophers, both in the justification of their assertions and in the clarification of the assumptions on which they rely.[3]

The role of logic and formalisation is indeed essential in Bulygin's legal philosophy. His main theoretical contribution, *Normative Systems*, co-authored with Alchourrón, is a paradigmatic example in which logic is used as a powerful instrument for legal analysis. In this book, taking advantage of some ideas proposed by Tarski, logic is used to reconstruct the central concept of normative system.[4] At the same time, logic is taken to be crucial for clarifying several problems usually put forward by legal practitioners, like normative conflicts, normative redundancy, different kinds of legal gaps and so forth. On this basis, one can be led to think that formal or logical analysis is the hallmark of Bulygin's legal positivism. In one sense, this view can be accepted because Bulygin explicitly supports the idea that the conceptual analysis that legal theorists should engage in

[2] See Bulygin 1980: 379–80; Bulygin 2009: 356. [3] See Bulygin 1980: 378–80.
[4] See Alchourrón and Bulygin 1971: 4.

implies an inquiry into the logical structure of our language. However, this view may also be misleading if we do not stress at least two aspects. Within Bulygin's theory, formal or logical analysis is always just an instrument to produce an accurate and fruitful reconstruction of the legal concepts we are interested in. Nevertheless, it can, and many times it should, remain implicit in the background of the analysis. Therefore, it would be incorrect to think that the objective of Bulygin's legal positivism is to offer a logical or formal understanding of the concept of law, or any other legal notion. Logic just gives support to any successful analysis of such concepts. As we shall see from some examples I will put forward, Bulygin's analysis of legal norms and interpretation is far from encouraging a formalist approach. In this regard, it should be noticed that Bulygin's conviction about the power of logic and formalisation is as explicit as his rejection of logical positivism.[5] This means that he is not committed to, and nothing in his legal theory requires, the acceptance of the strong theses proposed by this philosophical conception. To be precise, I am referring to the verificationist theory of truth and the idea that statements lacking truth value are meaningless. For instance, in Bulygin's view, normative contents are meaningful contents even if they have no truth value.

In order to depict Bulygin's position within the framework of contemporary philosophy, another important aspect deserves to be highlighted. Bulygin endorses an anti-realist and non-objectivist standpoint in meta-ethics.[6] His meta-ethical scepticism regarding the existence of objective moral facts and the possibility of objective moral justification is a concrete instance of his wide-ranging scepticism in the practical domain. In fact, according to Bulygin, there are no objective norms in general, be they moral, legal, religious and so forth. This conviction leads him to establish a clear distinction between any kind of practical enterprise, which could only be justified in terms of some subjective or intersubjective goal, and a theoretical enterprise, which instead can be objectively justified in terms of truth and falsity. This meta-ethical commitment is relevant to understanding several of his specific substantive theses, such as those regarding legal duties, internal legal statements, the concepts of legal validity and so forth.[7] And, in general, it explains why, contrary to a strong stream in

[5] See Bulygin 1980: 379. [6] See Caracciolo 1993: 509–511.

[7] In this regard, Bulygin follows John Mackie and Georg Henrik von Wright. See Bulygin 2006: 117.

current legal positivism, he does not think that legal philosophy should be developed assuming the perspective of practical philosophy.

According to Bulygin, a general theory of law must work by taking into account the lessons and using the instruments offered by philosophies of language and science. For instance, the developments in philosophy of language offer powerful arguments for rejecting certain wrong ideas about legal norms.[8] In this regard, independently of the debate on their ontological status, Bulygin thinks that treating them at a purely syntactical level (like sentences that correlate cases with solutions) 'has considerable advantages from a methodological point of view'.[9] Furthermore, the contribution of philosophy of language may be crucial to understanding the problems related to the semantic indeterminacy of legal norms, which is a problem that can be decisive for law enforcement.[10]

Similarly, legal theory has much more to learn from the debate about explanation and justification developed in philosophy of science than from the debate regarding explanation and justification developed in practical philosophy. Like the philosophy of science, legal philosophy is mainly focused on offering explicative models that are expected to be useful for specific goals. As we shall see, insofar as the goal of legal philosophy is the reconstruction of concepts, this enterprise is in a way – which I will explain later – also normative. Nevertheless, the (semantic) normativity of a conceptual analysis should not be confused with moral, political or legal normativity.

Summing up, Bulygin subscribes to an analytical conception of philosophy, and legal philosophy – or the general theory of law – is an example of analytical philosophy applied to the legal domain. Notwithstanding the similarity of labels, we should be particularly careful not to confuse this analytical conception of legal theory with Bentham's and Austin's 'analytical jurisprudence'.[11] Bulygin's legal theory is not an answer to

[8] Bulygin mentions, as an example, Kelsen's idea – based on Kantian philosophy – that norms are in a sense 'created' by legal science. In fact, once we take into account the philosophical contributions about the different functions of language, it is easy to admit that legal authorities can directly create legal norms by using prescriptive language without appealing either to transcendental categories or to any other kind of complex explanation. See Bulygin 1980: 376.

[9] See Alchourrón and Bulygin 1971: 5.

[10] Bulygin calls this problem 'gap of recognition'. See Alchourrón and Bulygin 1971: 33, 115, 146, 153.

[11] Bulygin 1980: 378.

a metaphysical question about what the law really is. But neither is it an attempt to describe the existing legal systems. In other words, his legal theory must be distinguished from legal science or legal dogmatics since it consists of conceptual analysis applied to the specific realm of law.

16.3 Bulygin's Position in the Context of the General Theory of Law

In order to have a full grasp of Bulygin's position within the general legal theory, it would be necessary to do something that is not possible to do here: to present the intense dialogue he has maintained with a great number of twentieth-century and contemporary legal theorists. To begin with, Bulygin analysed the ideas of legal philosophers who were considered authors of reference within both the European and the North-American contexts, mostly publishing in English (Kelsen, Ross, Hart, von Wright, Raz, Alexy, Paulson and so forth), and within the Latin context, mostly publishing in Romance languages (Guastini, Atienza, Ruiz Manero, Nino, Carrió, Garzón Valdés, Caracciolo and so forth). At the same time, he also discussed with, and has dedicated detailed contributions to, younger legal theorists, such as Juan Carlos Bayón, Fernando Atria and Jorge Rodríguez, whose work he found deeply impressive. Sometimes Bulygin picked up some specific ideas of these authors but, in general, he evaluated their theses and developed articulated criticisms.

There is no doubt that Bulygin puts forward a positivist legal theory. However, there are several ways of understanding this approach. When Bulygin analyses legal positivism in his essay 'El positivismo jurídico', he explicitly relies on a distinction proposed by Norberto Bobbio, which has been highly influential among legal philosophers within the Latin world.[12] According to Bobbio, there are three different ways in which legal positivism can be understood: as a theoretical, an ideological, or a methodological standpoint.[13] It is clear that, within this classification, Bulygin sees his own legal position as an example of methodological legal positivism. Nevertheless, as is the case with legal positivism in general, there are also different ways to understand this methodological approach. On this point,

[12] See Bulygin 2006: 69–73; also see Bobbio [1961]1996.
[13] See Bobbio [1961]1996: 246–50.

Bulygin moves away from Bobbio's exposition. In his view, methodological legal positivism is committed to the acceptance of three theses.[14] First, the separability thesis: the idea that legal validity does not imply moral validity and vice versa. Second, the social sources thesis: the idea according to which both the existence and the content of law depend on social facts. Third, the indeterminacy thesis: namely, that the law can be indeterminate and, when that is the case, judges have discretional power to create new law.[15] From this point of view, Bulygin's characterisation of legal positivism does not differ from the standard presentation that current legal philosophy offers.[16] In point of fact, the distinguishing trait of Bulygin's thought on this subject is related not to the theses that in his opinion legal positivism accepts but to the specific analytical method with which legal positivism contributes to legal science and legal practice.

Before presenting the central features of Bulygin's analytical legal positivism, a further ambiguity deserves to be pointed out. Unfortunately, the aforementioned three theses are controversial even among positivist authors. An important disagreement related to the social sources thesis is worth mentioning here.[17] According to what can be considered as a strong interpretation, whoever assumes the sources thesis has to define the law in empirical terms.[18] As a consequence, the law is not by itself normative, even though it aims or is believed to be such. A central reasoning that supports this position is roughly the following: (i) in virtue of the social sources thesis, the law is grounded in empirical facts (to be precise, on social practices, attitudes and beliefs); (ii) it is not possible to derive norms from empirical facts; (iii) ergo, in virtue of the social sources thesis, the law cannot consist of norms. It should be stressed that this reasoning can be misleading for different reasons, such as the ambiguity of the term 'norm'. The inference

[14] See Bulygin 2006: 73–4.

[15] In a different work, Bulygin asserts that legal positivism can be characterised by means of the two first theses: the sources thesis and the separability thesis; see Bulygin 2004: 302.

[16] See, e.g., Coleman and Leiter 1996: 241–60.

[17] Regarding the sources thesis, Bulygin also referred to the well-known disagreement between inclusive and exclusive legal positivism. Although Bulygin expressed his sympathy for exclusive legal positivism, he also admitted that this position is closely related to the Razian conception of authority, which he would not be willing to accept; see Bulygin 2007b: 203. Put briefly, Bulygin's theory is committed neither to inclusive nor to exclusive legal positivism. The methodological instruments of rational reconstruction that his theory purports to provide work in exactly the same way whichever of these two substantive theories is considered the best.

[18] See Nino 1984: 43–6. See also Schauer 1998: 65–78.

is obviously correct if norms are understood (as the norms of critical morality are usually understood) as standards the existence (or validity) of which is not derived from any social practice, attitude or belief. Instead, the same reasoning sounds absurd if the existence (or validity) of norms is conceived of as the result of a certain kind of human acts and beliefs.[19] To be sure, according to the supporters of the strong reading of the social sources thesis, our concept of norm is the first one.[20] Something would be a norm with justificatory power only if it were objectively binding. The so-called 'social norms' are not genuine norms. Actually, they are not able to justify behaviour.[21] In short, this view presupposes that normativity is a defining property of moral norms and once this is assumed, it would indeed be impossible for legal positivism to explain the normativity of law within its own framework, and coherently with the separability thesis.

By contrast, according to a weak interpretation of the social sources thesis, the law is surely based on social facts, but it cannot be defined in empirical terms because it is a set of norms. Bulygin is certainly committed to this weaker position.[22] In this respect, he is a strong supporter of the Kelsenian and the Hartian conceptions of law. These authors stress, with different strategies, the fact that law is normative and that in order to grasp legal normativity correctly, we should admit two things: first, that law cannot be defined in terms of sheer natural events; and second, that it depends entirely on social behaviour and attitudes. Therefore, legal norms cannot be confused with objective moral norms. From this point of view, it is not true that we have only one concept of normativity. We must distinguish legal from moral normativity. In sum, according to Bulygin, law is defined as a set of normative contents. However, he stresses that

[19] Bulygin stresses these two senses of the term normativity in Bulygin 2006: 98.

[20] These authors do not deny that the term 'norm' can also have other meanings. However, this is only a piece of not very interesting information about the fact that the word can be used in different ways. From this point of view, we should not confuse the concept of norm with the way in which the word 'norm' is generally used. See Raz 2004: 18–21.

[21] For instance, Dworkin (1977: 50–2) states a contrast between social rules and normative rules, implying that social rules are not normative. Joseph Raz also explicitly distinguishes between social and justified normativity. In this latter sense, 'to judge the law as normative is to judge it to be just and to admit that it ought to be obeyed' (Raz 1979: 137). According to C. S. Nino (1978: 373): 'As Raz says now, for Kelsen, as for natural law theorists, the only conceivable type of normativity is justified normativity.' See also Nino 1989: 30 and 115.

[22] According to this position, the statements about the law describe or inform us about the existence of a norm. In turn, the existence of a norm must be understood in empirical terms. See Bulygin 1981: 138–41.

these normative contents are not objectively binding standards.[23] Legal normativity should be analysed in terms of individual or social actions and beliefs. In Bulygin's words, the facts that make statements about the law true 'are complex institutional facts, such as the practices (customs) or actions of certain persons'.[24] At any rate, it is one thing to explain legal normativity and quite another thing to explain moral normativity. Once one has assumed this view, it is clear that legal positivism has no problem to explain the normativity of law within its own framework.

16.4 Bulygin's Analytical Legal Positivism: The Central Methodological Theses

16.4.1 An Analytical Approach

The identity mark of Bulygin's methodological legal positivism is given by the fact that it is conceived of as an analytical approach. This conception presupposes a clear distinction among three different enterprises and levels of discourses: first, the object-language of the law's practice, which is normally normative; second, the metalanguage of legal science and legal dogmatics that directly refers to the law or legal reality; and third, the analytical meta-discourse of legal philosophy or general legal theory, which, as mentioned already, refers directly not to legal reality but to legal concepts.

In Bulygin's view, conceptual analysis is the way in which legal philosophy contributes to legal science and legal practice. Actually, it is possible to read all of Bulygin's contributions as conceptual analysis of different concepts that he considers central to legal science and practice. In *Normative Systems*, which is one of his finest contributions to legal theory, we can find the analysis of the concepts of normative system, completeness, normative gaps, consistency, contradictory norms, redundancy, derogation, axiological gaps and so forth.[25] The same method is applied

[23] According to Bulygin (2006: 119): 'For a coherent form of positivism there are no objectively binding norms because the objective validity of a norm amounts to its truth, and there are no true norms' (my translation). See also Bulygin 2004: 302–10.

[24] Bulygin 2004: 304.

[25] Among these subjects, the specific conception of normative systems proposed by Alchourrón and Bulygin has been one of the most influential and deeply discussed by legal theorists. A very brief résumé of this conception can be found in Rodriguez 2007: 82. See also Navarro 2015: 6–7.

to many other concepts in Bulygin's single-authored works, such as legal validity, applicability, efficacy, legal order, judicial decision, power-conferring norms, human rights, legal statements and so on.

Bulygin has a very precise view about the kind of analytical contribution that legal positivism can make to legal science and legal practice. Together with Carlos Alchourrón, he proposed a well-defined model of conceptual analysis. According to this method, we explain a concept (the *explicandum*) through a rational reconstruction of it (the *explicatum*). The rational reconstruction of a concept is defined by two internal traits, which are (1) the clarification of the *explicandum* and (2) the construction of the *explicatum*.[26] In any case, the relevance of these two steps relies on the assumption that they are a rational way to make the concepts that legal science and practice are interested in more precise. It is worth noting that the two moments of the conceptual reconstruction are not conceived of as mutually independent. The first step (clarification of a concept) is necessary in order to accomplish the second step properly (the construction of a more precise and fruitful concept). In fact, the second step is subject to a set of adequacy criteria that aims to guarantee that the new concept is 'capable of performing with greater efficiency the function' of the one it should replace. For this to be possible, 'it is necessary, first, to clarify as far as possible the meaning of the *explicandum*; and this clarification may be achieved by different methods, such as providing examples and descriptions of the use of the concept in different contexts'.[27] Roughly, the requirements that the second reconstructive step must satisfy are the following four: (1) the *explicatum* must be as exact as possible; (2) it must be fruitful, in the sense that it must enable the formulation of as many universal statements as possible; (3) the extensions of the *explicatum* and the *explicandum* must be as much alike as possible; (4) simplicity. The first two requirements are the most important. The third is subordinate to the first two, whereas the fourth is less significant and not strictly necessary since a more complex *explicatum* is to be preferred to a simpler one if it is more exact or fruitful.

As we can see, the method just described constitutes a *model* of explanation. To the extent that it is a model, it does not explain anything. It sets a meta-meta-theoretical framework or scheme that any conceptual explanation – which is already an instance of meta-theoretical discourse – should satisfy.

[26] See Alchourrón and Bulygin 1971: 7–8. [27] See Alchourrón and Bulygin 1971: 8.

According to this model, explanation proceeds by abstraction and does not allow us to capture the *explicandum* in all its facets. Indeed, it grasps only some aspects of it. This limit is not a shortcoming of this method but a feature of any kind of explanation. As Bulygin highlights: 'No abstract model can depict the total reality, but there is no aspect of reality that could not be depicted in some model. Thus, for every concept we are interested in, an adequate *explicatum* can be constructed.'[28]

Regarding this methodological approach, one last point deserves to be highlighted. There are two senses in which a rational reconstruction can be said to be normative. On the one hand, it is clear that the second constructive step of conceptual analysis (the rational reconstruction) amounts to a normative proposal. Actually, it is a kind of stipulation subject to several adequacy criteria. In other words, even if the reconstruction yields a partially new concept, this normative move is not left to the unbound discretion of the theorist. The meta-meta-theoretical model imposes four specific requirements on it. On the other hand, a rational reconstruction can be said to be normative because its object is always a concept, and, according to Bulygin, concepts are nothing but the content of a specific kind of conventional constitutive rules: conceptual rules. Later on, I will return to Bulygin's analysis of this kind of norms.

16.4.2 Norms and Propositions

A presentation of the most prominent features of Bulygin's methodological view must mention his continuing insistence on the distinction between norms and propositions.[29] Bulygin argued about the relevance of this point by making explicit the many problems that arise when it is not taken into account. For instance, along with Carlos Alchourrón, Bulygin showed the importance of the distinction between a logic of norms and a logic of norm propositions.[30] In single-authored papers, Bulygin emphasised the difficulties that arise from some of Kelsen's

[28] See Alchourrón and Bulygin 1971: 9.

[29] Alchourrón and Bulygin (1992: 265) note that 'historically, the distinction between norms and normative propositions can be traced back to Bentham. It appears in different forms in such authors as Kelsen, Hedenius, and Alf Ross and has been clearly elaborated in von Wright.' See also Bulygin 1999a: 289–90.

[30] For instance, Alchourrón and Bulygin 1973/89: 103–15; Alchourrón and Bulygin 1988: 230–7.

theses as far as that Kelsen does not clearly see the difference between norms and normative propositions.[31] The same occurs with the Hartian distinction between external and internal statements to the extent that it is not clearly established whether they have to be understood as instances of descriptive or directive discourse.[32]

In other words, like every classical positivist legal theorist, Bulygin is a strong supporter of the logically unbridgeable gap between descriptive and normative discourses. What is especially interesting in his theory is that it puts forward that any normative discourse or utterance within the legal domain can be, in turn, subject to a descriptive or a prescriptive reading. For instance, a deontic sentence like (a) 'John has the obligation to pay his debt' has two possible meanings and ways of being analysed. On the one hand, it can be interpreted as a descriptive statement expressing a proposition, for instance, that a social group accepts that John must pay his debt, or that there is a norm in the legal system imposing on John the payment of his debt. On the other hand, the same sentence can be understood as a prescription or a norm. In this case, it can mean, for instance, that John is legally obliged to pay his debt or that it is morally binding for him to do so. It is worth noting that, according to Bulygin, the same descriptive/prescriptive ambiguity that affects deontic legal formulations can also affect isolated legal terms. In other words, some terms can express within a legal context both descriptive and normative concepts. In general, a descriptive concept includes among its defining features only empirical properties. A normative concept, instead, includes among its defining features some practical property or requirement. In section 16.5.1, I will take into account the descriptive and normative meanings of the terms 'existence' and 'validity' of legal norms.

It is important to emphasise that although the legal language is affected by this particular kind of descriptive/normative ambiguity, according to Bulygin, it has to be used in a descriptive sense within a positivist legal theory.[33] The justification of this thesis must be found in the fact that, otherwise, the theory would no longer be descriptive. It would be prescribing or justifying a certain kind of behaviour.[34] For this reason, the deontic sentence (a) must be analysed, in Bulygin's view, as the assertion that there

[31] See, e.g., Bulygin 1981: 136–45; Bulygin 1982: 188–206.
[32] See, e.g., Bulygin 1982: 200–6. [33] See Bulygin 1990: 246, 251; Bulygin 2009: 357.
[34] On this point, Bulygin is following A. Ross. See Ross 1961: 46–93.

is a norm imposing on John the obligation to pay his debt. In turn, that a norm exists must be understood in terms of empirical facts: it means, for instance, that such a norm has been enacted by a certain authority. In short, a proposition asserting that a certain act is legally obligatory or prohibited can be reduced, at the end of the day, to an empirical proposition.[35]

According to Bulygin, the claim that normative propositions (theoretical statements) are descriptive of certain empirical facts is implied by legal positivism. He calls this claim 'a weak reductive semantic thesis'.[36] In my view, it must be stressed that this semantic thesis, as Bulygin states, is weak and can be understood only with an important proviso: as we have seen, Bulygin claims that the law is a set of norms, and norms are not empirical entities. That is to say, Bulygin endorses a normativist stance regarding the law, and the empirical reduction enters the picture only in a second moment. It is true that Bulygin has offered two different analyses of the concept of norm. According to the hyletic conception, norms are semantic meanings. According to the expressivist conception, norms are understood as linguistic acts.[37] The interesting point is that, whatever ontology we prefer to ascribe to norms, legal systems are to be conceived of as sets of (at least some) normative contents. It is really important to see that Bulygin supports a normativist conception of law, otherwise we cannot grasp how he takes distance from those theories, such as certain forms of legal realism, that reject the existence of norms and define the law as an empirical practice or a set of judicial decisions. In a nutshell, according to Bulygin, only after having stressed that the law is a set of general normative contents, legal theory should show that these normative contents can be considered legally valid or existent only because some empirical facts took place.

16.4.3 On Internal and External Statements

Bulygin has applied the contrast between norms and normative propositions to analyse the Hartian distinction between internal and external statements. According to Bulygin, there is no doubt about the relevance of the Hartian distinction as long as the options are understood as mutually

[35] See Alchourrón and Bulygin 1973/89: 104. [36] Bulygin 1981: 139.

[37] See Alchourrón and Bulygin 1981: 147–51.

exclusive and jointly exhaustive.[38] In other words, a legal statement cannot be at the same time internal and external. It must be either internal or external, *tertium non datur.* Understood in this way, Hartian language can be used to express Bulygin's idea by saying that the one and the same deontic sentence can be interpreted as either an internal or an external statement.

The proposed reading of the Hartian distinction determines a well-defined disparity, on the one hand, between Bulygin and some authors – like Dworkin, for instance – who do not admit a clear-cut gap between descriptive and normative discourses and allow for a language that has both statuses simultaneously. On the other hand, it also determines a clear disparity between Bulygin and those authors – like Raz, for instance – who propose a third category of statements: the so-called 'detached statements', which would be necessary for legal scientists to be able to identify legal norms without accepting them. From Bulygin's point of view, both positions must be rejected. The Dworkinian position is a source of confusions and problems insofar as an appropriate methodology must maintain a sharp separation between description and prescription.[39] The Razian proposal of detached discourse is unnecessary insofar as the Hartian distinction between internal and external statements is sufficient to do all the work.[40] Hartian internal statements are normative and, as any normative statement, they are an expression of the subjective practical attitudes of the speaker. An internal statement cannot be evaluated as true or false: it is an example of directive discourse aiming at guiding or justifying, not at describing. By contrast, external statements are descriptive, they express true or false propositions and, as Hart has clearly stated and Bulygin recalls, this is so even when what is described is a normative object. For this reason, in order to identify or describe the content of a legal system or any other kind of legal object, legal science does not need any additional kind of statement other than the external ones. An external statement is always detached and this is so even when it refers to norms and expresses a normative proposition. As I have already said, the propositions referring to normative contents are true or false in virtue of complex institutional facts.[41]

[38] See Bulygin 1981: 139–40; Bulygin 1982: 196–206. [39] See Bulygin 1982: 203–6.
[40] See Bulygin 1981: 144. [41] See Bulygin 2004: 304.

Summing up, Bulygin accepts the opposition between external and internal statements as far as it is understood as a different presentation of the classical distinction between propositions and norms, or between cognitive and practical discourses. However, Bulygin emphatically rejects the contrast between external and internal statements when this is understood as two variants within the cognitive or assertive discourse. There is no such thing as internal knowledge. A cognitive discourse is necessarily external while internal statements do not admit a cognitive reading. As we can see, Bulygin does not follow the current interpretation of Hart's methodological proposal according to which, in order to grasp its normative object, a legal theory must adopt an internal point of view and use internal statements. Actually, Bulygin understands Hart's proposal as saying that legal theory must not adopt the internal point of view but rather take it into account from an external one.

16.5 Bulygin's Analytical Legal Positivism: Some Substantive Ideas

In this section, I will examine three specific issues analysed by Bulygin. Taking into account the general substantive theses he subscribes to each case, I will try to show, on the one hand, how they differ from some recurrent proposals in contemporary legal philosophy; and, on the other, how they are not only coherent but intimately related to the methodological theses that characterise his approach. First, I will refer to Bulygin's analysis of legal validity; second, to Bulygin's position regarding legal interpretation and meaning; last, to his thesis about the relation between regulative and constitutive norms.

16.5.1 The Analysis of Legal Validity

Regarding legal validity, Bulygin analysed theories of various authors.[42] On this basis, he stressed the ambiguity of the expression and concentrated his attention on three concepts of validity.[43] First, the concept of systemic validity or validity as membership. In this sense, a norm is legally valid if,

[42] See, e.g., Bulygin 1990: 243–6; Bulygin 1999a: 284–92; Bulygin 2005: 311–23.
[43] See Bulygin 1999a: 285–8.

and only if, it belongs to a legal system. Second, validity as binding force or obligatoriness. In this case, a norm is legally valid if, and only if, its addressees have an obligation to behave in the way prescribed by the norm. Third, what Wróblewski called factual validity and Bulygin prefers to call efficacy or law in force. In this sense, legal validity refers to a relation between a norm and the actual behaviour of its addressees or norm-subjects. What I find interesting to note regarding this subject is that Bulygin develops two classifications. On the one hand, he distinguishes between descriptive and normative concepts of legal validity. On the other hand, he highlights the distinction between relative and absolute concepts of legal validity.[44] For instance, according to the first criterion of classification, systemic and factual validity are clearly descriptive concepts. They do not include any normative property, but only empirical properties. By contrast, obligatoriness or binding force is a normative concept. If a norm has this property, it means that the addressees ought to act, or not to act, in a certain way.

In the first stage of his work, Bulygin agreed with Alf Ross on the thesis that a positivist legal theory can identify both descriptive and normative concepts of validity, although it should not itself make use of the normative concept of validity.[45] Bulygin accepted this conclusion on the basis that the theorist using a normative concept of validity would be stating that the addressees are morally obliged to do what the legal norms ask them to do. Certainly, by endorsing this idea, a positivist theorist – expected to offer a purely descriptive theory – could be justly accused – like Kelsen was – of falling into contradiction.

I find the fact that Bulygin later explicitly recanted this opinion quite remarkable.[46] According to his new standpoint, it is important to see that we have two normative concepts of validity (obligatoriness or bindingness): a relative and an absolute one. His reasoning is based on the assumption that there is a clear discontinuity between legal and moral obligation, and this difference is captured by his distinction between the relative and the absolute concepts of legal validity. The descriptive concepts of validity are certainly relative, but so is the normative concept of *legal* obligation. On the contrary, the normative concept of *moral* obligation is an absolute concept. That a norm is morally obligatory, binding or valid means that, by itself, it imposes a duty to act in accordance with it.

[44] See Bulygin 1990: 245. [45] See Bulygin 1990: 250–1. [46] See Bulygin 2005: 318.

This is an intrinsic, not a relative property of norms. Therefore, to the extent that validity is understood as based on, or imposed by, positive norms, it is a relative property. That a given norm is valid, binding or obligatory in this latter sense means that there is a positive meta-norm authorising or prescribing its application. Bulygin calls these meta-norms that confer power or prescribe the application of other norms 'application norms', and he uses the expression 'applicability' to refer to this normative sense of validity as obligatoriness. In any case, as Bulygin asserts: 'For reasons of logic, there must be ultimate application norms [in every legal system] that are neither applicable nor inapplicable. The question of their applicability is simply meaningless.'[47] If someone asserts that these ultimate rules are applicable or valid, they are using the expressions in a non-relative sense.

Certainly, validity understood as applicability is a normative concept. If norms are valid in this sense, they bind their addressees and succeed in imposing legal duties or granting legal permissions. However, such duties and permissions are relative to a given normative system and established by given, positive legal norms. What is worth stressing here is that, in this new perspective, a normative concept of validity is necessary to explain how legal norms create duties. If a legal theory could not use this normative concept of validity, it would not be able to explain the concept of legal obligation. Therefore, due to the modification of his position on the normative concept of legal validity, Bulygin is committed to introducing a slight change in his ideas regarding a positivist legal theory. In contrast with what he claimed earlier, he now must accept that a positivist legal theory not only *can* use a normative concept of validity but *has* to do so. What a positivist legal theory cannot use is an absolute normative concept, that is, a moral one. For reasons of logic, the theory has to employ a normative and relative concept of validity. Otherwise, it could not account for the difference between legal and moral obligation. We can see once again regarding this point that there is a sharp difference between Bulygin's position and the contemporary trend in the positivist legal theory where it is usually assumed, first, that we have only one concept of obligation and, second, that this single concept is a moral one. In Bulygin's view, a legal positivist must admit that there are at least two normative concepts of validity. In other words, there are two concepts of

[47] Bulygin 2005: 322.

bindingness or obligatoriness. The legal bindingness of a norm is based on a given set of ultimate application norms. Consequently, legal norms can be said to be binding, obligatory or valid in a normative, though not a moral, sense.

16.5.2 On Legal Interpretation

Regarding legal interpretation and meaning, on the one hand, Bulygin discussed and rejected scepticism or extreme subjectivism.[48] The meaning of legal texts does not depend – or, at least, does not always depend – on legal interpreters' choices or, to be more precise, on choices made by judges. Bulygin subscribes to a conventionalist theory of meaning. In his view, concepts are determined by the social use of language. To be sure, linguistic conventions are usually indeterminate in different ways. Regarding a given predicate, for instance, it is possible that (1) there is no established use at all, that is, there is no semantic rule, (2) there are different established uses, that is, there is more than one semantic rule, or (3) there are rules that leave the limits of the extension of the predicate undetermined (this gives us cases of vagueness and open texture).[49] Consequently, two kinds of cases should be distinguished: those in which there is an established linguistic usage, and those where the use is not determined. 'The crucial difference between the two cases is that in the one case the judge discovers an existent semantic rule and in the other, it is he who stipulates the rule.'[50] In any case, judges base their decisions on interpretive sentences. 'Interpretation may be viewed as the process of rendering the semantic rules of language explicit.'[51] Hence, interpretative sentences are analytic because their truth depends on the meaning of the relevant terms alone. In easy cases, interpretative statements refer to the already given rules. In hard cases, they refer to a stipulated rule made up by the interpreters themselves. In a few words, regarding legal interpretation,

[48] On this issue, Bulygin has specifically argued against the sceptical thesis according to which every linguistic expression is ambiguous so that the identification of its meaning always depends on the interpreter. In his view, the sceptical thesis leads to an infinite regress. On this basis, Bulygin (2004: 308–9) asserts: 'An essential feature of language is that at least some of its expressions must be univocal. A language that does not meet this condition is useless as a tool for communication . . . [I]n a given context there must be some univocal expressions.' See also Bulygin 1999b: 183–91.

[49] See Bulygin 1995: 35. [50] Bulygin 1995: 34. [51] Ibid.

Bulygin adopts a kind of Hartian, intermediate position that rejects both the formalist and the sceptical approaches.[52]

Coherently, on the other hand, Bulygin also rejected the thesis opposite to the sceptical position. Within a discussion regarding specifically the concept of law, he argued against the essentialist trend now fashionable in legal philosophy and mainly represented by Joseph Raz's ideas. The deep disagreement between Bulygin and Raz relies on the fact that, for this author, concepts are determined by the essential properties of those things they are the concepts of, and, in the case of cultural or social concepts, such essential properties only partially depend on how the concept is used. By contrast, from the conventionalist point of view assumed by Bulygin, concepts are determined only by how they are used. Something has essential properties only in relation to a concept.[53] In other words, it is the concept that determines its nature or its essential properties, not the other way around. In this sense, contrary to Raz's opinion, and in accordance with Hart, Bulygin contends that there is no difference between explaining the concept of something and explaining the nature of such a thing. On this basis, Bulygin stresses that the question 'what is the law?', for instance, amounts to asking for a definition of law, and asking for the essence or the nature of law is just an obscure variant of the same question.[54] The essential properties of the law are obviously not the same according to Aquinas, Austin, Holmes, Kelsen, Dworkin or Hart. These multiple concepts of law are, in a certain sense, products of the theory of law.[55] In any case, in order to clarify in which sense the concept of law may depend on legal theory, we must remember Bulygin's conception of conceptual analysis. In his view, legal theorists always reconstruct concepts – the concept of law among others. From this premise, it is correct to say that Aquinas, Austin, Kelsen and so forth have yielded different concepts of law.

It is easy to see how Bulygin's view on interpretation and meaning has repercussions also on other, more specific substantive theses regarding the power of judges to determine and create the content of the law. By supporting the thesis of the partial indeterminacy of conventional meanings, Bulygin admits both the interstitial creative power of judges' decisions and the limited reconstructive power of legal theory.

[52] See Bulygin 1992: 11–30. [53] See Bulygin 2007a: 102. [54] See Bulygin 2007a: 107.
[55] Ibid.

16.5.3 On Regulative and Constitutive Norms

According to Bulygin, there is a 'radical difference between two kinds of rules', that is, prescriptive and power-conferring norms.[56] In his view, prescriptive norms regulate behaviour: they prescribe, prohibit or permit certain actions. By contrast, power-conferring norms must be analysed as determinative rules (in von Wright's sense). Bulygin calls them conceptual rules. These rules 'do not prescribe certain behaviour as obligatory, prohibited or permitted. What they do is *define* concepts.'[57] Nonetheless, it must be clear that, first, determinative or conceptual rules are rules. That is to say, they do not describe anything and allow us to evaluate certain states or results as correct or incorrect. Second, as has just been said, they do not oblige or permit us to bring about these results; they only constitute the power to produce them.

It is interesting to see that, from this standpoint, one relevant difference between prescriptive and conceptual rules is that they do not belong to the same level of language. While the formulation of a prescriptive norm belongs to the first level of language directly referring to human actions, the formulation of a conceptual norm that defines or determines concepts is always metalinguistic. The fact that conceptual norms are metalinguistic may suggest that they regulate linguistic behaviour. However, Bulygin is very clear on this point: conceptual rules only constitute concepts; they neither impose nor allow the use of these concepts.

On this issue, Bulygin rejects the widely shared position according to which constitutive and regulative rules are necessarily dependent on one another, particularly, because any constitutive norm would also regulate behaviour or, vice versa, because any regulative norm in a certain sense would also constitute and allow to identify a new type of action. Thereby, he distances himself once again from a majoritarian trend among contemporary legal theorists, be they legal positivists or natural law theorists. Bulygin assumes part of Hart's argument in favour of the distinction between these kinds of rules. According to it, the provision of a nullity is part of a conceptual or power-conferring rule in a way in which the penalty

[56] See Bulygin 1992: 282.

[57] Bulygin 1992: 280 (italics in the original). Bulygin associates conceptual rules with those that John Searle has called constitutive rules. However, he criticises Searle's account, according to which constitutive rules also regulate the activities constituted by them.

attached to a duty-imposing rule is not.[58] Without sanctions, we can still have obligations and regulatory norms. Without nullity, there would be no definitions or conceptual rules. To be sure, it is not necessary to accept this argument in order to establish the sharp distinction that both Hart and Bulygin are trying to establish. For instance, we could admit that a certain kind of sanction is necessarily linked to regulatory norms just as a nullity is necessarily linked to conceptual norms. In any event, we can insist that, as Hart suggests, nullity and sanction are independent concepts and give rise to independent kinds of norms.

The admission of a sharp difference between conceptual and regulative norms has far-reaching consequences. In particular, it is relevant regarding an apparently distant methodological debate about how we understand legal theory. If the independence between conceptual and regulative rules is sound, then there is room for the kind of research that Bulygin's positivist legal theory intends to do (research on legal concepts or conceptual rules) without entering a discussion regarding which actions are permitted or prohibited. As we have seen, in Bulygin's perspective, general legal theory offers a metalinguistic conceptual analysis and does not directly refer to legal norms. In other words, it says nothing about what we (legally or morally) ought to do. On the contrary, for those who deny the independence between conceptual and regulative rules, the identification of legal concepts implies the identification of specific duty-imposing rules. If this position were sound, it would mean that Bulygin is wrong in more than one respect. In general, there would be no hope for conceptual research or analysis as Bulygin understands it. This is so because any conceptual analysis would be, at the same time, an inquiry into some regulative norms. Specifically, it would mean that there is no possibility of establishing a distinction – as Bulygin does – between descriptive and normative legal concepts. This would be so because all legal notions would be normative and necessarily connected to specific regulative rules. As Ronald Dworkin has suggested, legal philosophy should be understood as a substantive theoretical reflection, even if highly abstract, on normative (interpretive) concepts necessarily connected to duty-imposing rules. To be sure, if this were the case, according to Bulygin, legal theory can still be a cognitive or descriptive enterprise.

58 Ibid.

The point is that the theory's object would be legal reality; in other words, it would no longer consist only 'in the analysis of the conceptual (logical) components of the experience through which human beings know, or cope with, reality'.[59]

Nevertheless, we should stress that Dworkin's conclusion regarding legal philosophy is based on two controversial assumptions: on the one hand, the assumption that there is a single right answer or correct explanation about the way in which constitutive and regulative rules are related; on the other hand, the assumption that, according to the correct explanation, these kinds of rule are necessarily linked. By contrast, in Bulygin's view, there is no such thing as a single correct explanation. Moreover, according to the rational reconstruction he provides, it is fruitful to admit that, in the legal field, conceptual and regulative rules are only contingently related. This means that, as a matter of fact, there can be specific instances of conceptual norms that do entail regulative norms and others that do not. For instance, validity understood as a morally binding force is a normative concept of the first kind; it entails the duty to act according to the valid norm. Instead, the concept of validity as membership in a legal system is a descriptive concept of the second kind; it does not entail any duty-imposing norm.

It is worth noting that, if Bulygin's reconstruction were not appropriate, and any constitutive norm necessarily regulates behaviour or implies regulative norms, the problems that arise would not only affect Bulygin's legal theory. As a matter of fact, this conclusion would affect the general methodological idea according to which the analytical enterprise of legal philosophy can be conceived as a semantic enquiry, which does not refer directly to specific regulations in a given law. In other words, the research programme and the discourse of legal philosophy are not only more abstract than those of legal science and legal dogmatics; they are also of a different kind. Even in the event that we disagree with Bulygin's semantic approach, there is no doubt that his substantive theses on prescriptive and power-conferring norms are entirely coherent with the methodological premises that he assumes. Bulygin is committed to rejecting the necessary connection between conceptual and regulative norms. If there were such a necessary connection, Bulygin's analytical conception of legal positivism could not hold.

[59] See Bulygin 1980: 379.

References

Alchourrón, C. A. and Bulygin, E. 1971. *Normative Systems.* Springer-Verlag.

Alchourrón, C. A. and Bulygin, E. 1981. 'The Expressive Conception of Norms'. In Bulygin, E. 2015: 146–70.

Alchourrón, C. A. and Bulygin, E. 1988. 'Perils of Level Confusions in Normative Discourse: A Replay to K. Opalek and J. Wolenski'. *Rechtstheorie* 19: 230–7.

Alchourrón, C. A. and Bulygin, E. 1973/89. 'Von Wright on Deontic Logic and the Philosophy of Law'. In Bulygin, E. 2015: 88–116.

Alchourrón, C. A. and Bulygin, E. 1991. *Análisis Lógico y Derecho.* Centro de Estudios Constitucionales.

Alchourrón, C. A. and Bulygin, E. 1992. 'Limits of Logic and Legal Reasoning'. In Bulygin, E. 2015: 252–71.

Bobbio, N. [1961]1996. *Il positivismo giuridico.* Giappichelli.

Bulygin, E. 1980. 'Kant y la Filosofía del derecho contemporánea'. Alchourrón, C. A. and Bulygin, E. 1991: 371–82.

Bulygin, E. 1981. 'Legal Statements and Positivism: A Reply to Joseph Raz'. In Bulygin, E. 2015: 136–45.

Bulygin, E. 1982. 'Norms, Normative Propositions and Legal Statements'. In Bulygin, E. 2015: 188–206.

Bulygin, E. 1990. 'An Antinomy in Kelsen's Legal Theory of Law'. In Bulygin, E. 2015: 235–51.

Bulygin, E. 1992. 'Sull'interpretazione giuridica'. In P. Comanducci and R. Guastini (eds.). *Analisi e diritto 1992. Ricerche di giurisprudenza analitica.* Giappichelli: 11–30.

Bulygin, E. 1995: 'Cognition and Interpretation of Law'. In L. Gianformaggio and S. Paulson (eds.). *Cognition and Interpretation of Law.* Giappichelli: 11–35.

Bulygin, E. 1999a. 'Valid Law and Law in Force'. In Bulygin, E. 2015: 284–92.

Bulygin, E. 1999b. 'True and False statements in Normative Discourse'. In R. Egidi (ed.). *In Search of a New Humanism: The Philosophy of Henrik von Wright.* Kluwer: 183–91.

Bulygin, E. 2004. 'The Objectivity of Law'. In Bulygin, E. 2015: 302–10.

Bulygin, E. 2005. 'The Problem of Legal Validity in Kelsen's Pure Theory of Law'. In Bulygin, E. 2015: 311–23.

Bulygin, E. 2006. *El positivismo jurídico.* Fontamara.

Bulygin, E. 2007a. 'Raz y la teoría del derecho. Comentarios sobre *¿Puede haber una teoría del derecho?* de Joseph Raz'. In J. Raz, R. Alexy, and E. Bulygin. *Una discusión sobre la teoría del derecho.* Marcial Pons: 99–110.

Bulygin, E. 2007b. 'María Cristina Redondo sobre distintos tipos de positivismo'. In J. J. Moreso and C. Redondo (eds.) *Un dialogo con la teoría del derecho de Eugenio Bulygin.* Marcial Pons: 201–3.

Bulygin, E. 2009. 'My View of the Philosophy of Law'. In Bulygin, E. 2015: 355–9.

Bulygin, E. 2015. *Essays in Legal Philosophy*. Eds. C. Bernal, C. Huerta, T. Mazzarese, J. J. Moreso, P. E. Navarro and S. L. Paulson. Oxford University Press.

Caracciolo, R. 1993. 'Entrevista a Eugenio Bulygin'. *Doxa* 14: 499–513.

Coleman, L. and Leiter, B. 1996. 'Legal Positivism'. In D. Patterson (ed.). *A Companion to Philosophy of Law and Legal Theory*. Blackwell: 241–60.

Dworkin, R. 1977. 'The Model of Rules II'. In R. Dworkin. *Taking Rights Seriously*. Harvard University Press: 46–80.

Navarro, P. 2015. 'Normative Systems and Legal Positivism'. In Bulygin, E. 2015: 1–21.

Nino, C. S. 1978. 'Some Confusions Surrounding Kelsen's Concept of Validity'. *ARSP* 64: 357–77.

Nino, C. S. 1984. *Introducción al análisis del derecho*. 2nd ed. Astrea.

Nino, C. S. 1989. *El constructivismo ético*. Centro de Estudios Constitucionales.

Raz, J. 2004. 'Can There Be a Theory of Law?' in J. Raz. 2009. *Between Authority and Interpretation: On the Theory of Law and Practical Reason*. Oxford University Press: 17–46.

Rodríguez, J. 2007. 'Un breve balance de la teoría de los sistemas normativos'. In J. J. Moreso and M. C. Redondo (eds.). *Un diálogo con la teoría del derecho de Eugenio Bulygin*. Marcial Pons: 81–8.

Ross, A. 1961. 'Validity and the Conflict of Legal Positivism and Natural Law'. *Revista jurídica de Buenos Aires* IV: 46–93.

Schauer, F. 1998. 'Positivism through Thick and Thin'. In B. Bix (ed.). *Analyzing Law: New Essays in Legal Theory*. Clarendon Press: 65–78.

Part IV

Main Tenets

17 Social-Practice Legal Positivism and the Normativity Thesis

Stefano Bertea

17.1 Introduction

As much as legal positivism may be a traditional school of legal thought, it does not command any single definition that everyone is prepared to accept.[1] But this should not come as a surprise. After all, we should not expect to necessarily be able to identify a common denominator among research programmes spanning over centuries and pursued by theorists with (even radically) different philosophical backgrounds. Nonetheless, its semantic plurality may be an obstacle to a systematic discussion of legal positivism. And this is why I introduce my argument by making explicit what I take legal positivism to mean.

Throughout this contribution I will define legal positivism (at least in its contemporary instantiations) as the family of legal theories essentially shaped by the so-called social thesis. The social thesis states that law is fundamentally a matter of social facts, to the effect that what counts as law in any society can be established independently of evaluative considerations.[2] The social thesis, as I understand it, is a claim about the *nature* of law, as opposed to being a claim about its *validity*. Accordingly, legal positivism, insofar as it is essentially defined in terms of the social thesis (as I interpret this thesis), is to be viewed as a theory of *law*, as against

[1] This research was supported by a Deutsche Forschungsgemeinschaft Research Grant. I would like to thank Patricia Mindus, Jorge H. Sanchez Perez, Torben Spaak and the participants in the 'Conference on Legal Positivism 1' (University of Stockholm, 13–15 November 2018) for their comments on an earlier draft of this work. Needless to say, responsibility for the views expressed herein, as well as for any error of form or content, rests solely with me.

[2] For this reason, this thesis is also referred to in the literature as the 'social fact thesis'. A definition of legal positivism in terms of the social thesis (or at least primarily and essentially in terms of this thesis) can be found in Coleman 2001a: 145–7; Coleman and Leiter: 1996; Green 2018; Himma 2004: 126–9; Postema 1982: 167–8; Raz 1979: 37; Perry 2009: 315–8; Shapiro 2011: 27–30.

an account of *legal validity*.[3] Legal positivism, in other words, is not exclusively concerned with establishing the conditions under which certain norms belong to a legal system (and in this sense are legally valid); rather, legal positivism is more ambitiously interested in determining what is distinctive to law, or what the features of law are that on the one hand specifically and essentially characterise the artefact singled out by the term 'law', and on the other hand distinguish the law from the vast plurality of other artefacts we enter into contact with in the practical sphere. On this interpretation, then, legal positivism does not simply address the question 'How is it that we can determine whether a provision belongs to a legal system'? It also seeks to explain the law as a *distinct* domain, one that may bear similarities to other human practices and yet is ultimately irreducible to them.

As a theory of law seeking to explain what makes a subset of the practical directives that apply to us legal (as opposed to generically social, political, moral, to do with religion, or whatever), legal positivism may be construed as a set of (a) normative claims, (b) empirical claims, or (c) conceptual claims. In this chapter, I will be concerned with the last of the three, that is, with the *conceptual* reading of legal positivism; and so only a given form of legal positivism – *conceptual* legal positivism – will fall within the scope of the discussion that follows. Conceptual legal positivism is a distinctive (and influential) contribution to *general jurisprudence*, namely, to the legal-theoretical tradition proposing to arrive at a *descriptive* account of law, and one that 'is not tied to any particular legal system or legal culture'.[4] Within this tradition of legal studies, jurisprudence is regarded as a discipline whose fundamental feature is that it is not only *conceptual* – jurisprudence is concerned with *defining* concepts and their mutual relationships – but also *intuition-based*, in that jurisprudence proceeds from widely shared ideas about law, which are in turn taken to be plain truths about the legal domain, and uses these as bases on which to conceptualise the law and other fundamental legal concepts. Once conceptual legal positivism is understood as a contribution to, and an

[3] Thus, whereas some legal positivists (such as Gardner 2001: 199) regard themselves as putting forward only an account of the *validity* of law, I take legal positivism to embody a more ambitious set of claims and hence a philosophically more intriguing as well as theoretically more provoking one. Views similar to mine can be found in Bix 2005: 29–32 and Spaak 2018: 472–6, among others.

[4] Hart [1961] 1994: 239.

interpretation of, the programme of general jurisprudence, it should be expected to yield a theory of the *nature* (the *essence* or *concept*) of law, and so a theory aimed at arriving at a list of fundamental, prominent, and theoretically interesting properties by which law is defined.[5]

The claims just introduced set the boundaries of my engagement with legal positivism in this chapter, where I intend to assess the theoretical soundness of only one account of legal positivism, namely, the conceptual view of the nature of law based on the social thesis. For want of a better expression, I will refer to the specific account that will be discussed here as 'social-practice legal positivism'. This variant of legal positivism will be introduced in Section 17.2, where we will look at its two main current instantiations, namely, legal conventionalism (Section 17.2.1) and the conception of law as a shared activity (Section 17.2.2). Then, in Section 17.3, I will argue that social-practice legal positivism is incompatible with the recognition that law is intrinsically an obligation-engendering social practice. Section 17.4 concludes.

17.2 Social-Practice Legal Positivism: The Overarching Idea

In this chapter, as mentioned, I will not be engaging with legal positivism in general but rather with a specific variant of this broad theoretical view, namely, what I am calling 'social-practice legal positivism'. Since that is the specific target of the argument deployed in what follows, and the expression is not in any wide use in the literature, I should begin by giving this brand of positivism an introduction, however much in broad strokes.

By social-practice legal positivism I mean the distinct and original interpretation of the legal positivist project premised on the view that law essentially rests on a *social practice*. Whereas some variants of legal positivism explain the concept of law largely without appealing to the idea of a social practice,[6] social-practice legal positivism seeks to explain the

[5] For a characterisation of legal positivism along these lines, as a specific instantiation of general jurisprudence, see Coleman 2001b: 175–217 and Spaak 2018: 470–1.

[6] An influential variant of legal positivism that cannot be qualified as social-practice legal positivism is Hans Kelsen's, where the basic norm structuring the legal system is not so much a *practice* – one the relevant social group actually *follows* – as it is an *idea*, one the group *presupposes* to exist in its relation to the law. See, e.g., Kelsen 1934, 1945, 1967. Less clear is whether in social-practice legal positivism we can include Joseph Raz's legal

law – its nature and essential features – by pointing to the existence of (a) an institutional manner of behaviour that is regularly practised by a group and (b) a shared attitude that, within this group, and particularly among legal officials, informs the way individuals relate specifically to that mode or pattern of behaviour. And since those two features are essential, as well as specific to law, they act as necessary conditions for something to count as law, while distinguishing law from other normative phenomena. This means, in summary, that law would not even be possible without an underlying practice – the common social practice that obtains among officials, coupled with their attitude towards that practice – and that the same practice at the same time distinguishes law from other social activities.

If we take a survey of contemporary literature we should, I believe, find that two basic forms of social-practice legal positivism have been theorised: legal conventionalism and the conception of law as a shared activity. And even though, as forms of social-practice legal-positivism, they share the same foundation, their accounts of the nature of law differ significantly in several details. For this reason, these two conceptions will be taken up in two separate sections, providing a brief statement of them while highlighting their differences.

17.2.1 Legal Conventionalism

As a variant of social-practice legal positivism, legal conventionalism can be traced back to H. L. A. Hart's account of the nature of law. Hart is widely

positivism. In a sense we can, to the extent that legal systems are conceived by Raz as deeply shaped by certain practices that officials collectively follow. But in order to arrive at such a conclusion, we would have to discount the central role that Raz assigns to authority. Which is to say that not only does Raz make authority an essential component of law as a concept, but he also proceeds to fault both non-positivism and alternative variants of legal positivism for failing to provide an adequate account of authority in that role (see Raz 1979, 1986, 1994, 1999, 2009, among other works). Indeed, law is conceived by Raz as an essentially *authoritative* institution, such that no account of the nature of law can sidestep the question of its authority. And, since in Raz's view no general theory of law is better equipped to explain its authority than legal positivism and arguably Raz's own legal positivist theory offers an original account of authority understood as essential to an account of its nature, it follows that his legal positivism is better understood as a kind of 'authority-based' legal positivism and, as such, that it cannot be reduced to social-practice legal positivism, as I define it here. This reading of Raz's legal theory may be contentious, to be sure, but for a similar reading, see Coleman 2001a: 99–105.

understood to have invoked a conventionalist understanding of the rule of recognition – the social practice he lies at the foundation of law – especially in his Postscript to *The Concept of Law*, where he responds to Ronald Dworkin's critique of his theory of rules. In the Postscript, Hart re-fashions that theory as a theory specifically and exclusively concerned with *social* rules, as against rules in general – and social rules, Hart claims, owe their status as rules to their being conventional. Now, considering how influential Hart's theses about the concept of law have been in contemporary Anglo-American jurisprudence, his conventionalist turn encouraged legal philosophers of an analytic persuasion to explore the possibility of providing a conventionalist account of the nature of law as a practice grounded in a social rule.

Initially, legal conventionalists characterised the rule of recognition as a *coordinative* convention, namely, a regularity of behaviour that emerges as a practical solution to recurrent coordination problems. Thus, in a seminal article, Gerald Postema[7] argues that the notion of a (coordinative) convention is key to explaining law as a concept.[8] Conventions, according to this theory, arise as the solution that a social group finds in coping with persistent coordination problems. The most effective strategy by which to address these problems, Postema claims, is to establish patterns of conduct that all members of the social group involved are prepared to accept and follow. This mechanism in turn gives rise to a web of expectations that within the group are widely recognised as both legitimate and induced. Since the expectations associated with relevant socially practised patterns of behaviour are widely regarded by the group's members as legitimate and induced, they will not only act as reasons for action but will also, under certain circumstances, give rise to obligations for legal subjects generally.[9] By framing the rule of recognition as a coordinative convention, then, Postema's theory seeks to provide a comprehensive account of both the social existence of law and its bindingness.[10]

It was not long before this form of legal conventionalism, compelling though it may seem, began to attract critical scrutiny that forced it to take

[7] See Postema 1982.
[8] Variations of this form of legal conventionalism can also be found in Coleman 2001a: esp. 114–21; den Hartog 2002; Lagerspetz 1995.
[9] This argument is presented in Postema 1982: 179–82.
[10] On this point, see Postema 1982: 197–203.

a harder look at its own argument.[11] In fact, even some of the original proponents of legal conventionalism ultimately came to the realisation that coordinative conventions can go only so far in explaining the concept of law.[12] Nonetheless, owing especially to the sophisticated and systematic effort of Andrei Marmor, legal conventionalism survived this criticism, and transformed itself in the process, by relinquishing the view that coordinative conventions alone can explain the nature of law. Indeed, Marmor is critical of the attempt to reduce all conventions to social patterns through which to secure the uniformity of behaviour needed to solve coordination problems. Conventions, he points out, emerge for a variety of other reasons, too. To begin with, they can be introduced to establish hitherto inexistent practices and thus can serve a constitutive function, as opposed to a coordinative one. These constitutive conventions, as Marmor calls them, have a separate existence from coordinative ones and a distinct normativity, and so cannot be reduced to the latter.[13] There is also a further type of convention that Marmor considers to be important for a correct understanding of law. Which is to say that coordinative and constitutive conventions, for all their differences, are alike in being *surface* conventions. And, typically, surface conventions are not stand-alone normative practices: In a number of cases they operate on top of a more abstract conventional layer, where we find what Marmor calls *deep* conventions.[14]

This general theory of conventions carries implications that bear directly on the way in which law ought to be conceptualised. Law, Marmor argues, has a distinctively multi-layered conventional structure. Thus, on a surface layer, we find legal provisions that act as coordinative conventions, since they are introduced to deal with recurrent coordination problems. On a deeper layer, we find a rule of recognition that Marmor reinterprets as a structured constitutive convention shared by legal officials. Finally, on

[11] An acute critic of this form of legal conventionalism is Leslie Green: see in particular Green 1983, 1985; Green 1988: 89–121; Green 1999. Sharp critical remarks can also be found in Marmor 2006: 353–63.

[12] Among those who backtracked from legal conventionalism figures Coleman. See, in particular, Coleman 2001b: 94, where he claims that 'it would place an arbitrary and baseless constraint on our concept of law to stipulate that the social practice among officials necessary for the existence of a Rule of Recognition must always be representable as a game of partial conflict', namely, as the situation that coordinative conventions are associated with.

[13] On the notion of a constitutive convention, see Marmor 2009: 31–57.

[14] Deep conventions are discussed in Marmor 2007 and Marmor 2009: 58–78.

a deeper layer still, the law can be observed to rest on the deep conventions just mentioned, corresponding to the different legal traditions. The picture that emerges from Marmor's account, then, is one in which the law is fundamentally shaped by a set of conventional social practices that differ in kind, occupy different layers, and perform distinct functions.

17.2.2 The Conception of Law as a Shared Activity

The other main form of social-practice legal positivism – the conception of law as a shared activity – revolves around the claim that law is best explained as a collective effort undertaken by persons acting in a certain capacity, namely, as legal officials, and that their activity carries implications for the whole community of individuals who live under the jurisdiction of a legal system. From this organising idea of a shared activity, we in turn get the two-sided claim, at once positive and negative, that forms the core of this conception, stating that (a) law is an activity *jointly* carried out by a group of individuals, each of whom contributes in a distinct way to the collective enterprise; and (b) this activity cannot without distortion be interpreted as the outcome of the practices of a collection of *separately* acting individuals. In short, the law is what emerges from the collective action of a social group, and more specifically from what certain qualified individuals do when acting on behalf of the group as a whole.

This twofold idea is inflected in different ways by different proponents of the conception of law as a shared activity, especially when it comes to describing the collective undertaking that distinctly characterises the law as a concept. More to the point, we can detect a 'thick' account of this collective undertaking and a 'thin' one. In the first camp we can locate Jules Coleman, who constructs a theoretically robust and demanding account of law as a shared activity by conceiving the latter as a shared *cooperative* activity, an idea that Coleman borrows from Michael Bratman and uses to describe the rule of recognition.[15] At the core of any system of laws, Coleman argues, we find a cooperative practice jointly undertaken by those entrusted with administering the legal system. As a result, the legal system is, on this account, the outcome of a shared project that legal officials pursue *cooperatively*. It is the idea that this project is undertaken *cooperatively* that makes Coleman's account of law as a shared activity

[15] See especially Coleman 2001a: 114–21; Coleman 2001b: 74–102.

robust: In taking part in the activities out of which the law emerges, legal officials are not just doing their own job but are committed to supporting one another in the shared effort they devote to the legal system.

The *thin* conception of law as a shared activity has instead been advanced by Scott Shapiro, with an account of law that significantly revises the positivist stance from within. What sets this thin approach apart from other positivist theories is the idea of joint activity as a 'massively shared agency with authority'.[16] This idea draws on Bratman's model of shared agency but makes significant changes to it. For it is Shapiro's view that Bratman's model of shared agency – the model Coleman substantially endorses and applies to the legal domain *directly* – cannot be so applied to legal institutions straightaway, since it does not recognise the role that impersonal authority and hierarchy play in the governance of social affairs. In Shapiro's revised notion, then, shared agency can be said to hold even when (a) some agents in the group stand in a relationship of superiority to the others; (b) not everyone in the group cooperates or is even committed to the joint enterprise; and, relatedly, (c) coercion is used as a backup strategy to promote general conformism.[17]

By building on the notion of massively shared agency with authority, Shapiro sets out his 'planning theory of law', which frames law as a form of social planning.[18] This collective planning activity, and so the law as a whole, is in turn described as 'an incremental process whose function is to guide, organize, and monitor behaviour through the settling of normative questions and which disposes its addressees to comply under normal conditions'.[19] In this conceptual framework, then, law is a large-scale, hierarchically structured enterprise carried out by legal officials who are entrusted with the task of planning for the wider community. Accordingly,

[16] Shapiro 2011: 195.

[17] See Shapiro 2011: 161–73. This characterisation further illustrates the way Shapiro's notions of shared agency and collective undertaking are substantially thinner than, and indeed irreducible to, Bratman's or Coleman's (and I include Coleman because, as I understand him, he wholeheartedly embraces and fully commits to Bratman's theory of shared agency). Indeed, Bratman and Coleman, alike, define these two notions by incorporating into them features that Shapiro does not regard as necessary, such as a cooperative attitude, personality, the absence of hierarchy and the irrelevance of coercion as a means by which to achieve and preserve conformism. Other versions of the conception of law as a shared activity have been developed that build on thin assumptions about such an activity: examples can be found in Kutz 2001 and Sanchez Brigido 2009.

[18] For a summary statement of this legal theory, see Shapiro 2011: 193–233.

[19] Shapiro 2011: 203.

Shapiro's planning theory[20] reconstructs (a) legal systems as institutions of social planning; (b) legal rules as plans or plan-like norms; and, consequently, (c) legal officials as planners who, by creating, implementing and enforcing collective plans, guide the behaviour of individuals and groups, thus helping them to 'lower their deliberation, negotiation, and bargaining costs, increase predictability of behaviour, compensate for ignorance and bad character, and provide methods of accountability'.[21]

At this point, we can make explicit what keeps the conception of law as a shared activity apart from the other main strand of social-practice legal positivism, namely, legal conventionalism: While both approaches construct the law as a *social* practice (this is what makes them two variants of social-practice legal positivism), only on the latter is the conventional element understood to be *inherent* in that practice; on the former approach, by contrast, this element is *not* inherent in the idea of the shared activity in terms of which the law is conceived, for it is not a necessary part of this activity. The conventional element may be present, to be sure, but it does not *define* the activity, since people may participate collectively in a social practice without believing that this is required of them under a social convention, and this is understood to also apply to people who take part in the collective practices by which the law is defined.[22]

In conclusion, the key thesis underpinning the conception of law as a shared activity can be stated thus: Law is best characterised as a practice that consists in a group acting together and subscribing to a common goal. However, as much as those who act together in the legal domain do so in view of a common goal, they are not claimed to necessarily adhere to any set of social conventions. Hence, while, on this conception, sociality figures as an essential element of law, conventionality does not. And therein lies the difference between the conception of law as a shared activity and legal conventionalism, for on the latter theory the social practices constitutive of law *are*, by contrast, understood to be inherently conventional.

One final point bears mention in regard to this distinction before we move on. Which is to say that the distinction, while neat as a matter of principle, may turn out to be almost impalpable in practice, for even if a collective enterprise (as theorised by the conception of law as a shared

[20] See Shapiro 2011: 200. [21] Ibid.
[22] This is a point that is made clear in Bratman 2002: 515–16.

activity) does not necessarily rest on a convention, the mutual commitment to a goal that it *does* necessarily involve is likely to be accompanied by some form of commitment to more than just the means necessary for achieving that goal. This suggests that collective enterprises (joint or shared activities) and conventional practices alike are characterised by widespread social conformism. Which in turn means that joint activities, as a matter of fact, tend to look very much like conventional practices. Still, the phenomenological similarity that holds between shared activities and conventional behaviour should not obscure their *conceptual* distinction: Acting together is a constitutively social and yet not inherently conventional undertaking, meaning that there may well be collective practices that are not conventional, or that may be undertaken without an underlying convention – hence the conceptual difference between collective enterprises (which are social and yet not necessarily conventional) and conventional practices (which are not just generically social but specifically conventional).[23]

17.3 The Scope of the Normativity Thesis in Social-Practice Legal Positivism

From the premise that law is shaped by a collective pattern of behaviour, social-practice legal positivism derives the conclusion that, as a *social* fact, law is also a *normative* institution.[24] The social practice on which the law fundamentally rests, in other words, includes a normative component. Thus, on the one hand, social-practice legal positivism conceptualises the law as a social fact – this is the *social thesis*, and what makes this approach legal-positivist to begin with; on the other hand, the social fact regarded as essential to the definition of the law – be it a shared practice or a conventional one – is distinctly at the same time normative, and this is the *normativity thesis*.

Importantly, this normativity thesis is a thesis not about the *language* of law but about the law *itself*: It is pointing out a *property* of law, and

[23] I should like to thank Torben Spaak for discussing this point with me. Any error that may have been made in this statement of it should be attributed entirely to me.

[24] For statements of this tenor, see Coleman 2001a: 105, 114; Coleman 2001b: 67–73, 134–48; Shapiro 2002; Shapiro 2011: 113–15.

so conceived (as a thesis about the *nature* of law rather than about the language used in carrying out the legal enterprise) it can be interpreted in at least a couple of ways and given a narrower or broader scope. I will thus be pointing out a narrower, weaker or 'understated' interpretation and a broader, or robust, one. In the first case, the law is said to be normative in the sense that, through its provisions, it can *guide* the action of those who are subject to it, and since this is something the law does by providing *reasons* for acting as instructed,[25] the normativity thesis (on this understated interpretation) states that the law is normative essentially as a practice through which reasons are given for acting in keeping with the law itself.

On its robust interpretation, by contrast, the normativity thesis ascribes to law an intrinsic ability to give rise to *obligations*, in addition to generically giving *reasons* for action. The law, in other words, is understood to be endowed with an ability to make its prescriptions *obligatory*, rather than simply giving reasons why those who are subject to these prescriptions should comply. Moreover, on this interpretation, even if these obligations are legal in the sense that they are set forth in the law and are legally enforceable, they are understood to be grounded in rationality: their scope overlaps with that of practical rationality, and they are in this sense genuinely practical, without the qualification that they bind only within the confines of the law – which in turn means that they state what legal subjects ought to do *generally*, rather than only what they are *legally* required to do.[26]

[25] Or at least this is a widespread understanding of the way through which the law's action-guiding function is provided. As Raz (1999: 67) puts it, 'the normativity of all that is normative [including, on the normativity thesis, the law] consists in the way it is, or provides, or is otherwise related to reasons'.

[26] Throughout this chapter, when describing an obligation as *genuine*, or grounded in or bound up with *practical rationality*, or again as *general*, *full-blooded* or *unqualified*, I am highlighting different aspects of the same idea, namely, the idea just introduced that in stating what we are required to do by law, legal obligations set forth prescriptions understood to apply even outside the domain of law, precisely because they are backed up by reasons that hold good in the practical sphere generally and are thus genuine reasons. This nexus is underscored in Coleman 2001b: 143, which states that the 'reasons, along with the associated obligations' engendered by the law

> are not tied to the institution [of law] in the way, for example, many of rights and duties created by the rules of a game are ... Legal duties arise in law, but they are duties that figure in our determination of what we ought to do generally and not just in our deliberations about what we ought to do in playing the game "law".

On either interpretation of the normativity thesis, then, law is recognised to have a dual nature. Therefore, if social-practice legal positivism is to be consistent with its own premises, and if its account of the nature of law is to be comprehensive, it must be able to explain the law not only as a *factual* phenomenon (a social practice) but also as a *normative* one,[27] that is, it must explain how the law as a social practice can give its addresses genuine *reasons* for acting as prescribed (on the understated interpretation of the normativity thesis) or (on the robust interpretation) how it can give rise to genuine *obligations* (ones we are bound to fulfil unqualifiedly, regardless of whether they happen to be obligations imposed on us as legal subjects). If we can determine how well these two questions are answered by social-practice legal positivism, then we will have a reasonable assessment of this theory, for we will have assessed it on its own terms, and by this test – that is, by attempting, through this theory, to explain how the law can give rise to *genuine* norms and obligations, or how *norms* of general practical import and *obligations* grounded in or bound up with practical rationality can arise out of the *social facts* that the law (on this theory) is understood to ultimately consist of – we will also be able to appreciate whether the theory succeeds in explaining the normativity of law.

This is the assessment I will be making in the rest of this section, where I will confine myself to testing the stronger claim that law has an inherent ability to give rise to obligations that bind those who are subject to its jurisdiction, or at least that the provisions of law, by an inherent ability of the law itself, can be made mandatory for the bulk of that population – this is the robust interpretation of the normativity thesis. In this context, I will specifically argue that this ability ascribed to the law cannot be explained on the basis of social-practice legal positivism. This will mean that the normativity thesis espoused by this theory can be accepted only in its 'understated' sense, or that we cannot, on the basis of this theory, support the robust interpretation of this thesis.

[27] This point is clearly stated in Postema 1987: 81. See also Postema 1982: 165–6, which points out that the two dimensions of law (its sociality and its normativity) 'set the agenda for much of philosophical jurisprudence, both because they seem fundamental and because they are potentially in conflict . . . The history of philosophical jurisprudence is, in part, the history of attempts to modify and interpret these theses [i.e., the normativity and social theses] in the hope of reconciling them in a coherent general theory of law', since 'no historically important theory of law completely rejects either thesis; each tries to come to terms with and explain the intuitive appeal of both'. For a similar statement, see Perry 2009: 324.

I begin the argument by noticing that there are fundamentally two ways in which social-practice legal positivists conceptualise legal obligation, namely, as a *genuine* requirement set forth in the law or as a *perspectival* requirement, one we are to comply with only so long as we take the viewpoint of the legal enterprise itself. For a brief statement of both strategies, we can look at the work of the theory's main proponents. Let us consider Shapiro's theory first. In Shapiro's work, we find an account of law's ability to generate obligations of general practical scope. For Shapiro, these obligations, while genuine, bind only those who are specifically committed to the legal enterprise – or, rather, to the 'master plan' or rule of recognition laying at the foundation of law – that is, legal officials. The idea is that by the very act of joining the legal enterprise as legal officials, people make a commitment to the law that requires them to act as the law prescribes. This commitment makes that obligation genuine in combination with two further principles that kick in: These are the principles of instrumental rationality and personal integrity, or individual consistency. Stated in the negative, once a commitment is made to the social practice that the legal enterprise consists of, it would be both *irrational* and *inconsistent* to disregard that commitment: irrational because someone disregarding such commitment would be someone resolving to do something only to subsequently proceed along a course that fails to implement such choice without changing commitments; inconsistent because someone disregarding such commitment would be someone acting against, and thus contradicting, the very plan that they have had a part in designing in an official capacity and are still committed to.[28] In summary, to act in a legal capacity is to (a) make a commitment to the legal enterprise understood as a shared plan, in such a way that to violate that commitment would amount to violating the principles of (b) instrumental rationality and (c) personal integrity that necessarily accompany it. It is in this way that a legal official's obligation to act in keeping with the law is shown by Shapiro to be at once distinctly legal and genuine (grounded in principles of practical rationality).[29]

[28] As Shapiro (2011: 142) puts it, if a 'subject has accepted the shared plan', then 'he is bound to heed the plan' as a matter of instrumental rationality. And this is why 'legal officials are rationally required to conform to their shared plan' – the plan constitutive of law as a distinctive activity (Shapiro 2011: 182).

[29] This is only a snapshot of Shapiro's account, to be sure, but two points bear comment. First, this combination of elements – (a) through (c) – may not suffice to explain law's ability to give rise to legal obligations in a genuine sense: to this end, it may be necessary to bring in

Here, it should be emphasised that this account explains legal obligation only such as it applies to those who have made a commitment to the shared activity of shaping and maintaining the law. That is, the account covers only legal officials, leaving out the bulk of the population, namely, private individuals, or non-officials, who cannot be *presumed* to have made a commitment to the law as a shared practice, nor can such a commitment be *implicitly attributed* to them, nor can they be *expected* to make one. Therefore, to the extent that social-practice legal positivism can show how legal obligation can be genuinely binding, the account can apply only to that comparatively small portion of the population that works in an official legal capacity (at least in Shapiro's work).

This takes us to the second strategy that social-practice legal positivism uses to explain law's ability to give rise to obligations, that is, by conceiving legal obligations in a perspectival sense, in which obligation applies to us not as legal officials but as ordinary legal subjects. Indeed, in acknowledging that legal subjects are not covered by the shared-activity argument for the existence of genuine legal obligations, Shapiro also claims that we may come under a legal obligation not in virtue of any broad principle of practical rationality but in virtue of taking a standpoint associated with the legal system itself: It is in this perspectival sense that legal obligation applies to us regardless of whether we are actually participating in the legal enterprise as legal officials.[30]

Shapiro's account finds echoes among legal conventionalists in that they, too, can be said not to press beyond the claim that law can engender merely perspectival obligations for legal subjects at large. Consider Marmor's account of legal obligation. Marmor starts out by defining obligation through the concept of a normative, or justificatory, reason:[31] We have an obligation insofar as certain justificatory reasons of a particular kind apply to us (following Raz, Marmor calls them protected reasons). On the basis of this concept Marmor then distinguishes two broad

some other elements, such as (d) the principle that if it is reasonable for others to form social expectations about us, then those expectations should be honoured (by us) and, most importantly, (e) the condition that in order for a social practice to give rise to genuine legal obligations, it must also be recognised to conform to other basic standards of rationality. Second, it is not clear that these elements – (a) through (e) – are *inherent* in social practices and can thus be *reduced* to such practices. Neither of these two lines of criticism will be addressed here, but a full discussion can be found in Bertea 2019: ch. 3.

[30] See for instance Shapiro 2011: 182. [31] See Marmor 2011: 496–7.

classes of obligation: external and internal.[32] External obligations invoke protected reasons why we should *participate* in a given practice; internal obligations instead invoke protected reasons why we should act in a particular way *within* the relevant practice, on (and against the background of) the assumption that this person has some independent reason to take part in that practice. The distinction between external and internal obligations is key to Marmor's explanation of the nature of legal obligation. The law is conceived by Marmor as a conventional practice, and while conventions typically do not give rise to external obligations, they have the resources needed to impose internal ones. Therefore, once we have reasons for committing to the law, we thereby come under a legal obligation, understood as an internal obligation to act as the conventions constitutive of the law require.

Now, this construction can plausibly be understood to be a conception of legal obligation as a perspectival requirement. In fact, for Marmor the binding force of legal obligations is conditional on there being certain considerations external to the law itself. In Marmor's theory, however, these considerations are simply assumed as given: they are framed as unavoidable frameworks providing a fixed perspective from which flows the entire discourse about legal obligations. In his theory, therefore, legal obligations can be binding only on condition of there being a stance or perspective from which they issue and which secures their binding force. Which is to say that, for Marmor, legal obligation is an internal obligation, for it binds us only if we take the *point of view* of the legal system. And this is a paradigmatic statement of *perspectival* obligation.

In sum, in showing how legal obligation should bind not just legal officials but also the generality of legal subjects, the conception of law as a shared activity and legal conventionalism (particularly in the work of Shapiro and Marmor, respectively) can charitably and reasonably be interpreted as reducible to the claim that we are subject to legal obligations by virtue of either having a *reason* to take the perspective of the law (Marmor) or being *committed* to that perspective (Shapiro). Hence, social-practice legal positivism can be said to state that legal obligations conceptually also apply to private citizens at large, and not just to them when acting as legal

[32] This distinction is introduced in Marmor 2001: 25–34 and further developed in Marmor 2009: 168–71.

officials, only insofar as legal obligation is conceived as a *perspectival* statement.

At this point, however, we need to ask whether legal obligation in this perspectival sense is normative to begin with. I believe it is not. In claiming that *from a given perspective* (that of the law) a legal subject ought to act in such and such a way, we are not *directing* this person to act that way (as stated in the law itself) but are rather *describing* the normative standards (or 'oughts') that apply to such persons once they take that perspective. Perspectival obligations, in other words, may have a *normative object* – which consists in their concerning the *norms* of law – but in their quality, or broader framing, they are *descriptive*. Which is to say that perspectival legal obligations can be said to have the status of a *report*: They inform us of the fact that, barring interfering circumstances, individuals who take a given perspective view themselves as being under a requirement to act in a certain way. And, as reports about what is obligatory in accordance with the law – namely, as statements that lay out the condition or state of affairs of someone who embraces the point of view of the legal system – perspectival legal obligations are descriptive through and through.[33]

This conclusion is significant because it brings out an important implication of social-practice legal positivism: On this conception, the law must be understood as constitutively lacking a *general* capacity to impose unqualified obligations. Indeed, if (i) the obligations the law imposes on legal subjects at large are perspectival and (ii) perspectival obligations are descriptive, then the vast majority of the obligations that the law imposes cannot (on this conception) be qualified as normative or, a fortiori, as genuine. So, in the theoretical framework of social-practice legal positivism, for one thing, the normative dimension of law does not encompass any far-reaching capacity to impose genuine obligations, and, for another, general-practical bindingess cannot be ascribed to law as one of its inherent properties. Otherwise stated, law is theorised by social-practice legal positivism as conceptually non-normative in the robust sense. Relatedly, on this conception, while

[33] This descriptive status of perspectival obligation is acknowledged in Shapiro 2011: 184–8. See also Hershovitz 2015: 1167–73. In the context of a broader discussion, Scott Hershovitz emphasizes that an obligation from the law's point of view is 'a descriptive claim, not a normative one' and, relatedly, that 'claims about legal obligations are, on this picture, quasi normative; they appear to be normative, but they are not really' (Hershovitz 2015: 1169).

sociality is a *constitutive* component of law, the same is not true of *robust* normativity, in the sense of a full-blooded obligatoriness applying to all legal subjects – for this is rather understood as an epiphenomenon, a secondary and non-necessary element of law. I take this to be a deep theoretical implication, as it means that ultimately the proponents of social-practice legal positivism conceptualise law as a social institution incorporating a *contained* and *confined* normative dimension. This in turn means that we should not expect this approach to give us an account of law as an intrinsically obligation-engendering institution.

Note that this aspect of the approach does not make it inconsistent. In fact, from the standpoint of social-practice legal positivism, there is nothing amiss about conceptualising law as a practice that is systematically unable to give rise to unqualified obligations that bind the generality of legal subjects. There is nothing theoretically unobjectionable, in other words, about a theory that can only ground the normativity of law in its weaker, understated sense, so long as that is the view explicitly endorsed by the theory itself. And, indeed, that is precisely the argument that social-practice legal positivism makes. The view espoused by social-practice legal positivism, in short, is that robust normativity is not a defining, or constitutive, trait of law, and, precisely for that reason, a legal system still counts as a non-defective legal system even if the obligations it engenders are not genuine in quality.

Nonetheless, the theoretical import of embracing social-practice legal positivism is noteworthy and can best be appreciated by considering the relation between the two fundamental theses about the concept of law – the social thesis and the normativity thesis – as they are framed by social-practice legal positivism. In the conceptual framework associated with social-practice legal positivism, whereas the social thesis finds a comprehensive and unreserved recognition, the normativity thesis is subject to a considerable limitation in that law is asserted to possess no general unqualified-obligation-engendering capacity. So, while the social thesis is fully embraced within social-practice legal positivism, where it takes centre stage, the normativity thesis comes into this conception with a great many qualifications and is pushed into the background.

This point can be radicalised as follows. Insofar as they do not regard law as intrinsically normative in the sense of essentially being able to issue mandatory norms for the population living under its jurisdiction, social-practice legal positivists ultimately call into question the very possibility of asserting in a meaningful and wide-ranging sense that law is both a social phenomenon and a normative institution. For, whereas those espousing social-practice legal positivism endorse the view that law has a dual nature – social and normative – and provide detailed accounts for the social dimension of law, they do not offer any comparatively comprehensive elucidation of the normative component of law. In fact, they end up having no explanation of a key dimension of law qua a normative institution: its *general* capacity to impose *rationality-related* obligations. And this capacity should be considered a focal component of legal normativity, once legal normativity is understood in a far-reaching meaning.

Now, one may be tempted to think that social-practice legal positivists have no reason to be uncomfortable with such statement, which plays down the obligatory dimension of law, since the statement by itself does not force them to altogether abandon the normativity thesis; it entails only the conclusion that the normative dimension of law should be narrowly defined, as it is confined to the non-genuinely obligatory instantiations of what is normative. Accordingly, social-practice legal positivists can stick to the claim that law is a normative social institution, once the normativity of law is taken to be limited to single out the capacity to provide genuine *reasons* for action without necessarily extending to encompass the aptness to set forth *mandatory standards* (but for a small minority of legal subjects).

However, the view of law as a social institution constitutively unable to engender genuine obligations for the legal community at large is at odds with the widespread intuition that law is normative (also) in the sense of being an institution capable of issuing mandatory norms (or obligations in a genuine sense, as opposed to a perspectival sense) that apply as well to those living in the relevant jurisdiction who are not legal officials.[34] Such counterintuitive quality of the resulting theory of law – a theory that programmatically refrains from explaining how the law intrinsically can at least sometimes obligate in a genuine sense those who are not legal officials – is potentially problematic. The fact that the claim, while consistent within the theory, sits poorly with a widespread intuition is a problem for a twofold reason. To begin with, we should expect a theory of law to make sense of, rather than contradict, our common-sense understanding of the law. To continue, social-practice legal positivism is cast

[34] So widespread is this view that it can be argued to find recognition even among some of the proponents of the conception of law as a shared activity. See, e.g., Shapiro 2011: 113–15.

within the paradigm of analytical jurisprudence and, within this paradigm, ordinary intuitions and common assumptions are recognised as playing a prominent role.[35] Accordingly, the fact that several legal scholars and practitioners alike (not to mention lay people) see a strict connection between law and rationality-related obligation is a concern that social-practice legal positivists should take seriously.

The reason why the theory of legal obligation put forward by the proponents of social-practice legal positivism should strike us as questionable can be reformulated in the following terms. Setting forth obligations is commonly regarded as a typical way for law to provide guidance – it may not be seen as the only way, but it is seen by many as one of the essential ways. An account of the action-guiding function of law, therefore, can hardly be found to be sufficiently comprehensive and widely appealing unless it explains the sense in which the obligations that the law engenders are practical-general obligations for the totality, or at least the vast majority, of those living under a legal system. Social-practice legal positivism fails precisely in that respect: It allows for the possibility only that legal obligations genuinely bind a minority of legal subjects, which means that the very statements through which the law sets out obligations play no direct action-guiding role in relation to the community at large. Likewise, in the legal theory of the advocates of social-practice legal positivism for a significant part of the population, the action-guiding function of law will have to be fulfilled through mechanisms that do not involve recourse to obligations. And this is a picture running contrary to the commonly held view that law goes hand in hand with obligations qua mandatory normative statements; namely, it is a picture that does not accommodate the broadly accepted idea that the law is capable of *generally* shaping the behaviour of those under its jurisdiction, and one fundamental and paradigmatic way in which the law fulfils such general guidance function is *by setting forth obligations* for them. For this reason, not only lay people but also jurists, legal practitioners and legal philosophers, even if they are not averse to the broader legal-positivist project of which the theory is a part, could well find unpalatable social-practice legal positivism qua a conception that does not come to terms with the pervasive idea of law as an institution affecting the normative status of all legal subjects by means of the obligations it engenders.

[35] For a detailed account of this role, see Shapiro 2011: 13–22, among others.

17.4 Conclusion

This chapter was conceived as a reasoned and critical introduction to social-practice legal positivism. I considered the appeal that this approach may have as a form of legal positivism, but I also came upon a counterintuitive theoretical implication of proceeding from it in an attempt to explain the normativity of law. In the latter context, I argued that social-practice legal positivism cannot fully explain the capacity that the law is broadly acknowledged to have in giving rise to practical standards that are both *genuinely* and *generally* binding – genuinely binding in the sense that legal obligations are ultimately rooted in practical rationality, generally binding in the sense that they apply to all legal subjects and not just to those who play a role in enacting, administering and interpreting laws. Related to this, I claimed that social-practice legal positivism conceptualises legal obligation, qua a demand addressing the population living within the jurisdiction of a legal system, as a perspectival statement of what is obligatory under the law. And such conceptualisation of legal obligation as a perspectival demand runs contrary to the common-sense and widely held view that the law guides and governs action in part by issuing obligations, understood as statements of what is *required* of us, regardless of the role we may play as legal subjects. This suggests that, while social-practice legal positivism acknowledges that in law the social is combined with the normative, it cannot adequately explain the dual nature of law. Or, stated otherwise: In building on the insight that law is not entirely or reductively social – for there is always a normative dimension to it – social-practice legal positivism fails to extract from the law's social make-up the kind of robust normativity it is understood to have in shaping the behaviour of those who are subject to it even if they are not legal officials.

References

Bertea, S. 2019. *A Theory of Legal Obligation*. Cambridge University Press: 74–103.

Bix, B. 2005. 'Legal Positivism'. In M. Golding and W. Edmundson (eds.). *The Blackwell Guide to the Philosophy of Law and Legal Theory*. Blackwell: 29–49.

Bratman, M. 2002. 'Shapiro on Legal Positivism and Jointly Intentional Activity'. *Legal Theory* 8(4): 511–17.

Coleman, J. 2001a. 'Incorporationism, Conventionality, and the Practical Difference Thesis'. In J. Coleman. *Hart's Postscript.* Oxford University Press: 99–147.
Coleman, J. 2001b. *The Practice of Principle.* Oxford University Press.
Coleman, J. and Leiter, B. 1996. 'Legal Positivism'. In D. Patterson (ed.). *A Companion to the Philosophy of Law and Legal Theory.* Blackwell: 241–60.
Den Hartog, G. 2002. *Mutual Expectations.* Kluwer.
Gardner, J. 2001. 'Legal Positivism: 5½ Myths'. *American Journal of Jurisprudence* 46: 199–227.
Green, L. 1983. 'Law, Co-ordination and the Common Good'. *Oxford Journal of Legal Studies* 3: 299–324.
Green, L. 1985. 'Authority and Convention'. *Philosophical Quarterly* 35: 329–46.
Green, L. 1988. *The Authority of the State.* Oxford University Press.
Green, L. 1999 'Positivism and Conventionalism'. *Canadian Journal of Law and Jurisprudence* 12: 35–52.
Green, L. 2018. 'Legal Positivism'. In E. N. Zalta (ed.). *Stanford Encyclopedia of Philosophy.* https://plato.stanford.edu/archives/spr2018/entries/legal-positivism/.
Hart, H. L. A. [1961]1994. *The Concept of Law.* 2nd ed. With a Postscript. Clarendon Press.
Hershovitz, S. 2015. 'The End of Jurisprudence'. *The Yale law Journal* 124(4): 1160–1204.
Himma, K. E. 2004. 'Inclusive legal Positivism'. In J. Coleman and S. Shapiro (eds.). *The Oxford Handbook of Jurisprudence and Philosophy of Law.* Oxford University Press: 126–65.
Kelsen, H. 1934. 'The Pure Theory of Law'. *The Law Quarterly Review* 50: 474–98.
Kelsen, H. 1945. *General Theory of Law and State.* Harvard University Press.
Kelsen, H. 1967. *Pure Theory of Law.* University of California Press.
Kutz, C. 2001. 'The Judicial Community'. *Philosophical Issues* 11: 442–69.
Lagerspetz, E. 1995. *The Opposite Mirror.* Kluwer.
Marmor, A. 2001. *Positive Law and Objective Values.* Oxford University Press.
Marmor, A. 2006. 'How Law Is Like Chess'. *Legal Theory* 12: 347–71.
Marmor, A. 2007. 'Deep Conventions'. *Philosophy and Phenomenological Research* 74: 586–610.
Marmor, A. 2009. *Social Conventions: From Language to Law.* Princeton University Press.
Marmor, A. 2011. *Philosophy of Law.* Princeton University Press.
Perry, S. 2009. 'Beyond the Distinction between Positivism and Non-positivism'. *Ratio Juris* 22: 311–25.
Postema, G. 1982. 'Coordination and Convention at the Foundations of Law'. *Journal of Legal Studies* 11: 165–203.)
Postema, G. 1987. 'The Normativity of Law'. In R. Gavison (ed.). *Issues in Contemporary Legal Philosophy.* Oxford University Press: 81–104.
Raz, J. 1979. *The Authority of Law: Essays on Law and Morality.* Oxford University Press.
Raz, J. 1986. *The Morality of Freedom.* Oxford University Press.

Raz, J. 1994. *Ethics in the Public Domain: Essays in the Morality of Law and Politics*. Clarendon Press.

Raz, J. 1999. *Engaging Reason*. Oxford University Press.

Raz, J. 2009. *Between Authority and Interpretation*. Oxford University Press.

Sanchez Brigido, R. 2009. 'Collective Intentional Activities and the Law'. *Oxford Journal of Legal Studies* 29: 309–24.

Shapiro, S. 2002. 'Law, Plans, and Practical Reason', *Legal Theory* 8: 387–441.

Shapiro, S. 2011. *Legality*. Cambridge University Press.

Spaak, T. 2018. 'Legal Positivism, Conventionalism, and the Normativity of Law'. *Jurisprudence* 9: 1–26.

18 Social Facts and Legal Facts: Perils of Hume's Guillotine

Tomasz Gizbert-Studnicki *

18.1 Introduction

The social thesis claiming that law is a matter of social facts is the fundamental thesis of legal positivism. This thesis, however, has at least three versions:

(i) the social sources thesis (SST), in which 'the existence of law requires some form of social practice that includes judges and ordinary citizens, and this social practice determines, in any given legal system, the ultimate sources of law, or the ultimate criteria or ultimate tests for legal validity';[1]

(ii) the sources thesis (ST), in which 'in any legal system, whether a given norm is legally valid, and hence whether it forms part of the law of that system, depends on its sources, not its merits';[2] and

(iii) the social fact thesis (SFT), in which 'legal facts are ultimately determined by social facts alone'.[3]

Comparison of these three versions of the social thesis leads to the conclusion that the three levels need to be distinguished: (i) the level of social facts (social practice), (ii) the level of the sources of law and (iii) the level of legal facts (or legal content). The SST is a claim regarding the relationship between the first and second levels; the ST is a claim regarding the relationship between the second and third levels; the SFT is a claim regarding the relationship between the first and third levels. In this chapter,

* Thanks to Torben Spaak and Adam Dyrda for helpful extensive comments and to the participants of the Stockholm Conference in November 2018 for their suggestions.

[1] Hart 2016: 461.

[2] Gardner 2001: 199. This thesis can also be read as a version of the separation thesis. See Marmor 2011: ch. X.

[3] Shapiro 2011: 269.

I will focus exclusively on the SFT as it seems to be stronger than the ST and the SST in the sense that it encompasses both.

18.2 Legal Facts and Social Facts

18.2.1 Legal Facts

The concept of a legal fact is not unproblematic.[4] The simple mode or reasoning behind it is as follows: We want to say that certain legal propositions are true; for example, it is true that a car driver should not drive at a speed exceeding a certain limit, or it is true that Jones legally owes $100 to Smith. If these propositions are true, then there must exist an extralinguistic item that renders them true. Such an item is a legal fact.

Shapiro defines the concept of a legal fact as follows: '[A] legal fact is a fact about either the existence or the content of a particular legal system. It is a legal fact, for example, that Bulgaria has a legal system. Similarly, it is a legal fact that the law in California prohibits driving in excess of 65 miles per hour.'[5] I will leave aside the question of whether the existence of a legal system should be considered as a legal fact and I will deal exclusively with legal facts as facts about legal content.

Legal facts are normative since they encompass duties, rights, privileges, powers and so forth. They cannot be described without the use of deontic words such as 'ought to', 'is entitled to' and so forth. Two senses of the normativity of legal facts should be distinguished. In the weak sense, 'being normative' means 'being relative to a norm'. A norm is a rule or a standard with which something either does or does not conform.[6] The proposition 'driving with excess speed is prohibited' simply says that such driving does not conform to a valid rule of a certain legal system.

In the strong sense, normativity is linked to reason-giving. A fact is normative if it encompasses the reasons for action.[7] The proposition 'driving with excess speed is prohibited' describes a normative fact in the strong sense if it means that drivers have reasons not to exceed the speed limit. The metaphysical question here concerns whether and how normative facts in this strong sense exist. Realists claim that there exist normative facts that render the corresponding normative propositions true; however,

[4] See, e.g., Gkouvas 2016. [5] Shapiro 2011: 25. [6] See Finley 2010: 332. [7] Ibid.

antirealists claim that normativity is only a feature of our concepts and not a part of the furniture of the world.[8] For the purposes of this chapter, I will assume the realist position that legal facts are normative in the strong sense.

18.2.2 Social Facts

Social facts can be stated in purely descriptive terms, without the use of any moral (*good, bad, fair*) or deontic (for example, *obligation, right, entitlement*) terms. In order to be social, a fact must involve a human being.[9] Social facts encompass instances of human actions, human beliefs, attitudes and dispositions), as well as the existence of certain products of human actions, such as facts regarding the meaning of utterances.[10] Social facts must involve intentionality.

Legal positivists contrast social facts with moral facts. 'One who thinks that moral facts play some role in the ultimate determination of legal content is by definition a natural lawyer.'[11] The very idea of a moral fact is controversial since talking about moral facts assumes moral realism. Moral realism is the view that moral claims report facts and they are true if they get the facts right. If one wishes to avoid commitment to moral realism, Shapiro's thesis can be reformulated by replacing 'moral facts' with 'moral merits'. The 'social facts/moral facts' distinction, however, does not suffice. Positivism generally rejects the claim that the existence of law depends on *any* merits, including moral, economic, aesthetic or instrumental merits.[12]

18.2.3 Brute and Institutional Facts

Important in the context of the SFT is the distinction between brute and institutional social facts.[13] The fact that I met John on the street is a brute fact. The fact that I have a $20 bill in my pocket is an institutional fact. It is not equivalent to the brute fact that a certain piece of paper is in my pocket.

[8] See Finley 2010: 334.

[9] Toh 2008: 446 defines social facts as empirical facts about human psychology and behaviour.

[10] See Marmor 2013: 214; Plunkett 2012: 145. [11] Shapiro 2011: 270.

[12] See Gardner 2001: 224.

[13] See Searle 2006: 57 – institutional facts are a subset of social facts.

Such a piece of paper is a dollar bill on the basis of certain rules that ascribe the feature of being a $20 bill to this particular piece of paper. These rules create the institution of money and ascribe to this piece of paper a certain function (for example, I can exchange the piece of paper for a book). The rules that create a given institution (constitutive rules) take the following form: 'X counts as Y in context C.'[14] The fact that I have a $20 bill in my pocket is an institutional fact. Institutional facts are logically dependent on constitutive rules.

A question arises regarding whether the reference to social facts in the SFT encompasses both sorts of facts or only brute facts. If the reference encompasses both sorts of facts, then the following problem arises: Institutional facts depend on the existence of constitutive rules. It is sometimes said that a social fact that determines legal facts (the content of law) can be described as follows: The parliament passed a certain statute. The social fact so described is a complex institutional fact that may arise only on the basis of constitutive rules (including the rules contained in the constitution and procedural rules governing the parliament). The rules in question are legal rules.

If a set of social facts that determine legal facts encompasses institutional facts, then the SFT turns out to be trivial. The obtaining of institutional facts presupposes the existence of rules. Therefore, legal facts ultimately depend on rules. Therefore, it is important to demonstrate that the constitutive rules on the basis of which such institutional facts arise are ultimately fully determined by brute social facts.

18.3 The Rule of Recognition and the Practice Theory of Rules

Famously, Hart claimed that the foundation of any legal system is a rule of recognition (RoR), which is a social rule. Pursuant to Hart's practice theory of social rules, a social rule R exists in a group G, provided that the following conditions are satisfied:

1. Most of the members of G regularly conform in their behaviour to the content of R.

[14] Searle 2006: 58.

2. Most of the members of G accept R as a rule, which means that:
   (a) for most of the members of G, regular conformity with R creates a reason to act in accordance with R;
   (b) most of the members of G regard R as a standard of criticism concerning the behaviour of the members of G and are hence apt to put pressure on other members of G to conform.[15]

The existence of a social rule is a matter of social facts.[16] Such facts encompass the regular behaviour, beliefs and attitudes of the members of a social group, but what does it mean that the existence of a social rule is a matter of social facts? Are social rules identical to social practices? Are social practices aggregates of brute social facts or do they also encompass institutional facts?

The view prevails that social rules cannot be identified with social practices, which are conceived of as aggregates of concrete events. Rules are abstract entities, so practices and rules metaphysically belong to different categories.[17]

Pursuant to Hart, an RoR is a social rule that sets out the criteria for the recognition of other rules as being legally valid. A rule is legally valid if it originates in a (brute or institutional) fact indicated by the RoR as a source of law.[18] There is a specific RoR for each particular legal system.

An RoR is the ultimate rule.[19] It provides the criteria for the assessment of the validity of other rules, although there are no criteria for the assessment of the validity of an RoR; it simply exists as a matter of social facts.[20]

Therefore, if Hart's central claims are true (first, that an RoR is a social rule and, second, that the existence and content of social rules are exclusively a matter of social practice, which is in turn composed exclusively of brute social facts), then Hart was successful in establishing that legal facts are ultimately determined by (brute) social facts (provided that we know what 'being a matter of' or 'being determined' mean). We need nothing more than the observance of a certain social practice in order to ascertain that a certain RoR exists, and by using the criteria set out by such an RoR

[15] See Hart 2012: 255. I use the summary of the practice theory proposed by Marmor 2011: 52.
[16] Hart 2012: 245.
[17] See Shapiro 2011: 80. On the relationship between rules and practices, see Green 2020; Kramer 2018: 16; Toh 2014: 3.
[18] See Hart 2012: 94. [19] See Hart 2012: 105. [20] See Hart 2012: 108–9.

we can determine what the sources of law are. Further, by reference to such sources, we can establish which rules are legally valid, which allows us to establish legal facts, such as 'driving in excess of 60 m/h is prohibited'. As explained, at the first level we only deal with the brute social facts that determine an RoR. At the second level, we deal with the sources of law, which are institutional facts. An RoR ascribes to certain social facts the status function of a source of law, and in this way institutional facts (such as the adoption of a statute by parliament) become possible. In turn, such institutional facts create valid legal rules on the basis of which legal facts are established.

Hart claims: '[T]he assertion that it [the rule of recognition] exists can only be an external statement of fact ... [T]he rule of recognition exists only as a complex, but normally concordant, practice of the courts, officials, and private persons in identifying the law by reference to certain criteria. Its existence is a matter of fact.'[21]

The necessary condition for an RoR to exist is that the criteria for the identification of the law set out by it are shared and followed by the 'officials' of a given legal system.[22] According to Hart, two conditions are necessary for the existence of a legal system: (i) the bulk of the population must obey the laws and (ii) the officials working within the system must accept and follow the validity criteria. Such acceptance must be mutual in the sense that it is collective in the 'we-mode' as opposed to the 'I-mode'.[23]

The problematic issue here is the use of the word 'officials'. The fact that X is an official of the system may only come into existence on the basis of the rules of that system. X is a judge because certain rules of a given legal system confer such a status on X. Being a judge is a legal institutional fact. Spaak summed this up neatly:

> [I]t is the behavior precisely of judges (together with the internal point of view) that constitutes the rules of recognition. More specifically, in order to have rules of recognition, we need to have judges; in order to have judges, we need to have rules of adjudication; and in order to have rules of adjudication, we need to have rules of recognition.[24]

Various proposals on how to solve this issue have been offered, but limited space does not allow me to discuss them.[25]

[21] Hart 2012: 110. [22] Hart 2012: 114. [23] Burazin 2018: 119. [24] Spaak 2018: 3.
[25] See, e.g., Coleman 2001: 101.

18.4 The SFT and Hume's Guillotine

Famously, David Hume refuted any reasoning based on a set of descriptive premises that results in a conclusion that contains a normative claim (Hume's Guillotine).[26] Hume did not claim that normative propositions are not truth-apt; rather, he claimed that normative conclusions do not logically follow from solely descriptive premises.

The SFT implies that since legal facts are determined solely by social facts, the derivation of a conclusion stating a legal fact from premises that exclusively state social facts is possible. If, however, legal facts are normative, such a conclusion must contain words such as 'ought to'. The premises do not contain such words, therefore the SFT seems to fall within the remit of Hume's Guillotine.

18.4.1 The Social Thesis and the Normativity Thesis

This fundamental problem of the positivist theory of law has been formulated by Postema as a question concerning the compatibility of the two key positivist claims:

(i) the normativity thesis (the NT), in which 'law is a form of practical reasoning; like morality and prudence, it defines a general framework for practical reasoning. We understand law only if we understand how it is that laws give members of a community, officials and law-subjects alike, reasons for acting'; and
(ii) the social thesis, in which 'law is a social fact; what is and what is not to count as law is a matter of fact about human social behavior and institutions which can be described in terms which do not entail any evaluation of the behavior of the institutions'.[27]

The basic question is, thus, whether the SFT can be reconciled with the NT; the answer to this question may depend on the adopted understanding of the NT.

Some legal positivists argue that the explanation of the normativity of law (that is, its power to generate reasons for action) is a sort of

[26] See Hume 1960: 496. [27] Postema 1982: 165.

'pseudoproblem'[28] and is actually equivalent to the question 'Is there a moral obligation to obey the law?'.[29] This question is a matter of moral philosophy and not of a descriptive legal theory.

Those who identify genuine reasons for action with moral reasons believe that – as law is a matter of social facts alone – there is no necessary link between law and morality. Therefore, law does not necessarily generate moral reasons. The task of legal theory might be – at the most – to explain the ability of law to make moral claims (to claim moral authority), although such claims of law are frequently untrue.[30] Again, the question of whether a specific moral claim made by law is true is a matter of moral philosophy.

Those who maintain that legal reasons are specific reasons for action that are different from and not reducible to moral reasons are directly confronted with the perils of Hume's Guillotine. They cannot argue that the answer to the question of how social facts are able to generate legal reasons belongs to the realm of moral philosophy.

I will assume that legal reasons are specific reasons that are different from moral reasons. I think that this was the position of Hart, although *The Concept of Law* is unclear in this respect. It is true that Hart claimed that people may obey the law for various reasons (fear of punishment, conformity, prudence, morality and so forth). However, in this context, Hart had in mind motivating reasons and not justificatory (normative reasons). On the other hand, Hart maintained that legal obligation is a specific kind of obligation that is different from moral obligation.[31] If there are specific legal obligations, there must be specific legal justificatory reasons that are not reducible to moral and other reasons.

18.4.2 Justificatory and Metaphysical Interpretations of the SFT

In its justificatory interpretation, the SFT claims that propositions describing legal facts can be derived from propositions that describe exclusively social facts.[32] In the formula of the SFT, the word 'determined' means 'entailed' or 'derivable'. Thus, such an interpretation focuses on the relationship between two sorts of proposition: propositions describing social facts do not contain any deontic words (such as 'ought to'), while

[28] Enoch 2011b; Schauer 2017. [29] Schauer 2017. [30] See Raz 1979.
[31] See Hart 2012: 167–80. [32] See Levenbook 2013: 77.

propositions describing legal facts do contain such words. The SFT means that propositions about social facts ('is' propositions) logically entail propositions about legal facts ('ought' propositions). Thus, the SFT triggers a logical fallacy.[33]

Such a critique of the SFT is based on identifying justification with deduction; however, we frequently accept certain conclusions that are not based on deductive reasoning. Obviously, the truth of such conclusions is not warranted by the truth of the premises. 'Ought' statements do not deductively follow from 'is' statements, but they may be somehow supported by them.

If we, however, adopt such a weak version of the SFT, it will be reduced to a triviality. Nobody denies that normative claims are (non-deductively) supported by descriptive claims. Certain theories of natural law that claim that the basis of natural law is the biological nature of human beings would certainly not deny that; therefore, the conflict between the positivist theories of law and the natural law theories would disappear, since both types of theory would justify statements relating to legal facts by appeal to statements of certain social or natural facts. The only difference would be that different facts were referred to.

Further, reasoning that leads from factual premises to normative conclusions seems to be inherently enthymematic since it assumes certain tacit premises.[34] If we say, for example, that the nature of being human is the pursuit of happiness and, therefore, every human being should pursue happiness, we tacitly adopt the normative premise that a human being ought to pursue their nature.[35] Our normative conclusion is actually supported by a set of premises containing both descriptive and normative items.[36]

In its metaphysical interpretation, the SFT claims that a certain relation of determination holds between social and legal facts. Such a determination should be conceived of as a sort of non-causal metaphysical dependence. Metaphysical dependence is a relation between entities or beings, including facts, and not between propositions about such entities: '[T]here are various ways in which one being may be said to depend upon one or

33 See Toh 2008. 34 See Toh 2008: 474.

35 The same applies to the 'background norms' referred to by Levenbook (2013) in her defense of the justificatory interpretation of the SFT.

36 See Toh 2008: 464.

more other beings, in a sense of "depend" that is distinctly metaphysical in character and that may be contrasted, thus, with various causal senses of this word.'[37] The key question is what sort of dependence holds between social and legal facts. It is a question *de re*, as opposed to a question *de dicto*.

Legal positivists tacitly assume that a metaphysical dependence holds, although they rarely ask what sort of dependence it is.[38] Two basic sorts of metaphysical dependence should be distinguished: existential dependence, which is defined by stating that 'x depends upon y for its existence means that, necessarily, x only exists because y exists'; and essential dependence, which is defined by stating that 'x depends upon y for its existence means that it is part of the essence of x that x exists only if y exists'.[39]

If we apply these concepts to the SFT, we obtain the following theses:

Existential dependence

(i) Necessarily, legal facts exist only if (certain) social facts exist.
Obviously, this wording is unsatisfactory since natural law theories do not deny that legal facts depend in this sense on social facts. Therefore, legal positivism must also accept that:

(ii) It is not true that legal facts necessarily exist only if (certain) moral facts exist.
If the SFT claims the existential dependence of legal facts upon social facts, it is equivalent to the conjunction of (i) and (ii).

Essential dependence

(i) It is part of the essence of legal facts that they exist only if (certain) social facts exist.

For the reason given, (i) must be supplemented with:

(ii) It is not part of the essence of legal facts that they exist only if (certain) moral facts exist.

If the SFT claims the essential dependence of legal facts upon social facts, it is equivalent to the conjunction of (i) and (ii).

Both of these interpretations of the SFT are problematic. The former interpretation refers to the controversial concept of necessity; indeed, most legal positivists claim that the task of legal theory is to identify the

[37] Tahko and Lowe 2016. [38] See Greenberg 2004: 158. [39] See Tahko and Lowe 2016.

necessary features of law. One such feature could be that legal facts necessarily and exclusively depend upon social facts. It is, however, unclear what 'necessity' in this context means.[40] The latter interpretation refers to another controversial concept of essence. Legal positivists tend to instead use the concept of the 'nature of law'. I will leave the question of whether the SFT implies the existential or the essential dependence of legal facts upon social facts unanswered.

18.5 Types of Metaphysical Dependence

The claim that legal facts metaphysically depend on social facts will remain ambiguous so long as we do not identify the sort of metaphysical dependence being referred to.[41] I will discuss three alternative accounts: (i) legal facts are reducible to social facts, (ii) legal facts supervene on social facts and (iii) legal facts are grounded in social facts. This list of possible accounts is probably not exhaustive.

18.5.1 Reduction

Marmor claims that Hart's theory is a reductive enterprise: 'The hallmark of Hart's theory is the idea that social rules are at the foundations of law, and that social rules, in turn, can be explained reductively in terms of people's actual conduct, beliefs and attitudes.'[42] Pursuant to Marmor, positivistic legal theories are engaged in metaphysical reduction: '[T]he idea of metaphysical reduction is to show that a distinct type of phenomenon is actually constituted by, and fully reducible to, some other, more fundamental type of phenomenon.'[43] Marmor argues that both Austin's project and Hart's project are reductionist in this sense. They both explain the law in terms of something more fundamental in nature, namely, in terms of brute social facts. Legal theory, therefore, is about the reduction of law to more fundamental social facts. Legal theory is concerned with the nature of things, and not with the content of our concepts. Marmor invokes a comparison to the reductionist projects of natural sciences. An example

[40] See Gizbert-Studnicki 2017.

[41] This section (Section 18.5) is based (with major modifications) on Gizbert-Studnicki 2016.

[42] Marmor 2013: 214. [43] Marmor 2013: 216.

of such a reduction is the reduction of biological phenomena to physical phenomena, which is successful if we can fully explain the biological phenomena in terms of physical properties.[44]

The key issue is the determination of the criteria for the success of a reductive project. As far as the natural sciences are concerned, the answer (in a simplified form) is as follows: a reduction is successful if it is based on empirical data and causal laws. Biological phenomena will be successfully reduced to physical phenomena if we demonstrate how they can be fully explained in terms of physical phenomena. This would mean that biological phenomena are nothing other than and nothing over and above physical phenomena.

If the same criteria were applied to legal theory, it would become a purely empirical enterprise. Assuming that the reduction of legal facts to social facts is based on empirical data and causal laws, legal theory would be reduced to legal sociology, and its task would consist in the exploration of the causal links between various sorts of fact. Legal theory would hence be fully naturalised, but this is not Marmor's intention, since he certainly does not opt for the naturalisation of legal theory.[45]

As Marmor expressly refers to metaphysical reduction, he means the reduction of one world item to another – namely, the reduction of legal facts to social facts. The intuition linked to reduction is that if entity x reduces to entity y, then y is more basic than x and x fully depends upon it. This implies that x is nothing more than y and nothing over and above y. X and Y are the same fact but under different descriptions.

This implies that the following requirement should be imposed: a reduction must not leave any aspect of the item unexplained. In other words, legal facts must be fully reducible to social facts. It must be demonstrated that a given legal fact and the corresponding social fact are the same fact but under different descriptions. Even if it is demonstrated that legal facts depend solely on social facts, this does not entail that legal facts are reducible to social facts. Kramer, in his critique of Marmor's reductionism, invokes the following example: Rules of syntax are constituted by the behaviour of members of a linguistic community since they are fully dependent on their behaviour. Yet, rules of syntax and linguistic behaviour are not the same world item under different descriptions.[46]

[44] Ibid. [45] See Marmor 2013: 217. [46] See Kramer 2018: 6.

Demonstration that a certain fact F_1 depends (in any sense of this word) on another fact F_2 is not sufficient to justify the thesis that F_1 is reducible to F_2. Metaphorically speaking, F_2 may be something over and above F_1.

> The reductionist about a given area of discourse ('A-discourse') maintains that its characteristic statements ('A-statements') are reducible to – analyzable or translatable – without loss of content into statements of some other type ('B-statements') . . . The reductionist accepts that there are objective facts stated by A-statements but denies that such statements report any facts over and above those stated in B-statements. A-facts are just B-facts in disguise.[47]

If Marmor is right, then any statements regarding legal facts must be translatable without loss of content into statements regarding social facts. However, I do not think that this is the case, at least when we assume that legal facts are normative in the strong sense. A description of social facts can be given without any deontic words, whereas a description of legal facts must involve deontic words. Obviously, the truth of any statement of a legal fact depends on the holding of certain social facts. This, however, does not mean that legal facts are reducible to social facts. Legal facts are 'over and above' social facts since they encompass the 'ought' that is not present in social facts. So, even if legal facts ultimately depend on social facts, legal facts are not just social facts in disguise.

18.5.2 Supervenience

Supervenience is defined as follows: a set of properties A supervenes on another set B if no two things can differ with respect to their A-properties without also differing with respect to their B-properties. Commonly, the notion of supervenience is expressed by the saying 'There cannot be an A-difference without a B-difference.' The supervenience relation is weak in the sense that it is instantiated in numerous cases, since it may hold true between properties that are not related in any other way. 'Supervenience claims, by themselves, do nothing more than state that certain patterns of property (or fact) variation hold. They are silent about why those patterns hold and about the precise nature of the dependency involved.'[48] Supervenience is not ontologically innocent. The supervening property may

[47] Hale 2019. [48] McLaughlin and Bennett 2018: 13–14.

be ontologically something over and above the properties on which it supervenes.

A question arises as to whether the relation between social and legal facts can be explained in terms of supervenience. Obviously, supervenience holds between legal facts (as supervenient) and social facts (as subvenient). This is compatible with the claim that legal facts are something over and above social facts since they are metaphysically different; they have certain properties (normativity) that social facts do not have. Hume's Guillotine does not apply here since we do not derive 'ought' from 'is'; we claim only that normativity supervenes on facticity. The problem, however, is that the account of the relation between legal and social facts – as portrayed by the notion of supervenience – does not have explanatory force. 'Supervenience itself is not an explanatory relation. It is not a "deep" metaphysical relation: rather, it is only a "surface" relation that reports a pattern of property covariation, suggesting the presence of an interesting dependency relation that may explain it.'[49]

This is the basis of the following argument:

> The antipositivist says that the legal facts supervene on the moral and the social facts taken together; but, of course the positivist will agree. The positivist says that the legal facts supervene on the social facts alone – the possible worlds cannot differ in legal respects without differing in social respects. But the antipositivist need not deny this. For he may think that whenever two worlds are alike in social respects – whenever they involve the same actions, habits and responses of human being – they must also agree in moral respects, since the moral facts themselves supervene on the social facts broadly conceived. But in that case the parties will accept the same supervenience claims. And yet they differ on an important issue, viz. whether the moral facts play a role in making the law to be as it is.[50]

The key point of this argument is contained in the last sentence. The dispute between positivists and non-positivists cannot be reduced to a question of supervenience. The question is whether social facts alone (positivist view) or social facts together with moral facts (non-positivist view) play a role in making law what it is. The mere fact that fact F_1 supervenes on fact F_2

[49] Kim 1993: 167.

[50] Rosen 2010: 113–14 (emphasis added). Chilovi and Pavlakos (2019: 63) state: '[I]f the moral facts are necessary . . ., anti-positivism will be true just in case any variation in legal facts requires a variation in social facts, just as positivism is.'

does not yet mean that F_2 plays any role in making F_1 what it is. The dispute between positivism and non-positivism does not relate to the co-variance between social, moral and legal facts but rather to the question of what makes law what it is.[51]

18.5.3 Grounding

Over the past ten or fifteen years, the conception of 'grounding' has become popular in analytic metaphysics.[52] Supposedly, Mark Greenberg was the first to use the conception of grounding in the context of the SFT: 'A preliminary point is that the determination relation with which we are concerned is primarily a metaphysical, or constitutive, one and only secondarily an epistemic one; the law-determining practices make the content of the law what it is. To put it in another way, facts about the content of the law ... obtain in virtue of the law-determining practices.'[53] Space does not allow me to offer a full picture of the discussion around grounding. The basic intuition underlying this conception is that there exists a certain non-causal relation of dependence that is usually expressed by 'in virtue of'. We say, for example, that a complex whole has certain properties in virtue of the arrangements of its parts, or that a sculpture has certain aesthetic properties in virtue of its physical properties, or that a person has reason to adopt a certain belief in virtue of their sensual perception. Grounding refers to a certain sort of metaphysical dependence that is different from causal determination. 'Grounding is something like metaphysical causation. Roughly speaking, just as causation links the world across time, grounding links the world across levels.'[54] The fundamental issue is whether the concept of grounding is primitive or if it may be subject to a reductive definition. The prevailing view is that grounding is primitive.

Grounding has different formal properties from supervenience. Grounding is asymmetric (if F_1 grounds F_2, F_2 does not ground F_1), irreflexive (no fact grounds itself) and transitive (if F_1 grounds F_2 and F_2 grounds F_3, F_1 also grounds F_3).[55] Supervenience is non-symmetric, reflexive and transitive. The grounding relation has an explanatory function. The statement 'F_1 grounds

[51] Pavlakos 2017: 143.

[52] The history of the notion of grounding is described in Correira and Schnieder 2012.

[53] Greenberg 2004: 158. [54] Schaffer 2012: 122. [55] See Trogdon 2013: 8.

F_2' constitutes an attempt to explain F_2.[56] Obviously, this is not a causal explanation. A statue has certain aesthetic properties in virtue of having certain physical properties; however, these two facts (having physical properties and having aesthetic properties) are not causally related. 'If we recognize these cases as genuine explanations, and we agree that explanations require non-explanatory relations underlying their correctness, then we are committed to recognizing non-causal relations at work in these explanations.'[57] One fact F_1 may be grounded in more than one other fact ($F_2 \ldots F_n$). Taken together, these other facts fully ground F_1, and each of F_2 to F_n partly grounds F_1 when taken separately.

The SFT claims that legal facts are ultimately determined by social facts. This may mean that legal facts hold in virtue of certain social facts alone and, therefore, that social facts fully ground legal facts. We may refer to this relation as 'normative grounding'.

The SFT requires that social facts fully ground legal facts; otherwise, there would be no difference between positivism and non-positivism. Non-positivists would certainly accept the partial grounding of legal facts in social facts since they do not deny that social facts play a role in the determination of legal facts. The thesis of positivism is that legal facts are fully grounded in social facts. Legal facts hold solely in virtue of social facts, with the exclusion of any moral facts. The SFT refers to ultimate determination; therefore, it does not deny that legal facts may be grounded non-ultimately in moral facts, provided that the relevance of moral facts to the determination of legal facts is in turn determined by social facts alone. The SFT does not deny that the criteria for legal validity may be moral, provided that an RoR that sets out such criteria is wholly grounded in social facts. Therefore, the SFT is compatible with both hard and soft positivism.

A question arises as to what sort of explanatory force may be attributed to the use of the idioms of 'grounding' and 'in virtue of' with regard to the SFT. If grounding is a primitive notion that cannot be further analysed, then replacing the phrase 'determined by' in the wording of the SFT with the phrase 'grounded in' does not move us forward as it does not hermeneutically illuminate the relationship between social and legal facts.

I do not think that such an objection is sound.

[56] See Audi 2012: 687. [57] Audi 2012: 687–8.

> We do not know how to say in more basic terms what it is for one fact to obtain in virtue of another ... But that is obviously no reason for regarding the idiom as unclear or unintelligible. Many of our best notions – the words we deem fully acceptable for rigorous exposition – do not admit of definition, the notion of metaphysical necessity being one pertinent example.[58]

However, even if we accept the philosophical legitimacy of the notion of grounding, specific objections relating to its application in the field of legal theory arise.

The positivist explanation of how legal facts come into existence in virtue of social facts alone cannot be delivered by recourse to normative facts as part of the *explanandum*, since such an explanation would be self-defeating. Indeed, legal theory would have to admit that the existence of such pre-legal or extralegal normative facts is a condition for the existence of legal facts. Therefore, the SFT must be read as a claim that social facts fully ground legal facts.[59]

The question arises as to whether the grounding account of the relation between social facts and legal facts does not fall victim to Hume's Guillotine. The famous passage from Hume indicates that he had in mind relations of entailment between sentences or propositions.[60] His claim is that 'is' propositions do not logically entail 'ought' propositions (Hume's Guillotine). However, grounding is not the same as logical entailment since it is a metaphysical relation that holds between facts. The metaphysical question is whether grounding can hold between social facts (which are descriptive) and legal facts (which are normative). Does Hume's Guillotine also apply to such a relation? Space does not allow me to discuss this question in full, and in particular to analyse the concept of metaphysical entailment. I am able to offer only a few brief observations.

It is generally accepted in metaphysics that the relation of supervenience may hold between natural (descriptive) and normative facts.

> There can be necessary relations between distinct existences, at least when the distinct existences are normative on one side, and natural on the other. Asking how this could be is another way of asking how there could be moral (and other) norms that are of maximal jurisdiction. I do not have an answer to this question, but I do not feel the need to give one.[61]

58 Rosen 2010: 113.

59 For analysis of various problems with normative grounding, see Vayrynen 2013.

60 See Hume 1960: 496. 61 See Enoch 2011a: 147.

The citation refers to supervenience. If supervenience, which is a modal relation, can hold, why can grounding not hold? Supervenience, as described is not an explanatory relation: it relates to patterns of co-variance and not to determination, but this does not matter in this context as supervenience claims require justification and obviously grounding claims also require justification. Both claims are metaphysical, so their justification should be delivered by use of metaphysical methods. In metaphysics, we must rely on our intuitions, analysis of possible cases and thought experiments. The starting point of any metaphysical analysis is certain platitudes (folk beliefs) about the matter in question. Analysis of the concept of law in analytic legal theories is a modest conceptual analysis; it does not strive to discover the true nature of mind-independent reality but rather attempts to make sense of common platitudes about law. Such platitudes also include beliefs about which social facts are normatively relevant in the sense of triggering normative facts.

Obviously, any social (non-normative) fact can ground a normative fact only as far as such a non-normative fact is normatively relevant. Therefore, if grounding is to have an explanatory function, we must admit that any explanation of normative facts has to acknowledge that there is at least one fact with normative relevance among the grounding facts.[62] This may mean that normative facts cannot be fully grounded in non-normative facts. This objection against the grounding account of the SFT is based on the assumption that the normative relevance of a non-normative fact is itself a normative fact. It is true that 'ordinary empirical facts cannot determine their own relevance to legal facts'.[63]

But this does not necessarily mean that normatively relevant facts are by themselves normative. The fact that a certain action causes harm is certainly a normatively relevant fact, but by itself it does not encompass reasons for actions. How do we know that a certain fact is normatively relevant? As far as morality is concerned, we can rely only on our intuitions, which are expressions of certain moral platitudes. How can we know that a certain social fact is (legally) normatively relevant? We can rely only on our intuitions, which are also expressions of certain platitudes that are parts of the folk theory of law.

[62] See Vayrynen 2013: 159. [63] Greenberg 2006: 14.

The claim that normative legal facts hold in virtue of non-normative social facts is not subject to Hume's Guillotine. The scheme of our reasoning about legal facts is as follows:

(i) A social fact that S is the case obtains.
(ii) Social facts of the type to which S belongs are normatively relevant and in particular ground a legal fact F.
(iii) Therefore, a legal fact F obtains.

This does not trigger Hume's Guillotine. We do not derive a normative conclusion from purely descriptive premises since the element of normativity is already contained in premise (ii). This premise is justified by folk intuitions on the same basis as any other grounding claims.

18.6 Conclusions

Local and general normative grounding should be distinguished. The claim of general normative grounding is that legal facts are grounded in social facts; in other words, any law (actual or possible) is ultimately grounded in certain social facts in such a way that is constant across jurisdictions. The claim of local normative grounding is that certain particular legal facts are grounded in certain particular social facts in a specific jurisdiction. The SFT refers to general normative grounding. Legal theory makes universal claims related to the necessary properties of law but not to the contingent properties of any specific legal system. The SFT is an example of such a universal claim. For general legal theory, the problem is in virtue of what law exists. The answer provided by legal positivism is that law ultimately exists in virtue of social facts alone.[64] It is not the task of general legal theory to determine particular social facts grounding any particular legal facts within a specific legal system. The only claim that the SFT makes is that grounding facts must necessarily belong to the category of social facts (as opposed to moral or other normative facts).

The SFT should be read together with another core positivist thesis that claims that each legal system is based on an RoR as a matter of necessity. The function of an RoR is to set out the criteria of validity and, in particular, to ascribe the status of sources of law to certain social facts. Once such facts

[64] For other arguments in favor of grounding, see Chilovi and Pavlakos 2019.

(sources of law) occur, legally valid rules are created. Each RoR is both a constitutive rule (since it confers the status of a source of law on certain facts) and a rule imposing on the officials of a given legal system the duty to recognise certain facts as sources of law. At first glance, once we explain the normativity of an RoR (that is, its ability to generate reasons for action on the part of legal officials), we are able to explain the normativity of legal facts, provided that we are able to derive the normativity of legal facts (their ability to generate reasons for action for the addressees of legal rules) from the normativity of an RoR. This derivation is, however, problematic.

Grounding helps us to explain the normativity of the RoR. Pursuant to legal positivism, an RoR is ‘a matter of social facts’. The practice theory of social rules does not claim that any social rule (including an RoR) can be reduced to a set of brute facts. The relationship between social facts (the conforming behaviour of officials, their internal attitude) and the RoR of a particular legal system can be explained as metaphysical grounding. An RoR is normative, and the social facts grounding a particular RoR are descriptive.

The application of the conception of grounding allows us to explain the normativity of the RoR, which is understood as its ability to generate reasons for action. This, however, does not explain per se the normativity of legal facts (legal content). The fact that legal officials have reason to follow an RoR does not entail that subjects of law have reason to follow legal rules.[65] Social facts that ground an RoR do not (at least directly) ground legal facts. Two problems arise here.

First, lest us assume that an RoR grounded in social facts confers on a certain other fact the status function of a source of law (for example, certain actions of certain people count as adoption of a statute). The existence of an RoR does not trigger per se any legal facts encompassing reasons for ordinary citizens. Such reasons will be created when this group of people actually adopts a statute. The rules contained in the statute will create legal content (for example, driving with excess speed is prohibited) and, thus, a legal fact will come into existence. The social facts grounding an RoR do not determine this legal fact because the legal content depends on the decision of the people referred to above. Such facts *via* an RoR are a necessary condition only for the obtaining of any legal facts (in the

[65] ‘The normative force of the rule of recognition cannot be transmitted down to the lower levels of Stufenbau’ (Spaak 2005: 412).

absence of an RoR, no legal facts could obtain). Further, a statute as such does not fully determine the legal content, at least when the statute requires interpretation. What the legal facts eventually are (facts about legal content) depends (or at least may depend) on the method of interpretation.[66] Therefore, facts about legal content are not fully and ultimately grounded in brute social facts, at least when legal rules require interpretation.

Second, reasons encompassed by facts about legal content seem to be different from the reasons to follow an RoR. What sort of reasons do legal officials have to follow an RoR? Without going into the details of the dispute between the externalist and the internalist accounts of reasons, let me offer a few brief observations. Hart emphasised that the mere regularity of the behaviour of officials does not suffice for the existence of an RoR. In addition, officials must adopt the internal point of view with regard to an RoR, which means that they must accept the RoR and agree to use it as a guide for their behaviour. Therefore, the reasons for following the RoR must be actual internal reasons that the legal officials must be aware of and that must play a certain role in their motivation. The objectivist (externalist or counterfactual internalist) account of legal reasons does not allow for the explanation of the normativity of the RoR. Legal officials' reasons must be actual internal reasons that play a role in the officials' motivation.[67] These reasons are both motivational and justificatory.

Yet, legal reasons generated by facts about legal content have different characteristics. 'I ought to pay taxes' means that I have a legal reason to pay taxes, even if I am unaware of the valid legal rule imposing such a duty on me. Legal reasons do not have to play a role in my actual motivation since legal duties are independent of what I know or desire. Therefore, actual internalism is not an account of the reasons for action that is able to explain the normativity of legal content; such an explanation can be delivered only by externalism or counterfactual internalism.[68]

If this is true, then the reasons generated by an RoR are of a different type to the reasons encompassed by facts about legal content. This means that

[66] See Chapter 19 in this volume. [67] See Dyrda 2015: 237.

[68] Externalism explains normative reasons without reference to motivations and desires. Actual internalism claims that normative reasons always bear some relation to actual motivation and/or desire. Counterfactual internalism claims that if an agent has a reason to do A, then it necessarily follows that they would be motivated to some degree or desire to do A, provided that their rational deliberations are based on the possession of full information.

the normativity of an RoR differs from the normativity of legal content established on the basis of legal rules. This does not seem surprising in the context of Hart's theory. The status of an RoR is different from the status of legal rules. Although an RoR represents the foundation of every legal system, according to Hart's theory it is not a legal rule or, at least, the question of the legal validity of an RoR does not arise.[69] The reasons generated by an RoR are not legal reasons; therefore, the explanation of the normativity of an RoR as a social rule cannot be designed in the same way as the explanation of the normativity of valid legal rules.

This, however, triggers a couple of difficult questions. First, if an RoR is not a valid legal rule, then the duty of legal officials to apply it is not a legal duty, which seems paradoxical. Second, if the normativity of an RoR is not legal normativity, then how is it able to generate the ability of legal rules to produce legal content encompassing legal reasons for action? In other words, how can the internal subjective reasons of officials generate objective reasons for the addressees of legal rules that do not depend on the actual knowledge and motivation of an agent?

References

Audi, P. 2012. 'Grounding: Towards a Theory of the In-Virtue-Of Relation'. *Journal of Philosophy* CIX 12: 685–711.

Levenbook, B. 2013. 'How to Hold the Social Fact Thesis: A Reply to Greenberg and Toh'. In L. Green and B. Leiter (eds.). *Oxford Studies in Philosophy of Law* vol. 2. Oxford University Press: 75–103.

Burazin, L. 2018. 'Legal Systems as Abstract Institutional Artifacts'. In L. Burazin, K. E. Himma and C. Roversi (eds.). *Law as an Artifact*. Oxford University Press: 112–35.

Chilovi, C. and Pavlakos, G. 2019. 'Law-Determination as Grounding: A Common Grounding Framework for Jurisprudence'. *Legal Theory* 25: 53–76.

Coleman, J. 2001. *The Practice of Principles*. Oxford University Press.

Correira, F. and Schnieder, B. 2012. 'Grounding: An Opinionated Introduction'. In F. Correira and B. Schnieder (eds.). *Metaphysical Grounding: Understanding the Structure of Reality*. Cambridge University Press: 2–10.

Dyrda, A. 2015. 'Are Fundamental Legal Reasons Internal? A Few Remarks on the Hartian Idea of Internal Point of View'. In M. Araszkiewicz, P. Banas, T. Gizbert-

[69] See Hart 2012: 109.

Studnicki and K. Pleszka (eds.). *Problems of Normativity, Rules and Rule-Following*. Springer: 229–42.

Enoch, D. 2011a. *Taking Morality Seriously: A Defence of Robust Realism*. Oxford University Press.

Enoch, D. 2011b. 'Reason Giving and the Law'. In L. Green and B. Leiter (eds.). *Oxford Studies in Philosophy of Law* vol. I. Oxford University Press: 1–38.

Finley, S. 2010. 'Recent Work on Normativity'. *Analysis* 70 (2): 331–46.

Gardner, J. 2001. 'Legal Positivism: 5½ Myths'. *The American Journal of Jurisprudence* 46: 199–227.

Gizbert-Studnicki, T. 2016. 'The Social Sources Thesis, Metaphysics and Metaphilosophy'. In P. Banas, A. Dyrda and T. Gizbert-Studnicki (eds.). *Metaphilosophy of Law*. Hart: 121–46.

Gizbert-Studnicki, T. 2017. *Legal Theory's Claim to Necessity*. http://dx.doi.org/10.2139/ssrn.3050442.

Gkouvas, T. 2016. 'Legal Truth without Legal Fact: A Metaontological Argument'. In A. F. L. de Paula, A. S. Santacoloma and G. F. Rosas (eds.). *Truth and Objectivity in Law and Morals* II. ARSP Beiheft, Band 151: 25–48.

Green, M. S. 2020. 'The Semantic Thesis in Legal Positivism'. In P. Mindus and T. Spaak (eds.). *The Cambridge Companion to Legal Positivism*. Cambridge University Press.

Greenberg, M. 2004. 'How Facts Make Law'. *Legal Theory* 10: 157–98.

Greenberg, M. 2006. 'Hartian Positivism and Normative Facts: How Facts Make Law II'. In S. Hershovitz (ed.). *Exploring Law's Empire: The Jurisprudence of Ronald Dworkin*. Oxford University Press: 265–90.

Hale, B. 2019. 'Realism/Philosophy'. *Encyclopedia Britannica*. www.britannica.com/topic/realism-philosophy.

Hart, H. L. A. 2012. *The Concept of Law*. 3rd ed. Clarendon Press.

Hart, H. L. A. [1979]2016. 'The New Challenge to Legal Positivism'. *Oxford Journal of Legal Studies* 36: 459–75.

Hume, D. 1960. *A Treatise on Human Nature*. Clarendon Press.

Kim, J. 1993. 'Postscripts on Supervenience'. In J. Kim. *Supervenience and Mind: Selected Philosophical Essays*. Cambridge University Press: 161–73.

Kramer, M. 2018. *Hart and the Metaphysics and Semantics of Legal Normativity*. http://dx.doi.org/10.2139/ssrn.3116861.

Marmor, A. 2011. *Philosophy of Law*. Princeton University Press.

Marmor, A. 2013. 'Farewell to Conceptual Analysis'. In W. Waluchow and S. Sciaraffa (eds.). *Philosophical Foundations of the Nature of Law*. Oxford University Press: 209–29.

McLaughlin, B. and Bennett, K. 2018. 'Supervenience'. In E. N. Zalta (ed.). *Stanford Encyclopedia of Philosophy*. https://plato.stanford.edu/archives/spr2018/entries/supervenience/.

Pavlakos, G. 2017. 'The Metaphysics of Law: From Supervenience to Rational Justification'. In B. Brozek, A. Rotolo and J. Stelmach (eds.). *Supervenience and Normativity*. Springer: 139–60.

Plunkett, D. 2012. 'A Positivistic Route for Explaining How Facts Make Law'. *Legal Theory* 18: 139–207.

Postema, G. 1982. 'Coordination and Convention at the Foundations of Law'. *Journal of Legal Studies* XI: 165–203.

Raz, J. 1979. *The Authority of Law*. Clarendon Press.

Rosen, G. 2010. 'Metaphysical Dependence: Grounding and Reduction'. In B. Hale and A. Hoffman (eds.). *Modality: Metaphysics, Logic and Epistemology*. Oxford University Press: 109–35.

Searle, J. 2006. 'Social Ontology: Some Basic Principles'. *Anthropological Theory* 6(1): 12–29.

Schaffer, J. 2012. 'Grounding, Transitivity, and Contrastivity'. In F. Correira and B. Schnieder (eds.). *Metaphysical Grounding: Understanding the Structure of Reality*. Cambridge University Press: 122–38.

Shapiro, S. 2011. *Legality*. Harvard University Press.

Schauer, F. 2017. *Deconstructing Law's Normativity*. https://papers.ssrn.com/sol3/papers.cfm?abstract_id=3080437.

Spaak, T. 2005. 'Kelsen and Hart on the Normativity of Law'. In P. Wahlgren and M. Zamboni (eds.). *Perspectives on Jurisprudence: Essays in Honour of Jes Bjarup*. Stockholm Institute for Scandinavian Law: 397–414.

Spaak, T. 2018. 'Legal Positivism, Conventionalism and the Normativity of Law'. *Jurisprudence* 9(2): 319–44.

Tahko, T. and Lowe, E. J. 2016. 'Ontological Dependence'. In E. N. Zalta (ed.). *Stanford Encyclopedia of Philosophy*. https://plato.stanford.edu/archives/win2016/entries/dependence-ontological/.

Toh, K. 2008. 'An Argument against the Social Fact Thesis (and Some Additional Preliminary Steps Towards a New Conception of Legal Positivism'. *Law and Philosophy* 27: 445–504.

Toh, K. 2014. 'Four Neglected Prescriptions of Hartian Legal Philosophy'. *Law and Philosophy* 33: 689–724.

Trogdon, K. 2013. 'An Introduction to Grounding'. In M. Hoeltje, M. Schnieder and A. Steinberg (eds.). *Varieties of Dependence: Ontological Dependence, Grounding, Supervenience, Response-Dependence (Basic Philosophical Concepts)*. Philosophia Verlag: 97–122.

Vayrynen, P. 2013. 'Grounding and Normative Explanation'. *Proceedings of Aristotelian Society* (Supplementary Volume) 87: 155–78.

19 The Scope of Legal Positivism: Validity or Interpretation?

Torben Spaak *

19.1 Introduction

The theory of legal positivism has been much discussed over the years, and able writers have defended competing versions of it. These writers disagree not just about details but about the interpretation of the main tenets of legal positivism: the social thesis, the separation thesis and the thesis of social efficacy. As a result, there is some uncertainty about the scope of legal positivism. There is, in particular, the question of whether the social thesis applies not only to the level of sources of law but also to the level of interpretation and application of the law. In this chapter, I am going to argue (A) that legal positivists have reason to conceive of the social thesis as a thesis about sources of law only, (i) because if they do, inclusive legal positivists will not have to assume that legal statements can be true or false in a non-relative way, and exclusive legal positivists will not have to hold that judges create new law as soon as they invoke moral considerations in their reasoning, and (ii) because doing so will undermine Ronald Dworkin's well-known theoretical disagreement objection. I am also going to argue (B) that legal positivism, conceived along the lines of (A), will still be a significant theory.

I begin by briefly explaining, in Section 19.2, how I understand the main tenets of legal positivism, giving special consideration to the social thesis. In Section 19.3, I then introduce the distinction between the level of

* I would like to thank Staffan Carlshamre and Luka Burazin; the participants in the Cambridge Companion to Legal Positivism Conference 1 at Stockholm University, 13–15 November 2018, especially Brian Leiter and Kevin Toh; the participants in the advanced seminar in practical philosophy at the Department of Philosophy, Uppsala University; and the participants in the workshop on legal philosophy at the Philosophy Days, Uppsala University, 25 August 2017, for a number of helpful comments on this chapter in its various stages. Finally, I would like to thank Robert Carroll for checking my English. The usual caveat applies, of course: The author alone is responsible for any remaining mistakes and imperfections.

sources of law and the level of interpretation and application of the law and proceed to argue, in Sections 19.4–19.6, that if legal positivists conceive of the social thesis as a thesis about sources of law only, they can avoid the difficulties mentioned in (Ai). Next, in Section 19.7, I consider and reject Ronald Dworkin's well-known theoretical disagreement objection, on the grounds that the instances of theoretical disagreement that Dworkin identifies belong on the level of interpretation and application of the law, not on the level of sources of law. Having done that, in Section 19.8, I consider and reject a possible objection to my account, namely, that the very distinction between the existence and the interpretation of legal norms cannot be upheld. The chapter concludes, in Section 19.9, with a consideration of the significance of legal positivism, featuring the social thesis conceived as a thesis about sources of law.

19.2 Legal Positivism

Legal positivism, as I see it, is a theory of law (in a wide sense of the term 'theory') of the type defended by legal thinkers such as John Austin,[1] Hans Kelsen,[2] Alf Ross,[3] H. L. A. Hart,[4] Joseph Raz,[5] Neil MacCormick[6] and Jules Coleman,[7] not a theory telling the judge how he should decide hard cases or when civil disobedience is justified. What legal positivism thus conceived does is to lay down conditions that have to be satisfied by anything that purports to be a correct theory of law – if *X* does not satisfy the relevant conditions, *X* will not and cannot be a correct theory of law.

Although legal positivists differ on a number of issues, almost all of them accept three central tenets, namely, the social thesis, the separation thesis and the thesis of social efficacy.[8] In addition, some legal positivists accept a fourth thesis, namely, the semantic thesis.[9] Crudely put: the social thesis has it that what is law and what is not is a matter of social fact; the

[1] See Austin [1832]1998. [2] See Kelsen [1934]1994; 1960; [1945]1999.
[3] See Ross [1961]1998. [4] See Hart 1961; 1982. [5] See Raz [1979]2009; [1985]1994.
[6] See MacCormick 1985–6. [7] See Coleman 2001.
[8] Raz is an exception. He accepts the social thesis but rejects the separation thesis (and the semantic thesis). See Raz [1979]2009: 38–9. Note also that different writers may refer to essentially the same tenets in slightly different ways. For example, Coleman 2001: 75, 104 calls the social thesis the 'social fact thesis' and the separation thesis the 'separability thesis'.
[9] See, e.g., Kelsen [1945]1999: 60 and Hart 1982: 159–60. See also Holmes 1896–7: 461.

separation thesis says that there is no necessary connection between law and (true) morality; the thesis of social efficacy says that the validity (or existence) of law presupposes that it is socially efficacious; and the semantic thesis (in its most common form) has it that legal normative or evaluative terms have a different meaning (sense) from the corresponding moral terms, if there are any.

Like Raz,[10] Coleman,[11] Simmonds[12] and others, I believe that the backbone of legal positivism is to be found in the social thesis. The precise meaning of this thesis has been debated by legal positivists in the past thirty years or so, however. While exclusive legal positivists argue that, properly understood, the social thesis requires (in a conceptual sense) the use of *exclusively* factual criteria of legal validity, and that any reference to moral values is best understood as granting the judge power and discretion to create new law,[13] inclusive legal positivists maintain instead that the criteria of validity can, but need not, be of a moral nature, provided that they are grounded in facts.[14] That is to say, whereas inclusive legal positivists insist on a distinction between the basis and the content of criteria of validity and hold that the social thesis is satisfied if the basis of such criteria is (exclusively) factual, even if the content is not, exclusive legal positivists maintain that both the basis and the content need to be exclusively factual. We may express the strong and the weak social theses, respectively, in the language of first-order quantificational modal logic as follows:

The strong social thesis: $\Box(\forall x)(Nx \supset (\exists y)(Sy \,\&\, (\exists z)(Fz \,\&\, Dxyz)))$. (Necessarily, for any legal norm, *x*, there is a source of law, *y*, and there is a set of exclusively factual considerations, *z*, and *x* is determined with the help of *y* on the basis of *z*.)

The weak social thesis: $\Box(\forall x)(Nx \supset (\exists y)(Sy \,\&\, ((\exists z)(Fz \,\&\, Dxyz) \vee (\exists w)(Mw \,\&\, Dxyw)))$. (Necessarily, for any legal norm, *x*, there is a source of law, *y*, and there is a set of exclusively factual considerations, *z*, and *x* is determined with the help of *y* on the basis of *z*, or there is a set of moral considerations that have an exclusively factual basis, *w*, and *x* is determined with the help of *y* on the basis of *w*.)

Note that inclusive legal positivists must reasonably presuppose that moral judgements are, or can be, true or false in a non-relative sense – if they did not, they could not plausibly maintain that a judge who is making a moral

[10] See Raz [1979]2009: 38. [11] See Coleman 2001: 75; Coleman 2009: 383.
[12] See Simmonds 2002: 127–31. [13] See Raz 1986: 1110.
[14] See Coleman 2001: ch. 7; Hart 1994: 247–8, 250–1; Waluchow 1994.

judgement is determining what the law *is*, but would have to say instead that such a judge is creating new law. For, if moral judgements cannot be true or false at all (expressivism), or if they are all false (error theory), then there will be no moral properties at all and hence no such property that a valid legal norm will or will not have; and if moral judgements can be true or false only in a relative sense (meta-ethical relativism), there will be no non-relative answer to the question of whether the legal norm has the relevant property. Thus, it seems that if one rejects the view that moral judgements can be true or false in a non-relative sense, one will have to reject inclusive legal positivism.[15]

19.3 Two Levels of Legal Thinking

The pros and cons of legal positivism, as well as legal positivism's relation to natural law theory and other theories that emphasise a necessary connection between law and morality, have been discussed for many years, but it seems to me that the participants in these debates have, on the whole, failed to consider the implications of a very natural distinction between two levels of legal thinking. The idea is simply that it is one question whether a given norm (rule, principle, standard and so forth) is legally valid, that is, exists as a legal norm, and another question just how this legally valid norm is to be interpreted and applied. To determine whether a norm is legally valid, one consults the (traditional) sources of law: legislation, custom and precedent. And to determine how this legally valid norm is to be understood and applied, one makes use of the tools of the legal method (as it is called in the Nordic countries), such as the interpretive arguments (textual, systemic, intentionalist or teleological interpretive arguments), the modalities of decision (plain application, *contra legem* decision, liberal interpretation, strict interpretation, analogy, *argumentum contrario*), as I call them, the rule of lenity, the principle of legality, interpretive presumptions, such as 'courts should accept agency interpretations unless they are obviously wrong', conflict-solving maxims

[15] Interestingly, Hart 1982: 159–60 was a non-cognitivist who accepted inclusive legal positivism (Hart 1994: 250). The solution to the problem is perhaps that Hart was a *hybrid* non-cognitivist in the sense proposed by Raz 1993: 147–9 or in that proposed by Toh 2005: 85–91.

such as *lex superior*, *lex posterior* and *lex specialis*, and more.[16] Accordingly, we make a distinction between the level of sources of law (validity, existence) and the level of interpretation and application of the law (interpretation, content).

As I have said, I find the distinction between these two levels of legal thinking very natural. We might think of it as a distinction between the determination of the object of interpretation and the determination of the (correct) interpretation of the object of interpretation – if you do not know precisely what the object of interpretation is, how can you carry out the process of interpretation (and application) in a rational way? Moreover, the distinction appears to be generally accepted by legal scholars, including philosophers of law. For example, discussing the components that go into a full-fledged theory of legal reasoning, Michael Moore distinguishes between the question of whether some text is a legal text, that is, belongs to the law, and the question of how this text is to be interpreted.[17] Similarly, Alf Ross in his book *On Law and Justice* makes a distinction between what he refers to as the doctrine of the sources of law and the method(s) of interpretation, arguing that the former provides us with valid legal rules, whereas the latter tells us how to interpret and apply such valid legal rules.[18] Ross also points out that legislation, precedent and custom, conceived as sources of law, differ in an important way: Whereas legislation provides us with finished products, as he puts it, that is, ready-made legal norms (rules), precedent and custom provide us only with semi-finished products that will have to be completed by the judge.[19] The difference identified by Ross between legislation, on the one hand, and precedent and custom (and reason), on the other, is of interest in this context, because it is clearly more natural to distinguish between validity and interpretation of legal norms when they come more or less ready-made from a source of law than when they have to be constructed in some fashion by the judge on the basis of a certain legal raw-material. For, in the former case but not in the latter, one can plausibly maintain that there is something that in many cases can guide human behaviour as it stands, and the capacity to guide human behaviour is surely a central function of legal norms. The reason why ready-made legal norms in many cases can guide human behaviour as they stand is simply that law-appliers can

[16] I discuss the legal method in Spaak 2007: ch. 3. [17] See Moore 1985: 283.
[18] See Ross 1959: chs. 3–4. [19] See Ross 1959: 76–7.

typically (but not invariably) be relied on to respect their wording – if law-appliers did not reliably respect the wording of legal norms, the latter could not guide behaviour without having first been interpreted by the former, since the law-subjects would otherwise have no idea what the norms require of them.

19.4 The Social Thesis: Its Content and Scope I

Against this background, it is easy to see that Kelsen's and Hart's primary interest was in the question of the *validity* (or existence) of law; they actually had very little to say about the interpretation and application of the law. Thus, Kelsen devotes 8 of about 350 pages in the second edition of *Reine Rechtslehre* to legal interpretation,[20] and Hart devotes 1 chapter of *The Concept of Law* and 1 section of his 1958 article on legal positivism to rebutting the positions known as formalism and rule-scepticism.[21] Accordingly, Kelsen and Hart understood the social thesis to be a thesis about sources of law in the (traditional) sense identified by Raz (see Section 19.5), namely, legislation, precedent and custom, which concern precisely the validity of legal norms. It is, however, worth noting that, unlike Hart, Kelsen paid very little attention to the social thesis in his writings and rather took it for granted.

Kelsen explains that any theory that recognises nothing but positive law as law is a legal-positivistic theory, and that the idea of positivity is precisely that the *validity* of law in the sense of bindingness and, indirectly, in the sense of membership in the system depends on *facts* (*Tatsachen*).[22] These facts, he explains, are of two types, namely, (i) enactment or, more broadly, creation (*Erzeugung*) and (ii) social efficacy (*Wirksamkeit*). Whereas (i) is the idea of the social thesis, (ii) is the idea of the thesis of social efficacy. Our concern here is with (i), however, and Kelsen takes it to require that the acts through which law is created be *human* acts: 'Vom Standpunkt des Rechtspositivismus aus müssen die Akte, durch die das Recht gesetzt (*ius positivum*) oder, wie man figürlich sagt, "erzeugt" wird, Akte von *Menschen* sein. Nur durch Menschen gesetztes Recht ist positives

[20] See Kelsen 1960. [21] See Hart 1958: 606–15; Hart 1961.

[22] Kelsen 1965: 465. On Kelsen's analysis, positivity is a necessary, but not a sufficient, condition for validity.

Recht.'[23] And, he continues, we distinguish as regards *general* norms between posited (or enacted) norms and customary norms; and as regards *particular* norms, we take into account only one type of norm, namely, court decisions. Accordingly, Kelsen takes into account three different types of source of law: (a) legislation, (b) custom and (c) precedent.

Hart, for his part, speaks of the *rule of recognition*, not the social thesis, explaining that the rule of recognition is a judicial customary rule that identifies (I would say, constitutes *and* identifies) the sources of law:

Whenever such a rule of recognition is accepted, both private persons and officials are provided with authoritative criteria for identifying primary rules of obligation. The criteria so provided may . . . take any one or more of a variety of forms: these include reference to an authoritative text; to legislative enactment; to customary practice; to general declarations of specified persons, or to past judicial decisions in particular cases.[24]

Note also that Ronald Dworkin, in his early critique of legal positivism by means of a critique of Hart's theory of law, appears to have understood the social thesis in the same way as Kelsen and Hart did, namely, so that it concerns precisely the *validity* of law, not its interpretation and application:

The law of a community is a set of special rules used by the community directly or indirectly for the purpose of determining which behavior will be punished or coerced by the public power. These special rules can be identified and distinguished by specific criteria, by tests having to do not with their content but with their *pedigree* or the manner in which they were adopted or developed. These tests of pedigree can be used to distinguish legal rules from spurious legal rules (rules which lawyers and litigants wrongly argue are rules of law) and also from other sorts of social rules (generally lumped together as 'moral rules') that the community follows but does not enforce through public power.[25]

Dworkin maintains, as is well known, that Hart's theory of law and, therefore, legal positivism fails because, although it can account for the existence of legal *rules*, it cannot account for the existence of legal *principles*. As he puts it, '[p]ositivism . . . is a model of and for a system of rules, and its central notion of a single fundamental test for law forces us to miss the important roles of these standards that are not rules'.[26] And he clearly assumes here that the rule of recognition lays down exclusively factual

[23] Ibid. [24] Hart 1961: 97. [25] Dworkin [1967]1978:17. [26] Dworkin [1967]1978: 22.

criteria of legal validity. For he maintains that legal rules 'can be identified and distinguished by specific criteria, by tests having to do not with their content but with their *pedigree* or the manner in which they were adopted or developed' (in the quotation mentioned), and that the reason why the rule of recognition cannot capture legal principles is that legal principles – as distinguished from legal rules – are *legal* principles because of their *content*, not because of their origin (or pedigree).[27] I believe that it is clear that Dworkin is concerned here precisely with the question of the law's validity, not the question of its interpretation and application. As he sees it, Hart's rule of recognition cannot account for the *existence* of legal principles – the question of the interpretation and application of such principles is not at issue here.

19.5 The Social Thesis: Its Content and Scope II

In any case, some prominent legal philosophers have taken the view that the social thesis is applicable not only to the level of sources of law but also to the level of interpretation and application of the law. Thus, Joseph Raz makes a distinction between the weak social thesis, according to which, necessarily, we determine the existence and content of law using factual *or* moral criteria, provided that such moral criteria have a factual basis, and the strong social thesis, or the *sources thesis*, according to which, necessarily, we determine the existence and content of law using *exclusively* factual criteria; and he explains that he means by a 'source of law' something that provides the judge with factual arguments or considerations that help the judge establish not only the existence of a law but also its content, and that this sense of a 'source of law' is wider than the traditional sense of a 'source of law', which provides the judge with (factual) arguments or considerations that help him establish the validity of laws, though not their (precise) content.[28]

The idea that the social thesis is applicable not only to the level of sources of law but also to the level of interpretation and application of the law is also manifest in the writings of W. J. Waluchow, who is careful to distinguish in his explanation of the distinction between inclusive and

[27] Dworkin [1967]1978: 40. [28] See Raz [1979]2009: 47–8.

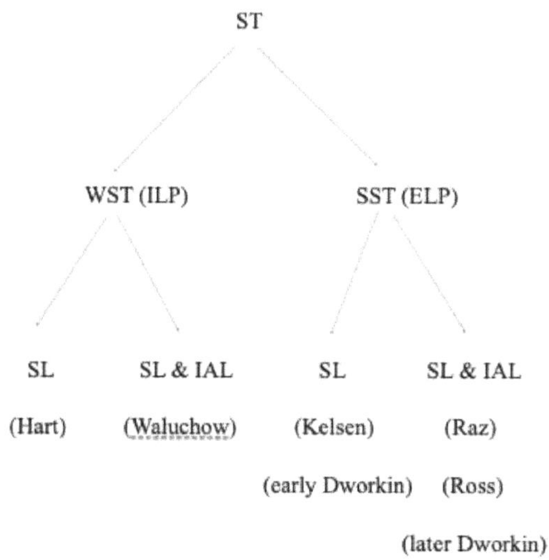

Figure 19.1 Interpretations of the social thesis

exclusive legal positivism between the existence of a legal rule, on the one hand, and the content and application of the same rule, on the other.[29]

It is worth noting here that, like Raz, Alf Ross appears to have espoused the strong social thesis (the sources thesis) and to have thought of this as a thesis not only about sources of law but also about interpretation and application of the law. For, in an article on the conflict between natural law theory and legal positivism, he explains that while the first main tenet of legal positivism is that there is only positive law and no natural law,[30] the second main tenet (the social thesis) has it that it is possible to 'establish the existence and describ[e] the content of the law of a certain country at a certain time in purely factual, empirical terms based on the observation and interpretation of social facts (human behavior and attitudes)'.[31]

Figure 19.1 makes clear the various alternative interpretations of the social thesis that we have discussed thus far.[32]

[29] Waluchow 1994: 81–2 (footnote omitted). [30] Ross [1961]1998: 149.

[31] Ross [1961]1998: 149–50.

[32] Here *ST* means 'the social thesis', *WST* means 'the weak social thesis', *SST* means 'the strong social thesis', *ILP* means 'inclusive legal positivism', *ELP* means 'exclusive legal positivism', *SL* means 'sources of law', and *IAL* means 'interpretation and application of the law'. I will explain the later Dworkin's position in Section 19.8.

19.6 Two Difficulties: Moral Objectivity and the Separation of Powers

Who is right about the scope of the social thesis and, therefore, about the scope of legal positivism – Kelsen, Hart and the early Dworkin, or Raz, Ross, Waluchow and the later Dworkin? To be able to discuss this question in an illuminating way, we need to begin by spelling out the implications of the two competing views.

To say that the criteria of *validity* are factual or, indeed, exclusively factual seems to be in keeping with legal practice because, in almost all legal systems, such criteria do seem to be exclusively factual, such as enactment by a certain organ, the existence of a custom, or a decision by the supreme court. But what, exactly, does it mean to say that the *interpretation and application* of a valid legal rule is or is not a matter of (exclusively) factual criteria? According to Raz, the question is whether 'one has to resort to moral arguments to identify the law'.[33] Waluchow explains that Raz's position is that the existence of a legal rule 'is solely a function of whether it has the appropriate source in . . . matters of pure social fact . . . which can be established independently of moral factors' and that the content of a legal rule 'can be determined . . . by establishing facts about human beings . . . that can be ascertained without the use of moral arguments'.[34]

But this view is problematic. While it may be possible – at least in principle – to determine the plain meaning of a word or a phrase, or the intention of a person, perhaps even of a collective body, without resorting to moral arguments, it does not follow that one can determine the content or application of a legal norm without resorting to moral arguments. For the question of which interpretive factor carries more weight (in general or in the particular case) is, in most cases, not a factual but an evaluative, typically, a moral, question. Suppose a judge reasons that, generally speaking, predictability is a more important value than legislative efficiency, and that therefore one should decide cases on the basis of the plain meaning of the relevant statutory provision instead of on the basis of its purpose, as it appears in the preparatory works. As I see it, this judge is adducing a moral argument – that predictability is a more important moral, or morally

[33] Raz [1979]2009: 46; see also Section 19.5. [34] Waluchow 1994: 82.

relevant, value than is legislative efficiency – in order to determine the content and application of the provision. The reason why I think of the choice to decide the case one way rather than the other, including the choice between competing interpretive arguments, as a moral choice is that it will typically have a considerable impact on the lives of the people concerned.[35] This is so even though the problem of determining (in keeping with the textual approach) what, exactly, is discrimination, a boxing match, and so forth, is *not* a moral problem.

If this is so, we face the following question: Should we say that, in determining the content and application of the provision pursuant to the textual interpretive argument, the judge in our example (i) is applying pre-existing law, as inclusive legal positivists would have it, or (ii) is creating new law using a discretionary power to do so conferred on him by the rule of recognition or, in some cases, by the legal norm itself, as exclusive legal positivists would say? In my view, neither position is appealing. The problem with (i), as we have seen, is that it assumes that moral judgements can be true (or false) in a non-relative sense, and while this assumption does not come to the fore when we are concerned with questions of legal validity, it does come to the fore once we are concerned with the interpretation and application of the law. For, as I have said, moral considerations are ubiquitous on the level of interpretation and application. The problem with (ii) is, instead, that we will have to say what many do not believe, namely, that judges are often not applying pre-existing law at all but are creating new law using a discretionary power to do so; and if this is so, it seems that we need to reconsider the relevance to legal thinking of the separation of powers doctrine and conclude that, since judges are creating new law almost every day, we should stop worrying about the distinction between creating and applying the law.

If I am right that the interpretation and application of law is typically a species of moral reasoning, then both inclusive and exclusive legal positivists face a problem, if and insofar as they take the social thesis to apply also to the level of the interpretation and application of the law. I therefore conclude that legal positivists of both the inclusive and the exclusive type have reason to limit the application of the social thesis to the level of the sources of law.

[35] On this, see Shapiro 2011: 113–15.

19.7 Theoretical Disagreement

Dworkin maintains in *Law's Empire*[36] that legal positivists overlook the interpretive nature of legal reasoning because they overlook the existence of *theoretical disagreement* in law, and that they overlook the existence of theoretical disagreement because they mistakenly believe that it is part of the *meaning* of the word 'law' that the truth of propositions of law (first-order legal statements) depends on shared criteria, the existence of which rules out the possibility of theoretical disagreement – if judges and attorneys share criteria, they cannot also disagree about them. He adds that they view the meaning of 'law' in this way because they (mistakenly) assume that disagreement would not be possible, unless the discussants shared criteria for determining the truth of propositions of law. Accordingly, he objects to legal positivism on the bases that it cannot account for theoretical disagreement in law, that this is so because the rule of recognition is a conventional rule the existence of which presupposes agreement, and that the result is that legal positivism is an inadequate theory of law.

I believe that Dworkin overshoots the mark here, however. First, the idea of a rule of recognition is not a necessary part of legal positivism. So even though the rule of recognition is undoubtedly a conventional rule that requires agreement about the relevant criteria, it does not follow that a critique of Hart's theory, specifically the theory of the rule of recognition, is a critique of the social thesis and therefore of legal positivism. For example, Jeremy Bentham and John Austin took the view that law is what the sovereign commands, and this means that their theories of law, too, are in conformity with the social thesis. Their theories do not, however, include any conventionalist component, and this means that the theoretical disagreement objection does not apply to them.

Second, if we assume, for the sake of argument, that the idea of a rule of recognition is a necessary part of legal positivism, my objection to the theoretical disagreement objection will be that, contrary to what he held in *The Model of Rules*, Dworkin is here tacitly assuming that the rule of recognition (and, indirectly, the social thesis or, as Dworkin refers to it, the plain-fact view of legal grounds) applies not only to the level of the sources of law but also to the level of interpretation and application of

36 See Dworkin 1986: ch. 2.

the law. For the instances of theoretical disagreement in law that he identifies – in Elmer's case, in the snail darter case, in *McLoughlin*, and in *Brown* – clearly belong not on the level of the sources of law (existence) but on the level of the interpretation and application of law (content).[37] For example, in both Elmer's case and the snail darter case, the court aims to avoid an absurd result that it predicts would follow from a literal application of the relevant statutory provision. What is this, if it is not theoretical disagreement on the level of the interpretation and application of the law? Hart might therefore reasonably object to Dworkin's criticism that such theoretical disagreement as there undoubtedly is in law is to be found only on a level of legal thinking to which the theory of legal positivism (in the shape of the plain-fact view or the social thesis) does not apply, and that therefore he does not *as a legal positivist* have to account for such disagreement at all.

I should like to emphasise that the existence of theoretical disagreement on the level of the interpretation and application of the law is a well-known phenomenon, which we cannot explain away. The main reason why there is such disagreement, it seems to me, is that judges typically wish to achieve reasonable results, or at least avoid absurd or manifestly unjust results, such that there is no agreed and firm ranking of the various interpretive arguments because this would lead to judicial inflexibility, which, in turn, would mean that, in at least some, perhaps quite a few, cases, it is not a factual matter whether, say, the plain meaning or the purpose of the provision carries more weight. As a result, the process of interpreting and applying the law will typically involve moral reasoning about what is and what is not an acceptable result, and about which interpretive argument of the ones involved should carry most weight either in general or in the case at bar.

It is interesting to note that Hart has considered and rejected Dworkin's theoretical disagreement objection, arguing that it rests on a misunderstanding of the function of the rule of recognition. As Hart sees it, whereas Dworkin appears to assume that the function of the rule of recognition is to 'determine completely' the conditions that correct legal decisions must satisfy, in reality its function is only to 'determine the general conditions' that such decisions must satisfy. Hart writes:

[37] Dworkin 1986: 15–30.

> It [Dworkin's theoretical disagreement objection] assumes that the rule [of recognition] is meant to determine completely the legal result in particular cases, so that any legal issue arising in any case could simply be solved by mere appeal to the criteria or tests provided by the rule. But this is a misconception: the function of the rule is to determine only the general conditions which correct legal decisions must satisfy in modern systems of law. The rule does this most often by supplying criteria of validity which Dworkin calls matters of pedigree and which refer not to the content of the law but to the manner and form in which the laws are created and adopted; but as I have said . . . in addition to such pedigree matters[,] the rule of recognition may supply tests relating not to the factual content of laws but to their conformity with substantive moral values or principles. Of course[,] in particular cases judges may disagree as to whether such tests are satisfied or not and a moral test in the rule of recognition will not resolve such disagreement. Judges may be agreed on the relevance of such tests as something settled by established judicial practice even though they disagree as to what the tests require in particular cases. To the rule of recognition viewed in this way[,] the practice theory of rules is fully applicable.[38]

Hart means to say, I think, first, that the distinction between the validity of legal rules, on the one hand, and the interpretation and application of such rules, on the other, is relevant here, and, second, that if the criteria laid down in the rule of recognition are partly *moral*, and if judges disagree about what such moral criteria require in the concrete case, they might nevertheless agree about the relevance (that is, the existence) of the criteria in question; and if this is so, the judicial agreement required by the conventionality of the rule of recognition is at hand. My idea, then, is that Hart is here first making a general claim about the function of the rule of recognition ('to determine only the general conditions'). and then discussing a particular problem that might arise when the rule of recognition is fulfilling its function, namely, the problem of interpreting moral criteria.

Dworkin objects to the distinction drawn by Hart (and Jules Coleman, who follows Hart) that it all depends on what level of abstraction is

[38] Hart 1994: 258–9. Jules Coleman 2009: 376 has raised the very same objection to Dworkin's theoretical disagreement objection. Having explained that Dworkin objects to Hart's theory, that the rule of recognition cannot account for legal (theoretical) disagreement, Coleman follows Hart (without saying so) and points out that what is necessary for the existence of the rule of recognition is judicial agreement about the relevance of certain tests for legality (or validity), not judicial agreement about what the relevant test requires in the particular case.

appropriate when one describes (dis)agreement.[39] For example, Dworkin points out, if it turns out that judges disagree about whether a statute criminalising homosexual acts is legally valid under the constitution, Coleman might adopt a *strategy of abstraction* and argue that the reality of it is that judges agree about an abstract convention providing that unfair or immoral statutes are legally invalid, although they disagree about the interpretation and application of that convention to this particular case. Dworkin's objection, then, is that Coleman can always make use of this abstraction strategy and insist that any disagreement is, in reality, not a disagreement about the existence of a given convention but a disagreement about the interpretation and application of that abstract convention to particular cases, and that this is absurd.[40]

The important question, of course, is how much room there is for a theorist to argue (as Hart and Coleman might wish to do) that a given disagreement is not about the existence (or validity) of a certain criterion but about the interpretation and application of a more abstract criterion. I believe that this strategy will be available only in rather few cases, however, because I believe that it will, typically, be reasonably clear what the relevant criterion is, say, equal protection, and that, therefore, Dworkin's critique of the abstraction strategy does not undermine Hart's (and Coleman's) objection.

It is in any case clear that Hart's (and Coleman's) objection is different from my objection. Whereas Hart and Coleman are primarily concerned with the distinction between existence and content as applied to a moral criterion in the rule of recognition, I am concerned with the distinction between existence and content as applied to legal norms that have been identified with the help of the rule of recognition, in particular statutory provisions. Hart and Coleman object to Dworkin's reasoning that while judges may disagree about the interpretation and application of a given moral criterion in the rule of recognition, they rarely disagree about the existence of that criterion – if they did, there would be no such criterion – and that this means that the occurrence of theoretical disagreement does not, contrary to what Dworkin believes, threaten the conventionality of the rule of recognition. I, for my part, agree with Hart and Coleman about this,

[39] Dworkin 2001–2: 1658–61. Dworkin focuses on Coleman's, not Hart's, discussion of the theoretical disagreement objection.

[40] Dworkin 2001–2: 1660.

but I also want to object to Dworkin's theoretical disagreement objection that, while judges may well disagree about the interpretation and application of a given legal norm, they will typically agree about the validity (or existence) of that legal norm, and that this means that the occurrence of theoretical disagreement that there undoubtedly is in law does not threaten the conventionality of the rule of recognition. So even though both Hart and Coleman's objection and my objection capitalise on a general distinction between the validity (or existence) and the interpretation (or content) of something, *X*, we differ as regards the choice of *X*: whereas Hart and Coleman take *X* to be a moral criterion of validity laid down in the rule of recognition, I take *X* to be a legal norm identified by the rule of recognition.

One might be tempted to object to my line of argument that the reason why judges or others may disagree about the interpretation and application of a given legal norm will be precisely that a certain interpretation, C_1, of the relevant moral criterion of validity in the rule of recognition will lead to a certain interpretation, N_1, of the legal norm in question, whereas another interpretation, C_2, of the criterion of validity will lead to a different interpretation, N_2, of the relevant legal norm. However, this would be a mistake. For the suggested reason is, of course, just *one* reason why there may be theoretical disagreement about the interpretation and application of a legal norm. Other instances of such disagreement can be explained instead by reference to independent moral disagreement on the part of judges or other law-appliers about the reasonableness of a given outcome or about the relative weight of the relevant interpretive arguments and need have nothing whatsoever to do with any interpretive disagreement about a moral (or a factual) criterion in the rule of recognition. For this reason, it is worth keeping apart these two, somewhat similar, objections to Dworkin's theoretical disagreement objection.

19.8 Existence and Interpretation

The distinction I have defended between (i) validity (or existence) and (ii) interpretation and application assumes, then, that we can speak coherently of legal norms (or rules) in an 'uninterpreted' shape and maintain that there is indeed such and such a legal norm, although its precise meaning is unclear. But this presupposes that there is an acceptable answer to the question 'What is the "uninterpreted" norm?' My own view is that, in the case of *enacted* norms, a legal norm is more or less identical with its formulation.[41] For example, we may coherently maintain, say, that Article 36 of the Swedish Contracts Act provides that the terms of a contract can be modified or be declared invalid by a court, if the court finds that the terms are unreasonable in light of the content of the contract, the circumstances when the contract was concluded, later circumstances, or other circumstances, even though Article 36 clearly needs interpretation in order for the judge to see precisely what it means and how it is to be applied in a given case. But, as we saw in Section 19.3, when it comes to *custom* and *precedent*, things change. For there is, in the case of such legal norms, usually no canonical formulation available, so that it is somewhat unclear what they say; and this, in turn, means that they cannot easily guide behaviour. As a result, it becomes more difficult to maintain that such norms exist in an uninterpreted shape.

Some authors appear to reject the very distinction between existence and interpretation, however. Stanley Fish,[42] for example, objects, in his debate with Owen Fiss about the possibility of objectivity in legal interpretation, that Fiss assumes that one first *has* a rule and then *interprets* it, and that this assumption is untenable. Fiss postulates the existence of interpretive communities, which are made up of people who share (what Fiss calls) *disciplining rules*, and maintains that, although there may well be disputes about the application of disciplining rules, we may still hold that the members of the interpretive community share them and are constrained by them – if this were not so, there wouldn't be any interpretive community (as regards *these* disciplining rules).[43] He argues, more specifically, that whereas some disputes about disciplining rules concern the legitimacy (or existence) of said rules, other disputes pose only 'issues of application'. And in regard to the latter type of dispute, he maintains that the authority (and, of course, the existence) of a given rule can be maintained, even though the rule is disputed, which is to say that he makes a distinction between the existence of the rule and its interpretation and application.[44]

Fish does not see things this way, however, arguing as he does that if the shape of the rule could be had without interpretation, interpretation would

[41] For a brief discussion of the question of what a legal rule is, see Hart 1958: 606–15. He, too, appears to take the view that a rule is identical with its formulation; Hart 1958: 614. See also Schauer 1985.

[42] Fish 1984: 1327. [43] Fiss 1981–2: 744–8. [44] Fiss 1981–2: 747.

be superfluous, that interpretation clearly is not superfluous, and that this means that rules cannot be had without interpretation, or, if you will, that we have rules only in an interpreted shape. That is to say, Fish rejects the very distinction between existence and interpretation that Fiss (tacitly) invokes. His argument, as I understand it, is that 'uninterpreted' rules cannot be said to exist because they cannot guide human behaviour: 'a so-called "disciplining rule" cannot be said to act as a constraint on interpretation because it is . . . the product of an interpretation'.[45]

I do not, however, agree with Fish that all rules, including disciplining rules, need interpretation, unless he means by 'interpretation' nothing more than the intellectual act of comprehending what the rule says (interpretation *sensu largo*). If, by 'interpretation', he means instead the act of solving a problem (interpretation *sensu stricto*), I would object that, in many cases, there is no problem of interpretation.[46] In any case, as my example featuring Article 36 of the Swedish Contracts Act shows, it makes good sense to say that we 'have' this rule, even though there may be disagreement about its precise content. For while it is not obvious how to apply this rule to some scenarios, the rule is sufficiently clear that it can guide behaviour in many cases.

As we have seen, the type of rule discussed by Fish and Fiss in this case is a rule of the legal method, that is, a judicial customary rule. As such, it will not have a canonical formulation, and this means that Fish's critique is more apt in this case than it would have been in the case of enacted rules. Indeed, even if Fish is right about the distinction between existence and interpretation in the case of disciplining rules, he could not successfully make the same claim in the case of enacted rules. And since enacted rules make up the overwhelming majority of legal norms, we may allow ourselves to take Fish's claim about the impossibility of upholding a distinction between the existence and the interpretation and application of rules rather lightly.

19.9 Significance

Having argued that the social thesis should be taken to concern the level of sources of law only, I need to consider a possible objection to legal

[45] Fish 1984: 1327. [46] On this, see Schauer 1985.

positivism understood in this more narrow sense, namely, that it is not a very interesting theory. From a legal point of view, one might well argue that the really interesting questions concern the interpretation and application of the law. How, exactly, are we to understand and apply legal norms concerning fundamental rights, bankruptcy, taxation and so forth? If legal positivism does not speak to questions of interpretation and application of the law, how interesting is it?

My own view is that legal positivism, narrowly conceived, is indeed an interesting theory. As is well known, prominent defenders of legal positivism have argued that a highly valuable feature of this theory is that it makes it possible for us to present the law of the land in a morally neutral way, so as not to lead us to take it for granted that we have a moral obligation to obey the law. For example, Jeremy Bentham objected to William Blackstone's *Commentaries on the Law of England* on the basis that Blackstone expounded English law as if it were flowing from a set of natural rights, and that this meant that citizens, and perhaps also lawyers and judges, ran the risk of being duped into believing that the law of England was automatically morally binding on them.[47] Bentham's recipe for clear thinking was instead to maintain a conceptual distinction between what the law is, which is the topic of expository jurisprudence, and what the law should be, which is the topic of censorial jurisprudence.[48]

Kelsen, too, maintains that on (what he refers to as) the natural law analysis, there is a risk that citizens (and legal officials) may take the moral authority of their own legal order for granted and may forget to examine it from a moral point of view:

> The thesis that law in its essence is moral – i.e. that only a moral social system is law – is rejected by the Pure Theory of Law not only because this thesis presupposes a true morality, but also because in its actual application through the dominant jurisprudence of a certain legal community[,] it amounts to an uncritical legitimization of the governmental coercive order that constitutes this community. For it is assumed as self-evident that one's own coercive order is law. . . . But if one's own coercive order is law, it follows from the thesis that it is also moral.[49]

[47] Bentham [1776]1988: preface. [48] Bentham [1776]1988: 7–8.

[49] Kelsen 1960: 71 (translated into English by Robert Carroll). The German text reads:

> Die These, daß das Recht seinem Wesen nach moralisch ist, das heißt: daß nur eine moralische Gesellschaftsordnung Recht ist, wird von der reinen Rechtslehre nicht nur abgelehnt, weil diese These eine absolute Moral voraussetzt, sondern auch darum, weil sie in ihrer tatsächlichen Anwendung durch die in einer bestimmten Rechtsgemeinschaft

Discussing Bentham's position on the separation thesis, Hart observes that 'there are therefore two dangers between which the insistence on this distinction [that is, between the law as it is and the law as it should be] will help us steer: the danger that law and its authority may be dissolved in man's conception of what law ought to be and the danger that the existing law may supplant morality as a final test of conduct and so escape criticism'.[50] And when faced with the claim that legal positivism (in the sense of the separation thesis) may lead to tyranny, and in fact did lead to tyranny in Germany before and during World War II, he says in regard to the latter danger, '[s]urely the truly liberal answer to any sinister use of the slogan "law is law" or of the distinction between law and morals is, "Very well, but that does not conclude the question. Law is not morality; do not let it supplant morality."'[51]

Legal positivism, narrowly conceived, retains this highly valuable feature. For, as we saw in Section 19.8, although what is really of interest to those whose behaviour is subject to legal regulation is what the norms, properly interpreted, require of them, 'uninterpreted' norms rules can and do guide human behaviour for the simple reason that law-appliers in general rarely deviate from the plain meaning of the norms. In my view, this is what is characteristic of easy cases, including (potential) cases that never reach the courts.[52] If things were to change, however, so that citizens could no longer predict in most cases what the law requires of them by simply looking at the text of the relevant rule, the value of legal positivism, narrowly conceived, would be undermined, and one could no longer defend its significance along these lines. That is to say, my defence of legal positivism, conceived as a theory about sources of law, depends on certain assumptions about human beings and the world they live in, in particular the assumption that judges and other legal officials rarely deviate from the plain meaning of legal norms. As Hart explains, when discussing the nature of law, one should make a distinction between conceptual (or logical) necessity (and possibility) and what we might call natural necessity (or possibility) and focus on the former.[53] But when we

herrschenden Jurisprudenz auf eine unkritische Legitimierung der diese Gemeinschaft konstituierenden staatlichen Zwangsordnung hinausläuft. Denn daß die eigene staatliche Zwangsordnung Recht sei, wird als selbstverstendlich vorausgesetzt. [. . .] Da aber die eigene Zwangsordnung Recht sei, muß sie, der These zufolge, auch moralisch sein.

[50] Kelsen 1960: 598. [51] Kelsen 1960: 618. See also Kelsen 1960:71.
[52] On easy cases, see Schauer 1985. [53] Hart 1958: 621–4.

are discussing not the truth of legal positivism but its significance, I see no reason to ignore questions of natural, as distinguished from conceptual, necessity (and possibility) or questions of fact.

References

Austin, J. [1832]1998. *The Province of Jurisprudence Determined and The Uses of the Study of Jurisprudence.* Introduction by H. L. A. Hart. Hackett.

Bentham, J. [1776]1988. *A Fragment on Government: The New Authoritative Edition by J.H. Burns and H.L.A. Hart. With an Introduction by Ross Harrison.* Cambridge University Press.

Coleman, J. L. 2001. *The Practice of Principle.* Oxford University Press.

Coleman, J. L. 2009. 'Beyond Inclusive Legal Positivism'. *Ratio Juris* 22: 359–94.

Dworkin, R. [1967]1978. 'The Model of Rules I'. In R. Dworkin. *Taking Rights Seriously.* 2nd ed. Duckworth: 14–45.

Dworkin, R. 1986. *Law's Empire.* Harvard University Press.

Dworkin, R. 2001–2. 'Thirty Years On'. *Harvard Law Review* 115: 1655–87.

Fish, S. 1984. 'Fish v. Fiss'. *Stanford Law Review* 36: 1325–47.

Fiss, O. 1981–2. 'Objectivity and Interpretation'. *Stanford Law Review* 34: 739–63.

Hart, H. L. A. 1958. 'Positivism and the Separation of Law and Morals'. *Harvard Law Review* 71: 593–629.

Hart, H. L. A. 1961. *The Concept of Law.* Clarendon Press.

Hart, H. L. A. 1982. 'Legal Duty and Obligation'. In H. L. A. Hart. *Essays on Bentham.* Oxford University Press: 127–61.

Hart, H. L. A. 1994. *The Concept of Law.* With a Postscript. 2nd ed. Eds. P. A. Bulloch and J. Raz. Clarendon Press.

Holmes, O. W. 1896–7. 'The Path of the Law'. *Harvard Law Review* 10: 457–78.

Kelsen, H. 1960. *Reine Rechtslehre* [*The Pure Theory of Law*]. 2nd ed. Österreichische Staatsdruckerei.

Kelsen, H. 1965. 'Was ist juristischer Positivismus?' [What Is Legal Positivism?]. *Juristenzeitung* [*Journal for Jurists*] 15/16: 465–9.

Kelsen, H. [1934]1994. *Reine Rechtslehre.* Scientia Verlag.

Kelsen, H. [1945]1999. *General Theory of Law and State.* Trans. A. Wedberg. The Lawbook Exchange.

MacCormick, N. 1985–6. 'A Moralistic Case for A-Moralistic Law?'. *Valparaiso University Law Review* 20: 1–41.

Moore, M. S. 1985. 'A Natural Law Theory of Interpretation'. *Southern California Law Review* 58: 277–398.

Raz, J. 1986. 'Dworkin: A New Link in the Chain'. *California Law Review* 74: 1103–19.

Raz, J. 1993. 'H. L. A. Hart (1907–1992)'. *Utilitas* 5: 145–56.

Raz, J. [1985]1994. 'Authority, Law and Morality'. In J. Raz. *Ethics in the Public Domain.* Revised ed. Clarendon Press: 210–37.

Raz, J. [1979]2009. 'Legal Positivism and the Sources of Law'. In J. Raz. *The Authority of Law.* 2nd ed. Oxford University Press: 37–52.

Ross, A. 1959. *On Law and Justice.* University of California Press.

Ross, A. [1961]1998. 'Validity and the Conflict between Positivism and Natural Law'. In S. L. Paulson and B. Litschewski Paulson (eds.). *Normativity and Norms: Critical Perspectives on Kelsenian Themes.* Clarendon Press: 147–63.

Schauer, F. 1985. 'Easy Cases'. *Southern California Law Review* 58: 399–440.

Shapiro, S. J. 2011. *Legality.* Belknap Press.

Simmonds, N. E. 2002. *Central Issues in Jurisprudence: Justice, Law and Rights.* 2nd ed. Sweet & Maxwell.

Spaak, T. 2007. *Guidance and Constraint: The Action-Guiding Capacity of Theories of Legal Reasoning.* Iustus.

Toh, K. 2005. 'Hart's Expressivism and His Benthamite Project'. *Legal Theory* 11: 75–125.

Waluchow, W. J. 1994. *Inclusive Legal Positivism.* Oxford University Press.

20 What *Is* Law and What *Counts* as Law? The Separation Thesis in Context

Andrei Marmor *

20.1 Introduction

There are not many philosophical theses that have generated as much confusion and misunderstanding as the so-called 'separation thesis' in legal philosophy. John Austin's famous dictum that 'the existence of the law is one thing; its merit or demerit is another' may not have actually engendered this confusion, but it is certainly associated with it.[1] The tradition of legal positivism of which Austin is a founder is sometimes characterised by espousing the idea that there is no necessary connection between law and morality. Yet of course there are many essential connections between law and morality, some of them quite plausibly necessary connections, and legal positivists have never denied it.[2] But then, detractors claim, if law and morality are necessarily linked, what is left of the separation thesis? I want to begin my discussion with John Gardner's excellent answer to this question, and show that it needs some modifications and further elaboration.[3] Along the way, I hope to show what is the main philosophical challenge here, and why it is important. I also hope to show that a proper construal of the separation thesis goes a long way towards supporting Austin's main philosophical insight.

* I am grateful to the participants of the conference on this volume held at Stockholm University (November 2018) and to Torben Spaak for helpful comments on an earlier draft.

[1] See Austin [1832]1995: 157.

[2] For example, it is plausible to assume that there is going to be, and necessarily so, a substantial overlap between the concerns of morality and those of law; that law is bound to regulate some issues on moral grounds (or, at least, on what is perceived to be moral grounds); that law is necessarily going to promote or to protect some goods that we consider morally desirable, and so on and so forth.

[3] See Gardner 2001.

20.2 The Metaphysical Grounding of Legality

The separation thesis amounts to the claim that there is a fundamental aspect of law, its 'existence' in Austin's formulation, that does not depend on morality. The first question that arises here is: What is it that legal positivists mean by this fundamental aspect? What is it for a law 'to exist' in a way that is independent of its merit? Gardner claims, and rightly so in my mind, that the separation thesis pertains to one, and only one, aspect of law: the conditions of legal validity or, as I would prefer to put it, the metaphysical grounding of legality. Gardner's formulation of this idea, which he takes to be the core commitment of the legal positivist (LP) tradition, is the following proposition:

(LP) In any legal system, whether a given norm is legally valid, and hence whether it forms part of the law of that system, depends on its sources, not its merits.[4]

(LP) is in need of two adjustments, one of which Gardner provides and the other he omits. The latter concerns the distinction between legal validity and membership of norms in a legal system. The formulation of (LP) suggests that if a norm is legally valid in legal system S, it is 'part of the law of' S. But, as Joseph Raz pointed out, this is not true; membership of norms in a legal system is more restricted than legal validity in the system. For example, legal systems often recognise as valid some laws of other legal systems and, under certain conditions, would apply those norms to resolve a dispute, but the foreign norms do not thereby gain membership in the system that recognises them.[5] Having said this, I will leave the issue aside, and focus, as Gardner does, on the idea of legal validity.

The second modification bears directly on the proper articulation of the separation thesis. To explain it, I will use an example different from Gardner's but in the same spirit. Thus, consider a small tribal society in which people believe that they are, and ought to be, guided by the spirits of their ancestors. And they believe that the Grand Shaman is the only one who communicates with the ancestors, and therefore regard the Grand Shaman's directives as the law of their land. Now, when you think about

[4] See Gardner 2001: 199. I do not know if Gardner means by 'merit' only the moral kind; probably not, and there is no reason to confine the notion of merit to moral concerns. Anything within the domain of what ought to be the case can count as 'merit' in this context.

[5] See Raz 2009: 193–4.

the application of (LP) to this society, you might think that there is a problem. After all, it matters to the people who regard the Grand Shaman's directives as law that the Grand Shaman is, as they believe, a conduit to the ancestors' spirits. In other words, the Grand Shaman's directives are law only if, and in so far as, the Grand Shaman conveys the will of the spirits. Therefore, if there were any doubts about that, if the population were to learn, for example, that the Shaman is a fraud, they would no longer regard his directives as legally binding. It would no longer be law. Or suppose that a different kind of doubt were to creep in: suppose that members of this population began to doubt that they are bound by the spirits' will or, maybe, even began to doubt that the spirits exist. You would think that this would lead them to doubt the legitimacy of the Grand Shaman's authority. And then they might no longer think that the Grand Shaman's directives were legally valid. Would that refute (LP)? After all, we seem to see here how beliefs about legitimacy affect legal validity. The latter seems to depend, inter alia, on considerations of merit, not source.

The question, to generalise, is whether the moral legitimacy of legal authority bears on the conditions of legal validity. According to Gardner, (LP) is to be understood as answering this question in the negative. The whole point of (LP), according to Gardner, is to deny that the conditions of legal validity depend on anything but sources; considerations of merit, either the merit of particular norms or the merit of the authority issuing those norms, have no bearing on the question of whether the norms are legally valid or not. Thus, he reformulates (LP) to capture this idea:

> (LP*) In any legal system, whether a given norm is legally valid, and hence whether it forms part of the law of that system, depends on its sources, not its merits (where its merits, in the relevant sense, include the merits of its sources).

Now there is something right and something a bit trickier about (LP*). It seems quite right to claim that as long as the relevant population *regards* the Grand Shaman's directives as law, it is law, irrespective of the reasons they may have, or not have, for so regarding it. And if, for whatever reason, the relevant population no longer regards the Grand Shaman's directives as law, then the Shaman's directives are not legally valid. In other words, legal validity does not depend on people's reasons for regarding it as legally valid. And this view gains a lot of support from the idea that the legal validity of a norm or a directive does not necessarily entail that the subjects of the norm ought to comply. There are many legally valid norms that ought to be ignored or sometimes even deliberately violated. Legal validity is no guarantee of moral soundness. That much, at least, we can all agree on.

And yet, this is a bit more complicated. Consider an analogy with promises:[6] a promise is valid, morally binding, regardless of the reason that the promisor may have had for making the promise. If you made a promise, you have a reason to keep it, and you would have this reason even if your reason for making the promise was not a good one. But this holds only up to a point. If the promise was made under duress, or extracted by fraud, and things like that, it is not a binding one. So, it is not entirely accurate to say that the reasons for making a promise are always irrelevant to the question of whether a valid, or binding, promise has been made. If the uttering of a promise is tainted by some moral failures or fails some moral conditions, it may not amount to a real promise, as it were. Why would this be different in the legal case? Why cannot we say that if the making of a putative law fails certain moral conditions, it is not really law?

The answer is that promises, unlike the law, are entirely within the moral domain. It is true, and quite important, actually, that, in both cases, the making of a promise and the making of law, it normally takes a speech act to accomplish. And it is true in both cases that there are certain conditions that have to be met to enable us to recognise the relevant speech act as one of promising or law-making. But our reasons for treating certain speech acts as the making of a promise are moral reasons and the ramifications of it are determined by the moral considerations that apply. Law is much more complex than that. There are, no doubt, moral reasons to have law, and those reasons would have a bearing on what we expect law to accomplish. And this is true of law in general, as it is of particular laws. But the law is not a moral practice, like promising; it is an institutional one. And it is this social, institutional aspect of law that creates a gap between legal validity and moral validity. A valid promise cannot be anything else but a morally valid promise; a legally valid norm or directive can be morally invalid. In other words, promising is entirely a moral practice, whereas law is a social practice with moral aspects.

None of this proves, of course, that (LP*) is correct. In fact, there are at least two aspects of it that invite some pressure. So, let me mention them up

[6] This analogy and its main point are inspired by Raz's discussion of it; see Raz 2009: 178–9. I think that the point I make here is somewhat different from Raz's but in line with his argument.

front and then elaborate on one of them, which I take to be the core issue here. For one thing, Gardner tells us precious little about the kind of facts that would establish what the sources of law are in any given legal order, except that they are not merit-based. As Gardner puts it, a norm is legally valid in a system if at some point 'some relevant agent or agents announced it, practiced it, invoked it, enforced it, endorsed it, or otherwise engaged in it'.[7] And I certainly agree with that. Law, as I argued elsewhere in some detail, is an artefact, it has to be created, and its persistence as law depends on practice, on a population treating it as such.[8] Law is, to use Gardner's words, a product of human engagement. But we still need an answer to the question of what makes it the case, in any given society, that certain types of human engagement are legally significant and others are not. In other words, what constitutes the legal sources? Scholars in the legal positivist tradition have given different answers to this question; some suggested that it is a matter of social rules or social conventions, while others have reservations about the rule/convention-based account. But, perhaps, none of this matters for understanding the separation thesis. Gardner clearly thinks that the only commitment that legal positivists share or, at least, the only commitment embodied in the separation thesis is the idea that whatever makes it the case that something counts as law is not merit-based.

Fair enough, but then we must acknowledge that the core idea of (LP*) relies on the dichotomy between source and merit. And, according to Gardner, a dichotomy it is: 'The two categories . . . are jointly exhaustive of the possible conditions of validity for any norm.' Anything that can ground the legal validity of a norm 'counts as source-based if it is not merits based'.[9] But here we begin to run into serious difficulties. The idea that the validity of a norm is either source-based or merit-based sounds too dogmatic. Pressure on it comes from two directions. One, which Gardner mentions, is that there might be a conditional link: source-based norms might direct us to condition the validity of other norms on their merits. This is the position held by 'soft' or 'inclusive' legal positivism. This view takes legal validity to be foundationally source-based, but it allows for those sources to condition the validity of some subset of law on merit-based

7 Gardner 2001: 200.

8 See Marmor 2011: chs. 1–4; Marmor 2018: 473.

9 Gardner 2001: 200.

considerations.[10] Let us call this the question of incorporation. I will get to this problem in Section 20.5. The second, and more important, challenge is about the soundness of the dichotomy itself. According to critics, the distinction between source and merit is not nearly as sustainable as (LP*) would have it.

20.3 The Distinction between Source and Merit

The distinction between source and merit seems to be a very close relative of the familiar distinction between *is* and *ought*, or between description and prescription. It is rather uncontroversial that we can draw a distinction between propositional content that describes some aspect of the world, and propositional content that expresses a view about the way things ought to be from some normative vantage point. The former kind is rendered true or false by the way that things are, in the world. If I assert that 'P is Q', the proposition is true if P is, indeed, Q, and false if P is not Q. But if I assert that 'P ought to be Q', then the fact that P is not, actually, Q would not render my proposition false. It would be false only if P ought not to be Q. In other words, the source versus merit distinction heavily relies on the distinction between the *is* and the *ought*, between statements describing how things are and statements prescribing ways that things should or ought to be. Notice, however, that (LP*) is not committed to Hume's famous argument that ought cannot be derived from is.[11] It is committed only to the logical distinction underlying Hume's argument, namely, to the idea that there is a clear distinction between statements of a descriptive kind and statements of an evaluative kind. Whether Hume was correct to maintain that no evaluative conclusions can possibly follow from any set of statements that are only descriptive is rather doubtful, but, in any case, it is not something that needs to be settled; Hume's argument is not part of what makes (LP*) plausible.[12]

[10] See Gardner 2001: 202. The soft or inclusive version of legal positivism has been articulated by Jules Coleman 1982 and Wil Waluchow 1994. It has also been endorsed by many others, including, arguably, H. L. A. Hart ([1961]1997) in his postscript to *The Concept of Law*.

[11] See Hume [1740]1978: 469.

[12] With the exception, perhaps, of Kelsen's legal theory. As I explained elsewhere, Kelsen took the Humean argument very seriously and thought that it frames the challenge that any

One way to understand Dworkin's interpretative objection to the legal positivist tradition is to see it as a direct challenge to the idea that source and merit can be clearly distinguished as (LP*) presupposes.[13] Dworkin's argument is based on the nature of interpretative reasoning. Interpretation, by its very nature, involves an inextricable mix of the evaluative and the descriptive. And, since legal reasoning is profoundly interpretative, any conclusion about what the law is involves a mix of source-based and merit-based considerations. As I argued elsewhere in some detail, Dworkin's conclusion that the distinction between source and merit cannot be sustained rests on two premises, only one of which is sound.[14] Dworkin is quite right to maintain that typical interpretative reasoning relies on both descriptive and evaluative considerations. But this is not enough to refute (LP*). The separation thesis is in trouble only if it is also true that interpretative reasoning identifies or discovers, as it were, what the law had been prior to the interpretative reasoning. Proponents of (LP*) can readily admit that whenever the law is in need of interpretation, evaluative considerations and judgements have to play a role. But interpretation is employed by judges and other legal actors as a way of concretising, extending or modifying the law, changing it, or even creating new law, not as a way of identifying what the law is. Law is identified by its sources, and then, when it turns out that law thus identified is not sufficiently clear to settle the legal issue at hand, or otherwise leaves some questions unanswered, judges may need to engage in ways of modifying or expanding the law by interpretative reasoning.[15]

Thus, even if it is true, as I think it is, that interpretation typically involves a mix of descriptive and evaluative considerations, it does not follow that (LP*) is false. The separation thesis is threatened only if is also true that interpretation is employed to figure out what the law on this or that is. But this is precisely the thesis that (LP*) is committed to denying. To put the same idea differently, the dispute between Dworkin and legal

theory of law needs to answer, namely, the challenge of explaining how actions and events in the world can be construed to have normative force. See Marmor 2011: ch. 1. But all this pertains to the question of legal normativity; it does not have a direct bearing on the conditions of legal validity.

13 Dworkin 1986. 14 See Marmor 2011: ch. 4.

15 On these issues, articulating what, in my view, is quite right and important in Dworkin's theory of interpretation, and why I think that it is misapplied to the legal case, I have elaborated on several occasions. See, e.g., Marmor 2005; Marmor 2011: ch. 4; Marmor 2013.

positivism is not about the nature of interpretation but about the role that interpretation plays in determining what the law is. According to Dworkin, any conclusion about what the law on this or that is is a result of some interpretation or other. According to proponents of (LP*), however, interpretation is just one of the ways in which human engagement with the law modifies it and creates new law. When judges, in their official capacity, interpret the law and conclude that the correct interpretation of it is X, X may well be the law, but not because X is the correct interpretation; X becomes the law because judges *say* (viz, officially hold) that it is.

To be sure, none of the above was meant to be a conclusive argument against Dworkin's view; it was meant to show only that Dworkin's theory of interpretation, that is, of what interpretative reasoning necessarily involves, does not settle anything about the truth or falsehood of (LP*); it leaves the argument about it where it found it. But there may be an argument in the vicinity that does threaten (LP*) directly. It would have to be an argument about the role that interpretative reasoning plays in ways of determining whether something is an object of a certain type. So, this is the general thought: when we pose a question of the kind 'Is o an F?', we would normally expect the answer to be determined by the relevant properties of o and the relevant properties of the predicate, or category F. But sometimes things are not so simple; there are areas in which answering such questions necessarily involves evaluative considerations. Whether o is an F or not might depend on what it is about F that we value, appreciate or care about. The realm of art provides a very good example.

Suppose, for example, that you visit a contemporary art museum and see a rather mundane object, like a chair or a mirror, presented there as a work of art, and it makes you wonder, is this object really a work of art or not? Is o an F, where F stands for 'a work of art'? You can see the various arguments that one can deploy in both directions here. One can argue that a work of art needs to demonstrate some special talent or skills in its creation. Another can reply that there are many kinds of talent that might be in play; artistic talent might consist in the artist's ability to see something that others have not, not necessarily to do something that others cannot readily accomplish. And so on and so forth, one can keep arguing about this. But, of course, such arguments are very closely entangled with views about the values of art and what we think that makes art worthy of our appreciation. And then, of course, different evaluative views about the nature of art yield different answers to the question of whether the object in front of us is a work of art or not.

I hope you can see that if something similar applies to law, the separation thesis is in trouble. (LP*) tells us that an answer to the question of the type 'Is o an F?', where o is some norm and F is law in a given legal system, can always be answered by tracing o's sources, that is, without considerations of merit. But, as I just exemplified, in the realm of art, whether o is an F or not (where o is an object and F is a work of art) may well depend on the merit of F; it may depend on views about what makes F valuable and worthy of appreciation. If that is true of law as well, the source versus merit distinction that (LP*) presupposes cannot be sustained. Whether a norm is law or not may well depend, partly, on what values we find in law and what makes law, or laws of that kind, worthy of appreciation.

How can proponents of (LP*) respond to that? There are two ways to go here. One rather obvious route is to protest the analogy between law and art. We could say that law is not like art, at least not in this respect. The other way is to draw on the distinction between *what is an F* and *what counts as an F*. These two answers are not mutually exclusive.

Let me return to the question of whether an object is a work of art or not. So here there might be something that provides an easy answer: if one held the view that institutional recognition, instantiated by exhibit in museums and art galleries, supported by art dealership markets, and so forth, is constitutive of what is a work of art, then the fact that you see the object exhibited as a work of art in a museum would make it art. But this seems questionable. When curators pick an object to exhibit in an art gallery, they pick it because they think that it is a work of art; they would not think that it becomes art because they have exhibited it in the gallery. This, however, is precisely the point at which the analogy between law and art breaks down. In the legal case, institutional practices are constitutive of what is a legal norm. Legislatures do not enact something because they think that it is law already; they make it law by enacting it. Similarly, according to (LP*), when judges and other officials modify the law or apply it in certain ways, their engagement with the relevant norm is what makes it law. So, at least in this crucial respect, law is very much unlike art.

This rejoinder seems right as far as it goes. But it may not go far enough.[16] There might be a deeper sense in which identifying an object

[16] I have explained this argument and its limits in greater detail in Marmor 2019.

as a work of art is very similar to identifying a norm as legal. In both cases, where the proposition takes the form 'o is an F', the F in question, a work of art in one case, a legal norm in the other, is neither purely descriptive nor purely evaluative but an inextricable mixture of both. It is certainly plausible to argue that an attribution of artistic qualities to an artefact is not value-neutral; to view something as art is also to view it in some positive light, as something we would have reasons to pay attention to, to value in some respect, and so forth. And notice that this would still hold even if you think that the object you classify as art is not a successful exemplar, namely, that it's not good art. Which is partly what explains why an argument about whether a particular object is, or is not, a work of art is a sensible kind of argument. It is a sensible argument precisely because we think that even if the object is not good art, it being art endows it with some value, something that we appreciate. That is, even if, all things considered, the object is not artistically praiseworthy. Thus, to be fair to critics, one cannot dismiss out of hand a similar line of thought applied to law. Since we all admit that there are very good reasons to have law, that there are good reasons to have human interactions regulated by legal means, and good reasons to prefer legal regulation to many other alternatives, and so forth, there might be something to be said for the idea that there is some good in legality per se, even if, on particular occasions, all things considered, the law is not good.[17] So the idea is that, in certain cases, the F, in a 'o is an F' type of statement, is neither a purely descriptive predicate nor a purely evaluative one but a mix of both. And if that is true not just about art but about law as well, (LP*) might be false. If F has some evaluative aspects, then it would seem that an answer to the question of the type 'Is o an F?' would have to be sensitive to the values associated with F.

The obvious rejoinder on behalf of proponents of (LP*) is to deny the analogy again. That is, to deny that the F predicate, when construed strictly in terms of legal validity, has any evaluative dimensions. On this view, to say that a norm is legally valid in a given legal system is simply to point out a social fact, something that just happens to be the case somewhere at some time. It does not involve any positive or negative evaluative stance; unlike art, which may be inherently good in itself, legal validity is not. It is just something that occurs in a social context, something that happens to be the case.

[17] See n. 17. See also Raz 2009: ch. 6.

In order to strengthen this last point, proponents of (LP*) often dwell on the point that the legal validity of a norm does not entail a moral obligation to comply with it. Some may dispute that, but I won't; let us assume that the fact that there is a legally valid norm that applies to X at some point, and would require X to φ in those circumstances, does not necessarily give X a moral obligation to φ, even pro tanto. It may give X a reason to φ, but that is not saying much; anything can count as a reason for action. Facts that count in favour of doing (or not doing) something do not have to be the kind of things we value. We may value something else, and the fact in question counts in favour of doing something in light of the things we may want to accomplish or other things we need to do. Granted all this, and even if we assume that there is no general moral obligation to obey the law, some legal philosophers may still resist the idea that an attribution of legality to a norm or set of norms is totally devoid of a moral dimension. I do not share this view, but I will try to make my point here indirectly.[18] In other words, I will try to show that proponents of (LP*) do not need to focus on rebutting the analogy between art and law in this respect. What we need to show is that the 'Is o an F?' type of question depends on the particular theoretical context in which the question is asked. And then I will try to show that, in the theoretical context that gives rise to (LP*), it makes sense to construe the F predicate in purely descriptive terms.

20.4 A Reductive Explanation

Let us suppose that the question we ask is not 'Is o an F?' but a modified version of it; we ask 'What makes it the case that o *counts as* F in S?' or, more generally, 'What counts as an F in S?' (where S stands for a given society or some relevant population). So, for example, an art historian can ask what kind of artefacts were regarded as works of art in the twelfth-century Seljuk empire? Did they have a distinction between ornamental artefacts and works of art? Or what makes it the case that abstract compositions started to count as art in the early decades of the twentieth century in Europe? Obviously, these are different kinds of question from the one we discussed before, that is, whether the particular object in front of us is, or is

[18] For more direct considerations counting against the idea that attribution of legality entails some moral appraisal, see Marmor 2019.

not, a work of art. Crucially, when we focus on a question of the type 'What counts as an F in S?', we do not need to rely on our own views about what makes art valuable. We just seek an understanding of what makes people, in some relevant population, treat something as a work of art; what makes them believe that it is, how they respond to it, how they rationalise those reactions, and so forth. The question is, you might think, essentially sociological in nature, and thus the answer to it is expected in terms of some sociological explanation or other.[19]

Now I hope we can see that the separation thesis can be seen as an answer to this second type of question: What makes it the case that *o counts as an F in S*? On this interpretation, (LP*) should be seen as an answer to the question of what kind of things make it the case that a norm counts as legally valid in a certain society. On this reading of it, (LP*) provides a reductive explanation as the answer; it maintains that whatever it is that makes people regard norms as legally valid in their legal system can be fully articulated in terms of sources, not values. To be more precise, as I will explain in a moment, the explanation of legal validity on this reading can be given in terms of articulating people's actual conduct and attitudes (namely, beliefs, intentions, dispositions and so forth). But now you might think that we are cheating; of course, if you ask a sociological question, you are bound to seek a sociological answer. But why should we ask the question as one about social facts? Why should we confine our interest to what counts as an F in S, and not what makes it the case that an o is an F (in S)?

There is no cheating here. In order to see this, we need to understand the main theoretical motivation of the legal positivist tradition. When Austin talks about the existence of law as distinct from law's merit, he has a particular theoretical ambition in mind. The ambition is to explain the legal phenomenon, at least some important aspects of it, by way of a reductive explanation. What Austin sought to accomplish is to show that legal validity (and, on his account, the normative aspects of law as well) can be fully explained by reducing the surface phenomena to facts about people's conduct, beliefs and other attitudes. As I explained elsewhere in some detail, H. L. A. Hart shared the same theoretical ambition. His dispute

[19] I am not using the word sociology here to refer to the academic discipline of sociology; my use of the term should be understood in terms of the subject matter, concerning descriptions of social facts and social reality.

with Austin was not about the reductive nature of the explanation sought but about the particular building blocks that Austin had offered. Hart argued, and quite successfully, that Austin's building blocks are too crude and are inadequate to the task.[20] Nevertheless, Hart clearly shared Austin's theoretical ambition to explain some essential aspects of law by way of reducing them to more foundational facts about people's actual modes of conduct, the beliefs they share about them, and other attitudes that accompany those beliefs. In other words, the hallmark of Hart's theory of law is the idea that social rules are at the foundation of law, and that social rules, in turn, can be explained reductively in terms of people's overt conduct and attitudes accompanying it. And, as I argued in the past, with the exception of Kelsen, this project of trying to articulate a reductive explanation of law is characteristic of the legal positivist tradition.[21]

The idea of a reductive explanation, at least in the case of metaphysical reduction, is to show that a distinct type of phenomenon is actually constituted by, and thus fully explicable in terms of, some other, more foundational type of facts. The main criterion of success for a reductive explanation is its completeness.[22] A reductive explanation is successful only when it provides a complete explanation of the reduced class by the building blocks of the more foundational class. For example, think about the possibility of reduction of the biological to the chemical and physical aspects of the material world. It is not enough to show that chemistry and physics explain many aspects of biological phenomena. A reduction of biology to chemistry and physics is successful only if it is complete, only when all the biological aspects of the world are fully explicable by the laws and facts of chemistry and physics. And this, of course, is a tall order; reductive explanations are rather ambitious by their nature, and often remain questionable because they are incomplete.[23]

[20] See Hart [1961]1997: chs. 2–5. [21] See Marmor 2011: chs. 1–3; Marmor 2013.

[22] Which is not the case, by the way, with ontological dependence or even with metaphysical grounding; grounding can be incomplete and still tell us something of metaphysical interest. Reduction is successful only if it provides complete metaphysical grounding between the items in its relata.

[23] The relation between metaphysical reduction – which is what I mean here, not semantic reduction – and metaphysical grounding is difficult to articulate briefly. Both are forms of explanation, as opposed to supervenience, which is not, and both purport to capture a form of metaphysical constitution, trying to capture the kind of cases where A is X *in virtue of* B. In my view, which I cannot hope to defend here, reduction comes in two main forms: either as a type of identity claim (for example, in semantic reductions) whereby A *just is*

One of the main differences between scholars in the legal positivist tradition consists in the scope of their reductive ambitions. With the exception of Kelsen, I think that all legal positivists shared the assumption that legal validity is reducible to social facts; they differed, however, about the explanation of the normativity of law.[24] Austin applied his reductive explanation to the normativity of law as well, purporting to show that we can explain how law gives its subjects reasons for action in terms of people's desire to avoid unpleasant consequences from failure to comply with the law. Hart and other legal positivists have not shared this reductive ambition when applied to the normativity of law. But, as we have assumed here all along, the separation thesis is not about law's normativity; it is only about the conditions of legal validity.

Now I hope we can see that if the theoretical ambition is to offer a reductive explanation of legal validity, then the main issue here is not well captured by the question 'What is law?'. Law is, undoubtedly, a lot of things, some of them contingent, others essential or at least more central to what law is, and so on and so forth. No doubt, some essential aspects of law are of great moral significance, and people can have reasonable disagreements about them. Therefore, it should come as no surprise that the 'Is o an F?' type of question might well admit of different and incompatible answers, equally plausible, depending on what aspects of law one deems relevant, essential or important (including, if you will, morally important). The theoretical ambition of trying to articulate a reductive explanation of legal validity points in the direction of asking a different question; it points us to ask 'What counts as an F?' in a given society or a given legal system. In other words, the ambition is to try to articulate the conditions under which members of a given society identify the norms and directives that purport to govern them as distinctly legal norms and directives. And it is to this question that (LP*) purports to be the answer.

Now you might think that I am drawing the target around the arrow here. As if first we have an answer, given by (LP*), and then I formulate around it

B or as a type of metaphysical reduction, which is a form of grounding. Furthermore, reduction involves complete, not partial, grounding of the type: A is X in virtue of B. Thus, when I talk about reduction in the text here, I mean (complete) metaphysical grounding.

24 As I explained elsewhere in detail, though Kelsen was rather explicit in trying to avoid a reductive explanation of legal validity, he actually failed in that endeavour. See Marmor 2011: ch. 1. His explanation turns out to be reductive after all, which is precisely what makes his theory of law belong to the legal positivist tradition.

the kind of question it might be the answer to. But this is not really what I am suggesting. The suggestion is that there are various ways of formulating the question about the conditions of legal validity, and that the formulations should be sensitive to the theoretical framework in which they arise. If the theoretical ambition is to see how far a reductive explanation of legal validity can go, as I think it is, at least historically speaking, then it makes sense to focus on trying to figure out what makes people regard norms of this or that type as distinctly legal norms. In other words, it makes sense to focus on what people have to do and believe and what other attitudes they need to entertain or exhibit for them to say that this is law and that is not law.

You might suspect, however, that we have already committed ourselves to an (LP*) kind of answer just by asking the question in terms of 'What counts as an F in S?'. But that is not true. (LP*) amounts to denying that we ever need to rely on moral argument to determine whether an o counts as an F in S. And this is not something that automatically follows, as it were, from the formulation of the question in the way I suggest. In fact, it is precisely what renders the reductive explanation contestable and subject to disagreement.

In order to see this last point, consider Dworkin's early critique of Hart's legal positivism, in which he clearly rejects the reductive explanation of legal validity that Hart has given.[25] By introducing the idea of legal principles, Dworkin aimed to show that no reductive explanation is possible to answer the question of what *counts as an F in S*; and that is so because, at least when the legal validity of principles is in play, the facts that partly establish legal validity are moral facts, not just facts about people's conduct and attitudes. In this dispute about the idea of legal validity, Hart and Dworkin try to answer the same question; they both focus on the question of what counts as legally valid in a given legal system. Hart purported to show that we can provide the answer by way of a reductive explanation that takes social facts to be foundational, whereby those facts provide necessary and sufficient conditions for legal validity. Dworkin, on the other hand, argued that this reductive explanation is bound to be utterly incomplete because it cannot apply to ways in which judges and other legal actors come to regard certain principles to

[25] See Dworkin 1977: chs. 2–3.

have legal validity; the legal validity of principles, Dworkin argued, is, partly but necessarily, a matter of moral argument.

Dworkin's theory of legal principles is precisely the kind of argument that forms the relevant type of challenge to the reductive explanation embodied in (LP*). Remember that, according to Dworkin's argument, principles, as opposed to legal rules, gain their legal validity by way of a combination of source-based and merit-based considerations. A principle is legally valid if it forms part of the best moral justification (or, as he later claimed, interpretation) of some source-based law. Which means that a conclusion to the legal validity of a principle partly, but necessarily, depends on moral reasoning. Clearly, if this is true, (LP*) is false.

My aim in this chapter, however, is not to settle this particular debate; elsewhere, I presented in greater detail my arguments against Dworkin's theory of legal principles, and I will not repeat those arguments here.[26] I will just say, briefly, that the problem that Dworkin's theory faces here is essentially the same problem we mentioned earlier about the interpretative nature of law. Proponents of (LP*) can easily admit that when judges face a case that would seem to be unsettled by existing law, they might reason to the solution in the way that Dworkin describes, namely, they would look at the relevant body of existing law and try to figure out the best moral justification underlying the relevant legal material. And once they came up with a justifying principle, they would apply it to bear on the case at hand. So far, none of this would show that (LP*) is false, because none of it shows that the principle in play had been the law prior to, and irrespective of, the judicial decision that applied it. The principle becomes part of the law, as (LP*) would have it, only because and to the extent that judges engage with it, rely on it and apply it.

Dworkin's response to this kind of critique was to argue that it misses the ways in which judges and other legal actors rationalise their own decisions. On his view, an (LP*) type of explanation is just not the kind of explanation that judges can come to recognise as their own, as it were; it is just not the way they would think about it.[27] They would think that they apply a legal principle because it is the law, and not that it becomes law because they apply it. We can raise some doubts about the generality of

[26] See Marmor 2011: ch. 4.

[27] See, e.g., Dworkin 1986: chs. 1–3. The same theme is reiterated, even further emphasized, in Dworkin 2006. See also Stravopoulos 2012.

Dworkin's claim here, seeing that judges are often quite aware of the fact that they are modifying the law by their decisions, even if they claim otherwise.[28] But this is not the point that I would like to pursue here. The more general, methodological point is to question the relevance of rationalisation to the kind of reductive explanation that (LP*) aims to provide. Let me explain this briefly.

There are certain types of theoretical explanation of social phenomena that are subject to what we can call an *internal rationalisation constraint*; namely, they would have to be the kinds of explanation that the participants in the social practice explained could come to recognise as their own, so to speak, *rationalising for them* the relevant conduct they engage in and the attitudes they have about it. In other words, those are the explanations that, if successful, would create a kind of 'aha!' moment for the participants, enabling them to see more clearly what gives them reasons to do this or that or have the attitudes they do. The internal rationalisation constraint should be clearly distinguished, however, from what H. L. A. Hart labelled the 'internal point of view' of social practices.[29] Of course, any explanation of a social practice, be it reductionist or not, must explain, inter alia, the participants' internal point of view. The participants' beliefs about their reasons for action form an essential part of the data that needs to be explained. This is common ground between reductionists and anti-reductionists. The internal rationalisation constraint, however, pertains to the type of explanation that is offered about the internal point of view; it requires the explanation to be of a kind that the participants can endorse as something that rationalises for them, normatively speaking, the reasons for belief and the reasons for action they endorse as participants.

Dworkin clearly assumes that a theory about the nature of law is subject to the internal rationalisation constraint; it must provide the kind of explanation that would rationalise, *for the participants*, their reasons for engaging in the practice and the various attitudes they hold about it.[30] The

[28] Sometimes judges do not even claim this; Dworkin ignores the fact that judges often acknowledge, quite explicitly, that their decisions modify the law or even make new law.

[29] For my own take on Hart's account of the internal point of view, and how it fits with his reductionist project, see Marmor 2011: ch. 2. As I explain there in detail, part of what Hart says about the internal point of view is a critique of Kelsen, explicitly, not of Austin; his main point is that we can provide a full account of the internal point of view reductively, without postulating anything like a Basic Norm.

[30] Note that I mean normative reasons here, not motivating reasons or causes.

problem is that, generally speaking, a reductive explanation of a social practice is not committed to this internal rationalisation constraint. A reductive explanation is successful, as I mentioned earlier, if it is a complete reduction. But it does not have to rationalise the practice it purports to explain in a way that participants could come to recognise as their own explanation for engaging in it. The clearest example of this is a Marxist explanation of religion or, more generally, of ideology. It is, no doubt, a reductive explanation, and it might be a good or a bad one at that, but it does not have to be the kind of explanation that participants can employ to rationalise their engagement with the practice. If you are a religious person, you would not be inclined to endorse a Marxist explanation by way of trying to rationalise to yourself your system of beliefs; that's not going to work for you. But, of course, it would not show a Marxist explanation to be wrong; it just shows that it is the kind of explanation that is not subject to the internal rationalisation constraint. And I think that this is generally true of reductive explanations of social practices; they are not the kind of explanations that are subject to the internal rationalisation constraint. And if I am right about the proper construal of (LP*) as forming part of a reductive explanation, I think that we should not count as a possible counter-example to it the fact that it may not be the best tool to explain how participants in the legal practice, perhaps judges in particular, would rationalise their own engagement with the law. To be sure, we need to be able to explain why judges and other committed participants have the attitudes they do, and what makes them think that there are reasons for belief and for action where they see them, but not necessarily in a way that they could come to recognise as reasons and values they endorse.[31]

20.5 The Question of Incorporation

Gardner was right to claim that his formulation of (LP*) does not rule out the possibility that merit-based considerations bear on the legal validity of norms if, but only if, those merit-based considerations are source-based. In

[31] It may be worth bearing in mind that even Dworkin's legal theory does not quite comply with the internal rationalisation constraint when applied to various religious legal orders. Dworkin's theory of law may sit well with the common law tradition in this respect, but not really with anything like Canon Law or Sharia Law.

other words, (LP*) would seem to leave room for a construal that allows for source-based norms to condition or otherwise constrain the legal validity of some subset of putative norms on merits.[32] There are two ways in which this may come to be: on the view of so-called *soft* or *inclusive* legal positivism, those same factual criteria that establish the particular sources of law in a given legal system, such as, say, Hart's rules of recognition, may be such that they direct the conditions of legal validity as partly merit-based. On this view, we need to draw a distinction between two levels of 'sources': at a foundational level, we have social facts that constitute what counts as the sources of law in the particular jurisdiction in question; and then, based on these foundational sources, we have particular sources, such as acts of a legislature or decisions of higher courts, and so forth, as established sources of law in the system. According to soft legal positivism, there is nothing to prevent the foundational sources from mandating or recognising various types of merit considerations as particular sources of law. We may have a legal system, for example, in which the foundational sources of law condition some subset of norms' legal validity on certain moral conditions. So, this is one way in which merit may be part of the conditions of legal validity, that is, due to the foundational sources of law that happen to prevail in a given society.

The second way in which merit-based consideration may bear on legal validity, which is much more familiar to lawyers, is by way of explicit legal instruction. The clear cases are typically constitutional, whereby the constitution renders unconstitutional, and thus not legally valid, certain norms that violate moral-political principles, such as respect for freedom of speech or human dignity, and such. In other words, it seems that the law can incorporate, explicitly and perhaps sometimes implicitly, merit-based considerations as conditions on the legal validly of norms.[33]

These two types of incorporation of merit-based considerations as conditions of legal validity raise different questions, and we need to deal with them separately. Let me start with the second type since it is more focused and easier to handle. So, take, for example, part of the US Constitution's first amendment, saying that 'Congress shall make no law ... abridging the freedom of speech.' It would seem that this constitutional provision makes the legal validity of certain norms depend on the question of whether their content is such that they violate the moral-political right to

[32] Gardner 2001: 201. [33] Raz 2009: ch. 7.

free speech. If an act of Congress violates freedom of speech, it is not legally valid in the United States. Or so it seems that the Constitution prescribes. And, of course, whether an act of Congress violates freedom of speech or not is a matter of moral-political argument; it depends on the law's merit, as it were. But this portrayal of the constitutional provision is specious. What such constitutional provisions do, legally speaking, is grant legal power to the courts, the legal power to strike down acts of the legislature if the court finds them in violation of the rights to freedom of speech. To see the difference, just bear in mind that an act of Congress that violates the freedom of speech is not legally void unless, and until, a court with a final authority on the matter holds that it is.

There is nothing special about legal powers that direct the power holder to exercise the power on the basis of certain types of consideration or, as is more often the case, that direct the power holder to exclude from consideration certain types of reason. A legal power is always constrained in various ways. For example, by granting some official bureau the power to issue building permits, the power would be directed and limited in many ways. It would normally direct the relevant bureau to consider granting or withholding the permit on some set of grounds and excluding others. And some of those grounds may well involve considerations of merit; aesthetic merit, moral merit (for example, the needs of the community, fairness in the allocation of resources, and so forth), economic merit and so on and so forth. Legal powers are invariably constrained and there is nothing special about them being constrained by all sorts of merit-based consideration. In any case, and this is why incorporation is not a problem for proponents of (LP*), when a legal power is granted, law is modified only by the actual exercise of the power. Once again, a law abridging the freedom of speech is not law only if it is actually held to be unconstitutional by the court. And this, of course, is perfectly consistent with the content of (LP*).

The type of alleged incorporation of morality as a condition of legal validity espoused by soft legal positivism is theoretically very different. It is not about legal powers but about the nature of the sources thesis itself. There are many complicated issues involved here and I cannot do justice to the extensive literature on the topic in a few short paragraphs. But I will conclude this chapter by pointing to what, in my mind, is the main difficulty here.

Soft positivism would have us envisage the possibility that a fully reductive explanation of legal validity, along the lines formulated by

(LP*), is compatible, at least theoretically, with the idea that the legal validity of some norms actually depends on their merit. But this seems very unlikely on its face, unless we substitute 'depends on merit' with 'depends on what people in S take to be the merit'. The latter is fully compatible with a reductive explanation because it reduces the conditions of legal validity to people's conduct and attitudes. In other words, on this latter construal of the possible role of moral considerations in determining the legal validity of norms, what matters is not the soundness or truth of the relevant moral considerations but the mere fact, the social fact, that people, particularly judges and other legal officials, believe them to be true and treat them as constraints on legal validity. This is fine, and consistent with (LP*). But problems begin when we shift from beliefs and other attitudes to moral truths. Then the view is no longer consistent with any reductive explanation. Unless, of course, you think that there is nothing more to morality and moral truths than whatever it is that people believe to be morally right. I do not think that this questionable meta-ethical stance is what soft positivists want to adhere to. And even if there is a plausible meta-ethical stance that fits a fully reductionist account, it is very questionable that we would want a theory about the nature of law to depend on any particular, and rather controversial, meta-ethical position. In short, I think that the price tag for adhering to a soft kind of legal positivism consists in giving up the kind of reductionist project that legal positivism aimed to pursue. And then the problem is that if we give up the reductionist aspiration of legal positivism, we may also lose the theoretical motivation for its core commitments.

References

Austin, J. [1832]1995. *The Province of Jurisprudence Determined.* Ed. W. E. Rumble. Cambridge University Press.

Coleman, J. 1982. 'Negative and Positive Positivism'. *Journal of Legal Studies* 11: 139–64.

Dworkin, R. 1977. *Taking Rights Seriously.* Duckworth.

Dworkin, R. 1986. *Law's Empire.* Harvard University Press.

Dworkin, R. 2006. *Justice in Robes.* Harvard University Press.

Gardner, J. 2001. 'Legal Positivism: 5½ Myths'. *American Journal of Jurisprudence* 46: 199–227.

Hart, H. L. A. [1961]1997. *The Concept of Law*. 2nd ed. Eds. P. Bulloch and J. Raz. Oxford University Press.

Hume, D. [1740]1978. *A Treatise of Human Nature*. Ed. P. H. Nittich. Oxford University Press.

Marmor, A. 2005. *Interpretation and Legal Theory*. 2nd ed. Hart.

Marmor, A. 2011. *Philosophy of Law*. Princeton University Press.

Marmor, A. 2013. 'Farewell to Conceptual Analysis (in Jurisprudence)'. In W. Waluchow and S. Sciaraffa (eds.). *Philosophical Foundations of the Nature of Law*. Oxford University Press: 209–29.

Marmor, A. 2018. 'Law as Authoritative Fiction'. *Law and Philosophy* 37: 473–97.

Marmor, A. 2019. 'What's Left of General Jurisprudence? On Law's Ontology and Content'. *Jurisprudence* 10(2): 151–70.

Raz, J. 2009. *Between Authority and Interpretation*. Oxford University Press.

Stravopoulos, N. 2012. 'Obligations, Interpretivism and the Legal Point of View'. In A. Marmor (ed.). *The Routledge Companion to Philosophy of Law*. Routledge: 76–92.

Waluchow, W. 1994. *Inclusive Legal Positivism*. Oxford University Press.

The Origins of Inclusive Legal Positivism 21

W. J. Waluchow

21.1 Legal Positivism

Legal positivism (LP) is a family of theories about the fundamental nature of law. It is usually understood in terms of its commitment to two key tenets.

The social thesis

1. Law is, essentially, a social phenomenon or construct.
2. Law and legal validity are ultimately a function of special *social facts* (not moral or natural facts).
3. These special social facts (for example, acts of legislation, or judicial decisions and practices) constitute the *sources of law*.

The separation thesis

1. A norm L can be *legally valid* even if L *lacks moral validity or merit* – that is, even if it is unjust or unfair, or fails to treat citizens equally.
2. *Conceptually*, a law's *existence* is independent of its *merit*, or what it *ought* to be.
3. Law and morality are *conceptually distinct* phenomena.

The positivist's separation thesis is, arguably, an implication of the social thesis.[1] If the existence and validity of law ultimately depend exclusively

[1] There is at least one notable legal positivist, Joseph Raz, who seems to deny this implication. Raz (1979: 38–9) states: 'The claim that what is law and what is not is purely a matter of social fact still leaves it an open question whether or not those social facts by which we identify the law or determine its existence do or do not endow it with moral merit. If they do, it has of necessity a moral character.' It is important to note, however, that the moral character referred to by Raz is not equivalent to a degree of moral merit sufficient to establish a moral obligation to obey the law of any particular legal system. Nor is it sufficient to rule out sound moral arguments in favour of modifying or eliminating that legal system or any of its norms. Nor is Raz suggesting that the social facts by which we identify law do in fact endow it with moral merit. He is merely suggesting that the contrary – that they do not – does not follow.

on *social* facts – that is, facts about the beliefs, attitudes, actions and practices of members of some society – and if social facts are a matter of what *is* the case, not what morally *ought to be* the case, then there seems nothing in the social thesis itself that guarantees that laws have moral merit. One sees this clearly when one considers the ultimate social facts specified by John Austin: the *command of the sovereign.*[2]

In Austin's view, if one looks carefully at any legal system, one will notice certain social facts: there is always a *sovereign*, a person (or group of persons) who enjoys the habitual obedience of the bulk of the society in which that system exists, and who habitually obeys no one else. The general commands of this sovereign person (or group of persons) constitute the laws of the society over whom that sovereign governs; and to be under a legal obligation is to be liable to a sanction should one disobey one of the sovereign's general commands. It means nothing more and it means nothing less. It's important to stress that, for Austin, there is no talk of moral or political legitimacy when it comes to identifying the sovereign. The test of sovereignty is factual through and through. There are also no substantive, content-specific constraints, moral or otherwise, on what this sovereign might, as a matter of sheer social fact, command – and hence what counts as law in the society in question. Unlike on Aquinas's natural law theory (NLT), where law is claimed to be, in its very essence, an *ordinance of reason* and for the *common good* – that is, an expression of the natural law – the identity of human law is, for Austin, essentially *indifferent* to morality.[3] And this, according to Austin, is the lesson encapsulated in the separation thesis: the existence of law is one thing; its merit or demerit is another thing altogether.

So, according to legal positivists, human law is essentially a social entity and its content is exhausted by norms that arise ultimately by virtue of the relevant social facts. Of course, not all positivists believe that the relevant social facts consist in the commands of an Austinian sovereign. H. L. A. Hart developed an influential version of positivism that endorsed both the separation thesis and the social thesis, but he understood the latter quite differently from Austin. Hart's view was that the existence and the validity of law are a function not of a sovereign's commands but of a special set of *conventional social rules* accepted and practised by officials

[2] For Austin's theory, see Austin 1954.

[3] For Aquinas's theory, see his *Summa Theologica* I-II qu. 90–7.

of the legal system.[4] These social rules, the existence and content of which are also matters of pure social fact, determine that other social facts – for example acts of legislation or precedent-setting judicial decisions – result in the creation, modification, annulment and authoritative interpretation of legal norms. According to Hart, law is ultimately a function of such official practices of recognition, change and adjudication. And, as with Austin, the dependence of law's existence and validity on these ultimate social practices entails that laws can exist absent any moral merit.

In light of their endorsement of the separation thesis, one might think that, for positivists, morality has no bearing whatsoever on law. But this would be a serious mistake. The separation thesis has a very specific, limited meaning, one that is in fact consistent with recognition of countless points of connection between law and morality. In putting forward the separation thesis, positivists are keen to stress one fundamental point: there is nothing in the bare notion of law (or legality) that itself *guarantees* that a legal system or its laws have any degree of moral merit. There is nothing in the very notion of a sovereign's command, or of a norm valid because it satisfies the conventionally agreed criteria of validity included in Hart's rule of recognition, that guarantees that a law is morally worthy. As Hart remarked, the criterion of validity found in a rule of recognition could be as rudimentary as 'Whatever Rex 1 enacts is law.'[5] So the separation thesis has a very specific, limited meaning. And, understood in the manner intended, it is consistent with a multitude of other ways in which law and morality are or could be connected with one another. Here are some of them.

As Hart observed, the laws of a society often reflect the moral principles and values accepted within that community – a society's tax laws, for example, are often based on certain widespread notions of fairness. Hart also thought it quite possible that a system's rules of adjudication might impose a duty on judges to decide in accordance with what they thought morally best when they make decisions in difficult cases where, for some reason, the law's guidance appears to have run out. The judges would in this instance be instructed to appeal to morality as a source of justification,

[4] Hart calls these *rules of recognition*, which introduce criteria of legal validity; *rules of change*, which render possible the authoritative creation, alteration or elimination of legal rules; and *rules of adjudication*, which create and regulate the activities of what we refer to as the judiciary. See Hart 1994: 50–78.

[5] Hart 1994: 96.

not for a decision as to what the law already is on the relevant matter but for a discretionary decision regarding what the law shall henceforth be for that type of case. In other words, morality is sometimes endorsed as a source of justification for the judicial *creation*, as opposed to *discovery*, of law.[6] Hart is notable for taking this thought on the role of moral norms in judicial decision-making one very important step further – and in a way that saw him depart from some of his fellow positivists. He thought that a rule of recognition might include moral criteria of legal validity to which judges might be required to appeal in assessing legal validity.

> The law of every modern state shows at a thousand points the influence of both the accepted social morality and wider moral ideals. These influences enter into law either abruptly and avowedly though legislation, or silently and piecemeal though the judicial process. In some systems, as in the United States, the ultimate criteria of legal validity explicitly incorporate principles of justice or substantive moral values ... The further ways in which law mirrors morality are myriad, and still insufficiently studied.[7]

How one is to understand the so-called moral criteria of legal validity to which Hart makes reference here is a tricky theoretical question that divides positivists, and to which we will return shortly. But what is abundantly clear is that, in asserting their separation thesis, defenders of LP in no way wish to deny that law and morality can be related to one another in all kinds of ways.[8]

Despite endorsement of the many ways in which law and morality can be connected, positivists are united in rejecting the one connection that arguably defines NLT: the conceptually necessary dependence of legal validity on moral validity or merit. They reject, for instance, Aquinas's contention that a law is, by its very nature or essence, and independently of contingent human beliefs, attitudes and conventional practices, necessarily an ordinance of reason for the common good. And they reject what Aquinas took to be a logical implication of that statement: that an unjust law is 'no law at all'. So, despite the many issues on which they divide, what

[6] For Hart's thoughts on the desirability and necessity of judicial discretion to create new law in what he called *penumbral cases*, see Hart 1994: 124–54.

[7] Hart 1994: 203–4.

[8] For further discussion of these issues, see Green 2008: 1048. Green's article includes a careful and insightful articulation of the many ways in which the separation thesis is consistent with connections between law and morality.

unifies all positivists is their commitment to the social and the separation theses so understood. These, in combination with one another, entail this simple truth (as defenders of LP see it): the social nature of law entails the conceptual possibility that a valid human law may well be devoid of any and all moral merit.

21.2 Dworkin's Challenge

Ronald Dworkin, Hart's student and successor in the Chair of Jurisprudence at Oxford University, provided the first sustained, critical analysis of Hart's particular version of LP, which Dworkin called 'the ruling theory of the law'.[9] Dworkin agreed with Hart that law includes rules authoritatively adopted by a political community, perhaps in accordance with procedures sanctioned by something like Hart's rule of recognition. These he called the *settled law*. But he dramatically parted ways with Hart in insisting that this settled, positive law in no way exhausts the law. What Dworkin referred to as the *full law* also includes the *principles of political morality* that these settled rules embody.[10] In Dworkin's terms, it includes the set of principles of political morality that provide the settled law with its best explanation and moral justification – what Dworkin later came to call (in *Law's Empire*) its *best constructive interpretation*. These principles, together with the settled law, not only constitute the full law; they actually serve as the justificatory basis for all judicial decisions and the coercive state measures they license, even in easy cases that appear to involve nothing more than the simple application of a legal rule. Judicial decisions that enforce the full law exhibit a fundamental virtue that Dworkin called *integrity*. By integrity, Dworkin meant *consistency of principle* – the law treats people with integrity when it treats them consistently in accordance with the same underlying principles of political morality and the rights these establish. Legal decisions that appear simply to be the application of the relevant legal rules are justified not because they follow from these rules but because, and to the extent that, in deciding as these rules require, judges are enforcing the principles and rights of political morality that the

[9] Dworkin 1977: vii.

[10] Dworkin's early theory was developed in Dworkin 1977. The theory was later developed and grounded in an overall theory of interpretation, in Dworkin 1986.

settled law endorses and expresses in its more concrete legal rules and decisions.

An implication of Dworkin's integrity theory (LI) is that the connection between what law already *is* and what it *ought to be* is much stronger than the positivist's separation thesis would allow. Dworkin agrees with natural lawyers in rejecting the separation thesis. If law is by its very nature a justification for state coercion that stems from the underlying principles and rights of political morality that the settled law endorses, it follows that law is deeply connected to morality at the conceptual level. It further follows that the model of rules is a seriously defective, impoverished theory of law.

In defending his claim that law is deeply connected to morality in the way he supposes, Dworkin drew on a number of familiar features of modern Anglo-American legal practice, most notably the ways in which judges deal with hard cases. A hard case was understood by Dworkin as one of those difficult cases where the law fails to provide an easy or clear solution to a legal question upon which the case turns.[11] As noted in Section 21.1, Hart claimed that law is a system of legal rules validated by a foundational rule of recognition. He further asserted that this set of rules exhausts the law. But sometimes, Hart recognised, the guidance provided by this finite set of rules will run out. It might be clear that a particular valid rule is relevant to the case in question, but not so clear – perhaps even indeterminate – what it actually requires. In such cases, judges will have to use their own best judgement in deciding how the rule should be read and hence what the rule shall henceforth be taken to require. In other words, they will be forced to exercise *discretion*, and to create new law by supplementing or adding to the rule's determinate meaning. Of course, such discretionary decisions will have to be based on something other than the existing requirements of valid law because the law's guidance has run out in this kind of hard case. It follows that judges will have to step beyond the law, perhaps drawing on their own moral beliefs concerning how the relevant rule *ought* henceforth to be interpreted. They will then have to apply that newly created law to decide the legal case to which the settled law had failed to provide a solution.

[11] One of Dworkin's earliest and most influential articles was in fact entitled *Hard Cases*. See Dworkin 1975: 1057.

Dworkin found fault with Hart's account of hard cases and the role it assigned morality in dealing with them. As a result, he set out to develop his alternative, according to which principles of political morality are sometimes used, not to create new law in the manner suggested by Hart but to determine what the law already *is* – the legal rights and duties that the law *already* establishes in its seamless web of normative requirements. Among the implications of this view is that law is intimately connected to morality in ways denied by the positivist's separation thesis. If moral principles are invoked, as Hart said, not to create new law but to determine what the law already is, then quite clearly the existence of law cannot possibly be one thing and its moral merit another thing altogether. In short, we cannot separate law from morality in the way sanctioned by LP's separation thesis.

So seemingly obvious facts about Anglo-American legal practice were sufficient to establish, Dworkin thought, that LP and its separation thesis must be rejected. The fact that Anglo-American legal practice often makes the identity of existing law, and the legal rights and obligations it establishes, crucially dependent on principles of political morality served, in Dworkin's view, to undermine LP entirely. But did it? Not according to some positivists who insisted that there is nothing in the theoretical commitments of LP that precludes morality from playing something like the role Dworkin ascribes to it. It is to the development of this particular line of argument, and the distinctive legal theory it generated, that we now turn.

21.3 The Positivist Strikes Back

In answering Dworkin's challenge, some positivists denied his premise that the principles on which judges rely in hard cases are in fact genuine principles of *political morality*, as opposed to ordinary principles of law that bear a striking resemblance to them. Rolf Sartorius argued that the principles on which judges rely in many hard cases are considered appropriate grounds for decisions not, as Dworkin posited, because of their role in explaining and morally justifying the settled law. On the contrary, they are binding legal principles because of the degree of *institutional support* they enjoy.[12] To be sure, these legal principles – for example that

[12] See Sartorius 1975: 181–210. Dworkin's reply to Sartorius can be found in Dworkin 1977: 64–8.

no one should be permitted to profit from his own wrongdoing – often *resemble* corresponding moral principles. But they are no more examples of genuinely moral principles than an ordinary tax law adopted in light of the moral principles of fairness it respects. Institutional support is a content-neutral criterion of legal validity that depends exclusively on morally neutral social facts, like the number of times a principle has previously been invoked by judges and other legal officials in the furtherance of their professional duties. It is a content neutral, *social* criterion of validity that has the power to transform a moral principle into one that is legally valid independently of its moral merit.

Other philosophers took a decidedly different route. They accepted Dworkin's premise that genuinely moral principles of political morality can, and perhaps sometimes do, play a role in establishing the requirements of existing law, but they argued that this fact is perfectly compatible with the fundamental commitments of LP. In the view of these positivists, the facts of legal practice to which Dworkin drew our attention are in fact fully consistent with the social and the separation theses, *properly understood*. The initial focus of these particular positivists was on the separation thesis and its supposed implication that legal validity can never depend on a norm's conformity with genuine moral principles or values. They insisted that this is not, in fact, an implication of the separation thesis at all, and that Dworkin had simply misunderstood the message conveyed by it. In pursuance of this reply to Dworkin, these positivists went on to develop what came to be known as *inclusive legal positivism* (ILP).[13] In so doing, they distinguished themselves from those defenders of LP who shared Dworkin's understanding of the separation thesis and who, as a result, endorsed what came to be known as *exclusive legal positivism* (ELP). Let's begin with ILP.

Inclusive positivists argued that Dworkin failed to distinguish two crucially different theses:

The separation thesis: As a matter of conceptual necessity, the legal validity of a norm can never depend on its consistency with moral norms.[14]

[13] The theory was also known by a number of different labels: *soft positivism*, *incorporationism*, and the *weak social thesis*. Common usage has, however, settled on *inclusive legal positivism* and its contrasting term *exclusive legal positivism*.

[14] Henceforth, we will refer to this thesis simply as the *separation thesis*, leaving unanswered whether the traditional separation thesis endorsed by Austin is to be read in this way or as asserting the weaker separability thesis.

The separability thesis: It is conceptually possible, but by no means necessary, that the legal validity of a norm can depend on its consistency with moral norms.

According to the separation thesis, legality and morality are *necessarily separate* from one another; consistency with a moral norm can never, as a matter of conceptual necessity, be a condition of what the law is. It can only be a condition of justifiable law creation, possibly by a judge in the exercise of her discretion. In other words, one very good reason to create, extend or supplement existing law in one way rather than another might be that this is the only way to remain consistent with some important moral principle, value or rule. The moral norm provides guidance to the law creator not in determining what the law is but in deciding what it henceforth ought to and will be. According to the *separability thesis*, on the other hand, legality and morality are only separable, that is, capable of being separated from one another, but not necessarily so. Though the two can, in practice, be separated from one another, it remains conceptually possible that they can be brought together *if the right social conditions prevail*. Among these conditions is the system's rule of recognition specifying conformity with a particular moral norm, such as a principle of fairness, as a condition of legal validity in that particular system.[15] In short, defenders of ILP reject the separation thesis but fully endorse the separability thesis. In response to Dworkin's claim that sometimes an appeal to moral norms figures in attempts to determine the requirements of existing law, defenders of ILP reply: Yes, but this is *not necessarily* so. Although there is nothing in the essential nature of law, as characterised by the social and

[15] In suggesting that conformity with a moral norm can be a condition of legal validity, Hart endorsed a 'necessity' version of ILP according to which conformity with a moral norm can be a necessary, though not necessarily sufficient, condition of legal validity. Others, most notably Jules Coleman, came to endorse a sufficiency version according to which truth as a moral principle could also serve as a sufficient condition for legal validity. See, for example, Coleman 1998: 381. Coleman initially referred to his theory as *incorporationism* but came later to refer to it as a version of inclusive legal positivism. Matthew Kramer reserved the term *inclusive legal positivism* for the necessity version endorsed by Hart. Kramer also distinguished two versions of incorporationism: *extreme incorporationism* of the sort defended by Coleman, according to which conformity with a moral norm can be a sufficient condition for legal validity in any sort of case, and Kramer's own *moderate incorporationism* according to which a rule of recognition could 'establish . . . that moral worthiness is a sufficient condition for the status of norms as legal norms [only] in hard cases that cannot be resolved by reference to legal norms from other [non-moral] sources' (Kramer 2004: 28). In this entry, the term *inclusive legal positivism* should, unless otherwise indicated, be understood to refer to any of these types of theory.

(now) the separability theses, *requiring* appeal to moral norms to determine existing legal requirements (as there arguably is with LI and with NLT of the sort espoused by Aquinas), there is nothing that *prohibits* this possibility either. This is something that Hart clearly recognised, long before Dworkin made the acceptance or denial of this possibility into a central issue. Hart was adamant in all of his writings on the issue that his rule of recognition can be as austere as *Whatever the Queen in Parliament enacts is law*, a rule that clearly separates legal validity from any and all moral conditions. But he was equally clear that '[i]n some systems [of law], as in the United States, the ultimate criteria of legal validity explicitly incorporate principles of justice or substantive moral values'.[16] Such criteria render the American rule of recognition one in which the conceptually separable properties of legality and morality are, as a matter of contingent social practice, brought together, the latter being a condition of the former.[17]

There are, in fact, many legal systems that stipulate conformity with moral principle as a condition of legal validity. Article 5 of the Brazilian Constitution specifies that 'All persons are equal before the law, without any distinction whatsoever.' Any act of Congress that results in a denial of equality before the law can be rejected by the courts as unconstitutional. The Fourteenth Amendment of the US Constitution asserts that no state may 'deprive any person of life, liberty, or property, without due process of law; nor deny to any person within its jurisdiction the equal protection of the laws'. The phrases 'due process of law' and 'equal protection' have generally come to be understood, in the United States, as requiring basic

[16] Hart 1994: 204.

[17] In what follows, we will focus on this particular connection between law and morality: the dependence of legal validity on conformity with moral norms. This is but one possible connection that legal practice might sanction. Here is another example. Common law jurisdictions often embrace what is traditionally called *the golden rule* of statutory interpretation. According to this rule, the otherwise obvious, ordinary meaning of a statute is to be rejected in favour of an alternative reading if failure to do so would lead to a 'manifest absurdity or repugnance'. In *Becke* v. *Smith* (1836) 2 M&W 195, Judge Parke summed up the rule as follows: 'It is a very useful rule in the construction of a statute to adhere to the ordinary meaning of the words used, and to the grammatical construction, unless that is at variance with the intention of the legislature to be collected from the statute itself, or leads to any manifest absurdity or repugnance, in which case the language may be varied or modified so as to avoid such inconvenience but no further.' Since repugnance is a decidedly moral notion, any legal practice that accepts the golden rule accepts a role for morality in helping to determine the legal norm for which a statute stands. What the law *is* partly depends on what it *ought* morally to be.

fairness. If a congressional statute is viewed by an American court as fundamentally unfair to some person or group of persons, then it is licensed to strike it down, to declare it legally invalid on grounds of unconstitutionality. And so on. The important point, for our purposes, is not the (highly significant) fact that these constitutional instruments recognise important principles of political morality and the rights to which they give legal standing. Rather, it is that they appear to require conformity with these principles and rights *as conditions of legal validity.*

So, the key move by defenders of ILP was to distinguish the separation and the separability theses and insist that LP is committed only to the latter. But what of the social thesis? In accepting the separability thesis, had defenders of ILP abandoned their claim that law is fundamentally a social entity and that the existence of law ultimately depends on the right social facts obtaining? Not necessarily. In order to see why this is so, we need to bring to light the crucial insight underlying the move made by those who introduced ILP as a distinct version of LP. What ILP insists on is the importance of distinguishing two questions:

(a) whether an *individual law, L,* has an appropriate social source; and
(b) whether a *criterion of validity, C,* has an appropriate social source.

According to ILP, the social thesis does not require that the validity of a law necessarily depends exclusively on whether it has the appropriate social sources in, for example, legislative enactment, executive action or judicial decision.[18] Rather, it says that what counts as a *criterion of legal validity* depends exclusively on whether *it* has the appropriate social source. Following Hart, most contemporary positivists identify the relevant social source with *acceptance* and use of the criterion by the officials of the legal system, most notably its judges. The fact that the officials of the Canadian legal system accept conformity with the moral principles and values specified in their Charter of Rights and Freedoms as a criterion of valid law in Canada establishes that those principles and values do in fact serve that role within Canadian law.

We might summarise this key point in terms of the following characterisations of the theoretical commitments of ILP and ELP.

[18] Or, in Austin's view, the command of the sovereign.

ELP

1. C is a criterion of legal validity of some law, L, only if C has the appropriate social source (in acceptance by officials of the system).
2. L is a valid law if and only if L itself has an appropriate social source (for example, in legislative enactment or judicial decision).

On this ELP reading of the social thesis, no criterion, C, can be moral in nature. It must not deal with L's moral content or merit but only with L's *pedigree.*[19] Not only must all criteria of validity have social sources; so too must all the individual laws validated by those criteria.

ILP

1. C is a criterion of legal validity only if C has the appropriate social source (in acceptance by officials of the system)'
2. C might – though it need not – be a moral condition of legal validity.

Therefore:

3. It is possible that an individual law, L, is legally valid only if L satisfies a non-pedigree, moral criterion of validity, C.

On this ILP reading of the social thesis, any criterion, C, can indeed be moral in nature. In other words, it can make reference to L's moral merit (or lack thereof), not merely its pedigree. Though it is true that what counts as a *criterion of validity*, C, can be established by nothing more than whether C has the right social source, the same is *not* necessarily true of all laws valid in virtue of C. If a system, like that of the United States, Brazil or Canada, has adopted moral criteria of legal validity, then more than a law's social source can count in establishing its legal validity. This sets defenders of ILP apart, not only from their ELP cousins but also from Dworkin and defenders of NLT who assert that the union of law with morality is *necessary* in light of the very nature or concept of law. The crucial differences among these three theories might usefully be summarised as follows:

NLT and LI: Conformity with moral principle is a *necessary* condition of legal validity.

ELP: Conformity with moral principle is *necessarily not* a condition of legal validity.

[19] Dworkin was the first to introduce the notion of *pedigree* in discussing the theoretical commitments of LP. See Dworkin 1977: 17.

ILP: Conformity with moral principle is a *possible, though not necessary*, condition of legal validity (it depends on the relevant social practices).

So defenders of ILP rejected the separation thesis and Dworkin's assertion that it reflects the theoretical commitments of LP.[20] Defenders of ELP, on the other hand, agreed with Dworkin on the theoretical commitments of LP and set out to defend their theory, ELP, both against Dworkin's critique of LP and against the claim of their ILP counterparts that the separability thesis provides a sufficient account of LP's theoretical commitments. In response to Dworkin, defenders of ELP accepted that many principles that resemble principles of political morality do indeed figure as binding law, but they were resolute in maintaining that the legal status of these principles is perfectly explicable in terms of morally neutral criteria of validity that make no mention of moral merit or worth. Sartorius developed the notion of institutional support to serve as the relevant criteria, while other philosophers noted other ways in which legal principles that resemble principles of political morality come into existence. In a very early response to Dworkin, for example, Joseph Raz noted that some principles gain their legal status via enactment in the preambles to statutes and constitutions.[21]

Yet another crucial strategy pursued by defenders of ELP (against both ILP and LI) was to distinguish between (a) criteria of validity and (b) criteria for the exercise of the Hohfeldian legal power to invalidate. This latter strategy constitutes the most plausible and powerful one pursued by ELP's defenders. As such it merits the careful examination provided in Section 21.5; but, before we get to that, we should consider why defenders of ELP were not prepared to go along with ILP's central claim that there is nothing in the nature of law that excludes the possibility of moral criteria of validity. Why, one might ask, were defenders of ELP so insistent that consistency with moral norms simply cannot, under any circumstances, be a condition of legal validity? One influential answer arose from the idea that permitting legal validity to depend on consistency with moral norms would undermine one of law's essential features – namely, its claim to authority. That ILP is supposedly inconsistent with law's claim to authority served as the key

[20] Recall that we have distinguished between the separation thesis – which denies that legal validity could ever depend on satisfaction of moral criteria – and the separability thesis – which denies that legal validity *must* depend on satisfaction of moral criteria.

[21] See Raz 1972: 823.

premise in what we will call Raz's *authority argument*. It is to that argument that we now turn.[22]

21.4 ILP and the Authoritative Nature of Law

According to Raz, it is in the very nature of a legal system that it claims justified practical authority over a population – it claims the right to issue binding directives on which (it claims) members of that population have a moral duty to act. Now if these claims are to be at all intelligible, a legal system must at the very least be the kind of thing that is conceptually capable of being practically authoritative, in the way that a person can possibly possess this trait but a tree cannot. As an avowed defender of LP, Raz denies, of course, that law necessarily possesses the justified practical authority it necessarily claims for itself. Its directives might, after all, be of little or no merit, moral or otherwise, in which case the claim to be authoritative would likely be false. But the law has to *make* this claim. And, once again, if that claim is to be at all intelligible, the law must be the kind of thing that is *capable*, conceptually speaking, of possessing practical authority. But what would it be actually to have authority? In answering this fundamental question, Raz developed his highly influential *service conception of authority* according to which (normally) A has authority over S to the extent that S's acting on A's directives renders it more likely that S's actions will be in conformity with the dictates of right reason than if S were to attempt to achieve that on their own.[23] The role of an authority is to provide us with this service. In order to see how law might fulfil this role, consider the following.

Each of us is constantly faced with the question 'What should I do?'. In answering this question, we often appeal to reasons for doing one thing rather than another. Typically, these reasons are either prudential or moral.

[22] Though Raz's authority argument was (and continues to be) the most influential argument against ILP, there were others. Scott Shapiro, for example, argued that ILP robs law of its ability to provide practical guidance. See Shapiro 1998, 2000. For an extended critique of Shapiro's argument, see Kramer 2004: 45–75. See also Waluchow 2000.

[23] A further condition of justified authority is that it is more important that one act in accordance with right reason than that one choose freely how to act. This condition Raz calls the *independence condition*, and, for the purposes of this chapter, I will set it aside. For Raz's service conception of authority, see, e.g., Raz 1979, 1985a, 1985b, 1986.

In deciding whether to finish this chapter or go to a party, I might balance my moral duty to meet the agreed deadline against the considerable enjoyment I would experience were I to go to the party instead. Raz calls the kinds of reasons involved in this example *first-order reasons for action*. In many situations in which we are faced with a choice, we weigh the applicable first-order reasons against one another and act on what we take to be the right balance of reasons.

Sometimes, however, reason suggests that we pursue a different strategy – that we should not, in this way, attempt ourselves to judge and act *directly* on the balance of first-order reasons but that we do so indirectly. This is where authority comes in. Sometimes right reason dictates that I act in accordance with a *second-order reason* that reflects someone else's judgement about the relevant first-order reasons that apply to me. Often the relevant second-order reason will be a directive to act in a particular way issued by an authority, say a financial counsellor if we are making investment decisions, or a trusted friend if we are attempting to answer a difficult moral question. In Raz's view, S is justified (normally) in accepting and acting on A's directives as authoritative when S is more likely to act in accordance with right reason by following those directives than by attempting themselves to act directly on the balance of first-order reasons. This Raz calls the *normal justification thesis* (NJT). Authority provides a kind of second-order *exclusionary reason* that not only purports to give me reason to act in a particular way – such as staying at home to finish the chapter instead of going to the party – but also aims to exclude, and replace, the relevant first-order reasons in my practical deliberations. When the conditions of the NJT are met, right reason suggests that we should act on the authoritative directive rather than directly on (what we ourselves take to be) the proper balance of first-order reasons. In Raz's view, it is the normal role of a practical authority to provide this service. And we are normally justified in accepting this service when the authority successfully fulfils its role – that is, issues second-order reasons that are more likely than our own judgements to reflect the proper balance of first-order reasons.[24]

It follows from this analysis of practical authority that if the law necessarily claims practical authority, and if this claim is to be at all intelligible,

[24] This is but a brief, necessarily incomplete summary of a very complex theory. And, again, I have set aside the independence condition. For further details, see Raz 1979, 1985a, 1985b, 1986.

then the law must at least be the kind of thing that is capable of providing the service that practical authorities are meant to provide. That is, it must be capable of issuing directives (laws) that provide us with second-order reasons capable of excluding and replacing the relevant first-order reasons. And importantly, as we will see later in this section, it must be capable of issuing directives the identity and content of which we can determine without ourselves being forced to consider the relevant first-order reasons the law's directives were meant to exclude and replace.

But why precisely would right reason suggest that we adopt legal institutions and that we follow their directives as opposed to acting directly on our own practical judgments? There are at least two important reasons. First, sometimes we all have first-order reasons to contribute to the realisation of certain public goods – such as education, health care and security – whose realisation requires a kind of coordinated, collective action that is almost impossible to achieve in the absence of directives issued by public institutions created and governed by law. In other words, we are often better able to achieve our collective goals if we act on the basis of second-order reasons established by publicly accessible and enforceable legal directives. When these directives are well designed and administered, we are far more likely to achieve what right reason demands of us – contributing towards the provision of decent levels of education, health and security – if we follow them instead of trying to act outside the law's coordinating framework. In such circumstances, the NJT entails that the law has authority over us, and we are justified in submitting to its authority.

A second reason for wanting a system of legal directives is that sometimes the law simply knows best because it has the time, energy, expertise and resources to determine what is best for us to do. Just as I might be justified in acting on the advice of my financial advisor instead of attempting myself to divine the mysteries of the market, I might be justified in being guided by the law's attempt, on my behalf, to discern the relevant requirements of right reason in relation to things like self-defence or the wearing of seatbelts.

Now comes a crucial step in Raz's authority argument against ILP. If authoritative legal directives are to serve their role in guiding us towards compliance with right reason, their identification and interpretation cannot depend on our having to consider the first-order reasons they were meant to exclude and replace. But this is precisely what happens, Raz thinks, if we accept ILP. Take a statute, for instance. As a second-order, authoritative directive, it is meant to exclude and replace whatever reasons of prudence and morality apply to us in the situations over which it governs. But if the statute's identity as a valid legal directive depends on its conformity with a moral principle such as fairness – a moral reason that is sometimes relevant in many situations governed by laws – then its identity as an authoritative directive may well depend on the very reasons, fairness included, it was meant to exclude and replace. We will have to deliberate on at least some of those first-order reasons in order to determine whether the statute is valid and therefore authoritative. But if so, then we might just as well have dispensed with the statute altogether and instead acted directly on the relevant first-order reasons, including the relevant reason of fairness. Hence, Raz concludes, ILP is incompatible with the law's claim to authority.

Inclusive positivists mounted vigorous and multifaceted replies to Raz's authority argument. Coleman and Waluchow pointed out, for example, that the moral reasons excluded by a legal directive need not be identical with the moral factors invoked in challenging its validity.[25] In its landmark abortion case, *R.* v. *Morgentaler*, the Canadian Supreme Court declared Canadian Criminal Code rules governing abortions unconstitutional because they violated the moral rights to procedural fairness guaranteed by the Canadian Charter of Rights.[26] And whatever the first-order moral reasons underlying those abortion rules might have been (for example, the right to life versus rights to bodily integrity and autonomy), they were not reasons of procedural fairness. Coleman further attempted to meet Raz's challenge by distinguishing between two functions of a rule of recognition: an *identification* function and a *validation* function, suggesting that Raz's authority argument requires only that the rules for identifying valid law employed by 'ordinary folk' make no reference to excluded moral reasons.[27] Since a rule of recognition is seldom used directly by any ordinary person to identify valid laws, the fact that it might require appeal to excluded first-order reasons poses no threat to the law's authority. Waluchow, for his part, took direct aim at Raz's conception of authority, arguing that there is nothing in the nature of an authoritative directive that precludes us from ever having to consult any of the relevant first-order reasons. It is possible that at least some of the relevant first-order reasons

[25] See Coleman 1998; Waluchow 1994, 2000.

[26] *R.* v. *Morgentaler* 1985: Supreme Court Reports 30. [27] See Coleman 1998.

might in various ways figure in attempts to determine the identity and content of a directive that remains authoritative nevertheless. Authoritative guidance can be partial guidance, Waluchow suggested.[28]

21.5 Constitutional Rights and Directed Powers

So, defenders of ELP strongly resisted efforts on the part of their ILP cousins to accommodate Dworkin's insights into the role of moral principles in legal practice. In their view, accepting that legal validity might depend on moral merit flies in the face of an essential feature of law – its necessary claim to practical authority. But a serious puzzle remained. If ILP is rejected, how can LP be made consistent with the obvious facts of legal practice relied on by Dworkin? And what about Hart's claim in *The Concept of Law* that 'In some systems, as in the United States, the ultimate criteria of legal validity explicitly incorporate principles of justice or substantive moral values'?[29] How, in other words, could defenders of ELP accommodate what look like challenges to legal validity based on rights of political morality recognised in constitutional bills and charters of rights?

There were at least two possible routes one could take in response to this puzzle. One would be to deny that provisions like the Fourteenth Amendment of the US Constitution make reference to genuine moral norms – moral norms that are valid or true independently of their acceptance by any particular person or society, for example. But if true morality is not the reference, then what is? The obvious answer is what Austin called *positive morality* and what Hart referred to as *accepted social morality*. By these terms, Hart and Austin meant the set of moral norms identifiable by their acceptance and practice among a particular social group, such as the Canadian or Swedish population. The reason that this option is attractive should be obvious. The existence and the content of such moral norms are arguably matters of social fact – precisely the kind of fact upon which positivists claim that law ultimately depends. There are two difficulties with the option, however. First, it is not obvious that this really is the kind of morality to which constitutional rights provisions are always taken to make reference. When, for example, the US Supreme Court ruled, in a seven-to-ten split decision and amidst much fanfare and controversy,

[28] See Waluchow 1994, 2000. [29] Hart 1994: 204.

in favour of elective abortions in *Roe* v. *Wade*, it did so on grounds of a right to privacy under the due process clause of the Fourteenth Amendment. Yet it is far from clear that a moral right to privacy, as encompassing access to elective abortions, was widely accepted at the time within the United States. Instead, the court arguably drew on what it viewed as moral truth – that individuals in democratic societies retain a moral right to control over fundamental issues affecting their lives. A second difficulty is the possibility of cases where social consensus on a moral principle or right exists, but it fails to extend to the case in hand. There can be widespread agreement on an abstract moral norm but deep disagreement on the meaning and concrete implications of that norm. Arguably, this was true in *Roe*. It might also have been true of the right to equality at play when the US Supreme Court ruled against segregated schools in *Brown* v. *Board of Education*. If such cases are to be decided, the court cannot point to the relevant social consensus to support its claim that a constitutional moral right has been violated. There often is no such consensus.

So, appealing to positive or social morality will not always work. A second possibility is one taken up by Raz, who invoked the concept of a *directed power*.[30] The due process clause does not, in Raz's view, include conformity with the moral principle of fairness as a condition of legal validity in the United States. Rather, it directs and obligates judges to exercise a legal power to *invalidate* any law that is inconsistent with that moral principle. The difference between Raz's account of constitutional rights and that proposed by ILP is analogous to the difference between a void and a voidable contract under the common law of contract. A contract to perform an illegal act is *void* – that is, it never was valid and never had any legal force or effect. Since there never was a valid contract to begin with, the court, in refusing to enforce the illegal bargain, is simply refusing to enforce nonexistent contractual rights and obligations. The status of a voidable contract, on the other hand, is very different. A voidable contract, say a contract that one of the parties later determines was the product of a deception, may indeed be valid. However, it can be invalidated, that is, *made invalid* if the deceived party triggers the exercise of a legal power to make it so. This may be done by requesting that a court exercise its power to invalidate the contract. It is the judicial act of invalidation that results in invalidity, not the presence of deception.

[30] See Raz 1996: 242.

Putting the point another way, absence of deception is not a condition of validity; rather, it is a condition under which a contractor has grounds to request invalidation by a court. It follows that, until such time as the power to void is triggered by the deceived party and acted upon by a court, the voidable contract is binding, valid law. This despite the fact that it was the product of deception and is hence vulnerable to invalidation – and despite the fact that the contract will remain valid if the power to invalidate is not exercised.

On the ILP account of constitutional rights, a statute's conflict with a constitutional right means that the statute is already invalid in virtue of the conflict. It's the fact that the statute stands in conflict with a right established in superior, constitutional law that renders it invalid, not any act on the part of a court to invalidate it. In this respect, it is like a void contract, not a voidable one. According to the ELP account, on the other hand, this fact – that there is a conflict between the statute and the constitutional right – does *not* establish the invalidity of the former. It means only that the statute is subject to invalidation. It means that conditions exist that can trigger the court's duty to exercise its power to invalidate. This, according to defenders of ELP, is the only account of constitutional rights that is consistent with the separation thesis, because invalidity is not due to the violation of a moral condition of validity. Rather, it is due to the performance of a judicial act of invalidation undertaken in response to violation of a moral principle. And the fact that such an act of invalidation has occurred is a non-moral *social fact* of the sort that can easily serve to establish legal invalidity in a manner fully consistent with the separation thesis. That a court has exercised its power to invalidate a statute is a social fact, on a par with analogous social facts that result in the passage of legislation.

So, the directed powers account of constitutional rights allowed the defender of ELP to maintain their commitment to the separation thesis and the particular understanding of the social thesis with which it is associated. The end result was that each side, ELP and ILP, had an account of constitutional rights that accords with its own rendering of the social and separation/separability theses.[31] But were these two accounts equally

[31] It is worth noting that, on ELP's picture of law, the directed powers account applies equally to any situation, not just those involving constitutional rights, in which the law directs or permits courts to apply moral principles in deciding legal cases. Consider, for instance, the

plausible? ILP's defenders offered at least two arguments purporting to show that their view was superior. The first tackles the directed powers account head on. The second returns us to the positivist's social thesis and the claim that legal systems are based on social practices of recognition according to criteria of validity.

21.5.1 The Argument from Descriptive Adequacy

According to some defenders of ILP, their theory better and more easily accounts for the ways in which moral and legal validity seem to interact with each other in modern constitutional democracies.[32] More specifically, it provides a better account of common legal practices within these jurisdictions, and with the conceptual understandings of these practices seemingly shared by its participants. Recall the main idea behind ELP's directed powers account of constitutional rights. Constitutional rights provisions do not, on this theory, establish fundamental legal rights the violation of which by a government measure renders said measure legally invalid. Rather, they establish moral conditions under which courts are required to invalidate any such measure. And should no court exercise its power to invalidate, the measure remains legally valid. All this despite the fact that the conflicting norm violates the relevant constitutionally recognised right. The Argument from Descriptive Adequacy (ADA) points out how this account of constitutional rights cases is in tension with the manner in which constitutional rights are typically conceived and framed in modern constitutional democracies. Consider the following provisions of Canada's Constitutional Charter of Rights and Freedoms:

> 15. (1) Every individual is equal before and under the law and has the right to the equal protection and equal benefit of the law without discrimination and, in particular, without discrimination based on race, national or ethnic origin, colour, religion, sex, age or mental or physical disability.

aforementioned golden rule of interpretation, according to which courts are permitted to substitute, for the conventionally understood meaning of a legal rule, one that allows it to avoid a 'manifest absurdity or moral repugnance'. On the Razian directed powers account, a court that interprets so as to avoid a moral repugnance is exercising its power to consult non-legal moral reasons in the service of changing the law. The law is changed when the court displaces the conventionally understood meaning for one that is morally superior. In this way, the court creates new law.

[32] See, e.g., Waluchow 1994, 2000.

52. (1) The Constitution of Canada is the supreme law of Canada, and any law that is inconsistent with the provisions of the Constitution is, to the extent of the inconsistency, of no force or effect.

Section 15 guarantees citizens a moral right to equality. And section 52 (1) makes explicit the result should a conflict arise between that right and an enactment on the part of the government. It does not say that the law is subject to invalidation by a court. Rather, it says quite explicitly that that law *is of no force or effect.* The most natural interpretation of section 52, one we should presumably accept absent a good reason to prefer an alternative interpretation, is that the offending measure is *already* invalid owing to its inconsistency with the moral right to equality specified in section 15. The courts are not required to *make* the offending measure invalid. Rather, they are required to *recognise* that it already is invalid and to decide accordingly.

This Canadian understanding of constitutional rights seems shared by many other jurisdictions. The US Supreme Court once said in *Norton* v. *Shelby* (1886) that 'An unconstitutional act is not a law; it confers no rights; it imposes no duties; it affords no protection; it creates no office; it is, in legal contemplation, *as inoperative as though it had never been passed.*'[33] In other words, an act of government that stands in conflict with a constitutional right is, in virtue of that fact, invalid. It is 'not a law'. It is 'as inoperative as though it had never been passed'. Legal validity is clearly conceived as sometimes depending on moral validity.

Thus, an unfortunate implication of ELP's directed powers account is that it is in tension with how constitutional rights appear to be conceived in some jurisdictions. A second, related implication is its inconsistency with a good deal of legal practice. Consider a case where a citizen, S, is ruled to have acted at time t1 in violation of a criminal statute, C, that is later, at time t2, ruled to be unconstitutional. Let's suppose further that the court accepts S's claim that C does indeed violate S's constitutional rights. How should the conduct that prompted S's prosecution be viewed on the directed powers account? The short answer is that S's conduct should be viewed as having been illegal. After all, the statute was valid at t1 – the time of S's conduct – and *became invalid* only after that conduct occurred, that is, at t2. But this is not how courts typically treat a defendant's actions in this

[33] *Norton* v. *Shelby County* 1886: 118 US 425 (emphasis added).

kind of case. Most courts will routinely treat S as having done nothing legally wrong at t1. In other words, S will typically be exonerated on the ground that the statute under which their actions were deemed illegal is – and was at the time of their conduct – legally invalid, and that S did not, therefore, act contrary to valid law. That is, S did nothing illegal. The consequence is that S's conviction will invariably be deemed void, as will any subsequent attempt at prosecution under the impugned statute.

21.5.2 The Argument from Convention

LP's social thesis asserts that law is fundamentally a matter of social practice. As Ken Himma nicely puts it: 'The most fundamental of positivism's core commitments is the idea that law is, in essence, a social creation or artifact.'[34] Furthermore, on modern renditions of that theory, it is a social creation that rests on conventional foundations. It 'is the emphasis on law's *conventionality* that distinguishes positivism from other conceptual theories of law'.[35] In Hart's theory, the conventional social practice most essential to establishing a legal system's existence is, of course, acceptance, by its officials, of a rule of recognition setting out the system's criteria of legal validity. As Coleman put it: 'The rule of recognition must be a social rule; it expresses or represents a convention of a certain kind.'[36] Coleman not only stressed this core commitment of positivism; he also drew attention to an important implication of it for debates between defenders and critics of ILP. For, Coleman states, 'The key move for the Incorporationist is the claim that positivism imposes no constraint on the criteria of validity. Whether a particular rule of recognition does so depends on the practice of officials.'[37] Further, Coleman explains that the 'rule of recognition expresses a social practice among officials to treat certain standards as criteria of legal validity. *There is nothing in this conception of it that imposes any constraints on the conditions of validity* ... For the Incorporationist, what matters in the rule recognition is not the criteria of validity set forth, but its existence conditions.'[38]

[34] Himma 2002: 1152. [35] Himma 2001: 286.

[36] Coleman 1998: 407. What kind of convention a rule of recognition is – whether it is, for example, a coordinating convention, or what Andrei Marmor calls a *constituent convention* – is a matter of some dispute. But all positivists seem agreed that it represents a convention of some kind. See Marmor 2007: 154–82; Postema 1982.

[37] Coleman 1998: 407. [38] Coleman 1998: 406–7 (emphasis added).

So, according to LP, law rests essentially on a conventional social practice of recognition according to agreed criteria of validity. And there is nothing in this conception of law's foundations that mandates or entails constraints, over and above agreement, on what can count as a criterion of validity. Now if, as positivism maintains, (1) the key to understanding the social nature of law is to acknowledge the fact that it rests on conventional practices of recognition according to agreed criteria of validity; and (2) the concept of a convention of recognition according to agreed criteria in and of itself neither entails nor requires any substantive constraints on the nature of those agreed criteria; then (3) any theory, such as ELP, that dictates substantive constraints – beyond agreement and shared practice – on eligible criteria of validity obscures the fundamental conventional nature of law. At the very least, (4) such a theory shoulders the burden of showing precisely why we must restrict criteria of validity to the type it specifies: for example, pure pedigree criteria. By way of contrast, ILP shoulders no such burden. And this is because ILP imposes no substantive constraints on eligible conditions of validity.[39] As Coleman observed: 'The Incorporationist sees no reason for assuming that these conditions cannot in principle include criteria making moral value or merit a condition of legality, at least for some norms.'[40] It is up to the legal system itself to define its own limits, to decide which criteria of validity for membership it wishes to adopt and practise – a point, ironically enough, stressed by Raz: '"Law regulates its own creation", said Kelsen. The law itself determines which facts create laws and which abrogate them.'[41]

So the fact that it respects, highlights and emphasises the point that law ultimately rests on conventional practices of recognition constitutes a strong reason for thinking ILP superior to ELP (and NLT). Unlike its two major competitors, ILP rejects substantive constraints on validity save those required to sustain the conventional practices of recognition essential to the existence of a legal system.

[39] Kramer does point to at least one substantive constraint, over and above agreement and shared practice. A criterion of validity that validates norms selected through a process of throwing dice would not be acceptable. But this is for reasons tied directly to the conventionality of law. Settling cases in accordance with such a criterion would result in 'a bewildering higgledy-piggledy welter of conflicting signals'. And '[u]nless legal positivists are comfortable with designating such a regime as a legal system, they ought to insist that that there are in fact some constraints on the sorts of criteria that can form a Rule of Recognition. No such rule can consist solely of criteria that fail to secure the minimum of regularity which is prerequisite to the existence of a legal system' (Kramer 2004: 26).

[40] Coleman 1998: 407. [41] Raz 1979: 151–2.

References

Aquinas, St Thomas. 1485. *Summa Theologica*. Various editions.

Austin, J. 1954. *The Providence of Jurisprudence Determined*. Weidenfeld and Nicholson.

Coleman, J. 1998. 'Incorporationism, Conventionality, and the Practical Difference Thesis'. *Legal Theory* 4: 381–426.

Dworkin, R. 1975. 'Hard Cases'. *Harvard Law Review* 88: 1057–1109.

Dworkin, R. 1977. *Taking Rights Seriously*. Duckworth.

Dworkin, R. 1986. *Law's Empire*. Harvard University Press.

Green, L. 2008. 'Positivism and the Inseparability of Law and Morals'. *New York University Law Review* 83: 1035–58.

Hart, H. L. A. 1994. *The Concept of Law*. 2nd ed. Oxford University Press.

Himma, K. 2001. 'Law's Claim of Legitimate Authority'. In J. Coleman (ed.). *Hart's Postscript*. Oxford University Press: 271–310.

Himma, K. 2002. 'Substance and Method in Conceptual Jurisprudence and Theory'. *Virginia Law Review* 88: 1120–1208.

Kramer, M. 2004. *Where Law and Morality Meet*. Oxford University Press.

Marmor, A. 2007. *Law in the Age of Moral Pluralism*. Oxford University Press.

Postema, G. J. 1982. 'Coordination and Convention at the Foundations of Law'. *Journal of Legal Studies* 11: 165–203.

Raz, J. 1972. 'Legal Principles and the Limits of Law'. *Yale Law Journal* 81: 823–54.

Raz, J. 1979. *The Authority of Law*. Oxford University Press.

Raz, J. 1985a. 'Authority and Justification'. *Philosophy and Public Affairs* 14: 3–29.

Raz, J. 1985b. 'Authority, Law and Morality'. *The Monist* 3: 295–324.

Raz, J, 1986. *The Morality of Freedom*. Clarendon Press.

Raz, J. 1996. 'The Inner Logic of the Law'. In J. Raz. *Ethics in the Public Domain: Essays in the Morality of Law and Politics*. Revised ed. Clarendon Press: 238–53.

Sartorius, R. 1975. *Individual Conduct and Social Norms*. Dickenson Publishing Company.

Shapiro, S. 1998. 'On Hart's Way Out'. *Legal Theory* 4: 469–507.

Shapiro, S. 2000. 'Law, Morality, and the Guidance of Conduct'. *Legal Theory* 6: 127–70.

Waluchow, W. J. 1994. *Inclusive Legal Positivism*. Clarendon Press.

Waluchow, W. J. 2000. 'Authority and the Practical Difference Thesis: A Defence of Inclusive Legal Positivism'. *Legal Theory* 6: 45–81.

22 Disruptive Implications of Legal Positivism's Social Efficacy Thesis

Brian Z. Tamanaha*

22.1 Introduction

The social efficacy thesis holds that for law to exist it must be generally obeyed by the populace. Accepted by virtually all legal positivists, this is the most neglected thesis of legal positivism. H. L. A. Hart identified general obedience of the rules of behaviour as a 'necessary' condition for the existence of a legal system, but he said little about what this entails.[1] Joseph Raz acknowledged that social efficacy is 'the least studied and least understood' condition for the existence of law, though he failed to elaborate beyond tentative, summary assertions.[2] 'Suffice it that all agree that a legal system is not the law in force in a certain community unless it is generally adhered to and is accepted or internalized by at least certain sections of the population,'[3] Hans Kelsen declared, 'a legal order is regarded as valid, if its norms are *by and large* effective (that is, actually applied and obeyed)';[4] he made a few pre-emptory comments about this requirement.

The efficacy thesis is little explored perhaps because legal theorists consider it plainly evident that law exists only if it is largely obeyed by the populace. A normative system would be 'meaningless' if people did not behave in accordance with it.[5] 'For that reason,' Kelsen asserted, 'a normative system to which reality no longer corresponds to a certain degree will necessarily lose its validity.'[6] Raz analogised the efficacy of law to morality: '[N]o morality is the social morality of a population unless it is generally conformed to and accepted by that population.'[7] Since legal theorists uniformly assert that the function of law is to control and guide

* I thank Toni Mullenix, Stanley Paulsen and Torben Spaak for their critical comments on earlier drafts.

[1] See Hart 1961/1994: 113. [2] See Raz 1980: 203–8; Raz 2009: 42. [3] Raz 2009: 43.
[4] Kelsen 1967: 212. [5] See Kelsen 1992: 60. [6] Ibid. [7] Raz 2009: 43.

conduct,[8] it would seem to necessarily follow that law cannot be said to exist unless this function is actually served.

Despite its nigh universal acceptance by theorists, however, the efficacy thesis is surrounded with unanswered questions with significant implications. Several questions immediately come to mind: How widespread must conformity to law be? What must people conform to (all areas of law)? Who must conform (legal officials, government officials, the entire populace, significant groups)? What does conformity entail (normatively, knowingly, behaviourally but unknowingly)? This chapter explores these issues and a few others, revealing a number of disruptive implications of the efficacy thesis for legal positivist theory. Most significantly, I draw on the empirical reality of legal efficacy to cast doubt on the monopoly, unified view of law incorporated within concepts of law as well as on the purported guidance function of law. In the course of the analysis, I address the implications of legal pluralism for the social efficacy thesis, I show that the grounds of efficacy vary and have changed over time, and I offer an account of efficacy in modern societies that is not grounded on guidance or obedience.

22.2 Why Questions of Obedience Arise

Let us start by identifying the underlying reason why issues of obedience arise: legal institutions and prevailing social behaviour within groups have separate grounds for existence. That is, what gives rise to legal institutions and the laws they produce in a given society is distinct from what gives rise to prevailing social behaviour. Legal institutions are constituted by ongoing practices by legal actors revolving around the creation and effectuation of norms. Prevailing social behaviour is the product of a complex of sources – habits, customs, morals, socialisation, reciprocal obligations, mutual understandings, agreements, goal-oriented purposive actions, naturalistic impulses, and more, including the actions of legal institutions. Since their grounds of existence differ, the relationship between the two is contingent and varying: they may influence one another, they may coincide, they may diverge, they may be disconnected.

[8] See Hart 1961/1994: 39.

Two familiar propositions are manifestations of this separateness: gaps may exist between law and social behaviour,[9] and a norm may remain valid law within a legal system although people widely disregard or breach it.[10] Unpacking these two propositions reveals that *three* separate realms are involved: rules recognised as valid within legal institutions (enactment); what legal officials actually do in connection with recognised rules (enforcement and application); and how people actually behave with respect to conduct addressed by the rules.[11] A simple illustration of their separation is a legally imposed speed limit of 60 miles per hour along a particular stretch of highway; though police typically ticket only people driving in excess of 65 miles per hour on that stretch, while drivers routinely go 60 to 70 miles per hour (with an eye out for police). Valid legal rules are one thing; what those tasked with carrying out the rules are actually doing with respect to those rules is another thing; and the actual behaviour of the group purportedly governed by the rules is yet another thing. Thus, general compliance with legal rules refers to legal officials themselves (are they enforcing and applying them?), as well as to the social group addressed by the rules (are they abiding by them?). Owing to their separate grounds of existence, it is theoretically possible for a coordinated complex of legal officials to recognise, change, enforce and apply legal rules with respect to a social group that behaves in ways wholly contrary to what the legal rules require.[12] Individual legal norms inconsistent with social behaviour remain valid as long as they are recognised as such by legal officials, so it follows that all legal norms in the aggregate applicable to a social group may remain valid notwithstanding a lack of general social conformity. What is critical to the existence of the legal system itself is that legal officials coordinate *their* behaviour to recognise, change, enforce and apply legal rules – that is akin to Hart's second condition for the existence of a legal system.[13]

[9] See Pound 1910. [10] See Kelsen 1992: 62.

[11] For simplicity, I use the term rules in this discussion, though legal norms more broadly include standards, principles, orders and other types of legal declaration.

[12] Raz's analogy of law to morality overlooks a key distinction. Morality typically lacks an institutionalised system for the creation and enforcement of norms, so the only sense in which moral norms can be efficacious is if they are actually invoked in social life. Legal systems can exist even if their norms are not generally adhered to in society because an institutionalised legal system has its own grounds for existence distinct from social norms; a legal system that lacks social efficacy will have a limited impact, but it will still exist.

[13] See Hart 1961/1994: 113. My term 'coordinate' does not include Hart's internal acceptance requirement.

But legal positivists insist on a further condition for the existence of law. 'Legal theorists almost all agree that efficacy [within society] is [a] necessary condition for the existence of a legal system.'[14] Whether this requirement is conceptual or empirical is unclear. Asserting that efficacy 'distinguishes between effective and non-effective law and not between legal and non-legal systems',[15] Raz suggests that securing general obedience is an empirical condition for the existence of law. It appears that Hart 'took the general conformity condition to be a conceptually necessary condition of the existence of a legal system'.[16] A legal system not followed by the populace seems unreal to theorists; 'at best . . . a possible, hypothetical, or virtual legal system, but not a real one',[17] Gerald Postema asserts.

As I demonstrate shortly, legal systems not followed by the general populace not only are very real but also are plentiful. First, I should identify a notion about law held by many legal theorists: the image of a monopolistic, unitary legal system governing society as a whole. Reflecting this assumption, Raz states, 'in a nutshell', that a legal system is 'a system of guidance and adjudication claiming supreme authority within a certain society and therefore, where efficacious, also enjoying such effective authority'.[18] This monopoly view of law, however, about which more follows, often does not comport with reality.

22.3 Systematic Divergence between Law and Social Behaviour

Situations exist in which the rules produced and enforced by the legal system systematically diverge from the norms followed by large portions of society. A recent World Bank report found:

> In many developing countries, customary systems operating outside of the state regime are often the dominant form of regulation and dispute resolution, covering up to 90% of the population in parts of Africa. In Sierra Leone, for example, approximately 85% of the population falls under the jurisdiction of customary law, defined under the Constitution as 'the rules which, by custom, are applicable to particular communities in Sierra Leone'. Customary tenure covers 75% of land in most African countries, affecting 90% of land transactions in countries like

[14] Shiner 1990: 82. [15] Raz 2009: 43. [16] Postema 2008: 48. [17] Postema 2008: 49.
[18] Raz 2009: 43.

Mozambique and Ghana . . . In many of these countries, systems of justice seem to operate almost completely independently of the official state system.[19]

This situation can be found in parts of Africa, the Middle East, Asia and the Pacific, particularly in rural areas. People in these communities do not resort to state law for a variety of reasons: it may be distant, corrupt, slow, too expensive or inscrutable to people. State law may be set forth in a language they do not understand – never mind the additional barrier posed by technical legal language. State law norms and institutions have been transplanted from elsewhere and are alien to and apart from their way of life. People live their lives in accordance with local customary and religious laws and institutions that shape and reflect their social and cultural existence, from which state laws and institutions frequently diverge in content and operation.[20]

As many as a billion people around the globe, according to one estimate, claim property rights and conduct property arrangements on terms inconsistent with official state law, ranging from urban settlements where families have lived without official titles for generations to rural areas where people follow customary land tenure.[21] State law typically provides freehold alienable property, whereas customary land tenure often is collectively held, confers use and consultation rights to various parties, and social relations are tied to the land. One study explains: 'Some property claimants may resist or ignore [state] law simply because it is the product of a distant centralist state, or a state they perceive as lacking in reliability, legitimacy or probity. Others may prefer local mechanisms for coordinating property relations that are embedded in long-standing mechanisms of social organization.'[22] A closer look at one such situation sheds additional light:

Yap had a legal system, with a legislature, a handful of judges and attorneys, a small police department, and a complete legal code based in its entirety on laws transplanted from the USA. But vast portions of the code had never been applied, few lay people had any knowledge of the content of the laws or [the] operation of the legal system, a large proportion of social problems were dealt with through traditional means without participation of the state legal system, and[,] indeed[,] on most of the islands there was no legal presence at all. The day-to-day behavior of the people was not governed by state law, but by their own cultural norms. Social

[19] Chirayath, Sage and Woolcock 2005: 3. [20] See Tamanaha 2008; 2011.
[21] See Fitzpatrick 2016: 137. [22] Fitzpatrick 2016: 165.

order was maintained by sources other than state law ... While they did not routinely act in conflict with the law (with the major exception that their culture perpetuated a thriving caste system, while the law prohibited discrimination), it could not be said that they were obeying or complying with the primary rules in Hart's terms, since they were ignorant of these rules and paid them almost no heed.[23]

While members of the social community followed customary laws and institutions, Yap had a functioning state legal system 'mostly occupied with the affairs of running a government. The existence of state law in Yap was a social fact, based upon the activities of legal officials.[24] Variations of situations like this exist around the world, it bears repeating, so they cannot be dismissed by theorists as marginal.

These situations help test assumptions about law and social efficacy that are common among legal theorists – but do not always hold. The state legal system functioned in Yap mainly in relation to government actions, notwithstanding that most members of the community had not 'accepted or internalized' the legal rules in the sense that Raz states, and they did not generally obey the law in the sense that Hart requires. The polity itself, the structure of government, was constructed by, and operated through, law. Governmental legal actions mainly involved authorising and carrying out instrumental activities, like supplying social services, maintaining electrification, building roads and harbours, providing education, and more, little of which involved maintaining the social order of the community. At the same time, the customary law system in Yap handled the bulk of social ordering; the population had 'accepted and internalized' this body of law and lived in accordance therewith. Two forms of law thus coexisted in Yap and were operative on mostly different matters – one in the realm of government actions and the other in community life – with some overlap.

These situations perhaps can be reconciled with the monopoly, unified view of legal systems by pointing to provisions recognising customary or religious law (subject to limits) included in many state legal systems in the Global South. Based on this official recognition, it might be said that state law still controls notwithstanding that its legal institutions and declared

23 Tamanaha 2001: 12. I witnessed this first-hand when working for almost two years as Assistant Attorney General of Yap, and later returning to work as legal counsel at the 1990 Constitutional Convention of the Federated States of Micronesia. I discuss this situation in the past tense because I have not confirmed that it remains the same today.

24 Ibid.

norms are not reflected in social conduct. But there are two problems with this construal. First, situations exist in which the coexisting systems are not recognised by state law, such as Taliban imposed Sharia in Afghanistan, which held sway across swaths of the countryside while the Taliban were at war with the state.[25] The second problem is that, in many situations, the customary and religious systems operate apart from state legal systems and people perceive them to be in contradistinction; their norms are often directly contrary to what state law requires, particularly on property and family law matters, and regularly contravene specified limits.[26] Forms of customary and religious law have existed in these areas for centuries, if not millennia (evolving over time), long prior to the development of state legal regimes, which are relatively recent transplants with limited power.[27] These indigenous legal forms have been de facto law all along, albeit undergoing adjustments when state law regimes were introduced. Affirmative state law recognition of customary and religious law – a practice that first began with colonisation[28] – is a face-saving gesture by the state to officially 'permit' thriving pre-existing forms of law within society, which it lacks the power to control, eliminate or supplant.

The social reality is that, in situations like this, declared state legal norms are not by and large obeyed by the populace. This has manifold implications for the social efficacy thesis as well as for the concept of law.

22.4 Serial Existence and Simultaneous Coexistence

When discussing the efficacy requirement, legal theorists have largely focused on problems of serial existence – on when legal systems come into and go out of existence, whether through revolution, civil war, enemy occupation, breakdown or anarchy.[29] Kelsen used revolutionary transformations or a wholly new constitutional order as his examples;[30] Raz mainly addressed revolutions or a changeover in legal system upon independence from colonisation.[31] During revolutionary shifts, particularly during a transitional period or when the outcome is not yet determined, questions arise about which legal system exists and when.

[25] See Yassari and Saboory 2010. [26] See Tamanaha 2008, 2011. [27] See Kahn 2015.
[28] See Hooker 1975. [29] See Hart 1961/1994: 114–16. [30] See Kelsen 1967: 208–11.
[31] See Raz 1970: 205–8. He also briefly mentions the coexistence of religious legal systems.

These discussions presuppose that, although more than one legal system may be *efficacious* in different respects during a transitional or contested period, only one can *exist* within a given society. As Raz put it, 'given two putative legal systems that are both efficacious in a certain society and are also incompatible, it is for the test of exclusion to determine which of them exists in that society'.[32] The test of exclusion, he tells us, looks at people's attitudes and intentions to see whether their following or disregarding one system or the other is out of allegiance, and looks at relative efficacy in the capacity of the legal organs to carry out their actions. This is a 'comparative test'. 'Of the competing legal systems, the one that comes out best is the existing one. In certain cases[,] two competing systems may have roughly equal claim and the case must be judged unsettled.'[33]

This way of putting it renders *efficacy* an empirical question of actual social impact, while *existence* is a conceptually infused notion tied to what it means to be a legal system. Legal systems are characterised by three features, according to Raz: they claim authority to regulate any type of behaviour (are comprehensive); they claim supremacy over all other institutionalised systems; and they are open in the sense that they purport to give binding force within the system to externally generated norms.[34] Understood in this way, 'A legal system exists if and only if it is in force. The significance of the point is that it brings out that normative systems are existing legal systems because of their impact on the behavior of individuals, because of their role in the organization of social life.'[35] More than one legal system may be present, in his account, because more than one can *claim* comprehensive authority and supremacy, but only one legal system can actually exist – be in force – because presumably only one legal system at any given time can actually carry through comprehensive and supreme ordering in social life. 'We would regard an institutionalized system as a legal system only if it is necessarily in some respect the most important institutionalized system which can exist in that society.'[36] Hence, efficacy is necessary to existence, but existence entails comprehensiveness and supremacy, and if none of the competing systems comes out best, as Raz put it, the case must be judged unsettled.

To say that two legal systems may be efficacious within a given society, though neither exists, is an odd locution. Why not simply say that if two

[32] Raz 1970: 207. [33] Raz 1970: 208. [34] See Raz 2009: 116–20. [35] Raz 2009: 104.
[36] Raz 2009: 116.

legal systems are simultaneously efficacious in various respects within a society then *both* exist? Raz is driven to his awkward assertion because he identifies the necessary features of legal systems in terms of the monopoly, unitary view of state law. This amounts to a conceptual stipulation that *only one* legal system can exist in a given society. This position makes it difficult to account for a society like Yap, in which two legal systems functioned side by side on different matters; or geographically based side-by-side systems, like Afghanistan, for example, wherein state law exists mainly in the cities, while people in the vast rural areas of the country follow tribal customary law and in other areas follow Sharia imposed by the Taliban. Closer to home, it is inconsistent with the sovereign status of Native American tribes that divide aspects of supremacy with individual states and the nation.

The most straightforward way to account for these situations is to recognise that multiple efficacious legal systems may coexist in the same society.

22.5 Implications of Efficacy for Concepts of Law

Several implications for concepts of law follow. A focus on social efficacy in situations of coexisting forms of law provides reasons to reject Raz's assertion that necessary features of legal systems include claims to comprehensiveness and supremacy. The monopoly view of law – a construction of contemporary theorists – is inconsistent with many legal regimes throughout history and today. Coexisting legal systems were normal in medieval Europe, continuing up through the modern consolidation of state law, and even thereafter pockets of coexisting law remained in many societies.[37] Nor is it clear that comprehensiveness and supremacy fit Europe today. European citizens are subject to national law as well as European Union law – with unsettled claims of supremacy on various issues – as well as human rights, private and public international law, various forms of transnational law, and religious law for adherents. The monopoly view of law is an idealised formulation of state law unthinkingly assumed by legal theorists. Given ample reasons to doubt it, significant justifications must be provided for it to be incorporated in analyses of law and efficacy.

[37] See Tamanaha 2017: 105–9.

A problematic correlative of the monopoly view is that law applies as a unity to 'society', 'citizens' or 'population' defined in territorial terms. This is indicated in Hart's assertion that a condition for the existence of a legal system is that rules of behaviour 'must be generally obeyed' by 'citizens'.[38] As Kelsen put it, 'to say . . . that the state is the sovereign legal system means, in particular, that it has the capacity, unrestricted by any higher legal system, to extend its validity territorially as well as materially'.[39] This proposition seems obvious when one assumes the monopoly view of state law, but it obscures potential distinctions among types of legal norm and realms of addressees. A legal system may be effective even when it is limited to certain spheres of application or when its geographical reach is partial.

Two distinguishable sets of legal norms exist that apply to different spheres: government officials carrying out government functions, and citizens and entities engaged in interaction.[40] In modern bureaucratic governments, laws applying to government officials provide the structure of government and the legal framework for the administrative apparatus, producing substantial bodies of law tied to the operation of government and furthering its objectives; to wit, legislators secure revenue, approve projects and authorise appropriations; executives and agencies carry them out; courts preside over disputes in connection therewith; and so forth, including the legal construction of their respective roles and powers. As Ed Rubin remarked in his critique of Hart's exclusive references to social behaviour, 'a great deal of legislation regulates the behavior of government agencies, not the conduct of private parties'.[41] In contrast, laws covering daily social interaction include property law, contract law, tort law, family law, criminal law and other bodies of law that relate to the routine interaction among people and entities. It is conceptually and realistically sound to conclude that a legal system exists if the rules are 'generally obeyed' within one of these spheres of addressees, though not the other, because it would have efficacious consequences within that realm. Law would be socially efficacious in the additional sense that projects advanced by government officials through legal means have real consequences, often socially beneficial, albeit not social ordering per se. A legal system would exist if the government were to operate through state law in carrying out its

[38] Hart 1961/1994: 113. [39] Kelsen 1992: 100. [40] See Tamanaha 2017: 118–50.
[41] Rubin 1989: 375.

instrumental objectives notwithstanding that social ordering is effectuated by other means – that was the situation in Yap.

The efficacy of legal systems can also divide along geographical lines within a territory, for example urban versus rural, or different regions. Assertions by theorists about obedience to legal rules by citizens, the population or society are presented as if the entire society must be covered, but a legal system would exist if it were effective in one area though not others – that was the situation in Afghanistan.

Yet another implication for concepts of law follows from this analysis. In a society in which a legal system is generally obeyed by government officials but not the populace, or is generally obeyed by people in cities but not in rural areas, or in certain regions but not in others, other legal orders presumably will be operative for the realms or populations not covered. As indicated earlier, these other legal orders may be customary or religious law, or an internal rival to the state; other forms of law may exist as well, including international and transnational law, and human rights. Because they effectively satisfy legal functions, legal theorists must consider these other forms of law when producing accounts of the features of law.

This would precipitate a profound theoretical shift – since heretofore theories of law have been based almost exclusively on the state law paradigm. Raz heads in this direction in a recent essay, 'Why the State?':

> Even though much of legal philosophy takes state law as its starting point, writers are aware of the existence of other kinds of law, and I do not mean laws of nature, mathematics, or grammar. I mean laws that are uncontroversially normative. They include international law, or the law of organizations like the European Union, but also Canon Law, Sharia law, Scottish law, the law of native nations, the rules and regulations governing the activities of voluntary associations, or those of legally recognized corporations, and more, including very transient phenomena, like neighborhood gangs.[42]

Focusing on forms of law other than state law promises significantly to alter understandings about concepts of law because their features differ from those of state law. For instance, as Raz has observed, 'Many, if not all, legal philosophers have been agreed that one of the defining features of law is that it is an institutionalized normative system.'[43] This is true in

[42] Raz 2017: 138. [43] Raz 2009: 105.

connection with state law but not with respect to all forms of customary law. Another core assumption is that 'What *is* law?' requires a singular answer, whereas this new focus leads to the identification of multiple forms of law, each with its own set of (perhaps overlapping) characteristic features.[44]

In sum, focusing on efficacy suggests that whether law has a monopoly within a territory is a contingent matter that should not be conceptually presupposed; comprehensiveness and supremacy are not necessary features of law; legal systems may exist and be effective within limited spheres and regions even though the entire citizenry does not generally obey the law; a plurality of legal forms may operate in the same social space; not all forms of law need be institutionalised; and there may be multiple forms of law with their own distinctive features. Although these are tentative assertions that require further examination, they show that the implications of the efficacy thesis for concepts of law are multiple and penetrating.

22.6 What Obedience Entails

The assertion that citizens must generally obey rules of behaviour for a legal system to exist requires an explanation of what 'obedience' entails. For Hart, thin obedience suffices:

> The first condition is the only one which private citizens *need* satisfy: they may obey each 'for his part only' and from any motive whatever; though in a healthy society they will in fact often accept these rules as common standards of behavior and acknowledge an obligation to obey them, or even trace this obligation to a more general obligation to respect the constitution.[45]
>
> The ordinary citizen manifests his acceptance largely by acquiescence in the results of these official operations. He keeps the law which is made and identified in this way, and also makes claims and exercises power conferred by it. But he may know little of its origin or its makers: some may know nothing more about laws than that they are 'the law'.[46]

Obedience is thin in the sense that the citizens need not normatively accept or like the legal rules – what matters is that they generally obey the legal rules.

[44] See Tamanaha 2001; 2017. [45] Hart 1961/1994: 113. [46] Hart 1961/1994: 60.

A striking implication of Hart's thin obedience is that the populace (including legal officials in their private capacities) need not normatively accept the rules of behaviour of the legal system, as long as legal officials accept the secondary rules when conducting their legal actions.[47] This would include a rapacious legal system that has subjugated its populace – much like former colonial legal systems and dictatorships throughout history – a Gunman writ large that relies on coercion, fear and passive acquiescence to effectuate obedience.[48] Hart recognised that law 'may be a narrow and exclusive system run in the interests of the dominant group'.[49]

Critics have argued that a richer notion of obedience is required, one involving genuine normative acceptance of the rules of behaviour, amounting to widespread belief in the legitimacy of law, at least for a stable legal system that persists over time. Roger Shiner, for example, suggests that the populace must exhibit a thick habit involving 'a disposition to display law-abiding behavior', which is grounded in fairness, justice and the common good provided by the system.[50] The thrust of his argument is that, to secure general obedience, law must be good and right, or at least be seen as such by the populace, so the efficacy requirement points legal positivism in a non-positivist direction.

This assertion, it must be noted, rests on the questionable proposition that a legal system cannot maintain enduring general obedience solely through coercion in the absence of genuine normative acceptance by the populace. This assumption has not been established and would be difficult to prove. History shows that exploitative systems can persist for lengthy periods (consider past colonial regimes or North Korea today). Furthermore, attitudes about what entitles a legal system to legitimacy vary. Rudolf von Jhering remarked that societies have existed in which 'people did not look upon force with our own eyes; they saw nothing improper in such a condition; nought detestable and damnable, but only what was natural and self-evident. Force as such made an impression on them and was the only kind of greatness they could appreciate.'[51]

Even thin obedience at a minimum requires that people consciously orient their behaviour in relation to what the law requires. This is because,

[47] See Payne 1982. [48] See Shiner 1990: 87–9.
[49] Hart 1961/1994: 197; see also Tamanaha 2017: 93–105. [50] See Shiner 1990: 106.
[51] See Jhering 1968: 191.

theorists uniformly declare, the function of law is to guide human conduct. Hart observed that 'it is quite vain to seek any more specific purpose which law as such serves beyond providing guides to human conduct and standards of criticism of such conduct'.[52] Raz hinges the existence of a legal system on providing effective normative guidance: 'a legal system exists if and only if it is in force. The significance of the point is that it brings out that normative systems are existing legal systems *because of their impact on the behavior* of individuals, because of their role in the organization of social life.'[53] If people do not consciously orient their behaviour in relation to law, the legal system will be inert, not fulfilling its social function. 'The core *modus operandi* of law', Gerald Postema observes, 'is to guide the actions of intelligent self-directing agents by addressing to them general norms to which their actions are expected to comply'.[54]

The purported guidance function of law, however, is dogged by a puzzle that legal theorists regularly ignore or wave away. On the one hand, 'people can only be guided by rules or prescriptions if they know about the existence of the rule or prescription'; on the other hand, 'most people do not know the vast majority of the laws of their country'.[55] Law is a highly specialised body of technical language, concepts, practices and institutions that people without legal training cannot fully comprehend. What also renders full knowledge of law beyond reach, including for lawyers, is that modern legal systems issue mountainous volumes of rules and regulations, with complex and obscure sub-areas. Studies have found that lay beliefs about law on important matters are incorrect a significant percentage of time across a range of legal subjects.[56] People often believe that the law *is* what they think the law *should* be, without checking the law to confirm whether this is correct.

This objection to the guidance function of law is 'beside the point', Andrei Marmor asserts, because most laws do not affect individuals in their daily affairs and they can hire a lawyer if they need to know the law on a given matter.[57] But most people do not routinely consult lawyers for guidance about the legal implication of their activities, and many forgo

[52] Hart 1961/1994: 249. [53] Raz 2009: 104 (emphasis added). [54] Postema 2008: 50.
[55] Marmor 2004: 5, 16.
[56] See Darley, Robinson and Carlsmith 2001; Kim 1998; Rowell 2017.
[57] See Marmor 2004: 16.

legal counsel owing to the prohibitive cost of legal services, resulting in a high rate of unmet legal needs in civil and criminal matters.[58]

Modern law is specialised, complex, obscure and extraordinarily voluminous; many people lack legal advice because they don't think they need it, or it is too costly and burdensome to acquire; and many people have mistaken views about what the law requires. A centuries-old common law maxim is that 'everyone is presumed to know the law'.[59] Jurists have acknowledged for over a century that this proposition 'is on its face absurd'.[60] The justification for the maxim is not factual accuracy but a prudential policy that incentivises people to know the law and holds them responsible regardless.[61] Legal positivist theorists who assert that legal rules guide the populace are in effect positing as true what has long been acknowledged to be a convenient fiction.

Commercial actors and wealthy people often actively use law and consult lawyers, but this is not the bulk of the population. Lay people in general know basic matters such as that murder, battery and theft are illegal, contracts are binding, traffic laws impose fines, and taxes must be paid, though the details of applicable doctrines and defences are beyond their ken. Many people don't murder, batter or steal from others not because of legal prohibitions but because they consider these actions abhorrent or unthinkable. Many people conduct their affairs hardly thinking about law, or holding assumptions about law that they do not verify. If their routine behaviour seldom takes law into account and they largely do not know the law anyway, people are not being normatively *guided* by law. As Postema remarks, there being 'merely coincidental correlations of behavior with standing legal norms fails to manifest law's effectiveness. To do so, it must be possible to attribute the behavior to law's efforts and operations, traced to properties or powers of law.'[62]

A crucial clarification is in order. A major difference exists between these situations and those described earlier with respect to coexisting forms of law in the global South. In the latter, official state law has a limited role in ordering social intercourse and responding to disruptions for large portions of the population, particularly in rural areas, who live by different legal orders. The discussion here, in contrast, is about law in advanced

[58] See Tamanaha 2017; Hadfield and Heine 2016. [59] Kohler 1935: 113.
[60] Keedy 1908: 91; see also Cass 1976: 691; Hall and Seligman 1941: 641.
[61] See Hall and Seligman 1941: 646–52. [62] Postema 2008: 50.

capitalist societies familiar to legal positivists – wherein law does serve a substantial role in the ordering of social life and law is generally effective across all spheres and regions (approximating the monopoly view of law). The point is that, contrary to repeated assertions by theorists, this social ordering does not come about through guiding people in their daily behaviour. A different conception of efficacy is required to capture how law works.

22.7 Efficacy Not Grounded on Guidance or Obedience

Gerald Postema faces these issues head on in an illuminating essay, 'Conformity, Custom, and Congruence: Rethinking the Efficacy of Law'. 'Rarely do citizens have more than a rudimentary grasp of much of the law, and certainly little or no grasp of its more technical features', he recognizes; hence 'it is difficult to maintain that ordinary citizens can be said to accept these normative propositions, treating them as common standards for their conduct and that of their fellow citizens'.[63] Postema offers a different way of understanding efficacy based on two key modifications to the assertion that law guides conduct.

First, he shifts the focus from specific individuals to people acting in networks of interaction, and from particular legal norms to law as a system; then he clarifies that people are not directly guided by the law but instead are subject to *indirect* guidance.[64] 'The law addresses law-subjects as a system, and the normative guidance it offers takes the form of providing a framework of practical reasoning rather than that of a discrete general command.'[65] The legal framework has a directive mode (what to do), an evaluative mode (standards by which to evaluate others) and a constitutive mode (constituting roles and relationships, such as employer–employee, marriage, citizens, and so forth). Legal guidance is indirect in the sense that it is mediated through social practices that are influenced by law as well as influence law, 'and individual law subjects are guided, in substantial part but not exclusively, through participating in those social practices'.[66] In other words, people conduct their activities within familiar social practices and networks of interaction that they

[63] Postema 2008: 52. [64] See Postema 2008: 53–6. [65] Postema 2008: 55.
[66] Postema 2008: 56.

understand, practices and networks that are reflected in law and in part produced through law.

Second, Postema identifies the efficacy of law in the existence of a substantial congruence between laws and legal processes and the customs, social practices and modes of reasoning and actions prevailing within society.[67] Congruence, for Postema, is not about legal rules directly mirroring social norms; instead, it entails that they generally work together, that they fit such that the products of legal activities comport or align with what people in society are doing. When congruence is lacking, law is not an efficacious normative system.

There is much more to his sophisticated account that cannot be conveyed here. What matters for present purposes is that Postema decisively shifts away from the implausible notion that people are normatively guided by legal rules in their social intercourse – implausible because most people most of the time seldom think about law and, even when it does enter their minds, do not know the law beyond general awareness of a few basic proscriptions – by fastening on how law actually comes into play in contexts of social action.

Let me now provide an alternative account with parallels to Postema's analysis that likewise eschews guidance of the populace. Rather than assume that people are normatively guided by law, instead, let us ask, how does law actually operate? Two main loci of legal production exist in modern societies: (1) government institutions control the production of official state law, which is used instrumentally in a multitude of ways to achieve government objectives; and (2) legally trained professionals exercise a relative monopoly over the operation of state law, mediating and carrying out legal operations. Government officials, the first locus, exercise legal authority in various roles: legislators and executive officials use their legal powers internally to construct and empower the government and instrumentally achieve desired purposes; police and prosecutors wield legal authority to maintain enforcement; judges apply law to situations; administrative officials utilise law in all these ways to effectuate designated objectives. Legal professionals, the second locus, engage in the wielding and tending of legal knowledge to carry through the legal activities of government officials, many of whom are legal professionals themselves, as well as the legal activities of private individuals and entities.

[67] See Postema 2008: 56–60.

Certain aspects of law-related action by government officials and legal professionals involve their being *guided* by law – as when carrying out legally imposed duties or remaining within legal limits – but much of it involves *utilising* law as a mechanism or tool to carry out activities and further aims (while deriving an income therefrom). And none of this necessarily involves that the people and entities being served are themselves actually guided by the law, though that may be the case in particular instances.

As mentioned in the earlier discussion of the Global South, even when it plays a marginal role in social ordering, law related to the actions of government officials is efficacious through structuring government and furthering instrumental objectives, which involve actions with social consequences. In advanced capitalist societies, law is socially efficacious in a third way as well: the aggregate result of the government production of law and the public and private utilisation of law, mediated through legal professionals, has been the emergence of a pervasive, relatively fixed background legal fabric that forms a backdrop for the entirety of social, cultural, economic and political activities.[68] The social efficacy of law lies in the presence of this background legal fabric, which people and entities rely on without specific knowledge of law and without being guided by law. Five factors in particular combined to produce this legal fabric, which will be briefly conveyed.[69]

The primary factor in the development of the legal fabric has been the growth and proliferation in the course of the nineteenth and twentieth centuries of law-utilising public and private organisations as the predominant vehicles of social action. 'It is the corporate actors, the organizations that draw their power from persons and employ that power to corporate ends, that are the primary actors in the social structure of modern society', social theorist James Coleman declared.[70] The proliferation of public and private organisations was wrought through law via enabling acts – the latter unleashed by the enactment of general incorporation laws – which in turn brought a proliferation of law within society through their activities. Organisations engage with law in a variety of ways: they are created by and structured through law; they use contracts with employees, customers, suppliers and sources of financing; they exercise property rights to acquire, preserve and

[68] See Tamanaha 2018. [69] See Tamanaha 2017: 139–42. [70] See Coleman 1973: 49.

transfer assets; tort law and criminal law apply to their actions; corporate law and securities law govern the operation of private corporations; various regulatory regimes cover organisations' relations with employees, the products and services they sell, the materials they extract and utilise, and so forth; and much more. The consolidation and multiplication of government legal institutions throughout this period was part and parcel of the growth of organisations more generally, increasing and enhancing the capacity of legal institutions to produce and process law.

A second factor, tied to the proliferation of organisations, is that fixed form contracts have become ubiquitous, including employment, purchases, mortgages, leases, insurance, credit cards, loans, bank accounts, telephone carriers, club and gym memberships, and so forth. Third, layers of laws and regulations imposed by government address a vast range of activities, setting minimum requirements, imposing obligations, and restricting options, from health and safety requirements, to licensing requirements, to pollution control, and an endless list of other matters (often incorporated in fixed form contracts). The fourth factor is the tendency within law to settle on, copy and repeat standard words, phrases and provisions, involving the formalisation of legal terminology in frequently utilised packets of settled meaning (also reflected in fixed form contracts).

The fifth factor merits emphasis because it undergirds the congruence emphasised by Postema: the lengthy co-evolution of law within society renders law an integrated aspect of social interaction, normalised as a taken-for-granted aspect of how things are. Social, cultural, economic and political affairs are built through, on top of and around law over time. Mortgages, for example, evolved over the course of several centuries from a limited device to occupy a pivotal place in real property financing, which cannot be abolished without wreaking economic havoc. The same is true of many other long-standing legal arrangements. What jurists centre on as the legal tradition in isolation is an interconnected aspect of an evolving holistic society that feeds into law and responds to law in various ways. The relations between law and society mentioned earlier in many parts of the global South are fundamentally different – one might say disjointed – precisely because their transplanted state legal systems did not co-evolve for a lengthy period within society, resulting in a lack of congruence between legal norms and the norms of social ordering.

The first four factors are the product of the combined activities of legal production by government officials and the workings of legal professionals consciously creating law and utilising law to serve the purposes of those who employ them. The fifth factor involves the interaction over time of government-produced law and the work of legal professionals with a limitless array of social, cultural, economic and political uses. The result is an omnipresent complex of legal arrangements between and across people and entities that courses through all aspects of society. Multiple factors contribute to the relative fixity of this legal fabric: pervasive uses of law by organisations; the ubiquity of standardised form contracts; that government regulations, once in place, are hard to dislodge; that legal knowledge is systematic; that law copies and repeats; and that law becomes entrenched over time as social, cultural, economic and political arrangements congeal around and through law. Though numerous aspects of the legal fabric are continually contested and altered, at any given time the bulk of it remains in place.

The efficacy of law fundamental to advanced capitalist societies constitutes a background infrastructure for innumerable social, cultural, economic and political activities that people engage in assuming the existence of this legal fabric. Only a small subset of this involves lay people actually being *guided* by law. (Think about the many detailed contracts that people enter into by signing or clicking on a box without reading a word – which they would struggle to apprehend anyway – contracts by which people unknowingly often waive various legal rights.) The bulk of this reliance involves people conducting their affairs with nary a thought about law, implicitly assuming that necessary legal arrangements are in place, whatever they might be, and that legal mechanisms for redress exist should things go wrong.

The claim here is not that people are never guided by law – but that people more often utilise law in ways that do not involve being *guided* by law or *obeying* the law. The common assumptions of legal theorists that the social efficacy of law lies largely in guidance and obedience are incorrect as applied to advanced capitalist societies. The social efficacy of law today lies primarily in the aggregate background legal fabric produced through legally empowered governmental officials utilising law instrumentally and the legal activities of legal professionals facilitating the objectives of individuals and entities (public and private) that employ them for legal services.

22.8 Implications of Variation and Change for Legal Positivism

The social efficacy thesis propounded by legal positivists appears to be neither entirely conceptual nor empirical but a mixture of the two. The conceptual component, as we have seen in the discussion of the monopoly view and the guidance function of law, is that legal theorists posit assumptions about what a legal system consists of and how it functions, with implications for what counts as efficacy. The empirical aspect is that knowledge about efficacy requires an examination of how law actually works.

This chapter uses the efficacy thesis to question a number of conceptual and empirical assumptions commonly held by theorists. Focusing on the empirical reality of legal systems exposes that legal positivist theorists have failed to recognise that even when citizens do not generally obey the law, the legal system can still be efficacious in different spheres or regions; recognition of this, in turn, has significant implications for concepts of law, as described. The most important implication is that the idealised monopoly view of law as comprehensive and supreme within society should be discarded from the concept of law. Focusing on how law is utilised also reveals that law is efficacious not primarily because it guides people in their actions but because it is used to structure government and to further the instrumental activities of government officials, and because, in advanced capitalist societies in the aggregate, it constitutes a background legal infrastructure – a kind of social connectivity – underlying countless activities by people and entities within society.

Two final lessons for legal positivist theory will be drawn from this exploration. The first lesson is that the relationship between law and social efficacy varies across societies. The relationship between law and social efficacy in post-colonial societies, wherein state law has been largely transplanted, creating an enduring legal pluralism alongside long-standing customary and religious law, is radically different from the relationship in advanced capitalist societies in the West, wherein law and society have co-evolved over centuries in an integrated fashion. Owing to these differences, legal positivist theorists must proceed with caution and greater awareness when uttering assertions about law purportedly applicable to all societies.

The second lesson is that the relationship between law and social efficacy changes over time. When Hart specified that primary rules are obligatory rules of behaviour that the populace must generally obey, he had in mind a view of law as a set of proscriptions directed at individuals. This paradigm fits a simple society with basic rules of social ordering – criminal law, property, contract, torts, family obligations and a few more – known by everyone, where legal institutions are accessible to and understood by most members of the community. Law has evolved away from this paradigm in two fundamental respects. First, in the last two centuries, the explosive increase of instrumental uses of law by government officials has brought into existence a major sphere of governmental legal activity that does not involve social ordering. Legal theorists who continue to discuss social efficacy solely in terms of citizens obeying legal rules have not caught up with this change. Second, following on the first, law has become exceedingly voluminous, technical and complex, a highly specialised discipline manned by legal professionals, beyond the knowledge of the populace. By way of analogy, in simpler societies, most everyone could understand commonly used implements in the community, whereas in contemporary society, physics, chemistry, medicine, technology and other areas of human knowledge are too specialised for people to understand, though the products of these specialisations are in everyday use. The same is true of law – which people widely rely on without knowledge of its details or how it works. Yet legal theorists continue to assert that people use law as if they understand it and are guided by it. In past societies, the efficacy of law operated directly on people, but today, significant aspects of law operate in the background.

Analytical jurisprudents seeking to identify essential and necessary features of law have difficulty accounting for variation and change. As this chapter demonstrates, theoretical work on the efficacy thesis requires close attention to the social reality of law. A broader implication of this chapter is that theorists in general tend to rely too heavily on untutored intuitions when engaging in conceptual analysis, smuggling in assumptions about law that often do not hold. Legal theorists must make greater efforts to become informed about, and to address, law as it actually exists within and across societies.

References

Cass, R. 1976. 'Ignorance of the Law: A Maxim Reexamined'. *William & Mary Law Review* 17: 671–700.

Chirayath, L., Sage, C. and Woolcock, M. 2005. *Customary Law and Policy Reform: Engaging with the Plurality of Justice Systems.* World Bank. http://documents.worldbank.org/curated/en/675681468178176738/Customary-law-and-policy-reform-engaging-with-the-plurality-of-justice-systems.

Coleman, J. S. 1973. *Power and Structure of Society.* W.W. Norton.

Darley, J. M., Robinson, P. H. and Carlsmith, K. M. 2001. 'The Ex Ante Function of the Criminal Law'. *Law and Society Review* 35: 165–90.

Fitzpatrick, D. 2016. 'Fragmented Property Systems'. *University of Pennsylvania Journal of International Law* 38: 137–93.

Hadfield, G. K. and Heine, J. 2016. 'Law in the Law-Thick World: The Legal Resource Landscape for Ordinary Americans'. In S. Estreicher and J. Radice (eds.). *Beyond Elite Law: Access to Civil Justice for Ordinary Americans.* Cambridge University Press.

Hall, L. and Seligman, S. J. 1941. 'Mistake of Law and Mens Rea'. *University of Chicago Law Review* 8: 641–83.

Hart, H. L. A. 1961/1994. *The Concept of Law.* Clarendon Press.

Hooker, M.B. 1975. *Legal Pluralism: An Introduction to Colonial and Neo-Colonial Laws.* Clarendon Press.

Jhering, R. V. 1968. *Law as a Means to an End.* Trans. I. Husik. A.M. Kelly Press.

Kahn, H. M. 2015. 'Islamic Law, Customary Law, and Afghan Informal Justice'. *Special Report* 363. United States Institute of Peace. www.usip.org/sites/default/files/SR363-Islamic-Law-CustomaryLaw-and-Afghan-Informal-Justice.pdf.

Keedy, E. R. 1908. 'Ignorance and Mistake in the Criminal Law'. *Harvard Law Review* 22: 75–96.

Kelsen, H. 1967. *Pure Theory of Law.* Trans. M. Knight. University of California Press.

Kelsen, H. 1992. *An Introduction to the Problems of Legal Theory.* Trans. B. Litschewski Paulson and S. L. Paulson. Clarendon Press.

Kim, P. T. 1998. 'Bargaining with Imperfect Information: A Study of Worker Perceptions of Legal Protections in an At-Will World'. *Cornell Law Review* 83: 105–56.

Kohler, R. E. 1935. 'Ignorance or Mistake of Law as a Defense in Criminal Cases'. *Dickinson Law Review* 40: 113–21.

Marmor, A. 2004. 'The Rule of Law and Its Limits'. *Law and Philosophy* 24:1–43.

Payne, M. 1982. 'Law Based on Accepted Authority'. *William & Mary Law Review* 23: 287–319.

Postema, G. J. 2008. 'Conformity, Custom, and Congruence: Rethinking the Efficacy of Law'. In M. H. Kramer, C. Grant, B. Coburn and A. Hatzistavrou (eds.). *The Legacy of H.L.A. Hart: Legal, Political, and Moral Philosophy.* Oxford University Press.

Pound, R. 1910. 'Law in Books and Law in Action'. *American Law Review* 44: 12–36.

Raz, J. 1970. *The Concept of a Legal System: An Introduction to the Theory of a Legal System.* Clarendon Press.

Raz, J. 2009. *The Authority of Law.* 2nd ed. Oxford University Press.

Raz, J. 2017. 'Why the State?'. In N. Roughan and A. Halpin (eds.). *In Pursuit of Pluralist Jurisprudence.* Cambridge University Press.

Rowell, A. 2017. 'Legal Knowledge, Belief, and Aspiration'. https://papers.ssrn.com/sol3/papers.cfm?abstract_id=2903049.

Rubin, E. 1989. 'Law and Legislation in the Administrative State'. *Columbia Law Review* 89: 369–426.

Shiner, R. A. 1990. 'The Acceptance of a Legal System'. *Canadian Journal of Law and Jurisprudence* 3: 81–106.

Tamanaha, B. Z. 2001. 'Socio-Legal Positivism and a General Jurisprudence'. *Oxford Journal of Legal Studies* 21: 1–32.

Tamanaha, B. Z. 2008. 'Understanding Legal Pluralism: Past to Present, Local to Global'. *Sydney Law Review* 30: 375–411.

Tamanaha, B. Z. 2011. 'The Primacy of Society and the Failures of Law and Development'. *Cornell International Law Journal* 44: 209–47.

Tamanaha, B. Z. 2017. *A Realistic Theory of Law.* Cambridge University Press.

Tamanaha, B. Z. 2018. 'Law's Evolving Emergent Phenomena: From Rules of Social Intercourse to Rule of Law Society'. *Washington University Law Review* 95: 1149–86.

Yassari, N. and Saboory, M. H. 2010. 'Sharia and National Law in Afghanistan'. *Jura Gentium.* www.juragentium.org/topics/islam/en/yassari.htm.

23 The Semantic Thesis in Legal Positivism

Michael S. Green*

23.1 Introduction

To be a legal positivist, in the sense in which current Anglophone philosophers of law usually use the term, is to accept what Joseph Raz calls the *social thesis*: the existence and content of the law are ultimately based solely in social facts about a community, not moral facts.[1] Under most positivist theories of law, the requisite social facts primarily concern the legal practices of the community's officials.

So described, the social thesis is ambiguous, however. On one reading, it states that a legal system and its laws are reducible to social facts, the way a traffic jam is reducible to facts about its constituent cars. Let us call this the *reduction version* of the thesis and those who accept this version *reduction positivists*. On another reading, a legal system and its laws are not social entities at all. They are abstract objects. But the grounds for assigning certain of these objects to a community – such that they are the legal system and laws of that community – are ultimately solely social facts about the community, not moral facts. Let us call this the *assignment version* of the thesis and those who accept this version *assignment positivists*.

Consider the following analogy. Philosophers of language accept their own social thesis: the existence and content of a language are based solely in social facts about a community. But some hold an assignment version of this thesis. In their view, a language is an abstract object – in particular, a function from things in the world (scribbles, phonemes) to propositions (which are themselves abstract objects). French takes one from 'le chat est

* Thanks to the participants in the Conference on Fundamentals of Legal Positivism at the University of Stockholm, with special thanks to Torben Spaak for his characteristically penetrating and detailed written criticisms. Thanks also to Stephen Finlay and Peter Hanks for essential help.

[1] See Raz 1994: 210.

sur le tapis' to the proposition that-the-cat-is-on-the-mat. Esperanto takes one from 'la kato estas sur la mato' to the same proposition. For such philosophers, these are necessary truths about French and Esperanto. They are not contingent truths dependent on social facts.[2]

But, for these philosophers, a language remains social in the following sense: the grounds for assigning a language to a community are solely social facts.[3] It is a contingent fact that the French speak French, rather than Esperanto. That they speak French is due solely to social facts about the French community.

Scott Shapiro has made it clear that he is an assignment positivist. Under his theory of law, laws are *plans*.[4] The master plan of a legal system specifies 'who has authority to plan with respect to what subject matter and over whom'.[5] The other laws of the legal system are the plans identified by the master plan. And what are plans? They are *norms*, understood as 'any standard ... that is supposed to guide conduct and serve as a basis for evaluation or criticism'.[6] And norms are 'abstract propositional entities' that exist outside space and time and that do not enter into causal relations with anything in the world, including human beings.[7]

It follows that facts about a legal system are not social. It is a necessary truth about the abstract object that is the English legal system that if the Queen-in-Parliament adopts the plan do-not-drive-above-70-kph, that plan is law.[8] It is not a contingent truth that depends upon social facts. But, for Shapiro, what connects a legal system to a community are solely social facts about the community, in particular its officials' adoption, through the psychological act of planning, of a master plan.[9] It is a contingent truth that the English have the English legal system. That

[2] See Schiffer 1993: 231–2. This assumes a static understanding of a language. If there is any change in the function (for example, because a word is added) one has a different language. A static language can usually be assigned to a community only at a particular moment in its history. Note that there may be an alternative understanding of a language as a set of static languages, each of which can be assigned to the same community at some point in its history. I thank Peter Hanks for identifying this issue.

[3] See Schiffer 1993. [4] See Shapiro 2011: 225. [5] Shapiro 2011: 204.

[6] Shapiro 2011: 41. [7] See Shapiro 2011: 41, 127; Green 2013: 350–3.

[8] This statement describes what follows from Shapiro's view that plans are abstract objects. It is not, to my knowledge, a position he explicitly endorses.

[9] See Shapiro 2011: 103. I ignore here the other social facts that are required to assign a legal system to a community under Shapiro's theory of law.

they have that system is due solely to social facts about the English, not moral facts.

Few legal positivists are as clear as Shapiro on the matter.[10] But many are best interpreted as assignment positivists. H. L. A. Hart is an example. Under this reading, Hart thought that a legal system is based in an abstract object – a norm he calls *a rule of recognition.*[11] According to this norm, officials ought to apply those norms (also abstract objects) that satisfy certain criteria.[12] The laws of a legal system are all the norms that satisfy the criteria in the rule. These facts about a legal system are not social.

Where social facts come into play is in determining which legal system is assigned to a community. A system is assigned to a community if the system's rule of recognition is accepted by the community's officials.[13] (Notice that such acceptance is probably not the same thing as the officials' adopting the rule of recognition as a master plan.) When they accept a rule of recognition, all the norms identified by the rule are the laws of that community.[14]

Because so many prominent legal positivists – including Shapiro, Hart and Raz –[15] accept (or are best interpreted as accepting) the assignment version of the social thesis, this chapter will focus on assignment positivism. When I speak of the social thesis, I will mean the assignment version of the thesis. I will only occasionally and tentatively speak of the consequences if reduction positivism is true.

[10] And even he is not as clear as he could be, for he sometimes conflates social or psychological facts about adopting plans with the plans adopted. See Green 2013: 347–57.

[11] Hart generally speaks of these objects as rules or standards, rather than norms. But norm is the more inclusive term because it does not suggest generality. See Shapiro 2011: 41. Since legal norms can be particular (for example, a court's judgment) as well as general, I will use the term norm here.

[12] See, e.g., Hart 1994: 108; Shapiro 2009: 239–42; Shapiro 2011: 40–2.

[13] I ignore here the other social facts that are required to assign a legal system to a community under Hart's theory of law. See Hart 1994: 116–17.

[14] In this reading of Hart, I attribute to him non-naturalism concerning norms. I may not be alone in doing so; see Sciaraffa 2011: 610. It is possible, however, that Hart had some naturalistic, or even social, conception of norms. But even if he did, he must have drawn a distinction between the social facts on the basis of which some norm is said to exist and the social facts – such as acceptance – that are the grounds for assigning the norm to a community. Otherwise, one could not distinguish between a community, or one of its members, thinking about a norm (say, to reject it) and their accepting it in a way that makes it a norm of the community. I thank Kevin Toh for motivating me to clarify this point.

[15] I think it is clear that Raz is an assignment positivist, although I will not argue for that conclusion here.

That said, some positivists do make it clear that they accept the reduction version of the social thesis. For the American legal realists, a legal system and its laws do not consist of abstract objects. They are instead constituted by social facts about the beliefs, attitudes and behaviour of a community's officials. Whereas assignment positivists would say that the Securities Exchange Act[16] is an abstract object that is assigned to the American community due to social facts, the realists would say the Act is itself a set of social facts about the beliefs, attitudes and behaviour of American officials.[17]

According to Hart, a rule of recognition might identify a norm as law only if it satisfies certain moral criteria. This is compatible with the social thesis, so long as the rule is assigned to a community solely on the basis of social facts about the community, not moral facts. Raz and Shapiro advocate a stronger social thesis – commonly called the *sources thesis* – under which a rule of recognition can identify norms as laws only on the basis of social facts.[18] But quite a few positivists disagree.[19] Solely to simplify discussion, I will assume that the sources thesis is correct throughout this chapter. (I believe that my argument would still work if the weaker social thesis is correct.) Thus, I will assume that, under the social thesis, it is not merely the case that only social facts determine which legal system should be assigned to a community – in addition, the assigned legal system must refer only to social facts when identifying the norms that are the laws of the system.

The social thesis is a *metaphysical* thesis about the nature of law. One might then wonder about the connection between this metaphysical thesis and a *semantic* thesis – a thesis about the semantic content of legal statements, especially those using normative terms like 'right' and 'duty'.

Raz has helpfully described a number of semantic theses sometimes held by positivists. One is that terms like 'right' and 'duty' cannot have the same meaning in legal and moral contexts.[20] Another stronger thesis – which entails the weaker thesis but is not entailed by it – is that legal statements are solely descriptions of social facts.[21] I will concentrate on the stronger semantic thesis in this chapter.

[16] 15 USC §78a ff. [17] See Green 2011: 409–16.

[18] See Raz 1994: 210–20; Shapiro 2011: 269–77. The sources thesis also applies to laws that are subordinate to the rule of recognition: they too can identify other norms as laws only on the basis of social facts.

[19] See, e.g., Waluchow 1994. [20] Raz 1979: 39. [21] See Raz 1979: 53; Raz 1998: 239.

We can distinguish two questions about this thesis. First, does it follow from the social thesis? Is it a consequence of the social thesis that legal statements describe only social facts and not, say, moral facts? The answer, as we shall see, is no.

The second question is this: Even if the semantic thesis does not follow from the social thesis, to what extent do legal statements actually conform to the semantic thesis? Many contemporary positivists – including Hart, Raz and Shapiro – argue that the semantic thesis mischaracterises legal statements. They are not solely descriptions of social facts.

One might think that, for assignment positivists like Hart, Raz and Shapiro, the reason is simple. A legal system and its laws are abstract objects. It should not be surprising, therefore, that legal statements would describe facts about these objects, not (or not solely) social facts. For example, the statement 'you (legally) ought not drive above 70 kph', when made in England, would describe a necessary truth about the abstract object that is the English legal system, namely that the abstract object do not-drive-above-70-kph is a law of that system, given that some social fact (say, an announcement by the Queen-in-Parliament) has obtained. The statement might be understood as *also* describing social facts, for example, the Queen-in-Parliament's announcement or the social facts that are the grounds for assigning the English legal system to the English community. But it describes facts about abstract objects as well. It is not solely a description of social facts.

I think that this simple account is the one that assignment positivists should adopt. Normative language is used in legal statements because the abstract objects described are norms in Shapiro's sense – they have the capacity to guide conduct. So understood, they are *formally* normative, meaning that they have this guiding capacity, the way the content of a shopping list does.[22] Normative terms like *obligated, permitted* or *authorised* are used in legal statements to identify the type of guidance that the relevant norms provide.

Formal normativity is usually considered cheap – too cheap to provide any interesting consequences in the philosophy of law.[23] Given that it

[22] For the distinction between formal and robust normativity, see McPherson 2011.

[23] See Finlay and Plunkett 2018: 67.

arguably requires non-natural objects, I am not sure that it is cheap.[24] But, in any event, it is not free. And assignment positivists should conclude that statements that solely describe social facts have not paid enough to be legal statements, for they do not describe anything with formal normativity. Such statements are like a shopping list that says 'many people believe they should buy milk'. The social fact described fails to guide conduct.

I believe that the simple account is the reason that Hart thought that legal statements do not conform to the semantic thesis. Unfortunately, many assignment positivists – and especially Raz – argue that the semantic thesis is false, not because legal statements describe the formally normative but because they describe the *robustly* normative. Robust normativity is the kind of normativity to which one appeals when speaking about what people *really* should do. Moral norms are paradigmatic examples. Although entities with robust normativity probably have formal normativity, the reverse is clearly not true: the fact that there is an abstract object that can guide one's behaviour does not mean that one really has a reason to conform one's behaviour to the object. There is, after all, an infinite number of such objects, telling one to do all kinds of crazy or evil things.

As we shall see, Raz is right that it is compatible with the social thesis that legal statements describe entities with robust normativity. That is the answer to the first question. But it is a mistake to conclude that they generally do so. In particular, the conclusion is not necessary to account for the use of normative language in legal statements. This mistake forces him and some other assignment positivists[25] into puzzling, and unnecessary, problems.

23.2 First Question: Does the Semantic Thesis Follow from the Social Thesis?

If the social thesis is true, does the semantic thesis follow, in the sense that legal statements, including those that use normative language, are solely

[24] For an account of how establishing a psychological relationship to a rule appears to commit one to anti-naturalism, see Boghossian 1989.

[25] I am thinking of Shapiro. Space considerations do not allow me to describe his position on the matter in detail here.

descriptions of social facts? In particular, could they still describe moral facts?

If the question is whether the social thesis *entails* the semantic thesis, it is easy to see that the answer is no. That we speak a certain language is a contingent fact, and there is no reason to believe that the meanings of our words necessarily track the world's metaphysical character. People might simply be confused about the metaphysical nature of law, and this confusion might express itself in their legal statements.[26]

But perhaps the semantic thesis follows from the social thesis in the weaker sense that the legal statements of those who are not confused about the nature of law (and so accept the social thesis) are solely descriptions of social facts, not moral facts. After all, if the fact that a norm is the law of a community does not depend upon moral facts, and people know this, why would their legal statements describe moral facts?

As Raz has shown, this argument is mistaken.[27] It is easy to imagine a scenario in which legal statements describe moral facts, without the social thesis being violated and without people being confused about the nature of law.

Imagine that a group of powerful people wish to systematically resolve the violent disagreements that arise in their community. They believe (wrongly) that once a practice for resolving disagreements is established, the members of the community will always have a moral duty to abide by the resolutions. They take it upon themselves to be the officials of the practice and accept a norm according to which they should enforce all the norms announced by one of them, whose name is Rex. After Rex announces that people should not drive above 55 mph, they describe that norm as a legal duty. By 'legal duty' they could easily mean a certain type of moral duty, namely one that is also law.

If so, we can understand their legal statement as describing moral facts (which is not to say that those facts obtain). That is compatible with the social thesis because it is still the case that the norm do-not-drive-above-55-mph (which the officials wrongly take to be a moral duty) is the law solely due to social facts, namely the officials' acceptance of a norm empowering Rex and Rex's announcement. Furthermore, the officials

26 For the same reason, the semantic thesis does not follow even from the reduction version of the social thesis.

27 See Raz 1979: 37–9, 153–9; Raz 1999: 170–7. See also Shapiro 2011: 113–15.

need not be confused about the nature of law because they can accept that the grounds for describing the moral duty not to drive above 55 mph as *legal* are solely those social facts.[28]

23.3 Second Question: To What Extent Do Legal Statements Satisfy the Semantic Thesis?

So, the first question has been answered. The semantic thesis does not follow from the social thesis. In particular, it is compatible with the social thesis that legal statements describe moral facts. Let us now move on to the second question. Do legal statements actually satisfy the semantic thesis? Are they solely descriptions of social facts?

Many positivists think that the answer is no because legal statements are normative.[29] To be sure, some legal statements – those Hart calls *external* – are solely descriptions of people's beliefs, attitudes and behaviour.[30] An example is:

1) In England, officials take themselves to be obligated to enforce norms announced by the Queen-in-Parliament.[31]

External legal statements satisfy the semantic thesis.

But most legal statements are what Hart calls *internal*. An example is:

2) One (legally) ought not drive above 55 mph.

Internal legal statements (ILSs) are commonly made by committed participants in the legal system and use normative language, such as 'ought' or 'duty'. Hart also speaks of statements as internal even when they do not use normative language, if they make use of norms, as when one describes a batter as out, using the norms of baseball.[32] Thus, legal statements that do not use normative language can be ILSs if they use a rule of recognition, or

[28] An assignment positivist can understand a moral duty as legal because the moral duty can also be considered as a formally normative abstract object, which is then assigned to a community solely due to social facts. By contrast, the semantic thesis arguably follows (in the weaker sense) from the reduction version of the social thesis, because a moral duty is not the sort of thing that can also be considered as a set of social facts. Thanks to Torben Spaak for bringing up this issue.

[29] For example, Hart 1983: 167. [30] Hart 1994: 89. [31] Hart 1994: 102.

[32] See Hart 1994: 102–3; see also Duarte d'Almeida 2016: 175.

norms identified as law by the rule, to assess a situation legally. An example is 'The Securities Exchange Act is law'.

23.3.1 Two Linguistic Phenomena

Despite their apparently normative character, it remains possible that a proper analysis of ILSs would show them to be solely descriptions of social facts. The positivist who rejects the semantic thesis must provide a credible semantic account of ILSs that explains why the thesis is false. This account must accommodate the variety of ways in which ILSs are appropriately used in legal discourse. Two linguistic phenomena are of particular concern.

The first is when an ILS is appropriately made by those who have no commitment to conformity with the law. If the ILS is solely a description of social facts, this would be unproblematic. One can describe social facts about legal practices without taking oneself to have reasons for conformity to those practices. But if ILSs are normative, such use is arguably a problem. It is commonly thought that those who make normative statements thereby take themselves to have a reason for action. Those who say one ought not drive above 55 mph take themselves to have a reason not to drive above 55 mph, meaning that they are committed, to some extent, to not driving above 55 mph. The fact that ILSs are made by those who are not committed to conformity with the law is thus a reason to think that they are not normative statements.

The second phenomenon concerns the inferences that may be made from ILSs. At this point, I will mention only one example. Consider the following:

3) If Rex announces a norm, then officials (legally) ought to enforce it.
4) Rex announces the norm do-not-drive-above-55-mph.
5) Officials (legally) ought to enforce the norm do-not-drive-above-55-mph.

It follows from 3's semantic content that it, in combination with 4, entails 5. If 3 and 4 are true, then 5 must be true. An account of ILSs should be able to explain why this is the case.

Such entailment suggests that ILSs are not solely descriptions of social facts (for example, facts about officials' acceptance of legal norms). Assume that the two ILSs in the inference – 3 and 5 – are such descriptions. The inference would look like the following:

6) Officials accept that if Rex announces a norm, then they (legally) ought to enforce it
7) Rex announces the norm do-not-drive-above-55-mph.
8) Officials accept that they (legally) ought to enforce the norm do-not-drive-above-55-mph.

The truth of 8 does not necessarily follow from the truth of 6 and 7.[33] Otherwise, it would be impossible for officials to fail to follow a norm that they have accepted.

23.3.2 The Prevailing Account: Expressivism

The most common semantic account of ILSs among positivists who reject the semantic thesis is probably expressivism.[34] To appreciate expressivist semantics, consider the sentence 'Hurrah, John!' The semantic function of 'hurrah' in this sentence is not to attribute the property of hurrahness to John. Otherwise, the sentence would be true or false depending upon whether John had that property. But 'Hurrah, John!', although meaningful, is neither true nor false. Rather than describing John, it expresses the speaker's positive attitude towards him. Its meaning can be understood in term of this expressive role.

In contrast to 'hurrah', descriptive terms, like 'bald', do attribute properties to the world. The assertion 'John is bald' is true or false depending upon whether John has the property of baldness. Two aspects of this assertion can be distinguished. The first is its propositional content: *that-John-is-bald*. This content is independent of its being asserted, for the same content can occur in an unasserted context, as when one says, 'If John is bald, then Jane is married to a bald man' or 'Joe believes that John is bald'. Although these two sentences also contain the propositional content *that-John-is-bald*, they do not assert that he is bald. The assertoric element of 'John is bald' comes from the way the propositional content is put to use in a particular type of speech act, namely an assertion. It follows that the meaning of an assertion cannot be explained solely in terms of its use in a speech act, for that would ignore its propositional content, which can occur in different speech acts, with different uses.

[33] See Mullins 2018b.
[34] Or, more accurately, non-cognitivist expressivism. See Toh 2005: 78–81; Gibbard 1990.

'Hurrah, John!', by contrast, cannot be understood through the model of propositional content and its use in a speech act. Indeed, 'Hurrah, John!' does not have propositional content at all, which explains why sentences like 'If Hurrah, John!, then . . .' or 'Joe believes Hurrah, John!' are meaningless. Unlike 'John is bald', the meaning of 'Hurrah, John!' can indeed be understood solely in terms of its use in a speech act, in particular, the expression of a positive attitude towards John.

Under an expressivist account of ILSs, their meaning is similar to 'Hurrah, John!' ILSs are speech acts that express one's acceptance of conformity with the relevant rule of recognition. Notice that because ILSs have expressive meaning, the semantic thesis is false. They are not, or not solely,[35] descriptions of social facts.

One advantage of an expressivist account is its ability to explain, in a suitably naturalistic manner, why those who make ILSs sometimes take themselves to thereby have reasons for action. The reasons are the affective states expressed. This avoids having to understand ILSs as describing the existence of mysterious robust reasons for action that are part of the fabric of the universe.

Expressivism is also the semantic account of ILSs most commonly attributed to Hart. This reading has been most fully developed by Kevin Toh.[36] As he has put Hart's view, one makes an ILS if and only if he:

(i) expresses his acceptance of the rule of recognition; and
(ii) presupposes that the rule of recognition is generally accepted and complied with by the members of his community.[37]

Notice that, for Hart, the acceptance expressed in ILSs is not necessarily moral.[38] Someone might accept a rule of recognition for prudential reasons, or simply due to mindless conformism.[39]

But expressivism has difficulty accounting for our two linguistic phenomena. First, if the meaning of an ILS is tied to the expression of the speaker's acceptance of the relevant rule of recognition, how are we to understand ILSs made by those who have no inclination to conform to the

[35] For the legal expressivist, ILSs might have both descriptive meaning and expressive meaning. This is Toh's position in Enoch and Toh 2013. Their descriptive meaning might solely concern social facts.

[36] See especially Toh 2005. I have attributed such a position to Hart myself, although I now think that this was a mistake. Green 2005: 1953–6.

[37] See Toh 2005: 88. [38] See Toh 2007: 414–20. [39] See Hart 1994: 203.

rule?[40] This is a problem not merely concerning ILSs made by those who do not accept the rule of recognition of their own legal system, but also ILSs concerning foreign, past and fictional legal systems.[41]

Second, expressivism cannot explain how 3 and 4 entail 5, that is, how 5 is true in all possible worlds in which 3 and 4 are true. For the legal expressivist, 3 and 5 do not have truth values at all. And there cannot, of course, be a necessary relationship between the attitude expressed by 3 and that expressed by 5. It is possible for someone to accept that if Rex announces a norm then officials (legally) ought to enforce it and believe that Rex announces the norm do-not-drive-above-55-mph and yet not accept that officials (legally) ought to enforce the norm do-not-drive-above-55-mph. If this were impossible, people could not fail to conform with norms that they have accepted.

But the problem for legal expressivism is broader than accounting for entailment concerning ILSs. It is the more general one of explaining how the semantic properties of ILSs depend upon their parts. Expressivism is threatened by the so-called *Frege-Geach problem.*

Consider the following moral inference:[42]

9) If tormenting the cat is bad, getting your little brother to do it is bad.
10) Tormenting the cat is bad.
11) Getting your little brother to torment the cat is bad.

The Frege-Geach problem concerning this inference is not explaining how 11 necessarily follows from 9 and 10. Rather, it is explaining how 'bad' contributes to the semantic properties of each of these sentences in a way that makes the inference appropriate in any sense. The expressivist would say that in 10 it (that is, 'bad') functions to express the speaker's negative attitude towards tormenting the cat. But it cannot have that function in the

40 Toh (2007: 414) argues that they express a psychological state that simulates an acceptance of the rule of recognition. For scepticism about the coherence of this account, see Duarte d'Alemeida 2011: 183 n. 105.

41 One might think that there is an additional problem concerning ILSs about past and fictional legal systems, which is that the relevant rule of recognition is not generally accepted by the members of the speaker's, or any existent, community. But under Toh's reading, an ILS does not describe that fact. It is instead presupposed by the person making the ILS, in the sense that one normally will utter an ILS about a legal system only if the fact obtains; Toh 2005: 86–7; compare Stalnaker 1999: 38. Because this presupposed fact is not part of the meaning of the ILS, the ILS may be appropriately uttered in its absence.

42 Geach 1972: 268.

antecedent of 9, for someone who utters 9 need not have such an attitude. Indeed, if 'bad' has expressive meaning, one would think that 9 should be meaningless, the way a conditional sentence with the antecedent 'If Hurrah, John! . . .' is meaningless.

Things would be different if 'bad' were a descriptive term, for then one could say that the antecedent of 9 has the same propositional content as 10, although it is being put to non-assertoric use in the former. But that avenue is unavailable to the moral expressivist.

The Frege-Geach problem applies with equal force to an expressivist account of ILSs, for normative legal terms can also be used in non-assertoric contexts. One can meaningfully say 'If one (legally) ought not drive above 55 mph then Joe has broken the law' or say 'Joe believes that one (legally) ought not drive above 55 mph'.

To repeat, the Frege-Geach problem is different from the problem of explaining entailment concerning ILSs. Let us assume that the expressivist can answer the Frege-Geach problem concerning the inference from 3 and 4 to 5, by identifying some complex attitude that 3 expresses, such that someone who utters 3 and also utters 4 would feel it appropriate to utter 5.[43] The psychological fact that someone feels it appropriate to utter 5 having accepted 3 and 4 does not mean that 3 and 4 entail 5. Indeed, because expressivists deny that ILSs have truth values, they must reject such entailment, for that requires that 5 be true in all possible worlds in which 3 and 4 are true. For the legal expressivist, 3 and 5 do not have truth values at all.

So even if legal expressivists answered the Frege-Geach problem, they still could not explain entailment concerning ILSs. But prospects for a legal expressivist answer to the Frege-Geach problem are themselves dim. Legal expressivists must explain how normative legal terms, although expressive, are not like 'hurrah', for they can meaningfully occur in complex sentences like conditionals and indirect reports. What is more, they just happen to contribute to the semantic properties of these complex sentences in a way that perfectly mimics the contribution they would make if they were descriptive. Given the incredible variety of complex sentences in which normative legal terms might appear, this is an impossibly tall order. It seems far simpler to simply accept that the terms are descriptive.

43 See Blackburn 1984: 189–96.

Of course, even if an expressivist account of ILSs is suspect, it might be the one offered by Hart. And there is evidence that he held something like expressivism in his 1953 work *Definition and Theory in Jurisprudence*.[44] But it is awkward, although not impossible, to attribute expressivism to Hart's major work, *The Concept of Law*. The difficulty is that the Frege-Geach problem was introduced by Peter Geach in response, in part, to Hart's 1953 work.[45] The fact that Hart conceded that Geach's criticism was correct in 1968, and probably was aware of it in 1960, when Geach published it, is a reason to think that Hart did not adopt an expressivist semantics of ILSs in 1961, when *The Concept of Law* was published.[46]

23.3.3 Raz's Account: Moral Norms

Joseph Raz, although also rejecting the semantic thesis, has offered an alternative account of ILSs that he believes avoids the inadequacies of legal expressivism.[47] As we have seen, Raz argues, rightly, that it is compatible with the social thesis that legal statements describe moral facts. In the statement 'you have a legal duty not to drive above 55 mph', the word 'duty' could be used with the same meaning that it has in a moral context. But Raz goes further and argues that the normative language in legal statements in fact describes moral reasons for action (which does not mean that such reasons for action exist).

As we have seen, Hart was intentionally vague about the underlying reasons an official might accept a rule of recognition. The reasons need not be moral. But Raz argues that only moral reasons can explain why an official would attribute legal duties to other officials or to the general population.[48] The fact that I get a paycheque if I use a rule of recognition explains only why I have a prudential reason to use the rule. It does not

[44] See Hart 1983: 21–48. It is more accurate to say that Hart's position in that work is not expressivism per se but a position that shares with expressivism the view that the semantic properties of certain legal terms are determined solely by their use in speech acts.

[45] Geach 1972: 270–7.

[46] See Kramer 2018: 181–203. Toh (2005: 103–5) recognises the difficulty, but argues that Hart might have thought that the Frege-Geach problem could be overcome.

[47] See Raz 1998: 248.

[48] See Raz 1984: 130–1; Raz 1998: 249; Raz 2004: 5–6. See also Shapiro 2011: 111–15.

explain why other officials have such a reason, or why the population as a whole has a reason to follow the norms identified as law by the rule.

Because Raz's account of ILSs treats them as descriptions of moral reasons for action, it does not suffer from the Frege-Geach problem. ILSs have propositional content that can occur in unasserted contexts. Raz's approach is also able to explain entailment concerning ILSs. In all possible worlds in which it is the case that if Rex announces a norm, then officials morally ought to enforce it and it is the case that Rex announces the norm do-not-drive-above-55-mph, it is also the case that officials morally ought to enforce the norm do-not-drive-above-55-mph. The truth of 5 follows necessarily from the truth of 3 and 4.

Where Raz's approach runs into problems is explaining ILSs made by those not committed to conformity with the rule of recognition. One difficulty is officials who, although committed to conformity, do not feel that it is demanded morally. They follow, say, for prudential reasons. Here, Raz generally argues that their ILSs, although still stating the existence of moral reasons for action, are insincere.[49]

Indeed, because it is questionable whether any official takes there to always be moral reasons for conformity with the law, Raz concedes that the only person who would always make sincere ILSs is hypothetical – the 'legal man'.[50] According to the legal man, all legal rights, duties, privileges and powers are moral rights, duties, privileges and powers. But even though there is no actual legal man, ILSs still describe the existence of these moral reasons for action.

The insincere character of so many ILSs made by officials is already a problem with Raz's position, for it does not appear that officials take their ILSs to be insincere. But the more substantial problem is accounting for those legal statements that Raz calls 'detached'.[51] Detached legal statements (DLSs), which are commonly made by lawyers, are not external legal statements, for – like ILSs – they usually are framed in normative language.[52] But they do not describe the existence of moral reasons for action. They communicate some other sort of normative fact.

Although Raz introduces DLSs by imagining those who have no commitment to conformity with the relevant rule of recognition, technically

49 See Raz 1979: 155; Raz 1984: 130; Raz 1998: 247.

50 Raz 1979: 140–3; Raz 1999: 171. See also Shapiro 2011: 186.

51 Raz 1999: 176.

52 See Raz 1979: 153.

their status as detached does not depend upon the attitudes of the person making them.[53] Rather, it is a consequence of the descriptive content of the statements themselves. Someone hearing a DLS and taking it to be true should not conclude that moral reasons for action exist. The DLS, although using the same language as an ILS, describes a different sort of normative fact. Thus, those who are morally committed to conformity with legal practices can also make a DLS, if they want to describe only that normative fact.[54]

But what is that normative fact? Raz's account of DLSs is not easy to follow. He speaks of them as describing moral reasons for action arrived at by adopting, without accepting, the legal point of view.[55] A DLS says the same thing as an ILS (that certain moral reasons for action exist), but the two have different truth-values because the DLS states that they exist only relative to the legal point of view, whereas the ILS says that they genuinely exist non-relativistically.

23.3.4 The Simple Account: Abstract Objects

Many philosophers have struggled to find a coherent account of DLSs as Raz understands them.[56] But, rather than delving into those details, let us take a step back and identify the characteristics of DLSs that Raz's account is attempting to accommodate. First, DLSs describe normative facts, not (or not solely) social facts. Second, they do not describe the genuine existence of moral reasons for action. Instead, they describe normative facts that follow – indeed, probably follow necessarily –[57] from legal norms considered independently of their capacity to generate genuine moral reasons. Third, the normative facts they communicate are of the sort that a lawyer might meaningfully wish to tell a client. What semantic account of DLSs could explain all this?

For assignment positivists, there is a very simple and straightforward answer. Since a legal system and its laws are abstract objects, DLSs describe facts about those objects.[58] This would explain why DLSs are not about

[53] See Duarte d'Almeida 2011: 179–80. [54] See Duarte d'Almeida 2011: 180.

[55] See Raz 1979: 140; Raz 1999: 171.

[56] For a careful account and criticism of Raz on DLSs, see Duarte d'Almeida 2011.

[57] I believe this is what Raz is getting at in Raz 1980: 235–6.

[58] Compare Duarte d'Almeida 2011: 198, who argues that all that is needed is for a DLS to communicate 'the content of a given set of legal materials'. Similar criticisms of Raz's position can be found in Silk 2019; Mullins 2018a.

social facts, since abstract objects are not social. It would also explain why someone making a DLS does not describe the existence of moral reasons for action. The relevant abstract objects are simply standards of conduct. There need not be any moral reasons for conformity to them.

Third, facts about these abstract objects are the sort that lawyers might wish to convey to their clients. For example, the statement 'you (legally) ought not drive above 70 kph', when made by an English lawyer, would describe an important necessary truth about the abstract object that is the English legal system, namely that the abstract object do-not-drive-above-70-kph is a law of that system, given that some social fact (say, an announcement by the Queen-in-Parliament) has obtained. This is something that a client might wish to know.

Rather than understanding a DLS as describing facts that follow from moral norms (albeit considered hypothetically or relativistically), as Raz does, it is much simpler and more intuitive to shift the object of the DLS to a real – not a hypothetical or relativised – abstract object. Furthermore, there is no reason not to offer the same account of ILSs. The putative reason to treat DLSs and ILSs differently was that those who make the former do not take their statements to describe the existence of genuine moral reasons for action. But, as we have seen, those who make ILSs are often not morally committed to conformity with the law either. The distinction between the two types of statement can therefore be abandoned. DLSs are simply ILSs. And ILSs describe facts about abstract objects, not moral reasons for action. Let us call this *the simple account* of ILSs' semantic content.

Raz has argued that ILSs must describe moral reasons for action, or one cannot explain why an ILS could attribute legal duties to other officials or to the general population. But the simple account can easily explain such attribution. If one is making an ILS about an abstract object that, by its formally normative content, is a duty that applies to other officials or the population as a whole, the ILS will speak of those people as having that duty. To refuse to attribute the duty to them would be to fail to acknowledge the character of the abstract object at issue. It would be equivalent to saying that a shopping list tells one to buy milk when it actually tells one to buy bread.

Notice that because, under the simple account, ILSs describe abstract objects, the semantic thesis is false. To be sure, ILSs might also describe social facts. 'You (legally) ought not drive above 70 kph' might describe the social fact that is the Queen-in-Parliament's announcement of that norm or the social facts that are the grounds for assigning the English legal system to the English community – although it seems to me more likely that these facts are presupposed rather than described. But even if social facts are described in an ILS, it is also a description of abstract objects. It is not solely a description of social facts.

Notice as well that the simple account easily accommodates our two linguistic phenomena. As we have seen, it explains why ILSs can be made by those not committed to conformity with the relevant rule of recognition. There is an infinite number of abstract objects. Most of them are not robustly normative. It is hardly surprising, therefore, that by talking about them, one does not commit oneself to conformity to the objects. The simple account also easily accommodates ILSs about foreign, past and fictional legal systems. Those legal systems are no less existent as abstract objects than the system that is assigned to one's own community.

Second, the simple account does not suffer from the Frege-Geach problem. Because ILSs are descriptions of abstract objects, they possess propositional content that can occur in unasserted contexts. What is more, the simple account can explain entailment concerning ILSs. When 3 and 5 are understood as descriptions of abstract objects, 5 is true in all possible worlds in which 3 and 4 are true.

I think that the simple account was Hart's view, for it explains nicely what he says about ILSs. First, it explains why he often speaks of ILSs as made by those who *use* legal norms.[59] To use a legal norm is to speak of facts that necessarily follow from the norm and other facts. That is what goes on when one concludes that 5 necessarily follows from 3 and 4. The same thing goes on when one says that a batter is out using the norms of baseball. That the batter is out is a necessary truth following from those norms and a fact about the pitch thrown.

The simple account also explains why Hart says that when officials start speaking of what rule of recognition they use, they have stopped making ILSs.[60] They have started talking about which abstract object should be assigned to their community, which is a question of social fact. They are no longer talking about the characteristics of the abstract object itself.

The simple account also explains why Hart says that someone who makes an ILS presupposes social facts about his community.[61] It is usually

[59] See Hart 1994: 102–3. [60] See Hart 1994: 107–8. [61] See Hart 1994: 102–3, 108.

because social facts assign a rule of recognition to one's community that one talks about facts concerning the rule. But the simple account also explains why Hart is not bothered by cases where people make ILSs about legal systems that cannot be assigned to their community, or any existent community (such as ILSs concerning the ancient Roman legal system or the legal system of the Kingdom of Gondor in Tolkien's *The Lord of the Rings*).[62] Hart does not see this as a problem, for those legal systems exist as abstract objects just as much as the legal systems assigned to actual communities do.

The simple account also explains why Hart understands an ILS as expressing acceptance of the rule of recognition.[63] Officials who describe facts about a rule of recognition are usually manifesting, but not describing, their acceptance of conformity to the rule. This is because, under usual circumstances, they will talk about such facts because they have accepted conformity. But to say that ILSs express acceptance of the rule of recognition is not to make a claim about their semantic character. ILSs are normative not because they express acceptance of the rule of recognition (they can be appropriately made in the absence of such expression) but because they describe facts about formally normative abstract objects.

Furthermore, the simple account makes it clear why Hart does not care about officials' reasons for accepting the rule of recognition – whether they are moral, prudential or no real reasons at all (that is, nothing but mindless conformity).[64] The reasons for acceptance do not make a difference to the content of one's ILS, which is always about the same abstract objects. And it is also understandable why Hart blithely described Raz's idea of a DLS as a 'valuable supplementation' to his views.[65] He was right to be unbothered by DLSs. Facts about the very same abstract objects are described in DLSs as in ILSs.

23.3.5 Pragmatic Expressivism

Recently, Stephen Finlay and David Plunkett have offered an account of ILSs, and of Hart's views on ILSs, that is very similar to the simple account presented here. Their primary focus is the role of acceptance of the rule of recognition. In contrast to Toh, they do not understand the semantic

[62] See Hart 1983: 167–8; Hart 1994: 104. [63] See Hart 1994: 102, 108.
[64] See Hart 1994: 203. [65] Hart 1982: 153–61; Toh 2007: 413.

character of ILSs as tied to the expression of this acceptance. Such expression is part of ILSs' pragmatics, rather than their semantics. But their semantic content is not that moral reasons for action exist, as Raz claims. Rather, it is that a rule satisfies the criteria of the rule of recognition of a legal system.[66]

Because they treat ILSs as having propositional content, Finlay and Plunkett avoid the Frege-Geach problem. Furthermore, their approach easily accommodates ILSs made by those with no commitment to conformity to the rule of recognition,[67] for ILSs have propositional content that can be appropriately asserted in the absence of any pragmatic expression.

But because their focus is on the expressive element of ILSs, they do not take a stand on whether the semantic thesis is true of them. Do ILSs describe social facts alone, social facts and facts about abstract objects, or facts about abstract objects alone? To be sure, they say that the semantic content of an ILS is that a rule satisfies the criteria of the relevant rule of recognition. And this certainly suggests that ILSs are the description of facts about the rule, understood as an abstract object. They are not the description of social facts. If so, Finlay and Plunkett, like Hart, should accept that ILSs can be about past or fictional legal systems (a possibility they do not discuss).

But there is some evidence that they understand ILSs as describing social facts (either partly or solely).[68] If ILSs are understood as solely descriptions of social facts, then their approach would be inadequate. What is described by ILSs has formal normativity. And statements about social facts do not describe anything formally normative. Social facts lack the capacity, on their own, to guide conduct.[69]

66 Finlay and Plunkett 2018: 55. Their account of the semantic content of ILSs as concerning only the relationship between rules and the rule of recognition is the result of their provisional adoption of a narrower understanding of ILSs than Hart's (Finlay and Plunkett 2018: 59). The set of facts about abstract objects described in ILSs as Hart understands them is broader.

67 They do not discuss the problem of DLSs in their article, however.

68 For example, they characterise their view as one in which ILSs are 'descriptive of social (or relational) facts' (Finlay and Plunkett 2018: 72). Relational facts are presumably facts about abstract objects. Social facts are not. They also argue that social facts 'are alone the ultimate grounds' of rules. On the other hand, they note that facts about relations to rules 'might arguably not themselves be "social facts" in a narrow sense' (Finlay and Plunkett 2018: 55). This seems to concede that they are facts about abstract objects.

69 Stephen Finlay has communicated to me privately that, for his part, relational facts are indeed facts about abstract objects, rather than being social.

Consider the fact that English officials take themselves to be obligated to enforce norms announced by the Queen-in-Parliament. From this social fact alone, one cannot discern a recommended course of action. It recommends action only in conjunction with a norm. Here is one possibility: do-not-enforce-what-English-officials-take-themselves-to-be-obligated-to-enforce. That norm, plus the social fact, recommend *not* enforcing norms announced by the Queen-in-Parliament.

It is easy to misunderstand the problem as concerning robust normativity. And it is true that the mere fact that people accept a norm does not give one a robust reason to follow the norm. But the problem is more fundamental. The social fact fails to suggest a course of action at all, even an evil one.

In addition, if it is their view that ILSs solely describe social facts, they cannot account for entailment concerning ILSs. The fact that officials accept a rule does not mean that they accept what necessarily follows from the rule. To explain entailment, ILSs must be about rules, understood as abstract objects, rather than social facts about rules' acceptance.

23.4 Conclusion

Our second question was this: Even though the semantic thesis does not follow from the social thesis, to what extent do ILSs actually conform to the semantic thesis? Are they solely descriptions of social facts? Raz was right to argue that the semantic thesis is descriptively false. And he was right to say that the problem is tied to the normative character of ILSs. But he was wrong to argue that ILSs describe the existence of robust reasons for action. It is, of course, possible that they do so. But, for assignment positivists, there is a simpler explanation, which is that they describe facts about abstract objects. In this area, Hart's account was superior to the positivists who followed him.

References

Blackburn, S. 1984. *Spreading the Word: Groundings in the Philosophy of Language.* Oxford University Press.

Boghossian, P. A. 1989. 'The Rule-Following Considerations'. *Mind* 98: 507–49.

Duarte d'Almeida, L. 2011. 'Legal Statements and Normative Language'. *Law and Philosophy* 30: 167–99.

Duarte d'Almeida, L. 2016. 'The Grounds of Law'. In W. Waluchow and S. Sciaraffa (eds.). *The Legacy of Ronald Dworkin.* Oxford University Press: 165–202.

Enoch, D. and Toh, K. 2013. 'Legal as a Thick Concept'. In W. Waluchow and S. Sciaraffa (eds.). *Philosophical Foundations of the Nature of Law.* Oxford University Press: 257–78.

Finlay, S. and Plunkett, D. 2018. 'Quasi-expressivism about Statements of Law: A Hartian Theory'. In J. Gardner, L. Green and B. Leiter (eds.). *Oxford Studies in Philosophy of Law* vol. 3. Oxford University Press: 49–86.

Geach, P. T. 1972. *Logic Matters.* Blackwell.

Gibbard, A. 1990. *Wise Choices, Apt Feelings.* Oxford University Press.

Green, M. S. 2005. 'Legal Realism as Theory of Law'. *William and Mary Law Review* 46: 1915–2000.

Green, M. S. 2011. 'Leiter on the Legal Realists'. *Law and Philosophy* 30: 381–418.

Green, M. S. 2013. 'On Hart's Category Mistake'. *Legal Theory* 19: 347–69.

Hart, H. L. A. 1982. *Essays on Bentham: Studies in Jurisprudence and Political Theory.* Oxford University Press.

Hart, H. L. A. 1983. *Essays in Jurisprudence and Philosophy.* Oxford University Press.

Hart, H. L. A. 1994. *The Concept of Law.* 2nd ed. Oxford University Press.

Kramer, M. H. 2018. *H.L.A. Hart.* Polity Press.

McPherson, T. 2011. Against Quietist Normative Realism. *Philosophical Studies* 154: 223–40.

Mullins, R. 2018a. 'Detachment and Deontic Language in Law'. *Law and Philosophy* 37: 351–84.

Mullins, R. 2018b. 'Legal Positivism and Deontic Detachment'. *Ratio Juris* 31: 4–8.

Raz, J. 1979. *The Authority of Law.* Oxford University Press.

Raz, J. 1980. *The Concept of a Legal System.* 2nd ed. Oxford University Press.

Raz, J. 1984. 'Hart on Moral Rights and Legal Duties'. *Oxford Journal of Legal Studies* 4: 123–31.

Raz, J. 1994. *Ethics in the Public Domain.* Oxford University Press.

Raz, J. 1998. 'Purity of the Pure Theory'. In S. L. Paulson and B. L. Paulson (eds.). *Normativity and Norms: Critical Perspectives on Kelsenian Themes.* Oxford University Press: 237–52.

Raz, J. 1999. *Practical Reasons and Norms.* 2nd ed. Oxford University Press.

Raz, J. 2004. 'Incorporation by Law'. *Legal Theory* 10: 1–17.

Schiffer, S. 1993. 'Actual-Language Relations'. *Philosophical Perspectives* 7: 231–58.

Sciaraffa, S. 2011. 'The Ineliminability of Hartian Social Rules'. *Oxford Journal of Legal Studies* 31: 603–23.

Shapiro, S. J. 2009. 'What Is the Rule of Recognition (and Does It Exist)?'. In M. D. Adler and K. E. Himma (eds.). *The Rule of Recognition and the U.S. Constitution.* Oxford University Press: 227–46.

Shapiro, S. J. 2011. *Legality*. Harvard University Press.

Silk, A. 2019. 'Normativity in Language and Law'. In D. Plunkett, S. Shapiro and K. Toh (eds.). *Dimensions of Normativity: New Essays on Metaethics and Jurisprudence*. Oxford University Press: 287–314.

Stalnaker, R. C. 1999. *Context and Content*. Oxford University Press.

Toh, K. 2005. 'Hart's Expressivism and His Benthamite Project'. *Legal Theory* 11: 75–123.

Toh, K. 2007. 'Raz on Detachment, Acceptance, and Describability'. *Oxford Journal of Legal Studies* 27: 403–27.

Waluchow, W. J. 1994. *Inclusive Legal Positivism*. Oxford University Press.

Part V

Normativity and Values

24 Legal Positivism and Meta-Ethics

Kevin Toh *

24.1 Three Questions

Larry is a junior lawyer working at a law firm. A senior partner of the firm comes into Larry's office one day, and asks him to write a memorandum answering the following question: Does a newspaper's publication of a photograph of a famous actress and her children at a public shopping mall amount to an illegal misuse of private information? This is a straightforward legal question of the sort that lawyers and judges are trained to answer, even if many would not know the answer to this particular question immediately without doing some research. We can also call it a '*first-order* legal question'.

Now, consider a different kind of question involving law. Anthea is a junior anthropologist who is a member of a team of anthropologists studying a community of people who have never been studied by outsiders before. The lead anthropologist comes into Anthea's tent one day, and assigns her the task of figuring out whether the people the team is studying have laws. Clearly, this question is very different from the kind that Larry is dealing with. It is not a question of the sort that lawyers and judges are trained to answer. It is not a *legal* question but an anthropological question.

In order to answer that anthropological question, Anthea first needs to answer a third kind of question: What are laws? We might say that she needs a theory about *the nature of law*. Presumably, the people her team is studying have all kinds of rules or norms that they follow. Most likely, they will have rules or norms of morality, prudence, religion, epistemic justification, etiquette, fashion, diction, various games, and so on. Anthea will

* I thank the members of the audience at the University of Stockholm where an early draft of this chapter was presented. Torben Spaak's very helpful written comments saved me from some mistakes.

need to think about how laws are similar to and different from these other kinds of rules or norms. In other words, in order to answer her anthropological question, Anthea will have to rely on a philosophical or *second-order* theory about the nature of law. We can expect Anthea to travel to a nearby village soon to dash off an email to her grad school friend Philippa seeking help.

24.2 The Double-Duty Presumption

To which question is legal positivism an answer? We can safely set aside the middle question in the above sequence, the anthropological question. Some influential contemporary formulations appear to say that legal positivism is an answer to both of the other two kinds of questions – that is, first-order legal questions and the second-order question about the nature of law. According to Joseph Raz, for example, '[i]t is common ground to all legal positivists that the law has social sources, i.e. that the content and existence of the law can be determined by reference to social facts and without relying on moral considerations'.[1]

In trying to figure out what the *content* of the law is on such and such issue, we are trying to figure out what the law is on that issue. In other words, content questions are first-order legal questions. We could be asking first-order legal questions also when we ask about the *existence* of laws. For example, we could ask whether there *exists* a law prohibiting publication of a photograph of an actress and her children at a public shopping mall. Presumably, however, Raz means different things by 'content' and 'existence', and that prompts reading his talk of existence of the law as implicating the second-order question about the nature of law. The idea is that the existence-conditions for laws would differ from those for other kinds of norms or rules, including those of morality. It appears then that Raz is conceiving legal positivism as an answer to both first-order legal questions and the second-order question about the nature of law. Legal positivism, in his view, is supposed to say that both kinds of questions should be answered by invoking only 'social facts', which is Raz's term for the various facts about what people do and think, and not any moral considerations.

[1] Raz 1979: 53.

I recently argued against the presumption, apparently shared by many contemporary legal philosophers, that a same set of facts or considerations should be invoked to answer both kinds of questions.[2] Let me call the presumption 'the double-duty presumption'.[3] Nowhere is the presumption plainer to see than in many legal philosophers' characterisations of the pre-eminent legal positivist theory in contemporary legal philosophy – namely, H. L. A. Hart's. Hart sums up his theory of the nature of law in chapter 6 of *The Concept of Law* as follows:

> There are therefore two minimum conditions necessary and sufficient for the existence of a legal system. On the one hand, those rules of behaviour which are valid according to the system's ultimate criteria of validity must be generally obeyed, and, on the other hand, its rules of recognition specifying the criteria of legal validity and its rules of change and adjudication must be effectively accepted as common public standards of official behaviour by its officials.[4]

At least since *Law's Empire* (1986), Ronald Dworkin has argued that Hart offers an analysis of the word 'law', and that this analysis specifies the grounds of first-order legal statements, or 'propositions of law'. In response to Hart's accusation that he is confusing the meaning of 'law' with the meaning of legal statements,[5] Dworkin says in a posthumously published paper:

> But in his book [Hart] seemed to say the opposite. He said that the presence of a rule of recognition accepted by officials, and obedience by the general public to other rules made valid by that rule of recognition, are "necessary and sufficient for the existence of a legal system" and that "[t]he assertion that a legal system exists is therefore a Janus-faced statement looking" toward the satisfaction of these two necessary and sufficient conditions. That is the language of semantics, and it does seem to declare that in every true legal system lawyers use the same criteria or truth conditions for identifying true propositions of law in that system.[6]

The second sentence of this passage summarises, and partially quotes, the same passage from *The Concept of Law* that I quoted earlier. And in the last sentence, we catch the double-duty presumption in action. Dworkin here moves straightaway from Hart's conception of the facts that amount to the existence of a legal system – that is, his second-order

[2] See Toh 2019. See also Toh 2013 and 2018, which were spinoffs of earlier drafts of Toh 2019.
[3] In Toh 2019, I spoke of 'the fallacy of double duty'. [4] Hart 1961/1994: 116.
[5] See Hart 1961/1994: 247. [6] Dworkin 1994/2017: 2106 (citations omitted).

theory – to an account of the grounds of first-order legal statements to which Hart is allegedly committed.

Dworkin is not alone in relying on the double-duty presumption in characterising Hart's legal theory. Here are two other legal philosophers' characterisations:

> [I]f Hart is correct, and social practices explain how legal systems are possible, then legal reasoning must always be traceable to a social rule of recognition. Arguments about who has authority to do what, what rights individuals have, which legal texts are authoritative, and the proper way to interpret them must ultimately be resolved by reference to the sociological facts of official practice.[7]

> [T]he Rule of Recognition, on Hart's view, is a social rule, meaning its content – that is, the criteria of legal validity – is fixed by a complex empirical fact, namely, the *actual practice* of officials (and the attitude they evince towards the practice). So it looks like the only dispute about the criteria of legal validity that is possible, on Hart's view, is an empirical or "heads count" dispute: namely, a dispute about what judges are doing, and how many of them are doing it, since it is *the actual practice of officials and their attitudes towards that practice* that fixes the criteria of legal validity according to the positivist.[8]

And it is not just in characterising Hart's legal theory that we see the double-duty presumption at work. Contemporary legal positivists have been carving out their respective positions by disagreeing with Hart about the kinds of social facts that amount to the existence of a legal system.[9] Despite their differences with Hart, and with each other, these philosophers have not deviated from the presumption that the same set of social facts that they delineate as amounting to the existence of a legal system in a community must also serve as the facts in virtue of which first-order legal statements are true or correct. In this respect, Raz's characterisation of legal positivism is entirely representative.

The double-duty presumption, however, is unwarranted. To be sure, the ideal of wide reflective equilibrium means that the results of our first-order legal theorising and those of our second-order theorising about the nature

[7] Shapiro 2011: 102. [8] Leiter 2009: 1222.

[9] For example, some (Postema 1982) have argued that the relevant facts amount to coordination conventions; some (Marmor 1998/2001, 2009) that they amount to what they call 'constitutive conventions'; some (Shapiro 2002, 2011) that they amount to shared plans or cooperative activities; and some of these same philosophers and many others have followed Raz 1985 in arguing that the relevant facts must enable treatments of laws as authoritative directives.

of law should mesh together. There is also a possibility that our best attempts at the two kinds of theorising will end up identifying the same set of facts or considerations as those in virtue of which both our first-order legal statements and our second-order statement about the existence of a legal system are true or correct. But that is merely a possible outcome, and its actualisation would be surprising. What is unwarranted is to begin with the presumption that there must be a single set of facts or considerations that answers both kinds of theorising. We should not handicap either kind of theorising with such a presumption. Nor should we saddle legal positivism with it. As I read him, Hart himself was not guilty of the double-duty presumption, and it is all the more unfortunate that he has generally been taken to prompt or license his many followers' reliance on it.[10] As indicated in the passage quoted earlier, Hart characterised the existence of a legal system in a community of people as consisting of certain social facts alone. And while he did not make any first-order legal statements in *The Concept of Law* and related works, he consistently characterised such statements, or what he called 'internal legal statements', as normative statements, which implies that the facts or considerations in virtue of which they are true or correct must include some normative considerations.[11] It follows that Raz's characterisation of legal positivism with which we began this section ill fits Hart's commitments.

24.3 Meta-Ethics

Meta-ethics helps us to get past the double-duty presumption in our legal theorising. The contemporary meta-ethical scene is not regulated by anything like the double-duty presumption. While recognising that any results in second-order theorising about the nature of morality or ethics may have important implications for first-order ethical thinking or theorising, meta-ethicists have varied widely in their views as to how strong or determinative such implications are.[12] Some have argued that the constraint is quite strong and determinative;[13] others that their meta-ethical theories have at most only some tendencies towards particular first-order

[10] There are some textual stumbling blocks to my reading, which I address in Toh 2014/15.

[11] As I argued at length explicitly in Toh 2008 and implicitly in Toh 2005.

[12] Here, I repeat some points made in Toh 2013. [13] See, e.g., Foot 1958–9; Hare 1981.

ethical views;[14] and there is a plethora of positions in between. The diversity of the meta-ethical terrain on this issue should make us suspicious of the simplicity of the jurisprudential terrain where the double-duty presumption sticks out like an unavoidable landmark.

We could broach many meta-ethical issues by raising a question that is analogous to the anthropological question we raised in Section 24.1. Instead of asking whether some people have laws, we could ask whether they have a morality or mores. And as the legal anthropological question prompts us to theorise about what kinds of facts in a community would amount to their having laws, the moral anthropological question prompts us to theorise about what kinds of facts in a community would amount to their having a morality or mores. The latter kind of theorising is clearly distinct from first-order moral or ethical theorising. As Peter Railton recently pointed out:

> [T]here is a broad conception of "morality" in which Kantians, Utilitarians, and virtue theorists take themselves to be offering accounts of a common subject matter, and so they concede that there is a perfectly legitimate sense of "morality" in which views they do not endorse on normative grounds are nonetheless moralities. For there to be such a common subject matter all sides must agree that there are certain features that distinguish moralities from other schemes of individual or social regulation – moralities, for example, involve standards or evaluations of personal and interpersonal conduct that are taken to be *objective*, *impartial*, *general*, *non-hypothetical*, etc. One of these features is *normativity* – the moral standards and evaluations *purport* to give reasons for thought and action with significant normative weight. A metaethicist might be engaged in trying to understand morality as a distinctive kind of normative scheme, without taking a stand on whether any candidate [first-order] moral theories live up to their normative purport.[15]

Now, imagine that we come across a community of people who evaluate personal and interpersonal conduct by a set of standards that they treat as objective, impartial, general, non-hypothetical, and normative. We could very well treat such people as having a morality. What is important is that we would not thereby be tempted to think of the same standards as the considerations in virtue of which their first-order moral or ethical judgements are true or correct.

[14] See e.g. Mackie 1977; Blackburn 1985: esp. s. 4.

[15] Railton 2019: 2–3.

There is then little temptation to think that the set of facts that amount to the existence of a morality in a community *must* be the same set of facts in virtue of which first-order moral statements are true or correct. It is a curious fact that legal philosophers have felt a great pull to think that the set of facts that amount to the existence of a legal system in a community *must* be the same set of facts in virtue of which first-order legal statements are true or correct.

24.4 Whither Legal Positivism?

Once we distinguish the two kinds of theorising, we can no longer be satisfied with any conception of legal positivism like Raz's. We should ask whether legal positivism is to be conceived as a first-order legal thesis, or as a second-order thesis about the nature of law.

There is much to be said for leaving first-order legal theorising to lawyers and legal scholars who study substantive law. American law students are familiar with the so-called hornbooks, which summarise and systematise substantive areas of the law of a jurisdiction. Instead of hornbooks covering only particular areas of the law, we can imagine one that covers all of the law of a jurisdiction. Such an *Überhornbook*, if accurate, would enumerate the most fundamental facts and considerations in virtue of which the rest of the law of the jurisdiction obtains. And those facts and considerations would be the ultimate legal grounds in that jurisdiction. Legal positivism, conceived as a first-order thesis, would be about those ultimate legal grounds.

Now, it may be tempting to think of such a first-order legal positivism as saying that the ultimate legal grounds of any jurisdiction consist only of social facts, and not of any moral or normative considerations. But that would be too hasty. First, while some meta-ethical theories portray norms and values as irreducibly normative items,[16] and some see them as dispensable in the best explanations of our normative thought and talk,[17] other theories portray them as consisting of the properties of the sort

[16] See e.g. Moore 1903/1993; Enoch 2011.

[17] Two kinds of theory fit this description. First, there are those that think of our normative thought and talk as in good standing despite not positing any norms and values. See, e.g., Stevenson 1937; Gibbard 1990. Second, there are those that deem them systematically defective because they falsely posit norms and values. See, e.g., Mackie 1977: ch. 1; Joyce 2001.

posited by natural and social sciences – that is, those that would make up social facts.[18] Second, social facts are behavioural and psychological facts, and an influential tradition in the philosophy of mind tells us that such facts are partly constituted by normative considerations.[19] Third, there are norms other than those of morality, and it is unobvious that all such norms – some with the normative purport of the sort that Railton talks about, and some without – can be reduced to social facts without any normative remainders. For these reasons, we cannot rely on any facile distinction between social facts on the one hand and moral or normative considerations on the other in conceiving legal positivism and anti-positivism. Instead, I believe, we should revert back to what is arguably *the* fundamental question for thinking about legal positivism and anti-positivism – namely, whether there are any moral or all-things-considered normative tests for first-order legal judgements. Following this thought, we should conceive first-order legal positivism as saying that ultimate legal grounds, consisting of some combination of social facts and normative considerations, do not impose such a moral or all-things-considered normative test. And first-order legal anti-positivism can be conceived as saying that ultimate legal grounds do impose such a test.

Of course, such conceptions are in need of many further specifications. I am inclined to think that we should proceed with such specifications to flesh out legal positivism and anti-positivism as first-order legal theses about ultimate legal grounds, and hence as analogues of normative ethical theories such as consequentialist and deontological theories, which are first-order *moral* theories aimed at specifying the ultimate moral grounds. But it may be complained that there would be something important missing in any resulting conceptions. For it may be thought that legal positivism and anti-positivism are not just views about what are, even *invariably* or *regularly*, the facts or considerations that make up ultimate legal grounds; instead, they are about what such ultimate legal grounds *must* or *can* include. Legal anti-positivism is usually understood as saying that ultimate legal grounds *must* include moral or normative considerations; and legal positivism, as saying that ultimate legal grounds *need not* or *must not* include such moral or normative considerations.[20] As I have just argued, such formulations need

[18] See, e.g., Boyd 1988; Lewis 1989. [19] As will be elaborated in Section 24.5.

[20] The two listed options are what go by the labels 'inclusive legal positivism' and 'exclusive legal positivism', respectively. See, e.g., Raz 1985; Waluchow 1994.

to be revised to move away from any facile distinction between moral and normative considerations on the one hand and social facts on the other. But the *modal constraints* contained in such formulations may need to be retained in whatever revised formulations we devise.

If we were to set out to capture such modal constraints, we should wonder what kind of modality is involved. We can follow Kit Fine (2002) in thinking that there are three basic kinds of necessity: metaphysical, natural or nomic, and normative.[21] In other words, the sources of the relevant modal constraints could be the nature of things, laws of nature, or norms and values. Let me bracket the second option until Sections 24.5 and 24.7 below. The third option is a non-starter for us. One possibility in fleshing out this third option would be to conceive the relevant norms as the laws of individual jurisdictions, which would be poor candidates for sources of modal constraints on the composition of ultimate legal grounds in general. The rest of the possibilities would involve moral or other non-legal norms or values as the ultimate or underived sources of the modal constraints, and what result from such lines of thinking would be theories of what laws should be, rather than theories of what laws are. If there were modal constraints of the sort that we are talking about, then they would most likely be metaphysical constraints, likely generated by the nature of law or of legal systems, which it is the business of second-order theorising to study. Given that we have abandoned the double-duty presumption, we should not begin expecting or requiring a theory of the nature of law or of legal systems to identify the facts and considerations in virtue of which first-order legal statements are true or correct. But we should still consider the possibility that the results of our second-order theorising would motivate or make plausible some modal constraints on the composition of ultimate legal grounds about which legal positivists and anti-positivists argue. In investigating this possibility, we can take additional cues from meta-ethics.

As I indicated, what we are after in our second-order theorising about the nature of law is a set of facts that would amount to a community's having laws or a legal system. As Hart conceives this task,[22] a plausible

[21] To be more precise, these are three kinds of *non-epistemic* necessity. Some may worry that conceptual necessity is missing from the list. I am here following Fine 2002: 237 in thinking that conceptual necessity can be explained in terms of metaphysical necessity.

[22] See Hart 1961/1994: ch. 1.

hypothesis should enable us to see how the facts that amount to a community's being governed by laws or a legal system are similar to and different from those that amount to a community's having a morality or a set of mores. Many meta-ethical theories could be conceived as offering hypotheses about this latter set of facts. This means that meta-ethical investigations can help in carrying out our second-order task of theorising about the nature of law. Instead of relying on intuitive or folk understanding of the nature of morality, we can discipline our thinking by relying on developed and vetted theories in contemporary meta-ethics.

There is another, more consequential way in which meta-ethics can aid our second-order investigation about the nature of law. Wilfrid Sellars long ago opined that the aim of philosophy 'is to understand how things in the broadest possible sense of the term hang together in the broadest possible sense of the term'.[23] And a good case can be made for thinking that something like this conception of philosophy should regulate second-order theorising in both meta-ethics and legal philosophy. Both kinds of theories should make use of resources made available by other areas of philosophy and related empirical disciplines, and should also be susceptible to constraints imposed by results in those areas and disciplines. Arguably, this is the kind of theorising that philosophers working in meta-ethics have done a far better job of carrying out in recent years than have legal philosophers. Following contemporary meta-ethicists' lead, in devising hypotheses about what kinds of facts or considerations amount to a community's having laws or a legal system, legal philosophers must take care to posit only those facts that are allowed by plausible metaphysics. The facts they posit surely would include some social facts, which in turn must be commensurate with our going philosophy of mind, psychology, and sociology. Legal philosophers also must themselves employ, and attribute to their subjects – that is, the members of the studied community – a plausible epistemology. A crucial part of such epistemology will concern how it is that the subjects manage their semantic access to legal facts, should there be any. All such theoretical considerations – that is, metaphysical, epistemological, psychological, sociological, and so on – are likely to motivate certain positions, for example, as to whether legal thought and language are factual or non-factual,

[23] Sellars 1962: 1.

whether there are legal facts, and if there are how they fit into our going conception of the world.

After much work along this line has been done, or at least along the way, we can consider the question of whether the facts we identify as amounting to a community's possession of laws or a legal system are of the sort that would impose any modal constraints on the composition of ultimate legal grounds.

24.5 Acceptances of Rules

Obviously, this chapter will not offer a full-scale investigation into the nature of law along the lines I have just sketched. In the meta-ethical literature, we see different philosophers pressing and pulling at different theoretical nodes in their attempts to contribute to theorising about the nature of morality. The hope is that the result of these various attempts will be progress in thinking about the nature of morality. We should expect something similar in legal philosophy.

With that end in view, in the balance of this chapter, I want to focus on the psychology of those whose thoughts and behaviour are regulated by laws.[24] Once again, the organising question for us is what kinds of facts amount to a community of people having laws or a legal system. As he sums up in the passage I quoted near the beginning of Section 24.2, Hart asserted that a legal system exists or prevails in a community if the officials of the community accept the secondary rules governing change, adjudication, and identification of the rules that make up the legal system, and the rest of the community at least follow the rules that are valid under the secondary rule for identification. At the centre of this account is the notion of *acceptance of rules*. In chapter 1 of his book, along with the questions of how law is different from coercion, and how law is different from morality, Hart raised the more fundamental question of what rules are, and what it takes for a person or group of people to be committed to rules.[25] And in chapters 2–4, the most fundamental point that Hart makes in his arguments

[24] My subsequent treatment of the psychological attitude of acceptance of rules should be read in conjunction with the discussion in Toh 2011 and forthcoming. Limitations of space prevented any attempt to provide a synthesis in this chapter.

[25] See Hart 1961/1994: 8.

against command theories of law is that people's thoughts and behaviour motivated by their acceptances of rules are fundamentally different from those motivated by fear, habit, or both. As Hart construes the notion, the members of a community accept a rule only if: (i) they think that they ought to, or have reasons to, do as the rule says; (ii) they criticise those who flout the rule; and (iii) they deem such criticisms to be justified.[26] This is Hart's answer to the fundamental question he raised in chapter 1, and it is the basic building block of his account of legal systems.

Notice that Hart's conception of acceptance of rules *by itself* imposes no real constraint on the contents of the rules that can be accepted by a group of people. In chapter 9 of his book, Hart argues that certain natural facts, or 'truisms', about human beings and the environments they live in – for example that human beings are roughly equal in their powers and are of limited altruism and rationality, and that the environments they inhabit are of scarce resources – make it the case that any legal system that has some staying power is likely to have rules with certain contents, which could be deemed to make up what he calls 'the minimum content of Natural Law'. These rules restrict violence; protect possessions; and enable transfer, exchange, and sale of possessions and services. Hart observes:

> [I]t is a truth of some importance that for the adequate description not only of law but of many other social institutions, a place must be reserved, besides definitions and ordinary statements of fact, for a third category of statements: those the truth of which is contingent on human beings and the world they live in retaining the salient characteristics which they have.[27]

In other words, although Hart's conceptions of acceptance of rules and of legal systems do not themselves impose any constraints on the contents of the rules accepted, certain natural facts about human beings and their environments do. Here, we see the relevance of the second kind of necessity, the natural or nomic kind, which we bracketed earlier in Section 24.4. Hart is here discussing metaphysically contingent but naturally necessary facts. These are implicated by the laws of nature – that is, those of psychology, biology, sociology, and so on – that necessitate legal systems having the kinds of rules that Hart enumerates.

A key point is that these modal constraints, which Hart is happy to acknowledge, are not sufficient to require legal systems to be moral or

[26] See Hart 1961/1994: 55–7. [27] Hart 1961/1994: 199–200.

just on the whole. The rules that make up the minimum content of Natural Law are geared towards survival and perhaps some degree of well-being but not really towards morality or justice.

24.6 Acceptances and *Verstehen*

Could it be that Hart is wrong about the modal implications of acceptances of rules which he thinks are at the centre of the workings of legal systems? Could it be that these psychological attitudes invariably impose much greater modal constraints on the contents of the rules accepted, ones that would far exceed those imposed by the natural facts about human beings and their environments we discussed above? And could these acceptance-derived modal constraints be powerful enough to imply some moral or all-things-considered normative tests on first-order legal judgements?

A very significant portion of legal philosophy of the last sixty years could be read as various attempts to thicken Hart's conception of acceptance of rules.[28] One line of thinking that has proved seductive for some legal philosophers has been prompted by the idea that human goings-on, unlike natural goings-on, are not susceptible to purely descriptive characterisations.[29] According to Donald Davidson's particular development of this line of thinking, for example, beliefs, intentions, and other psychological attitudes are constructs within an integrated theory that is structured by the principles of rationality, consistency, and coherence. Another way of putting the point is to say that psychological facts are infused with normative facts. It follows that in attributing psychological attitudes, interpreters need to deploy their own rationality and their own commitments to coherence and consistency to make sense of their interpretees by rendering them rational, coherent, and consistent to some degrees. In sum, psychological interpretation requires reliance on a *principle of charity*.

This line of thinking can be applied to attributions of acceptances of rules, as well as to attributions of other psychological attitudes. According

[28] In Toh 2007 and 2010, I argued against Raz's view that the psychological attitudes that Hart calls 'acceptances' must amount to moral endorsements.

[29] See, e.g., the papers collected in Davidson 1980 and 1984 and Dennett 1981 and 1989 for some influential developments of this idea in contemporary Anglophone philosophy.

to Davidson, the set of beliefs, intentions, and other psychological attitudes we attribute to a person must meet certain standards of rationality, coherence, and truth even to qualify as a system of psychological attitudes. If acceptances of rules are in the mix, then they too must be to some degree rational, coherent, and correct relative to the physical and behavioural evidence that interpreters deem available to interpretees, and to other attitudes they have. The question is whether this Davidsonian line of thinking can motivate a much more substantial modal constraint on the contents of the rules that are accepted than what Hart countenances. The idea is that some rules that could otherwise be accepted by subjects could be filtered out by charity because their behaviour would not make sense if they were thought to accept rules with certain kinds of contents.

Much here depends on how substantial the relevant principle of charity is for psychological attributions in general, or for attributions of acceptances of rules in particular. In the writings of some anti-positivist legal philosophers, the relevant principle is thought so substantial as to require interpreters to deploy their own first-order moral commitments in characterising the social facts that amount to legal practices, or some portions thereof that are deemed privileged instances of such facts.[30] Any such moves will require some arguments to show that we end up with less than full understanding, that we miss something crucial in the human goings-on that we are studying, unless we deploy a very substantial version of the principle of charity, which is to say unless interpreters deploy their own substantive first-order commitments. Favourite examples that some philosophers employ to motivate such a line of thinking outside legal philosophy are those dealing with colours and humour. The point is that we cannot understand some psychological attitudes as, for example, perceptions of red things or as finding something funny unless we deploy our own understanding of the phenomenology of seeing red or our own sense of humour.[31]

It would follow that in order to argue for more substantial modal constraints on the contents of the rules accepted than Hart countenances, one

[30] See, e.g., Finnis 1980: ch. 1; Dworkin 1986: ch. 2. Even some legal positivists appear to find such a line of thinking compelling. See, e.g., Raz 1983: 192–3; Raz 1985: 219–21; Postema 1986: s. 9.4.

[31] See, e.g., McDowell 1985; Wiggins 1987; Stroud 2000.

must point to something that we as interpreters would clearly miss unless our own first-order moral or all-things-considered normative commitments are deployed to filter the facts that amount to a community's having laws or a legal system. Is there something analogous to the phenomenology of seeing red or the humour of a joke? Instead of focusing on something that participants discern but that observers arguably miss, Finnis invokes another kind of explanandum:

> If there is a point of view in which legal obligation is treated as at least presumptively a moral obligation . . ., a viewpoint in which the establishment and maintenance of legal as distinct from discretionary or statistically customary order is regarded as a moral ideal if not a compelling demand of justice, then such a viewpoint will constitute the central case of the legal viewpoint. For only in such a viewpoint is it a matter of overriding importance that law as distinct from other forms of social order should come into being, and thus become an object of the theorist's description.[32]

But this argument fails. As Mark Murphy rightly points out, the task of explaining what it is for a legal system to exist and that of explaining how a legal system comes into being are two different tasks.[33] And without some other concrete explanandum to point to, we lack the incentive to thicken our conception of charity to the extent of requiring interpreters to deploy their own first-order moral or all-things-considered normative commitments. More generally, as many commentators on the Davidsonian programme have argued,[34] what interpreters should be deemed to be deploying is not their full-blown rationality, including their own first-order moral or all-things-considered normative commitments, but instead what could be called 'minimal rationality', which would allow interpretations that portray interpretees as making many mistakes and holding normative commitments at great variance with our own. Such a thin conception of the principle of charity is much likelier to be of help than thicker ones for our projects of understanding and predicting each other's behaviour.[35]

[32] Finnis 1980: 14–15.

[33] Murphy 2004: 24. We also have little reason to go along with Finnis's empirical conjecture about what induces creation of legal systems.

[34] See, e.g., Cherniak 1986; Railton 1997.

[35] As Railton has recently observed, the thought that psychological interpretations need to deploy a very substantial charity makes little evolutionary sense: 'Empathy was not designed simply to help us understand those who agree with us, but also to fathom our rivals and enemies, whose thoughts, feelings, and behaviors we must anticipate as best we can if we are

24.7 Regulatives and Evaluatives

In Railton's (2019) new contribution to legal philosophy, we have a new attempt, in many ways similar to Finnis's, to thicken our conception of acceptance of rules in a way that could warrant an inference of a substantial modal constraint on first-order legal judgements. I believe that Railton's arguments are superior to Finnis's, though I am not sure that they ultimately furnish the more substantial modal constraints of the sort we are considering.

Railton's approach in thinking about the nature of law is quite similar to Hart's. Railton too is after an account of what kinds of facts amount to a community's having laws or a legal system.[36] And at the centre of his account is a conception of a type of psychological motivation, which he calls 'normative guidance', that is contrasted with motivation by physical or biological constraints, habits or reflexes, and externally imposed force. Railton's normative guidance could be deemed a philosophically improved and empirically better-informed version of Hart's acceptance of rules.[37] There are many aspects of the notion that warrant close scrutiny and discussion, but let me single out for our consideration one particular aspect that clearly distinguishes Railton's normative guidance from Hart's acceptance of rules.

According to Railton, normative guidance *partly* consists of people's self-imposition of certain norms or constraints, which in turn involves their mental representations of the norms or constraints that mediate their thought and behaviour, and their dispositions to react to violations as not disconfirming the norms or constraints, nor as merely surprising, but as errors that call for corrections. So far, we have something strikingly similar to Hart's acceptance of rules. But the key word in the above formulation is 'partly'. For normative guidance, as Railton conceives it, does not consist solely of something like an acceptance of a rule. Instead, it consists of three

to meet the challenges they pose or to spot the occasional instance when they are willing to work together with us, even when *we* were not planning this' (Railton 2016: 242).

[36] In fact, instead of inquiring about the conditions for the existence of one kind of thing that is a legal system, as Hart does, Railton pursues the conditions for the existences of two different kinds of legal 'schemes'. But I shall ignore this difference for the moment to facilitate my exposition in this section.

[37] It is a component of a normative psychology that Railton has been building in recent years. Key outputs of this project include Railton 2006, 2012 and the chapters in Seligman, Railton, Baumeister and Sripada 2016.

distinct kinds of psychological attitudes working in tandem. In addition to such 'regulative' attitudes, as Railton calls them, there are 'evaluative' and 'deliberative' ones. The need for evaluative attitudes is highlighted by the facts that there is an indefinite number of rules or norms we might follow, and that rules or norms do not enforce themselves. Railton opines that people cannot participate in normative schemes in any sustained ways unless they are able to self-impose certain rules or norms; and they are not able to self-impose such rules or norms unless they can think, however tacitly or inchoately, that some value, purpose, or goals will be achieved or furthered by following them. People find some normative schemes *worthwhile*, and some not. And to judge something worthwhile is to make an evaluative judgement. Railton also observes that people must be able to decide or choose, however implicitly, to be guided by some rules or norms, and not others, in many cases in light of their evaluative judgements, and such decisions or choices are deliberative attitudes that are different from both regulative and evaluative ones. In sum, Railton argues that there has to be a division of labour among the three kinds of normative attitudes for genuine normative guidance to take place.

Let me set aside deliberative attitudes for the rest of my discussion, as I want to focus on the relation between regulative and evaluative attitudes. In bringing up power-conferring rules in law, Hart underscored the fact that laws not only may restrict our freedom but sometimes enhance it by enabling us to do things that we would not otherwise be able to do. Railton similarly observes that by imposing on ourselves certain rules or norms, and relying on each other to do the same, we restrict our freedom, and by so doing create 'opportunity paths' that would not otherwise exist. A particularly helpful illustrative example concerns linguistic rules – namely, the rules of phonetics, syntax, and semantics, as well as the more informal conversational norms (including, presumably, what Griceans call 'conversational maxims'). We as speakers regiment the sounds we make in many ways, thus restricting our freedoms, so that we as hearers can extract identifiable, repeatable, and re-combinable units that can be mapped to meanings. The payoffs here are communication and coordination. Clearly, there is an indefinite number of schemes of linguistic rules that we could have adopted, but we have chosen to adopt only certain kinds, for only some are effective means of securing and facilitating communication and coordination. We are not willing to self-impose others, as they would not create like opportunity paths. Similar stories could be told, Railton surmises, about other kinds of rules or norms, including laws, that regulate our lives in sustained ways.

The lesson is supposed to be that regulative attitudes, what Hart calls 'acceptances of rules', cannot operate in isolation but must work in tandem with evaluative attitudes in providing normative guidance. Railton at one point in a footnote compares his own view with Hart's as follows: 'The notion of *normative guidance* at work in the present chapter is an attempt to give an account of when and why, the kind of acceptance of rules that Hart discusses could have a genuinely normative character for the individuals concerned, and thus help us to understand [legal systems] as normative social schemes.'[38] Railton observes that when a group of people are motivated by their regulative attitudes without the accompanying evaluative attitudes, what is likely to result is *alienation* – that is, perception of the demands of the rules or norms as alien forces or mere legalism – or blind conformity that in the end may not be all that different from motivation by instinct or habit.[39] The real source of the tie between regulative and evaluative attitudes in this picture is human psychology. We are just not built to be regulated in a sustained way by a set of rules or norms unless we see, however implicitly, some values, a point, or a purpose that we endorse, again however implicitly, that gets furthered by such regulation. What we have here is perhaps another 'truism' about human beings that should be added to the stock that Hart listed in his argument for 'the minimum content of Natural Law'. Again, such truisms about human nature and the nature of the environments we inhabit are metaphysically contingent but naturally necessary facts that could be seen as imposing certain modal constraints on the composition of the ultimate grounds of the law of any human legal systems.

24.8 Implications?

Even if we follow Railton in thinking that regulative and evaluative attitudes naturally must go together, it is not obvious what the implications are for how we should think about the nature of law. We have been investigating this last issue by way of an organising question: what kinds of facts amount to a community's having laws or a legal system?

[38] Railton 2019: 15 n. 10. [39] See Railton 2019: 9.

Following Railton, we can say that at the centre of these facts is not just the psychological phenomenon of people accepting rules or norms, as Hart argued, but instead such acceptances accompanied by evaluative attitudes in support of those regulative attitudes. But one question that is not clearly answered by such an answer to the organising question is what kind of modal constraints on the truth- or correctness-conditions of first-order legal judgements this new answer to the organising question implies. Any constraints that this new answer imposes may not be any more substantial than the ones that are imposed by the truisms of human nature and the environments that humans inhabit that together imply what Hart calls 'the minimum content of Natural Law'. In other words, it may be the case that even quite unjust or immoral systems of rules may qualify as legal systems even after Railton's point about the naturally necessary packaging of regulative and evaluative attitudes is brought onboard.

Railton himself discusses two distinct kinds of normative social schemes that qualify as legal systems – *rule by law* and *rule of law*. Rule by law consists of a set of rules and procedures that are general, clear, transparent, stable, and prospective, which a group of people can be motivated to impose on themselves for the sake of protection, stability, economic efficiency, and the like. What rule *by* law does not have, and rule *of* law does, has to do with equality and autonomy. In rule by law, the members of a community need not be all equal before the law; some may be above, and some may even be below the law. In rule of law, by contrast, every member has the same status before the law. And a part of that equality is having an equal claim to participate in the law-making and law-enforcing activities, exercise of which would amount to self-government. The important point for our purposes is that both rule by law and rule of law are legal schemes that are built on Railton's conception of normative guidance, according to which regulative and evaluative (and also deliberative) attitudes necessarily go together by virtue of human psychology. But as many legal systems that comply with the minimum content of Natural Law may fall very much short of moral justification or justice, many legal schemes marked by rule by law would likely fall short of moral justification or justice. And there is no indication in Railton's arguments to suggest that rule by law is a defective or degenerate version of rule of law.

We can come back to the issue of the modal implications of Railton's conception of normative guidance by raising another question. Granting that regulative and evaluative attitudes need to go together in genuine normative guidance, we may wonder about the legal status of the values, points, or purposes that the relevant evaluative attitudes track. In other words, would they be parts of the law of the relevant jurisdiction, or would they be extralegal considerations that make people's self-impositions of laws possible? Here, a line of thinking that connects Railton's conception of normative guidance with some of Dworkin's early arguments suggests itself. In 'The Model of Rules I' (1967), Dworkin argued that judges deciding some cases appeal not just to rules but also to *principles*, and that they treat principles as parts of the law that they are bound to apply. Not much hangs on the particular terminology of 'rules' and 'principles' that Dworkin used.[40] To use the terminology that Hart (1987) used to characterise Dworkin's position, we can speak of the 'explicit law' of a jurisdiction, which consists of the standards that law-making and law-applying officials have explicitly recognised, and the 'implicit law', which consists of the standards that justify the explicit law. Dworkin does not think of the implicit law as consisting only of values, goals, or purposes; and Railton does not think of the values, goals, and purposes that evaluative attitudes track as necessarily moral ones. But overlooking this imperfect match, we could think of the values, goals, and purposes tracked by evaluative judgements as figuring in the workings of legal systems the way that Dworkin thinks of the standards that make up the implicit law. It makes sense to think: (i) that judges, in deciding some hard cases, will try to look behind the rules or norms of the explicit law, and to appeal to the values, goals, or purposes that consistent adherence to the rules or norms would realise; and (ii) that, as they do, they will think of those values, goals, or purposes as non-optional legal constraints on their decision-making. I am not sure that these values, goals, or purposes will always figure as parts of the law, but it appears a reasonable bet that at least sometimes they will.

Now, does this last conclusion enhance the prospect of Railton's conception of normative guidance generating some modal constraints on the composition of ultimate legal grounds? That does not appear to be the case. The fact is that the values, goals, or purposes that could potentially make up the implicit law of a jurisdiction may be ones that are morally

[40] 'Rules' in Hart's terminology cover all of what Dworkin calls 'standards', including principles. See Raz 1972: s. 2. Perry 1987 provides a nice unifying explanation of what Dworkin calls 'rules' and 'principles' in terms of reasons.

questionable or even objectionable. It should be remembered that it was considerations of charity that motivated Railton's view that regulative and evaluative attitudes need to go together. And as we noted at the end of Section 24.6, what we should be deploying in interpreting is not our full-blown rationality, including our own first-order moral or all-things-considered normative commitments, but instead what could be called 'minimal rationality', which allows room for interpretees to make many mistakes and to hold normative commitments at great variance with our own. It follows that we should allow the values, goals, or purposes that figure in people's evaluative attitudes to diverge from our own commitments, even quite markedly. In the Dworkinian picture we have been exploring, this means that the implicit law of a community may justify its explicit law only in the sense of providing support for it, and not in the sense of providing compelling moral or all-things-considered normative justification. And that outcome is consistent with the objection to Dworkin's conception of the nature of law that Hart (1966/1982 and 1987) and others have raised again and again, without eliciting from Dworkin a satisfying reply. That is that there could be, and in fact have been, legal systems the explicit laws of which are so unjust or immoral as to exclude the possibility of moral justification. We can deploy a thin principle of charity, one that calls for reliance on minimal rationality, to say that we can make sense of the participants in such immoral legal systems.

24.9 Conclusion

In the foregoing pages, I have sought some revision in the way that the debates about the nature of law and about legal positivism, one of the contending theoretical options, have been understood in the last sixty or so years. I believe that we would do well to abandon what I called 'the double-duty presumption'. I also explored in tentative ways some approaches for thinking that the correct conception of the nature of law will impose certain substantial modal constraints on the contents of the rules or norms that make up ultimate legal grounds. I did not succeed in identifying an approach that provides a plausible avenue for such a conclusion. But I hope that the way in which I have reconfigured the dialectic may prove helpful for future investigations in this theoretical neighbourhood.

References

Blackburn, S. 1985. 'Errors and the Phenomenology of Value'. Reprinted in S. Blackburn. *Essays in Quasi-Realism.* 1993. Oxford University Press: 149–65.

Boyd, R. 1988. 'How to be a Moral Realist'. In G. Sayre-McCord (ed.). *Essays on Moral Realism.* Cornell University Press: 181–228.

Cherniak, C. 1986. *Minimal Rationality.* MIT Press.

Davidson, D. 1980. *Essays on Actions and Events.* Clarendon Press.

Davidson, D. 1984. *Inquiries into Truth and Interpretation.* Clarendon Press.

Dennett, D. 1981. *Brainstorms: Philosophical Essays on Mind and Psychology.* MIT Press.

Dennett, D. 1989. *The Intentional Stance.* MIT Press.

Dworkin, R. 1967. 'The Model of Rules I'. In R. Dworkin. *Taking Rights Seriously.* 1977. Harvard University Press: 14–45.

Dworkin, R. 1986. *Law's Empire.* Harvard University Press.

Dworkin, R. 1994/2017. 'Hart's Posthumous Reply'. *Harvard Law Review* 130: 2096–2130.

Enoch, D. 2011. *Taking Morality Seriously.* Oxford University Press.

Fine, K. 2002. 'The Varieties of Necessity'. Reprinted in K. Fine. *Modality and Tense.* 2005. Clarendon Press: 235–60.

Finnis, J. 1980. *Natural Law and Natural Rights.* Clarendon Press.

Foot, P. 1958–9. 'Moral Beliefs'. Reprinted in P. Foot. *Virtues and Vices.* 1978. University of California Press: 110–31.

Gibbard, A. 1990. *Wise Choices, Apt Feelings.* Harvard University Press.

Hare, R. M. 1981. *Moral Thinking.* Clarendon Press.

Hart, H. L. A. 1961/1994. *The Concept of Law.* 2nd ed. Clarendon Press.

Hart, H. L. A. 1966. 'Legal Duty and Obligation'. Revised and reprinted in H. L. A. Hart. *Essays on Bentham.* 1982. Clarendon Press: 127–61.

Hart, H. L. A. 1987. 'Comment'. In R. Gavison (ed.). *Issues in Contemporary Legal Philosophy: The Influence of H.L.A. Hart.* Clarendon Press: 35–42.

Joyce, R. 2001. *The Myth of Morality.* Cambridge University Press.

Leiter, B. 2009. 'Explaining Theoretical Disagreements'. *University of Chicago Law Review* 76: 1215–50.

Lewis, D. 1989. 'Dispositional Theories of Value'. Reprinted in D. Lewis. *Papers in Ethics and Social Philosophy.* 1999. Cambridge University Press: 68–94.

Mackie, J. L. 1977. *Ethics: Inventing Right and Wrong.* Penguin Books.

Marmor, A. 1998. 'Constitutive Conventions'. Revised and reprinted in A. Marmor. *Positive Law and Objective Values.* 2001. Oxford University Press: 1–24.

Marmor, A. 2009. *Social Conventions: From Language to Law.* Princeton University Press.

McDowell, J. 1985. 'Values and Secondary Qualities'. Reprinted in J. McDowell. *Mind, Value, and Reality.* 1998. Harvard University Press: 131–50.

Moore, G. E. 1903/1993. *Principia Ethica.* 2nd ed. Cambridge University Press.

Murphy, M. 2004. 'Natural Law Theory'. In M. Golding and W. Edmundson (eds.). *The Blackwell Guide to the Philosophy of Law and Legal Theory.* Blackwell: 15–28.

Perry, S. 1987. 'Judicial Obligation, Precedent and the Common Law'. *Oxford Journal of Legal Studies* 7: 215–57.

Postema, G. 1982. 'Coordination and Convention at the Foundations of Law'. *Journal of Legal Studies* 11: 165–203.

Postema, G. 1986. *Bentham and the Common Law Tradition.* Clarendon Press.

Railton, P. 1997. 'Explanations Involving Rationality'. In J. Earman and J. Norton (eds.). *The Cosmos of Science: Essays of Exploration.* University of Pittsburgh Press: 530–70.

Railton, P. 2006. 'Normative Guidance'. In R. Shafer-Landau (ed.). *Oxford Studies in Metaethics* vol. 1. Oxford University Press: 1–33.

Railton, P. 2012. 'That Obscure Object, Desire'. *Proceedings and Addresses of the American Philosophical Association* 86: 22–46.

Railton, P. 2016. 'Morality and Prospection'. In M. Seligman, P. Railton, R. Baumeister, and C. Sripada. *Homo Prospectus.* Oxford University Press: 225–80.

Railton, P. 2019. '"We'll see you in court!": The Rule of Law as an Explanatory and Normative Kind'. In D. Plunkett, S. Shapiro, and K. Toh (eds.). *Dimensions of Normativity: New Essays on Metaethics and Jurisprudence.* Oxford University Press: 1–22.

Raz, J 1972. 'Legal Principles and the Limits of Law'. *Yale Law Journal* 81: 823–54.

Raz, J. 1979. 'Legal Reasons, Sources, and Gaps'. Reprinted in J. Raz. *The Authority of Law.* 1979. Clarendon Press: 53–77.

Raz, J. 1983. 'The Problem About the Nature of Law'. Reprinted in J. Raz, *Ethics in the Public Domain.* 1994. Clarendon Press: 179–93.

Raz, J. 1985. 'Authority, Law, and Morality'. Reprinted in J. Raz, *Ethics in the Public Domain.* 1994. Clarendon Press: 194–221.

Seligman, M., Railton, P., Baumeister, R. and Sripada, C. 2016. *Homo Prospectus.* Oxford University Press.

Sellars, W. 1962. 'Philosophy and the Scientific Image of Man'. Reprinted in W. Sellars. *Science, Perception and Reality.* 1963. Routledge & Kegan Paul: 1–40.

Shapiro, S. 2002. 'Law, Plans, and Practical Reason'. *Legal Theory* 8: 387–441.

Shapiro, S. 2011. *Legality.* Harvard University Press.

Stevenson, C. L. 1937. 'The Emotive Meaning of Ethical Terms'. *Mind* 46: 14–31.

Stroud, B. 2000. *The Quest for Reality: Subjectivism and the Metaphysics of Colour.* Oxford University Press.

Toh, K. 2005. 'Hart's Expressivism and His Benthamite Project'. *Legal Theory* 11: 75–123.

Toh, K. 2007. 'Raz on Detachment, Acceptance, and Describability'. *Oxford Journal of Legal Studies* 27: 403–27.

Toh, K. 2008. 'An Argument Against the Social Fact Thesis (and Some Additional Preliminary Steps Towards a New Conception of Legal Positivism)'. *Law and Philosophy* 27: 445–504.

Toh, K. 2010. 'Some Moving Parts of Jurisprudence'. *Texas Law Review* 88: 1283–1321.

Toh, K. 2011. 'Legal Judgments as Plural Acceptances of Norms'. In L. Green and B. Leiter (eds.). *Oxford Studies in Philosophy of Law* 1: 107–37.

Toh, K. 2013. 'Jurisprudential Theories and First-Order Legal Judgments'. *Philosophy Compass* 8: 457–71.

Toh, K. 2014/15. 'Four Neglected Prescriptions of Hartian Legal Philosophy'. *Law and Philosophy* 33: 689–724. Republished with corrections as 'Erratum to: Four Neglected Prescriptions of Hartian Legal Philosophy'. *Law and Philosophy* 34: 333–68.

Toh, K. 2018. 'Law, Morality, Art, the Works'. In L. Burazin, K. Himma, and C. Roversi (eds.). *Law as an Artifact*. Oxford University Press: 61–85.

Toh, K. 2019. 'Legal Philosophy à la carte'. In D. Plunkett, S. Shapiro, and K. Toh (eds.). *Dimensions of Normativity: New Essays on Metaethics and Jurisprudence*. Oxford University Press: 221–47.

Toh, K. (forthcoming). 'Law and Collectivity'. In T. Marques and C. Valentini (eds.). Collective Action, Philosophy and the Law. Routledge.

Waluchow, W. J. 1994. *Inclusive Legal Positivism*. Clarendon Press.

Wiggins, D. 1987. 'Sensible Subjectivism?'. In D. Wiggins. *Needs, Values, Truth*. Basil Blackwell: 185–214.

The Normativity of Law 25

Brian H. Bix

25.1 Introduction

Legal positivists (as well as other legal theorists) regularly claim that a primary task (if not *the* primary task) of legal theory is to 'explain the normativity of law'.[1] However, what is meant by 'the normativity of law', or even by 'explain', is often left uncertain or is defined in imprecise ways.[2] Additionally, however the terms are defined, there remains some doubt, on one hand, whether it is the proper task of legal theory (at least legal theory within the legal positivist tradition) to answer such questions.[3] An approach that generally asserts that there is no necessary moral content to individual legal norms or to whole legal systems seems, at the least, to be in tension with an analysis that assumes that law is normative in a robust sense. And even among those who accept that legal theory has the objective of explaining the normativity of law, some commentators doubt that any of the best-known legal positivist theories succeed at doing so (and some critics of legal positivism base their opposition to that school of thought precisely on what they view as its inevitable failure at this task).

In what follows, Section 25.2 analyses in general terms the task of explaining normativity, examining some conventional understandings of what normativity is, how law raises problems of normativity, the division between 'is' and 'ought', and the possibility of legal normativity as *sui generis*. Section 25.3 then offers an overview of some of the best-known explanations within the legal positivist tradition for law's normativity, looking at Hans Kelsen's Basic Norm, H. L. A. Hart and social conventions,

1 See, e.g., Coleman and Leiter 2010: 228–9; Postema 1982: 165; Raz 1990: 154–5, 166–70.

2 As Delacroix (2004: 504) points out, even the basic question of whether law's normativity is a simple given or not depends on whether one equates 'normativity' with law's *making* a claim on us or its *having* a (justified) claim.

3 See Marmor 2018: 95: 'Legal philosophers tend to talk about the normativity of law as if it is a central aspect of law that we need to explain . . . I think that this is a mistake.'

Scott Shapiro and plans, and David Enoch on triggering, as well as some other lines of responses. The end of Section 25.3 also briefly considers, by way of contrast, some of the more important non-positivist approaches to legal normativity. Section 25.4 concludes.

25.2 Assumptions and Tasks

25.2.1 The Problem

What does it mean to say that law is 'normative'?[4] Joseph Raz states that '[t]he problem of the normativity of law is the problem of explaining the use of normative language in describing the law or legal situations'.[5] In law, as in morality, we speak of 'rights', 'duties', 'authorisations' and 'powers'; though these terms can occasionally be found in other contexts, they are distinctive of normative discourse. However, in some ways, Raz's statement merely pushes the analysis back one step. Normative discourses (not merely law and morality but also everything from religion to etiquette to games to rationality) use normative terminology, but what does it mean to say that *law's* normativity *needs explanation*?

One common direction of further analysis would be to state that law is normative if it gives citizens reasons for action,[6] or citizens at least believe that it does.[7] Sylvie Delacroix suggests that, in the literature, the

[4] In some accounts, the 'normativity' of law is elaborated in terms of morality (for example, law as making moral claims, law as a subset of morality, or moral tests for legal validity). For example, Leslie Green (2003b: s. 4.2) argues that 'law purports to obligate us' in the sense that it makes 'moral demands on [us]'. However, the nature of morality is itself contested: the normativity of morality requires explanation, as does, indeed, the nature of normativity itself; Rosati 2016: 308–9; Copp 2015. These are large topics that take us far beyond the scope of the present chapter. For a recent view that tries to tie up in intriguing ways normativity, the nature of morality and the nature of law, see Copp 2019.

[5] Raz 1990: 170; see also Raz 2009: 3.

[6] This is meant in a justificatory sense (why an action should be done) rather than a causal, explanatory or motivational sense (why a particular person did a certain action); Marmor 2018: 96; see generally Dancy 2000.

[7] See Raz 1990: 170. See Marmor 2001: 25 (arguing that while the 'question about the normativity of law is a difficult one to define', at the least 'the idea that law is a normative social practice suggests that the law purports to give rise to reasons for action'). In general, discussions of the normativity of law focus, in one way or another, on *reasons for action*; in principle, law could be 'normative' in the sense of giving reasons *for belief*, but that would be an unusual position (though Hurd 1990 approaches a claim of this sort).

'normativity of law' has pointed both to guidance of behaviour and to the imposition of obligations, but that these paths are each problematic in their own way.[8] Yet another approach is offered by Triantafyllos Gkouvas who divides normativity into

(a) a metaphysical claim about which facts favour or mandate a particular response;
(b) an evaluative claim about which facts serve as standards for appraising an agent's exercise of their rational capacities; and
(c) an explanatory claim about which facts make normatively intelligible an event of intentional action.[9]

Thus, under this analysis, there are three different kinds of reason-giving fact. Rationality and morality both seem to be normative in all three ways.[10] What of law? The complication in answering that question comes from law's hybrid nature.[11] Law has an aspect that is descriptive, empirical, historical: the actions of (legal) officials in creating, promulgating and applying certain standards of behaviour. It also has an aspect that is prescriptive or constructive: law as a kind of practical reasoning that (legal) officials and citizens use in determining what to do and avoid doing. Due to this hybrid nature, law contrasts with other normative systems. Morality and rationality (at least as conventionally understood) create standards that are generally independent of individual and collective action, decision or judgement.[12] Law, by contrast, is largely a product of human choice, human fiat.[13] Additionally, law purports to create obligations whose bindingness does not depend on their merit or, indeed, their content: what some commentators have called 'content-independence'.[14]

[8] See Delacroix 2019: 17–18.

[9] Gkouvas 2018: 19. Robert Alexy's similar, but slightly different analysis speaks of the semantic, justificatory and motivational dimensions of normativity; Alexy 2011: 220.

[10] Though the connection between rationality and normativity is neither straightforward nor uncontroversial; see, e.g., Broome 2013.

[11] See, e.g., Finnis 2014: 95–6; Alexy 2013: 99–100.

[12] Obviously, that statement would require much qualification and elaboration, but it attempts to capture in rough form the conventional understanding.

[13] Of course, how large a role there is for non-posited sources in determining what is the current law is itself the center of much of the jurisprudential literature, not least the debates between legal positivism and its critics.

[14] See, e.g., L. Green 2003a: s. 1; Sciaraffa 2009. Law thus purports to have the sort of 'because I said so' quality often associated with parenting. See Edmundson 2013.

In describing norms, it is important to distinguish 'external' and 'internal' reasons – distinguishing reasons that *ought* to apply to our decisions as against the reasons that *actually motivated* our decisions.[15] Most scholars writing about the normativity of law seem to be referring to law as an external reason, a reason we *ought* to take into account, whether we do so or not. However, it is worth remembering that a central concept of one of the most important writers on law, H. L. A. Hart's 'internal point of view',[16] focuses on internal reasons (what actually motivates us), not external reasons.[17]

One function that the law has is guiding behaviour,[18] usually by imposing civil or criminal sanctions on behaviour that the government wants citizens to avoid doing. Law also encourages certain behaviour, through rewards or by offering processes for private enforcement. Of course, within most legal systems, the law has other roles as well, for example in creating legal powers (to make legally enforceable contracts, wills, trusts and so forth). The connection between those roles and action-guidance is indirect at best, but, in any event, the guidance of behaviour through sanctions remains a large part, if not the largest part, of what legal systems do. Those sanctions (and occasional monetary benefits, like tax deductions, offered to encourage certain behaviour) create prudential reasons for action. However, when theorists speak of the normativity of law, they generally mean something more than (or at least something different from) the prudential reasons that legal coercion and state benefits create for citizens.

Gerald Postema argues that both the role of law in practical reasoning and the social-fact nature of law seem essential elements for which any theory of law must be able to account, yet, as he points out, the two seem to be in sharp tension.[19] The social-fact nature of law invites the external perspective of the observer, or the social science scholar, and is more compatible with the legal positivist separation of the *existence* of law and legal norms and their evaluation. The aspect of law that touches on its giving citizens reasons for action (to whatever extent legal rules in fact do so) seems to fit less well with legal positivist approaches.

[15] See, e.g., Williams 1981: 101–13; Gizbert-Studnicki 2019: 31–5. Also refer back to n. 6.

[16] Hart 2012: 84–91. [17] See Gizbert-Studnicki 2019: 34–5.

[18] Commentators differ on what law's 'primary' or 'essential' or 'most important' function is, but no one doubts that guiding behaviour is among law's significant functions.

[19] See Postema 1982: 165–6.

The normativity of law is often equated with, or at least connected to, citizens' moral obligation to obey the law. For a long time, it was thought that whether citizens had this moral obligation to obey was simply the flip side of the question of whether the government was legitimate. It was assumed that if the government was legitimate, then citizens had a moral obligation to obey the laws.[20] In his well-known debate with H. L. A. Hart, Lon Fuller criticised legal positivism for not being able to explain the moral duty to obey the law.[21] More recent writers have separated the questions, holding that it is possible for a government to be legitimate, for its rules generally to be just, and for it to have the moral right to enforce its rules coercively, and yet citizens might still have no general moral obligation to obey the law. While this chapter will make no effort to prove that the moral status of government and the moral duties of citizens are independent in this way, the possibility of their separation will be assumed. That is, the chapter will focus on the citizens' obligation to obey, and will not assume that this can be shown simply by showing the actions of government to be legitimate.

25.2.2 The Nature of the Claim

What are the criteria of success for a theory of (the nature of) law, especially one that purports to 'explain the normativity of law'? Some theorists claim that we should seek a theory that explains how law gives us reasons for action, but this prompts the reasonable objection that we should not beg the question of whether law in fact *does* give us reasons for action. Joseph Raz asserts that law necessarily *claims* to be a practical authority (to give us reasons for action),[22] even if he elsewhere argues that it rarely achieves that status.[23] I will take as standard an analysis of 'the normativity of law' in terms of practical reasoning (reasons for action): does the law – do legal rules – give us reasons for action that we did not have without the law or those rules?[24] I see no reason to begin

[20] See, e.g., Smith 1973: 950; Raz 1986: 70–105. The question, more precisely, is whether there is a general, presumptive (defeasible) moral obligation to do what the law prescribes, simply because the law prescribes it.

[21] See Fuller 1958: 656. [22] See Raz 1994: 199. [23] See Raz 1994: 325–38.

[24] 'All normative phenomena are normative in as much as, and because, they provide reasons or are partly constituted by reasons' (Raz 2010: 5). For Raz (1990: 171, 191–4), those who

with the assumption that law *does* give us such reasons, or even with the assumption that it *claims* to do so.[25] (As already mentioned, there is a different, if related, sense of explaining the normativity of law: explaining the use of normative language by legal officials and citizens, or at least focusing on the fact of such use.)[26]

So, law can give prudential reasons for action by imposing sanctions on some behaviour and offering rewards (directly or indirectly) for other behaviour. Law can give reasons for action as a salient coordinator of behaviour (for example, stating on which side of the road cars should be driven). Law can give reasons to choose behaviours by creating bright lines to clarify or make more precise vague moral standards. Even without the law, we have an obligation to support a just state and to take care of the poor, but the state can determine what our precise tax burden should be. We have an obligation to drive safely, but the state can set precise speed limits. And so on.[27] Do these, individually or collectively, constitute the 'normativity of law' that theorists have tried, and continue to try, to explain? This will be explored in Section 25.3.

'act from the legal point of view' treat legal norms as 'exclusionary reasons'. An 'exclusionary reason is a second-order reason to refrain from acting for some reason' (Raz 1990: 39) and, for Raz (1990: 170–99), exclusionary reasons are distinctive to law and other forms of authoritative guidance. For present purposes, we need not enter the debates regarding exclusionary reasons and whether legal rules create such reasons. See, e.g., Raz 1990: 178–99.

25 And if the focus of this chapter is primarily on versions of legal positivism, that simply reflects the overall project of the present volume. There is no assumption here that legal positivism is the only or best approach to understanding law in general, or legal normativity in particular. There will be some discussion of non-positivist approaches in Section 25.3.6.

26 See Spaak 2018. He argues that this is the primary sense in which Hans Kelsen explained the normativity of law (Spaak 2018: 330–1). This sense also seems to be important for H. L. A. Hart. Kelsen's approach will be discussed in Section 25.3.2 and Hart in Section 25.3.3.

27 Additionally, legal rules can express opinions and offer information. They express opinion by reflecting the view of society regarding certain behaviours (as when adultery is made illegal: even though there is no real interest in the law prohibiting adultery being enforced, the legal rule serves to condemn that behaviour). Legal rules can also offer information (indirectly), by indicating what is thought to be safe and unsafe. The expression of opinion may not give us reasons for action (depending on one's view of the wisdom of the legislators), but the provision of information might.

25.2.3 Is / Ought: David Hume

A view often attributed first to David Hume (though questions remain as to the best understanding of Hume's text)[28] is that there is a sharp division between 'is' statements and 'ought' statements: in particular, that no conclusion about what one ought to do can be derived from propositions regarding what is the case. Thus, the argument goes, from the fact that 'the use of chemical XYZ will lead to the death of thousands of infants, while creating no significant benefits', one *cannot* derive the conclusion that 'one should not use chemical XYZ'. However, one *can* justify that same conclusion if one adds in the normative premise that 'one should not do anything that harms large numbers of infants, especially if that action creates no benefits'. Under this analysis, the normative premise needed for a normative conclusion need not be anything controversial, but, nonetheless, a normative premise is needed. And the point for the study of law is that the actions of legal officials are matters of description,[29] and so there is a mystery as to how such actions can ground normative conclusions about what citizens should and should not do. And 'do as legal officials prescribe' is not nearly as obvious or uncontroversial a normative premise as 'do not harm infants for no good reason'. A broad understanding of Hume's division of is and ought plays an especially significant role in Hans Kelsen's work (see Section 25.3.2), but the challenge of bridging 'is' and 'ought' can be seen as motivating aspects of many contemporary theories of law.

[28] Hume (1978: s. 3.1.1, at 469–70) wrote:

> In every system of morality, which I have hitherto met with, I have always remark'd, that the author proceeds for some time in the ordinary way of reasoning, and establishes the being of a God, or makes observations concerning human affairs; when of a sudden I am surpriz'd to find, that instead of the usual copulations of propositions, *is*, and *is not*, I meet with no proposition that is not connected with an *ought*, or an *ought not*. This change is imperceptible; but is, however, of the last consequence. For as this *ought*, or *ought not*, expresses some new relation or affirmation, 'tis necessary that it shou'd be observ'd and explain'd; and at the same time that a reason should be given, for what seems altogether inconceivable, how this new relation can be a deduction from others, which are entirely different from it . . . [I] am persuaded, that a small attention [to this point] wou'd subvert all the vulgar systems of morality, and let us see, that the distinction of vice and virtue is not founded merely on the relations of objects, nor is perceiv'd by reason.

On the controversy regarding the understanding of the text, see, e.g., Cohon 2018: s. 5.

[29] Bracketing for the moment the fact that what makes an individual a 'legal official' itself requires a normative framework.

While legal positivists sometimes accuse natural law theorists of ignoring the division of 'is' and 'ought',[30] John Finnis has argued that it is in fact the legal positivists who are the more egregious violators of the division between the two.[31] Finnis's argument tracks the discussion that follows: that many legal positivists have offered arguments that appear to ground law's giving us reasons for action ('ought' statements) on some combination of conventions, shared attitudes and other empirical grounds ('is' statements).

There are theorists who do not accept a strong version of the Humean division of 'is' and 'ought', including scholars who have worked to develop moral theories with a factual ('naturalist') grounding. In particular, there is a growing number of theorists who believe that Hume's ideas should be understood narrowly, as a constraint on logical deduction, rather than as a proof that one cannot bridge factual premises and normative conclusions.[32]

25.2.4 Legal Normativity as *Sui Generis*?

A few commentators have argued that law purports only to create '*legal* reasons', a category of reasons that reduces neither to mere prudential reasons nor to moral reasons.[33] Legal norms create *legal* rights and duties; any moral or prudential claims beyond that are secondary and not essential to law's nature. The view of legal normativity as *sui generis* is unconventional in modern legal philosophy; it is both somewhat difficult to articulate clearly and even more difficult to justify.[34] The basic view can only be outlined here. The idea of legal normativity seen on its own terms, and not

[30] And historically there are some grounds for this accusation, especially within the voluntarist strand of the natural law tradition, where some adherents purported to derive morality (what ought to be done) from various statements of what is the case (what God commanded, what role humanity has in the divine plan, or what human nature is). For one view of which strands of the natural law tradition are vulnerable to an is/ought critique and which parts are not, see Finnis 2011a: 33–48.

[31] See Finnis 2000.

[32] For older critiques of is/ought, see, e.g., the articles in Hudson 1969. For contemporary discussions, see Maguire 2018; Pigden 1991, 2016; Fine 2018. For a naturalist approach to moral philosophy, see, e.g., Copp 1995: 9–49.

[33] See Hart 1982: 262–8; Bix 2018: 34–40; Bix 2019; Finnis 2011b: 248–56; Finnis 2013: 553–6.

[34] For doubts about this approach, see, e.g., Rosati 2019; Raz 2009: 188 ('we cannot conceive of the law as a normatively valid point of view contrasting with morality').

reducible either to prudential considerations (as in the American legal realist equation of law with what officials will do)[35] or to morality, is part of what could be considered a deflationary or pluralistic approach generally to normative discourses.[36] Law creates 'law reasons' the same way that etiquette creates 'etiquette reasons', and chess 'chess reasons' (for those who choose to play that game).

The idea of legal normativity as *sui generis* takes seriously conventional ways of thinking (by both citizens and legal officials): that it is sensible, and indeed common, to distinguish legal from moral judgements (that even within generally just legal systems something can be legally permissible, or even legally required, and still be immoral, and that some deeply immoral actions are not subject to legal sanction, and so forth). Of course, such conventions of usage are far from conclusive on the topic, and one can also find linguistic habits that seem to point in a different direction, as when some people are reluctant to apply the label 'law' or 'legal' to rules or rule systems that are extremely unjust. There are also aspects of legal practice, for example when common law courts make new law, when the line between law and morality may seem quite thin.

25.3 Responses

25.3.1 Consequentialism

Thomas Hobbes, in his *Leviathan*, famously argued that everyone has an obligation to obey the law (at least if the government is effectively maintaining order). His argument was that disobedience leads to anarchy, 'a warre of every man against every man',[37] which is far worse (in Hobbes's view) even than the most unjust government. Thus, we have an obligation to obey the law because the consequences of not obeying would be so terrible.

David Hume offered a critique of the social contract approach to justifying government, in particular in John Locke's formulation of it.[38] For

[35] See, e.g., Holmes 1897: 461. The inadequacy of a purely prudential or purely predictive theory of law is clearly shown by H. L. A. Hart's example of the game of 'scorer's discretion' (Hart 2012: 142–5).

[36] See Scanlon 2014; Tiffany 2007. [37] Hobbes 1929: ch. 13, at 98.

[38] See Hume 1994. Another part of Hume's critique was that, historically, almost all governments were formed by 'usurpation or conquest, or both, without any pretence of fair

Hume, to say that our obligation to obey is grounded on a promise (or, even less persuasively, on 'tacit consent' to an arrangement) was simply to substitute one philosophical mechanism (promise, consent) for another (obligation to obey), where one is as much in need of justification as the other. For Hume, the obligation to obey the law would be justified in the same way as would the obligation to keep promises: it is justified to the extent that it operates for the greater good.[39]

Though Hobbes and Hume seemingly take different positions on social contract justifications of government, they can be seen to be agreeing on one matter: that whether we have an obligation to obey the law or not turns on the consequences of obedience and disobedience.[40] If many now disagree with Hobbes regarding whether there is a consequentialist-based general moral obligation to obey the law, it is because we doubt that the alternative to a general moral obligation to obey is inevitably 'the war of all against all'. The contrary evidence seems to be all around us: in many societies, there is pervasive disobedience to the law on speed limits, and fairly common disobedience to many other laws (for example, regarding tax payments, reporting requirements and so forth), yet with most nations, most of the time, society has not (yet) descended into lawlessness. This can be explained in various ways. As M. B. E. Smith argued, between the fact that legal rules frequently track our own moral views (most of us would not murder, rob or rape, even if the law no longer prohibited those actions) and the fact that we fear legal sanctions, society can maintain a sufficient level of order even if the population does not accept a general moral obligation to obey the law.[41]

Additionally, consequentialist justifications will always be an uneasy fit with a claim of a 'necessary' or 'universal' obligation, as consequentialist arguments are, by their nature, contingent.[42] The actions, rules or principles that are (most) beneficial under one set of circumstances may be less beneficial, or in fact harmful, under different circumstances.

consent' (Hume 1994: 189–90) and that consent has rarely played much of a role (Hume 1994: 189–95).

39 See Hume 1994: 196; see also Murphy 1978.

40 For a modern argument that depends in part on the bad consequences of citizens' not believing that they had a presumptive obligation to obey the law, see Honoré 1987: 115–38.

41 See Smith 1973: 968–9.

42 I am grateful to Torben Spaak for emphasising this point.

25.3.2 Presupposition of a Foundational Axiom: Kelsen

Hans Kelsen famously offered a 'Pure Theory of Law' (*reine Rechtslehre*), a theory of law purified of political, moral or sociological elements. Kelsen's analysis portrayed law as a hierarchical system of norms, with earlier and more general norms authorising later and more specific norms. Kelsen argued that a foundational norm, the 'Basic Norm' (*Grundnorm*) – something like 'act in accordance with the historically first constitution' – is presupposed whenever a legal scientist or other person views the actions of legal officials normatively.[43]

In this theory, Kelsen does not seem so much to be explaining why or in what way law is normative;[44] rather, he is explaining *what follows* from the fact that we treat law as normative.[45] Kelsen emphasises the division between 'is' and 'ought' (as discussed in Section 25.2.3). This naturally turns one's attention to how the actions of legal officials ('is') can give rise to legal norms ('ought'). The legal scientist understands legal officials' expressions of will in a normative way, as authorisations to officials to impose sanctions, but how can this be justified?

Kelsen's approach focused on the way that legal systems display both static and dynamic hierarchies: earlier legal norms authorise the creation of later legal norms, and more general or more basic legal norms are the justification for more specific legal norms. Either way, the analysis leads back to a most basic and historically first norm, the foundational 'ought' statement that can, or must, ground the rest of the system of norms.

Some writers, evaluating Kelsen's theory as a response to the problem of explaining normativity, have been highly critical. For example, Leslie Green wrote: '[I]f we are willing to tolerate the basic norm as a solution[,]

[43] Kelsen 1992: 55–8.

[44] Through most of this chapter, 'normative' and 'giving reasons for action' have been treated as largely interchangeable. However, some theorists have argued that, for Kelsen, 'normative' did not mean 'giving reasons for action'. See, e.g., M. S. Green 2016: 38 n. 13 and sources cited there. There is also significant controversy regarding whether normativity for Kelsen was 'justified normativity' (what others have called 'robust normativity': binding and not contingent, the way most people think about morality but not about games). See generally Paulson 2012.

[45] Kelsen's views changed dramatically over the decades of his writing; e.g. Paulson 2017. The present short discussion does not purport to cover the nuances of every variation of Kelsen's changing ideas; it focuses on the view presented in Kelsen's better-known middle period(s), as exemplified by Kelsen 1967, 1992. For a recent effort to track some of Kelsen's later changes in view in relation to law's normativity, see Spaak 2005: 402–7.

it is not clear why we thought there was a problem in the first place.'[46] That is, positing or presupposing a norm as a way across the is/ought divide seems like a cheat, a *deus ex machina*. However, when an analytical move from a well-known theorist seems this weak, it is good evidence that one has misunderstood the theorist's argument.[47] As discussed, Kelsen's Basic Norm is answering a different question: the neo-Kantian question of what follows from the fact that some view the actions of legal officials in a normative way.[48] Kelsen is working from the fact that legal scientists and many citizens view the actions of legal officials in a normative way, as creating reasons for action. He is not attempting to justify that view.[49]

25.3.3 Social Practices and Conventions: Hart

Gerald Postema argues that H. L. A. Hart's Rule of Recognition[50] could be seen as a coordinating convention among judges, and that this would explain why judges have a moral obligation to follow the Rule.[51] The Rule of Recognition is the standard for legal validity (including any hierarchy among legal sources) derived from the decisions and other actions of legal officials. Like Kelsen's Basic Norm, the Rule of Recognition functions as the foundational norm of the legal system. All other legal norms derive their validity ultimately from the Rule of Recognition; as a foundational norm, the Rule of Recognition can gain its validity only by acceptance by the officials of the system.

A convention (in David Lewis's understanding of conventions) is a rule that is followed in large part because one expects others to follow that same rule; it is arbitrary in the sense that there are alternative rules that also would have served the same purpose comparably well.[52] Postema argues that the Rule of Recognition is a 'coordination convention' because it is or reflects a 'regularity of behavior in recurring situations calling

[46] L. Green 2003b: s. 2. A similarly dismissive comment can be found in Marmor 2011: 146.
[47] With due respect to L. Green and Marmor (see note 46), who are generally among the best writers in contemporary jurisprudence.
[48] See, e.g., Paulson 2012. [49] See Paulson 2012; see also Spaak 2005: 402–5.
[50] See Hart 2012: 94–110.
[51] Hart did not refer to the rule of recognition as a convention in the original text of *The Concept of Law*, but he did use that label in his later, posthumously published Postscript. Hart 2012: 94–110, 256–9; see also Marmor 2009: 160–2.
[52] See generally Lewis 1969, Rescorla 2019; see also Marmor 2009: 1–30.

for coordination'.[53] Coordination conventions occur when it is more important that the parties agree on some behaviour or choice and less important on what it is they have agreed. A well-known example is road travel: it matters little whether all cars drive on the left side of the road (as in Britain) or on the right side (as in the United States); what *is* important is that all drivers make the same choice. Coordination of behaviour is important, expected and mutually relied upon. The relevant parties – in the case of law and the Rule of Recognition, judges – prefer conforming to the agreed solution (following a particular shared set of standards regarding the identification and application of legal rules) to any other path. In Postema's words, through coordination conventions one can 'construct . . . a bridge linking social facts of judicial practice to bona fide normative considerations, indeed, to a species of genuine official obligation'.[54]

Andrei Marmor claimed that it is important to distinguish coordination conventions from what he labelled 'constitutive conventions'.[55] The latter are conventions whose primary purpose is not solving a coordination problem but rather constituting social practices. These conventions 'determine what the practice is, and how one goes about engaging in it'.[56] For example, the rules of chess do not solve a coordination problem among players; they create the rules that constitute what it means to play chess.[57] Marmor argues that the Rule of Recognition is a constitutive convention that primarily constitutes the practice of law for a particular community, and the normativity of establishing and maintaining this practice must be 'determined on moral-political grounds'.[58]

[53] Postema 1982: 201; see also Postema 2011: 483–545; Postema 2012; Coleman 1998: 398 ('I . . . characterize the rule of recognition as a coordination convention. The rule of recognition solves the coordination problem of settling on a particular set of criteria of validity').

[54] Postema 1982: 199.

[55] For an intriguing argument that Hart's Rule of Recognition would be better analyzed through Ruth Millikan's understanding of conventions, rather than David Lewis's (or Andrei Marmor's), see Matczak 2019.

[56] Marmor 2002: 106.

[57] See Marmor 2009: 22–4. In another work, Marmor (2011: 154–7) distinguishes 'surface' and 'deep' conventions, but that distinction is not relevant for present purposes.

[58] Marmor 2009: 169; see also Marmor 2019. While Marmor argues (or perhaps assumes) that the Rule of Recognition cannot be both a coordinating and a constitutive convention, Torben Spaak (2018: 338–42) claims that the rule can in fact fill both roles.

Regardless of which kind of convention the Rule of Recognition is, the question remains whether it succeeds in crossing the is/ought divide, in creating reasons for action out of the actions of legal officials. There is a fairly strong argument that the Rule of Recognition, as a convention, creates reasons *for judges (and other officials)* to obey the rule.[59] There are straightforward reasons for judges to want to be in at least rough agreement on the legal standards they are applying, and this will depend, in turn, on their being in at least rough agreement on the criteria of legal validity and the hierarchy of legal sources. Additionally, it is probably more important that the judges be in agreement on such ultimate standards than that the standards be *this* set of criteria rather than *that* set.[60] However, it is far less clear that there is a convention-based argument for the view that the Rule of Recognition, or rules validated by the Rule of Recognition, create reasons *for citizens.*[61] Certainly, citizens have an interest in the consistent and predictable application of law, but it is less obvious that citizens have a general moral obligation to obey whatever rules have been authorised by the country's Rule of Recognition.

25.3.4 Plans: Shapiro

In his book, *Legality*,[62] Scott Shapiro attempts to explain law and legal normativity in terms adapted from the work of philosopher Michael Bratman.[63] Shapiro presents law as social planning, shared planning and plans about plans. Legal rules and procedures are the plans we collectively make (in part through agents – legal officials – but also through the actions of citizens, using legal powers delegated by the state) to coordinate behaviour and solve complex problems in society. For Shapiro, while many legal rules and procedures can be called plans literally, others might only be seen, metaphorically, as being 'plan-like'.[64]

59 There may be another ground for officials' moral obligation to obey the law, if, as part of their oath of office, they have promised to follow the law, but that is a separate issue.

60 That is, there is a range of comparably good, or at least comparably acceptable, ultimate standards, though there would certainly be potential ultimate standards so unjust (or bad in other ways) that no agreement would be preferable to agreement on those terms.

61 See generally L. Green 1999.

62 Shapiro 2011a; see also Shapiro 2011b.

63 See Bratman 1987; see also Bratman 2011.

64 Shapiro 2011a: 225–30.

Plans show one way that the bridge can be built from is to ought, from fact to norm.[65] When I (we) make a plan, I (we) have a reason to act consistently with that plan, and a reason not to act in ways that undermine the plan. As regards law, Shapiro seems to view that normativity as conditional. People who have made or 'accepted' an individual or shared plan are 'bound to heed the plan', though only 'from the point of view of instrumental rationality', not necessarily 'from the moral point of view'.[66] Plans – including the legal systems that are shared plans – thus can give reasons for action *to those who accept them*, but even then such reasons fall far short of moral reasons. And there remains the question of what reasons we have to accept (all) the plans that constitute our legal system.

25.3.5 Triggering: Enoch

David Enoch argues that when law gives us reasons for action, it does so by 'triggering' moral reasons that already apply to us.[67] To offer an analogy from a non-legal example, the cost of some product can warrant our buying less of it, where the changed price is a non-normative fact, triggering our existing reason to put limits on how much we spend. It is not that the fact of the higher-priced product 'created' the reason in some way that would violate the is/ought division; rather, the fact of the higher price is just part of the premise, along with an 'ought' premise (for example, never spend so much on food that one does not have enough left to pay the rent) that was already there but had not been invoked until the new fact (the higher price) was introduced. Similarly, Enoch argues, legal enactments and other official acts can trigger reasons for action that were always already there (for example, reasons to drive safely – on the side of the road designated by a salient source like the law).

[65] Shapiro also argues that his planning theory supports a legal positivist approach because '[s]hared plans must be determined exclusively by social facts *if they are to fulfill their function*' (Shapiro 2011b: 65 (emphasis in original)); see also Shapiro 2011a: 119, 176–8.

[66] Shapiro 2011a: 142–3. As Rosati (2016: 319–20) points out, this gives Shapiro's approach no advantage over Hart's: one could equally say that those who accept the Rule of Recognition comparably makes themselves subject to norms of instrumental rationality. Also, as Rosati (2016: 320) notes, there are questions as to whether instrumental rationality is sufficient on its own to give us reasons for action, if we cannot also show that our ends are morally worthy; on this last point, see also Korsgaard 2008: 27–68.

[67] See Enoch 2011b; see also Enoch 2011a.

The advantage of Enoch's approach is that it seems largely to dissolve the is/ought problem for law. Under this analysis, the actions of legal officials do not generally (or, perhaps, ever) create new (non-prudential) oughts. Rather, those actions are merely factors to feed into pre-existing (moral) obligations. However, some commentators have questioned Enoch's basic analytical structure, in particular arguing that Enoch's conditions for 'robust reason-giving'[68] (how governments or other entities might create entirely new reasons for action, rather than simply sometimes triggering our existing reasons) are too strong.[69]

25.3.6 A Note on Non-positivists

To help place the views of the legal positivists discussed in context, this section will offer a very brief overview of how some well-known non-positivist theorists have approached the problem of the normativity of law.

John Finnis is a natural law theorist working in the Thomistic tradition.[70] In analysing law, Finnis emphasises the moral reasons for establishing and maintaining a legal system,[71] and follows Aquinas in arguing that just laws created by proper procedures will generally (but not universally) create moral reasons for obedience by citizens.[72] Human-created ('positive') laws can create obligations when they make more determinate our general moral obligations:[73] how much money to pay in taxes to support the government and help the needy, which speed limit would best balance efficiency and safety, and so on.[74]

Ronald Dworkin[75] argued that law is the product of a constructive interpretation of the actions of legal officials, creating a moral constraint on, and a moral justification for, the application of state coercion.

68 Enoch 2011b: 4–14. 69 See, e.g., Edmundson 2013; see also Ehrenberg 2016: 148–79.

70 See, e.g., Finnis 2011a, 2011b. 71 See Finnis 2011b: 23–41.

72 See Finnis 2011a: 231–7; Finnis 2011b: 46–73; Finnis 2013: 553–6; Aquinas 1993: 321–329 (qu. 96, art. 4).

73 This is Aquinas's notion of *determinatio*. Finnis 2011a: 284–289; Aquinas 1993: 287–8 (qu. 95, art. 2).

74 The idea of legal norms giving us reasons for action because they make existing general norms workably specific is not confined to natural law thinkers. See, e.g., Marmor 2018: 100–1.

75 Dworkin's views changed in many ways over the decades that he was writing. This short summary is based on Dworkin's middle-period monograph on legal philosophy, *Law's Empire* (Dworkin 1986) and the interpretive theory elaborated in that work.

Constructive interpretation – interpretation sensitive to the purpose of an enterprise – is central to both legal practice and legal theory. The (constructive) interpretation that lawyers and legal officials undertake to determine what the law is itself involves moral analysis, as it entails the morally best understanding that also adequately fits the past actions of legal officials.[76]

Under Mark Greenberg's 'moral impact' theory, law is a part of morality, consisting of those moral obligations that follow from the actions of legal officials.[77] As with Dworkin, one has already crossed the is/ought division just to ascertain what the law is. And, as with Finnis and Enoch, the focus is on when the actions of legal officials alter our (moral) reasons for action.[78]

According to Robert Alexy's 'nonpositivistic concept of law',[79] law necessarily claims correctness, meaning moral legitimacy and justice. For Alexy, there are moral elements in determining the content of the law and its application (moral principles help to fill gaps, and extremely unjust rules lose their legal status),[80] but it is not clear whether Alexy believes that a general moral obligation to obey the law follows.

25.4 Conclusion

While many commentators claim that legal theory should explain the 'normativity of law', there is surprisingly little discussion, and even less agreement, on what is meant by law's 'normativity'. Legal systems purport to give us reasons for action, but what kind(s) of reason they are attempting to give, and what kind(s) of reason they actually succeed in giving, remain highly controversial matters. At one level, few disagree that law could, and often does, give us *prudential* reasons for action by offering rewards and punishments. Many commentators have asserted that law claims to, and

[76] See, e.g., Dworkin 1986: 87–101. Sometimes Dworkin spoke of morally best interpretation that adequately fit the pre-interpretive data, and sometimes he spoke of the best overall interpretation, taking into account both fit and moral value. The difference is not important for present purposes.

[77] See Greenberg 2011: 84, 88–9, 96–101; see also Greenberg 2014, 2017.

[78] And as with some legal realists, like John Chipman Gray, the actions of legal officials are not themselves law but only 'sources of law'; Gray 1909: 115–20.

[79] Alexy 2018: 255; see generally Alexy 2002.

[80] See Alexy 2007: 39. This is Alexy's adaptation of the Radbruch Formula; for the origins of the Formula, see Radbruch 2006.

perhaps frequently succeeds at, something more, the giving of *moral* reasons. However, for some there is then the response that not all legal rules lead to moral reasons, and that any moral reasons produced are simply the legal rules 'triggering' existing moral reasons. It is difficult, especially from within the legal positivist tradition, to establish that law creates entirely new moral obligations.

References

Alexy, R. 2002. *The Argument from Injustice: A Reply to Legal Positivism*. Trans. B. L. Paulson and S. L. Paulson. Clarendon Press.

Alexy, R. 2007. 'An Answer to Joseph Raz'. In G. Pavlakos (ed.). *Law, Rights, and Discourse*. Hart: 37–55.

Alexy, R. 2011. 'Normativity, Metaphysics and Decision'. In S. Bertea and G. Pavlakos (eds.). *New Essays on the Normativity of Law*. Hart: 219–28.

Alexy, R. 2013. 'Some Reflections on the Ideal Dimension of Law and on the Legal Philosophy of John Finnis'. *American Journal of Jurisprudence* 58: 97–110.

Alexy, R. 2018. 'The Special Case Thesis and the Dual Nature of Law'. *Ratio Juris* 31: 254–9.

Aquinas, T. 1993. *The Treatise on Law: St. Thomas Aquinas Summa Theologiae I–II; qq. 90–97*. Ed. R. J. Henle. University of Notre Dame Press.

Bix, B. H. 2018. 'Kelsen, Hart, and Legal Normativity'. *Revus* 34: 25–42.

Bix, B. H. 2019. 'On the Nature of Legal Normativity: Response to Commentators'. *Revus* 37: 83–91.

Bratman, M. E. 1987. *Intention, Plans, and Practical Reason*. Harvard University Press.

Bratman, M. E. 2011. 'Reflections on Law, Normativity and Plans'. In S. Bertea and G. Pavlakos (eds.). *New Essays on the Normativity of Law*. Hart: 73–85.

Broome, J. 2013. *Rationality Through Reasoning*. Wiley Blackwell.

Cohon, R. 2018. 'Hume's Moral Philosophy'. In E. N. Zalta (ed.). *Stanford Encyclopedia of Philosophy*. https://plato.stanford.edu/entries/hume-moral/.

Coleman, J. L. 1998. 'Incorporationism, Conventionality, and the Practical Difference Thesis'. *Legal Theory* 4: 381–425.

Coleman, J. L. and Leiter, B. 2010. 'Legal Positivism'. In D. Patterson (ed.). *A Companion to Philosophy of Law and Legal Theory*. Wiley-Blackwell: 228–48.

Copp, D. 1995. *Morality, Normativity, and Society*. Oxford University Press.

Copp, D. 2015. 'Explaining Normativity'. *Proceedings and Addresses of the American Philosophical Association* 89: 48–73.

Copp, D. 2019. 'Legal Teleology: A Naturalist Account of the Normativity of Law'. In D. Plunkett, S. J. Shapiro and K. Toh (eds.). *Dimensions of Normativity*. Oxford University Press: 45–64.

Dancy, J. 2000. *Practical Reality*. Oxford University Press.
Delacroix, S. 2004. 'Hart's and Kelsen's Concepts of Normativity Contrasted'. *Ratio Juris* 17: 501–20.
Delacroix, S. 2019. 'Understanding Normativity'. *Revus* 37: 17–28.
Dworkin, R. 1986. *Law's Empire*. Harvard University Press.
Edmundson, W. A. 2013. 'Because I Said So'. *Problema* 7: 41–61.
Ehrenberg, K. M. 2016. *The Functions of Law*. Oxford University Press.
Enoch, D. 2011a. 'Giving Practical Reasons'. *Philosophers' Imprint* 11(4): 1–22.
Enoch, D. 2011b. 'Reason-Giving and the Law'. In L. Green and B. Leiter (eds.). *Oxford Studies in Philosophy of Law* vol. 1. Oxford University Press: 1–38.
Fine, K. 2018. 'Truthmaking and the Is-Ought Gap'. *Synthese*. https://doi.org/10.1007/s11229-018-01996-8.
Finnis, J. 2000. 'On the Incoherence of Legal Positivism'. *Notre Dame Law Review* 75: 1597–1611.
Finnis, J. 2011a. *Natural Law and Natural Rights*. 2nd ed. Oxford University Press.
Finnis, J. 2011b. *Philosophy of Law: Collected Essays* vol. IV. Oxford University Press.
Finnis, J. 2013. 'Reflections and Responses'. In J. Keown and R. P. George (eds.). *Reason, Morality, and Law: The Philosophy of John Finnis*. Oxford University Press: 459–583.
Finnis, J. 2014. 'Law as Fact and as Reason for Action: A Response to Robert Alexy on Law's "Ideal Dimension"'. *American Journal of Jurisprudence* 59: 85–109.
Fuller, L. L. 1958. 'Positivism and Fidelity to Law: A Reply to Professor Hart'. *Harvard Law Review* 71: 630–72.
Gizbert-Studnicki, T. 2019. 'On Legal Things to Do: External and Internal Legal Reasons'. *Revus* 37: 29–38.
Gkouvas, T. 2018. 'The Metric Approach to Legal Normativity'. In K. E. Himma, M. Jovanavić and B. Spaić (eds.). *Unpacking Normativity*. Hart: 17–37.
Gray, J. C. 1909. *The Nature and Sources of the Law*. Columbia University Press.
Green, L. 1999. 'Positivism and Conventionalism'. *Canadian Journal of Law and Jurisprudence* 12: 35–52.
Green, L. 2003a. 'Legal Obligation and Authority'. In E. N. Zalta (ed.). *Stanford Encyclopedia of Philosophy*. https://plato.stanford.edu/entries/legal-obligation/.
Green, L. 2003b. 'Legal Positivism'. In E. N. Zalta (ed.). *Stanford Encyclopedia of Philosophy*. https://plato.stanford.edu/entries/legal-positivism/.
Green, M. S. 2016. 'Marmor's Kelsen. In D. A. J. Telman (ed.). *Hans Kelsen in America: Selective Affinities and the Mysteries of Academic Influence*. Springer: 31–55.
Greenberg, M. 2011. 'The Standard Picture and Its Discontents'. In L. Green and B. Leiter (eds.). *Oxford Studies in Philosophy of Law* vol. I. Oxford University Press: 39–106.
Greenberg, M. 2014. 'The Moral Impact Theory of Law'. *Yale Law Journal* 123: 1288–1342.
Greenberg, M. 2017. 'The Moral Impact Theory, the Dependence View and Natural Law'. In G. Duke and R. P. George (eds.). *The Cambridge Companion to Natural Law Jurisprudence*. Cambridge University Press: 275–313.

Hart, H. L. A. 1982. *Essays on Bentham: Jurisprudence and Political Theory.* Clarendon Press.

Hart, H. L. A. 2012. *The Concept of Law.* 3rd ed. Oxford University Press.

Hobbes, T. 1929. *Leviathan.* Clarendon Press.

Holmes, O. W., Jr. 1897. 'The Path of the Law'. *Harvard Law Review* 10: 457–78.

Honoré, T. 1987. *Making Law Bind.* Clarendon Press.

Hudson, W. D. 1969. *The Is-Ought Question.* Macmillan.

Hume, D. [1738]1978. *A Treatise of Human Nature.* 2nd ed. Ed. P. H. Nidditch. Clarendon Press.

Hume, D. [1748]1994. 'Of the Original Contract'. In *David Hume: Political Essays.* Ed. K. Haakonssen. Cambridge University Press.

Hurd, H. 1990. 'Sovereignty in Silence'. *Yale Law Journal* 99: 945–1028.

Kelsen, H. 1967. *Pure Theory of Law.* Trans. M. Knight. University of California Press.

Kelsen, H. 1992. *Introduction to the Problems of Legal Theory.* Trans. B. L. Paulson and S. L. Paulson. Clarendon Press.

Korsgaard, C. 2008. *The Constitution of Agency.* Oxford University Press.

Lewis, D. 1969. *Convention: A Philosophical Study.* Blackwell.

Maguire, B. 2018. 'The Autonomy of Ethics'. In T. McPherson and D. Plunkett (eds.). *The Routledge Handbook of Metaethics.* Routledge: 431–42.

Marmor, A. 2001. *Positive Law and Objective Values.* Oxford University Press.

Marmor, A. 2002. 'Exclusive Legal Positivism'. In J. Coleman and S. Shapiro (eds.). *The Oxford Handbook of Jurisprudence and Philosophy of Law.* Oxford University Press: 104–24.

Marmor, A. 2009. *Social Conventions.* Princeton University Press.

Marmor, A. 2011. 'The Conventional Foundations of Law'. In S. Bertea and G. Pavlakos (eds.). *New Essays on the Normativity of Law.* Hart: 143–57.

Marmor, A. 2018. 'Norms, Reasons, and the Law'. In K. E. Himma, M. Jovanavić and B. Spaić (eds.). *Unpacking Normativity.* Hart: 95–118.

Marmor, A. 2019. 'Conventions, Reasons, and the Law'. In L. Ramírez-Ludeña and J. M. Vilajosana (eds.). *Legal Conventionalism.* Springer: 47–63.

Matczak, M. 2019. 'Non-Lewisian Conventionalism and Law'. https://papers.ssrn.com/sol3/papers.cfm?abstract_id=3378565.

Murphy, J. G. 1978. 'Hume and Kant on the Social Contract'. *Philosophical Studies* 33: 65–79.

Paulson, S. L. 2012. 'A "Justified Normativity" Thesis in Hans Kelsen's Pure Theory of Law?' In M. Klatt (ed.). *Institutionalized Reason.* Oxford University Press: 61–111.

Paulson, S. L. 2017. 'Metamorphosis in Hans Kelsen's Legal Philosophy'. *Modern Law Review* 80: 860–94.

Pigden, C. R. 1991. 'Naturalism'. In P. Singer (ed.). *A Companion to Ethics.* Blackwell: 421–31.

Pigden, C. R. 2016. 'Hume on Is and Ought: Logic, Promises, and the Duke of Wellington'. In P. Russell (ed.). *The Oxford Handbook on Hume.* Oxford University Press: 401–15.

Postema, G. J. 1982. 'Coordination and Convention at the Foundations of Law'. *Journal of Legal Studies* 11: 165–203.

Postema, G. J. 2011. *Legal Philosophy in the Twentieth Century World: The Common Law World.* Springer.

Postema, G. J. 2012. 'Custom, Normative Practice, and the Law'. *Duke Law Journal* 62: 707–38.

Radbruch, G. 2006. 'Statutory Lawlessness and Supra-Statutory Law'. Trans. B. L. Paulson and S. L. Paulson. *Oxford Journal of Legal Studies* 26: 1–11.

Raz, J. 1986. *The Morality of Freedom.* Oxford University Press.

Raz, J. 1994. *Ethics in the Public Domain.* Clarendon Press.

Raz, J. 1990. *Practical Reason and Norms.* Oxford University Press.

Raz, J. 2009. *Between Authority and Interpretation.* Oxford University Press.

Raz, J. 2010. 'Reason, Reasons, and Normativity'. In R. Shafer-Landau (ed.). *Oxford Studies in Metaethics* vol. 5. Oxford University Press: 5–23.

Rescorla, M. 2019. 'Convention'. In E. N. Zalta (ed.). *Stanford Encyclopedia of Philosophy.* https://plato.stanford.edu/entries/convention/.

Rosati, C. S. 2016. 'Normativity and the Planning Theory of Law'. *Jurisprudence* 7: 307–24.

Rosati, C. S. 2019. 'Bix on the Normativity of Law'. *Revus* 37: 69–74.

Scanlon, T. M. 2014. *Being Realistic About Reasons.* Oxford University Press.

Sciaraffa, S. 2009. 'On Content-Independent Reason: It's Not in the Name'. *Law and Philosophy* 28: 233–60.

Shapiro, S. J. 2011a. *Legality.* Harvard University Press.

Shapiro, S. J. 2011b. 'Planning Agency and the Law'. In S. Bertea and G. Pavlakos (eds.). *New Essays on the Normativity of Law.* Hart.

Smith, M. B. E. 1973. 'Is There a Prima Facie Obligation to Obey the Law?'. *Yale Law Journal* 82: 950–76.

Spaak, T. 2005. 'Kelsen and Hart on the Normativity of Law'. In *Perspectives on Jurisprudence: Essays in Honour of Jes Bjarup.* Ed. P. Wahlgren. Stockholm Institute for Scandinavian Law: 397–414.

Spaak, T. 2018. 'Legal Positivism, Conventionalism, and the Normativity of Law'. *Jurisprudence* 9: 319–44.

Tiffany, E. 2007. 'Deflationary Normative Pluralism'. *Canadian Journal of Philosophy* supp. 33: 231–62.

Williams, B. 1981. *Moral Luck.* Cambridge University Press.

26 An Italian Path to Legal Positivism: Ferrajoli's *Garantismo*

J. J. Moreso *

> *There is no position which depends on clearer principles, than that every act of a delegated authority, contrary to the tenor of the commission under which it is exercised, is void. No legislative act, therefore, contrary to the Constitution, can be valid. To deny this, would be to affirm, that the deputy is greater than his principal; that the servant is above his master; that the representatives of the people are superior to the people themselves; that men acting by virtue of powers, may do not only what their powers do not authorize, but what they forbid.*[1]

26.1 Introduction

Over the last fifty years,[2] Luigi Ferrajoli has built an original and powerful theory of law, designed to account for certain features of contemporary constitutional democracies. The Italian expression 'garantismo' evokes a conception of law as a *system of guarantees* or *warranties*, 'an artificial system of warranties constitutionally established for the protection of

* I am very thankful to the participants of the conference on this volume at Stockholm University, November 2018: Patricia Mindus, Stefano Bertea, Michael S. Green, Cyril Holm, Brian Leiter, Andrei Marmor, Frederick Schauer, Tomasz Studnicki and, especially, Torben Spaak for such insightful and detailed comments. It was also presented in a seminar at the University of Roma Tre in April 2019 and I am also grateful to its participants: Arianna Colonna, Dario Ippolito, Fabrizio Mastromartino, Matija Žgur and, especially, my Roman host Giorgio Pino. The work has benefitted from two research grants: DER2016-80471-C2-1-R of the Spanish Government and 2017 SGR 00823 from the Generalitat of Catalonia.

1 Hamilton, Madison and Jay 1788: n. 78.

2 Maybe the three main moments are Ferrajoli 1970, 1989 and the monumental (with three volumes) 2007. However, other books and many papers complete his contribution.

human rights'.[3] Probably, 'garantismo' has become the usual way to refer to Ferrajoli's doctrine,[4] a work that offers a robust defence of a system of criminal law entirely faithful to rule of law: much less punitive and much more centred on the autonomy and freedom of citizens than the current criminal law systems tend to be.

Two main ideas articulate Ferrajoli's account: (1) the thesis of the separability of law and morality and (2) the distinction between *valid law* and *law in force*, in the sense that, in our constitutional systems, certain acts and other regulations can be applied and used in our jurisdictions even though they are in contradiction with the Constitution and, in accordance with Ferrajoli, they are in force, but they are invalid because unconstitutional.

In Sections 26.2 and 26.3, I shall present and comment on both of these theses. In Section 26.4, I shall distinguish between Ferrajoli's account and other contemporary defenders of constitutionalism (like Robert Alexy, Ronald Dworkin or Manuel Atienza), in what is called – in Latin jurisprudence – constitutionalism of guarantees (*costituzionalismo garantista*) against constitutionalism of principles – or, also, constitutionalism of rights – (*costituzionalismo principialista*). In Section 26.5, I shall conclude.

26.2 The Separability Thesis

The thesis of the separability between law and morals can be understood in a minimal sense, for instance in the sense endorsed by the following words of Hart:

> What both Bentham and Austin were anxious to assert were the following two simple things: first, in the absence of an expressed constitutional or legal provision, it could not follow from the mere fact that a rule violated standards of morality that it was not a rule of law; and, conversely, it could not follow from the mere fact that a rule was morally desirable that it was a rule of law.[5]

Obviously, this is not the only way of understanding the thesis that there is no necessary connection between law and morals. This thesis, understood in other ways, can be firmly rejected.[6]

[3] Ferrajoli 1999: 19. [4] See Ferrajoli 1989. [5] Hart 1958: 599.

[6] See, e.g., Gardner 2001. This thesis is also different from the thesis that the existence of law has always some moral value, e.g. Raz 2009: 318.

This thesis is clearly endorsed by Ferrajoli as a consequence of his rejection of moral objectivism. Ferrajoli argues: 'The existence or the validity of a legal norm does not in any way entail its justice, and its justice does not in any way entail its validity.'[7] According to Ferrajoli, this is the theoretical or descriptive reading of the separation thesis. For Ferrajoli, whereas saying that 'N is a valid legal norm' expresses a proposition, which can be true or false, saying that 'N is a valid moral norm' is not apt for truth; it does not express a proposition because 'the ultimate moral and political values . . . have nothing to do with either logical truth, [as] no demonstration of them is possible; or with the empirical truth, as no evidence can be given in their favour. Simply they are chosen, obviously grounded in their rational argumentation, and then, they are defended.'[8]

Moreover, this thesis has a normative or prescriptive reading because the author considers that meta-ethical realism or objectivism (he does not distinguish between them) entails intolerance and the negation of moral autonomy: 'this rejection (of intolerance) entails in fact, per *modus tollens*, the negation of their professed objectivism and their consequent ethical cognitivism'.[9]

This is a surprising thesis. On the one hand, it seems that meta-ethical claims have no normative consequences; on the other hand, only some normative ethics entails this lack of toleration. For instance, Ferrajoli mentions sometimes the morality of Catholic doctrine.[10] However, now Ferrajoli acknowledges that this disagreement may be only a verbal dispute,[11] given that 'objective' or 'true', as predicated of moral judgements, can be accepted if they mean only something like 'justified' or 'rationally acceptable'.

26.3 Constitutional Democracy and Legal Validity

Ferrajoli[12] considers that the changes in the democratic constitutions after World War II in continental Europe, with the introduction of entrenchment

[7] Ferrajoli 2011a: 36. See also Ferrajoli 1989: 203–10; Ferrajoli 2007 vol. 2: 309–21.

[8] Ferrajoli 2018: 69. [9] Ferrajoli 2018: 67.

[10] For instance Ferrajoli 2011a: 31: 'The moral objectivism and the cognitivism more coherent are, without doubt, those expressed by the catholic morality.' Perhaps Ferrajoli considers that the consequence of intolerance follows as a causal – and not conceptual – question from moral objectivism. This is an empirical issue, true in some contexts, false in others, I guess.

[11] See Ferrajoli 2018: 67 and n. 11. See also Ferrajoli 2012; Ferrajoli and Ruiz Manero 2012.

[12] For instance, Ferrajoli 2011c: 361.

of the Bill of Rights and a centralised model of judicial review, introduced a new model of democracy: *substantive or constitutional* democracy, different from the precedent *formal or majoritarian* democracy. In the formal democracy, the validity of rules depends only on being enacted in accordance with the formal mechanisms of authorisation. Nevertheless:

> The formal and procedural character of majority rule, though certainly necessary, it is not sufficient to define democracy: neither empirically, with reference to the experience of modern constitutional democracies, nor theoretically in relation to the very definition of political democracy. For a system to be democratic, the majority has at least to be deprived of the power of suppressing minorities - thus the power of future majorities must be curtailed. This is a substantive feature, dealing with the content of decisions, therefore contradicting the thesis that democracy consists entirely in a method: the procedural rules that ensure the popular representativeness of collective decisions through universal suffrage and majority rule. Substantive features, which guarantee democratic forms and methods, and their various and complex prerequisites, are therefore necessary for a theoretical definition of democracy with adequate explanatory power.[13]

Constitutional democracy has a set of substantive rules (mainly the Bill of Rights) that defines *the sphere of what cannot be decided*,[14] which has two parts: *what cannot be decided that*, delimited by the civil and political rights, and *what cannot be decided that not*, whose perimeter is established by social rights.

This change in the institutional design of our democracies demands that our legal theory allows for the possibility that legal authorities enact legal rules, which can be in force, in the sense that they can be efficacious, followed by citizens or applied by judges, even if incompatible with constitutional provisions. In this case, we have *invalid* legal rules.[15] On the versions of old legal positivism (which Ferrajoli called *paleo-legal positivism*), the notions of valid legal rule and legal rule in force were synonyms.[16] There can be legal norms that are in force but invalid. Furthermore, any time legal authorities enact a legal rule in contradiction with the content of constitutional rights, this legal rule exists but is invalid, and we have an *antinomy*. And each time legal authorities fail to enact

[13] Ferrajoli 2011c: 357. [14] See Ferrajoli 2001, 2007: vol. 2 ch. 13.
[15] See Ferrajoli 1989: 895–909; 2001: 18–22; 2007 vol. 1: 530–542.
[16] Ferrajoli 2016 considers this aspect, the Kelsenian idea that validity is the specific way of existence of legal norms, one of the main reasons for the failure of Kelsenian account.

legal rules for the protection and guarantee of social constitutional rights, they create a *lacuna* in the legal system.[17] In this sense, *legal ought* is introduced in the law as it is, because it can be that law as it is, is not as it ought to be. And, in this way,

> [t]he subordination of the law to the rule of law is the result of the incorporation in entrenched constitutions of ethical–political principles, such as the separation of powers, the principle of equality, and the various fundamental rights, which have been transformed from sources of political or external legitimacy (or, when infringed, lack of legitimacy) into juridical or internal sources of legitimacy.[18]

In order to grasp these features of constitutional systems, Ferrajoli[19] built an axiomatic monumental – three volume – and formal theory, the syntax and semantics of which define what now is known – in computer and information sciences – as a domain ontology,[20] that is to say, an explicit specification of a conceptualisation. The delimitation of a set of entities constitutes a certain universe of discourse in which several properties, relations and functions are defined. A set of formal axioms determines the interpretation and the adequate use of the introduced terms.

There are two kinds of axiom: *principia iuris et in iure*, which are the principles of deontic logic underlying legal systems, such as *obligatory* entails *permitted*. They also are *principia iuris tantum*, establishing – for instance – that low-level norms should be consistent with high-level norms. The first are logical principles, necessarily present in all systematisation; the second are normative principles whose presence is only contingent. They represent an *ideal* legal system, hierarchically ordered in accordance with the superior law of the constitution.

The first kind of principle draws the framework; the second kind allows us to make legal validity judgments.

The *primary guarantees* of constitutional rights are precisely the legal enactments (and the legal omissions) addressed to protect the rights. When these guarantees fail, then judges should use the *secondary guarantees*, overruling the laws that violate our rights and, if possible, introducing mechanisms to allow us the development of social rights.[21]

[17] Ferrajoli 2007 vol. 1: 685–6. [18] Ferrajoli 2011c: 365. [19] Ferrajoli 2007.
[20] See, e.g., Gruber 1993. Here Ferrajoli was maybe following the programme drawn by Bobbio 1950.
[21] Ferrajoli 2007 vol. 1: 668–95.

As you can see, the role of the judiciary in Ferrajoli's model is crucial. Even though Ferrajoli imagines judges to be subject to the constitution and legislation, limited to the adjudication of previous constitutional and legal rules, it is obvious that their function is highly relevant. The *least dangerous branch*, as Hamilton said, becomes less painless.[22]

Much can be shared in Ferrajoli's account. Here I would like to share three questions for discussion. First, Ferrajoli considers the distinction between legal validity and legal existence (in force) as the clue to the new legal positivism. Well, this position seems to neglect more than 200 years of US legal history and legal theory. This distinction is the key of Number 78 of *The Federalist*, quoted at the beginning of the chapter, where Hamilton reminds us that

> [t]he complete independence of the courts of justice is peculiarly essential in a limited Constitution. By a limited Constitution, I understand one which contains certain specified exceptions to the legislative authority; such, for instance, as that it shall pass no bills of attainder, no ex-post-facto laws, and the like. Limitations of this kind can be preserved in practice no other way than through the medium of courts of justice, whose duty it must be to declare all acts contrary to the manifest tenor of the Constitution void. Without this, all the reservations of particular rights or privileges would amount to nothing.[23]

One position was ratified in *Marbury* at the origins of American judicial review in 1803, with these very known words:

> Between these alternatives there is no middle ground. The constitution is either a superior, paramount law, unchangeable by ordinary means, or it is on a level with ordinary legislative acts, and like other acts, is alterable when the legislature shall please to alter it.
>
> If the former part of the alternative be true, then a legislative act contrary to the constitution is not law: if the latter part be true, then written constitutions are absurd attempts, on the part of the people, to limit a power in its own nature illimitable.
>
> Certainly all those who have framed written constitutions contemplate them as forming the fundamental and paramount law of the nation, and consequently the theory of every such government must be that an act of the legislature repugnant to the constitution is void.[24]

[22] Later I come back to the counter-majoritarian difficulty. Obviously, the reference is Bickel 1962.

[23] Hamilton, Madison and Jay 1788: n. 78.

[24] *Marbury* v. *Madison*, 5 US 137 1803.

It is rather odd to consider this doctrine a *new* doctrine, even if, admittedly, in continental Europe, the judicial review of legislation had to wait until the twentieth century.

Second, even though Ferrajoli often places Dworkin among the defenders of a constitutionalism of rights, against his own account, the Ferrajolian conception of constitutional democracy is very near to Dworkin's conception. Maybe it is sufficient here to quote Dworkin and to compare it with Ferrajoli's claims:

> The constitutional conception of democracy, in short, takes the following attitude to majoritarian government. Democracy means government subject to conditions – we might call these the 'democratic' conditions – of equal status for all citizens. When majoritarian institutions provide and respect the democratic conditions, then the verdicts of these institutions should be accepted by everyone for that reason. But when they do not, or when their provision or respect is defective, there can be no objection, in the name of democracy, to other procedures that protect and respect them better. The democratic conditions plainly include, for example, a requirement that public offices must in principle be open to members of all races and groups on equal terms. If some law provided that only members of one race were eligible for public office, then there would be no moral cost – no matter for moral regret at all – if a court that enjoyed the power to do so under a valid constitution struck down the law as unconstitutional.[25]

Third, it is also surprising that Ferrajoli never takes into account the counter-majoritarian difficulty. Although it is possible to endorse a conception of rights as *the sphere of what cannot be decided*, this position is not an answer to *who* should be the authority for deciding what is inside the sphere. The theory of rights is part of our theory of justice, but we also need a theory of authority. Ferrajoli seems to believe that if we are able to include the Bill of Rights in our Constitution, then judges shall only adjudicate the cases in accordance with the Constitution. But this claim neglects the issue of constitutional interpretation. Even though we can agree about what the Constitution says, we disagree about what the Constitution presupposes and, therefore, we often disagree about the right answer in constitutional cases. If we give the last word to the Supreme Court or the Constitutional Court, we take a controversial decision in our institutional design, a decision that should be justified. The most relevant

[25] Dworkin 1996: 17.

critics of judicial review[26] are not necessarily critics of a rights-based theory; they are critics of giving the last word to judges. It is not my opinion that there is no answer to this powerful objection,[27] but it cannot be ignored.

26.4 Constitutionalism of Guarantees versus Constitutionalism of Rights[28]

Ferrajoli distinguishes two kinds of constitutionalism: the constitutionalism of *guarantees* and that of *rights* (or, also, of *principles*).[29] The first is a kind of legal positivism that accepts the thesis of the separability between law and morality, maintains that there is no sharp distinction between rules and principles and, moreover, argues that constitutional provisions protecting constitutional rights should be interpreted as rules and, therefore, that balancing is not crucial in the adjudication of the Constitution, in which case subsumption would be the core of judicial reasoning. The second, contrariwise, is a kind of legal anti-positivism that restores in some sense the conceptual connection between law and morality, by insisting on the relevance of the difference between rules and principles and projecting this distinction onto the adjudication of law-making, balancing the core of constitutional reasoning.[30]

In this section, I intend to analyse the accuracy of this characterisation. First, if the separability thesis entails only that the legal validity of a norm does not necessarily entail its moral validity and that the moral validity of a norm does not necessarily entail its legal validity, this minimal thesis probably is not rejected by anyone, positivist or anti-positivist. Perhaps, today, the distinction between legal positivism and legal anti-positivism lies in the claim of whether moral facts figure or not among the *grounds* of law.[31] And, on the other hand, if Ferrajoli excludes some meta-ethical

[26] As Waldron 1998, 2006. In the Spanish world, you can see this position in, e.g., Gargarella 1996 and Bayón 2004.

[27] See Moreso 2009: chs. 4–6.

[28] In this paragraph I use some ideas presented in Moreso 2008, 2011, 2012a.

[29] See Ferrajoli 2011a, 2011b. It is a distinction that was made previously in Prieto Sanchís 2008.

[30] Here, Ferrajoli usually refers to Alexy, Atienza and Dworkin. See Alexy 1986; Atienza 1998; Atienza and Ruiz Manero 1996: ch. 1; Dworkin 1977: ch. 2.

[31] See, e.g., Greenberg 2004.

accounts, some specially robust forms of moral realism, this exclusion seems compatible with other meta-ethical positions (constructivism, objectivism without metaphysical commitment), which allows us to retain rationality and reasonableness in moral reasoning.

Second, Ferrajoli is afraid that the introduction of principles and balancing in judicial reasoning undermines the certainty in judicial reasoning. I intend to show – on the basis of Ferrajolian arguments – that we can incorporate moral considerations in judicial reasoning because constitutional and legal provisions refer to them in a way that is compatible with legal certainty. Thus, Ferrajoli argues:

> It would be appropriate that the legal constitutional culture, rather than to assume as inevitable the indeterminacy of constitutional language and the conflict of rights, and maybe indulging in both, supporting judicial activism, promotes the development of a more precise and rigorous legislative and constitutional language. Indeed, among the most important factors of judicial discretion and the increasing role of argumentation, is the crisis of legal language, which has become now a true dysfunction: in virtue of the imprecision and ambiguity of normative formulations, their obscurity and, sometimes, their contradictoriness, and also in virtue of the legislative inflation that has undermined the regulatory capacity of law.[32]

Ferrajoli reminds us of the importance that some of the great enlightened jurists – such as Jeremy Bentham, Gaetano Filangieri or Gian Domenico Romagnosi – conceded to the elaboration of a *science of legislation* apt to protect the precision and rigour of legislative language. It is the enlightened ideal of the *legal certainty.*[33]

But, although legal certainty is a value, we should identify the reasons for certainty in order to determine whether they are sufficiently important to defeat any kind of reasons against certainty. Most of the reasons for conferring value on legal certainty relate to the value of personal autonomy. One of the faces of personal autonomy is related to the capacity of choosing and carrying out our own life plan; only clear, precise and public laws allow us to choose and to plan our life in a reasonable way. But are there reasons to carry this enlightened ideal to extremes? I do not think so, because I consider that personal autonomy also requires that the addressees of rules should argue in favour of the justification of their conduct, when they do not follow these rules. For this reason, legal rules should, in

[32] Ferrajoli 2011a: 51.
[33] And Ferrajoli 1989 is the most relevant contemporary expression.

many situations, make it possible to have recourse to the underlying reasons (which are moral reasons) in order to apply them. In this way, for instance, criminal law treats the justifying and excusing conditions, and private law treats the invalidating conditions of certain civil transactions (for example, wills, gifts, contracts and marriages).[34] A criminal law without justifying conditions would display more certainty than our present criminal systems, but it would be more unjust because our personal autonomy would be weaker. Therefore, it is more respectful to personal autonomy to allow self-defence against an attack, even though that opens the door to a less certain terrain than the easier one of determining whether an individual has injured another person or not. Now we must determine if self-defence was reasonable, that is, if it was proportionate, if the attack was not the reaction to a previous unjust provocation, and so forth. Ferrajoli acknowledges with similar examples the role played by balancing in these cases:

A similar balancing can be found in other branches of law. Think, for instance, on the balancing required for the valuation of criminal justifications, as the necessity or self-defence, that the Italian Criminal Code acknowledges if they are judged 'proportional to the offense' (or 'to the danger'); or also the proportionality which is required by the principle of proportionality of punishment, abstractly or concretely, relative to the gravity of the committed crime, or also the valuation, again on the ground of balancing opposite interests, of the 'unjust' harm regulated in art. 2043 of the Italian Civil Code, as a presupposition of tort liability.[35]

It is a very pertinent observation: balancing occurs in adjudication in all branches of law. However, Ferrajoli insists here that balancing is not caused by the open texture of the formulation of principles and the tension between them[36] but by

the circumstances of fact expected by the rule in order to legally classify and to equitably connote the judged case. The norms, rules or principles, are always the same and they have always, for this reason, equal weight. It is the facts that change, the facts are always unrepeatable and unique and, therefore, the facts and the concrete situations should be weighted in order to determine the applicable norms.

[34] The analogy between excusing conditions in criminal law and invalidating conditions in private law comes from H. L. A. Hart 1968: 28–53.

[35] Ferrajoli 2011a: 48. [36] See Ferrajoli 2011a: 47–8.

But, in my view, this is only a *façon de parler*. Ferrajoli realises that in all branches of law there are, sometimes, opposite norms to be applied, that is, norms in conflict. When some authors defend that, in these cases, norms – rules or principles – are balanced in order to determine the norm applicable to a concrete case, obviously they mean that, in the factual circumstances at hand, a given norm is defeated by another and, in this sense, this norm loses its stringency. Each author generates his preferred lexicon; 'equitable connotation' is what, for instance, Alexy calls 'balancing'.[37] It is the same activity and, as Ferrajoli accepts, it is common in legal reasoning.

Furthermore, a private law without invalidating conditions would have much more certainty, but it would also be more unjust. If contracts were not void in the event of mistake or duress, then it would be clearer when we are under a contractual duty, as in the case of *stipulatio* in ancient Roman law.[38] Now, we must determine, for instance, the nature of the mistake, the injustice of the coercion and so forth. In brief, honouring personal autonomy, which confers value on legal certainty, requires us to make room for moral arguments, even though this sacrifices certainty to some extent. On our moral horizon, there are always values in conflict. How to fit them and weigh them is our task as moral agents. Therefore, the fact that the incorporation of moral concepts into law sometimes diminishes certainty should not be necessarily considered undesirable; on the contrary, often it is the only way to make law more respectful of our moral autonomy.

The same happens with the rules in our daily life. If I want to enjoy a morning of calm work, without being disturbed, in order to, for instance, finish this chapter, I can ask my secretary not to put any telephone calls through to me. It is a clear and precise rule, but if the secretary follows it without exceptions, then it could lead to bad effects: the president of the board of trustees of my university, who wants to talk to me urgently, may not be able to speak to me, or my wife may not be able to tell me that our daughter has been admitted to the hospital, and so forth. For this reason, we do not want secretaries to apply our orders mechanically. Sometimes we formulate explicitly the *defeater*, which makes the rule inapplicable: 'Please don't put any calls through to me this morning, unless it is very

[37] Alexy 2003a, 2003b. Another question, which cannot be developed here, is whether subsumption and balancing are alternative possibilities, as Alexy says, or, as I defended, whether balancing is only a previous stage for a final subsumption (see Moreso 2012b).

[38] The Roman *stipulatio* example is in the stimulating book Atria 2002: ch. 6.

important.' This second rule is less precise than the first. Even though some cases are clearly excluded by this second rule (my wife's call, for instance), in other cases the secretary will doubt and should exercise judgement in order to apply the rule. However, this second rule respects my autonomy to a greater extent than the first. Someone could still argue that it would be better to formulate a rule that includes clearly all exceptions. However, this is not possible: there are so many diverse circumstances that lead to the disapplication of a rule and we cannot enclose them in a canonical formulation without concepts of value.

Thus, my suggestion is that the law introduces moral concepts in a way analogous to the example of the secretary and, with the same arguments, in a justified way. The moral concepts incorporated in the law often work like *defeaters*, permitting certain conduct (self-defence) or forbidding certain regulations (cruel punishments). In my view, even if certainty is sacrificed to some extent, our moral autonomy is enhanced.

As Fredrick Schauer has argued,[39] the rules always suffer from *under-* and *over-inclusiveness* in relation to the reason that justifies them, to their *rationale*. A way of partially preserving the advantages of being governed by rules and taking the problem of under- and over-inclusion into account consists of the incorporation of some *defeaters* into the rules. This means that the rule-applying agencies have recourse to the underlying reasons in some cases, in order to put aside the rule in cases not covered by the underlying reason. It is clear that the inclusion of such *defeaters* affects the *semantic autonomy* of rules and, moreover, diminishes certainty. But this reduction of certainty is balanced by a more suitable justification of the mechanism of applying rules. We could return to the example of the secretary: if we do not include in the rule 'don't put through any phone calls this morning' the clause 'unless it is very important' and we try to specify the circumstances in which the rule should not apply, we will become mired in a casuistry that lead us to the infra-inclusion, because there will be circumstances not included in the defeater and not covered by the rationale of the rules, and because infra-inclusion in the defeater amounts to over-inclusion in the rule.

It is obvious that the culture of constitutionalism has increased the extent to which morality is incorporated into law. But the reason of this fact is that legal adjudication is more respectful of basic human rights.

[39] See Schauer 1991: 31–4.

However, morality does not float in the air; there are proper constitutional and legal norms that resort to morality, using moral concepts (often in the Bill of Rights, as the prohibition, for instance, of cruel, inhumane and degrading treatments), general clauses or concepts as reasonable, due care and so on. For instance, Francisco Laporta reminds us that probably it is in the field of criminal law where this incorporation is more visible, to the point that 'the norms of Criminal Law lead to be applied using a practical reasoning decidedly similar to moral reasoning', but, as the author warns:

> Moral norms in force inside the legal systems have not acquired their force *in virtue of* their moral character, that is to say, in virtue of their ethical relevance, but because a specifically legal norm in the system resort[s] to them. This warning allows us to maintain that there is no *necessary* connection between law and morals and, the idea that, however, legal norms in contemporary legal systems often incorporate moral content.[40]

My point does not consist in rejecting the distinction between the constitutionalism of guarantees and the constitutionalism of rights; my point is only to show that the constitutionalism of rights does not necessarily lead to unfettered judicial activism.

When, at the beginning of the chapter, I presented the Hartian thesis of the separation of law and morality, I quoted Hart: '[F]irst, in the absence of an expressed constitutional or legal provision, it could not follow from the mere fact that a rule violated standards of morality that it was not a rule of law.' It seems that, already early on, Hart considered that morality can be a test of legal validity if there is an expressed constitutional or legal provision with this effect.[41] This idea is developed, as is well known, in the Postcript to *The Concept of Law*.[42] This publication has become one of the crucial points in the debate between so-called *exclusive* legal positivism, according to which the identification of what law requires never depends on moral considerations,[43] and *inclusive* legal positivism, according to

[40] Laporta 1993: 61–2. [41] See Hart 1958. [42] See Hart 1994.

[43] This is the well-known position of, e.g., Raz 1979: ch. 3; Raz 1994: ch. 10; Raz 2004, as a consequence of his version of the so-called Social Thesis (the existence and the content of the law depends only on social facts, without resort to moral argument). See also Marmor 2002, 2011; Shapiro 1998: ch. 9; Shapiro 2011: 259–81. However, even though Ferrajoli considers that law is a human creation, he often repeats the Hobbesian sentence 'Auctoritas, non veritas facit legem' – e.g. Ferrajoli 1989: 17 – although he never refers to the contemporary debate about the scope of the Social Thesis.

which, when law resorts to morality, then moral argument is proper to identify the content of the law.[44]

This is not the place to venture into the deep waters of this debate. However, I could perhaps provide some arguments to characterise Ferrajoli as an inclusive legal positivist because he argues in favour of *the positivisation* of the Law of Reason, a way of incorporating morals in law. For instance, in Ferrajoli:

> In this way, the old and persistent contrast between Reason and Will, between Law of Reason and Law of Will, between Natural Law and Positive Law, between Antigone and Creon, which permeates legal and political philosophy, from Antiquity to the twentieth century, and which corresponds to the old and also permanent dilemma and contrast between a government of laws and a government of men, has been mainly solved by the current entrenched Constitutions through positivisation of the Law of Reason – even if historically determined and contingent – under the form of the principles and fundamental rights established in them, as limits and bonds to the Law of Will, which in democracy is the Law of numbers expressed by the will of majority.[45]

As you can see, this account is perfectly compatible with the incorporationist thesis, and Ferrajoli may, therefore, be counted among the inclusive legal positivists. His way to support this thesis is geared to avoid collapsing moral and legal argumentation into one another and, in this manner, restraining judicial activism. Well, this is precisely a way to defend the incorporation thesis.

It is true, however, that, in order to make this position stable, Ferrajoli should endorse a meta-ethical account able to ground rational reasoning about moral issues.

26.5 Concluding Remarks

In this light, it seems to me that none of the perils that Ferrajoli considered able to jeopardise the constitutionalism of rights are triggered: the incorporation of morality by law and the possibility of rationally ruling our moral considerations do not entail the rehabilitation of the ancient natural law doctrines. Especially, this fact does not entail in any way the

[44] See, e.g., Coleman 2001; Waluchow 1994. Two general presentations are in Moreso 2001 and Himma 2002.

[45] Ferrajoli 2011a: 25.

endorsement of perfectionist moralities without room for toleration. The distinction between rules and principles does not weaken the normative force of our Constitution, just as the presence of justifications and defences in our criminal codes – which have in their linguistic form the texture of principles or standards – does not weaken the normative force of our criminal legislation. Finally, it is clear that this adoption of moral considerations to some extent increases judicial discretion, as it is now possible to use moral reasoning to determine the way in which the law should be adjudicated, but this increase of judicial activism is necessary in order to respect the rights and moral autonomy of everyone. As Farnsworth points out: 'That is the general difference between a rule and a standard; the consequences of a rule are triggered once we settled the facts; a standard requires a judgment about the facts before it kicks in.'[46] Legal adjudication is not a mechanical activity; it does not follow predetermined algorithms; it is an activity in which judgement, reasonableness, practical wisdom and Aristotelian *phronesis* play a very prominent role.

I would like to end with the following suggestion: in the last years, as a consequence of the criticism against Hart's theory,[47] law is often conceived as a two-storey building: on the first floor, we find rules that provide us with protected reasons,[48] opaque to their justification; on the second floor, we find principles, transparent to their justification and able, for this reason, to expulse certain rules on the first floor.

Well, I would like to suggest, finally, the substitution of this image with the image of a single-storey building (with only the ground floor), in which rules and defeaters live together, defeaters being something like gargoyles that can modify, alter and make more accurate the rules through allowing the use of moral considerations and moral argument.

In my view, Ferrajoli – excessively anchored in Kelsenian and Bobbian legal positivism – seems to adopt a conception of the law as a book of rules, a set of self-applicable rules. Perhaps he is resisting the adoption of the two-storey building image because this image undermines the sovereignty of the law. Nevertheless, we can imagine rules living together with defeaters, which sometimes authorises the link with rules justifying reasons. In this sense, law demands a jurisprudence of rules *and* reasons.

46 Farnsworth 2008: 164.

47 Dworkin 1977: ch. 2; also Alexy 1986; Atienza and Ruiz Manero 1996: ch. 1.

48 See Raz 1975.

References

Alexy, R. 1986. *Theorie der Grundrechte*. Suhrkamp.

Alexy, R. 2003a. 'Constitutional Rights, Balancing, and Rationality'. *Ratio Iuris* 16: 131–40.

Alexy, R. 2003b. 'On Balancing and Subsumption: A Structural Comparison'. *Ratio Iuris* 16: 433–49.

Atienza, M. 1998. *El sentido del Derecho*. Ariel.

Atienza, M. and Ruiz Manero, J. 1996. *Las piezas del Derecho*. Ariel.

Atria, F. 2002. *On Law and Legal Reasoning*. Hart Publishing.

Bayón, J. C. 2004. 'Democracia y derechos: problemas de fundamentación del constitucionalismo'. In J. Betegón, F. Laporta, J. R. Páramo and L. Prieto Sanchís (eds.). *Constitución y derechos fundamentals*. Centro de Estudios Políticos y Constitucionales: 67–118.

Bickel, A. M. 1962. *The Least Dangerous Branch: The Supreme Court at the Bar of Politics*. Bobbs-Merrill.

Bobbio, N. 1950. 'Scienza del diritto e analisi del linguaggio'. *Rivista trimestrale di diritto e procedura civile* 4: 342–67.

Coleman, J. L. 2001. *The Practice of Principle*. Oxford University Press.

Dworkin, R. 1977. *Taking Rights Seriously*. Duckworth.

Dworkin, R. 1996. *Freedom's Law: The Moral Reading of the Constitution*. Oxford University Press.

Farnsworth, W. 2008. *The Legal Analyst: A Toolkit for Thinking about the Law*. University of Chicago Press.

Ferrajoli, L. 1970. *Teoria assiomatizzata del diritto. Parte generale*. Giuffrè.

Ferrajoli, L. 1989. *Diritto e Ragione. Teoria del garantismo penale*. Laterza.

Ferrajoli, L. 1999. *Derechos y garantías. La ley del más débil*. Trans. P. Andrés Ibáñez and A. Greppi. Trotta.

Ferrajoli, L. 2001. *Diritti fondamentali. Un dibattito teorico*. Ed. E. Vitale. Laterza.

Ferrajoli, L. 2007. *Principia Iuris. Teoria del diritto e della democrazia*. Laterza.

Ferrajoli, L. 2011a. 'Constitucionalismo principialista y constitucionalismo garantista'. *Doxa. Cuadernos de Filosofía del Derecho* 34: 15–53.

Ferrajoli, L. 2011b. 'El constitucionalismo garantista. Entre paleo-iuspositivimo y neo-iusnaturalismo'. *Doxa. Cuadernos de Filosofía del Derecho* 34: 311–62.

Ferrajoli, L. 2011c. 'The Normative Paradigm of Constitutional Democracy'. *Res Publica*. 17: 355–67.

Ferrajoli, L. 2012. 'La scelta come fondamento ultimo della morale'. *Teoria Politica* 2: 177–88.

Ferrajoli, L. 2016. *La logica del diritto. Dieci aporie nell'opera di Hans Kelsen*. Laterza.

Ferrajoli, L. 2018. *Manifesto per l'uguaglianza*. Laterza.

Ferrajoli, L. and Ruiz Manero, J. 2012. *Dos modelos de constitucionalismo. Una conversación*. Trotta.

Gardner, J. 2001. 'Legal Positivism: 5½ Myths'. *American Journal of Jurisprudence* 46: 199–226.

Gargarella, R. 1996. *La justicia frente al gobierno. Sobre el carácter contramayoritario del poder judicial.* Ariel.

Greenberg, M. 2004. 'How Facts Make Law'. *Legal Theory* 10: 157–98.

Gruber, T. R. 1993. 'A Translation Approach to Portable Ontologies'. *Knowledge Acquisition* 5: 199–220.

Hamilton, A., Madison, J. and Jay, J. 1788. *The Federalist: A Collection of Essays, Written in Favour of the New Constitution.* J. and A. M'Lean.

Hart, H. L. A. 1958. 'Positivism and the Separation of Law and Morals'. *Harvard Law Review* 71: 593–629.

Hart, H. L. A. 1968. 'Legal Excuses and Responsibility'. In H. L. A. Hart. *Punishment and Responsibility.* Oxford University Press.

Hart, H. L. A. 1994. *The Concept of Law.* With the Postscript. Eds. P. Bulloch and J. Raz. Oxford University Press.

Himma, K. E. 2002. 'Inclusive Legal Positivism'. In J. L. Coleman and S. J. Shapiro (eds.) *The Oxford Handbook of Jurisprudence and Philosophy of Law.* Oxford University Press: 125–65.

Laporta, F. 1993. *Entre el derecho y la moral.* Fontamara.

Marmor, A. 2002. 'Exclusive Legal Positivism'. In J. L. Coleman and S. J. Shapiro (eds.). *The Oxford Handbook of Jurisprudence and Philosophy of Law.* Oxford University Press: 104–24.

Marmor, A. 2011. *Philosophy of Law.* Princeton University Press.

Moreso, J. J. 2001. 'In Defense of Inclusive Legal Positivism'. In P. Chiassoni (ed.). *The Legal* Ought. Giappichelli: 37–64.

Moreso, J. J. 2008. 'Ferrajoli o el constitucionalismo optimista'. *Doxa* 31: 279–87.

Moreso, J. J. 2009. *La Constitución: modelo para armar.* Marcial Pons.

Moreso, J. J. 2011. 'Antígona como *defeater.* Sobre el constitucionalismo garantista de Ferrajoli'. *Doxa* 34: 183–99.

Moreso, J. J. 2012a. 'Legal Defeasibility and the Connection between Law and Morality'. In J. Ferrer Beltran and G. Battista Ratti (eds.). *The Logic of Legal Requirements. Essays on Defeasibility.* Oxford University Press: 225–37.

Moreso, J. J. 2012b. 'Ways of Solving Conflicts of Constitutional Rights: Proportionalism and Specificationism'. *Ratio Juris* 25: 31–46.

Prieto Sanchís, L. 2008. 'Derecho y democracia constitucional. Una discusión sobre *Principia iuris* de Luigi Ferrajoli'. *Doxa* 31: 325–53.

Raz, J. 1975. *Practical Reason and Norms.* Hutchinson.

Raz, J. 1979. *The Authority of Law.* Oxford University Press.

Raz, J. 1994. *Ethics in the Public Domain.* Oxford University Press.

Raz, J. 2004. 'Incorporation by Law'. *Legal Theory* 10: 1–17.

Raz, J. 2009. 'The Argument from Justice, or How Not to Reply to Legal Positivism'. In J. Raz. *The Authority of Law.* 2nd ed. Oxford University Press: 313–36.

Schauer, F. 1991. *Playing by the Rules.* Oxford University Press.

Shapiro, S. J. 1998. 'On Hart's Way Out'. *Legal Theory* 4: 469–508.

Shapiro, S. J. 2011. *Legality*. Harvard University Press.
Waldron, J. 1998. *Law and Disagreement*. Oxford University Press.
Waldron, J. 2006. 'The Core of the Case against Judicial Review'. *Yale Law Journal* 115: 1346–1406.
Waluchow, W. J. 1994. *Inclusive Legal Positivism*. Oxford University Press.

Part VI

Critique

Gustav Radbruch's Critique of Legal Positivism 27

Martin Borowski

27.1 Introduction

Gustav Radbruch is Germany's most important legal philosopher of the past 100 years, in terms of both theoretical significance and practical import. Hardly any other German-language text in the field of legal philosophy has been quoted more often than Radbruch's formula of 1946. German courts referred to the Radbruch formula in their attempts to come to terms with the morally outrageous legal consequences of the National Socialist regime[1] and the communist regime of former East Germany.[2]

Radbruch explicitly criticised legal positivism throughout his entire career. This explicit criticism was based, however, on an understanding of legal positivism as statutory positivism (*Gesetzespositivismus*) or as naturalism,[3] two familiar movements within positivism in the German debate in the first half of the twentieth century. This criticism is not, however, particularly telling against the backdrop of the modern understanding of 'legal positivism' qua separation thesis.[4]

From the point of view of the modern understanding of legal positivism qua separation thesis, Radbruch's legal philosophy offers important and pithy criticism. From the outset, there was, for Radbruch, a necessary connection between law and morality implied by his basal criterion, according to which 'law is the reality whose meaning is to serve justice'.[5] It is also clear that the Radbruch formula after World War II reflects a necessary connection between law and morality with respect to the criteria for the identification of valid law. It is less than clear, however,

[1] See Alexy 2002: 5–7.
[2] See Alexy 1997; H. Dreier 1997: 424–8; Seidel 1999: 17–21; with further references respectively.
[3] See Section 27.6. [4] On the separation thesis see, e.g., Alexy 2002: 3–4.
[5] Radbruch [1932]1950: 75, trans. altered following Paulson 2006: 19.

that he embraced this form of non-positivism before the war. Radbruch's basal criterion prima facie calls for moral correctness as a criterion for the identification of valid law. This is, however, a mere presumption rather than an implication, which would follow of necessity. On the contrary, the basal criterion also calls for legal certainty, which also represents, according to Radbruch, a requirement of justice. The argument from legal certainty is an argument on behalf of positivism with respect to the criteria for the identification of valid law.[6] This is to say that the basal criterion points to arguments for both non-positivism and positivism with respect to the criteria for the identification of valid law.[7] The tension between these arguments is crucial for a proper understanding of Radbruch's legal philosophy.

27.2 A Periodisation of Gustav Radbruch's Legal Philosophy

The first period of Radbruch's legal philosophy is characterised by the *Outlines of Legal Philosophy.*[8] In this book, he laid important foundations for his approach, among them the dual theory of validity.[9] The article 'The Problem of the Idea of Law' of 1924,[10] which introduces the idea of justice as equality, marks the beginning of the second period. This completes his system of the nature and the concept of law, which is then systematically and comprehensively explained in his main treatise *Legal Philosophy* in 1932.[11]

The third period commences shortly thereafter. Having emphasised relativism in his treatise from 1932, he qualifies it significantly in the article 'Relativism in Legal Philosophy' of 1934[12] and supports the idea of human rights in the article 'The Purpose of the Law' of 1937.[13] His famous post-World War II articles are the short piece 'Five Minutes of Legal Philosophy'[14] and the longer article 'Statutory Lawlessness and

[6] See, e.g., Alexy 2002: 51–3. [7] See Section 27.5.3.

[8] Radbruch [1914]1933. The translations of the titles of Radbruch's publications in German or French into English generally follow Paulson 2006. All other translations by M.B., unless stated otherwise. On the following periodisation, see generally Borowski 2015: 237.

[9] See Section 27.5.1. [10] Radbruch 1924. [11] Radbruch [1932]1973.

[12] Radbruch 1934; German in Radbruch 1957. [13] Radbruch 1937–8.

[14] Radbruch 1945; English in Radbruch 2006a.

Supra-Statutory Law'.[15] In addition, the article 'The Statute and the Law'[16] is important in the context of his explicit criticism of legal positivism. We have an outline of his general legal philosophy after the war owing to the *Primer in Legal Philosophy*,[17] a revised and authorised publication of lecture notes taken by two students in Radbruch's lecture on legal philosophy in Heidelberg in the summer semester 1947.

27.3 Conversion or Continuity?

In looking at the three periods, the question arises: what precisely changed and what do these changes mean against the backdrop of the dichotomy between positivism and non-positivism? Those who defend the *conversion thesis*, the prevailing view in the second half of the twentieth century, would have us believe that Radbruch had been a positivist before World War II and converted, having faced the horrors of the Third Reich, to non-positivism after the war.[18] If this is true, what then of his explicit and implicit critique of legal positivism throughout his career?

By contrast, those who defend the *thesis of non-positivistic continuity* claim that Radbruch was a non-positivist from the beginning.[19] Changes in Radbruch's legal philosophy may well modify the extent or kind of necessary connection between law and morality, but they do not mark a transition from positivism to non-positivism.

In what follows, I shall explain the non-positivistic nature of Radbruch's legal philosophy during the last period, from 1934 to 1949, this against the backdrop of legal positivism qua separation thesis. Here, the Radbruch formula is front and centre.[20] The interpretation of the formula will be confirmed by and contrasted with an interpretation of the second period of Radbruch's philosophy, from 1924 to 1932.[21] Finally, I invite attention to Radbruch's explicit criticism of 'legal positivism' throughout all periods of his *Oeuvre*.[22]

[15] Radbruch 1946; English in Radbruch 2006b. [16] Radbruch 1947. [17] Radbruch 1948.

[18] See, e.g., Hart 1958: 616; Alexy 1992: 80 (greater care in Alexy 2002: 45); Haldemann 2005: 164; Hoerster 2006: 79; for references from the early German literature, see Seidel 1999: 112–15.

[19] Borowski 2015: 264; R. Dreier 2011: 19, 43; R. Dreier 2015: 228; Paulson 2006: 19; Paulson 2008: 106; Paulson 2015; early supporters were Baratta 1959: 505, and Engisch 1949–50: 315.

[20] See Section 27.4. [21] See Section 27.5. [22] See Section 27.6.

27.4 The Non-positivism of Radbruch's Formula

There are three different kinds of necessary connection between law and morality in the final version of Radbruch's legal philosophy: a necessary connection between law and morality established by his basal criterion and two different kinds of necessary connection with respect to the criteria for the identification of valid law.

27.4.1 A Necessary Connection between Law and Morality Established by Radbruch's Basal Criterion

The basal criterion from his earlier writings, according to which 'law is the reality whose meaning is to serve justice',[23] is still prominent in the third period,[24] and it provides the justification of the criteria for the identification of valid law as characterised by the Radbruch formula. This necessary connection between law and morality in the justification of the criteria for the identification of valid law is not, however, evident, compared with the intolerability formula and the disavowal formula. I shall return at a later point to the character of this connection between law and morality and the sense in which it gives rise to non-positivism.[25]

27.4.2 Two Necessary Connections between Law and Morality with Respect to the Criteria for the Identification of Valid Law

Following the received opinion, Radbruch's formula can be summarised with the phrase 'Extreme injustice is no law.'[26] The phrase focuses on the first part of the Radbruch formula, the intolerability formula. The second part, the disavowal formula, is – again, as the received opinion has it – subjective in nature with little, if any, theoretical import or practical significance. Owing to the fact that the subjective requirements of the disavowal formula are very difficult to establish, it is usually quickly set aside and the focus is, then, completely on the intolerability formula.[27]

[23] Radbruch [1932]1950: 75, trans. altered following Paulson 2006: 19.
[24] See Radbruch 2006b: 7; Radbruch 1947: 99; Radbruch 1948: 32 (RGA vol. 3: 151).
[25] See Section 27.5.3.
[26] See, e.g., Alexy 1999: 17; Alexy 2008: 282; Dyzenhaus 2010: 16.
[27] See, e.g., R. Dreier 1993: 58; H. Dreier 1997: 423; Alexy 1999: 16; Haldemann 2005: 166; Bix 2011: 46–7.

This is not, however, a convincing reconstruction of the disavowal formula. Contrary to what the received opinion would have one believe, it is objective rather than subjective in nature; it refers to cases of extreme discrimination. What is more, it has escaped the notice of those supporting the received opinion that Radbruch uses the disavowal formula rather than the intolerability formula in his efforts to cope with the legal consequences of the regime of the National Socialists.

27.4.2.1 The Intolerability Formula

The phrase 'Extreme justice is no law' may actually serve as a plausible short form for the intolerability formula, albeit with one qualification: The expression 'is no law' must be taken to mean 'is no valid law'. The intolerability formula reads:

> The conflict between justice and legal certainty may well be resolved in this way: The positive law, secured by legislation and power, takes precedence even when its content is unjust and fails to benefit the people, unless the conflict between statute and justice reaches such an intolerable degree that the statute, as 'flawed law', must yield to justice. It is impossible to draw a sharper line between cases of statutory lawlessness and statutes that are valid despite their flaws.[28]

'Extreme injustice' can be understood as a synonym for an 'intolerable degree' of 'conflict between statute and justice'. The consequence of the intolerability formula – 'the statute, as "flawed law", must yield to justice' – is loss of validity. 'Flawed law' is invalid positive law.[29] What is more, Radbruch emphasises that it is very difficult to draw the line between cases in which the threshold is crossed and cases in which it is not: 'It is impossible to draw a sharper line.'

To be sure, the intolerability formula raises important questions, to wit: whether and how one can justify that there is a case of – in Radbruch's words – an 'intolerable degree' of 'conflict between statute and justice' or – in the modern short form – 'extreme injustice', and when precisely this threshold is crossed. It presupposes meta-ethical objectivism.[30] In his first post-World War II article, Radbruch refers to a 'far-reaching consensus in the so-called declarations of human and civil rights',[31] so that a qualified violation of human rights counts as a promising candidate for 'extreme

[28] Radbruch 2006b: 7. [29] This is confirmed in Radbruch 1948: 35 (RGA vol. 3: 154).
[30] See Spaak 2009: 266–75. [31] Radbruch 2006a.

injustice'. At any rate, Radbruch assumes that if the threshold of qualified immorality is crossed, the judge is empowered not to apply – and, indeed, has the obligation not to apply – the statute in question to the case at hand. This is to say that the intolerability formula implies non-positivism with respect to the criteria for the identification of valid law.

27.4.2.2 The Disavowal Formula

The second part of Radbruch's formula, the disavowal formula, runs as follows: 'One line of distinction, however, can be drawn with utmost clarity: Where there is not even an attempt at justice, where equality, the core of justice, is deliberately betrayed in the issuance of positive law, then the statute is not merely "flawed law", it lacks completely the very nature of law.'[32]

In short, positive law that 'deliberately betrays' or disavows equality as the core of justice lacks legal character. Lacking 'completely the very nature of law' is more than just a lack of validity; the statute in question does not even count as invalid law. This is corroborated in Radbruch's *Primer in Legal Philosophy*.[33] There, too, Radbruch emphasises that there is a 'clear boundary' (*scharfe Grenze*),[34] which echoes the phrase that a 'line ... can be drawn with utmost clarity' in the disavowal formula. This can hardly be reconciled with the subjective reading of the disavowal formula, which would render the application of the formula notoriously difficult and unclear. The key question, however, is what 'deliberately [to] betray justice' precisely means.

'[D]eliberately' in 'deliberately betrayed' points in a subjective direction. There are also subjective connotations in passages in which Radbruch assesses statutes of the Nazi regime against the backdrop of the disavowal formula.[35] This led Hans-Ulrich Evers to claim, in 1956, that the disavowal formula requires a subjective intent on the part of the lawgiver to 'disavow' or betray justice, and Evers went on to dismiss the disavowal formula on this reading as hardly relevant in the practical application of the Radbruch formula.[36] This view quickly became the received opinion[37] and has largely remained unchallenged ever since.

[32] Bix 2011: 53. [33] Radbruch 1948: 33 (RGA vol. 3: 151). [34] Ibid., trans. by M. B.

[35] Radbruch 2006b: 8: 'explicit intention'; see also Radbruch 1947: 6 (RGA vol. 3: 99): 'deliberately extricated'.

[36] See Evers 1956: 82–3. [37] See Seidel 1999: 174–5 with further references.

There are serious doubts as to whether a subjective reading of the disavowal formula can be reconciled with Radbruch's greater legal philosophy. The foundations of Radbruch's theory in neo-Kantian philosophy[38] count against a subjective reading, for 'meaning' in the neo-Kantian sense of Radbruch's basal criterion points in the direction of an objective meaning.[39] What is more, Radbruch's theory of interpretation is decidedly objective in nature.[40] These two arguments, counting against a subjective reading, are, in my view, convincing.[41] The question remains, however, how an objective meaning of 'deliberately betrayed' is to be understood. The roots of the disavowal formula in Radbruch's 'concept of law' – by contrast to his 'conception of legal validity' – suggest that extreme discrimination, extreme violations of equality, represent cases of the disavowal formula.

Although Radbruch emphasises relativism in *Legal Philosophy*,[42] his version of relativism was never all-encompassing. He stresses the formal character of equality as the core of justice.[43] There was, however, an – albeit thin and not easily recognised – substantive dimension of equality in his legal philosophy from an early point, namely, from 1924 on. In section 9 of *Legal Philosophy*, Radbruch explains that law is governed by three antinomies, namely, 'justice, purposiveness, and legal certainty'.[44] 'Justice' is characterised by the appeal to equality. The substantive standards for determining who and what is equal or unequal are provided by 'purposiveness'. Owing to relativism, rational cognition of these standards of 'purposiveness' is impossible.[45] There are, however, exceptions to relativistic 'purposiveness': '[T]here are a number of legal provisions that are dictated by no purposiveness at all but solely by justice or legal certainty. Equal protection of the laws or the prohibition of *ad hoc* tribunals, for instance, rests on requirements not of purposiveness but solely of justice.'[46]

The phrase 'for instance' makes clear that these two examples do not exhaust sorts of case that 'rest on requirements . . . solely of justice'. A third and telling example can be found in Radbruch's article of 1924, 'The Problem of the Idea of Law': 'A short series of fundamentally important

[38] See, generally, Wiegandt 2004; Paulson 2006: 29–32. [39] See Funke 2003: 3–16.
[40] See Seidel 1999: 176. [41] See, in greater detail, Borowski 2019: 41–3.
[42] See, e.g., Radbruch [1932]1950: 48, 57–9. [43] See, e.g., Radbruch [1932]1950: 74–5.
[44] Radbruch [1932]1950: 110, trans. amended. [45] Radbruch [1932]1950: 108.
[46] Radbruch [1932]1950: 111, trans. amended; see also Radbruch 1948: 25 (RGA vol. 3: 144).

provisions is, however, dictated by justice alone, for example equality before the law, *the equality of laws without regard to sex, birth, and class*, the prohibition of *ad hoc* tribunals.'[47]

The first phrase in italics contains a prohibition of discrimination on grounds of 'sex', 'birth' and 'class' as has become common in bills of rights at both the national and the international level. There is no obvious reason why the list of these three grounds of discrimination ought to be seen as exhaustive – 'for example' says that another prohibited ground of discrimination might well be added. For example, the provision respecting prohibited grounds of discrimination in modern bills of rights, such as Article 14 of the European Convention on Human Rights, boasts, among other things, of a prohibition on grounds of race. If one adds 'race' to Radbruch's list of prohibited grounds of discrimination, it becomes immediately clear why and how Radbruch uses the disavowal formula to address National Socialist statutes. These statutes represented extreme discrimination against Jews and other minorities, first and foremost on grounds of race. In those passages in which Radbruch explains why certain National Socialist statutes lacked the character of law from the outset, he emphasises extreme discrimination. A few lines after the disavowal formula, one reads:

> The explicit intention from the very beginning, then, was that National Socialist 'law' would extricate itself from the essential requirement of justice, namely, the equal treatment of equals. It thereby lacks completely the very nature of law; it is not merely flawed law, but rather no law at all . . . Legal character is also lacking in all the statutes that treated human beings as subhuman and denied them human rights.[48]

Nota bene, it is not the violation of the right to life or the right to liberty and property of the minority that represents the decisive problem for Radbruch; it is extreme discrimination, the extreme violation of the right to equality. National Socialist statutes sanctioned extreme discrimination. Some people were granted human rights while others (Jews and other minorities) were denied the same rights. This is confirmed in the article 'The Statute and the Law', in which Radbruch stresses the 'idea of *equal* human rights for everyone with a human countenance',[49] and in *Primer in Legal Philosophy*, where he states that a 'statute that denies to *certain* human

[47] Radbruch 1924: 49 (RGA vol. 2: 465) (emphasis added). [48] Radbruch 2006b: 8.
[49] Radbruch 1947: 6 (RGA vol. 3: 99) (emphasis added).

beings human rights' lacks legal character.[50] This is to say that the roots of the disavowal formula in Radbruch's substantive concept of law suggest the following objective reading: Positive law disavows justice if it represents a case of extreme discrimination, such as discrimination on grounds of sex, birth, class, race or on other comparable grounds.

If both parts of the Radbruch formula are objective in nature, the disavowal formula can actually be seen as a special case of the intolerability formula, for extreme discrimination such as the Holocaust also represents an instance of 'extreme injustice'. One might argue that the objective reading of the disavowal formula renders this part of the Radbruch formula futile – why not refer immediately to the intolerability formula if every case of the disavowal formula is a special case of the intolerability formula? This is a question about whether the most coherent reading of Radbruch's writings proves convincing in this respect. This question should not, however, be confused with the question as to what the most coherent reading of Radbruch's writings actually is. Radbruch saw two different kinds of moral limit on positive law, one stemming from the criteria for the 'concept of law' and another from the criteria for the validity of law. This difference was so important to him that he distinguished the consequences, lack of legal character and lack of legal validity. And he may actually have a point when he claims that cases of extreme discrimination can be more easily and more clearly established than (other) cases of extreme injustice. For example, among those who generally support the Radbruch formula, there was and is near consensus to the effect that the paradigmatic National Socialist statutes never were valid positive law, whereas there is less agreement respecting cases of the border shootings during the East German communist regime.[51] The former are a clear and flagrant violation of the prohibition on grounds of race, while the latter cannot easily be reconstructed as a violation of a classic prohibition of discrimination – they are cases of the intolerability formula rather than the disavowal formula.

At any rate, if and when the threshold of the disavowal formula, extreme discrimination, is crossed, a judge is empowered to forbear from applying the statute in question. Just as in the case of the intolerability formula, so likewise the disavowal formula presupposes a necessary connection with

[50] Radbruch 1948: 33 (RGA vol. 3: 151) (emphasis added).

[51] See Seidel 1999: 37–49 with further references.

respect to the criteria for the identification of valid law. In this sense, it implies non-positivism.

27.5 Non-positivism in Radbruch's Legal Philosophy up to 1932

The question arises as to which of the three kinds of necessary connection between law and morality[52] emerge only after 1932 and which were – and if so, to which extent – already present in the second period, from 1924 to 1932.[53]

27.5.1 Necessary Connections between Law and Morality Expressed in the Criteria for Legal Validity

Radbruch's theory of legal validity in section 10 of *Legal Philosophy*, 1932, provides for different criteria for legal validity, namely, stemming from two different standpoints, the standpoint of the judge and the standpoint of the citizen. It is possible, he grants, that intolerably unjust positive law proves invalid from the standpoint of the citizen: 'The individual conscience usually will, and properly may, deem an offense against positive law more objectionable than the sacrifice of the individual's own legal conviction, but there may be "laws endorsing matters shameful (*Schandgesetze*)" which conscience refuses to obey.'[54]

This is to say that 'laws endorsing matters shameful', which may be taken as a synonym for 'intolerably unjust laws' in the sense of the intolerability formula developed later, have – from the standpoint of the citizen – no legal validity. The law 'may prove its power but can never demonstrate its validity'.[55] Radbruch's theory of validity in 1932 resembles the intolerability formula in so far as the standpoint of the citizen is concerned, and this implies a necessary connection between law and morality.[56]

[52] As explained in Section 27.4.

[53] An inquiry into the transition from the first to the second period lies beyond the scope of this chapter.

[54] Radbruch [1932]1950: 118, trans. amended.

[55] Radbruch [1932]1950: 119.

[56] See R. Dreier 2011: 32; Borowski 2015: 262.

This standpoint, however, is different from the standpoint of the judge. The judge is under a strict obligation to enforce positive law:

> It is the professional duty of the judge to validate the law's claim to validity, to sacrifice his own sense of the right to the authoritative command of the law, to ask only what is legal and not whether it is also just. ... We despise the parson who preaches in a sense contrary to his conviction, but we respect the judge who does not permit himself to be diverted from his loyalty to the law by his conflicting sense of the right.[57]

It is not without reason that commentators who claim that Radbruch defended legal positivism in his *Legal Philosophy* of 1932 and, consequently, support the conversion thesis typically focus on this often quoted, indeed notorious passage. Radbruch's theory of validity from the standpoint of the judge precludes his embracing moral correctness as a criterion for identifying valid law. Seen for its own sake, it is 'positivistic' in nature.

Radbruch provides no solution for the 'truly tragic case', that in which a judge, under an obligation to enforce the statute independently of considerations of morality, faces a citizen for whom the statute counts as intolerably unjust.[58] Thus, from a practical point of view,[59] the non-positivistic theory of validity from the standpoint of the citizen is superseded by the 'positivistic' theory of validity from the standpoint of the judge. Whether the sanction is an expression of the law or of mere power, the citizen is faced with the sanction.

This is hardly a convincing reconstruction. If there is no valid law from the standpoint of the citizen in the case of an intolerably unjust statute, there is, from the citizen's standpoint, no legal obligation to obey the statute either. Does that mean that the citizen, for want of a legal obligation to acquiesce in an interference with his liberty, is legally entitled to engage in acts of self-defence against the state? Radbruch's reference to Socrates in the course of emphasising the importance of enforcing positive law suggests that he is hardly prepared to accept such a self-defence.[60] If, from the standpoint of the judge, the citizen is under an obligation to obey the law, does this not imply a legal obligation from an objective point

57 Radbruch [1932]1950: 119, trans. amended. 58 See Radbruch [1932]1950: 119.

59 Radbruch did not regard the theory of legal validity from the standpoint of the citizen as completely superseded by the theory of validity from the standpoint of the judge; see Radbruch [1932]1950: 111.

60 See Radbruch [1932]1950: 120.

of view? If so, is it then correct to say that imposing the sanction is a mere exercise of power?

Radbruch abandoned the dual theory of validity by adopting, in 1946, the intolerability formula. The distinction between the standpoint of the judge and the standpoint of the citizen is gone, so that the 'truly tragic case' can no longer arise. This represents a clear change in Radbruch's position in the transition from the second period to the third period.

Is this, however, a transition from positivism to non-positivism? Radbruch's dual theory of validity has a non-positivistic element, that is, from the standpoint of the citizen, moral correctness necessarily plays a role in identifying valid law. And the dual theory has a positivistic element, that is, from the standpoint of the judge, moral correctness plays no role in identifying valid law. A single non-positivistic element in a theory of law renders the overall theory non-positivistic.[61] What is more, there is also Radbruch's 'concept of law', which may be non-positivistic in nature.[62] Even if his theory of legal validity in 1932 were classified as positivistic in nature, a necessary connection with respect to the criteria for establishing the legal character of a norm would nevertheless render his legal philosophy non-positivistic.

It is worth emphasising again,[63] however, that the change in Radbruch's theory of legal validity had no practical implications for him. After World War II, he did not suggest that National Socialist statutes be denied legal validity owing to an intolerable degree of conflict between statute and justice. Rather, he suggested that such statutes were lacking in legal character from the outset, owing to the disavowal of justice through the extreme discrimination that they represent.

27.5.2 A Necessary Connection between Law and Morality in the Concept of Law?

Is the disavowal formula anticipated in Radbruch's legal philosophy in the second period, from 1924 to 1932? The answer is affirmative, that is, all theoretical foundations of the disavowal formula are already evident.

[61] See Borowski 2015: 240. [62] See Section 27.5.2. [63] See Section 27.4.2.2.

27.5.2.1 The Basal Criterion and the Limits of Relativism

In section 9 on *The Concept of Law* in Radbruch's *Legal Philosophy* of 1932, the basal criterion[64] is front and centre. It has already been explained[65] that there was, already in the second period, a limit in Radbruch's relativism, a limit to the effect that equality – the core of justice, according to Radbruch – manifests a modest substantive dimension. Owing to this modest substantive dimension of equality, a statute that represents extreme discrimination lacks legal character. In this context, the two passages on 'requirements not of purposiveness but solely of justice' that have already been quoted[66] are key. Against the backdrop of the basal criterion, this is to say that, for example, a statute that discriminates on grounds of birth – that reserves certain privileges to nobility – cannot be a 'reality whose meaning is to serve justice'. Justice, by definition, is not served by such a statute. If one replaces 'birth' with 'race', it becomes clear that the prohibition of discrimination on grounds of race 'rests on requirements ... solely of justice'. This points precisely in the direction of the disavowal formula, according to which statutes that provide for extreme discrimination lack legal character from the outset.

27.5.2.2 The Formal Concept of Law and Its Substantive Limits

In the *Primer of Legal Philosophy* of 1948, Radbruch refers to the disavowal formula in the context of his formal concept of law: '[L]aw can be defined as the epitome of general, positive norms for social life.'[67] He continues: '[W]here ... there is not even an attempt at justice, the directives thus created can only be expressions of power, never legal rules.'[68] A couple of lines further on, we read: '[A] statute that denies certain human beings human rights is not a legal rule. Here we have a clear boundary between law and non-law.'[69] This formal concept of law, which rests on Radbruch's basal criterion, was exactly the same in 1932: Law is 'positive and normative, both social and general. In this sense we define law as the complex of general precepts for the social life of human beings.'[70]

[64] See n. 23. [65] See Section 27.4.2.2. [66] Ibid.
[67] Radbruch 1948: 33 (RGA vol. 3: 151). [68] Ibid. [69] Ibid., trans. amended.
[70] Radbruch [1932]1950: 76, trans. amended (emphasis omitted).

27.5.2.3 Conclusion: The Continuity in the Concept of Law

Thus, by contrast to his theory of legal validity, Radbruch's concept of law in the third period has not changed from the second period at all. This suggests the conclusion that the disavowal formula was already implicitly contained in Radbruch's *Legal Philosophy* of 1932.

27.5.2.4 The Power of the Judge to Forbear from Applying Law that Disavows Equality

We have clear evidence in the post-World War II articles that Radbruch extends the power to the judge to forbear from applying a statute that 'disavows' equality.[71] Ulfrid Neumann has claimed that we do not have comparably clear textual evidence to the effect that he was prepared to extend such power to the judge in 1932.[72] This is true. But we also have no clear textual evidence to the effect that he was *not* prepared to extend such power to the judge. This is a matter of interpretation going beyond direct textual evidence. Neumann claims that up to 1932, the basal criterion was 'merely epistemological in nature' and that Radbruch accepted its 'normative-pragmatic relevance' only after the war.[73] Neumann refers to passages in which Radbruch accepts that a 'precept'[74] can lack legal character but can have legal validity.[75] This might suggest that a statute that disavows equality in 1932 could have been considered by Radbruch, running parallel to the theory of validity from the standpoint of the judge, as a measure that does not count as valid law but needs nevertheless to be enforced by the judge. It is, however, far from clear that this is a valid conclusion. To begin with, Radbruch distinguished clearly and consequently between the 'concept of law' and the validity of law throughout all the periods of his work. What is more, Radbruch develops his construction of 'measures without legal character, but legal validity' in the second period with an eye to the requirement of generality in his formal concept of law.[76] Radbruch is not prepared to accept the idea that there can be *individual norms*. He explains that 'as a matter of fact, we determine by the standard of

[71] See Section 27.4.2.2. [72] See Neumann 2015: 132. [73] See Neumann 2007: 17–20.

[74] See Radbruch [1932]1950: 76: 'precept'. Radbruch consciously uses '*Anordnung*' as opposed to '*Rechtsnorm*' or '*Rechtssatz*' in the German original, for his very point is that the 'precept' is not a legal norm.

[75] See Neumann 2007: 19–20; Neumann 2015: 140–2. [76] See Section 27.5.2.2.

purported justice alone whether a measure is legal in nature at all'.[77] In a footnote he continues: 'This, of course, does not prejudge their admissibility: thus, Art. 48 of the Reich Constitution authorizes "measures" that owing to their individual nature do not bear the character of law.'[78] This stands in sharp contrast to Hans Kelsen's Pure Theory of Law, according to which the process of interpretation of the constitution and of general norms culminates in individual norms.[79] It is far from clear that Radbruch was prepared to extend this particular construction of 'valid non-law' to general norms of positive law that call for extreme discrimination.[80]

Neumann's thesis leads to the inevitable assumption that a judge, according to Radbruch in 1932, was under an obligation to apply norms of positive law, even if the judge had correctly established that these norms lack legal character. The paradox that emerges here is the supposed obligation of judges to enforce 'valid non-law' ('measures' that lack legal character but have legal validity), whereas we usually assume that judges are committed to enforcing only valid law. Why should there be a legal obligation on the part of the judge to enforce 'valid non-law' if it is *clear* that the statute in question is not a 'reality whose meaning is to serve justice',[81] if it is by definition a factual rather than a legal phenomenon? This reconstruction is hardly plausible.[82]

These considerations suggest that there is no convincing reason why Radbruch had denied judges the power to forbear from applying statutes that called for extreme discrimination. At that time, Radbruch had no reason to expect that the National Socialist regime would later carry out the most extreme forms of discrimination in modern history.[83]

[77] Radbruch [1932]1950: 110, trans. amended.

[78] Radbruch [1932]1950: 110 n. 7, trans. amended (translator's notes omitted). See also Radbruch [1932]1950: 76.

[79] See Kelsen 1992: 67–70; Kelsen 1945: 134–42; Kelsen 1967: 232–67.

[80] Borowski 2015: 256.

[81] Radbruch [1932]1950: 75, trans. altered following Paulson 2006: 19.

[82] Neumann argues that Radbruch's theory actually has two different concepts of law: one philosophical, the other juridical; Neumann 2015: 142. That is true. There is, however, a 'programmatical congruence' between these two concepts; R. Dreier 2015: 195. Thus, there is hardly any textual evidence suggesting that Radbruch's theory boasts of a 'concept of law in its wide sense' that would require the judge to enforce norms that lack legal character according to a 'concept of law in its narrow sense' but are legally valid.

[83] See Paulson 2015: 182; Borowski 2015: 259.

27.5.2.5 Conclusion

If one assumes that Radbruch, in 1932, was prepared to grant to judges the power to forbear from applying positive law that lacks legal character, his position at that time is identical to the later non-positivistic position that he expresses with the disavowal formula.[84] The situation is less clear if one follows Neumann. Strictly speaking, even on this reading, the judge looks to morality for the identification of valid legal norms, for a statute that has the qualified moral defect of disavowing equality is refused the status of 'law' – this, too, counts as non-positivism with respect to the criteria for the identification of valid law, even though, according to Neumann, this lacks practical consequences.

27.5.3 The Necessary Connection between Law and Morality Established by Radbruch's Basal Criterion

Radbruch's basal criterion presupposes a necessary connection between law and morality from the very outset:

> Law can be understood only within the framework of the value-relating point of view. Law is a cultural phenomenon, that is, a fact related to value. The concept of law can be determined only as something given, the meaning of which is to realize the idea of law. Law may be unjust (*summum jus – summa injuria*), but it is law only because its meaning is to be just.[85]

A reality – a statute, authoritatively issued and socially effective – can be understood as 'law' only if it has the 'meaning to serve justice'. Law, 'as the very means for the realization of moral values[,] . . . partakes of the worthiness of its end'.[86] The 'value-relating point of view',[87] the idea that law is a means for moral ends along with Radbruch's emphasis on legal certainty, echoes Kant's moral obligation with his transition from the state of nature to the civic state, carried out by subjecting the individual to the law.[88] In his legal philosophy, Kant assumes the strict priority of positive law over moral considerations.[89] There is a debate as to whether this creates tension with Kant's moral philosophy, which may call for an interpretation

[84] See Section 27.4.2.2.
[85] Radbruch [1932] 1950: 52, trans. altered (emphasis in the original), note omitted.
[86] Radbruch [1932] 1950: 87.
[87] On Radbruch's 'value-relating point of view', see Paulson 2006: 29.
[88] Kant 1999: 116. [89] See, e.g., Kant 1996: 253.

according to which moral considerations can outweigh legal certainty in extreme cases.[90] Leaving this debate aside, one may ask whether Kant's thesis of a strict priority of positive law over moral considerations implies a positivistic position. According to Jeremy Waldron, Kant supports 'normative positivism'.[91] It is true that Kant argues against the very idea of making the identification of valid law depend on the moral correctness of positive law, which, *ceteris paribus*, would render his theory positivistic with respect to the criteria for the identification of valid law. If, however, one focuses on the necessary connection between law and morality established by the moral purpose of the law, this positivism turns out to be 'truncated non-positivism'.[92] Alexy claims that a position such as Kant's is non-positivistic in nature, owing to the qualifying connection that is established by the law's claim to correctness, and he terms such a position 'superinclusive non-positivism'.[93] This is to say that there is a necessary connection between law and morality even if a positivistic element acts with respect to the criteria for the identification of valid law.

Alexy grants that the law's claim to correctness and Radbruch's basal criterion have much in common,[94] and this prompts the suggestion that Radbruch's basal criterion implies a necessary connection between law and morality, independently of positivism and non-positivism with respect to the criteria for the identification of valid law. What is more, Radbruch places much emphasis on legal certainty, which counts as an argument *against* moral criteria for the identification of valid law. In 1932, legal certainty definitively outweighs substantive moral correctness in the theory of legal validity from the standpoint of the judge, whereas from 1946 on, legal certainty outweighs – from the standpoints of both the judge and the citizen – substantive moral correctness in all cases except those of extreme injustice. It is telling that Radbruch granted throughout all his periods of work that legal certainty is actually a requirement of justice.[95] This is to say that legal certainty is itself a moral value.[96] It is an argument on behalf of a positivistic set of criteria for the identification of valid law, but it is called for by Radbruch's basal

[90] See, e.g., R. Dreier 1981: 93; Alexy 2002: 120–1. [91] Waldron 1996: 1540–1.

[92] See Borowski 2018: 107: '*kupierter Nichtpositivismus*'. [93] Alexy 2008: 289–90.

[94] See Alexy 2002: 34 n. 64; Alexy 2018: 239–42.

[95] See Radbruch [1914]1933: 172, 183 (RGA 2: 162, 174); Radbruch [1932]1950: 108; Radbruch 1948: 30 (RGA vol. 3: 150).

[96] See, e.g., Spaak 2009: 270.

criterion, which presupposes, in and of itself, a necessary connection between law and morality.[97]

27.5.4 The Result

Radbruch's basal criterion, the idea of law as a 'reality whose meaning is to serve justice',[98] presupposes a necessary connection between law and morality. Radbruch's concept of law – the criteria for the identification of the legal character of norms – was fully developed in his second period (1924–32) and did not change after World War II. The only element that clearly changed was his theory of legal validity. To be sure, even his dual theory of legal validity had a non-positivistic dimension from the standpoint of the citizen. Owing to these non-positivistic elements of Radbruch's legal philosophy in 1932, his post-war articles cannot be seen as expressing a conversion from positivism to non-positivism. His legal philosophy never was positivistic in the modern sense, the sense of legal positivism qua separation thesis.

27.6 Radbruch's Explicit Criticism of Legal Positivism

Throughout all his periods, Radbruch explicitly criticised legal positivism. It might seem tempting from the standpoint of the thesis of non-positivistic continuity[99] to use this fact as an argument – how could Radbruch be classified as a legal positivist in 1932 if he criticised legal positivism at that time? To be sure, the modern distinction between positivism and non-positivism along the lines of the separation and connection theses was unknown in Germany during the first half of the twentieth century.[100] Radbruch used the term 'positivism' with two different readings, that of 'naturalism' and that of 'statutory positivism'.

27.6.1 Legal Positivism as Naturalism

Radbruch's initial criticism of legal positivism identifies it with naturalism. This criticism began early in the first period, at the beginning of his first

[97] See Borowski 2018: 105–6.
[98] Radbruch [1932]1950: 75, trans. altered following Paulson 2006: 19.
[99] See Section 27.3. [100] See, e.g., Paulson 2008: 107.

period in Heidelberg, in 1905,[101] and can also be found in *Outlines of Legal Philosophy* of 1914,[102] the Kiel lectures of 1919[103] and in his *Legal Philosophy* of 1932.[104] Radbruch criticises rather different versions of naturalism, for they are not compatible with the dualism of 'is' and 'ought' that he supported throughout.[105] Purporting to derive an 'ought' from an 'is' counts as the naturalistic fallacy: 'Statements concerning the *Sollen* or the "ought" may be established or proved only by other statements concerning the *Sollen* or the "ought".'[106] Notwithstanding Kelsen's elaborate reconstruction in order to avoid the naturalistic fallacy, Radbruch classified the Pure Theory of Law as still another instance of positivism qua naturalism. To be sure, this is hardly convincing.[107] But the important point lies elsewhere. Legal positivism as naturalism cannot be reconciled with Radbruch's basal criterion and the 'value-relating point of view'[108] on which it is based.

27.6.2 Statutory Positivism or *Gesetzespositivismus*

According to statutory positivism, the law is said to be identical with, and exhausted by, statutes. In the most thoroughgoing form of statutory positivism, statutes have no gaps, no open texture, and there is no other source of law.[109] Scarcely any author supported statutory positivism in this most thoroughgoing form, but there were more than a few who went quite far in this direction. This applies also to Radbruch with his *doctrine of judicial bindingness*[110] – the thesis, from 1932, that the judge is strictly bound by statutory law. This doctrine, however, clearly falls short of the most thoroughgoing form of statutory positivism.[111] Radbruch accepts customary law,[112] and the fact that statutes inevitably have gaps means that judges have to fill these gaps by means of a teleological method, which gives them a creative role.[113] The basal criterion is the key not only in identifying law but also in interpreting law:

[101] See Paulson 2006: 108 with further references.
[102] Radbruch [1914]1993: 14–18 (RGA vol. 2: 34–6). [103] See Radbruch 2003: 33.
[104] Radbruch [1932]1950: 111. [105] See, e.g., Radbruch [1932]1950: 53–5.
[106] Radbruch [1932]1950: 55. [107] See Paulson 2008: 110–11 with further references.
[108] Radbruch [1932]1950: 50, trans. amended. [109] See Schröder 2005: 572.
[110] See Paulson 2006: 36. [111] See Paulson 2008: 115.
[112] See Radbruch [1932]1950: 87.
[113] See, e.g., Radbruch [1914]1993: 190–4; Radbruch [1932]1950: 142–8; Radbruch 1948: 75–9 (RGA vol. 3: 193–7).

To understand means to apprehend a cultural phenomenon precisely as a cultural one, that is in its relation to the corresponding cultural value . . . Thus, legal interpretation, in particular, means: To embrace the law as a realization of the concept of law, i.e., as an entity, whose meaning is to realize the idea of law, i.e. an attempt at realizing the idea of law.[114]

The creative role is emphasised in the following passage on legal interpretation: 'It passes by imperceptible steps from interpretation in the spirit of the legislator to rules which the interpreter himself "would lay down as a legislator".'[115] Radbruch's theory of legal interpretation makes clear why he had to criticise 'statutory positivism',[116] which, in its most consequent form, would have us believe that statutes have no open texture and judges no creative role in the penumbra of doubt.

27.7 The Positivism Legend

Shortly after World War II, Radbruch raised a particularly controversial claim in his article 'Statutory Lawlessness and Supra-Statutory Law': 'Positivism, with its principle that "a law is a law", has in fact rendered the German legal profession defenseless against statutes that are arbitrary and criminal.'[117] This is repeated in *The Statute and the Law* of 1947:

'The statute and the law', in this phrase we believed we had said the same thing with two expressions. Every statute was law to us and every law statute, legal science was nothing other than the interpretation of the statute and adjudication exclusively the application of statutes. We called ourselves positivists, and positivism, regarding the statute alone as law, counts as the blame that German legal science has to bear for the state of the law during the years of National Socialism.[118]

The claim that Radbruch himself was a positivist before the war is surprising – on all readings of 'positivism'. With 'a law is a law' and '"[t]he statute and the law", with this phrase we believed we had said the same thing with two expressions', he is obviously referring to 'statutory positivism' rather than to 'legal positivism' in the sense of the modern separation thesis. The only element of his own theory that points in the direction of 'statutory positivism'

[114] Radbruch [1932]1950: 146–7, trans. amended. [115] Radbruch [1932]1950: 142.
[116] Radbruch 2003: 33; Radbruch 1948: 75–9 (RGA vol. 3: 193–7).
[117] Radbruch 2006b: 6. [118] Radbruch 1947: 5 (RGA vol. 3: 96).

is the doctrine of judicial bindingness already mentioned. This 'bindingness' is precisely the element of his theory that he changed.[119] And Radbruch had in fact criticised 'statutory positivism'.[120] Paulson speculates that, by including himself among those Germans who had to bear some blame by not resisting the National Socialist regime more decisively, Radbruch hoped to be taken seriously in his country, paving the way for a new beginning.[121] That he identified his own earlier theory with statutory positivism may well also count as an expression of the 'survivor-guilt-syndrome' – Radbruch surviving relatively unharmed, while many others had lost their lives. In 1946 and 1947, the horrors of the former regime had become fully apparent. It is not without reason that Radbruch would emphasise how much the experience of the unfathomable immorality of the National Socialists had influenced him.[122]

It has correctly been pointed out that the ostensibly empirical claim of the 'positivism legend', the claim that the National Socialists relied on the binding nature of statutes, is historically simply false. Of course, there were some notorious, morally outrageous statutes. Often, however, the regime pursued its aims by interpreting blanket clauses in the spirit of the new ideology or even with *contra legem* interpretations of statutes.[123]

27.8 Conclusion

Radbruch explicitly criticised legal positivism in the sense of naturalism and statutory positivism throughout his career. The most important criticism of legal positivism in the sense of the modern separation thesis is, however, his very own legal philosophy, in which he argues on behalf of different necessary connections between law and morality.

[119] See Section 27.5.1. [120] See Section 27.6.2. [121] See Paulson 2015: 179.

[122] See Radbruch 1999: 193 (RGA vol. 20: 25).

[123] See, e.g., Müller 1991: 219–34; Paulson 2006: 33–5; H. Dreier 2015: 10–12. Surprisingly, in s. 26 on the free law movement in the *Primer in Legal Philosophy* of 1948, Radbruch seems to be perfectly aware that the National Socialist regime systematically resorted to *contra legem* interpretations of statutes in pursuit of their aims; Radbruch 1948: 79 (RGA vol. 3: 196–7), which is difficult to reconcile with the ostensibly empirical claim of the positivism legend.

References

Alexy, R. 1992. *Begriff und Geltung des Rechts*. Alber.

Alexy, R. 1997. *Der Beschluß des Bundesverfassungsgerichts zu den Tötungen an der innerdeutschen Grenze vom 24. Oktober 1996*. Jungius.

Alexy, R. 1999. 'A Defence of Radbruch's Formula'. In D. Dyzenhaus (ed.). *Recrafting the Rule of Law: The Limits of Legal Order*. Hart: 15–39.

Alexy, R. 2002. *The Argument from Injustice: A Reply to Legal Positivism*. Trans. B. Litschewski Paulson and S. L. Paulson. Clarendon Press.

Alexy, R. 2008. 'On the Nature and the Concept of Law'. *Ratio Juris* 21: 281–99.

Alexy, R. 2018. 'Gustav Radbruchs Rechtsbegriff'. In A. von Arnauld, I. Augsberg and R. Meyer-Pritzl (eds.). *350 Jahre Rechtswissenschaftliche Fakultät der Christian-Albrechts-Universität zu Kiel*. Mohr Siebeck: 237–49.

Baratta, A. 1959. 'Relativismus und Naturrecht im Denken Gustav Radbruchs'. *Archives for Philosophy of Law and Social Philosophy* 45: 505–37.

Bix, B. 2011. 'Radbruch's Formula and Conceptual Analysis'. *American Journal of Jurisprudence* 56: 45–57.

Borowski, M. 2015. 'Begriff und Geltung des Rechts bei Gustav Radbruch'. In M. Borowski and S. L. Paulson (eds.). *Die Natur des Rechts bei Gustav Radbruch*. Mohr Siebeck: 229–65.

Borowski, M. 2018. *Grundrechte als Prinzipien*. 3rd ed. Nomos.

Borowski, M. 2019. 'Radbruch's Formula and Human Rights'. In M. La Torre, L. Niglia and M. Susi (eds.). *The Quest for Rights*. Edward Elgar: 27–48.

Dreier, H. 1997. 'Gustav Radbruch und die Mauerschützen'. *Juristenzeitung* 52: 421–34.

Dreier, H. 2015. 'Die Radbruchsche Formel – Erkenntnis oder Bekenntnis?'. In M. Borowski and S. L. Paulson (eds.). *Die Natur des Rechts bei Gustav Radbruch*. Mohr Siebeck: 1–22.

Dreier, R. 1981. 'Bemerkungen zur Rechtserkenntnistheorie'. In A. Aarnio, I. Niiniluoto and J. Uusitalo (eds.). *Methodologie und Erkenntnistheorie der juristischen Argumentation*. Duncker & Humblot: 89–105.

Dreier, R. 1993. 'Gesetzliches Unrecht im SED-Staat? Am Beispiel des DDR-Grenzgesetzes'. In F. Haft et al. (eds.). *Strafgerechtigkeit. Festschrift für Arthur Kaufmann*. C.F. Müller: 57–92.

Dreier, R. 2011. 'Gustav Radbruchs Rechtsbegriff'. In M. Mahlmann (ed.). *Gesellschaft und Gerechtigkeit. Festschrift für Hubert Rottleuthner*. Nomos: 17–44.

Dreier, R. 2015. 'Kontinuitäten und Diskontinuitäten in der Rechtsphilosophie Radbruchs'. In M. Borowski and S. L. Paulson (eds.). *Die Natur des Rechts bei Gustav Radbruch*. Mohr Siebeck: 183–228.

Dyzenhaus, D. 2010. *Hard Cases in Wicked Legal Systems*. 2nd ed. Oxford University Press.

Engisch, K. 1949–50. 'Gustav Radbruch als Rechtsphilosoph'. *Archives for Philosophy of Law and Social Philosophy* 38: 305–16.

Evers, H.-U. 1956. *Der Richter und das unsittliche Gesetz*. De Gruyter.
Funke, A. 2003. 'Überlegungen zu Gustav Radbruchs "Verleugnungsformel"'. *Archives for Philosophy of Law and Social Philosophy* 89: 1–16.
Haldemann, F. 2005. 'Gustav Radbruch vs. Hans Kelsen: A Debate on Nazi Law'. *Ratio Juris* 18: 162–78.
Hart, H. L. A. 1958. 'Positivism and the Separation of Law and Morals'. *Harvard Law Review* 74: 593–625.
Hoerster, N. 2006. *Was ist Recht?* C.H. Beck.
Kant, I. 1996. 'The Conflict of the Faculties'. Trans. M. J. Gregor and R. Anchor. In A. W. Wood, G. di Giovanni and I. Kant (eds.). *Religion and Rational Theology*. Cambridge University Press: 233–327.
Kant, I. [1797]1999. *Metaphysical Elements of Justice*. First part of the *Metaphysics of Morals*. Trans. J. Ladd. 2nd ed. Hackett.
Kelsen, H. 1945. *General Theory of Law and State*. Trans. A. Wedberg. Harvard University Press.
Kelsen, H. [1961]1967. *Pure Theory of Law*. Trans. M. Knight. University of California Press.
Kelsen, H. [1934]1992. *Introduction to the Problems of Legal Theory*. Trans. B. Litschewski Paulson and S. L. Paulson. Clarendon Press.
Müller, I. 1991. *Hitler's Justice: The Courts of the Third Reich*. Harvard University Press.
Neumann, U. 2007. 'Naturrecht und Positivismus im Denken Gustav Radbruchs. Kontinuitäten und Diskontinuitäten'. In W. Härle and B. Vogel (eds.). *Vom Rechte, das mit uns geboren ist. Aktuelle Probleme des Naturrechts*. Herder: 11–32.
Neumann, U. 2015. 'Zum Verhältnis von Rechtsgeltung und Rechtsbegriff'. In M. Borowski and S. L. Paulson (eds.). *Die Natur des Rechts bei Gustav Radbruch*. Mohr Siebeck: 129–49.
Paulson, S. L. 2006. 'On the Background and Significance of Gustav Radbruch's Post-War Papers'. *Oxford Journal of Legal Studies* 26: 17–40.
Paulson, S. L. 2008. 'Ein ewiger Mythos: Gustav Radbruch als Rechtspositivist'. *Juristenzeitung* 63: 105–15.
Paulson, S. L. 2015. 'Zur Kontinuität der nichtpositivistischen Rechtsphilosophie Gustav Radbruchs'. In M. Borowski and S. L. Paulson (eds.). *Die Natur des Rechts bei Gustav Radbruch*. Mohr Siebeck: 151–82.
Radbruch, G. [1914]1993 (RGA vol. 2). *Grundzüge der Rechtsphilosophie*. Quelle & Meyer. Reprinted in A. Kaufmann and G. Radbruch (eds.). *Gesamtausgabe* or Collected Works vol. 2: Rechtsphilosophie II. C.F. Müller: 9–204.
Radbruch, G. 1924. 'Die Problematik der Rechtsidee'. *Die Dioskuren. Jahrbuch für Geisteswissenschaften* 3: 43–50. Reprinted in RGA vol. 2: 460–7.
Radbruch, G. [1932]1973. *Rechtsphilosophie*. Eds. E. Wolf and H.-P. Schneider. 8th ed. Koehler. Reprinted in RGA vol. 2: 206–450.
Radbruch, G. [1932]1950. 'Legal Philosophy'. Trans. K. Wilk. In K. Wilk (ed.). *The Legal Philosophies of Lask, Radbruch, and Dabin*. Harvard University Press: 47–224.

Radbruch, G. 1934. 'Le Relativisme dans la Philosophie du Droit'. *Archives de Philosophie du Droit et de Sociologie Juridique* 4: 105–10.

Radbruch, G. 1937–8. 'Le But du Droit'. *Annuaire de l'Institut de Philosophie du Droit et de Sociologie*: 48–59.

Radbruch, G. 1945. 'Fünf Minuten Rechtsphilosophie'. *Rhein-Neckar-Zeitung* from 12 September. Reprinted in RGA vol. 3: 78–9.

Radbruch, G. 1946. 'Gesetzliches Unrecht und übergesetzliches Recht'. *Süddeutsche Juristenzeitung* 1: 105–8. Reprinted in RGA vol. 3: 83–93.

Radbruch, G. 1947. 'Gesetz und Recht'. *Stuttgarter Rundschau* January: 5–6. Reprinted in RGA vol. 3: 96–100.

Radbruch, G. 1948. *Vorschule der Rechtsphilosophie*. H. Schubert and J. Stoltzenburg (eds.). Scherer. Reprinted in RGA vol. 3: 121–227.

Radbruch, G. [1934]1957. 'Der Relativismus in der Rechtsphilosophie'. In G. Radbruch. *Der Mensch im Recht*. Vandenhoeck & Ruprecht: 80–7. Reprinted in RGA vol. 3: 17–22.

Radbruch, G. [1937]1957. 'Der Zweck des Rechts'. In G. Radbruch. *Der Mensch im Recht*. Vandenhoeck & Ruprecht: 88–104. Reprinted in RGA vol. 3: 39–50.

Radbruch, G. 1999. 'Nachwort-Entwurf'. In R. Dreier and S. L. Paulson (eds.). *Rechtsphilosophie. Studienausgabe*. C.F. Müller: 193–208. Reprinted in RGA vol. 2: 25–39.

Radbruch, G. 2003. *Rechtsphilosophische Tagesfragen*. Eds. H. Adachi and N. Teifke. Nomos.

Radbruch, G. 2006a. 'Five Minutes of Legal Philosophy'. Trans. B. Litschewski Paulson and S. L. Paulson. *Oxford Journal of Legal Studies* 26: 13–15.

Radbruch, G. 2006b. 'Statutory Lawlessness and Supra-Statutory Law'. Trans. B. Litschewski Paulson and S.L. Paulson. *Oxford Journal of Legal Studies* 26: 1–11.

Schröder, J. 2005. 'Gab es im deutschen Kaiserreich einen Gesetzespositivismus?'. In W. Baumann et al. (eds.). *Gesetz, Recht, Rechtsgeschichte. Festschrift für Gerhard Otte*. Sellier: 571–9.

Seidel, K. 1999. *Rechtsphilosophische Aspekte der 'Mauerschützen'-Prozesse*. Duncker & Humblot.

Spaak, T. 2009. 'Meta-ethics and Legal Theory: The Case of Gustav Radbruch'. *Law and Philosophy* 28: 261–90.

Waldron, J. 1996. 'Kant's Legal Positivism'. *Harvard Law Review* 109: 1535–66.

Wiegandt, M.-A. 2004. *Unrichtiges Recht*. Mohr Siebeck.

Good Order and Workable Arrangements: Lon Fuller's Critique of Legal Positivism 28

Kenneth Winston*

28.1 Introduction

Lon Fuller was a dialectical thinker. This temper is evident in his penchant for setting forth contrasting polarities – ideal and real, duty and aspiration, reason and fiat, freedom and planning – and exploring each side for the truth it contains. As a result, it is often difficult to pin him down as definitely affirming one or another doctrine or principle. Yet, against legal positivism, Fuller carried on a lifelong crusade.

Fuller had his own understanding of legal positivism and of what it implies, an understanding that aligns only in part with the contemporary literature. From Fuller's perspective, recent debates have constricted jurisprudential inquiry mainly to semantic or conceptual questions, and consequently lost sight of the core issues in political philosophy essential for grasping the place of law in a larger social order. In this chapter, I will be guided by Fuller's understanding, assisted by materials recently available in the Harvard Law School archives, as well as books and papers from Fuller's personal library.

In some writings, Fuller highlighted an *analytic* claim about the distinction between fact and value. Unlike many non-positivists, however, he was not inclined to make concepts do a lot of moral work – a difference that led to several fruitless exchanges with analytic philosophers for whom conceptual questions were primary. Fuller was, rather, mainly preoccupied by *methodological* and *governance* issues, in particular the adequacy of a scientific approach to understanding human society and a proper account of the purpose of legal ordering in civic life. Many legal positivists were of the view that the universe is governed by deterministic laws discoverable

* An early, longer draft was posted on SSRN, abstract #3165562. For written comments, I am indebted to Charles L. Barzun, Amy J. Cohen, Mark J. Osiel, Stanley L. Paulson, Torben Spaak and Kenneth P. Winkler.

by science, and that these laws apply to human life. Fuller saw implications in this view for jurisprudence – and *other* social sciences – which he felt duty-bound to challenge. For, if legal order is a moral endeavour, as he believed, it requires a conception of human beings as responsible agents, capable of purposive, self-directed, order-creating activity – a conception that positivists, either consciously or by implication, sought to undermine or deny.

Hence, the importance of the crusade.

28.2 Fact and Value

In its simplest version, legal positivism is distinguished by the separation of fact and value: what the law is and what it ought to be. Fuller discusses this analytic claim at length in *The Law in Quest of Itself* [hereafter *Quest*], which was his most sustained polemic against positivism.[1]

It is possible to argue that Fuller did not mean to deny the *distinction* between fact and value, only their separation. *Separation* is, indeed, the word he commonly uses. In *Quest*, for example, he says that the positivist's error lies 'in assuming that the taking of a distinction implies a kind of permanent bisection of the subject matter'.[2] In subsequent pages, the permanent bisection becomes a 'rigorous separation'.[3] Thus, recognising a distinction between fact and value is conceptual, while separating them is an activity, the work of an individual in making a decision or as part of an inquiry – specifically, the act of bracketing or setting value aside. Why would Fuller focus on the activity of separating, in contrast to the conceptual distinction? Where would separation be a source of mischief? Most obviously, in the decisions of judges.

Fuller spoke to this issue in exchanges with several prominent philosophers in the fifties, although unfortunately they argued almost completely at cross-purposes. The philosophers focused mainly on semantic or ontological issues, whereas Fuller attempted to stake out a claim about the duties of officials in legal institutions. In a letter to Samuel Mermin, he observes that 'the issue before [Ernest] Nagel and me was whether there is something that can be called "the collaborative articulation of shared purposes" – a process by which men by discussion can arrive at a better

[1] See Fuller 1940/1966. [2] Fuller 1940/1966: 58. [3] For example, Fuller 1940/1966: 60.

collective conception of both means and ends'.[4] This is a remarkable characterisation of a debate that appeared (to others) to be about *is* and *ought* – and whether *purpose* somehow brings about a fusion of the two.

What Fuller had in mind was a practical and professional question: Should a judge in the field of private law take as a model Holmes or Cardozo, Eldon or Mansfield?[5] This is what divides positivists and natural lawyers, he says. The first of each pair adopts a posture of deference to other officials as their primary duty and avoids what the other side calls legislating from the bench; the second adopts a more productive role and improves existing law while transmitting it. The blending of application and improvement is a blending of *is* and *ought.* Fuller consistently describes natural law judges as creative; they penetrate the 'face value' of precedents and statutes to get to 'underlying realities'. Positivist judges, instead, stick to the surface of the law, draw out the 'logical implications' of precedent and statute, and truncate inquiry into underlying purposes.[6] A straightforward example of 'collaborative articulation' would be judicial probing of legislative intent, when the text of a statute is uncertain. Rather than relying on their own judgement, judges attempt to determine what the legislators were trying to do. Think of it as constrained creativity. More paradigmatically, Fuller had in mind the collaborative activity of common law judges – colleagues in the shared enterprise of adapting the law to the needs of a new day and helping it to 'work itself pure'.[7]

Fuller formulates the same practical question for other legal professionals. Should a lawyer argue the rights of a client under existing rules, or the rightness of the client's case as a matter of justice? Should a legal scholar construct a theory to support decisions by judges who are too busy to explain themselves, or should the scholar 'anticipate the future by giving legal form to emergent ethical values'? This emphasis on addressing questions about professional obligation is characteristic of Fuller's writing as a whole. The point here is that Fuller offers these choices as illustrations of separating or, alternatively, merging *is* and *ought.*

To be sure, Fuller sometimes denies the analytic distinction altogether, not only the separation. As early as *Legal Fictions* (1930–1), he says 'there

[4] Letter to Samuel Mermin, 30 November 1959. [5] See Fuller 1940/1966: 12.

[6] See Fuller 1939: 12–13. In *Quest*, Fuller says that the judge 'ought to be proud that his contribution is such that it cannot be said with certainty whether it is something new or only the better telling of an old story'. Fuller 1940/1966: 140.

[7] Fuller 1940/1966: 114, 140.

is no such thing as a plain, brute "fact"'.[8] Nearly twenty years later, he attributes to 'the insights of [William] James and [John] Dewey' our ability to see the fallacy in the idea of 'a kind of pure fact of law'.[9] And in his personal copy of Richard von Mises's *Positivism*, Fuller put brackets around an epigraph from Goethe: 'Das Hochste ware zu begreifen, dass alles Faktische schon Theorie ist. The highest achievement would be to grasp that whatever we call a "fact" is already theory.'[10]

However, if there are no plain facts – no *pure fact* of law, no *law that is* – then positivism itself must be incoherent. That indeed was Fuller's view, but, importantly, this claim does not require a general denial of the fact/value distinction. At least, Fuller offers a different and more satisfactory way to support the claim of incoherence. Rather than worrying about a metaphysical dualism between *is* and *ought*, he takes note of how legal theorists employ moral criteria to identify an institutional arrangement as a legal system. He notes, for example, Hans Kelsen's reason for excluding considerations of justice from his 'pure theory' – namely, that justice (like other moral values) is an ideal without rational content. *Order*, on the other hand, is an object of cognition, which Kelsen regards as attainable by rational and purposive action. But Fuller asks: Is not order also an ideal? After all, Kelsen is willing to talk about legal order as bringing peace, security and certainty.[11] In another letter to Mermin, Fuller writes: 'When we talk about law as opposed to justice, we do not really have a datum on one side and an ideal on the other, but one ideal pitted against another . . . . [T]he ideal or goal or thing-to-be-aimed-at indicated by the word law [is order].' Fuller concludes: 'Law, considered merely as order, contains, then, its own implicit morality.'[12]

Fuller was aware that the argument is generalisable; it does not depend on Kelsen's peculiar view of the subjectivity (or cognitive emptiness) of morals. Different positivists offer different reasons for excluding morality, while including order as an ideal. In John Austin's case, it is his fear of 'disorder and disintegration', combined with his belief in the 'uncertainty, scantiness, and imperfection' of the moral rules that people generally espouse.[13] Fuller observed the same dynamic at work in H. L. A. Hart, as

[8] Fuller 1930–1/1967: 134. [9] Fuller 1949a: 503 n. 6. [10] Von Mises 1951: 101.
[11] Fuller 1940/1966: 85 nn. 90–1.
[12] Fuller 1958: 645. Letter to Mermin, 22 November 1950.
[13] See Fuller 1949b: 110. On Austin's fear of disorder, see Winston 1999: 56–8.

well, because, despite his professed aim of doing descriptive sociology, Hart deploys an ideal conception in articulating what it means for a legal order to exist. Roughly, it goes like this. For a legal order to exist, it must be efficacious, and it cannot be efficacious unless it is possible to provide determinate answers to legal subjects regarding their legal obligations – or at least to identify determinate persons with the authority to decide these questions. Thus, contrary to appearances, the judgment that a legal order exists is not a straightforward factual statement but a tacit appraisal of the capacity of a set of institutional arrangements to serve the required aim of determinateness. It is an evaluative judgment.[14]

Now, if positivism, too, sees an intimate connection between law and morality, what is the debate about? The obvious answer is that it centres on which ideal should take priority. Positivists value peace, order and certainty, while non-positivists insist on a more demanding ideal such as justice, freedom or human flourishing. Thus, the debate is about not simply comprehending the world but also shaping it. Legal inquiry is not purely descriptive but is constructive and evaluative. In more general terms, the human mind is not a passive register of pre-existing patterns but reconstructs a pliable reality to suit human purposes. This pragmatic – active, constructive – conception of human agency indicates how Fuller responded to the threat of scientific determinism. In moving to this topic, we do not leave the fact/value debate behind, but we get to what Fuller regarded as legal positivism 'in a more exact sense' –[15] an approach that examines legal phenomena in factual terms, in abstraction from human purpose, and aims to predict and control human events.

28.3 Positivism and (Social) Science

In the nineteenth and early twentieth centuries, it was common to speak of law as a science. The term has a long history in Anglo-American thought, but it was re-invigorated by university educators such as Christopher Langdell of Harvard, who argued for the value of a law degree by touting the superiority of academic training over apprenticeship in a law office as a route to success in legal practice. What was learned in a law office, Langdell said, could never be more than 'a species of handicraft', whereas

[14] See Winston 1988: 334–6. [15] Fuller 1970: vol. 13, 149.

university study could provide mastery of 'one of the greatest and most difficult of sciences'. Langdell's ambition was to give Harvard Law School the stature 'occupied by the law faculties in the universities of continental Europe', albeit without adopting their methods or state-centred orientation. Langdell shared the aspiration of contemporaneous European scholars to articulate universal principles of law, but by deriving these principles from common law cases (from the bottom up, as it were), rather than, as in the civil law tradition, from theoretical studies (top down).[16]

On both sides of the Atlantic, science was understood in broad terms. It had to do with the classification and arrangement of the whole body of legal materials, and the formulation of general principles and doctrines from which specific rules or decisions in particular cases could be derived. The focus was on method, and the goal was to make legal argument systematic, while isolating it from other academic disciplines. Langdell's vision was distinctly positivist. The task of the legal scholar is to locate the records of past judicial decisions within a domain (say, contracts) and assemble them in a treatise, thereby displaying distinct knowledge of *what the law is*. The assumption is that 'existing law' is sufficiently clear and consistent to be capable of an intelligible presentation, with an organisation that is somehow inherent in the materials. No intrusion by the scholar of social, ethical, philosophical or policy considerations is permitted, and it is taken for granted that none is needed.[17]

From the beginning of his career, Fuller resisted this model. The importance of jurisprudence – and its superiority over other social sciences – lies precisely in the practical experience (the 'handicraft') and the moral concerns that lawyers possess (and other social scientists lack), which Fuller believed should inform the whole field of legal studies. He believed, for example, that even the simplest problem of contract or tort law contains implicit within it issues concerning the place of law in society and the ethics of human conduct.[18] Taking up his anti-positivist crusade, he devoted several decades to making the case for the special status of jurisprudence.

In *Legal Fictions*, his first significant work, Fuller quotes with approval Karl Wurzel's assertion that jurisprudence is the first of the social sciences: 'Of all men, judges and legislators were the first that found themselves

[16] Langdell's words are quoted by Chase 1982: 23–46. [17] See Fuller 1939: 7–15.
[18] See Fuller 1949a: 500, 506.

compelled to seek a clear and conscious knowledge of the principles according to which human beings live together.'[19] In his own words, Fuller says: 'Indeed, the courts were compelled to investigate the successions and interrelations of social life long before the disciplines of sociology, economics, psychology, political science, and anthropology were pursued as separate studies.'[20] Here, Fuller gestures to the fact that, before the social sciences became distinct disciplines, the fields of natural jurisprudence, moral philosophy and political economy were closely intertwined. When the various 'separate studies' emerged in the nineteenth century, they challenged the status of jurisprudence. Could jurisprudence sustain itself any longer as an autonomous discipline? Indeed, do we need jurisprudence once these other sciences are available? Fuller's answer is yes, because these 'separate studies' – the 'other' social sciences – have a fatal weakness in helping us understand 'the principles according to which human beings live together'. What is the weakness? Crucially, they purge themselves of the concerns that are at the heart of legal ordering. They omit any reference to human purposes, fail to attend to natural laws of organisation (which involve the interplay of means and ends) and orient their students towards governance by means of legislation and bureaucracy. In the US context: 'American legal science gives evidence that it is on the verge of making an orthodoxy of the sterile and uninspired behavioristic philosophy which has worked such havoc in the other social sciences.'[21] This is a weighty indictment, and we will examine its parts as we proceed.

Fuller concedes that the advance of our knowledge of nature was accompanied by a gradual emancipation from anthropomorphic concepts. The crucial move was asking *how* things happen rather than *why* they happen – what Bertrand Russell refers to as 'the dethronement of purpose'. 'This idea', Friedrich Hayek observes, 'was later to become the leading theme of positivism and was ultimately misapplied to the science of man himself'.[22] Hayek's concern, like Fuller's, was the 'illegitimate extension to the phenomena of society of scientistic methods of thought'.[23] This extension begins in the nineteenth century, especially with the ambition of Auguste Comte to create an empirically grounded science of society in which moral and political questions would be subject to scientific determination. Comte advocated a rational approach to social problems

[19] Fuller 1930–1/1967: 131–2. [20] Ibid. [21] Fuller 1934: 443. [22] Hayek 1952: 106–7.
[23] Ibid. On page 106, Fuller wrote in the margin: 'Good on what is positivism'.

modelled on the natural sciences, with the aim of material and spiritual improvement. Of course, Fuller and Hayek were not pioneers in attacking scientism. As early as 1887, John Dewey warned that the physical interpretation of the universe 'necessarily shuts out those ideas and principles which are fundamental to ethics'. Dewey identifies three features of moral action that are 'incongruous and contradictory' to a purely physical philosophy: '(1) activity for an end, that which has a purpose or aim, in technical phrase teleological action; (2) activity from choice, from the decision of personality, volitional action; and (3) activity towards an ideal, that which is not, but which ought to be'. This is almost exactly what Fuller wanted to say about law – and felt still needed to be said in the thirties, forties and later.[24]

The so-called behavioural revolution in social science turned away from what officials should do in favour of what they actually do, and attempted to account for what they actually do in terms drawn mainly from psychology and economics. Legal realists like Karl Llewellyn, for example, proposed to inquire whether judges actually achieve the results they purport to aim at. In his terms, he wanted to compare facts with facts, objective data on what is claimed, what is done and what happens.[25] In Fuller's account, the positivist scholar studies the behaviour of judges and other officials the way a physicist studies gravity or the behaviour of atoms. 'The model of true science is taken to be the science of inanimate matter, and in that science it is a cardinal principle that no observed event shall be interpreted as though it were the expression of a purpose.'[26] The object of positivist legal science is to trace the patterns and effects of external forces.

The behaviourist strand of realism was not the sole, and perhaps not even the dominant, strand. And, among realists, Llewellyn is only one of half a dozen writers that Fuller targets, and not the most extreme. I mention Llewellyn, however, because of a tantalising hint that Fuller offers of a different approach, which occurred to him as he was reading Llewellyn and Hoebel's book *The Cheyenne Way*. On an onion skin page that Fuller inserted on page 127, where the authors relate the details of a property dispute (the case of Wolf Lies Down), Fuller suggests that the tribal chiefs' articulation of new rules to resolve the dispute can be understood as their

[24] On Dewey, see Wilson 1990: 68. Ross (1979: 107–38) describes the factors that led to 'a more rigorous scientism' after 1912.

[25] See Barzun 2017: 142. [26] Fuller 1955a: 1307.

discovery of the three reasons Thomas Aquinas offers for preferring a legal order built on individual rather than communal property. These reasons, which Aquinas characterises as 'necessary to human life', are (in Fuller's summary): providing incentives, preventing confusion about the permissible use of objects, and eliminating disputes caused by common ownership. Fuller says that these reasons 'were waiting there to be discovered, just as much as the psychological law that there is a small interval of time between a sensation and reaction to it'.[27]

Fuller does not discuss the case of Wolf Lies Down in his published work, but it reveals how he would respond to the behaviourist challenge. His comment shows, in outline, how a model of human action based on natural science can be displaced in favour of a humanistic model for understanding how and why social events occur. Instead of causal generalisations, it offers reasoned explanations. The story begins with the statement of a problem – a recurring, pervasive problem regarding ownership. Fuller then asks: what convinces the protagonists (the chiefs) to address the problem as they did? The aim is to show that what was done was the thing to have done – explaining how it was right or appropriate, taking into account the context, relevant constraints and assorted contingencies. Thus, a reasoned explanation makes human action intelligible in light of conditions, purposes and outcomes. The aim of inquiry – the social scientific aim – is to discover patterns in the relationships among these three elements.

The suggestion is that when we contemplate recurrent problems in human experience, we see that all persons, or at least all persons in a certain situation, benefit from the introduction of specific practices. The practices meet a common need, and thus (as Fuller often uses the phrase) are part of natural law – waiting to be discovered. If they were introduced simply because they were expedient or provided parochial advantages, the practices would be only a matter of positive law. Although he refers to Aquinas on the onion skin page, Fuller's language here is actually closer to that of David Hume, whom Fuller regarded as a 'great sociologist'. In his *Treatise*, Hume describes how human beings gradually come to recognise

[27] Llewellyn and Hoebel 1941. Fuller's source on Aquinas is Gilson 1925: 295–6, which consists of selected passages from the *Summa Theologica* with commentary. The passage on these pages is from Pt IIa–IIae, ques. 66, art. 2. Aquinas's three reasons are somewhat different from Fuller's summary.

the benefits of living together in communities and, in particular, how their peace and security depend on abiding by certain laws of property. The laws arise gradually and acquire force 'by a slow progression, and by our repeated experience of the inconveniences of transgressing [them]'.[28] Although a product of artifice, the laws are properly considered natural, understanding that to mean what is common to, and inseparable from, the species.[29]

28.4 Social Engineering versus Social Architecture

Along with their ambitions for social science, Comte and his followers were also anti-democratic. Their faith lay in elites who would govern society through social engineering. Comte's idea was that *sociocrats* – not democrats any more than they were aristocrats – would be a new priesthood, combining spiritual with secular power. Many of these features figured in twentieth-century despotisms based on an ideology of science, such as Marxism. They were also evident, Fuller believed, in less ominous, but nonetheless worrisome, form in democratic societies as *public policy*, in the guise of a trained elite designing programmes to bring about social harmony and prosperity through top-down control. Positivists view society as a kind of laboratory, an arena for scientific experimentation, manipulating human behaviour in the pursuit of desired goals. Jurisprudential inquiry, accordingly, is displaced by public policy studies.

Part of the Fullerian narrative is that the development of public policy as a discipline (and vocation) feeds the development of the bureaucratic/regulatory state. Policy experts staff the bureaucracies and legislative committees that have taken over from judges the task of managing the normative order of society. In this way, political science departments and schools of public administration displace law schools as the principal route to government service. Fuller's attack on 'policy science' as advocated by Harold Lasswell and Myres McDougall at Yale reflects his concern. Although their newfangled curriculum was developed for lawyers, they

[28] Hume 1739/1888: 484–95.

[29] Fuller's list of 'great sociologists' includes de Tocqueville, Burke, Hume, Adam Smith, Walter Bagehot and Henry Maine – writers (I surmise) who blend, rather than separate, descriptive and normative enquiry and who regard human beings as disposed to social, cooperative behaviour independently of law.

aimed to cultivate government technocrats who would engage in social engineering. Two aspects of their approach are of concern.[30] The first is positing a short list of 'social values', the achievement of which is meant to guide all government action. The list is sufficiently cryptic that it remains unclear whether anything important has been omitted, but, in any case, it is constructed without attention to how the values are to be implemented. Further, when they devote attention to the policy-making process, Lasswell and McDougall think of policy and institutional design as consisting in the creation of material incentives, motivating citizens to act so as to achieve the values set by policy-makers. As a result, they go wrong in two ways. They empower officials at the expense of citizens in determining how people are to live their lives, and they fail to understand the interplay between means and ends, which, as we will see, is the major failing of positivist social science. (In public policy schools today, this orientation is found most prominently among behavioural economists.)

Fuller had a different picture of how society works, or works best, more bottom up than top down. I will get to that in a moment. And he held on to the idea that the lawyer, properly educated, even while taking centre stage in social decision-making, does not act like a policy-maker, at least of the Lasswell and McDougall type. Fuller does not abandon the search for regularities in social phenomena, but he pursues it without the stress on uniform causation or technical manipulation from above.

Fuller wrote quite a lot on legal education. A central point is the need to get beyond the case-arguing and dispute-settling aspect of lawyers' work. The fundamental work of lawyers, he suggests, is *legislative* – understood in a special sense. Lawyers create rules and, in other ways, give structure to human relationships. Legislative work ranges from negotiating and drafting contracts and other private documents, to mediating collective bargaining agreements, to planning and drafting statutes. In all of this work, the lawyer finds ways of accommodating opposing interests and giving clear verbal expression to patterns of accommodation. In short, the lawyer facilitates effective collaboration among citizens. 'Every legal instrument is a kind of constitution establishing a framework for the future dealings of the affected parties.'[31] So, the lawyer is an architect – the chief architect – of social structure.

[30] For Fuller's critique, as well as a fine example of Fuller's wit, see Fuller 2001c: 271–81.
[31] Fuller 2001b: 265.

Fuller remarks that legal education almost totally neglects legislation so understood. But to attend to it would require a fundamental reorientation. Competence in legislative tasks requires the ability to synthesise many factors, to integrate legal and extralegal considerations, and thus to make use not only of law but also of the other social sciences. Unlike other social scientists, however, legal professionals are fiduciaries whose vocation is to help people meet each other on common ground, finding ways of living together. Lawyers are architects of *shared* social structures – they work to devise forms into which citizens' varied interests can be accommodated 'fairly, comfortably, and safely'. To do this well, lawyers need every skill and aptitude that affects the intellectual and moral life of human beings. What kind of pedagogy would this require? Fuller often wrote about the need to move beyond the traditional case method of teaching, which had been introduced by Langdell, in favour of what he called a problem-oriented pedagogy. But he was elusive as to details, and, to my knowledge, he never completely redesigned one of his own courses at Harvard to embody an alternative approach. In one of the few statements in his writings suggesting a different classroom experience, he remarks that the narrative case method employed at the Harvard Business School (HBS) 'would seem to be in order'.[32] Rather than using the decisions of appellate courts, with their condensed fact descriptions and narrow reasoning, HBS cases provide extended, richly detailed accounts of problematic situations in which protagonists – individuals or agencies – need to make crucial choices. It is then up to the students in class to bring to bear whatever analytic techniques, disciplinary knowledge and practical experience they have available to help the protagonists make a decision. Moral concerns are easily encompassed by this approach.

In sum, jurisprudence is saved from the threat posed by positivist social science by being integrated into legal education rightly conceived. But what constitutes an integrated law-and-social science? The only clear point is that Fuller envisions a science that is descriptive, explanatory and normative. In this regard, he shared a theoretical ambition entertained by other members of the legal process school. But what does it look like? Does it have a distinctive method? Does it rest on fundamental moral principles, and, if so, how are they derived? I return to these questions in the final sections; we will see that the special skill that lawyers have as

[32] Fuller 1948: 31.

architects of social structure – and that positivist social scientists lack – is the skill of actively (and prudentially) managing the interaction of means and ends. Before we turn to that, I want to set Fuller's critique of scientific positivism – and thus his disciplinary and theoretical preoccupations – in the context of his larger view of society.

28.5 Legal Order and Social Order

It is a distinctive aspect of Fuller's non-positivism that he was as much interested in informal (customary, moral) ways of acting as in formal (legal) arrangements, as much interested in natural practices as in planned institutions. In a marginal note, he observes: 'Many theorists seem to assume that without formally declared law[,] society would be displaced by chaos.' But the idea that order, structure and regularity must be imparted from above, by law, is a positivist idea. Legal regulation does not necessarily represent an improvement in human society.

To the contrary, too often it reflects the use of law as an instrument of power and control, a top-down projection from positions of authority. Although not as extreme as in authors like Austin or Bentham, this tendency is apparent in H. L. A. Hart's work. On the inside front cover of his personal copy of Hart's *Concept of Law*, Fuller notes: 'As with so much modern writing in the positivist mood, [Hart's] favorite term [is] "control", "direction". [Law is a] system of rules [used] as an "instrument of social control".' The latter passage was, I am sure, especially galling to Fuller. Without mentioning Fuller in the text, Hart concedes that, in 'any method of social control' consisting of general standards of conduct (thus law), the rules must satisfy the conditions of Fuller's internal morality. 'If this is what the necessary connexion of law and morality means, we may accept it,' Hart says. But rather than taking satisfaction in this concession on the analytic claim, Fuller complains about Hart's use of 'method of social control' and 'control by rules'. Framing the concession in this way demonstrates to Fuller that he and Hart are still very far apart. Indeed, Fuller's reaction suggests that the analytic point was less important than the underlying conception of governance. Law, in Fuller's view, is not a method of social control but sets baselines and provides guideposts for individual choice and self-directed action, thereby facilitating activities that occur independently of the law.

In short, Fuller proposes to turn the positivist picture of governance upside down. In his copy of Michael Polanyi's *The Logic of Liberty*, on an onion skin page inserted at page 29, Fuller says: 'By saying [that] A's rules are law, or that I regard them as law, I make a commitment, which helps [A] to achieve control, indeed, it is an aspect of [A's] power now ... [B]y the very fact of enough [people] making that commitment, control is achieved. / [This] may sound a little like Wm James, "By believing in God we may help him to exist." / But in human affairs this is not absurd.' Fuller is emphasising that whatever authority legal officeholders possess depends crucially on the authorisation they are granted by the consent of citizens. And citizens provide authorisation when they believe it is warranted, that is, when it is consistent with their values, expectations and commitments. Otherwise, control is coercive – a form of domination or manipulation. This is an insight that Fuller gained (or found reinforced) in the classic work of Chester Barnard on organisations. Barnard observes: 'The decision as to whether an order has authority or not lies with the persons to whom it is addressed, and does not reside in "persons of authority" or those who issue these orders.'[33] Authority, in other words, comes from below and reflects mutual consent. This means that granting authority to others does not entail suspension of one's own judgement, and the exercise of control is in need of continuing justification.

Fuller is able to suggest this because, like the anthropologist Bronislaw Malinowski, he believed that the bulk of social ordering occurs outside the law.[34] In such circumstances, what law aims to do is to provide frameworks within which the conduct of citizens may proceed more smoothly on its own. If legislators have a primary responsibility, it is not to exercise control; it is to respect people's capacity for agency and to facilitate the release of human energies by designing helpful mechanisms for social decision-making.

It needs to be stressed that Fuller's field of expertise was contract law, which at its best facilitates private activity. It is different from, say, criminal law, which aims to prevent certain acts from occurring in the first place – although criminal law still facilitates private ordering by

[33] Barnard 1938/1942: 163.

[34] See Fuller 1940/1966: 111. A central theme in Malinowski's work is how social order is achieved without central authority or written codes of conduct or police. The core mechanism is interaction based on reciprocity.

providing guideposts for action and decision. Also important was Fuller's attachment to the common law. In the traditional picture of common law adjudication, the judge is not a law-maker; decisions are based, rather, on custom. The expertise of the judge – exemplified, paradigmatically, in the jurisprudence of Benjamin Cardozo – lies in the ability to discern antecedent expectations and entrenched communal norms. The judge's task is to give official expression to these expectations and norms and perhaps to refine or update them. The upshot is not that the judge uses moral criteria to determine legal rights and duties; rather, the judge adopts a moral posture by placing respect for extralegal practices or social mores at the centre of the judicial task.

Why defer to custom? In brief, it is because custom embodies the way in which citizens work out their relationships with one another on their own, pursuing their own objectives collectively. In the background, we can detect Fuller's attachment to (or nostalgia for) the experience of his pioneer upbringing in California's Imperial Valley, where he felt

> a strong sense of community such as I have never experienced since ... [where] everyone had a sense of participation in the affairs of the district. We were all parts, one of another, and we knew it. One who has had this sort of experience will be left, as I have been, with a lasting skepticism toward the notion that the frontier was a place of 'individualism' where every man faced nature by himself.[35]

In different words, Fuller defers to custom for what we could call democratic reasons. Custom embodies the results of extended interactions and reflects what is accepted and regarded as legitimate. In line with this, Fuller says: Lawmaking that reinforces already existing interactional expectancies shows the greatest respect for citizens' capacity for self-direction.[36] Indeed, a proliferation of laws could be a sign of disorder. It could mean that the usual bases of social and moral order – customary norms or mores – are not functioning as they should. As de Tocqueville observes, it is a problem when 'too much importance is attached to laws and too little to mores'.[37] For Fuller, as for de Tocqueville, democracy is not simply an arrangement of political institutions; it is a certain type of society.

Positivists, then, make two mistakes. They believe that law is necessary when it is not, and they believe that law consists in a kind of social control, by designated officials. Fuller observes (in a personal note): 'My preference

[35] Fuller 2001a: 209. [36] See Fuller 2001a: 232–5. [37] De Tocqueville 1988: 308.

for morality or natural law against positive law is a preference for unorganized and not wholly rationalized control as against an over-organized, over-rationalized legal order.' And in another note: 'Kelsen says natural law [is] anarchistic in tendency; [yes,] precisely, it recognizes [the] anarchistic, natural order which grows with society. [It] recognizes that to a degree the order of a society grows, is "natural".' This note indicates why Fuller took a great interest in theories of spontaneous order – although, in the end, he did not believe that they applied without qualification to economic markets (unlike Hayek) or to the common law (unlike Polanyi). In any event, we should be clear that the preference for anarchy does not represent an attempt to transcend the need for order. Rather, order comes from somewhere other than law.

As Fuller sees it, positivists are prone to think of society as mere clay in law's hands, an inert substance that gains its shape from the operation of law as its active principle. Thus, where positivists see a need for social control – because otherwise people will engage in all kinds of mischief and society will fall apart – Fuller has a more sanguine view of the extralegal realm. This reflects his meliorism and confidence in the goodwill of ordinary people. Why, then, use law at all? How do legal structures relate to non-legal ordering? For Fuller, the move from an informal to an institutionalised world has to be an improvement of some kind. Yet his high regard for extralegal social ordering seems to preclude such a possibility. I will say more on the question of why use law at all. What is important here is that guideposts are not instruments of domination or control; they make ordered interaction possible where it otherwise might not occur. (Social architecture is not social engineering.) Accordingly, Fuller writes (in a personal note): 'We often tacitly assume that the more moralistic rules of law are most fundamental. But[,] from another point of view[,] rules with the guidepost function are the indispensable precondition for all other rules ... Driving carelessly so as to endanger others is immoral, but driving carefully is expedited by traffic signs.'

28.6 Positivist Deracination

These observations on social order help us to understand the distinctive thrust – as well as limitations – of Fuller's critique of legal positivism's approach to governance.

Beginning in the Progressive Era, the most important development in US public institutions in the twentieth century was the proliferation and consolidation of administrative agencies. As a faculty member at Harvard from 1939 on, Fuller was among colleagues who were deeply involved in shaping and staffing these agencies, addressing the issues raised in governing new areas of economic life and working diligently on structural innovations. It seems that this activity should have attracted the interest of a legal scholar who placed such emphasis on institutional values and their responsiveness to social problems. Yet Fuller cast doubt on the legitimacy of 'bureaucracy' throughout his life. He did not see how 'that form of government'[38] could defend itself against charges of being arbitrary and overbearing. He recognised that many administrative tasks are not justiciable, that is, manageable by ordinary judicial procedures. But rather than articulating an alternative decision model appropriate to this realm, he dismissed it as not *law* – he called it, instead, *managerial direction* – and decried its failure to meet all eight of the principles that make up the internal morality of law. The main worry that Fuller expressed, following Henry Sumner Maine, is that administrative agencies lack a moral foundation, the kind of deep acceptance as a legitimate form of decision-making that courts enjoy – and maybe legislatures, too – when they abide by the principles of the internal morality. (The eight principles of the internal morality are constraints on law-making, such as the requirements of clarity, generality and prospectivity. By following them, legislators display their respect for citizens' capacity for agency and self-direction.)[39]

Maine's picture of how society works aligns with that of Edmund Burke and Walter Bagehot, and all three were important influences on Fuller. For these authors, social change must be incremental because society is like an organism 'and can absorb and survive only so much surgery'.[40] Accordingly, Fuller invokes Maine's thesis that a society is liable to experience catastrophe if legal change occurs too rapidly. The examples Maine discusses are from ancient times, but it is clear that he also had in mind nineteenth-century England.[41] Fuller, for his part, was seriously worried that the United States was liable to this kind of danger during the New Deal

[38] Fuller 1940/1966: 134.

[39] See Winston 2005: 313–47. Rundle (2012) places moral agency at the center of her study of Fuller.

[40] Fuller 2001a: 335. [41] See Maine 1861/1963: especially ch. 4.

because advocates of large-scale reforms were impatient with the task of examining the conceptual structure of law to see what it really accomplishes and how it works. The result is insufficient thought on how social problems can or cannot be managed and by which processes. Thus, the danger is *positivist deracination*, ripping legal forms from their social and moral roots and treating them as self-sustaining, if not self-justifying, to be manipulated at will.

Fuller acknowledges that New Dealers are right to believe that major adjustments in the current economic and social order are necessary, and he concedes that they have the right goals. But, with only a few exceptions, they move too quickly, before they know how to achieve the goals effectively. Many of the changes are a product of legislative enactments and administrative decrees that come too close to pure fiat and, as a result, stretch thin the public's readiness to accept their legitimacy.[42] The New Dealers also do not understand the interaction of ends and means and thus how institutionalisation itself changes goals and limits what can – and should – be done. So, in this period of tremendous institutional innovation, Fuller saw a mishmash, without clear models of processes that possess integrity. As late as 1965, Fuller discusses the dangers in governments taking on tasks for which they are not prepared.[43]

How would the aims of administration as a legal form be determined? Where would the guiding norms come from? How could broad public support be engendered? These are good questions, but Fuller does not address them. It is possible that what worried Fuller about administrative agencies is 'their *potential* for continuous supervision and direct intervention' in the self-initiated activities of citizens.[44] Another possibility is that Fuller was disturbed by the apparent displacement of courts, which no longer have adequate resources for making sound judgements in economic and other matters. By relying on public policy experts, administrative agencies make more reliable judgements (so it would be claimed), and meanwhile are just as fair to the parties (or give a new meaning to fairness). In this sense, courts and administrative agencies could be thought of as rivals, not necessarily because one does

[42] See Fuller 1940/1966: 115–16.

[43] See Fuller 1965: 1021–42, reprinted in Winston 2001.

[44] See Chase 1982: 10.

better what the other does, but because what is needed is doing something different. Again, a new jurisprudence requires 'separate studies'.

Fuller had a different idea.

28.7 What Lawyers Know

I mentioned at the beginning of the chapter that Fuller's dialectical bent shows itself in his penchant for setting up contrasting polarities and exploring each side for the truth it contains. This bent is evident in the opposition between legal positivists (as proponents of fiat) and natural lawyers (as proponents of reason). What social order requires is a proper balance between reason and arbitrary will. Both are indispensable; both are 'imbedded in the very marrow [of law]'. Law 'is compounded of reason and fiat, or order discovered and order imposed ... [T]o attempt to eliminate either of these aspects of the law is to denature and falsify it.'[45] Yet, each side in this debate harbours illusions about its project. In emphasising law's foundation in arbitrary will, the positivist pretends to be engaged in a purely factual inquiry and hides the promotion of peace or order as an ethical desideratum. Meanwhile, the natural lawyer dismisses the inevitability of arbitrary will and believes that there is no limit to what reason can accomplish in regulating human relationships.[46] As a result, each side makes a mistake about the limits of law.

Consider the positivists. By focusing on will and its displacement of reason in regulating human relations, positivists come to believe in what Fuller calls the infinite pliability of institutions. This is a kind of social relativism applied to structural forms, and, as with other versions of relativism, the mistake the positivist makes is not in seeing variation among societies but in thinking that the variation is independent of objective factors. In particular, what the positivist misses are 'general principles of social order' and 'natural laws of organization'. Here, Fuller is reaching for large – not to say hugely ambitious – claims about non-contextual, potentially universal and perhaps necessary features of the social world; not fixed categories or mental structures but truths about social order whose compelling force emerges ineluctably and invariably in

[45] Fuller 1946: 382. [46] See Fuller 1940/1966: 109–10.

human experience. His comment on the case of Wolf Lies Down is an early illustration.

To it, Fuller adds what he refers to as 'the Gestalt idea' that means-end relationships are limited. When reflecting, in the mid-sixties, on the importance of Dewey, Fuller reports:

> I was at one time quite influenced by his thought, and the influence, I suspect, lingers on . . . His means-end continuum and his treatment of fact and value were of course generally congenial to me, and perhaps had a lot to do with my own thinking. What I missed, however, was the Gestalt idea, that means-end relations fall into a limited number of patterns – what I call forms of social order.[47]

The 'Gestalt idea' is Fuller's response to the positivist assumption of infinite pliability. He sees, rather, certain 'natural laws of organization', which he variously describes as the components of a procedural or technological or institutional natural law. They represent inherent limits or constraints, including moral constraints, in constructing human institutions – to be discovered and respected, even as they are utilised. (A quick example: '[A]djudication loses its whole reason for being if we have no restriction against the bribing of judges.')[48] These constraints are like social science discoveries about what makes institutions and social arrangements work effectively, or not. Legal professionals, in crucial situations, must often conform their creative activity to an external order rather than impose an order on others to which they must conform. The external order is practical and has both moral and technical dimensions, including the state of social invention, the limits of available resources, and general features of communal life.

To this extent, then, natural lawyers make a valid point against positivists. However, they, too, are prone to error about the interaction of means and ends. Specifically, in suggesting that reason yields clear statements of value and correspondingly firm, incorrigible rules, natural lawyers fail to consider how ideas become reality. Fuller often identifies natural law with the claim that ethical standards are independent of time, place and circumstance. More specifically, it presumes that ethical ends can and must be selected in abstraction from means. In other words, natural lawyers neglect problems of implementation – and thus fail to realise that such problems have implications for any initial statement of ends. 'They lay down rules

[47] Letter to Philip Selznick, 18 August 1965. [48] Fuller 1955b: 916.

about what is right,' he observes, 'and leave to someone else the problem of how you get there'.[49] The ethical life, rather, involves reciprocal adjustment. When a decision-maker modifies an initial (abstract) statement of principle or policy in light of issues of implementation, this is a sign not of compromise but of mature deliberation about how ideals relate to the real world. Ends are rightly modified or redefined in light of feasible means.

In both views, then, there is confusion about the interplay of means and ends and thus how institutions work. We are not free to follow 'our whims and impulses of the moment . . . [W]e must understand and respect those laws that naturally govern the reality we seek to mold.' At the same time, there is an element of irreducible contingency that stems from the social and historical reality with which we are confronted. Constructing social institutions is not just about autonomous choice, but neither is it about the discovery of a pre-existing natural order. And that is what lawyers know. From their long experience as social architects, lawyers have developed a special competence for assessing the interaction of means and ends and bringing that knowledge to bear in practical decision-making – knowledge unavailable in other disciplines. 'Current ethical theory', for example, 'offers almost no guidance for the conduct of this vital procedure of reciprocal adjustment'.[50] And similarly for positivist social science.

Since it is lawyers who have direct experience of the process of adjusting ends and means, and managing the technologies of implementation, it is they who understand best how institutions succeed or fail in achieving social purposes. Lawyers think about the good but also about what can be done and what is likely to happen. At their best, lawyers possess a wisdom that comes from cumulative, experiential learning. They are skilled at discerning what is appropriate in the circumstances, which is the virtue that Aristotle identified as *prudence*. Although Fuller does not use the term here, I think he would have welcomed it. It is not a matter of logical demonstration or purely technical skill. Prudence is practical reasoning involving complex judgements about ends and means. It is the capacity to judge reliably about such matters in situations of conflict, uncertainty and

[49] Letter to B. R. Inagaki, 9 April 1968.

[50] Fuller 1955b: 916. Fuller's conception of the lawyer's craft is presented with great clarity in his remarks at a conference on the teaching of law in liberal arts colleges. See Berman 1956: 37–43, 50–4, 61–4.

risk. The good lawyer has the ability to weigh how contextual factors – local knowledge and tacit understandings, for example – make a difference for accurate diagnosis and successful resolution of a problematic situation.

Fuller summarises: 'I believe . . . [that] the law school's special contribution to the student's development is that it teaches him to think in context.'[51]

This conclusion may seem deflationary, or at least disappointing, after such a sustained critique of positivism. Yet, it points to Fuller's ultimate commitments. During the fifties, Fuller realised that what he was ready to say about human nature was not nearly as robust as he had originally thought. Social and historical context, and the stage of technological and institutional development, are crucial determinants of warranted ends and valid ethical norms. More importantly, Fuller came to realise the difficulty in assuming that any political principle is fixed independently of experience, rather than arising out of uncoerced human interaction. In a marginal note, he writes: '[Regarding] "natural law" – [compare] say[ing] [the] object of law is to impose [the] best order vs. [saying the] object of law is to enable men to achieve [the] order they want. [The latter allows for] technological change – developing insight – experience with new satisfactions, etc.'[52] This note reflects Fuller's most provocative idea about legal order, namely, that law should be thought of primarily as a vehicle (a set of modalities) for enabling human freedom, that is, the ability of citizens to exercise effectively their capacity to be purposive, choosing, creative beings. Importantly, freedom in this sense is achieved not by increasing the range of choice but by providing formal structures – the 'forms of social order' – by which choices can be carried over into the larger society.

The focus on freedom brings human nature back in, albeit in a different way. In *The Morality of Law*, Fuller says that the internal morality of law is neutral over a wide range of ethical issues but not regarding its view of human beings.[53] Ultimately, what this signifies for Fuller is the importance of law's recognition of each citizens' capacity for moral agency. Thus, when explaining the inclusion of generality as a key feature of the internal morality of law, Fuller says that we must ask why law takes the form of general rules. 'The answer is a relatively simple one: The law does not tell

[51] Fuller 1955b: 916.

[52] Fuller 1955a: 1311–12; see Winston 2001: Introduction to the revised edition.

[53] Fuller 1969: 162–3.

a man what he should do to accomplish specific ends set by the lawgiver; it furnishes him with baselines against which to organize his life with his fellows.'[54] If people are to live together harmoniously in the same world, as Fuller is confident that they can, they must work out an accommodation – fair terms of cooperation – from the ground up.

28.8 Practising Non-positivism

So, is a lawyer's knowledge a matter of science, or is it knowledge of a craft? Knowing that? Or knowing how? Thinking dialectically, we can discern some truth in each side. From my reading of Fuller, I would emphasise that his writings exemplify – and encourage in others – the practitioner's craft of engaging in continuous, incremental and iterative reasoning about means and ends. This approach to the study of forms of order – 'the science of Where-do-we-go-from-here?', in his Harvard colleague Henry Hart's lovely oxymoron – depends on the successful integration of normative and descriptive inquiry, which is still a work in progress.

References

Barnard, C. I. 1938/1942. *The Functions of the Executive*. Harvard University Press.

Barzun, C. L. 2017. 'Jerome Frank, Lon Fuller, and a Romantic Pragmatism'. *Yale Journal of Law and the Humanities* 29: 129–76.

Berman, H. J. 1956. *On the Teaching of Law in the Liberal Arts Curriculum*. Foundation Press.

Chase, W. C. 1982. *The American Law School and the Rise of Administrative Government*. University of Wisconsin Press.

De Tocqueville, A. 1988. *Democracy in America*. Harper Perennial.

Fuller, L. 1930–1/1967. *Legal Fictions*. Illinois Law Review 25/Stanford University Press.

Fuller, L. 1934. 'American Legal Realism'. *University of Pennsylvania Law Review* 82: 429–62.

Fuller, L. 1939. 'Williston on Contracts'. *North Carolina Law Review* 18: 1–15.

Fuller, L. 1940/1966. *The Law in Quest of Itself*. Northwestern University Press/ Beacon Press.

Fuller, L. 1946. 'Reason and Fiat in Case Law'. *Harvard Law Review* 59: 376–95.

[54] See Fuller 2001a: 234.

Fuller, L. 1948. 'What the Law Schools Can Contribute to the Making of Lawyers'. In *Education for Professional Responsibility.* Carnegie Press.
Fuller, L. 1949a. 'The Place and Uses of Jurisprudence in the Law School Curriculum'. *Journal of Legal Education* 1: 495–507.
Fuller, L. 1949b. *The Problems of Jurisprudence.* Temporary ed. Foundation Press.
Fuller, L. 1955a. 'Freedom: A Suggested Analysis'. *Harvard Law Review* 68: 1305–25.
Fuller, L. 1955b. 'The Philosophy of Codes of Ethics'. *Electrical Engineering* 74: 916–18.
Fuller, L. 1958. 'Positivism and Fidelity to Law: A Reply to Professor Hart'. *Harvard Law Review* 71: 630–72.
Fuller, L. 1965. 'Irrigation and Tyranny'. *Stanford Law Review* 17: 1021–42.
Fuller, L. 1969. *The Morality of Law.* Revised ed. Yale University Press.
Fuller, L. 1970. 'Jurisprudence'. *Encyclopedia Britannica.* 14th ed.
Fuller, L. 2001a. 'Human Interaction and the Law'. In K. Winston (ed.) *The Principles of Social Order: Selected Essays of Lon L. Fuller.* Revised ed. Hart Publishing: 211–48.
Fuller, L. 2001b. 'The Lawyer as an Architect of Social Structures'. In K. Winston (ed.) *The Principles of Social Order: Selected Essays of Lon L. Fuller.* Revised ed. Hart Publishing: 264–70.
Fuller, L. 2001c. 'On Legal Education'. In K. Winston (ed.) *The Principles of Social Order: Selected Essays of Lon L. Fuller.* Revised ed. Hart Publishing: 271–81.
Gilson, E. 1925. *Saint Thomas D'Aquin.* 2nd ed. Librairie Victor Lecoffre.
Hayek, F. 1952. *The Counter-Revolution of Science.* Free Press.
Hume, D. 1739/1888. *A Treatise of Human Nature.* Oxford University Press.
Llewellyn, K. N. and Hoebel, E. A. 1941. *The Cheyenne Way.* University of Oklahoma Press.
Maine, H. S. 1861/1963. *Ancient Law.* Beacon Press.
Ross, D. 1979. 'The Development of the Social Sciences'. In A. Oleson and J. Voss (eds.). *The Organization of Knowledge in Modern America, 1860–1920.* Johns Hopkins University Press.
Rundle, K. 2012. *Forms Liberate: Reclaiming the Jurisprudence of Lon L Fuller.* Hart Publishing.
Von Mises, R. 1951. *Positivism: A Study in Human Understanding.* Harvard University Press.
Wilson, D. J. 1990. *Science, Community, and the Transformation of American Philosophy, 1860–1930.* University of Chicago Press.
Winston, K. 1988. 'Is/Ought Redux: The Pragmatist Context of Lon Fuller's Conception of Law'. *Oxford Journal of Legal Studies* 8: 329–49.
Winston, K. 1999. 'Three Models for the Study of Law'. In W. J. Witteveen and W. van der Burg (eds.). *Rediscovering Fuller.* Amsterdam University Press: 51–77.
Winston, K. (ed.) 2001. *The Principles of Social Order: Selected Essays of Lon L. Fuller.* Revised ed. Hart Publishing.
Winston, K. 2005. 'The Internal Morality of Chinese Legalism'. *Singapore Journal of Legal Studies*: 313–47.

Dworkin's Critique of Hart's Positivism 29

Dennis Patterson*

29.1 Introduction

Ronald Dworkin was a major figure in the world of legal philosophy. His work, which spanned the better part of the second half of the twentieth century, was diverse and controversial. Dworkin wrote primarily about two things: general jurisprudence and political philosophy. It is fair to say that Dworkin thought of jurisprudence as a part of political philosophy. As an anti-positivist,[1] Dworkin rejected the separation between law and morality. In fact, Dworkin thought that legal questions could only properly be answered by connecting them with the more abstract considerations found in moral and political philosophy.

This chapter will focus on one portion of Dworkin's *oeuvre*, that is, his critique of H. L. A. Hart's legal positivism. Dworkin was a lifelong critic of legal positivism. From the first essay he published in the *University of Chicago Law Review* until his final days, Dworkin remained a persistent and unyielding critic of all forms of legal positivism.[2]

* Thanks to John Oberdiek and Urszula Kosielinska for very helpful suggestions for improving this chapter. I benefitted greatly from a seminar on a draft of the chapter in Uppsala in May of 2018. Special thanks to Patricia Mindus and Torben Spaak. Miriam Sheikh provided research assistance. All errors are my own.

[1] This chapter focuses on Dworkin's criticisms of the positivism of H. L. A. Hart. When Dworkin needed a specific target for a critique of positivism, he consistently chose Hart's work.

[2] Dworkin 2008 arguably contains a small concession to positivism. In the Introduction, Dworkin distinguishes between doctrinal positivism ('moral facts cannot figure, at least fundamentally, in the truth conditions of propositions of law') and taxonomic positivism ('moral principles and legal principles are distinct and therefore the law does not include any moral principles'); he states: 'My writings about positivism have taken doctrinal positivism as their target' (Dworkin 2008: 26–7). Later in the book, in a chapter titled 'The Concepts of Law' (Dworkin 2008: 234), he writes: 'I did not mean to make . . . the fallacious taxonomic argument that everything that figures among those truth conditions should be counted as belonging to a distinct set of rules or principles called legal . . . I therefore do not believe that the replies [like Shapiro's] that took me to make a taxonomic claim actually provided any answer at all to the arguments I actually made. Perhaps a great deal of time

Much has been written over the years about Dworkin's various attacks on legal positivism. To be sure, Dworkin altered his stance on positivism as a result of replies to his criticisms largely from defenders of Hart's positivism. A review of this literature would, perhaps, be a useful exercise, but that is not the purpose of this chapter. Instead, this chapter will identify a narrative thread in Dworkin's thought that reveals a consistent, albeit complex, approach to his misgivings about Hart's legal positivism. It is not inconceivable to suggest that Dworkin's own conception of general jurisprudence was forged in reaction to Hart's positivism and the responses received from Hart's defenders.[3] In this regard, the present chapter can be added to the already voluminous literature on the long-running and much-discussed 'Hart–Dworkin debate'.

29.2 General Jurisprudence and Philosophy

Ronald Dworkin graduated from Harvard Law School. After completing law school, Dworkin clerked for Judge Learned Hand of the Second Circuit Court of Appeals. While Dworkin did not take a PhD, his year as a Rhodes Scholar at Oxford was so successful that he was brought to the attention of H. L. A. Hart, whom Dworkin would later succeed at Oxford.[4]

Notwithstanding a lack of formal philosophical training, Dworkin began his career at Oxford (in 1969)[5] by addressing deep philosophical questions as they related to law. From 1973 to 1975, Dworkin led a series of seminars at Oxford with the late Gareth Evans on the topic of objectivity in law and morals. As Stephen Guest recalls it,[6] the seminar took up the question of truth and its demonstrability. The question was whether the truth of propositions was greater than their demonstrability. In other words, are there at least some propositions that are true without their truth being demonstrable?[7]

has been wasted.' Here, arguably, Dworkin concedes that the taxonomic point – and so taxonomic positivism – is correct. But he was never trying to argue against that: he was criticising doctrinal positivism. My thanks to John Oberdiek for reminding me of Dworkin's discussion.

[3] Those responses would ultimately take the form of two forms of positivism, inclusive and exclusive.

[4] Hart actively promoted Dworkin's candidacy as his replacement.

[5] See Liptak 2013.

[6] See Guest 2012: 15–16.

[7] Dworkin would make precisely this claim about the truth of propositions of law. See Dworkin 2011: 116, 153–4, 173.

Professors from a variety of disciplines were brought to the seminar room for the purpose of exploring the ways in which truth and its demonstrability proceeded in disciplines other than law. This seminar experience seemingly had a profound impact on Dworkin's thought: he would spend his career repeatedly returning to the question of the truth of legal propositions.[8]

In 1977, Dworkin published an edited collection of papers on the philosophy of law.[9] In the Introduction to the book, Dworkin said this about the relationship between general jurisprudence and philosophy: 'Even the debate about the nature of law, which has dominated legal philosophy for some decades, is, at bottom, a debate within the philosophy of language and metaphysics.'[10] About this sentence, two things are salient. First, it shows that, early in his career, Dworkin believed that philosophy of law or general jurisprudence had to consider its problems from the point of view of more traditional and mainstream philosophical sub-disciplines like philosophy of language and metaphysics. Second, this sentence articulates a theme that would captivate Dworkin's thought for his entire career.

29.3 The Model of Rules

Dworkin's first sustained critique of Hart's positivism was his 1967 article 'The Model of Rules 1'.[11] In that piece, Dworkin articulates three theses that he thinks captures the essence of positivism, including that of Hart:

(1) 'The law of a community can be identified and distinguished by specific criteria, by tests having to do not with their content but with their pedigree or the manner in which they were adopted or developed.'
(2) 'The set of these valid legal rules is exhaustive of "the law", so that if someone's case is not clearly covered by such a rule (because there is none that seem appropriate, or those that seem appropriate are vague, or for some other reason) then that case cannot be decided by "applying

[8] Of course, it is possible that the seminar merely reinforced pre-existing interests on Dworkin's part. I suspect that exposure to a mind like that of Evans at this early stage of Dworkin's career explains, at least in part, his continuing interest in questions of truth and its demonstrability.
[9] See Dworkin 1977. [10] Dworkin 1977: 1.
[11] Originally published as Dworkin 1967 and subsequently reprinted in Dworkin 1978.

the law". It must be decided by some official, like a judge, "exercising his discretion".'

(3) 'To say that someone has a "legal obligation" is to say that his case falls under a valid legal rule that requires him to do or to forbear from doing something.'[12]

The first thesis has been dubbed the 'pedigree thesis'.[13] As Scott Shapiro has commented, the thesis states a composite claim.[14] First is the claim that, in any legal system, there is a master rule that distinguishes law from non-law. The second claim is that this master rule sets out criteria of legality that refer only to social facts. Importantly, the master rule may not articulate criteria of legality that depend on the moral worth of a norm: the master rule may never require legality to be conditional on morality.

Does the pedigree thesis capture Hart's concept of the rule of recognition? Not really. Dworkin's central claim is that a test of pedigree is the central feature of the rule of recognition. But Hart nowhere imposes such a requirement. In fact, he states that the rule of recognition may make explicit reference to moral considerations.[15]

The second thesis is the discretion thesis. Law, for Hart, is a phenomenon composed of primary and secondary rules. Dworkin argued that Hart was simply incorrect about legal norms because he famously failed to take account of legal principles. Rules, Dworkin argued, apply in an 'all or nothing fashion' whereas principles have a dimension of weight or importance.[16] If a case does not fall under an existing legal rule, then the judge must exercise discretion to resolve the dispute.[17] The third thesis is a corollary of the second. If legal obligations can only be generated by legal rules then, in the absence of an extant legal rule, no obligation can be found.

[12] Dworkin 1967: 25. [13] See Shapiro 2007. [14] See Shapiro 2007.

[15] See Hart 2012: 204. As we will see shortly, so-called 'soft' or 'inclusive' positivism provides a further riposte to Dworkin's critique.

[16] See Dworkin 1978: 25, 27. Dworkin described the difference between rules and principles as a 'logical' one: 'The difference between legal principles and legal rules is a logical distinction. Both sets of standards point to particular decisions about legal obligation in particular circumstances, but they differ in the character of the direction they give. Rules are applicable in an all-or-nothing fashion' (Dworkin 1978: 25). 'Principles have a dimension that rules do not – the dimension of weight or importance' (Dworkin 1978: 27).

[17] 'Positivists hold that when a case is not covered by a clear rule, a judge must exercise his discretion to decide that case by what amounts to a fresh piece of legislation' (Dworkin 1978: 31).

In the Postscript to *The Concept of Law*,[18] Hart admitted that he should have said more about the role of principles in law. But that admission does not extend to an admission that Dworkin is right about the role of discretion in law.[19] Dworkin employed a number of cases to sustain the claim that principles play a role in legal reasoning. No one seriously disputed this[20] and, more importantly, Dworkin's own account of the binding quality of principles did little to undermine the central claim of Hart, to wit, that the criteria of legality are the product of intersubjective agreement among officials. Dworkin writes:

> The origin of [legal principles] lies not in a particular decision of some legislature or court, but in a sense of appropriateness developed in the profession and the public over time. Their continued power depends upon this sense being sustained. If it no longer seemed unfair to allow people to profit by their wrongs, or fair to place special burdens upon oligopolies that manufacture potentially dangerous machines, these principles would no longer play much role in new cases, even if they had never been overruled or repealed.[21]

From Dworkin's point of view, the pedigree thesis (whether it is advanced by Hart or not) cannot be plausible because legal principles are sometimes binding on judges in virtue of their intrinsic moral worth.[22] Accordingly, judges are not free to ignore the force of binding principles, especially in cases where no legal rule seems to apply: they have no discretion.[23]

[18] Hart 2012: 238–76. [19] For more on this topic, see the paragraph containing n. 24.

[20] Recall that it was Dworkin who maintained that rules and principles are 'logically distinct'. As many pointed out, it is not at all clear that Hart's conception of 'rule' would, in principle, preclude inclusion of principles.

[21] Dworkin 1978: 40.

[22] See Dworkin 1978: 32–40. Given that, for Dworkin, the origin of principles lies in a 'sense of appropriateness developed in the profession' (p. 40), it seems that belief in the moral worth of principles is at least as important as the fact of their moral worth.

[23] As Dworkin (1978: 45) states:

> This theory holds that a legal obligation exists when (and only when) an established rule of law imposes such an obligation. It follows from this that in a hard case – when no such established rule can be found – there is no legal obligation until the judge creates a new rule for the future. The judge may apply that new rule to the parties in the case, but this is *ex post facto* legislation, not the enforcement of an existing obligation. The positivists' doctrine of discretion (in the strong sense) required this view of legal obligation, because if a judge has discretion there can be no legal right or obligation – no entitlement – that he must enforce. Once we abandon that doctrine, however, and treat principles as law, we raise the possibility that a legal obligation might be imposed by a constellation of principles as well as by an established rule. We might want to say that a legal obligation

Dworkin's attack on Hart's account of judicial discretion is mounted in terms that are not fair to the way in which Hart formulated his thesis. Perhaps owing to the influence of Wittgenstein and Oxford ordinary language philosophy,[24] Hart's thesis about judicial discretion is not grounded in a theory of law as rules. Rather, it is driven by a conception of law that is primarily social and linguistic in character. Law, for Hart, is a special sort of social practice. In that practice, certain acts have special significance. Among these are acts of legislation and prior legal decisions (precedents). Judicial discretion is the inevitable consequence of the vagueness both of language and of authoritative directives.[25] It is precisely Hart's conception of law as a social practice that Dworkin seeks to deny.

Dworkin has maintained since the beginning of his work in legal philosophy that there are binding moral norms that judges are duty-bound to apply. His entire engagement with Hart's positivism is a clash of visions over the nature of law.

It was not until the Postscript that Hart directly responded to Dworkin's criticisms.[26] But Hart had defenders who mounted sophisticated rejoinders to Dworkin. In any complete account of Dworkin's criticisms of Hart's positivism, we must discuss these positions if only to have a full picture of Dworkin's target.

There are two main responses to Dworkin's initial critique of positivism. These are exclusive and inclusive legal positivism. Exclusive (or 'hard') positivists, represented by Joseph Raz, distinguish law from non-law by a pedigree test: the test of legality is social facts. Law is grounded in social facts and, more importantly, these sources are applied without resort to

exists whenever the case supporting such an obligation, in terms of binding legal principles of different sorts, is stronger than the case against it.

24 What the Postscript in Hart 2012: 297 n. 17 calls an '[o]pen texture of verbally formulated rules'. For the idea of open texture, see Waismann 1945/1951: 117–30. For its relevance to legal reasoning, see Dewey 1924; Hart 1955; 1958; Stone 1946.

25 As Hart (2012: 127) states:

> Faced with the question whether the rule prohibiting the use of vehicles in the park is applicable to some combination of circumstances in which it appears indeterminate, all that the person called upon to answer can do is to consider (as does one who makes use of a precedent) whether the present case resembles the plain case 'sufficiently' in 'relevant' respects. The discretion thus left to him by language may be very wide; so that if he applies the rule, the conclusion, even though it may not be arbitrary or irrational, is in effect a choice.

26 However, Hart did criticise Dworkin's positions on several occasions; see Hart 1977, 1982 and 1983. Also see Gavison 1987.

moral considerations.[27] Grounding the law/non-law distinction in sources runs afoul of Dworkin's persistent claim that judges often feel obligated to apply novel moral principles to the cases before them.[28] In a withering riposte, Raz argued that Dworkin mistakenly assumed that the law of a given legal system consists solely in those standards that judges are required to apply.[29] According to Raz, when pedigreed legal standards run out, judges are obligated to apply the morally best extralegal standards.[30]

Inclusive or 'soft' positivism has attracted more adherents than exclusive positivism.[31] In addition, the position won the endorsement of Hart.[32] A central feature of inclusive positivism is the claim that positivism does not prohibit moral tests for law.[33] More specifically, inclusive legal positivism has two primary claims. First is the separability thesis, which is the denial of any necessary connection between legal validity and moral truth. The second thesis is the social fact thesis: legal facts are grounded on social, not moral, facts.

27 See Raz 2009.

28 This was the case in *Henningsen* v. *Bloomfield Motors, Inc* (1960), for example; 161 A.2d 69 (N.J. 1960).

29 See Raz 1983. 30 See, e.g., Raz 1983: 50:

> If a legal question is not answered by standards deriving from legal sources then it lacks a legal answer – the law on the question is unsettled. In deciding such cases[,] courts inevitably break new (legal) ground and their decision develops the law (at least in precedent-based legal systems). Naturally, their decisions in such cases rely at least partly on moral and other extra-legal considerations.

31 I have received some strong disagreements about this sentence. There are many prominent hard positivists. But the larger nominal number of self-described positivists in my universe are of the soft variety. Yes, that's anecdotal, but the other side can do no better.

32 See the Postscript in Hart 2012: 250–1:

> Dworkin, in attributing to me a doctrine of 'plain-fact positivism', has mistakenly treated my theory as not only requiring (as it does) that the existence and authority of the rule of recognition should depend on the fact of its acceptance by the courts, but also as requiring (as it does not) that the criteria of legal validity which the rule provides should consist exclusively of the specific kind of plain fact which he calls 'pedigree' matters and which concern the manner and form of law-creation or adoption. This is doubly mistaken. First, it ignores my explicit acknowledgement that the rule of recognition may incorporate as criteria of legal validity conformity with moral principles or substantive values; so my doctrine is what has been called 'soft positivism' and not as in Dworkin's version of it 'plain-fact' positivism. Secondly, there is nothing in my book to suggest that the plain-fact criteria provided by the rule of recognition must be solely matters of pedigree; they may instead be substantive constraints on the content of legislation such as the Sixteenth or Nineteenth Amendments to the United States Constitution respecting the establishment of religion or abridgements of the right to vote.

33 Jules Coleman has persuasively developed this position; see Coleman 1988.

The separability thesis does not rule out tests for law that include moral criteria. The claim is simply that such tests need not be moral. But would not moral tests run afoul of the social fact thesis? Not if those tests had a basis in social facts. Dworkin took issue with the claim that the rule of recognition could require judges to resolve hard cases by resort to moral rules without conceding that such rules could be social in nature. The reason he offered (in 'The Model of Rules II')[34] is the inclusive positivist's claim that social rules rest on agreement. In cases of conflict, where there is no agreement, the social fact thesis necessarily failed.

In one of the most important articles written on this issue,[35] Jules Coleman argued that the matter required a better understanding of disagreement. Coleman maintained that there are two kinds of disagreement about the rule of recognition. The first are 'content' disputes. The second type of dispute – application disputes – presupposed consensus about the content of a rule. Hard cases, Coleman argued, were best understood as disputes over the correct application of the rule of recognition and not a dispute about its content.[36] As Scott Shapiro put it (paraphrasing Coleman), '[a]ll judges agree ... that the rule of recognition requires them to look toward moral principles in adjudication, thereby making these principles valid law. They simply disagree about which principles are moral principles (and hence legal principles).'[37] With Hart's endorsement, inclusive positivism has become a widely adopted account of positivism in the analytic tradition.[38] After years of struggle with Dworkin's critiques of Hart's positivism, a consensus developed that Dworkin had not dealt Hart's positivism any fatal blows. The stage was thus set for the next and final encounter between Dworkin and positivism.

[34] Reproduced in Dworkin 1978.

[35] See Coleman 1988. Coleman elaborated his view in Coleman 2001.

[36] In his review of Coleman 2001, Dworkin maintained that Coleman's 'inclusive positivism' was not positivism at all. Dworkin argued that Coleman's description of adjudication was precisely that of Hercules. See Dworkin 2002: 1657 ('This does not sound like positivism: it sounds like Hercules and his colleagues at work').

[37] Shapiro 2007: 34.

[38] Although Raz's exclusive positivism has many followers. For a critique of Raz's claims regarding authority, see Leiter's Chapter 4 in this volume: '[O]f course law *claims authority* in the sense of claiming the right to tell those subject to its jurisdiction what they must do, but the idea that this claim to authority is a claim to Raz's Service Conception looks like ideological obfuscation.'

29.4 Theoretical Disagreement

When Dworkin published the essay 'The Model of Rules' in 1967, it felt as if Hart's positivism had sustained a deep blow.[39] Part of the success of Dworkin's critique was a function of its elegant simplicity. Utilising just a few cases, Dworkin was able to demonstrate that principles play an important role in law, particularly in hard cases. A case as simple as *Riggs* v. *Palmer*[40] showed that Hart's description of law as a system of rules was simply inaccurate. It would take some time for Hart's followers to take in Dworkin's criticism and mount a persuasive reply. After a decade of replies, the conventional wisdom was that positivism could accommodate Dworkin's claim that moral principles played a role in law. Inclusive legal positivism was the result of Dworkin's critique.

Some have observed that Dworkin himself must have felt this[41] because Dworkin's next assault on Hart's positivism was much more thorough and fundamental. As Dworkin puts it in the opening pages of *Law's Empire*,[42] his focus shifts from phenomenology to interpretation. In addition, Dworkin adopts explicit metaphysical language. His concern – as he says – is with truth, specifically the truth of propositions of law.

For the purposes of this chapter, the most important aspect of *Law's Empire*[43] is Dworkin's discussion of disagreement in law.[44] Two ideas are central: propositions of law and truth.[45] Dworkin describes propositions of

[39] The arguments that follow draw upon Patterson 2016; 2018.

[40] *Riggs* v. *Palmer* [1889] 115 NY 506 (Court of Appeals of New York).

[41] See Shapiro 2007: 35. [42] See Dworkin 1986: viii. [43] See Dworkin 1986: 3–6.

[44] Dworkin's argument from theoretical disagreement is different from his Semantic Sting argument (see Dworkin 1986: n. 35 and pp. 43–4). As Dworkin sees it, positivists are committed to a 'criterial semantics' in their account of the concept of 'law'. It is uncontroversial that, for Hart, intersubjective consensus among officials is a key feature of the Rule of Recognition. Dworkin claims that this emphasis on consensus commits positivists to a 'criterial semantics' whereby consensus proceeds from shared criteria for application of the concept 'law'. But, Dworkin avers, if agreement in criteria for the concept of law is a central feature of legal practice, positivists are unable to account for disagreement in law. This is the so-called 'semantic sting'. As Scott Shapiro observes, Dworkin's argument is no objection to positivism if positivists are not committed to a criterial semantics; see Shapiro 2007: 54 n. 58. The consensus is that this aspect of Dworkin's attack on Hart's positivism misses the mark. See, e.g., Coleman and Simchen 2003.

[45] Dworkin's interest in the propositional character of law and the concept of truth was longstanding; see Dworkin 1977: 1: 'Even the debate about the nature of law, which has dominated legal philosophy for some decades, is, at bottom, a debate within the philosophy of language and metaphysics.'

law as 'all the various statements people make about what the law allows or prohibits or entitles them to have'.[46] He provides the following examples: '[T]he Fourteenth Amendment to the US Constitution forbids denial of equal protection of the laws to anyone' to '[T]he law requires Acme Corporation to compensate John Smith for the injury he suffered in its employ last February.'[47]

Propositions of law, which are either true or false, are 'made true' or are 'true in virtue of' other propositions. This, at least, is what '[e]veryone thinks'.[48] On this model of truth, we are concerned with the truthmaker, namely, that in virtue of which a proposition of law is true. As we will see, the truthmaker will be synonymous with a 'ground of law'. As a simple example, the proposition 'The speed limit in California is 55 miles an hour' is true just in case the California legislature has enacted a statute to that effect. It is the statute properly passed by the legislature that 'makes' the proposition regarding the speed limit true.

Of course, lawyers sometimes disagree whether a source exists that settles a dispute about the current state of the law. This is a factual disagreement, one that can be resolved by consulting the appropriate statutory reference. But this sort of disagreement – Dworkin calls it 'empirical disagreement' – is not the only type of disagreement that lawyers sometimes have about law. Of much greater importance than empirical disagreement is what Dworkin terms theoretical disagreement (hereafter, TD). This type of disagreement is not one about facts (that is, sources of law); it is disagreement over what Dworkin calls 'the true grounds of law'.[49] Unlike empirical disagreement, TD cannot be resolved 'by looking in the books where the record of institutional decisions are kept';[50] more is required.[51]

TD is a fundamental feature of legal practice, one that Dworkin believes that positivists cannot account for.[52] More importantly, positivism has 'no plausible theory of theoretical disagreement'.[53] Here it is important to be clear about the nature of TD: what is disagreement about and how is it properly resolved? Dworkin states that such disagreements are 'about whether statute books and judicial decisions exhaust the pertinent grounds

[46] Dworkin 1986: 4. [47] Dworkin 1986: 4–5. [48] Dworkin 1986: 4.
[49] Dworkin 1986: 6. [50] Dworkin 1986: 7.
[51] As with the Semantic Sting argument, Dworkin will claim that the positivist reliance on consensus precludes a defensible account of theoretical disagreement.
[52] See Dworkin 1986: 42–3. [53] Dworkin 1986: 6.

of law'.[54] As we will see, there is more to TD than simply grounds of law. Much of Dworkin's dispute with Hart on the question of TD is not only about the pertinent grounds of law but also about their application in a given case.

To illustrate his thesis about TD, Dworkin employs one of his favourite cases, that being the New York case of *Riggs* v. *Palmer* 1889. The question in *Riggs* was whether a grandson who poisoned his grandfather could benefit under the grandfather's will. The dispute between the majority and the dissenting judges was over how to interpret the New York Statute of Wills. The majority took the view that the meaning of the statute could be answered by a counterfactual: what would the legislature have done had it been presented with the question then before the court? The dissent made a simple 'plain meaning' argument: because the requisites of the New York Statute of Wills had been satisfied, Elmer was entitled to his legacy as per his grandfather's will, his crime notwithstanding.

Let us succinctly recap Dworkin's central claims regarding TD. Propositions of law – claims about the current state of the law – are true in virtue of the grounds of law. TD is disagreement over the grounds of law.[55] Thus, disagreement over the grounds of law is disagreement over the truthmaker for propositions of law. Because positivism lacks the resources even to make sense of debates about the grounds of law, it must be rejected as a proper account of the nature of law.

How does Dworkin use *Riggs* to illustrate his claims regarding TD? He begins with a startling claim: for positivists, TD 'is an illusion'.[56] The following, Dworkin argues, are the main theses of the positivist view of the grounds of law:

(1) The law is only a matter of what legal institutions, like legislatures and city councils and courts, have decided in the past.
(2) Questions of law can always be answered by looking in the books where the records of institutional decisions are kept.

[54] Dworkin 1986: 5.

[55] There are at least two sorts of disagreement that lawyers can have about the grounds of law. The first is whether particular sources exhaust the grounds of law. An example is the question of whether a controlling precedent exhausts the grounds of law. The second, illustrated by the *Riggs* case, is which ground of law (among several) controls. For Dworkin, the answer to this question – indeed, the answer to all questions about the grounds of law – turns on the demands of political morality.

[56] Dworkin 1986: 7.

(3) When lawyers and judges disagree in the theoretical way about what the law is, they are really disagreeing about what it should be. Their disagreement is really over issues of morality and fidelity, not law.[57]

Dworkin maintains that Hart and positivists generally have a 'plain fact' view of law. The view has two core components. First, the grounds of law are fixed by consensus among officials. If everyone believes that *x*, *y* and *z* are the grounds of law, then they are. The question 'What are the grounds of law?' is a factual question. For the positivist, the law 'is only a matter of what legal institutions like legislatures and city councils and courts have decided in the past'.[58] The only sort of disagreement that positivists can account for is factual disagreement.

Scott Shapiro finds Dworkin's argument for TD convincing.[59] Framed in Dworkin's terms, he has to be right. If the only sort of disagreement recognised is factual disagreement, then it seems that positivism cannot account for TD. Two points are salient. Positivism assumes that all officials agree on the grounds of law. Second, whatever judges are doing when they debate the grounds of law, they are clearly not debating matters of fact.

Both of these points are easily accommodated. First, it is perfectly plausible to maintain that judges agree, as in *Riggs*, that both grounds of law (represented by the majority and the dissent) are part of the rule of recognition. Echoing a point made by Coleman, while judges agree on the content of the rule of recognition, they may disagree about its application. That, it seems, is precisely what was going on in *Riggs*. Second, when positivists debate the grounds of law, they are clearly not debating matters of fact. But that does not mean that they are engaged in 'constructive interpretation'. If not, then what are positivists doing when they debate the grounds of law?

Brian Leiter has a clever answer to this question.[60] First, parties (usually judges) to a dispute like the one in *Riggs* are simply trying to change the existing state of the law. They are, as Dworkin puts it, disagreeing about 'what [the law] should be', not 'what the law is'.[61] Second, parties to TDs may simply be wrong in their belief that there is a fact of the matter about the true state of the law. The culprit is the lack of convergent behaviour that is the touchstone of the positivist position.

[57] Ibid. [58] Ibid. [59] See Shapiro 2007: 37. [60] See Leiter 2009.
[61] Dworkin 1986: 7.

Neither of these explanations is especially attractive nor, I maintain, exhaustive of the options available to positivists. We cannot truly understand disagreement in law until we understand the phenomenon of agreement, specifically agreement in legal judgments. To put the point more strongly, disagreement can occur only against the background of pervasive agreement in judgment.[62] Thus, Dworkin starts in the wrong place[63] and, as a result, vastly overstates the significance of TD.

Brian Leiter's critique of Dworkin's claims for TD starts with the observation that 'there is massive and pervasive agreement about the law throughout the system'.[64] If, indeed, there is agreement, how is it to be explained? There are two aspects to this pervasive 'agreement in judgment'[65] that merit attention. In general, lawyers, judges and other institutional officials usually agree about what is the case as a matter of law. Indeed, it is difficult to see how there could be a functioning legal system without pervasive agreement. The second, and perhaps more important, issue is the question of whether or not they agree for the same reasons.[66]

[62] See Schauer 1985: 399. 'A theory, or at least a set of insights, about easy cases is the necessary first step toward development of a theory for dealing with hard cases' (Schauer 1985: 407). Postema (1987: 316) adds: 'Disagreement, even substantial disagreement, then, has a place in a world of common meanings.'

[63] See Leiter 2009: 1220. I agree completely with Leiter's remark that Dworkin's theory exhibits 'a curious dialectical structure' by starting with a few hotly disputed cases and using them to illuminate the more quotidian aspects of law.

[64] Leiter 2009: 1227; see also Patterson 1996: 92: 'Much of the lawyer's work involves no sort of "interpretation" or "theory" whatsoever.'

[65] See Wittgenstein 2010: section 242.

[66] One objection to this argument is that it turns on 'number counting' and, thus, cannot be right. This is a mistake. Intersubjective agreement turns on more than just numbers. Again, Postema (1987: 318–19 and n. 66) states what is at stake:

> Conflict always presupposes consensus, but the consensus, on this view, does not take the form of agreement on a discrete set of formal, constitutive rules, nor on the behavioral 'data' of the practice. Instead, consensus takes the form of a shared discipline and a thick continuity of experience of the common world of the practice. This consensus does not obviate the need for interpretations, nor does it guarantee univocality of the interpretations. But it does decisively shape the spirit in which interpretations are constructed and debated. Controversy, then, is possible, even at what we might call the 'constitutional' level of the practice, without jeopardizing the practice as a whole (and it may even be healthy for it). It is possible because there is a deeper and broader continuity of experience and discipline. Where this continuity is threatened or weakened, there the practice itself is threatened.

Some disagreement notwithstanding, there is pervasive sociological, academic and institutional evidence for the proposition that, in the vast majority of cases, there is little, if any, question about the state of the law.[67] When I speak of 'cases', I do not mean to refer solely to litigated cases (that is, appellate cases), for these account for a minuscule portion of the total number of instances where, on a quotidian basis, lawyers and legal officials answer the question 'What is the law on this question?'. I think that it is fair to say that anyone making the case for global indeterminacy is fighting an uphill battle.

Now to the second point. A key feature of the rule of recognition is that it supplies a 'test for law'. But for a test to be adequate, participants cannot be applying different criteria to reach the same result. In other words, agreement in legal judgment has to be motivated by the same materials applied in the same way for the rule of recognition to be as explanatorily efficacious as Hart imagined.

When we look at the ordinary work of lawyers, we see a practice (indeed, as Dworkin argues, an argumentative practice) suffused by a thick web of mutual intelligibility.[68] Consider contract interpretation. Every dispute over the terms of a written contract starts with the text. The ordinary meaning of terms is given prima facie authority. This is rarely the end of the argument, but it is the normal point of departure. This process is not limited to contracts. Statutes are consulted (often without argument) for all manner of rules from conveyancing to tax and regulatory matters. Even the US Constitution, about which there is so much controversy, exhibits a discernible structure of principle.[69]

To give Dworkin his due (although he does not make this point), it is not enough for a rule of recognition simply to identify valid sources of law.[70]

[67] Again, there is disagreement on this point among legal philosophers.

[68] This is the central insight in Postema 1987: 318–19. [69] See Schauer 1985: 403–4.

[70] Leiter (2019), 251 n.1 mentions this issue but fails to provide an answer that would further the positivist position:

> Timothy Macklem presses on me a different kind of positivist response, namely, that a rule of recognition (RR) identifies the sources of law, but does not adjudicate among all the ways of interpreting them. Here I agree, I take it, with Dworkin (as well as Shapiro): namely, that this austere conception of the rule of recognition would be inadequate to discharge the functions of a RR as Hart originally conceived them, namely, eliminating some (if not all) uncertainty about the valid [*sic*] legal norms are in a particular system. I thus agree (infrequent as that may be) with Dworkin that saying the duly enacted statute is a source of law is not enough for a RR that resolves uncertainty: it is necessary that the RR provide

Once valid sources have been identified, they must be construed (that is, interpreted). Neither Hart nor any of his followers has ever addressed this issue with the kind of focus it deserves. Only such an account of interpretation will provide the needed reply to Dworkin. Nevertheless, Dworkin overplays the role of TD in legal practice. To overcome this exaggeration and give positivism what it needs by way of a defensible account of interpretation, we need to consider the very idea of interpretation.[71]

There are many reasons why the need for interpretation arises in a practice. In this regard, law is not special, but it does have unique interpretive problems. But what was the problem in *Riggs*? Was it not simply the case that the need for interpretation arose from the fact of the murder of the testator by his grandson? We may legitimately ask why this event generated the need for interpretation. The majority opinion answers this by explaining the significance of the murder against the background of an unproblematic probate of a will. The majority shows how understanding (that is, the unreflective act of probating the will in the normal course of things) broke down as the court tried to come to terms with the significance of the murder as the event that precipitated the need for interpretation.[72]

In *Riggs*, the majority made the case for the common law maxim 'No man shall profit from his own wrong'[73] as a constitutive feature of law beyond just the New York law of wills. This was the basis for the majority's

guidance as to what norms the statute enacts as legally valid. This, of course, can be done by content-neutral criteria: e.g., the intent of the legislature, the plain meaning of the text, and so on. And, indeed, these content-neutral criteria can come in hierarchical orderings, such that some sources trump others. But a RR that did not resolve some number of TDs would not, in fact, be adequate to support a functioning legal system.

71 Although it borders on speculation, one plausible explanation for the staying power of the debate over TD is the fact that positivists have simply failed to mount a credible account of legal interpretation. One unfamiliar with the jurisprudential literature may find this claim implausible, but it is, in fact, the case. Timothy Macklem (see Leiter, Chapter 4 in this volume, n. 1) makes just this point. Positivism must have some account of how to adjudicate among conflicting interpretations. Without such an account, TD will remain a viable account of interpretive disputes.

72 The distinction I am drawing is Wittgenstein's distinction between understanding and interpretation; see Wittgenstein 2010. For Wittgenstein, interpretation arises against a settled background of practice. Dworkin's account of interpretation inverts this. For Dworkin, interpretation is primary. As I have argued elsewhere, this is philosophically problematic. See Patterson 1996. Dworkin was not completely unaware of the philosophical dimensions of interpretation, but it is unclear how much he paid attention to the subtleties. One must recall that all the endnotes on this topic – indeed, all the endnotes to *Law's Empire* – were written by students. See Dworkin 1986: 417–53.

73 See Dworkin 1986: 20.

conclusion that the murder made a straightforward reading of the statute impossible. Having shown how the 'No man shall profit from his own wrong' principle is a constitutive feature of law in the most general way, Judge Earl then demonstrated the reach of the principle throughout varied departments of law.[74]

One could uncharitably describe Judge Gray's dissent as proceeding from a wooden reading of the statute. In claiming that the court was 'bound by the rigid rules of law',[75] Gray maintained that Elmer was twice being punished for his offence, first for the murder and second in being denied his inheritance. In a clever (and seemingly unnoticed) rebuttal to Judge Gray, the majority pointed out that he begged the question whether Elmer was entitled to receive his victim's property under the will. Gray's dissent lacked the subtlety and persuasive power of the majority opinion. Does this explain why the majority won the argument?

Before answering that question, we need to ask what *Riggs* teaches us in general about interpretation in law. I begin with the observation that, in the absence of the murder, the text of the New York statute of wills is decisive (that is, it is an easy case). Positivism can explain this outcome in simple, straightforward terms, making no use of interpretation. Dworkin, on the other hand, engages in a baroque explanation of the outcome as the product of multiple interpretations converging on the same outcome.

Where does this leave legal positivism, specifically Hart's account? Agreement in judgment is a central feature of legal practice and, perhaps, the most important social fact that any account of law must explain.[76] Positivists have focused on valid sources of law and have concluded, rightly, that validity is a function of intersubjective agreement. The validity of the Constitution proceeds from the fact that everyone from lawyers and judges to politicians regards it as such. Validity is best explained as

[74] Citing cases from the law of wills and insurance, Earl made a strong case for the proposition that precedents both directly on point (that is, the law of wills) and from related departments of law support an exception to the ordinary meaning of the words of the statute. See *Riggs* v. *Palmer* 115 N.Y. 506 (1889): 509–10.

[75] *Riggs* v. *Palmer* 115 N.Y. 506 (1889): 515(Gray J. dissenting).

[76] As I have already argued, this is a fundamental weakness in the Dworkinian position. As Postema noted, since Dworkin's conception of participants in legal practice is that of the windowless monad, it can only be a miracle that, in most cases, private acts of interpretation end in the same judgment regarding the state of the law. Dworkinians have no plausible explanation for this phenomenon.

a psycho-social phenomenon. Perhaps this is what Hart had in mind when he described *Concept* as a work in 'descriptive sociology'.[77]

The fact remains that Hart and his followers simply have not gone far enough in generating a proper account of legal interpretation.[78] But this is not impossible. Validity is not just a matter of sources of law. It applies to their construal as well. There has to be a reason why the majority garnered sufficient votes for their position. Of course, we can speculate that it is a matter of sotto voce agendas,[79] but a simpler explanation may be more persuasive.

As I have argued elsewhere,[80] the key question in *Riggs* is 'How did Judge Earl persuade enough of his colleagues to see the law as he did?' Three factors suggest themselves. First, in articulating the reasons for its decision, the majority opinion did no damage to the existing state of the law. I will call this interpretive norm 'minimal mutilation'.[81] In other words, deciding against Elmer did not put in question the efficacy of any other element of the New York Statute of Wills. Second, through its decision, the majority demonstrated that its conclusion was consistent with everything else it knew to be true about the law of wills. I shall refer to this as coherence.[82] Finally, the opinion shows how a decision against Elmer comports with similar decisions in other departments of law. I shall

[77] Hart 2012: v. In an interview conducted by David Sugarman (2005), Hart admits that his intention was to 'put the stick in an anthill'; sociology – as such – he did not take too seriously.

[78] Hart (2012: 259) acknowledges Dworkin's claims regarding TD; additionally, he states that 'the rule of recognition may supply tests relating not to the factual content of laws but to their conformity with substantive moral values or principles'. Of course, he continues, judges may disagree about the relevance of such tests as well as 'what the tests require in particular cases' (Hart 2012: 259). My thanks to Torben Spaak for reminding me of this passage. I have profited from reading MacCormick 2003.

[79] This is Leiter's suggestion. See Leiter 2009: 1218.

[80] I have argued for such an account of interpretation in Patterson 1996.

[81] See Ullian and Quine 1978: 66–7 discussing the virtue of conservatism; see also Harman and Thomson (1996: 12): 'It is rational to make the least change in one's view that is necessary in order to obtain greater coherence in what one believes' (citations omitted); and see H. M. Hart and Sacks 1994: 140 discussing reasoned elaboration.

[82] The idea of coherence is apt. '[A]t its most general level, coherence refers to the ways in which parts are interconnected to form a whole; and at a similar level of generality, the appraisive category of coherence is an abridgment of the range of questions one asks of a text in terms of its parts and the closeness of their interrelationships' (Condren 2014: 148). While Dworkin maintains that coherence is a central feature of his theory of law, there is reason to doubt this; see Raz 1995.

refer to this aspect as generality.[83] Taken together, minimal mutilation, coherence and generality are the three aspects of the majority's opinion that support the notion that its interpretation of the law is more persuasive[84] than that offered by the dissenting opinion.[85]

In thinking about the relationship between argument and persuasion, one can do no better than this observation by the great American logician and philosopher Willard Quine: 'We convince someone of something by appealing to beliefs he already holds and by combining these to induce further beliefs in him, step by step, until the belief we wanted finally to inculcate in him is inculcated.'[86] I think that this is a fine explanation of what happens when lawyers interpret the law. It explains what happened in the *Riggs* case and I believe it to be a sound basis from which to build a positivist account of interpretation in law.

29.5 Conclusion

The focus of this chapter is Dworkin's criticisms of Hart's positivism. As we have seen, it is not possible to properly consider Dworkin's critique of Hart without assessing the merits of Dworkin's own conception of the nature of law. Dworkin's mature critique of Hart is more about what Dworkin sees as Hart's failure to take account of the interpretive nature of legal practice. But, as I have endeavoured to show, Dworkin inflates this point well beyond the realm of plausibility. It is true that Hart did not think deeply enough about legal interpretation. But this is a problem that can be solved. Dworkin's criticisms of Hart were always interesting, but, in the end, Hart's view of the nature of law survived Dworkin's critique.

[83] Ullian and Quine 1978: 73: 'The wider the range of application of a hypothesis, the more general it is.'

[84] The basis for my comparative claim is the fact that the Dissent fails to engage the points made by the Majority.

[85] While I acknowledge that more work needs to be done (for example, lexical ordering of the three in any particular case), I do believe that the *Riggs* opinion is sufficient to identify the basic contours of a positivist account of interpretation. Minimal mutilation, coherence and generality are three interpretative norms that one finds in virtually every account of legal interpretation. These three norms will find diverse expression in different departments of law; but all three will be present and are a quotidian feature of law.

[86] Ullian and Quine 1978: 77.

References

Coleman, J. L. 1988. 'Negative and Positive Positivism'. In J. Coleman. *Markets, Morals and the Law.* Cambridge University Press: 3–27.

Coleman, J. L. 2001. *The Practice of Principle: In Defense of a Pragmatist Approach to Legal Theory.* Oxford University Press.

Coleman, J. L. and Simchen, O. 2003. 'Law'. *Legal Theory* 1(1): 1–41.

Condren, C. 2014. *The Status and Appraisal of Classic Texts.* Princeton University Press.

Dewey, J. 1924. 'Logical Method and Law'. *Cornell Law Quarterly* 10: 17–27.

Dworkin, R. 1967. 'The Model of Rules I'. *University of Chicago Law Review* 35(1): 14–46.

Dworkin, R. 1977. *The Philosophy of Law.* Oxford University Press.

Dworkin, R. 1978. *Taking Rights Seriously.* Harvard University Press.

Dworkin, R. 1986. *Law's Empire.* Harvard University Press.

Dworkin, R. 2002. 'Thirty Years On'. *Harvard Law Review* 115: 1655–87.

Dworkin, R. 2008. *Justice in Robes.* Harvard University Press.

Dworkin, R. 2011. *Justice for Hedgehogs.* Harvard University Press.

Gavison, R. 1987. 'Comment' [on Dworkin, 'Legal Theory and the Problem of Sense']. In R. Gavison (ed.). *Issues in Contemporary Legal Philosophy: The Influence of H.L.A. Hart.* Clarendon Press: 21–34.

Guest, S. 2012. *Ronald Dworkin.* 3rd ed. Stanford Law Books.

Harman, G. and Thomson, J. 1996. *Moral Relativism and Moral Objectivity.* Wiley-Blackwell.

Hart, H. L. A. 1955. 'Theory and Definition in Jurisprudence'. *Proceedings of the Aristotelian Society,* Suppl. 29: 259–64.

Hart, H. L. A. 1958. 'Positivism and the Separation of Law and Morals', *Harvard Law Review* 71: 606–12.

Hart, H. L. A. 1977. 'American Jurisprudence through English Eyes: The Nightmare and the Noble Dream'. *Sibley Lecture Series.* 33: 137–41. http://digitalcommons.law.uga.edu/cgi/viewcontent.cgi?article=1032&context=lectures_pre_arch_lectures_sibley.

Hart, H. L. A. 1982. 'Legal Duty and Obligation'. In H. L. A. Hart. *Essays on Bentham.* Oxford University Press: 147–53.

Hart, H. L. A. 1983. 'Law in the Perspective of Philosophy' in H.L.A. Hart. *Essays in Jurisprudence and Philosophy.* Clarendon Press: 153–8.

Hart, H. L. A. 2012. *The Concept of Law.* 3rd ed. Introduction by L. Green, eds. J. Raz and P. Bulloch. Oxford University Press.

Hart, H. M. and Sacks, A. M. 1994. *The Legal Process: Basic Problems in the Making and Application of Law.* Eds. W. N. Eskridge and P. P. Frickey. Foundation Press.

Leiter, B. 2009. 'Explaining Theoretical Disagreement'. *University of Chicago Law Review* 76: 1215–50.

Liptak, A. 2013. 'Ronald Dworkin, Scholar of the Law, Is Dead at 81: Dworkin Came to Oxford from the Yale Law School'. *New York Times*. www.nytimes.com/2013/02/15/us/ronald-dworkin-legal-philosopher-dies-at-81.html?pagewanted=all.

MacCormick, N. 2003. 'Argumentation and Interpretation in Law'. *Ratio Juris* 16(4): 469–85.

Patterson D. 1996. *Law as Interpretation: The Jurisprudence of Ronald Dworkin*. Oxford University Press.

Patterson, D. 2016. 'Can We Please Stop Doing This? By the Way, Postema Was Right'. In T. Gizbert-Studnicki (ed.). *Metaphilosophy of Law*. Hart Publishing: 49–60.

Patterson, D. 2018. 'Theoretical Disagreement, Legal Positivism and Interpretation'. *Ratio Juris* 31: 260–75.

Postema, G. J. 1987. '"Protestant" Interpretation and Social Practices'. *Law and Philosophy* 6: 283–319.

Raz, J. 1983. 'Postscript to *Legal Principles and the Limits of Law*'. In M. Cohen (ed.). *Ronald Dworkin and Contemporary Jurisprudence*. Rowman & Allanheld: 84–5.

Raz, J. 1995. 'The Relevance of Coherence'. In J. Raz. *Ethics in the Public Domain*. Oxford University Press: 277–325.

Raz, J. 2009. 'Legal Positivism and the Sources of Law'. In J. Raz. *The Authority of Law*. 2nd ed. Oxford University Press: 37–52.

Schauer, F. 1985. 'Easy Cases Interpretation Symposium: Philosophy of Language and Legal Interpretation'. *Southern California Law Review* 58: 399–407.

Shapiro, S. J. 2007 'The "Hart-Dworkin" Debate: A Short Guide for the Perplexed'. *Public Law and Legal Theory Working Paper* 77(7). In A. Ripstein (ed.). *Ronald Dworkin*. Cambridge University Press: 22–55.

Stone, J. 1946. *The Province and Function of Law*. Harvard University Press.

Sugarman, D. 2005. 'Hart Interviewed: H.L.A. Hart in Conversation with David Sugarman'. *Journal of Law and Society* 32(2): 267–93.

Ullian J. S. and Quine W. V. 1978. *The Web of Belief*. 2nd ed. McGraw-Hill Education.

Waismann, F. 1945/1951. 'Verifiability'. In A. Flew (ed.). *Essays on Logic and Language I*. Philosophical Library: 11–30.

Wittgenstein, L. 2010. *Philosophical Investigations*. Trans. G. E. M. Anscombe, P. M. S. Hacker and J. Schulte. 4th ed. John Wiley & Sons.

30 Tracing Finnis's Criticism of Hart's Internal Point of View: Instability and the 'Point' of Human Action in Law

Veronica Rodriguez-Blanco*

30.1 Introduction

Much ink has been spilled on Hart's internal point of view[1] and its role in understanding and defining the so-called rule of recognition. Surprisingly, however, there has not been much attempt to unpack and further develop the criticism advanced by Finnis that Hart's internal point of view is *instable*. Finnis agrees with Raz and Hart that the internal perspective is key to elucidating the character of law; however, he states that Hart's internal point of view cannot do the job that it aims to do due to its *instability*. Finnis then adds that there is a remedy to this *instability*, that is, that law should be understood from the point of view of the agent who possesses practical reason. Let me explain.

Finnis (and also to a certain extent Dworkin) advances a methodology in which the practical point of view enables us to identify and determine the subject matter of jurisprudence. Unlike Dworkin, however, Finnis acknowledges that there are both social and evaluative facts that play an important role in any descriptive-explanatory approach. Finnis advocates the view that any description and explanation of what law is should be done from the point of view of the man who possesses practical reasonableness.[2] In other words, practical reasonableness allows us to understand the unique qualities of law and the ways in which it can assist in fulfilling the basic

* I am grateful to Torben Spaak for his very helpful comments that enabled me to improve the chapter. The usual disclaimer applies.

[1] In the last ten years, there has been an important body of literature that discusses Hart's idea of the 'internal point of view'. See Adler 2009; Coleman 2001; Holton 1998; Patterson 1999; Perry 1995, 2000, 2006; Schauer 1994;Shapiro 2000, 2006; Zipursky 2006.

[2] 'Practical reasonableness' is the term introduced by Finnis (2011: chapter V).

goods in our lives. How does Finnis reconcile a descriptive-explanatory method and the view that there is a privileged point of view which is the point of view of practical reasonableness without falling prey to the strong version of normative jurisprudence advocated by Ronald Dworkin?[3]

Finnis resorts to the Aristotelian idea, later well developed by Aquinas and medieval scholars, of 'focal' meaning or 'central' case, which is the view that the central case of law is the conception of law advocated by the man who possesses practical reasonableness.[4] This methodology enables legal theorists, Finnis argues, to differentiate the defective or marginal legal systems from the ones that approximate the ideals of justice. In other words, multiplicity and unification can be reconciled because both the common belief and the legal-positivist approach that wicked legal systems are law, together with the view that law serves ideals of justice, can be coherently unified.

Finnis is following Aristotle's insight: for Aristotle, a successful criticism of Plato's theory of the forms needed to show that there is multiplicity, but also unity, in key concepts such as 'being', 'good', 'democracy' and so on. The point of view of the man who possesses practical reasonableness, Finnis tells us, will explain why we consider to be law legal systems that do not possess desirable features such as pursuing the common good. Moreover, the legal theorist will simultaneously be able to explain why we consider law legal systems that do embrace the ideals of justice. If Finnis's argument succeeds, then Finnis's new natural law theory, as opposed to Dworkin's strong normative jurisprudence, might be a fruitful path towards answering the main question of substantive jurisprudence, that is, what law is.

Finnis's methodological claims are intriguing and complex because one can identify two aspects in his methodology: an explanatory aspect and a practical one. The first aspect involves a descriptive-explanatory methodology; this means that he aims to describe legal concepts but believes that description cannot take place without considering the central case of jurisprudence, the point of view of the man who possesses practical reasonableness. According to this view, the legal theorist needs to explain and describe both the marginal cases of law and the core case of law as conceived by the practical point of view. This task cannot be done,

[3] See Dworkin 1986.

[4] For the use of Finnis's methodology in legal interpretation, see Endicott 2001.

however, without taking the point of view of the participant, that is, the point of view of the man who has habits, social practices, values, intentions and beliefs in a given community. Finnis emphasises the role of anthropology, statistical analysis and so on to expand the understanding of the participant's point of view. However, he tells us that such data only help us to understand the degrees of perfection or defectiveness of the practical point of view and the principles of practical reasonableness in different cultures and social practice. It is the task of the intellect to grasp what is practically reasonable.[5] In other words, what is practically reasonable cannot be derived from the empirical data of human nature; the formation of a concept depends on grasping '*men's practical viewpoint*'.

On the other hand, Finnis rejects Dworkin's view that our starting point should be our own moral and political beliefs, since, according to Finnis, these beliefs can be false or affected by our prejudices. We need to stand outside these beliefs and revise them in order to reach the 'right' reasons.[6]

For Dworkin, by contrast, the practical question needs to be answered in terms of a theoretical question: what I ought to do requires an answer to the question of what I ought *to believe* about the grounds of law. The practitioner, the judge, the legislator and the lawyer need to engage in an inquiry into the grounds of law that make legal propositions true, and this search will be a constructive task that will require us to take into account the practitioner's and the theorist's moral convictions.[7] True, it is integrity that will guide the practitioner in constructing the best possible interpretation of what the law is, and the requirement of fit with the bulk of the legal material will enable the practitioner to reach a balance between moral soundness and legal precedent. But it is a theoretically justificatory enterprise, characterised by determining the grounds of law.

The second aspect of Finnis's methodology is the practical one. At the core of Finnis's inquiry is the practical question of what one ought to do according to the principles of practical reasonableness. For Finnis, the theorist needs to explain the practical viewpoint, but once the practical

[5] See Finnis 2011: 17–18.

[6] Finnis 2011: 17. See also Finnis 1987. For a criticism of Dworkin's methodology as a failure to see the importance of practical reason, see Rodriguez-Blanco 2016b.

[7] Ronald Dworkin asserts in several passages of *Law's Empire* that the interpretive task requires the substantive convictions of the theorist and the judge in order to determine which interpretation best fits the past legal materials and is morally sound. See Dworkin 1986: 67, 87–8.

viewpoint has been identified, it impinges on all of us: the theorist and the participant. It is because the practical viewpoint impinges on all of us that we must act according to the principles of practical reasonableness, and the law needs to be shaped according both to such principles and to the basic values.

From the viewpoint of the theorist, according to Finnis, the explanatory task precedes the justificatory task. There is, however, a mutual interdependence between the explanatory and the justificatory enterprises. Practical deliberation requires knowledge of the human situation, but, at the same time, evaluation from the point of view of the man who possesses practical reasonableness determines which descriptions are illuminating and significant.[8]

The concept of law, Finnis tells us, is used in different ways and in different contexts; in spite of this multiplicity, however, 'law' refers to a single concept and, consequently, the different conceptions of law refer to a primary source, which is the point of view of the man who possesses practical reasonableness. Hence, Finnis's argument shows that multiplicity can be unified by a central case of law. Let us scrutinise the two key roles of the 'central case' identified by Finnis.

First, Finnis begins with the idea that a descriptive-explanatory method needs to be aware of the different conceptions and self-interpretations of the people whose conduct and dispositions shape the concept to be investigated.

Complete understanding of an *action or practice entails an understanding of the point of the action or practice.* The agent who executes the action or the participant *who participates in the practice gives the action or practice its point or value.* Therefore, only through understanding the self-interpretations of participants does the theorist understand the

[8] Finnis (2011: 19) asserts that there is an interplay and interdependence between evaluating with the view of acting reasonably well and describing and he puts this as follows:

> There is thus a mutual though not quite symmetrical interdependence between the project of describing human affairs by way of theory and the project of evaluating human options with a view, at least remotely, to acting reasonably and well. The evaluations are in no way deduced from the descriptions; but one whose knowledge of the facts of the human situation is very limited is very unlikely to judge well in discerning the practical implications of the basic values. Equally, the descriptions are not deduced from the evaluations; but without the evaluations one cannot determine what descriptions are really illuminating and significant.

attributed value or point.[9] The theorist is confronted, however, by the problem of a variety of conceptions about the value or point of the practice and action. The point of a practice changes from person to person and from society to society.[10]

How can the theorist organise these conflicting and different self-interpretations and conceptions? Theorists in the human sciences resort to the identification of a common factor that will unify the variety of conceptions about the point or value of a practice and action. This strategy is criticised by Finnis, and we now turn to this point.

The unifying role constitutes the second role identified by 'central case' methodology. Finding an answer to the multiplicity of conceptions and self-interpretations about the point of actions and practices means searching for a common factor that covers all these different self-interpretations and conceptions.[11] Kelsen, according to Finnis, is aware that the point or function of an activity is fundamental to the success of the descriptive-explanatory task of the subject matter. Kelsen, Finnis tells us, advances the view that the theorist needs to find one thing in common or the one feature that characterises and explains the subject matter.[12] This view presupposes that the concept 'law' is connected to one single feature.

Raz and Hart, Finnis tells us, break the 'naïve' methodology of Austin and Kelsen and argue that Austin and Kelsen are mistaken on the function attributed to law. Hart explains the concept of law by appealing to the practical point of the components of the concept. Both Raz and Hart emphasise that law provides reasons for actions and aims to guide the conduct of the legal participants. They also believe, according to Finnis, in the idea that these different conceptions have a principle or rationale that unifies them.[13]

Finnis criticises Kelsen because he presupposes that there is a common factor or one thing in common to all the different conceptions of law. But he also criticises Raz and Hart: although they abandon the idea that there is one thing in common to all instances of the concept of law, they adopt an *unstable* or unsatisfactory 'practical point of view'.[14] Finnis uses the term 'practical point of view' to refer to a point of view that addresses decision

[9] See Finnis 2011: 13. [10] See Finnis 2011: 15.

[11] There is a parallel motivation in Aristotle's introduction of the idea of 'focal meaning'. See Irwin 1981: 540.

[12] See Finnis 2011: 6. [13] See Finnis 2011: 10.

[14] Finnis 2011: 13. We discuss this key point later in this and subsequent sections.

and action.[15] Thus, Raz[16] adopts the 'ordinary man's point of view' and, in a later work, refers to the 'legal point of view',[17] whereas Hart adopts the 'internal point of view', namely, the point of view of the man who uses the rules as a standard for evaluating his own and others' actions. Raz's and Hart's practical points of view, Finnis tells us, represent steps forward from Austin and Kelsen, who presuppose that man who merely acquiesces in the law because of fear of punishment.

However, Finnis finds both Raz's and Hart's internal points of view *unstable* and unsatisfactory because they cannot explain the distinction between different points of view such as that between the anarchist and the ideal law-abiding citizen. Legal theorists need a principle or rationale that will enable them to discriminate between points of view and to identify what is significant or relevant when organising the different self-interpretations and conceptions of law.

In the current literature, Finnis's criticism of Hart's and Raz's methodologies has ignited discussions about the differences between central or focal cases of law[18] and defective instances of law.[19] Finnis's criticism of Hart's internal point of view focuses on its problematic character in unifying the different self-conceptions and self-interpretations of law. However, a further explanation of the problematic character of Hart's internal point of view can be found in the following quotation: '[B]ut all this is unstable and unsatisfactory because it involves a refusal to attribute significances to differences that any actor in the field (whether the subversive anarchist or his opponent the ideal law-abiding citizen) would count as practically significant.'[20]

In other words, Finnis tells us, any participant in legal practice, for example a citizen, a judge, a lawyer, is engaged with the law and is interested in distinguishing between a good and a *not so* good norm, between a just directive and an unjust directive, between a rational court decision and a non-rational court decision. Hart's internal point of view

[15] Finnis 2011: 12.

[16] For a discussion on the differences between Raz's and Finnis's methodologies, see Dickson 2001.

[17] See Raz 1999.

[18] For an alternative view on central case or focal meaning, see Rodriguez-Blanco 2007.

[19] Murphy (2006) develops a defence of Finnis's methodology. By contrast, Julie Dickson (2001) engages in a distinction between direct and indirect evaluation and argues that Finnis's methodology is close to the former.

[20] Finnis 2011: 13.

refuses to make further distinctions between the peripheral and the central cases of law, and this brings *instability* to the concept.

Hart's internal point of view as unstable can be traced to a more fundamental criticism, that is, Hart's internal point of view cannot be used to understand the point of human actions and therefore we cannot rely on Hart's internal point of view to identify *significance differences that any actor in the field can make*. In the 'methodology' literature, this argument on *instability* is overlooked and its premises have not been carefully examined. In this chapter, I will try to show that the idea that the internal point of view is unstable is key to both understanding the limits of Hart's legal theory and shedding further light on the view that law should be conceived in terms of a central or focal case.

We could infer that, for Finnis, placing practical reason at the core of the concept of law provides the anchor that gives stability to the concept of law and enables us to grasp it correctly. But why does practical reason constitute the paradigmatic or 'central case' of law? Why should it have priority over other internal points of view, for example the point of view of the bad man or woman, or the point of view of the legal anarchist? *Furthermore, why does it provide stability? What kind of stability is Finnis talking about?* Finnis,[21] Grisez[22] and Tollefsen[23] have defended the priority of the practical reason viewpoint using Aquinas's conception of intentional action and the four orders of nature. However, the sceptical theorist, the critical legal theorist and the Holmesian bad woman remain indifferent to this defence and are unpersuaded by the arguments of Finnis, Grisez or Tollefsen. Furthermore, they do not seem to understand the verdict of instability advanced by Finnis against Hart's internal point of view.

I will explain why this instability arises, although I will not rely *exclusively* on the notion of intentional action, which I have defended elsewhere, advocated by Aristotle, Aquinas, Anscombe, Grisez, Finnis and Tollefsen, or on the four orders of nature. My key argumentative strategy is a negative one that is intended to show that Hart's model of action cannot account for the point of human actions in law.

I will defend three claims:

(1) Understanding a human action in law involves understanding what that action aims to achieve that is its point.

[21] See Finnis 1998, 2003. [22] See Grisez 1967. [23] See Tollefsen 2018.

(2) Hart's internal point of view cannot be used to understand the point/s of the action. His position shows only what the mental state, that is, the belief, of the agent who performs an action might be when they follow the rule of recognition and/or legal rules in general.

(c) Understanding the internal mental state of the action is not understanding the point of the action. Understanding the mental state of the agent might or might not provide an understanding of the point of the action, but if it does so it can be considered mere fluke. Therefore, Hart's internal point of view is *unstable.*

I will presuppose that (1) is uncontroversial as the 'point' of an action can be construed widely to include motives, interests and values. In order to show that mental states, that is, beliefs, cannot capture the point of an action and its eventual content (2), I will use a theory of intentional action defended by Anscombe. I will argue that when we observe an action from the third-person perspective, we do not capture the mental state of the performer nor provide an interpretation of the bodily movements that are the physical marks of the action. We are trying to 'see the point' of the action, to give meaning to it. If we cannot see the point/s of the action, it is because we are not exercising certain capacities[24] and dispositions, that is, practical reason and practical imagination, and these capacities are learned through language-games embedded in human forms of life.

Arguably, we are blind to some aspects of the point of an action. It is tempting to theoretically replace this blindness with a theory of mental states, for example the belief that an action corresponds to the type of action that is legal, or other fictions that obscure the understanding of human actions. Finally, I will argue that the instability is produced because we need to rely on *remembering* our mental states and we might or might not be able to remember our beliefs about legal rules. I might remember my mental state of belief in the rule of recognition or legal rules in general, but this is *mere fluke*. There is no route that guarantees my remembering and grasping the meaning or point of an action. By contrast, in order to 'see the point of an action', whereby certain capacities and dispositions are exercised, we need to exercise the capacity of recognising actions learned

[24] I understand capacities as the abilities of human beings to engage in different operations. (See Aquinas ST I: 75–83.) A full discussion of capacities and dispositions will go beyond the central argument of this chapter. For a discussion of capacities as actualisation of potentialities with special focus on practical reasoning, see Rodriguez-Blanco 2016a).

in language-games. We should not obscure the 'point of an action' with fictions like mental states as, in doing so, we lose the agent and the action itself.

The chapter is divided into two main sections: in Section 30.2, I use Anscombe's theory of intentional action to shed light on 'seeing the point of a human action' and I discuss learning the *logos* of social practice as the exercising of our capacities within specific forms of life. In Section 30.3, I delve further into Finnis's criticism of the instability of the internal point of view and defend the Finnisian claim that the exercise of our capacity of practical reason is the central case of human action and therefore of human action in law. Section 30.4 concludes the chapter.

30.2 'Seeing the Point of an Action' and a Theory of Intentional Action

Our actions are not merely physical movements or the representations of one or more mental states; our actions have an inner dimension that gives them unity. More precisely, this unity results from the agent's choice and intention.

The choice that expresses itself in the physical realm in certain movements makes it a certain kind of action or constitutes its nature or species.[25] This being so, it is incumbent upon us to ask how this inner dimension can be intelligible to third persons. For example, when I see someone sitting at a desk and tracing lines with certain features on to a sheet of paper, I can understand that they are writing a letter *if and only* if I grasp what they intend to do. This inner dimension is intelligible because the *logos of intentional actions* – in other words, the reasons behind actions – can be understood through the specific context of the exterior performance. I understand the letter writer's intentions, for example, because I recognise objects with the typical features of stationery on their desk and I know what is required by the practice of writing letters.

Anscombe discusses this relationship between the exterior performance of actions and the institutional facts or contexts in which they occur in her

[25] In what follows, I develop an argument that I outlined (with Pilar Zambrano) in Rodriguez-Blanco and Zambrano 2018.

1958 article *On Brute Facts.*[26] In what my co-author and I have termed her *institutional transparency thesis*, Anscombe argues that while a factual description of an action A *is not a description of the institution behind* A,[27] the *existence* of a factual description of action A does *presuppose* an institution A. Put in the context of intelligibility, understanding the inner dimension (that is, the intention or choice) of a third person's actions requires understanding the social or institutional context in which those actions occur. To understand that the utterance of certain words by someone is a promise, for example, I need to know how promises are institutionalised in my community, even if – and this is the transparency thesis – I do not need to think about that while I promise or when I recognise a promise. Furthermore, the intelligibility of these actions occurs not at the level of the theoretical but at the level of the practical.

To explain further, we must ask what the *institution behind the description* is. Anscombe offers an example – 'I owe the grocer five pounds for the potatoes he has supplied to me' – that we can use as a starting point.

Let us say that I order five kilograms of potatoes from the grocer and that the grocer loads the potatoes into his delivery van, drives to my house, rings my doorbell, unloads the potatoes from his delivery van and gives me a bill for five pounds. You observe both my actions and those of the grocer. You conclude, as an observer, that I owe the grocer five pounds. You reach this conclusion, but how? Do you reach this conclusion because you ask me what am I doing and I tell you? But you would ask this question only when what I am doing is unintelligible to you. You understand both the way I move my body and the reasons *why* I am moving my body *as a unity*. Unless you already possess the concepts necessary to understand the reasons *why* I move my body – concepts such as *supplying, owing* and *five pounds* – simply observing the way the grocer and I move our bodies as I receive the potatoes and the bill for five pounds does not tell you that I owe the grocer five pounds for the potatoes he has supplied. The obligation of owing becomes intelligible to you only if you already understand the action of supplying as the reason for the obligation of *owing*. In that case, you already grasped concepts such as *supplying, owing* and *five pounds* prior to the bodily movements between the grocer and me. You, me and the grocer had previously learned that set of concepts within the context of the social institution of *buying and selling*. We learned that set of

[26] Anscombe 1958. [27] Anscombe 1958: 72.

concepts when we were young and learned that the exchange of goods in our society creates obligations. We learned *as a unity* the bodily movements and the *reasons why* we buy, sell and satisfy our obligations in the exchange of goods. My bodily movements, the bodily movements of the grocer and the reasons *why* we perform those actions, in other words, the *logos* of those actions, are understood as a whole in Anscombe's example. Your understanding, as an observer, of the unity of bodily movements and the reasons *why* those bodily movements were performed does not describe the institution of *buying and selling*.

Because the *action is practical, it should be understood as practical*. We can say that the action is 'practical' because it is about the intentions of both the grocer and the buyer. The grocer and the buyer intend to produce a certain state of affairs and they know *why they are doing what they are doing*.

Would, Anscombe asks, the same bodily movements in a film where one actor supplies the potatoes and another actor receives the potatoes be different from the example above? Despite the actors' bodily movements in the film, they do not intend to create a purchasing contract or the obligation to satisfy such a contract. And the observer, who understands the difference between the background institutions in each situation, understands the difference between those two situations.

To further understand this subtle and difficult point, we need to understand Anscombe's conception of intentional action, which rejects actions as a two-link causal-effect chain composed of an interior act, that is, mental states such as beliefs and desires that *cause* an action, and the exterior action, that is, the *effect* of the interior act. Like Aquinas, Anscombe does not separate the physical action and the answer to the question of *why* the agent is acting in the way they are. If the question of *why* cannot be applied to the physical action, then, more than likely, the action was not intentional. Which is to say that there are not two actions, an interior and an exterior, but only one action. Different perspectives can analyse that action, but the exterior action is one and the same as, and not essentially different from, the interior will. The one action is its performance and manifestation.[28]

What, then, is the choice or will that is performed and manifested by the exterior action? Do all voluntary actions involve a choice?[29]

[28] Aquinas (2006) ST I–II 17, a. 4.

[29] See Aquinas (2006) ST I–II 18, particularly aa. 2 and 7; Finnis 1988: 65–6; Rhonheimer 2008: 41.

Consider two different examples. In one, I want to move my arm but, instead, my foot moves. In another, I want to move my arm and my arm in fact moves. My actions are voluntary in both examples; however, my action does not perform my choice in the first example. We can make a distinction, then, between a merely volitional act, that is, an act initiated by a person, and a wilful act, that is, a volitional act that actually fulfils a choice. That said, how can a third-person observer know whether the act is volitional or wilful? Observers can see that I move my foot or my arm, but they cannot know my choice, so they cannot, from observation alone, know that only my arm moved intentionally.

Arguably, the way to determine whether or not an action is willed is to ask the agent to describe the action. However, agents are only very rarely asked to describe their actions because, in most cases, the institutional background or language-games in combination with the physical movements of the action are sufficient to make such a determination.

A theoretical engagement with human action is closer to an explanation than to a form of understanding. In theoretical or metaphysical knowledge, actions are individuated through a cognitive process that focuses not on identifying *choices* performed in actions but on identifying actions as effects of previous events. Donald Davidson, in his account of intentional action, defends this causal theory of action and the correlative theory of the interpretation of concrete actions.[30]

For Davidson, intentional actions are understood in terms of the reasons that the agent gives when describing what they did. The goal is to rationalise the action. Furthermore, the agent can be said to have a reason if (a) the agent has a pro-attitude towards the action and (b) the agent believes (or knows, remembers, notices, perceives) that their action is of that kind.[31] Davidson calls this pairing of belief and desire a primary reason and he claims that 'a primary reason for an action is its cause'.[32]

In Davidson's account, beliefs and desires are mental events that (may) *cause* an exterior action, which is a subsequent and corresponding event. The relationship between mental events and actions is causal, specifically a kind of causal relationship between facts.[33] So, my desire to flip a switch and my belief that my action is of that kind causes the action *I flip the switch*. Furthermore, observation of the action allows us to infer the cause. Even though we only observe the effect, that is, the action, which in this

[30] See Davidson 1963. [31] See Davidson 1963: 685. [32] Ibid. [33] Ibid.

case is the flipping of the switch, we can infer the cause, that is, the mental events that caused the effect.

Davidson denies that there are psychophysical laws that connect actions and reasons, saying that if there are laws, they ought to be neurological, chemical or physical.[34] In the last forty years, his account of intentional action has exerted great influence. In that time, practical reasoning has tended to be assimilated into intentional action as a mental state.[35] The assimilation of practical reasoning as a mental state offers two advantages over competing accounts like Anscombe's. One, this assimilation allows neo-Humeans[36] to advance the Humean view that desires or pro-attitudes motivate and explain intentional actions. Two, this assimilation is compatible with a descriptive, scientifically neutral understanding of action as caused by mental events. Despite these advantages, Davidson's view contains a notable flaw; namely, it has no way to guarantee that the causal link between a reason and the corresponding action is right.[37]

There are other problems that affect the standard model of intentional action. If an intention to act is a mental state, it entails that I can remember my mental state and can reflect upon it. Unfortunately, however, it seems that the memory of or ability to reflect on my intention as a mental state can vanish. If intentions are purely mental states that can vanish, we might not remember them correctly, they might not endure, and then our intentional action might also vanish.

In conclusion, putting human actions on the same level as physical/theoretical or metaphysical events, or putting the understanding of human actions on the same level as the explanation of effective causal relationships, fails to guarantee the individuation of actions.

As previously discussed, the best way to determine whether an agent willed an action is to ask them for a description of their action. We can prompt a description of the action by asking the agent *why* they performed an action.[38] Prompting a description in this way is known as the *why-question*

34 Ibid.

35 See, e.g., Wallace 2014: 'Practical reasoning gives rise not to bodily movements *per se*, but to intentional actions, and these are intelligible as such only to the extent [that] they reflect our mental states.'

36 See Blackburn 1998; Harman 1986a, 1986b; Smith 1994.

37 Chisholm (1976: 28) was the first scholar to write about deviant causal chains. Other, more radical scholars go further and deny that intentional actions are causes; see, e.g., Dancy 2000.

38 See Anscombe 1963.

methodology and is the key method in Anscombe's *Intention* for clarifying the connections between our actions and our practical reasoning.[39] Fully understanding this methodology requires accounting for the facts that (a) paradigmatically, an intentional action is a sequence of actions aimed towards the action's final end and (b) we know that the explanation finishes because the last step is described in terms of good-making characteristics that make intelligible and illuminate as a coherent whole the successive steps of the action. With these considerations in mind, we can now explain the why-question methodology.

Anscombe begins *Intention* by stating that the subject of the book should be studied under three headings – expression of an intention, intentional action, and intention in acting[40] – and that all three should be understood as interdependent. Thus, my expression of an intention cannot be understood as a prediction about my future acts or as an introspective explanation of an intention such as desires, wants and so forth. If I utter 'This afternoon I will go for a walk' as an expression of an intention, the utterance cannot be understood as a forecast of the future. Indeed, the intention is rightly expressed by the utterance, even if it then turns out that as a forecast it would have been false, since a friend comes to visit and I cannot leave home. Nor can the utterance be an expression of desires or wants. I might intend to walk even if I have no desire whatsoever to do it: for example, I might need to walk to a friend's house to return a book, even if I would rather do something else. Anscombe tells us, however, that people formulate expressions of intentions about the future and they usually turn out to be correct.[41] How is this possible?

To answer this question, she tries to explain the way in which we can identify intentional acts and separate them from non-intentional actions. Doing this requires taking the logical step of trying to understand what it means when I say that 'I have acted with an intention'. For Anscombe, acting intentionally means acting for a reason or being able to provide *reasons for actions*, with the understanding that the question *why* can be said to apply to such actions.[42] All of which is to say that we act

[39] Anscombe's exposition follows Aquinas's explanation of intentional action very closely (Anscombe 1963). Notably, Kenny (1979) argues that Aquinas's model would be better understood more as a Gestalt psychology.

[40] Moran and Stone (2009: 37) explain the transformation of these three headings in the post-*Intention* literature.

[41] See Anscombe 1963: ss. 3–4. [42] See Anscombe 1963: ss. 4–6.

intentionally when we act for reasons, which in turn entails us to be responsive and sensitive to a framework of justification for our actions. If I perform an action φ, am asked why I have performed φ and give a genuine answer, for example 'I was not aware I was doing Φ' or 'I did not know I was performing φ', the action cannot be said to be intentional or directed by reasons. The action might be voluntary, but it is not intentional.[43] On the other hand, if the answer takes the form 'because φ' or 'in order to φ', then it might be a prima facie case for an intentional action, which is to say an action directed by reasons. Reasons demonstrate themselves, so to speak, in intentional actions, and reasons demonstrate that they operate as a part of the practical reasoning of an agent.

The problem for the understanding of action is whether or not, when asked *why* we have performed an action, we are in control of the truthfulness of intentions. A further problem presents itself: whether or not we can give a plausible answer without relying on the testimony of the agent of the action.

Anscombe notes that a set of *contextual conditions* allows us to determine whether or not the agent has given their genuine intentions in response to the question *why*.[44] This set of contextual conditions contains those concepts learned at a young age through social context. For example, we learn that money is necessary to purchase goods and that if we order goods for home delivery then we owe the seller money. In our example of a film scene in which a grocer delivers potatoes, we know from the contextual conditions that when the actor-buyer says that he owes the actor-grocer five pounds, the actor-buyer's words are not genuine.

Intentional actions, or actions performed for reasons, require a sequence of steps or actions and, therefore, a sequence of reasons that explain each action-step. If somebody writes a letter and has a reason to do it (for example, greeting a friend), they do so by taking a sheet of paper and a pen and by tracing letters with the pen on the paper. Writing the letter is their reason for tracing lines on the sheet and the latter is their reason for taking the sheet from the drawer. This being the case, the question arises as to how we can know when the explanation is complete and the agent can stop giving justifications. Anscombe argues that the justification stops when the agent describes the endpoint of the action with regard to what is desirable or good for itself. The endpoint of the action is, then, a state of

[43] See Anscombe 1963: s. 17. [44] See Anscombe 1963: s. 25.

affairs, a fact, an object or an event that the agent appears to consider desirable or good. The state of affairs, fact, object or event is considered by the agent to be a good sort of thing. This explanation is commonsensical and arguably the most *naive explanation of our actions.*[45]

To return to our initial discussion, how can the intention/choice of the agent become intelligible to an observer and allow the observer to individuate that intention/choice? Intelligibility requires (i) that both the agent and the observer hold a mutual understanding of what good-making characteristics may be intended or chosen by the agent in performing an action, and (ii) that the good-making characteristics intended by the agent are manifest in the action. The first condition requires that good-making characteristics neither exist purely through convention nor are discoverable through empirical methods but are, at least to some extent, the objects of human intelligence. The second condition requires that the intended good-making characteristics of an action be a specific instance of the good-making characteristics of the institutional background or social practices that give actions their final form or *logos.*[46]

With these conditions in mind, the primary aim of the why-question methodology is to highlight the articulation or structure of an intentional action.[47] In our potatoes example, the grocer does not reflect on why he is doing what he is doing at each concrete action-step. Rather, the grocer understood the sequence of action-steps necessary for buying and selling and the good-making characteristics that explain *why we human beings* buy and sell in the social context.

The concern, then, is not to discover the propositional attitudes – the desires and beliefs that explain buying and selling – *nor even to explicitly describe the institution* of buying and selling, nor to discover the nature of the human action in terms of a given good. The concern is to understand whether or not the action is intentional and to understand what choice the agent intends in the performance of the action. Putting the testimony of the agent aside for the moment, it is only possible to understand the agent's choice when their action is understood as a specific instance within a social practice and justified by the good-making characteristics of that social practice. Only once those understandings are in place can the observer

[45] See Grisez 1967: 177.
[46] See Grisez 1967: 174. These arguments are further developed in Zambrano 2015.
[47] See Vogler 2001.

grasp the intentional action as a unity of physical movements and the answer to the question *why*, or *the grounding logos* of the action.

30.3 Rescuing the Concept of Law: Finnis's Defence of Practical Reason as the Central Case

Having unpacked the idea that intentional actions become intelligible due to institutional transparency and the language-games in which they are inserted, and the idea of a *logos* in the form of values and good-making characteristics that underlie intentional actions, which presupposes the exercise of our capacity of practical reason, we shall now examine whether this conception of intentional action sheds any light on Finnis's criticism of Hart's internal point of view.

Finnis aims to establish that Hart's internal point of view is unstable and that a remedy for such instability is the recognition that the central case of law arises from women and men exercising their practical reasoning capacities as they engage with the law. But there is a lack of clarity as to *why* there is instability and *how* our capacity as practical reasoners provides an adequate solution to the diagnosed instability.

Hart tells us that when women and men see legal rules from their *internal* aspect, there is an acceptance of such rules, which entails that:

1. The behavior in question is seen as the general standard to be followed by the group.
2. There is a critical attitude among the women and men towards this pattern of behavior. The general standard applies to all participants in the social practice and there is consequently ample use of critical expressions in normative language such as 'you ought to', 'that is right', and so forth.[48]

These two key features enable us to distinguish legal rules from habits and orders backed by threats. Interestingly, Hart also distinguishes between the idea of social rules as having an *active* aspect, that is, the internal perspective, and that of their having a passive aspect, that is, habitual obedience orders backed by threats. It is worthwhile quoting his explanation in full:

[48] Hart 1994: 54–61 (here summarised).

> The weakness of the doctrine is that it obscures or distorts the other relatively *active aspect*, which is seen primarily, though not exclusively, in the law-making, law-identifying, and law-applying operations of the officials or experts of the system. Both aspects must be kept in view if we are to see this complex social phenomenon for what it actually is.[49]

Unfortunately, the internal aspect as mere acceptance of a standard and reflective criticism is not sufficient to establish the *active/passive distinction* that Hart is so eager to show as evidenced.[50] When we accept legal rules and these rules are observed as the standard and any deviation can be the subject of reflective criticism, then there is only a difference of degree and *not in kind* of our engagement with the law. According to Hart, the action of the legal participant is captured by an observer through the following mechanism: they recognise a pattern of external behaviour that criticises any deviation of the standard that has previously been accepted by the participant. If this is so, I would like to argue, then it is a mere fluke if the observer can connect the mental state, that is, the desires and beliefs, of the legal participant with the observed pattern of behaviour of the legal participant. *This is the core of the so-called instability of Hart's internal point of view*. Let me explain.

The mental state of belief, that is, acceptance of the legal rule, produces a pattern of behaviour, but we cannot be certain that this particular pattern of behaviour is always accompanied by the *correct* mental state of belief, that is, understanding the point of the action of the participant and engaging with the action because of its point. Consequently, and unsurprisingly, then, the anarchist and the bad woman could have a certain pattern of behaviour and have the belief of acceptance because they can accept the legal rule *for any reason or motive*. However, neither the anarchist nor the bad woman would see any valuable point in actions that engage with the law, nor can we make intelligible *why* they reject the law unless we understand that they *have chosen* to do so. But once we introduce the notion of 'choice', we need to think about an intentional action that is guided by a *logos* as good-making characteristics from the point of view of the agent; for example, the anarchist gives prevalence to their radical autonomy and freedom and this gives a point to their actions against the

[49] Hart 1994: 61 (my emphasis).

[50] See Gardner 2001 for an attempt to defend the 'active' element of Hart's legal theory. For a criticism of this position, see Rodriguez-Blanco and Zambrano 2018.

law. Furthermore, once we introduce 'choice' and reflect on the intelligibility of the choice, then the idea of *a pattern of behaviour becomes theoretically unnecessary.* It does not do any work as all the work is done by our understanding of intentional action. Let me explain this point further.

Hart's idea that we accept legal rules from an internal perspective presupposes an inward-looking approach to action as opposed to an outward-looking approach. The latter examines intentional actions as a series of actions that are justified in terms of other actions and in view of the purpose or end of the intentional action as a good-making characteristic, for example to put the kettle on in order to boil the water, in order to make tea *because* it is pleasant to drink tea. The former examines the mental states that rationalise the actions. The mental states consist of the belief/pro-attitude towards the action.

If the 'acceptance thesis' is the correct interpretation of Hart's central idea concerning the internal point of view towards legal rules, then criticisms that are levelled against inward-looking approaches of intentional actions also apply to Hart's internal point of view and its 'acceptance thesis'. The main criticism that has been raised against the idea that the belief/pro-attitude pairing can explain intentional actions is the view that it cannot explain deviations from the causal chain[51] between mental states and actions.

Let us suppose that you intend to kill your enemy by running over him with your vehicle this afternoon when you will meet him at his house. Some hours before you intend to kill your enemy, you drive to the supermarket, you see your enemy walking on the pavement and you suffer a nervous spasm that causes you to suddenly turn the wheel and run over your enemy. In this example, according to the belief/pro-attitude view, there is an intentional action if you desire to kill your enemy and you believe that the action of killing your enemy, under a certain description, has that property. Ontologically, the theory would establish that you had both the desire to kill your enemy and the belief that this action has the property 'killing your enemy'. Thus, this mental state has caused the action and there is an intentional action. The problem with this view is that it needs to specify the *appropriate causal route.* Davidson has made much effort to specify the 'attitudes that cause the action if they are to rationalize

[51] The first person to discuss deviant causal chains was Chisholm 1976.

the action'.[52] Davidson seems to fear that the idea of attitudes causing action might lead to *infinite regress* and he struggles with his own proposal.[53] He asks *how attitudes must cause actions if they are to rationalise actions.* Davidson's model of intentional action does not help us to determine whether there is an intentional action, it only helps us to determine the *conditions* that would explain the existence of an intentional action. The intentional action is already *given.* A similar criticism is applicable to the 'acceptance thesis' and to this we now turn.

Let us suppose that I intend to go to the park in my car; however, I read a sign at the entrance of the park that states 'Vehicles are not allowed to park in the park' so I turn the wheel of my vehicle, reverse my car and park a few streets away. You ask me *why* I turned the wheel of my vehicle, reversed and parked a few streets away from the park; I answer that I carried out these actions because there is a rule that states 'Vehicles are not allowed to park in the park'. According to the 'acceptance thesis', my desire to follow the pattern of behaviour indicated by the rule and my belief that turning the wheel of my vehicle, reversing my car and not parking in the park are the type of action or *pattern* of behaviour indicated by the rule. However, let us suppose that I desire to avoid parking in the park and have the respective belief. In other words, I accept 'not parking in the park'. On my way to the park, however, while following directions to the park, I take a wrong turning and end up parking just outside the park entrance. Even though the two criteria of the 'acceptance thesis' have been met, this was not a case of following the legal rule by acceptance since I comply with the rule *by accident.*

The problem with the 'acceptance thesis' is that it does not consider the action from the deliberative point of view, that is, as it is seen from the point of view of the agent or deliberator. In the self-understanding of their own actions, the agent does not examine their own mental actions; rather, they look outwards to the vehicle, the park, the sign and so on. The reasons for actions, that is, turning the wheel to reverse the vehicle, then parking outside the park to follow the rule, are self-evident or *transparent* to the agent. But then, an objector might advance, what is the good-making characteristic of a rule that is the goal of the action of avoiding parking in the park. My reply is as follows. When the driver is asked why they are

[52] Davidson 1980: 79.
[53] For an illuminating discussion of this point, see Vogler 2007: 347.

turning the wheel and reversing the vehicle, their answer will be 'because it is the rule'. But this is still not completely *intelligible* unless we *assume* or *know* that the driver is a law-abiding citizen or that they believe in the general fairness of legal rules, and so forth. We can still ask them 'Why, because of the rule, do you do this?' Their answer would need to be in terms of reasons as good-making characteristics for them, in order to make intelligible their intentional action. They will probably reply that they have reasons to follow the legal rule because it is the best way of preserving the peace of the park, or that they have reasons to follow legal rules in general because it is the best way of preserving coordination[54] among the members of a community. In a nutshell, the agent or deliberator needs to provide the reasons for the action in terms of good-making characteristics and the end or reason of the action provides the *intelligible form of the action.*

Furthermore, in evil or benevolent regimes, if we follow Hart's model, officials criticise any deviation from the rules and expect rule-following as standard, but we can observe this same pattern of official conduct in both evil and benevolent regimes. In Hart's methodology, we are thus not able to differentiate between evil and benevolent regimes, or this differentiation becomes irrelevant as long as there is a pattern of conduct and any deviation from the standard of conduct is criticised. This seems paradoxical as the lay woman who engages with the intelligibility of action within the specific legal language-game, as illustrated in the example 'buying and selling potatoes', is able to make this basic distinction but the legal theorist equipped with Hart's methodology is not. As a result, criticism of the participant in the social practice who deviates from the standard is random, unintelligible and/or arbitrary because it is not guided by the *logos as* good-making characteristics or the values that determine *the choice of the participant.*

The idea of legal action produced by a legal agent engaged with the *logos* as good-making characteristics and exercising their capacities in circumstances of known institutional contexts and language-games sharply contrasts with the idea that we understand legal action through grasping the pattern of action that reflects criticism of deviation from the legal rule. The view defended by Hart reduces the richness of the *active aspect of*

[54] See Anscombe 1981 for an argument of authority as practical necessity.

the actions of the legal participant and offers a change in degree – but not in kind – to the passivity represented by law as orders backed by threats.

The kind of active engagement with the law is phenomenologically distinctive. There is reflective criticism not because of deviation from the accepted standard but rather because a breach of legal rules undermines the *logos as values or good-making characteristics* that underlies the legal rule or the law in general. For Finnis, it undermines the aim of the common good that the law aims to achieve. The complexity of the active aspect of the law entails a *change in kind* and cannot be grasped by the two key features of the internal aspect adumbrated by Hart. Consequently, for Finnis, there is a need for a more complex way of identifying the action that engages with the law.

30.4 Conclusions

During the last fifty years, legal philosophical debates in the English-speaking world have concentrated on Dworkin's criticism of Hart's *Concept of Law*, including the much-debated distinction between semantic and theoretical disagreements. In my view, this concentration of intellectual resources on a single debate has been at the cost of understanding a more arresting and insightful critique by Finnis, which would have taken legal philosophy into a realm of inquiry into practical reason and theory of action in law. Arguably, debates on normative ethics cannot be soundly understood without understanding *what action is* and more specifically what right and good actions are. Had Finnis's critique been taken seriously, legal theorists would have been ahead of the game in debates on normative questions and much clarity would have been gained on the nature of law and its relation to agency, reasons for actions and goodness.

Finnis tells us that the participant in legal practice, for example the citizen, the judge, the lawyer, is engaged with the law and is interested in distinguishing between a good and a *not so* good norm, between a just directive and an unjust directive, between a rational court decision and a non-rational court decision. Hart's internal point of view refuses to make further distinctions between the peripheral and the central cases of law and this brings *instability* to the concept.

Hart's internal point of view as unstable can be traced to a more fundamental criticism, that is, Hart's internal point of view cannot be used to understand the point of human actions and therefore we cannot rely on Hart's internal point of view to identify *significance differences that any actor in the field can make.*

At the core of Finnis's inquiry is the practical question of what one ought to do according to the principles of practical reasonableness. For Finnis, the theorist needs to explain the practical viewpoint, but once the practical viewpoint has been identified, it impinges on all of us: the theorist and the participant.

Complete understanding of an *action or practice entails an understanding of the point of the action or practice.* The agent who executes the action or the participant *who participates in the practice gives the action or practice its point or value.*

I have shown that Hart's internal point of view depends on a flawed conception of human action that relies on the mental states, that is, beliefs, desires, attitudes, that cause actions. The chapter has demonstrated that this theory cannot explain the point of human action and practice that Hart was so eager to emphasise. I have contrasted Hart's conception of human action with Anscombe's view on action, which relies on the 'why-question methodology', reasons for actions as good-making characteristics and contextual conditions in which we learn the *logos* of social practices. This last has illuminated Finnis's point that only if we locate law as practical reason as the central case of law are we able to identify *significance differences that any actor in the field can make.*

References

Adler, M. 2009. 'Social Facts, Constitutional Interpretation and the Rule of Recognition'. In ed. M. D. Adler and K. E. Himma (eds.). *The Rule of Recognition and the U.S. Constitution.* Oxford University Press: 193–233.

Anscombe, E. 1958. 'On Brute Facts'. *Analysis* 18(3): 69–72.

Anscombe, E. 1963. *Intention.* 2nd ed. Blackwell.

Anscombe, E. 1981. 'On the Source of Authority of the State'. *Ethics, Religion and Politics: Collected Philosophical Papers of GEM Anscombe.* Blackwell.

Aquinas, T. 2006. *Summa Theologiae* I-II. Cambridge University Press.

Blackburn, S. 1998. *Ruling Passions.* Clarendon Press.

Chisholm, R. 1976. 'Freedom and Action'. In K. Lehrer (ed.). *Freedom and Determinism.* Random House: 11–44.

Coleman. J, 2001. *The Practice of Principles.* Oxford University Press.

Dancy, J. 2000. *Practical Reality.* Oxford University Press.
Dickson, J. 2001. *Evaluation and Legal Theory.* Hart Publishing.
Davidson, D. 1963. 'Actions, Reasons and Causes'. *Journal of Philosophy* 60(23): 685–700.
Davidson, D. 1980. 'Freedom to Act'. In D. Davidson. *Essays on Actions and Events.* Clarendon Press: 63–81.
Dworkin, R. 1986. *Law's Empire.* Harvard University Press.
Endicott, T. 2001. 'How to Speak the Truth'. *American Journal of Jurisprudence* 46: 229–48.
Finnis, J. 1987. 'On Reason and Authority in Law's Empire'. *Law and Philosophy* 6(3): 357–80.
Finnis, J. 1988. *Moral Absolutes: Tradition, Revision, and Truth.* Catholic University of America Press.
Finnis, J. 1998. *Aquinas.* Oxford University Press.
Finnis, J. 2003. 'Law and What I Truly Should Decide'. *American Journal of Jurisprudence* 48: 107–29.
Finnis, J. 2011. *Natural Law and Natural Rights.* 2nd ed. Oxford University Press.
Gardner, J. 2001. 'Legal Positivism: 5½ Myths'. *American Journal of Jurisprudence* 46: 199–227.
Grisez, G. 1967. 'The First Principles of Practical Reasons: A Commentary on the *Summa Theologiae*, 1–2, Question 94, Article 2'. *Natural Law Forum* 10: 168–201.
Harman, G. 1986a. *Change in View.* MIT Press.
Harman, G. 1986b. 'Willing and Intending'. In R. Grandy and R. Warner (eds.). *Philosophical Grounds of Rationality.* Oxford University Press: 363–80.
Hart, H. L. A. 1994. *The Concept of Law.* Oxford University Press.
Holton, R. 1998. 'Positivism and the Internal Point of View'. *Law and Philosophy* 17: 597–625.
Irwin, T. 1981. *'Homonym in Aristotle'. The Review of Metaphysics* 34(3): 523–44.
Kenny, A. 1979. *Aristotle's Theory of the Will.* Yale University Press.
Moran, R. and Stone, M. 2009. 'Anscombe on Expression of Intention'. In C. Sandis (ed.). *New Essays in the Explanation of Action.* Palgrave MacMillan.
Murphy, M. 2006. *Natural Law in Jurisprudence and Politics.* Cambridge University Press.
Patterson, D. 1999. 'Explicating the Internal Point of View'. *Southern Methodist University Law Review* 52: 67–74.
Perry, S. 1995. 'Interpretation and Methodology in Legal Theory'. In A. Marmor (ed.). *Law and Interpretation.* Clarendon Press: 97–135.
Perry, S. 2000. 'Holmes versus Hart: The Bad Man in Legal Theory'. In S. Burton Jr. (ed.). *The Path of Law and Its Influence: The Legacy of Oliver Wendell Holmes.* Cambridge University Press: 158–96.
Perry, S. 2006. 'Hart on Social Rules and the Foundations of Law: Liberating the Internal Point of View'. *Fordham Law Review* 75: 1171–1209.
Raz, J. 1999. *Practical Reason and Norms.* Oxford University Press

Rhonheimer, M. 2008. *Perspective of the Acting Person: Essays in the Renewal of Thomistic Moral Philosophy.* Catholic University of America Press.

Rodriguez-Blanco, V. 2007. 'Is Finnis Wrong?'. *Legal Theory* 13: 257–83.

Rodriguez-Blanco, V. 2016a. *Law and Authority under the Guise of the Good.* Hart-Bloomsbury.

Rodriguez-Blanco, V. 2016b. 'Action in Law's Empire: Judging in the Deliberative Mode'. *Canadian Journal of Law and Jurisprudence* 29(2): 431–56.

Rodriguez-Blanco, V. and Zambrano, P. 2018. 'One Myth of the Classical Law Theory: Reflecting on the "Thin" View of Legal Positivism'. *Ratio Juris* 31: 9–32.

Schauer, F. 1994. 'Fuller's Internal Point of View'. *Law and Philosophy* 13: 285–312.

Shapiro, S. 2000. 'The Bad Man and the Internal Point of View'. In S. Burton Jr. (ed.). *The Path of Law and Its Influence: The Legacy of Oliver Wendell Holmes.* Cambridge University Press: 158–96.

Shapiro, S. 2006. 'What Is the Internal Point of View?'. *Fordham Law Review* 75: 1157–70.

Smith, M. 1994. *The Moral Problem.* Blackwell.

Tollefsen, C. 2018. 'Aquinas's Four Orders, Normativity, and Human Nature'. *Journal of Value Inquiry* 52(3): 243–56.

Vogler, C. 2001. 'Anscombe on Practical Inference'. In E. Millgram (ed.). *Varieties of Practical Reasoning.* MIT Press.

Vogler, C. 2007. 'Modern Moral Philosophy Again: Isolating the Promulgation Problem'. *Proceedings of the Aristotelian Society*: 347–62.

Wallace, R. J. 2014. 'Practical Reason'. In E. N. Zalta (ed.). *Stanford Encyclopedia of Philosophy.* https://plato.stanford.edu/entries/practical-reason/.

Zambrano, P. 2015. 'Fundamental Principles, Realist Semantics and Human Action'. *Rechtstheorie*: 323–45.

Zipursky, B. 2006. 'Legal Obligations and the Internal Aspect of Rules'. *Fordham Law Review* 75: 1229–53.

31 Alexy's Critique of Legal Positivism

Jan Sieckmann*

31.1 Introduction

Robert Alexy is one of the most prominent representatives of contemporary legal non-positivism. He defends the thesis of the necessary connection between law and morality,[1] which follows from law's necessary claim to correctness and implies the dual nature of law.[2] The thesis of the dual nature of law proposes that law necessarily includes a factual as well as an ideal dimension.[3] The factual dimension includes authoritative issuance and social efficacy, the ideal dimension moral correctness. Therefore, the concept of law comprises as a necessary element also moral correctness and is, hence, non-positivistic.

The connection thesis is the crucial point of Alexy's critique of legal positivism. By contrast, Alexy characterises legal positivism by means of the separation thesis,[4] that is, the denial that there is a conceptually necessary connection between law and morality.[5] Alexy offers three arguments for the connection thesis: the argument from injustice, the argument from principles,

* I am greatly indebted to Stanley Paulson for corrections and improvements in the English of my text.

[1] See Alexy 2002a: 23. [2] See Alexy 2015: 441–2. [3] See Alexy 2010: 167.

[4] The question of whether necessary conceptual relations between law and morality exist has long been common ground in the dispute on legal positivism and natural law. See Hart 1983: 50; Hart 1994: 185; Raz 1999: 162; Marmor 2001: 71. However, Raz (2007: 21) objected to Alexy's opposition of the connection thesis and the separation thesis, stating that there are many undisputed conceptually necessary relations between law and morality and therefore one cannot distinguish positivism and non-positivism by these theses. See also Gardner 2012: 48. In the ongoing debate, it has been made clear that not just any logical relation is of interest, but only those concerning the moral merits of law – see Gardner 2012: 19, 49; Alexy 2007: 43 – or the criteria of determining what the law is – Raz 2007: 22; Marmor 2001: 71. In fact, Hart (1994: 185) already understood the separation thesis as concerning the criteria of legal validity.

[5] See Alexy 2002a: 3.

and the argument of the necessary claim of law to correctness. All of them highlight aspects of the dual nature of law, which has evolved as the overarching idea of Alexy's non-positivist theory of law.

31.2 Alexy's Non-positivism

31.2.1 The Connection Thesis

In his book *The Argument from Injustice*, Alexy has developed the connection thesis by means of a comprehensive analysis of the conceptual relations between law and morality. He introduces a conceptual framework including five distinctions, which lead to a set of thirty-two possible combinations and corresponding connection theses.[6] The distinctions are:

- concepts of law omitting or embracing validity (the latter is chosen by Alexy, for if the concept of law were not related to validity, the question of whether a necessary connection between law and morality exists would become trivial);[7]
- legal systems as systems of norms or of procedures;
- the participant's or the observer's perspective;
- classifying or qualifying connections between law and morality; and
- conceptually necessary or normatively necessary connections between law and morality.

In addition, Alexy distinguishes individual norms and legal systems, both with regard to the observer's[8] and the participant's perspectives,[9] and with regard to the weak and strong connection theses,[10] depending on whether a connection of law is stated in regard to just any morality or in regard to a correct morality. Alexy makes clear that the weak connection thesis is not sufficient[11] but that it also does not refer to a single correct morality. Instead, he claims a connection of law with the idea of a correct morality[12] that includes basic human rights and the rules of practical discourse.[13]

[6] Alexy 2002a: 23–6. [7] See Alexy 2002a: 24. [8] See Alexy 2002a: 28.
[9] See Alexy 2002a: 40. [10] See Alexy 2002a: 75; see also Alexy 2013a: 234.
[11] See Alexy 2013a: 235. [12] See Alexy 2002a: 80–1. [13] See Alexy 2013a: 235.

31.2.1.1 The Participant's Point of View

Alexy's main argument for the connection thesis concerns the participant's perspective, that is, the perspective of someone who asks what the correct legal answer to a legal question is.[14] In this perspective, Alexy proposes

- an analytically founded qualifying connection between law and morality with regard to individual norms;
- an analytically founded classifying connection regarding legal systems; and
- a normatively founded classifying connection regarding individual norms.[15]

The analytical foundation rests on the thesis that the necessary claim of law to correctness renders violations of moral requirements also legally defective. With regard to individual norms, this leads to a qualifying connection, that is, the respective norm is legally faulty but not invalid. Regarding legal systems, the claim to correctness also constitutes a classifying connection,[16] distinguishing bandit systems, which do not raise a claim to correctness, from legal systems, which do.

Alexy argues with two examples, which are meant to display a performative contradiction in case the law denies its claim to correctness:

(i) A constitutional provision 'X is a sovereign, federal, and unjust republic' is conceptually defective. The claim to correctness, in this case, to justice, is necessarily attached to the act of framing a constitution.[17]

(ii) The decision of a judge 'The accused is sentenced to life imprisonment, which is an incorrect interpretation of prevailing law' would be a performative contradiction and hence conceptually defective.[18]

The absurdity of these examples shows, according to Alexy, that law necessarily implies a claim to correctness for analytical reasons.

[14] Alexy 2013b: 228.

[15] Bulygin has objected against Alexy's analytical/normative distinction that the latter would be either superfluous if analytical reasons existed or useless if they did not (see Bulygin 2013: 50). However, it seems that the arguments can be combined: an analytical argument in favour of the necessity of law's claim to correctness with a normative argument that this requires inclusion of moral elements in the concept of law (the argument from injustice). See Alexy 2013a: 226.

[16] Alexy 2002a: 36. [17] Alexy 2002a: 37. [18] Alexy 2002a: 38–9.

The normative foundation of the connection thesis follows, first, regarding individual norms, from the thesis that extreme injustice cannot be law.[19] The violation of its own claim to correctness does not necessarily result in the invalidity of the respective norm. However, in extreme cases its legal validity must be denied. Alexy defends this thesis against eight arguments (language, clarity, effectiveness, legal certainty, relativism, democracy, dispensability, candour) with regard to individual norms. Second, with regard to legal systems, Alexy suggests that the injustice of the whole system does not lead to consequences that go beyond the consequences of applying the argument to individual norms.[20]

Another connection follows from the principles thesis and the need to adduce non-positive arguments in open or hard cases.[21] Alexy regards this connection as analytically founded.[22] However, the argument is complex. The thesis is based on the distinction between rules and principles. Three theses are advanced in order to show the connection of law and morality: The 'incorporation thesis', the 'morality thesis' and the 'correctness thesis'. The 'incorporation thesis' states that each minimally developed legal system necessarily comprises principles.[23] The 'morality thesis' claims that the existence of principles in a legal system leads to a necessary connection between law and some morality or other.[24] The 'correctness thesis' maintains that the existence of legal principles leads to a necessary connection between law and correct morality.[25] This connection is taken for granted where legal principles are morally required or at least permitted. However, even if legal principles are morally wrong, a judge applying such principles lays claim to the correctness of his decision. This implies a claim to justifiability according to a correct morality.[26] However, it does not determine a particular content of morality, but rather links law with the idea of correct morality as a regulative idea.[27]

31.2.1.2 The Observer's Point of View

Alexy discusses the connection thesis not only from the point of view of the participant but also from the observer's perspective of someone who asks what legal decisions have actually been taken.[28] With respect to

[19] Alexy 2002a: 40. [20] See Alexy 2002a: 68. [21] See Alexy 2002a: 68–70.
[22] See Alexy 2002a: 70. [23] Alexy 2002a: 74. [24] Alexy 2002a: 75.
[25] Alexy 2002a: 77. [26] See Alexy 2002a: 78.
[27] See Alexy 2002a: 80–1; Alexy 2013a: 235. [28] See Alexy 2013b: 228.

individual norms, he accepts the separation thesis, arguing with an example regarding a Nazi law depriving Jews of their German citizenship. According to Alexy, one would understand a jurist's statement

(1) 'X has been deprived of citizenship according to German law',

but it would be incorrect or misleading to state

(2) 'X has not been deprived of citizenship according to German law.'[29]

In the observer's perspective, it would even be conceptually impossible to include moral elements in the concept of law.[30]

With regard to legal systems, Alexy insists that they necessarily raise a claim to correctness and therefore that a necessary connection between law and morality exists.[31] Two kinds of social order cannot qualify as law: a senseless order, where there is no consistent purpose of the rulers or no consistent rules are discernible, and a predatory order, where rules serve the purpose only of exploiting the subjects of the order.[32] A third type is the governor system, which exploits its subjects but strives to acquire legitimacy.[33] It can be called a legal system. The difference is its claim to correctness.[34]

[29] Alexy 2002a: 29.

[30] Alexy 2002a: 30. Bulygin (2013: 58) and Finnis (2014: 90) argue that this concession is all a positivist needs. However, one might doubt that this is correct. If all participants must raise a claim to correctness and an observer correctly describes a legal system in which all participants raise a claim to correctness, a connection between law and what is regarded as the correct morality by the participants must be stated from the observer's perspective. An observer cannot judge what the correct morality is, but must state that the interpretation of law includes the issue of what is morally correct.

[31] This thesis is not quite clear. It might include that in a legal system someone must claim for some norm that it be morally correct. However, if in the participant's perspective the claim to correctness is analytically necessary, then each participant must raise this claim for each individual norm, and an observer will state this for each norm. By contrast, if the connection were normative, the requirement that a participant must claim the correctness of a norm stated to be legally valid might be violated in some cases. But one might claim that it cannot be violated in all cases. That is, some participants will claim for some legal norms that they are just. On the other hand, one might refer not to the claim to correctness (the qualifying connection) but to the correctness of the norm itself (the classifying connection). This would amount to the thesis that there may be unjust norms but that not all norms of a legal system can be unjust.

[32] See Alexy 2002a: 32–3. [33] See Alexy 2002a: 33. [34] See Alexy 2002a: 34.

31.2.2 The Dual Nature Thesis

Alexy expresses the connection of law and morality also by means of his thesis of the dual nature of law.[35] This thesis presents a reformulation rather than an independent justification of the connection thesis. One can justify the connection thesis without reference to the dual nature thesis, but not the reverse. The dual nature thesis offers, however, a closer analysis of the relation between morality and positivity in law. Alexy develops the dual nature thesis in a theory of law as institutionalised reason, explaining the ideal dimension, the real dimension and the reconciliation of the ideal with the real.

The ideal dimension is based on the thesis of the necessary claim of law to correctness, including a claim to moral correctness.[36] This presupposes that there can be knowledge as to what is morally correct. This is possible, according to discourse theory, by means of a practical discourse.[37] The insufficiency of this discourse as a decision procedure necessitates as its complement the existence of a real, that is, positive dimension of law.[38] However, the necessity of positivity does not imply its exclusive character.[39] The institutionalisation of law does not eliminate the claim to substantive correctness, which, according to Alexy, is first-order correctness. Second-order correctness refers to both the ideal and the real dimension, and comprises requirements of justice as well as of legal certainty. The principles of justice and legal certainty can collide. Thus, second-order correctness is a matter of balancing.[40] It is a matter of the institutionalisation of reason, which again has a substantive and a procedural aspect.

The substantive aspect consists of the outermost borders of law following from its claim to moral correctness. Law cannot have just any content whatever. Extreme injustice cannot be law.[41] The procedural aspect consists of the political form of a democratic or discursive constitutionalism, which connects positivity and correctness inside a legal system.[42] Discourse theory requires democracy and constitutional rights, both of which have a dual nature. Democracy can be conceived of as a decision procedure or as an

[35] See Alexy 2010: 167; also see Alexy 2007: 37, on the notion that the relation between law as fact and law as an ideal is the most important issue in explaining its nature.

[36] See Alexy 2010: 168.

[37] See Alexy 2010: 172. As to the connection of the necessary claim of law to moral correctness with discourse theory, see Alexy 2015: 442.

[38] See Alexy 2010: 173. [39] See Alexy 2010: 174. [40] Ibid. [41] See Alexy 2010: 175.

[42] See Alexy 2010: 177.

argumentative procedure, the first reflecting the positive dimension, the second the ideal dimension.[43] Constitutional rights are intended to transform human rights into positive law. Human rights as moral rights belong exclusively to the ideal dimension of law. Their transformation into positive rights reflects the effort to connect the ideal with the real dimension.[44]

31.3 Discussion

The connection thesis and the corresponding dual nature thesis do not concern primarily the criteria of legal validity. Rather, they present a more general analysis of the nature of law.[45] Their core is the necessary claim of law to correctness, which, in the first place, leads to qualifying connections between law and morality. Thus, Alexy has changed the focus of the contemporary debate on positivism,[46] which began with Dworkin's critique of Hart's legal positivism and took the identification of law as the central issue of contention between positivism and non-positivism.[47] In this view, the connection of law and morality is to be found at the level of legal validity. By contrast, Alexy's approach also allows one to consider relations between law and morality that do not concern the classification of a norm as legally valid. Therefore, a first issue that is raised by Alexy's theory concerns the concept of legal positivism.

31.3.1 The Concept of Legal Positivism

31.3.1.1 The Nature of Law and the Criteria of Identification

Alexy's theory is not merely a theory of legal validity but one about the nature of law. His claim to have presented a thesis about the nature of law is, however, disputed. The fruitfulness of arguments about conceptual

[43] Ibid.

[44] Alexy 2010: 178. In addition, Alexy points to the dual nature of legal argumentation, which is reflected by the 'special case thesis' (Alexy 2010: 179). Finally, the dual nature of law is to be found in the distinction between the real and the ideal 'ought', which underlies the distinction between rules and principles (Alexy 2010: 180).

[45] See also Alexy 2007: 37.

[46] One should note, however, that Raz (1999: 162–3) had already presented a more differentiated account of the connection thesis.

[47] Dworkin 1978: 17 (test of pedigree), 60.

necessities is cast into doubt in general,[48] for such arguments may well express mere intuitions with regard to borderline cases. Therefore, one might prefer a straightforward normative approach as more promising. However, this critique can be assessed only by considering the arguments that Alexy actually offers.

Another objection is that one must distinguish between a theory of law and one of adjudication, which is concerned with the question of how judges should decide.[49] This objection presupposes a particular concept of law, which separates law from adjudication. By contrast, the point of view of a judge is crucial for Alexy's theory of law. Law is defined in a way that tells judges how they are to decide. Which of these conceptions of law is more adequate is exactly the point of dispute and cannot be taken for granted.

Still, one might have doubts about whether Alexy's thesis can be a thesis about the nature of law; for it presupposes the participant's perspective. From the perspective of an observer, the alleged conceptual connection between law and morality does not exist. As a consequence, an observer cannot recognise the nature of law and, therefore, law is a phenomenon that exists only from the participant's perspective of individuals who ask how one ought correctly to decide within a particular legal system.[50] However, law might include aspects that are not recognisable from the perspective of a participant. A participant asking how one should correctly decide will consider those facts and legal norms relevant for this decision but not the whole legal system. What is not directly relevant as a legal argument will remain beyond the participant's perspective. Therefore, there may be facts about the legal system that cannot be recognised from a participant's perspective. Should we then assume that there are diverse natures of law? This would not correspond to the definition of the nature of law as giving expression to necessary conditions of law. It seems that the thesis of the dual nature of law implies that law is to be defined from the perspective of a participant, and cannot be adequately defined from the perspective of an observer.[51]

[48] See Finnis 2014: 90. By contrast, Finnis suggests to ask for the basic needs that make law a reason for action: see Finnis 2014: 9.

[49] See Bix 2006: 139, 145; see also Bulygin 2013: 58.

[50] The existence of the legal system might, again, be discernible only from the perspective of an observer.

[51] This would be in line with Dworkin's thesis that law is an interpretive concept that cannot adequately be understood from a purely descriptive perspective. See Dworkin 1986: 87.

31.3.1.2 New Classifications

Alexy's change of focus in the debate over positivism shakes up the usual classifications of positivist and non-positivist theories. Following Alexy, the essential connection of law and morality consists in law's claim to moral correctness. Following these lines, Raz, for example, might qualify as a non-positivist owing to his thesis that law rests on authority, which must claim to be morally legitimate.[52] Even a Kelsenian theory might be regarded as non-positivist. For Kelsen accepts the need for justification, with the consequence that someone making a legal statement necessarily presupposes a basic norm in order to transform a system of power into a normative system.[53] Alas, it is a matter of dispute whether Kelsen understood normativity as moral validity,[54] and, in any case, the 'basic norm' for Kelsen was an epistemological presupposition, not a moral demand. However, one might reconstruct Kelsen's theory in such a way that the basic norm turns out to be the consequence of a moral justification. Would such a theory be non-positivist owing to its entailing a necessary connection between law and morality?

Alexy clarifies his connection thesis, granting that no logical relation is of interest; rather, the issue is whether moral merits of the law are legally relevant.[55] Interpreting moral merits as a form of justification, one can distinguish, accordingly, whether one accepts the need for justification, whether it must be a moral justification, and whether such a justification would belong to the legal system.[56] In addition, one might ask whether the need for justification holds for all norms of a legal system, or whether it is the case that a moral justification must be available for only some legal norms. Accordingly, one can distinguish diverse forms of legal non-positivism and positivism. In particular, one can distinguish:

- the thesis that law includes a moral justification, leading to the inclusion of moral correctness as a criterion of legal validity;
- the thesis that law includes a moral justification, however, rejecting the conceptual inclusion of moral correctness as a criterion of legal validity; and

[52] See Raz 2007: 21. [53] See Kelsen 1960: 7–8, 205–6.
[54] See Paulson 2012: 173; Paulson 2017: 592. [55] See Alexy 2007: 44; Alexy 2013b: 98.
[56] One could, in addition, distinguish whether the justification must be sound or defensible, or any claim to justification would suffice.

- the thesis that law needs a moral justification, which, however, is not included in the legal system but leads to the inclusion of moral correctness as a criterion of legal validity.[57]

Positivism, too, can take diverse forms. A positivist might hold the thesis that law needs a moral justification, which, however, is not part of the law, and moral correctness is not a criterion of legal validity. A positivist might accept the claim that law needs some form of justification, but not a moral justification. A positivist might reject the need of any justification whatever for law.

One might further distinguish diverse meanings of *moral*. In the widest sense, it might mean merely that the justification is substantive, that is, it refers to the content of the norm and not merely to a positive law enactment. In a narrow sense, one might connect moral justification with the criterion of universalisability.[58]

The weakest connection thesis would then be that for each legal system, each participant will claim a substantive justification for some legal norm. Alexy, however, not only supports the weakest form of a connection thesis but suggests that each participant will require a substantive justification for each norm of a legal system (wherever this demand makes sense), and that, in cases of extreme injustice, the lack of a substantive justification excludes legal validity.

31.3.1.3 Alexy's Systematisation: Exclusive, Inclusive and Super-Inclusive

Alexy's analysis of the conceptual relations between law and morality has opened the field for investigations of possible positivist and non-positivist conceptions of law. Alexy himself offers a systematisation of positivist and non-positivist theories of law, distinguishing exclusive and inclusive legal positivism on the one hand, and exclusive, inclusive and super-inclusive non-positivism on the other. The distinction between positivism and non-positivism is made according to whether a theory of law includes moral correctness as an element of law, and this pertains to the justification of law, not to the criteria of validity. Positivist theories might then exclude moral correctness from law in all cases (exclusive positivism), or regard moral defects as legally relevant in some cases, depending on whether

57 For example, one might assume that judges have the competence to deny legal validity to a norm that they regard as immoral.

58 See, e.g., Habermas 1994: 139.

a legal system says so (inclusive positivism). For non-positivism, Alexy distinguishes three positions with regard to the effect of moral defects: Legal validity is lost in all cases of moral defect (exclusive non-positivism), or only in some cases (inclusive non-positivism), or it is not affected at all (super-inclusive non-positivism).[59]

One might ask whether this approach is adequate as a means of distinguishing positivist and non-positivist theories. In particular, it is puzzling that the favoured position is characterised only in a negative form, as non-positivism, and is not identified by means of its central characteristics.[60] The point of requiring a moral justification of law is that law is normative, and that normativity, thus understood, can exist only if it is able to count on a moral justification.[61] If, however, the crucial point is the normativity of law, it would then be appropriate to distinguish normative and non-normative theories of law according to whether they claim and attempt to justify an obligation to follow and apply the law or at least attempt to justify that the application of law is morally permitted.[62] It would not be appropriate to identify this distinction with that of positivism or non-positivism.

Also, one might use the label of 'normative positivism' for theories of law that insist upon strict validity for positive law.[63] Kant's theory of law may well be an example.[64] By contrast, Alexy suggests that Kant's combination of the postulate of 'unconditional submission' to the positive law with the subjugation of positive law to non-positive law can be regarded as a form of 'super-inclusive non-positivism'.[65] However, there is no need to call such a position non-positivistic. Also the consequence that one has to distinguish among non-positivist theories those that are positivist and those that are non-positivist does not seem to be congenial.

[59] See Alexy 2012: 5; Alexy 2008: 286–8. [60] See also Finnis 2014: 96.
[61] Some theories deny this, such as Hart's conception of normativity based on social rules (Hart 1994: 82–91), but they can be regarded as mistaken; see Dworkin 1978: 22, 48–58.
[62] See Dworkin 1986: 190–2.
[63] In this sense, see Sieckmann 1990: 129–30. One should note that there are diverse uses of the term 'normative positivism'. Waldron distinguishes theories that regard law as a system of norms from theories that regard the separation of law and morals as desirable; Waldron 2001: 410.
[64] See Waldron 1996: 1566.
[65] Alexy 2012: 6; see also Alexy 2008: 288–90; Alexy 2010: 174.

31.3.2 The Claim to Correctness

The thesis of the necessary claim of law to moral correctness is Alexy's specific contribution to non-positivism,[66] but also a disputed one. Alexy does not speak of moral correctness in any specific sense but as justifiability by means of practical reasoning.[67] Still, it is more than a claim to correctness that – according to Raz –[68] every agent must necessarily raise for his actions.

31.3.2.1 Raising a Claim

A first objection is that law itself cannot raise a claim.[69] This is answered by Alexy's granting that the claim to correctness is raised by human beings, but acting as representatives of law.[70] Then, however, the question arises as to what is 'the law' that the participants are representing. From the perspective of participants, law is what the participant believes to be law. The participant does not represent the law, but they do make judgments as to what the law is. Law might be an object of representation from the perspective of an observer. Now one might maintain the idea that participants also act as observers of the law, so that it is possible for them to combine both perspectives. The question remains: What is the contribution of the thesis that law raises a claim, instead of ascribing such claims to the participants themselves?

One ought to grant, in any case, that law's claim to correctness[71] is a matter of degree, for it is not the case that each representative of law must necessarily raise a claim to moral justification for his legal actions. If law, however, exists, then some representatives must raise such a claim, and this must be done to a degree that is sufficient to characterise the legal system as a normative system.

31.3.2.2 The Notion of a Participant

The notion of the participant in a legal system has been cast into doubt, too.[72] What defines the participant's perspective, and how is it different

[66] The injustice thesis goes back to Radbruch, the principles thesis to Dworkin.
[67] See Alexy 2013b: 99. [68] See Raz 2007: 27. [69] MacCormick 2007: 59, 63.
[70] See Alexy 2010: 168.
[71] That is, understood as a conceptually necessary claim. As a normative claim, it may be upheld strictly.
[72] See Raz 2007: 23; Bulygin 2013: 53.

from an observer's perspective? A common objection is that people are usually observers as well as participants of a legal system. Alexy, however, rejects this objection, for the distinction is not between persons but between perspectives, and the participant's and the observer's respective perspectives are clearly distinct according to the corresponding questions as to what the correct legal answer is and what legal decisions have actually been taken.[73]

Not all of Alexy's explications of the respective perspectives of observers and participants are clear, however. The participant's perspective is first introduced in a rather elusive way, as being 'adopted by one who, within the legal system, participates in disputation about what is commanded, forbidden, and permitted in the legal system, and to what end this legal system confers power'.[74] However, it is made more precise in later writings. In short, the difference is that participants ask a normative question, while observers do not: '[T]he participant asks and adduces arguments on behalf of what he deems to be the correct answer to a legal question in the legal system in which he is found, whereas the observer asks and adduces arguments on behalf of a position that reflects how legal questions are actually decided in that legal system.'[75] Regarding a question of interpretation, the observer cannot engage in argument on the question as to which answer is correct. The participant's context is defined by the question 'What is the correct legal answer?', the observer's by the question 'How are legal decisions actually taken?'[76] The reason why participants and observers must use different legal concepts is that the answer of a participant to the question as to what the law is might involve considerations about what the law ought to be, whereas the observer's answer cannot take up this issue.[77] In this sense, the participant's and the observer's perspectives are clearly distinct.

31.3.2.3 The Content of the Claim to Correctness

Another issue is the question of what is the content of the claim to correctness, which precedes the crucial question of whether such a claim is really necessary. According to Alexy, the claim is one of moral correctness. In the first place, the claim to correctness must claim objectivity, that is, with regard to law it must claim to be acceptable to all who take the point

[73] See Alexy 2013b: 228. [74] Alexy 2002a: 25. [75] Alexy 2007: 45.
[76] Alexy 2007: 46. [77] See Alexy 2007: 48.

of view of the legal system in question.[78] In addition, the claim must be moral in the sense of being justifiable by practical reasoning.

31.3.2.4 The Necessity of the Claim to Correctness

In order to show that law necessarily raises a claim to correctness, Alexy argues with the performative contradiction that would arise if legal norms or decisions were claimed to be unjust (as noted). One might concede this, but the impossibility of explicitly denying that law is just does not imply that law cannot remain indifferent to justice. A constitution might declare that matters of justice without any backing from the positive law are not valid legal arguments and must not be considered by the courts. A judge might declare that a judgment is required by positive law although it is unjust. What constitutional or ordinary legislators or judges cannot do is declare that they are taking a decision that they actually ought not to take. That is, they cannot deny the claim to the legitimacy of their decisions. On which reasons the legitimacy of these decisions is grounded remains an open question.

As a consequence, a claim to moral correctness might be necessary if one understands 'moral' in the sense of being justified by practical reasoning. However, this does not connect law to morality in any specific sense.[79]

The question remains: Why must moral justification, understood in a wider sense, form a part of the law? One might argue that a participant will have a twofold task: As a participant in a legal system he has to offer legally correct judgments, and as a morally responsible person he must not violate moral obligations. His judgment must integrate both requirements. Since his judgment will count, however, as a legal judgment, moral reasons must belong to the justification of legal judgments and will determine what is legally correct. Whatever determines what is legally correct belongs to the law.

Plausible as it is, doubt remains as to whether the inclusion of moral reasons in the law is necessary. One must presuppose that the participants have to judge according to law and must not change the law. With this presupposition, the inclusion of moral reason in the law seems to be

[78] See Alexy 2007: 49.

[79] Still, this claim to practical rationality includes more than the thesis that any action whatever has some intention and is regarded by the agent as correct relative to this intention. It retains correctness as an abstract, contentless idea.

necessary. Still, this presupposition might not be necessary. It corresponds to the traditional definition of the role of judges in modern legal systems, in particular systems with a division of powers that separates legislative and judicial power. One might think of legal systems with a different structure. What is more, the question remains as to whether it is adequate to see judges as strictly bound by law. An alternative would be to ascribe to them the normative power to change the law for moral reasons.[80] The point of view of a judge whose task is nothing other than applying the law, so that whatever the judge ought to apply as law counts as law, is certainly a fruitful starting point for developing a theory of law, but it is not the only possible starting point. As a consequence, there will be a necessary connection between law and morality if a certain point of view is presupposed but other conceptions of law remain possible.

31.3.2.5 The Hypocrisy Objection

Against Alexy's connection thesis, Eugenio Bulygin has objected that an unjust system that claims to be just amounts to hypocrisy, and this would be worse than an openly unjust system.[81] Alexy agrees, but he replies that the claim to correctness, hypocritical or not, includes a risk for the legal system.[82] The possible risks for a dictatorial system that might result from a claim to correctness do not, however, seem to be the crucial point.[83] One ought to concede that a hypocritical system is, in moral respects, worse than an openly unjust system. This implies only, however, that law does not necessarily have moral value. The necessary connection between law and morality resulting from its claim to correctness does not guarantee that this claim is met. As a consequence, the connection between law and morality does not render law immune against critique but enhances the possibility of legal critique.

31.3.3 The Argument from Injustice

The argument from injustice is already found in Radbruch's formula, claiming that in general one must recognise the validity of positive law, but positive law can be unjust to such a degree that one must deny its validity or even its character as law.[84] Alexy's slogan 'Extreme injustice is

[80] See also Alexy 2013b: 231. [81] See Bulygin 2013: 52. [82] See Alexy 2013b: 230.
[83] See also Finnis 2014: 92; Finnis 1980: 274. [84] See Radbruch 1946: 106.

not law' is a short form of this position. Alexy explains that if law includes the principle of legal certainty as well as that of justice, the participant must strike a balance between these principles. Although legal certainty will in general have priority, one cannot exclude the possibility that the moral reasons on the side of legal certainty will be outweighed by the moral reasons on the side of justice.[85]

One can hardly deny the correctness of this thesis if anything at all can be known in moral affairs. A matter of dispute might simply be the limit of extreme justice that must be reached in order to deny legal validity. One must address, however, the objection that there might be no moral knowledge at all, and in this case no necessary moral elements in law would exist.[86] Alexy refers to discourse theory and in particular to his justification of human rights as necessary elements of law.[87] Indeed, discourse theory shows that one cannot exclude the possibility of moral knowledge.

On the other hand, we must also consider the objection that law's connection with morality goes much further than the criterion of extreme injustice suggests.[88] The interpretation of law depends on moral argument, which may take priority over arguments in favour of particular positive laws even before the limit of extreme justice is reached, depending on the strength of the pertinent competing arguments. Thus, moral principles may demand the invalidity of positive legal norms even before the limit of extreme justice is reached.

This points to a constructive problem in Alexy's account of the dual nature of law. This duality is explained as the coexistence of facts and ideals in the law. It seems that law primarily is an institutional fact and hence the notion of law as a fact is an adequate account of law in general, which needs only a marginal modification by means of principles of justice. However, the principle of legal certainty is not a fact but an ideal, which indeed forms a part of the principle of justice in a wider sense.[89] In addition, facts are also relevant to the application of the principle of justice in a narrower sense. The specific relevance of facts suggested by the principle of legal certainty is that existing authoritative decisions or rules should be regarded as binding. However, the bindingness of such decisions or rules is not a value in itself. The authority behind them or the value of their existence requires a normative justification. This justification might

[85] See Alexy 2007: 53. [86] See Alexy 2012: 2: 'existence problem'. [87] Alexy 2012: 9.
[88] See also the critique of Allan 2017: 89–90. [89] See also Finnis 2014: 101.

follow from principles of justice or from other principles of political morality. Then, however, the factual aspect of law represented by existing decisions or rules is not a principle that might counter a principle of justice but only a factor in the balancing of principles of justice. The conflict is not one between the factual and the ideal dimension of law, but one within the ideal dimension.

In addition, authoritative decisions themselves will be required to take into account principles of justice. Arbitrary decisions cannot command bindingness. Thus, such decisions are subordinated to the principles of justice. The issue is whether, owing to the defect of decisions that do not comply with demands of justice, one must deny that they are binding, despite some legitimation that they might find in other principles. This problem, however, is grasped better by turning to the distinction of formal and material principles, which Alexy introduced in his *Theory of Constitutional Rights*.[90] Hence, the problem of positivism does not concern only marginal cases of extreme injustice but pervades the whole legal system.

Some objections refer to the problem of retroactivity. One of them is that to regard unjust laws as not being law at all is unnecessary, for retroactive legislation would be possible.[91] Alexy rightly objects that this will not be possible in all cases. For example, retroactive legislation might be prohibited in matters of penal law.[92] Therefore, one cannot avoid the issue of whether an extremely unjust law should be treated as valid. If one is to regard such a law as invalid, one has to recognise that this in fact amounts to a form of retroactivity, for what was once recognised and applied as law is later no longer regarded as law. Alexy answers that in cases of extremely unjust laws, no one could have believed that this was law.[93] Indeed, the issue is a matter of balancing. Although the limits of extreme justice may be in doubt, one cannot rule out the possibility that one will have to regard as invalid positive law a norm that is extremely unjust.

31.3.4 The Argument from Principles

The argument from principles is twofold: from a legal point of view, participants have to assess legal decisions according to principles of

[90] Alexy 2002b: 58, 82, 414–25. [91] See Hart 1983: 76. [92] See Alexy 2002a: 51, 56–8.
[93] See Alexy 2002a: 56–8.

political morality, which cannot be identified by formal criteria of validity alone; and the balancing of principles requires judgements regarding the concrete weight of principles, which cannot be justified merely on grounds of positive law. Hence, principles connect law with morality but do not determine a classification of which norms are legally valid or cannot be legally valid. Accordingly, the argument from principles presupposes the perspective of a participant, is conceptual and leads to a qualifying connection between law and morality.[94]

The thesis that principles belong to the legal system is fundamentally attacked by those who deny that principles form a category of norms on their own, or that the existence of principles is incompatible with legal positivism.[95] Indeed, Alexy's notion of principles as requirements of optimisation, or as the objects of such requirements, is not suitable to establish a difference between principles as reasons for balancing and rules as the results of a balancing.[96] Also, it is not clear why legal principles as requirements of optimisation should not be identifiable, from the perspective of an observer, by means of formal criteria.[97]

Nevertheless, the argument from principles is a decisive argument against positivism. First, one cannot seriously deny the logical difference of, on the one hand, norms that are definitively valid and applied by means of subsumption and deduction and, on the other hand, norms that present normative arguments to be balanced against competing arguments. Definitive norms are the content of normative statements that purport to present normative facts, excluding the definitive validity of incompatible norms. Normative arguments, or principles, purport to present normative requirements, demanding a certain result of a balancing but granting the validity of competing principles.[98]

Second, it is indeed impossible to identify principles in the above sense of normative arguments by means of formal criteria of validity. The argument is that principles present intrinsic values, carrying with them the source of their own validity. This is owing to their structure as reiterated requirements of validity.[99] Thus, recognition of the validity of such a principle implies that its validity does not depend on positive sources.

[94] See Alexy 2002a: 70. [95] See Sieckmann 1990: 52–3, 178–98.
[96] See Sieckmann 1990: 62–7. [97] See García Figueroa 1998: 388–9.
[98] See Sieckmann 2012: 30, 45–8. [99] See Sieckmann 2012: 47.

Still, there is an objection. Even though moral principles may be relevant for adjudication, this does not imply that they belong to the legal system.[100] Judges may be under an obligation to apply norms from a different legal system, as in international private law. Alexy answers that, in the case of moral principles, there is no need for incorporation; these principles belong to the legal system in any case.[101] Indeed, the need for normative justification requires a theory that also includes substantive criteria of legal validity.

31.4 Conclusion

Alexy's main innovative contribution to the debate on legal positivism is the thesis of law's necessary claim to correctness. This claim serves to establish a necessary connection between law and morality, not only in a classifying sense with regard to the identification of valid law but also as a qualifying connection that renders laws that are morally wrong also legally defective. The presupposition of the argument for the necessary claim to correctness is the participant's perspective.

From the participant's perspective, law has a justificatory structure, manifested by its claim to moral correctness (argument from correctness). This structure cannot be represented adequately in a positivist manner (argument from principles). One must also recognise the limits of legal validity in cases of extreme injustice (argument from injustice).

The existence of a justificatory structure in the law seems to be a conceptual necessity. It does not imply, however, that each legal system refers to substantive moral criteria in order to justify its claim to legitimacy. Therefore, a positivist theory of law, taking an observer's perspective, remains possible. Kelsen's theory of law might be untenable for a reasonable participant, but it is not impossible to conceive of law in this way. Although in general one can expect that participants connect law with acceptable criteria of legal validity, the possibility remains that they do not. An observer will always present statements about law as descriptions of what is going on in a legal system. It seems possible to present these social facts as law. The observer's perspective cannot be eliminated.

[100] See Raz 2007: 34. [101] See Alexy 2007: 55.

To grant the observer's perspective alongside the participant's perspective leaves room for legal positivism. The argument respecting legal positivism versus non-positivism seems to be a matter of choice, and it depends on the type of theory that one is interested in. Alas, observers must correctly present the views of the participants of a legal system. In particular, they must recognise that participants raise a claim to correctness, which, if one understands morality in a broad sense of judgements about what one ought to do, establishes a connection between law and morality. This does not imply, however, that the identification of law itself depends on moral claims. Observers can describe the content of the participant's view of law.

The possibility of conceiving law from an observer's perspective raises doubts with regard to Alexy's dual nature thesis, maintaining, as he does, the idea that the ideal dimension of law and hence its connection to morality is an essential element of the concept of law. A consequence of Alexy's dual nature thesis seems to be that law can be adequately defined only from the participants' perspective, a thesis that, however, remains doubtful.

Alexy's classification of exclusive, inclusive and super-inclusive non-positivism also raises doubts. Although one might regard as a form of non-positivism the idea that one accepts the need of law for moral justification, it is not convincing to classify as non-positivist a theory that grants as criteria of legal validity only positive criteria. If one insists on the demarcation of positivist and non-positivist theories of law, the crucial difference still seems to be whether one regards moral correctness as a criterion of legal validity.

When all is said and done, Alexy has presented a powerful critique of legal positivism and developed an impressive non-positivist theory of law. Even though it might well fail to refute the very possibility of legal positivism, it makes clear that, for those interested in law as a normative, action-guiding system, legal positivism is not an adequate theory of law. The fact that Joseph Raz, as an outstanding representative of legal positivism, doubts that legal positivism still counts as an illuminating category with regard to the nature of law[102] may well be regarded as a sign of the retreat from legal positivism.

[102] See Raz 2007: 35.

References

Alexy, R. 2002a. *The Argument from Injustice*. Trans. S. Paulson and B. Paulson. Oxford University Press.

Alexy, R. 2002b. *A Theory of Constitutional Rights*. Trans. J. Rivers. Oxford University Press.

Alexy, R. 2007. 'An Answer to Joseph Raz'. In G. Pavlakos (ed.). *Law, Rights and Discourse*. Hart: 37–55.

Alexy, R. 2008. 'On the Concept and the Nature of Law'. *Ratio Juris* 21: 281–99.

Alexy, R. 2010. 'The Dual Nature of Law'. *Ratio Juris* 23: 167–82.

Alexy, R. 2012. 'Law, Morality, and the Existence of Human Rights'. *Ratio Juris* 24: 2–14.

Alexy, R. 2013a. 'Between Positivism and Non-positivism: A Third Reply to Bulygin'. In J. Ferrer Beltrán, J. J. Moreso and D. M. Papayannis (eds.). *Neutrality and Theory of Law*. Springer: 225–38.

Alexy, R. 2013b. 'Some Reflections on the Ideal Dimension of Law and on the Legal Philosophy of John Finnis'. *American Journal of Jurisprudence* 58: 97–110.

Alexy, R. 2015. 'Legal Certainty and Correctness'. *Ratio Juris* 28: 441–51.

Allan, T. R. S. 2017. 'In Defence of Radbruch's Formula: Injustice, Interpretation, and Invalidity'. In M. Borowski, S. Paulson and J. Sieckmann (eds.). *Rechtsphilosophie und Grundrechtstheorie*. Mohr Siebeck: 87–104.

Bix, B. 2006. 'Robert Alexy's Radbruch Formula and the Nature of Law'. *Rechtstheorie* 37: 139–49.

Bulygin, E. 2013. 'Alexy between Positivism and Non-positivism'. In J. Ferrer Beltrán, J. J. Moreso and D. M. Papayannis (eds.). *Neutrality and Theory of Law*. Springer: 49–59.

Dworkin, R. 1978. *Taking Rights Seriously*. 2nd ed. Harvard University Press.

Dworkin, R. 1986. *Law's Empire*. Fontana Press.

Finnis, J. 1980. *Natural Law and Natural Rights*. Clarendon Press.

Finnis, J. 2014. 'Law as Fact and as Reason for Action: A Response to Robert Alexy on Law's Ideal Dimension'. *American Journal of Jurisprudence* 59: 85–109.

García Figueroa, A. 1998. *Principios y positivismo jurídico*. Centro de estudios políticos y constitucionales.

Gardner, J. 2012. 'Legal Positivism: 5½ Myths'. In J. Gardner. *Law as a Leap of Faith*. Oxford University Press: 19–53.

Habermas, J. 1994. *Faktizität und Geltung*. 4th ed. Suhrkamp.

Hart, H. L. A. 1983. 'Positivism and the Separation of Law and Morals'. In H. L. A. Hart. *Essays in Jurisprudence and Philosophy*. Clarendon Press: 49–87.

Hart, H. L. A. 1994, *The Concept of Law*. 2nd ed. Clarendon Press.

Kelsen, H. 1960. *Reine Rechtslehre*. Deuticke.

MacCormick, N. 2007. 'Why Law Makes No Claims'. In G. Pavlakos (ed.). *Law, Rights, and Discourse*. Hart: 59–67.

Marmor, A. 2001. *Positive Law and Objective Values*. Clarendon Press.

Paulson, S. 2012. 'Justified Normativity'. In M. Klatt (ed.). *The Institutionalization of Reason.* Oxford University Press: 61–111.

Paulson, S. 2017. 'The Makings of a Radical Norm Theory: Hans Kelsen's Theory of the Sanction-Norm as Empowering Norm'. In M. Borowski, S. Paulson and J. Sieckmann (eds.). *Rechtsphilosophie und Grundrechtstheorie.* Mohr Siebeck: 589–630.

Radbruch, G. 1946. 'Gesetzliches Recht und übergesetzliches Unrecht'. *Süddeutsche Juristenzeitung*: 105–8.

Raz, J. 1999. *Practical Reason and Norms.* 3rd ed. Clarendon Press.

Raz, J. 2007. 'The Argument from Injustice, or How Not to Reply to Legal Positivism'. In G. Pavlakos (ed.). *Law, Rights, and Discourse.* Hart: 17–35.

Sieckmann, J. 1990. *Regelmodelle und Prinzipienmodelle des Rechtsystems.* Nomos.

Sieckmann, J. 2012. *The Logic of Autonomy.* Hart.

Waldron, J. 1996. 'Kant's Legal Positivism'. *Harvard Law Review* 109: 1535–66.

Waldron, J. 2001. 'Normative (or Ethical) Positivism'. In J. Coleman (ed.). *Hart's Postscript: Essays on the Postscript to the Concept of Law.* Oxford University Press: 410–33.

32 Mark Greenberg on Legal Positivism

Barbara Baum Levenbook*

32.1 Situating Greenberg

Commentators differ over whether legal positivism involves a metaphysical position, yet it is clear that many legal positivists have adopted one. Either they think that law is a complex social fact, or they hold that law is ultimately grounded in social facts. The latter view, held by legal positivists such as Hart, Raz, Shapiro and Coleman,[1] entails that the content of law can be fundamentally explained by reference to social facts, as opposed to moral facts or facts of practical reasonableness. This second metaphysical position thus calls for a general theory of legal content, one that shows precisely how legal content is ultimately grounded in social facts. (As I am using the term, a *general theory of content* is a metaphysical theory, not a theory about how to recognise or know the content of law in legal systems.)

Attempts by proponents of the grounding thesis to complete this task have been less than compelling. Hart claims that a social rule of recognition ultimately picks out the valid laws in a municipal legal system.[2] Though Hart does not say this, the alleged pathway from the social rule of recognition to these other laws in the legal system could run at points through rules of law for retrieval of (the content of) valid rules of law from legal texts and authoritative pronouncements. Such a view would require an explanation of how the content of rules for retrieval of legal content is itself determined. However, any such view, as well as Hart's explicit contention, appears to be embarrassed by the existence of so-called 'theoretical disagreement' famously insisted upon by Dworkin, at least in one of its versions.[3] Raz has said that established 'conventions of

* I am indebted to Patricia Mindus, Torben Spaak, Michael Pendlebury, John Carroll and Robert Mabrito for comments on earlier drafts.

[1] See Hart 1994; Raz 1979; Shapiro 2011; Coleman 2001. [2] See Chapter 9.

[3] See Chapter 27. See especially Shapiro's 2007 version of the argument.

interpretation' determine the content of legislation and allow modification to that antecedent content. It is noteworthy that he does not distinguish between conventions for retrieving *ex ante* legal content and conventions for modifying it, since he believes that they cannot be distinguished.[4] The idea that the content of legislation is determined by conventions of interpretation also appears vulnerable to one version of Dworkin's theoretical disagreement argument.[5] When it comes to law from non-authoritative sources, the record is no better. Hart claimed, without offering specifics, that a rule of recognition could pick out customary law; but this claim has been powerfully challenged by Dworkin.[6]

Against this background, there is a default theory of legal content that many legal positivists – and non-positivists – accept. It is the idea that the legal content of texts, or of authoritative pronouncements in general, is their ('ordinary') linguistic content. The theory is compatible with legal positivism; for linguistic rules can be entirely explained by social facts.

Mark Greenberg challenges legal positivism on this default legal theory of content. He does so by claiming that it is often combined with a view that he calls *Atomism*: individual legal norms are 'explanatorily prior' to the total content of the law.[7] The linguistic thesis and Atomism are two prongs of a three-pronged 'Standard Picture' that Greenberg opposes.[8]

The Standard Picture has its own difficulty with disagreement. It cannot explain the existence of dissenting opinions in appellate cases, as Greenberg notes. For presumably, each of the dissenters is equally skilled in discerning linguistic content and in applying it to the agreed facts of the case. Moreover, the Standard Picture has further problems. Greenberg's best point against the Standard Picture is that it is at odds with certain established practices for the identification of legal content. His examples include the identification of legal content in precedent cases in the Anglo-American legal systems and the interpretation of the content of criminal statutes in those systems as modified by Model Penal Code commentary, principles of interpretation and common law doctrines.[9] Some might also

[4] Raz 2009b: 288; Raz 2009a: 120–2. Raz thinks that it is also unnecessary to do so.

[5] See Levenbook 2015. [6] See Dworkin 1977: 41–3. [7] Greenberg 2011: 50.

[8] Greenberg takes 'Explanatory Directness', the view that the existence of a legal norm is directly explained by its authoritative pronouncement, not its content or 'impact on the law', as the third and most important prong.

[9] See Greenberg 2011: 73–6. See also Greenberg 2014: 1316. Greenberg provides a summary of criticisms of the Standard Picture in Greenberg 2017: 301–5.

claim that the Standard Picture cannot explain the fact that, in the United States, statutes with clear linguistic content have no legal content if they violate certain clauses of the Constitution. They have no legal force and contribute nothing to the law; hence, they have no legal content.

The argument against the Standard Picture upon which Greenberg places greatest weight, however, relies on what he calls *the bindingness hypothesis.* That hypothesis, which is 'relatively uncontroversial', Greenberg claims, is that it is part of the 'nature of law' that it is 'supposed to operate' so as to 'arrange matters' to 'reliably ensure' that its legal obligations are genuinely, all-things-considered, binding.[10] Greenberg demonstrates that on the Standard Picture, legal systems would not be able to 'reliably ensure' such a thing. So, on this picture of legal content, it is generally not true that legal systems can 'operate as they are supposed to'.[11] This, he thinks, raises doubts about the Standard Picture. Insofar as legal positivism purports to be a theory about the nature of law, Greenberg thinks that it raises doubts about legal positivism; for legal positivism omits this alleged normative property of law in its account.

The bindingness hypothesis is a particularly strong claim, requiring all-things-considered binding obligation. A weaker form may be a more plausible basis for criticism of legal positivism. A familiar and attractive idea is that genuinely being obligated to do something entails a good reason to do it. On this view, legal positivism has a problem explaining how all legal obligations and legal claim-rights deserve to be considered real obligations and real rights. In contrast, Greenberg develops and defends a theory that satisfies the bindingness hypothesis and, in so doing, satisfies this weaker constraint on legal obligations.

It is called the Moral Impact Theory of law. Greenberg coins the phrase *the moral profile* to stand for the totality of our moral rights, duties,

[10] Greenberg 2011: 90. See also his later characterisation of this hypothesis: '[By their nature] legal norms are supposed to be binding (or, at least, . . . legal norms are supposed to be such that it is morally permissible to force people to comply with them)' (Greenberg 2017: 292). With this statement of the hypothesis, Greenberg appears to assume that saying that a person P has a legal obligation to A is equivalent to, or entails, that someone in the legal system is morally permitted to force P to comply. As Nozick 1974 argues, the assumption is not true for moral obligations, even all-things-considered ones.

[11] Greenberg 2011: 96. Greenberg later asserts, without demonstration, that, on his own theory of legal content, 'the contribution of an authoritative text will often be close to its linguistic meaning' (Greenberg 2017: 310).

immunities, powers and so on.[12] According to the Moral Impact Theory, 'the content of the law is that part of the moral profile that obtains in virtue of the actions of legal institutions'.[13] Another way to put this is: the content of the law is 'the moral impact of certain decisions of legal institutions'.[14] This makes 'legal obligations ... a certain subset of moral obligations'.[15] (He means all-things-considered moral obligations.)[16]

The connection to the actions of legal institutions must be of the right sort, the obligations arising in the 'legally proper way'. Moral obligations to 'mitigate' the effects of or 'remedy' morally bad statutes, for instance, do not count as legal obligations on this theory.[17]

The idea is that an act by a legal institution – say, the enactment of a statute by the legislature or a decision by an appellate court – can alter the *ex ante* moral profile for law subjects, 'by changing people's expectations, providing new options, or bestowing the blessing of the people's representatives on particular schemes'[18] that solve coordination problems. One should add 'or in other ways'; he says that the content of law is 'determined by all relevant values'.[19] In this way, Greenberg's theory satisfies the bindingness hypothesis and preserves the idea that legal obligations are necessarily connected to good reasons for action.

Greenberg does not merely expose the failure of a particular theory of legal content and offer an alternative; he launches a transcendental attack on the grounding thesis itself.[20] The very nature of law, he claims, requires a particular kind of rational connection – which he calls *rational intelligibility* – between the metaphysical determinants of legal facts and legal facts themselves. Social facts cannot satisfy this requirement, but normative, especially moral, facts can.[21] The argument is as follows: Law is metaphysically dependent on simpler facts. Law is also reason-apt; it cannot be just a 'brute fact' that certain social facts result in a law with

[12] See Greenberg 2011: 56–7.

[13] Greenberg 2014: 1341. Several legal philosophers, including Raz, have noted that law can change the moral profile. For an account, see Bix 2014: 3–4.

[14] Greenberg 2017: 294. [15] Greenberg 2014: 1290. [16] See Greenberg 2014: 1293–4.

[17] Greenberg 2014: 1322. And see Greenberg 2017: 281–2 for another improper way in which actions of legal institutions might give rise to moral obligations.

[18] Greenberg 2014: 1290. [19] Greenberg 2017: 276.

[20] See Greenberg 2004: 157–98 ånd its sequel, Greenberg 2006: 265–90.

[21] Levenbook 2013: 80–1 n. 12. This is to assume that social facts cannot be normative facts. However, if legal facts are just complex social facts, the language for describing these social facts is non-normative, not the facts themselves.

a specific content, as opposed to its contradictory or its contrary. There must be an explanation in terms of reasons why just these social facts determine just this legal content. It must make rational sense when one focuses on a particular set of base facts that a particular proposition of law, and not its contradictory or contrary, holds or, as Greenberg would put it, is true. However, no function from social facts alone has this feature.[22] Hence, the base facts are not confined to social facts, and social facts alone cannot be the ultimate grounds of law.

In sum, Greenberg's challenge to legal positivism is important for three reasons: Greenberg makes a transcendental attack on the grounding thesis, he presses legal positivism at a point of perceived vulnerability – the failure of grounding theorists to develop and defend a compelling theory of legal content – and he preserves a necessary connection between legal obligations and good reasons for action.

32.2 Assessing Greenberg's Transcendental Argument

Taking Greenberg's contributions in chronological order, consider the transcendental attack on the grounding thesis. Greenberg is correct that a metaphysical theory of law needs a defence. The theory must be rationally defensible. What cannot be just a 'brute fact' is the theory itself. (However, a theory might claim that it *is* just a brute fact that legal fact L is constituted by function F of social facts 1 . . . N.) Such a theory might turn out to be rationally defensible – on grounds, we might say, *external* to it. Because of the theory, the relationship between L and the social facts in question will make sense. The theory will make it clear why it must be L and not something else that is created by the social facts in question.

Greenberg tries to demonstrate that no successful defence of Hart's theory of law – and, by extension, any social fact theory of law – can be constructed. His case relies at points on his chief mistake, which is to insist that a defence of a constitutive theory of law must come from inside the theory in the following way: the connection between the alleged base facts and the legal facts must be explained entirely by the base facts. The base facts jointly must wear their relevance to the legal content on their faces.[23]

[22] Greenberg 2004: 178–85; Greenberg 2006: 270–3.

[23] Greenberg 2004: 164. Greenberg says that this is to be 'transparent'.

(This is the demand of 'rational intelligibility'.) Simply put, this demand is ad hoc, as is easily seen by imagining it made upon a theory of the metaphysical dependency of mental states on physical states.[24]

So why is law different? Greenberg's main response confuses the established practice among legal theorists and jurists (which we see only in contested cases) of offering (or demanding) reasons for legal conclusions that legally justify them with a very different practice of naming (or demanding) metaphysical determinants of legal facts. This is to confuse, as Sellars, citing Aristotle, terms it, the *order of knowing* with the *order of being*.[25] We may know, for example, that someone is in a psychological state, based on behaviour, and it may be the normal practice to use behaviour as a justification for a claim about someone's psychological state, but it does not follow that the metaphysical determinant of that psychological state is behaviour (rather than, for example, a particular physical state of the brain).[26]

Let us provisionally suppose that legal justification is always aimed at justifying claims about *ex ante* law. Legal justification aids knowledge, and, like all justification, it comes to an end. Explicitly, judges in a particular legal system may end with an appeal to a statute and an established canon of interpretation of it. Legal theorists usually suggest that there is a further, implicit end. According to Hart, for instance, the line of justification can be traced back further to a rule of recognition. It picks out rules of change that pick out the statute in question. However, beyond the rule of recognition, on Hart's theory, legal justification ends. What fixes the rule of recognition, according to Hart, is official practice. But official practice is not part of the chain of legal justification; it is part of the philosophical explanation, which, given the theory, epistemically justifies a particular claim about the law in a particular legal system.

That the practice of officials has a certain metaphysical role in fixing legal facts is not, of course, meant to be self-explanatory. As Greenberg correctly notes, the claim that a social practice of any sort fixes legal facts in such-and-such a manner is not self-explanatory. However, it need not be, as long as the whole theory of law is rationally defensible (so that it can be shown to be true or a better alternative than other theories) and the

[24] I thank Michael Pendlebury for bringing this point to my attention.

[25] See Sellars 1991: 14 n. 4. [26] I am indebted to Michael Pendlebury for the example.

precise manner in which official practice does this fixing is rationally discoverable.

Greenberg, on the contrary, assumes that the chain of justification must end with reference to a metaphysical constituent whose role as a metaphysical constituent is self-explanatory. This demand does not follow from anything we observe in the practice of legal justification and legal argumentation. When reasons given in legal argumentation are challenged, the grounds are rarely, if ever, that they do not wear their metaphysical relevance to legal content on their face. For all of these reasons, Greenberg's assumption of rational intelligibility is wholly unwarranted.

It is also so rigorous that Greenberg's own selected base facts cannot satisfy it.[27] For example, Greenberg names fairness as a moral fact that serves as one of the base facts in a true constitutive theory of legal content.[28] Consider the claim that the legal content of a statute is L because L is only fair (given the statute's plain public meaning and the practice of relying on plain meaning in the past). This claim fails to furnish an explanation because it is not obvious why what's only fair, given the statute's plain meaning, helps to determine the content of the positive law. In other words, the role of fairness as a determinant of legal content is not self-explanatory. There is no rational transparency in the claim that it has this role. The theory that it is because of the fairness of applying a statute in this way (as opposed to because it is the practice of applying a statute in this way), that this is the way it *ex ante* applies, requires, as does Hart's theory, an external defence.

That defence cannot, moreover, be successfully mounted on the bindingness hypothesis. Recall that the bindingness hypothesis is that from the nature of law, the normative demand follows that law 'reliably ensures' that its obligations are genuinely, all-things-considered, binding. The main problem is that this hypothesis cannot be used to raise doubts about any theory of legal content or theory of law or to support any such

[27] I may be echoing earlier unpublished comments by Gideon Rosen, as reported by Greenberg 2006: 285; Greenberg's main response, same page, is: 'On the face of it, facts about how law practices should contribute to the content of the law make rationally intelligible how the law practices do contribute to the content of the law.' This is not the least plausible unless one starts equivocating on the idea of rational intelligibility, conflating an explanatory sense of 'make rationally intelligible' – make comprehensible – with a normative sense – practically justify.

[28] See Greenberg 2006: 275–6. In a later work, he cites 'the fact that, on balance, the relevant [moral] values support' the relevance of an S as another (Greenberg 2017: 305).

theory for anyone who rejects it. It is hardly uncontroversial, as Greenberg claims. It needs a defence.

In partial defence of the bindingness hypothesis, Greenberg borrows from Mark Murphy's argument that there is something defective about law if it does not have what it claims to have. Greenberg maintains that those who accept Raz's view that law 'necessarily claims legitimate authority' hold an unsustainable position if they stop short of the bindingness hypothesis.[29] Greenberg also adds a corollary argument: the legal system typically treats its demands as all-things-considered obligations, not as subordinate to morality.[30] Greenberg thinks that it follows that it is part of the nature of law that law is supposed to create all-things-considered obligations.

For those who reject Raz's view because they do not think that law can claim anything, all that is left to answer here is Greenberg's corollary argument. This argument is not a good one, whether it is intended to be deductive or inductive. For law is not the only system of practical reasoning that treats its alleged obligations as dispositive. Consider an example from Shapiro,[31] the organised crime syndicate known as the Yakuza. Doubtless when orders are given to subordinates, they are expected to be followed without exception, and failure to do so is punished severely. Excuses from morality, law or any other source are considered irrelevant. One might, with as much justification as in the case of law, say that, in Yakuza thinking, Yakuza demands are all-things-considered obligations. One might go on to say that it ought to be that these demands are genuine all-things-considered obligations, within the bounds of morality. Yet, even if the Yakuza are in this way representative of all criminal syndicates, one cannot conclude that it is part of the nature of criminal syndicates, understood properly, that they aim at genuine all-things-considered obligations and are defective as criminal syndicates wherever they fail. Such a notion is absurd.

Greenberg further claims that 'we' treat law as providing exclusionary reasons against every other consideration. This is a weak defence of the bindingness hypothesis, as 'we' could be mistaken. He offers no evidence for the empirical clam; and it may be false of the broader public beyond officials, bureaucrats and those who give legal advice. The generalisation has notable exceptions, even among those inclined to be law-abiding. For

[29] See Greenberg 2011: 90. [30] See Greenberg 2011: 93–4. [31] See Shapiro 2011: 215.

example, the vast majority of motorists in the United States treat what they know to be the speed limit laws as subordinate to certain practical considerations (and desires), and are known to obey the speed limits only when they fear imminent enforcement. In the United States recently, a significant subset of individuals has laid claim to the supremacy of their religious convictions over certain legal obligations they recognise,[32] thus treating law as failing to exclude some considerations.

In short, Greenberg's defence of the bindingness hypothesis fails. This leaves the case for the Moral Impact Theory to be made on other grounds.

32.3 The Moral Impact Theory

The Moral Impact Theory is developed and defended as a challenge to that branch of legal positivism that accepts the grounding thesis. How viable is this challenge? We can begin by noting some problems in the characterisation of the theory. Greenberg presents it as a 'constitutive' theory of law.[33] That is, he presents it as an account of upon what more metaphysically basic facts legal content facts are grounded, or dependent.[34] Yet Greenberg disclaims presenting a theory for 'all possible legal systems' and contends instead that his theory is meant to apply only to 'theoretically interesting' legal systems such as those in the United States and the United Kingdom.[35] This combination of contentions makes no sense; a theory of metaphysical constituents of law applies to all possible legal systems.

Moreover, Greenberg claims that legal obligations are moral obligations arising in a certain way. This is a contention of identity, from which it follows that moral obligations cannot be constituents or metaphysical determinants of legal obligations.

Or can they? Recall that the obligations identical to legal obligations are supposed to be all-things-considered obligations. Suppose Greenberg holds that the metaphysical determinants of them include pro tanto

[32] Such as the obligation on the part of magistrates to conduct marriages of same-sex couples.

[33] See Greenberg 2014: 1296. [34] See Greenberg 2017: 275.

[35] Greenberg 2017: 287. See also Greenberg 2017: 302: 'I want to allow ... that different fundamental accounts [accounts of how law is determined at a fundamental level] could be true of different legal systems.' This suggests that he does not understand what a theory of metaphysical determinants is.

ex ante moral obligations.[36] The trouble with this idea is that, although all-things-considered obligations are justificatorily more complex than pro tanto obligations, it does not follow that they are metaphysically more complex. Indeed, the claim that one obligation can be metaphysically more complex than another is opaque; it may be incoherent. What would it be like to have one obligation metaphysically simpler or more complex than another? What would it be like to have one moral fact metaphysically simpler than another, or one value metaphysically simpler than another?

These problems of characterisation are relatively minor. What is more important is the case that Greenberg makes for the Moral Impact Theory. Since relying on the bindingness hypothesis is not a viable option, it is well that Greenberg proffers three other defences.[37]

First, he argues that his Moral Impact Theory promotes clarity about legal obligations. He does this by illustrating a clear difference between the Standard Picture and his own theory with respect to statutory law:

> Suppose that a community faces a problem for which there are multiple solutions, and there is no agreement on which solution would be better. As things are, though there is a moral obligation to help others, there is no obligation to participate in any particular scheme for solving the problem . . .. Nothing determines which scheme is the one that people should participate in. In addition, there is no mechanism for people to join together in a common scheme.
>
> Suppose that, in response to the problem, the legislature enacts a statute. The statute's linguistic meaning clearly designates a particular scheme, call it scheme A . . .. As it happens, however, the scheme that becomes salient and that a majority of people are likely to participate in – scheme B – is subtly but significantly different from scheme A. This could come about in various ways, perhaps because a private company that is a dominant player in the relevant industry misinterprets the statute early on, or because a widespread psychological tendency makes it unlikely that people would adhere to scheme A. In this kind of situation, different reasons support A and B. For example, democratic reasons may militate in favour of A, while reasons of fairness, helping others and solving the community problem

[36] He also uses what could be metaphysical language to make the following claim: '[T]he content of the law depends on the moral circumstance of the fact that the legal institution took the action in question' (Greenberg 2014: 1317). Greenberg also describes other determinants in 'the morally relevant (background) circumstances', including other acts of officials but not institutions (Greenberg 2014: 1318).

[37] He does, however, claim that the bindingness hypothesis is 'a natural part of the background to the Moral Impact Theory' (Greenberg 2017: 292).

> may militate in favour of B. Suppose that, in the circumstances, the effect of the enactment of the statute, all things considered, is to generate a (genuine) obligation to participate in scheme B, not scheme A . . ..
>
> . . . According to the Moral Impact Theory . . . there is a legal obligation to participate in scheme B.[38]

In response to those theories choosing scheme A as designated in the legal content of the statute, Greenberg contends that since cooperating in scheme A is not a genuine all-things-considered obligation for anyone, 'it is hard to see why using the term "obligation" [to designate the apparent requirement to cooperate in scheme A as a legal obligation] promotes clarity. It seems at least as clear a use of language to use the term "legal obligation" for the genuine obligation to cooperate in scheme B.'[39] In this way, his Moral Impact Theory preserves 'the commonsense view that a legal obligation is a kind of [real] obligation'.[40]

The foregoing would be a strong argument provided that (1) there is no other way to preserve the idea about legal obligation, (2) this idea is deeply entrenched and theoretically important to retain, and (3) the price that the Moral Impact Theory pays for its method of preservation is not too steep. One may well doubt that the first condition is satisfied. As to the third condition, an examination of the price that the Moral Impact Theory pays is reserved for the last section of this chapter (Section 32.4).

Second, Greenberg asserts that his Moral Impact Theory makes it easy to account for our 'dominating concern with law',[41] with the implication that legal positivism cannot so easily account for that concern. However, as Leiter points out, legal positivism has no trouble accounting for a concern for law, both on prudential grounds and on the grounds that, occasionally, law really does alter one's moral profile.[42]

Third, Greenberg claims that his Moral Impact Theory fits appellate practice better than some views, perhaps best. This is to make a familiar mistake, one that Dworkin makes. That mistake is to indiscriminately take what judges and lawyers appeal to in appellate cases in textual interpretation, and the reasons they present in a rationale on common law and precedent, as always bearing on antecedent legal content.

Recall that Greenberg has an argument for doing so in his earlier works, in connection with the bindingness hypothesis. It goes as follows: Those

[38] Greenberg 2017: 289–90. Note omitted. [39] Greenberg 2017: 290.
[40] Greenberg 2014: 1304. [41] Ibid. [42] See Leiter 2014.

working out the content of law, such as judges and legal theorists, give reasons for their conclusions. They take themselves to be citing reasons that make the legal content what it is.[43] That is, they take themselves not to be offering mere heuristic devices or epistemic evidence but to be alluding to the metaphysical constituents of the legal content. Therefore, they must be citing such reasons. (It remains for a natural law theorist such as Greenberg only to note that the set of reasons offered at the appellate level sometimes includes moral reasons.)

This argument is invalid. Even if the premises are true, the appellate judges may simply be confusing the order of being and the order of knowing. Moreover, there are at least two other problems with the argument.

The first is that appellate cases are ones in which there has been some problem in straightforwardly applying a legal text, common law doctrine or precedent. Leiter reminds us that most of the interpretation of legal texts, in the form of applying them to specific cases, occurs well outside the court system.[44] What is true of a small minority of cases, namely appellate cases, cannot be reliably generalised to all cases. To do so is to commit the fallacy known as hasty generalisation. One must first show that one's sample is unbiased and representative, a task that Greenberg (and Dworkin) does not attempt.

The second problem is that there is reason to doubt the previous provisional assumption that appellate cases are always about working out the *ex ante* content of the law, even epistemically. There are several possibilities. For legal texts, they are appellate decisions aimed (i) at discerning the full linguistic content of an authoritative text, (ii) at discerning the contribution to law that the authoritative text makes, and (iii) at assigning or extending a meaning to it by way of repair of its content. (The linguistic content may be inconsistent, indeterminate or otherwise incomplete or unsatisfactory in other ways, such that compliance with it would have absurd results.) For decisions concerning precedent in common law, they are appellate decisions aimed (i') at discovering how the original precedent case's decision applies to the current case and (ii') at discerning whether law permits or requires its application to the case. If an account of

43 See Greenberg 2006: 239. See also Greenberg 2014: 1304: '[I]t is plausible that moral reasoning has a place in legal interpretation.'

44 See Leiter 2009: 1215–50.

precedent I offered elsewhere is correct, there is a third possibility: that they are appellate decisions aimed (iii') at making more determinate the inchoate categories of the example that the original precedent established.[45] To assume that in all or most appellate reasoning only activities (ii) or (ii') are being pursued is to beg important questions.

For all of these reasons, Greenberg's second and third arguments for the Moral Impact Theory are inadequate.

32.4 The Price of the Moral Impact Theory

What about the first argument – the one that claims that the Moral Impact Theory rescues the idea of legal obligation as genuine obligation? Unfortunately, the Moral Impact Theory does so at a very steep price. For Greenberg's theory of law has five problems, which may be presented in order of increasing seriousness.

The first problem is that the Moral Impact Theory cannot account for legal permissions. It cannot, that is, if legal permissions are what Hohfeld termed *privileges*. Privileges are the opposite of duties, or obligations, on Hohfeld's schema.[46] Yet Greenberg cannot agree. For if legal permissions are the opposite of legal obligations, then whenever law fails to generate a legal obligation, there is a legal permission. This is how most lawyers view the matter. For instance, they say that I have a legal permission to use my savings to invest in a speculative stock or, even if it will empty my bank account, to buy that red Maserati or the lovely diamond pendant on offer. I have this legal permission even if, in my case, it would be wildly imprudent to do so. If prudence is a relevant value, it seems that, all things considered, I ought not to do these things. It would follow, on Greenberg's account, that I do not have a legal permission to do them. So the absence of a legal obligation to the contrary does not, on his theory, generate a legal permission.

The second, related problem with Greenberg's Moral Impact Theory is that it follows that there is much less legal content in the systems important to Greenberg – those of the United States and the United Kingdom – than he, and everyone else, thinks. In addition to accounting in general for legal permissions, Greenberg has a problem accounting for the legal permission,

[45] See Levenbook 2000. [46] See, e.g., Hohfeld 1978.

or perhaps the legal duty, allegedly held by certain government officials, to inflict punishment on convicted criminals. Greenberg assumes that by supplying notice of a specific punishment for conduct, legal systems might create an all-things-considered moral permission to impose that punishment.[47] The problem is that although legal systems might do this, they will do so under conditions that do not seem prevalent in the target legal systems.

To see why, consider the strongest scenario for Greenberg's contention, where the conduct in question is *ex ante* morally wrong (or, as lawyers in the common law system say, *mala in se*), the perpetrator's act was fully voluntary and informed, and the perpetrator has no moral excuse or justification. Even under those conditions, a government does not gain moral permission to do terrible things to people who have done what they *ex ante* should not have done simply by warning them what would happen to them if they did and then carrying out the threat. Thinking otherwise greatly underestimates the difficulties of justifying criminal punishment, as familiarity with the vast literature on this subject reveals. Consider the case in which the punishment warned of is morally disproportionate to the offence, so that it is far more than the criminal deserves. This situation can plausibly be asserted to obtain frequently in the enforcement of statutes setting mandatory sentences, particularly for non-violent drug offences, enacted in the era of 'getting tough on crime' in the United States at the end of the previous century. Consider the case in which the government lacks moral legitimacy. Consider the case in which the perpetrator has not benefitted from the scheme of criminal law whereas others have, so that the benefits of enforcement of the criminal law have not been justly distributed. Many poor criminals from disadvantaged backgrounds might qualify as examples. Consider the case in which there is an alternative response to the perpetrator that would have, on balance, better consequences. One could extend the list.

Some familiar alleged legal obligations do not fare any better on Greenberg's picture. Recall the speed limit example from Section 32.2. One can make a good case on the basis of *ex ante* moral considerations that if a motorist is in moderate traffic flowing at the rate permitted by the speed limit, it would be, under normal circumstances, all-things-considered wrong to speed. Given expectations, speeding would unjustifiably jeopardise life

[47] See Greenberg 2017: 288.

and property. Yet the matter looks different if the motorist is alone on the road, the weather is excellent with good visibility, the motorist has good reflexes and good hand-eye coordination, and the vehicle has perfect brakes. Add that the motorist is late for an important appointment – say, the start of a class he or she is to teach. Now it is much harder to generate an all-things-considered moral obligation for that motorist to obey the speed limit.

Greenberg does not help. Recall that Greenberg describes legal obligations as arising from some function of 'all [the] relevant values'.[48] In addition to fairness, Greenberg often names democracy as contributing to changing the moral profile. (He sometimes refers to democracy as the state of affairs of having had an equal chance to participate in 'the procedures of governance'.)[49] Democracy is at a very abstract level some form of collective decision-making based on some form of political equality. In any system other than one of direct democracy, collective decision-making along democratic lines must be properly institutionalised through (among other things) the legislature, and the statutes produced in the way designated as proper. There may be other conditions to be met for democracy to yield obligations for its law subjects, for 'the blessing of the people's representatives' to carry moral weight. For instance, some political philosophers think that the democracy must be deliberative, or discursive, to be (morally) legitimate, that is, to yield moral obligations on the part of law subjects and moral rights on the part of legislators and other officials.

Democratic considerations do not generate obligations for the citizenry under morally defective political conditions. Unfortunately, we find these defective conditions all too often. Our motorist may be in them. In the United States alone, there are states in which suffrage is restricted discriminatorily, legislators do not follow established rules, bills are not given to legislators until the last minute and, for other reasons, legislators and judges do not reflect the will of the people. (One may wonder what the moral consequences are when the impact of votes is manipulated through partisan gerrymandering – also rife in parts of the United States – so that it appears that the legislators are selecting their electors.)[50] So it looks as if

[48] Greenberg 2017: 276.

[49] Greenberg 2014: 1313. He refers to this as 'democratic considerations'.

[50] Political scientists working on the Electoral Integrity Project have devised a test to measure the degree of democracy in elections. The result of applying it to alleged democracies was that some of them in developing countries were regarded as 'failed democracies'. One member of the team of political scientists has applied the test to my home state, North

democratic reasons will be irrelevant to the existence of the motorist's legal obligations if he or she lives in the United States, especially in certain states.

If this is correct, it is likely that no appeal to democracy will generate a moral reason for a citizen of such a state to obey the speed limit under the conditions of the thought experiment. Will fairness do so? Greenberg never clarifies the kind of fairness he has in mind. Perhaps he thinks that some laws – for example, those that solve coordination problems such as speed limit laws – create a duty of fair play for individual law subjects to do their part in the selected cooperative scheme. Unfortunately, a duty of fair play does not attach unless either one has actively accepted the benefits of the scheme and they are greater to one than the costs of complying or one has actually consented to the cooperative scheme.[51]

Let us call the motorist Smith, and suppose that Smith has not consented to the posted speed limit, as is true of many motorists. Under these circumstances, Smith's costs of complying may be greater than the benefits that Smith has received if in fact virtually no one around Smith drives at the speed limit. The benefits that Smith has received would then have come from motorists around Smith driving alike at a steady speed, whatever it is. Smith discerns that rate of speed, and this gives him or her enough information to form expectations and take actions that increase Smith's motoring safety.

Though this discussion has hardly canvassed all of the possible relevant moral considerations, it appears that, in all of the circumstances envisaged, motorist Smith does not have what Greenberg would consider to be a legal obligation to obey the speed limit regulation. Quite the contrary; it may begin to appear that, all things considered, Smith (morally) ought to violate the speed limit regulation. (After all, Smith has a moral obligation to meet that class on time.)

Many alleged legal obligations of law subjects are like the speed limit example. These legal obligations are thought to obtain across a large class of instances, even in situations in which the balance of considerations does not tip in favour of compliance with them. Schauer puts the point this way:

Carolina. His conclusion is that North Carolina is no longer a 'fully functioning democracy'. There are many reasons why. See Reynolds 2016 and the follow-up article, Reynolds 2018.

51 See Nozick 1974: 93–5.

with respect to their background justifications, entrenched rules (including those setting requirements such as we find in law) are over-inclusive.[52]

We should note that some considerations of fairness seem to be more applicable to judges deciding cases or to officials enforcing decrees than to individuals complying with requirements. Yet Greenberg's appeal to fairness does not put him in a stronger position with regard to alleged legal obligations of officials, particularly judges. Perhaps Greenberg thinks that treating like cases alike is a principle of fairness applying to judges in applying statutes or following precedent, particularly in common law cases. Unfortunately, treating like cases alike, where likeness is arbitrarily set by a statute or a precedent, is just a formal principle. It has no moral bite, as Lyons pointed out many years ago.[53]

Suppose that Greenberg is assuming that the categories of likeness are set by morality, so that fairness is a reason for reaching the same judicial decision or applying a statute the same way in a case that is in morally relevant respects the same as a prior case. Setting aside considerations of detrimental reliance, fairness is not even a pro tanto reason if the initial decision or application was morally wrong.[54] Suppose, for example, that it was morally wrong to set aside Beardsley's conviction for manslaughter (*People* v. *Beardsley*)[55] on the grounds that the woman in his home for whom he failed to summon medical aid wasn't his wife. The alleged fairness of treating morally relevant like cases alike provides no reason to decide this way again in a similar subsequent case.[56]

Finally, perhaps Greenberg is thinking about the fairness of meeting expectations among law subjects that a promulgated statute will be applied as announced[57] or that a practice of interpreting a statute a certain way will be continued by the courts. This is a very limited consideration because disappointing expectations is not in itself unfair and does not constitute a pro tanto reason to meet them. As several philosophers have pointed out, there was no reason for Kant to continue

52 See Schauer 1991: 47–9. 53 See, e.g., Lyons 1973: 833–61.

54 Greenberg seems inclined to agree in the case of 'evil laws', whatever they are, but not in the case of merely 'morally defective laws' (Greenberg 2017: 294).

55 150 Mich. 206, 113 (1907).

56 There is also the difficulty that legislatures have the power to be unfair in this sense, to draw morally arbitrary lines between what or whom they will privilege or exempt in their statutes.

57 See Fuller 1969: 81–91.

his daily walks at the same hour and minute to meet the expectations of his neighbours, even though his past behaviour had set those expectations and he could have foreseen them, or perhaps did foresee them.[58] Adding detrimental reliance does not provide a pro tanto reason, even when the expectations are reasonable. The people of Kant's town are said to have set their watches by his walks; so the day he does not take a walk, their reliance is detrimental. However, there is still no reason to think that Kant would have done anything pro tanto wrong in breaking his habit without announcement. The point is that there are many conditions to be satisfied for meeting expectations to furnish a pro tanto reason to act. Short of working them out, one can only be sceptical that they are met very often in the legal systems that Greenberg has in mind.[59]

For these reasons, there seems to be a lot less legal content on Greenberg's theory than most of us suppose there to be. If so, on the Moral Impact Theory, whatever legal officials and so-called law-abiding law subjects think and say they are doing, much of the time they are not obeying, acting in accordance with, exercising legal rights under, applying or enforcing the content of the law. That makes Greenberg's theory of legal content radically counterintuitive.

A third problem with Greenberg's Moral Impact Theory is that legal content on his view becomes relative to individuals and situations, despite what rules seem to say or how they are applied. Individuals differ in their moral circumstances, which vary not only from individual to individual but also from time to time for the same individual. This is not merely to say that, on Greenberg's view, a law subject might have an all-things considered (legal) obligation that a judge is not obligated (or even not morally – and, thus, legally – permitted) to enforce. Greenberg is happy to admit that this can be the case.[60] Nor is it to say that some individuals have special legal obligations, privileges or permissions (because of their professions or legal status) that other people do not have and that trump more common legal obligations. It is to say that you may have an all-things-considered obligation to repay credit card debt, whereas your single neighbour may not, in spite of statutory language and accepted legal doctrine, simply

[58] See, e.g., Simmons 2001: 76.

[59] One can be more sceptical that they are met in all the past and present types of legal system.

[60] See Greenberg 2017: 286. A legal official might also have an all-things-considered moral obligation to enforce a rule against someone who does not have an all-things-considered obligation to obey it.

because her alternative involves living in a car with her two small children. Note that, in this case, she lacks an all-things-considered obligation to repay the debt in advance of filing bankruptcy and going through discharge. On Greenberg's account, her legal obligation – if she had one initially – disappears well before virtually any practising lawyer would say it does.

There are other consequences of this relativity. You might have had a legal obligation under a statute yesterday; however, today, because of something that has happened in your life outside of a legal institution, not named or recognised as an exception by any legally authoritative source or anticipated in any way by precedential cases – for example, new religious convictions, a crisis in the life of someone to whom you are emotionally committed – you do not.[61]

One way to avoid the relativity problem is to change the view and hold that a law is a norm created (in the proper way, if this can be specified without circularity) by the actions of legal institutions that changes the moral profile of somebody – official or law subject. There are, however, reasons to doubt that Greenberg's theory can do justice to the idea of a legal norm.

Legal norms come, on Greenberg's view, from legal institutions; but Greenberg's assumption that there are legal institutions, and that some of their actions are relevant to generating the content of law, cannot be accommodated by his theory of legal content.[62] This is the fourth problem with the Moral Impact Theory. Greenberg supplies no account of what makes an institution a legal institution beyond a necessary condition.[63] A legal institution is one that is created by law. The laws that do this are constitutive rules or norms, and they have legal content. Greenberg has no account of the determinants of their content. Constitutive rules do not set obligations. There are also rules for what counts as an act of a particular legal institution, some of them rules of the institution. It is not plausible to see these rules as altering a moral profile, even under the best circumstances. Therefore, Greenberg's account of legal content must at the very

[61] Brian Bix (2014: 6) makes a related point against Greenberg. My point may have been anticipated by Scott Hershovitz's 'worry that the impact of our legal practices on our moral rights and obligations is . . . widespread and varied' (Hershovitz 2015: n. 66).

[62] Leiter 2014 anticipates this criticism.

[63] Greenberg 2014: 1324: 'an organization that, by its nature, is supposed to improve the moral situation' [note omitted].

least be amended, or it will not be a comprehensive account of legal content.

Further trouble appears when we recall the person-specific nature of all-things-considered obligations and their dependency on fluctuating normative factors in a person's circumstances. Recall, too, that, on Greenberg's view, you have a legal profile (legal obligation, legal power and so forth) just in case you have a corresponding moral profile that has been altered or created (by the actions of legal institutions).[64] The law is, then, the set of all-things-considered obligations, powers, immunities and so forth held by a shifting set of individuals. These obligations, powers and so on can change even in the absence of fresh action by legal institutions. They will change when the relevant normative circumstances of an individual change. How, then, would a law be individuated? As the set of such things traceable to a single legal institutional action? An affirmative answer will not work well for the development of the common law through precedent.

Consider what norm can be formulated for an alleged individual law on this picture. Let us take a prohibition based on a statute. At best, the norm is something like, 'It is prohibited to A unless you have a justification (based on all normative factors) for Aing or there is no reason for you to refrain from A at all (because the enactment did not even pro tanto change your moral profile).' Alternately, perhaps it is: 'All those who, all things considered, including the enactment of the statute, ought not to A are legally prohibited from Aing.' These proposed standards are less like legal norms and more like instantiated statements of the Moral Impact Theory itself.

So – and this is the fifth problem – Greenberg's view amounts to a challenge to the prevailing assumption that individual statutes at least sometimes, if not usually, introduce individual norms into law. He sometimes writes as if his challenge does not go this far, permitting himself to talk about legal standards that become law.[65] At one point, he claims that sometimes on his Moral Impact Theory, 'the legislative enactment of a statute' may '[add] to the content of law a norm that is more or less captured by the linguistic content of the legislation'.[66] At another point, he writes: 'When legal institutions take actions that change the moral profile in certain characteristic ways, they thereby create legal norms.'[67]

[64] For example, Greenberg (2014: 1340) maintains that the establishing of a side of the road to drive on alters your moral profile.

[65] See Greenberg 2017: 294. [66] Greenberg 2014: 1342. [67] Greenberg 2017: 311.

However, on his Moral Impact Theory of law, if we mean by 'law' the legal content, then law is not a system of norms.[68] Instead, law is composed of diachronically shifting sets of genuine obligations, powers, permissions, rights and so on belonging to particular individuals at a moment and created by the actions of legal institutions.[69] Legal content consists in momentary normative tokens, not types.

For all of these reasons, the price that the Moral Impact Theory pays to preserve the idea that an obligation entails a good reason for action is unacceptable. The Moral Impact Theory thus fails to constitute a viable alternative to legal positivism.

References

Bix, B. 2014. 'When Law Becomes Morality: Comments on Mark Greenberg's Moral Impact Theory of Law'. https://papers.ssrn.com/sol3/papers.cfm?abstract_id=2434075.

Coleman, J. 2001. *The Practice of Principle*. Oxford University Press.

Dworkin, R. 1977. *Taking Rights Seriously*. Harvard University Press.

Fuller, L. 1969. *The Morality of Law*. Yale University Press.

Greenberg, M. 2004. 'How Facts Make Law'. *Legal Theory* 10: 157–98.

Greenberg, M. 2006. 'Hartian Positivism and Normative Facts: How Facts Make Law II'. In S. Hershovitz (ed.). *Exploring Law's Empire*. Oxford University Press: 265–90.

Greenberg, M. 2011. 'The Standard Picture and Its Discontents'. In L. Green and B. Leiter (eds.). *Oxford Studies in Philosophy of Law*, vol. 1. Oxford University Press: 39–106.

Greenberg, M. 2014. 'The Moral Impact Theory of Law'. *Yale Law Journal* 123: 1288–1342.

Greenberg, M. 2017. 'The Moral Impact Theory, the Dependence View, and Natural Law'. In G. Duke and R. George (eds.). *Cambridge Companion to Natural Law Jurisprudence*. Cambridge University Press: 275–313.

Hart, H. L. A. 1994. *The Concept of Law*. 2nd ed. Oxford University Press.

Hershovitz, S. 2015. 'The End of Jurisprudence'. *Yale Law Journal* 124: 1160–1204.

Hohfeld, W. 1978. *Fundamental Legal Conceptions*. Ed. A. Corbin. Greenwood Press.

[68] Once again, Hershovitz (2015) seems to anticipate this point.

[69] '[T]he law is the moral impact or effect of certain actions of legal institutions – i.e., the moral obligations [and powers and rights and so on] that obtain in light of those actions' (Greenberg 2014: 1301).

Leiter, B. 2009. 'Explaining Theoretical Disagreement'. *University of Chicago Law Review* 76: 1215–50.

Leiter, B. 2014. 'Some Questions and Doubts about Greenberg's "Moral Impact Theory of Law"'. https://leiterreports.typepad.com/brianleiterlaw/2014/05/some-questions-and-doubts-about-greenbergs-moral-impact-theory-of-law.html.

Levenbook, B. B. 2000. 'The Meaning of a Precedent'. *Legal Theory* 6: 185–240.

Levenbook, B. B. 2013. 'How to Hold the Social Fact Thesis: A Reply to Greenberg and Toh'. In L. Green and B. Leiter (eds.). *Oxford Studies in Philosophy of Law*, vol. 2. Oxford University Press: 75–102.

Levenbook, B. B. 2015. 'Dworkin's Theoretical Disagreement Argument'. *Philosophy Compass* 10: 1–9.

Lyons, D. 1973. 'On Formal Justice'. *Cornell Law Review* 58: 833–61.

Nozick, R. 1974. *Anarchy, State and Utopia*. Basic Books.

Raz, J. 1979. 'Legal Positivism and the Source of Law'. In J. Raz. *The Authority of Law*. Oxford University Press: 37–52.

Raz, J. 2009a. 'On the Nature of Law'. In J. Raz. *Between Authority and Interpretation*. Oxford University Press: 91–125.

Raz, J. 2009b. 'Intention in Interpretation'. In J. Raz. *Between Authority and Interpretation*. Oxford University Press: 265–98.

Reynolds, A. 2016. 'North Carolina Is No Longer Classified as a Democracy'. *New Observer*. www.newsobserver.com/opinion/op-ed/article122593759.html.

Reynolds, A. 2018. 'North Carolina's Democracy Was Bad at the Start of 2017. A Year Later It's Much Worse'. *New Observer*. www.newsobserver.com/opinion/op-ed/article198165644.html.

Schauer, F. 1991. *Playing by the Rules*. Oxford University Press.

Sellars, W. 1991. 'Reply to Aune'. *Wilfrid F. Sellars Papers*. Archives of Scientific Philosophy, Archives and Special Collections, University of Pittsburgh Library System: 1–19.

Shapiro, S. 2007. 'The "Hart-Dworkin" Debate: A Short Guide for the Perplexed'. In A. Ripstein (ed.). *Ronald Dworkin*. Cambridge University Press: 22–55.

Shapiro, S. 2011. *Legality*. Harvard University Press.

Simmons, A. J. 2001. *Justification and Legitimacy: Essays on Rights and Obligations*. Cambridge University Press.

33 Positivism and Totalitarianism

David Dyzenhaus*

33.1 Introduction

Critics of legal positivism have charged it with a propensity to encourage totalitarianism or at least to weaken resistance to it. Totalitarian leaders govern in the name of only that part of the people that fits their ideas of the substantive good. Once in power, such leaders tolerate liberal democratic institutions only for as long as these serve their interests. This is a rough definition. But it captures what the Nazi and fascist regimes have in common with the post-war dictatorships of Latin America, the apartheid state, as well as the 'illiberal democracies' of today.

Debate over this propensity is fundamentally shaped by H. L. A. Hart, *Positivism and the Separation of Law and Morals* (hereinafter *Positivism*).[1] It also shaped the whole course of legal philosophy, though there is little recognition of the philosophical impact of Hart's attempt to refute the charge that a positivistic 'insistence on the separation of law as it is from law as it ought to be' had 'powerfully contributed to the horrors'[2] of the Nazi regime by encouraging German lawyers to think that anything with the form of law should be obeyed. Indeed, although Hart presented the essay as a defence of the 'separation thesis' that there is no necessary conceptual connection between law and morality, and argued that positivism stiffens resistance to totalitarianism, his students have taken to claiming that positivism accepts several necessary connections between law and morality, and even deny that Hart ever subscribed to the separation thesis.[3]

* I thank the participants in the legal philosophy workshop of Uppsala University and for helpful written comments and correspondence: Nicola Lacey, Patricia Mindus, Thomas Mertens, Torben Spaak and Kenneth Winston. I also thank Ken Winston for providing me with the translation of Gustav Radbruch in Lon L. Fuller's Jurisprudence Materials, i.e. the materials he prepared for his course at the time H. L. A. Hart was visiting Harvard.

[1] Hart 1983. [2] Hart 1983: 81. [3] See, e.g., Gardner 2012: 221.

Positivism began as a lecture at Harvard Law School in 1957 and, as Hart pointed out, the 'stink' of totalitarian societies was still in 'our nostrils'.[4] He was thus concerned about the impact of a charge that came from the 'testimony' of those who had lived through the 'terrible experience' of Nazi terror – who had 'descended into' an earthly 'Hell' and 'brought back a message for human beings'.[5] Hart thought it easy to demonstrate that the charge was 'stark nonsense' precisely because of the light shed by the separation thesis.[6] But, in this demonstration, he brought Gustav Radbruch – the scholar who attracted Hart's ire – to the attention of philosophy of law outside Germany and provoked the debate about the link between positivism and totalitarianism.

For Radbruch's charge was from a natural law position that asserts a necessary moral quality to law and neither the charge nor natural law disappeared in the wake of Hart's 'refutation'. Lon L. Fuller argued that legal order has an 'inner morality'[7] and reinstated the charge. Ronald Dworkin argued that judges who sought a principled basis for their interpretations within the positive law would make the law morally better, while positivistic judges would make it worse, with the latter argument supported by work on apartheid South Africa.[8] Robert Alexy sought to rehabilitate Radbruch's position in the context of the legal response to the activities of the East German regime in the wake of German reunification.[9] Finally, Carlos Nino argued on the basis of his experience of totalitarian regimes in Latin America that 'ideological positivism' contributes to totalitarianism. This doctrine holds that 'all power justifies itself and that the prescriptions enacted by those who enjoy the monopoly of force in a society are in and of themselves reasons for justifying action'.[10]

Nino recognised that positivists reject the claim that 'all power justifies itself', which raises the question of why the charge persists. The answer is as follows. First, Hart claims that law is no more than positive law with the content it happens to have, which helps the good liberal citizen to avoid the natural law traps of supposing either that merely because X is the law, X has a moral quality to it, or that X fails to be a law simply because it is morally bad. Second, he claims that law must be understood as a matter of authority. As Hart explained his move away from his positivist

[4] Hart 1983: 81. [5] Hart 1983: 72. [6] See Hart 1983: 73. [7] Fuller 1958.
[8] See Dworkin 1986, and for South Africa, see Dyzenhaus 2010. [9] See Alexy 2002.
[10] Nino 1996: 156.

predecessors and their command theory of law: 'Law surely is not the gunman situation writ large.'[11]

But Hart thus set legal positivism the following puzzle: How can one consistently deny a necessary connection between law and morality and assert a necessary connection between law and authority? For if the latter is the case, it seems that positivism is ideological positivism. Those subject to the power of a de facto sovereign must understand that sovereign's law as authoritative, whatever its content.

In later work, Hart frankly confessed that he lacked the resources to deal with the puzzle, but he insisted that the authority of law is not moral.[12] That suggestion relies on the claim in both *Positivism* and later work that there is no *conceptually* necessary connection between law and morality. Any concessions to natural law depend on contingent facts about human beings and the world we happen to live in.

I will argue that the puzzle presented Hart and his students with a dilemma: Either accept the force of the charge that positivism encourages totalitarianism or accept that the authority of law is always to some extent legitimate. The second horn of the dilemma requires forgoing not only the separation thesis but also a hard and fast distinction between de facto and de jure, or legitimate, authority; and that distinction remains central to the work of even those among Hart's students who claim to disavow the separation thesis.

To show that there is this dilemma, I recover principled resources in Hart's own theory – his version of an inner morality of law – that go far beyond the necessary connections between law and morality announced by Hart's students. It is only if these resources move from the margins of Hart's theory, where he kept them for safety's sake, to its centre that Hart and legal positivism can avoid the slide into ideological positivism. These resources have been occluded, first, by Hart's insistence on the separation thesis and, second, by the way he structured his argument in *Positivism.*

For Hart postponed his discussion of the natural law challenge to legal positivism at the most general level to the penultimate part of his essay (part 5). However, when the subject matter of part 3 – how to understand the role of a theory of adjudication within a general theory of law – and that of part 4 – how judges should respond to unjust law – are placed within the context of the natural law challenge at the most general level, his

[11] Hart 1983: 59. [12] See Hart 1982: 266–8.

arguments against natural law positions in parts 3 and 4 become ineffective. In other words, Hart's argumentative strategy made it much easier to present his counters to natural law positions as refutations, as he treated each as distinct from the others, so that he could 'refute' them one by one in isolation. But it also led to the conclusion that the law has authority, whatever its content.

33.2 Fuller as the Foil of 'Positivism'

Part 1 of *Positivism* sets out the moral virtues of the separation thesis as the central idea of the positivist tradition bequeathed by Bentham and Austin to their heirs. Part 2 argues that legal theory must move away from their command theory of law, not only because law is not a giant gunman but also because the idea of law as the commands of a legally unlimited sovereign fails to explain much of legal order, including the fact that 'nothing which legislators do makes law unless they comply with fundamental rules specifying the essential law-making procedures'.[13]

Because Hart's lecture was to an audience at Harvard Law School, in part 3 he responded to the argument of American legal realists against an allegedly positivist view of judicial interpretation that judges should use formal, deductive methods to reveal what the law as a matter of fact requires. However, the realists were not natural lawyers, and they did not argue that their critique of such approaches to adjudication shows a necessary connection between law and morality. Hart's main response to them relates to the separation thesis only insofar as he argues, first, that the positivist distinction between law as it is and law as it ought to be does not entail a view that judicial interpretation is a matter of judges determining facts about what the law requires. Rather, because in such 'penumbral' cases there is no fact of the matter about what the law requires, judges must rely on their own sense of right and wrong and legislate an answer. The other 'core' cases – where people know what the law as a matter of fact requires – do not for that reason get to court, which is why law can do its job of organising our lives. This feature of law leads to Hart's second point – that realists tend to equate law with penumbral cases that, though

[13] Hart 1983: 59.

the 'daily diet' of law schools, should not be confused with the 'hard core of settled meaning' that is 'law in some centrally important sense'.[14]

It is, then, Hart's other aim in part 3 that is important to a defence of the separation thesis. He wanted to nip in the bud the kind of natural law position that Fuller was developing, which does not make moral standards that are external to law the test for the validity of law, since it relies on an argument about principles internal to legal order that condition the content of law. While Hart mentions Fuller in the text only at the very end, his position is the implicit target throughout. He is the main foil of part 3 because his account of adjudication adopts the premise that judicial interpretation in the penumbra is based on values, but he denies that the action takes place in a penumbra.[15] As Dworkin was to elaborate this kind of argument, the judge is making explicit what had hitherto been implicit – the moral resources the law contains that are fully capable of answering the question posed to the judge. Hart's response was and remained that social values are not the same as morality. If the law is commonly used as the instrument of morally obnoxious aims, the values inherent in it will be obnoxious.[16]

In addition, it was Fuller's early hints that there is an internal morality to law with which law must comply that preoccupied Hart in part 5[17] and it was his critique of legal positivism that most disturbed Hart. For when Hart began his defence of the separation thesis by portraying legal positivism as under attack for its tendencies to blind 'men to the true nature of law and its roots in social life', to be 'corrupting in practice', 'at its worst apt to weaken resistance to state tyranny or absolutism', 'at its best apt to bring law into disrepute',[18] he could cite very little evidence for this proposition besides Fuller's *The Law in Quest of Itself* and a short essay by him,[19] as well as two short essays by Radbruch.[20]

I shall now argue that the distance between Hart's version of positivism and a modern, secular natural law theory, with Radbruch as the exemplar, reduces to vanishing point once legal positivism properly confronts the natural law spectre who haunts *Positivism.* We can then reconfigure Hart's legal theory in a way that preserves its most important elements while

[14] Hart 1983: 71. [15] See Hart 1983: 68–71. [16] See Hart 1983: 69–70.
[17] Fuller 1940: 34–41. [18] Hart 1983: 50–1. [19] Fuller 1956.
[20] Gustav Radbruch, 'Die Erneuerung des Rechts', 1947 and 'Gesetzliches Unrecht und Übergesetzliches Recht', 1946. The latter is translated as Radbruch 2006.

explaining why, in the absence of this reconfiguration, positivism as a theory of law that insists on the separation thesis becomes ideological positivism.

33.3 Hart on Radbruch

Radbruch argued that the positivist slogan 'law is law' was adopted by German lawyers and that it explains their complicity in the Nazi rise to power. His antidote, which became known as the 'Radbruch Formula', was the thesis that extreme injustice is no law. Hart vehemently rejected Radbruch's claims. On his understanding, Radbruch, because of his experience of National Socialism, had recanted his pre-war commitment to legal positivism and 'naïvely' embraced a natural law position, which Hart set out as follows:

> His considered reflections led him to the doctrine that the fundamental principles of humanitarian morality were part of the very concept of *Recht* or Legality and that no positive enactment or statute, however clearly it was expressed and however clearly it conformed with the formal criteria of validity of a given legal system, could be valid if it contravened basic principles of morality.[21]

Hart added that this 'doctrine can be appreciated fully only if the nuances imported by the German word *Recht* are grasped'. He had in mind the distinction that English elides between enacted law, *Gesetz*, and *Recht* with its connotation of legal right or justice. But he did not think it worthwhile to explore these nuances in part 4, as he thought that Austin had shown that natural law positions are 'stark nonsense' by the example of a man condemned to death for a trivial offence, who claims that the law is not law because immoral, but who is refuted because 'the court of justice will demonstrate the inconclusiveness' of his 'reasoning by hanging' him 'in pursuance of the law of which [he had] impugned the validity'.[22]

Just in case his readers were not persuaded by this 'academic discussion',[23] Hart offered the example of a post-war German court's decision that he thought showed both the ills of deploying the Formula and the virtues of an approach based on the separation thesis. In this case, a court found guilty of the crime of illegal deprivation of liberty a 'grudge

[21] Hart 1983: 74. [22] Hart 1983: 73. [23] Hart 1983: 75.

informer' – a woman who had turned in her husband to the authorities during the war because he had said insulting things about Nazis, an act made criminal by two Nazi statutes. Hart's view, based on an incorrect report of the decision, was that the court deployed the Radbruch Formula to deny validity to the statutes, thus both circumventing the argument that what the woman did was perfectly legal and obscuring the fact that the court was offending against the 'very precious principle of morality endorsed by most legal systems' –[24] the rule against retrospective punishment. If, Hart argued, one thought that the grudge informer should be punished, the only way to do this honestly was to face up to the fact that the Nazi statutes were valid law. That would require the legislature to enact a 'frankly retrospective law' making criminal the act of informing.[25] That the Formula obscured this dilemma by pretending that a valid law is not a law simply because of its injustice was, in Hart's view, conclusive reason to reject it; and he proceeded to his discussion of the nuances of 'legality' in the next part of his essay as if it were a distinct topic.

This was a consequential deferral. Hart's argument depends on ridding Radbruch's position of its nuances by conceiving it as Hart's legal positivism with a minus sign: the law of a legal order is its positive law, as certified by the criteria of legal validity in its most fundamental rules, minus those positive laws that we judge to be extremely unjust by the standards of a moral position external to the law. Radbruch would, then, differ from Hart only in that Hart says that citizens should disobey extremely unjust laws, while for Radbruch there is no law to be disobeyed, which makes him prey to the dire confusions that can be avoided only if we 'speak plainly' in saying 'that laws may be law but too evil to be obeyed'.[26]

But Hart was not responding to Radbruch's actual position. In his Formula, Radbruch asserted three main propositions and I will insert 'Recht', 'Unrecht' and their derivatives in square brackets to indicate where Radbruch deliberately wished to convey law in the sense of legal justice or right.

(1) 'The positive law [*Recht*] secured by legislation and power takes precedence even when its content is unjust [*ungerecht*] and fails to benefit the people, unless the conflict between statute and justice [*Gerechtigkeit*] reaches such an intolerable degree that the statute, as "flawed law" [*unrichtiges Recht*], must yield to justice.'

[24] Hart 1983: 77. [25] See Hart 1983: 77. [26] Hart 1983: 77.

(2) 'Where there is not even an attempt at justice [*Gerechtigkeit*], where equality, the core of justice [*Gerechtigkeit*], is deliberately betrayed in the issuance of positive law [*positiven Recht*], then the law is not merely "flawed law" [*unrichtiges Recht*]; it lacks completely the very nature of law [*Rechtsnatur*].'

(3) 'For law, including positive law [*positives Recht*], cannot be otherwise defined than as a system and an institution whose very meaning is to serve justice [*Gerechtigkeit*].'[27]

Discussion of the Formula is often preoccupied with the question of whether propositions (1) and (2) contain distinct formulas, the first having to do with the tricky issue of whether enacted law has a content so extremely unjust that it should not be applied, the second with enacted law that explicitly states its commitment to injustice of a kind that clearly betrays law's 'core' mission of protecting equality, in which case it fails to be law. But attention to Radbruch's use of *Recht*, set in the context of the discussion that immediately precedes it, suggests that these two propositions may be better understood as the two ends of a continuum of legality.

When Radbruch complained that positivistic thinking had dominated lawyers in Nazi Germany, he had in mind ideological positivism, the view that 'law is law' and thus anything that has the form of law ought to be enforced or obeyed. This view, he said, excluded the ideas of 'statutory lawlessness' [*Unrecht*] and 'supra-statutory law' [*Recht*]. But, he pointed out, obligation and validity cannot be based simply on power and compulsion. They must be based 'on a value inherent in the statute'.[28]

This is the value of justice, which is the reason we value the certainty that statutes afford us. Even the fact that we value the certainty that only enacted law can achieve must be understood as a requirement of justice – as serving the public good of legal subjects – because without the certainty that enacted law brings, we could not have that service. This good Radbruch named 'purposiveness'. But, he emphasised, 'what benefits the people is, in the long run, only that which law is, namely, that which creates legal certainty and strives towards justice'.[29] As proposition (3) states, part of law's striving for justice is that 'equality' – the 'very core of justice' – is respected.

[27] Radbruch 2006: 7. For the German original, see Radbruch 1973: 345–6.
[28] Radbruch 2006: 6. [29] Ibid.

Hence, Radbruch finds three values inherent in law – certainty, purposiveness and justice – with certainty occupying a 'curious middle place' since it is there to bring about both purposiveness and justice.[30] Propositions (1) and (2) may not then so much set out distinct formulas as presuppose a continuum of value conflicts from minor to major; and it is only in the exceptional case of blatant extreme injustice that a judge should make justice the test for the validity of law. What gives the exceptional case its character is that the law is not interpretable in a way that can avoid finding that its purpose is to be an instrument of extreme injustice. Up to that point, the judge will attempt to find an interpretation that reconciles the certainty that positive law brings with the demands of justice in so far as this is possible, thus preserving equality, the 'core of justice'.

My claim here is supported, first, by the fact that, within proposition (1), Radbruch refers to 'the positive *Recht* secured by statute and power'. The translation of 'das positive, durch Satzung und Macht gesicherte Recht'[31] as 'the positive law secured by legislation and power' not only makes this part of the sentence redundant by reading it as the 'positive law secured by positive law' but also rids it exactly of the nuances of *Recht* that Radbruch sought to preserve. Radbruch's point was that law that we might condemn as unjust because our general moral position finds it to be so remains law only as long the content of the law can be understood as preserving some element of legal justice.

Second, Radbruch wished to understand from a juridical point of view the arguments that German lawyers and judges were already engaged in making, which did not rely on the claim that extreme injustice is no law but rather sought to find an interpretation of the law that permitted them to reach what they regarded as both legally and morally justified conclusions.[32] They sought to find in German law the interpretative resources necessary to get to the conclusion that served justice, but without invalidating Nazi statutes. In this light, Radbruch was not so much providing a 'formula' for judicial use as trying to make juridical sense of judicial arguments in response to past injustice.

These arguments were set out in a long extract that Radbruch quoted from the legal opinion of a prosecutor in a grudge informer case and that formed part of the materials that Hart read in preparing his lecture.[33]

[30] Ibid. [31] Radbruch 2006: 345–6.

[32] For discussion of the actual cases, see Dyzenhaus 2008 and Pappe 1960.

[33] See Radbruch 2006: 2–4.

There is an interesting question, then, about why Hart distorted not only Radbruch's position by ridding it of its nuances but also the situation that faced German lawyers and judges in post-war Germany. In addition, had Hart consulted Radbruch's *Philosophy of Law* of 1930, available in a translation of 1950, he would have found that Radbruch, far from recanting his pre-war positivism, did little more than bring out an implication of it, in which he had already stated that 'even the validity of positive law that is unjust and wrong cannot be maintained unqualifiedly; hence the question of validity may be considered not only from the standpoint of legal certainty but also [from] that of justice and [purposiveness]'.[34]

Fuller thought that Hart had misread both Radbruch and the situation because he simply did not see that there was more wrong with Nazi law than that it was used as the instrument of evil ends. Hart did not appreciate that the Nazi system was so marked by abuses of legality that it was plausible to suppose that it was not really a legal order.[35] There is much to this point. But even more remarkable is that Hart, in part 5 of *Positivism*, could not help but recognise that a secular natural law position like Radbruch's is required if one wishes to understand law as a matter of authority, though he stopped short of a full recognition because that would have led to an abandonment of the separation thesis.

33.4 Hart's Natural Law Theory

In part 5 of *Positivism*, Hart explored the challenge to the separation thesis that arises when one analyses a 'legal system considered as a whole'.[36] Quoting Austin, he said that there are certain 'fundamental notions' that are 'necessary' and 'bottomed in the common nature of man' and that any legal system must take into account. They amount, in Hart's view, to 'simple statements of fact', for example, that a legal system must 'provide sanctions for certain of its rules' and that 'the normally fulfilled assumption that a legal system aims at some form of justice colours the whole way

[34] Radbruch 1950. The translator has 'expediency' for Radbruch's *Zweckmässigkeit* (Radbruch 1950: 168–9) and I prefer 'purposiveness' from the translation in Radbruch 2006. Hart refers to this work in the German fourth edition of 1950 in Hart 1983: 50 n. 8, but only as a source for the postwar essays that he discussed in part 3, using the translation in Fuller's Jurisprudence Materials.

[35] See Fuller 1958: 650–7, 660. [36] Hart 1983: 78.

in which we interpret specific rules in particular cases', so that 'if this normally fulfilled assumption were not fulfilled[,] no one would have any reason to obey except fear (and probably not that) and still less, of course, any moral obligation to obey'.[37] As a result, '[t]he connection between law and moral standards and principles of justice is ... as little arbitrary and as "necessary" as the connection between law and sanctions, and the pursuit of the question [of] whether this necessity is logical (part of the "meaning" of law) or merely factual or causal can safely be left as an innocent pastime for philosophers'.[38]

Hart said that he wished to 'go further' by identifying two more characteristics of legal order. First, given facts about human vulnerability and needs, one will find in any legal order rules 'forbidding the free use of violence and rules constituting the minimum form of property'. Such 'fundamental' rules 'overlap with basic moral principles ... and so we can add to the factual statement that all legal systems in fact coincide with morality at such vital points, the statement that this is, in this sense, necessarily so'.[39] However, Hart thought that he could still easily distinguish his position from natural law because the latter wishes to 'push the argument' yet 'further' than one about 'survival' and 'assert that human beings are equally devoted to and united in their conception of aims', for example, 'the pursuit of knowledge, justice to their fellow men'. Hart retorted that the 'purposes men have for living in society are too conflicting and varying'[40] to support such an extension.

The second characteristic is that there is, 'in the very notion of law consisting of general rules, something which prevents us from treating it as if morally it is utterly neutral'. Generality, Hart said, requires '[n]atural procedural justice', which consists of 'principles of objectivity and impartiality in the administration of the law' that

> are designed to ensure that rules are applied only to what are genuine cases of the rule or at least to minimize the risks of inequalities in this sense .... This is justice in the administration of the law, not justice of the law. So there is, in the very notion of law consisting of general rules, something which prevents us from treating it as if morally it is utterly neutral, without any necessary contact with moral principles.[41]

[37] Hart 1983: 79. [38] Ibid. [39] Hart 1983: 80. [40] Hart 1983: 81–2.
[41] Hart 1983: 81.

But that does not threaten the separation thesis because:

> a legal system that satisfied these minimum requirements might apply, with the most pedantic impartiality as between the persons affected, laws which were hideously oppressive, and might deny to a vast rightless slave population the minimum benefits of protection from violence and theft. The stink of such societies is, after all, still in our nostrils and to argue that they have (or had) no legal system would only involve the repetition of the argument. Only if the rules failed to provide these essential benefits and protection for any one – even for a slave-owning group – would the minimum be unsatisfied and the system sink to the status of a set of meaningless taboos. Of course no one denied those benefits would have any reason to obey except fear and would have every moral reason to revolt.[42]

But, contrary to its intent, this passage in fact pushes Hart's argument 'further' than one about 'survival' in the direction of 'the pursuit of justice' precisely because that move is required given that the 'purposes men have for living in society' are so 'conflicting and varying'. For why should we think that law, on the assumption that it, more than the gunman situation writ large, governs the lives of those in the group that get no protection and who are deprived of it by 'hideously oppressive commands' backed by force?

Moreover, if there are juridical reasons for thinking that, in the normal case, 'some form of justice colours the whole way in which we interpret specific rules in particular cases', it seems to follow that judges confronted by an unjust law face a *legal* problem, not merely a clash between legal and moral duty. Such a problem requires them to ask whether the law really has that content although the legislature seems in fact to have stipulated it. If their answer is 'yes', they are driven by legal duty to confront Radbruch's situation of extreme injustice, since if they apply that content to the oppressed group, they are carrying out the gunman's commands, not implementing law.

Such questions become even sharper when Hart says, late in *The Concept of Law*, in chapter 9 on 'Laws and Morals', that 'a minimum of justice is realized whenever human behaviour is controlled by general rules publicly announced and judicially applied'; if law is to function as a system of social control, its rules 'must be intelligible and within the capacity of most to obey, and in general they must not be retrospective'.[43] He argues that both

[42] Hart 1983: 624. [43] Hart 1994: 206–7.

law and morals must have a 'minimum content' if they are to 'forward the minimum purpose of survival which men have in associating with each other' and that 'in the absence of this content', men would have 'no reason for obeying voluntarily any rules'.[44] The point about reason is important because we have to understand law as operating with reasons, not causes.[45] These reasons must be addressed at least to the natural facts of human vulnerability, approximate equality, limited resources and limited understanding and will.[46] This 'natural necessity', he thus says, has to qualify the 'positivist thesis that "law may have any content"'.[47]

Hart also says that judges 'may often display' what he calls 'characteristic judicial virtues': 'impartiality and neutrality in surveying the alternatives; consideration for the interest of all who will be affected; and a concern to deploy some acceptable principle as a reasoned basis for decision'.[48] Hart is, I think, deliberately coy about the status of these virtues within his general argument about the necessary minimum content of natural law, just as in *Positivism* he referred to the principle against retrospective punishment as 'a very precious principle of morality endorsed by most legal systems'. That description allowed him to avoid recognising it as a very precious *legal* principle, which, if a legal order failed to endorse, would give us grounds for supposing that the order had a shaky claim to be legal. But I assume that he sees the virtues as the characteristics of the role of a judge who understands himself as operating in a system of authority rather than a gunman situation, and who understands his legal order as catering to the minimum content of natural law.

On Hart's account in part 5 of 'Positivism', as developed in *The Concept of Law*, such judges should come up with an answer to the legal question that meets two criteria. First, it shows how the law responds to legal subjects in a way that respects their subjectivity – their ability to respond to reasons. Second, the answer rests on a justice-like general principle supported by the relevant legal materials, a principle that shows that the legal subjects are such because they are not outside the class whose interests the law protects, even if the protection is minimal.

Now imagine such a judge confronted by a law requiring the inequitable treatment of a whole group of people, for example one of the segregationist statutes of the apartheid regime.[49] As a matter of legal

[44] Hart 1994: 193. [45] See Hart 1994: 194. [46] See Hart 1994: 194–200.
[47] Hart 1994: 199. [48] Hart 1994: 205. [49] See Dyzenhaus 2010.

duty, the judge must struggle to find an interpretation that displays both consideration for the interest of all those who will be affected and a concern to deploy some acceptable general principle, derived from the relevant legal materials, as a reasoned basis for decision. It is a struggle because a law that institutionalises inequality on its face does not display such consideration and is hard to interpret in a way that displays some acceptable general principle. That creates a tension internal to the legal perspective of the judge, since the judicial virtues are prominent among the norms that define the judicial role. Put most concretely, the judge will have a hard time answering the legal subject who asks: 'But, how can that be law for me?'

One may paraphrase these passages by saying that if the commands of the powerful are incapable of sustaining a claim to be exercised with legal right on those within their power, the commands lack authority and therefore start to lose their grip on their claim to legal status. For such commands undermine the mutual relationship between protection and obedience that Hobbes outlined at the end of *Leviathan*[50] and that Hart depicts as follows, in giving a snapshot in chapter 8 of *The Concept of Law* of his argument to come in chapter 9:

> It seems clear that the sacrifice of personal interest which such rules *demand* is the price that must be paid in a world such as ours for living with others, and the protection they *afford* is the minimum which, for beings such as ourselves, makes living with others worthwhile. These simple facts constitute ... a core of indisputable truth in the doctrines of Natural Law.[51]

Hart's own treatment of this issue relied on a clear distinction between an in-group that gets protection from the law and an out-group that does not. In *The Concept of Law*, he suggested that the in-group could be small, confined to the officials of the system, and the system would still be a legal system, albeit in a 'deplorable' state.[52] Only if there were no one in the in-group at all would the system become one in which there was the appearance of law but what passed for law had sunk to 'the status of a set of meaningless taboos'. Hart thus did not attend to the important issues that arise for legal philosophy when one is in the

[50] Hobbes 1997: 491. [51] Hart 1994: 181, his emphasis.
[52] Hart 1994: 117. Compare 90–1.

in-group for some purposes but not for others; when, that is, one is a second-class citizen.[53]

Yet, it seems fair to say that Hart must hold the view that the normal case of a legal order is one in which power is exercised authoritatively. To be a first-class citizen, or full legal subject, in such an order is to be able to accept that the legal order as a whole and its particular laws offer one the kinds of reason that are understandable as addressing one's interests. Even when such subjects strongly disagree with the content of the law, they must be able to recognise that the legal order serves the interests that are in the character of a legal order to serve and that its laws are interpretable in light of those interests. When they ask the question 'But, how can that be law for me?', a judge mindful of the judicial virtues can give an answer.

If the only answer available is that the person must understand that they are a second-class citizen, then, as suggested, judges are put in a problematic position because it is not clear that they can play their role as judges, which, as I have also suggested, also makes problematic the claim that the person is governed by law. At this point, precisely Radbruch's limit situation of extreme injustice, the problematic nature of the relationship of that person to their fellow first-class citizens raises questions not only about 'justice in the administration of the law' but also about the 'justice of the law', questions that go to the law's status as law.

This argument may seem undermined by Hart's insistence that in any case in which the judge must display these virtues in responding to a legal question raised by the parties, the judge must exercise extralegal discretion as such a question will arise precisely because the judge is in the 'penumbra' where the 'core' of the positive law determines no answer. These issues were the preoccupation in the debates in legal theory that Dworkin initiated about 'hard cases'. He sought to show that ultimately at stake in

[53] Indeed, he did not seem to think that there was an issue – see his treatment of a segregationist law in Hart 1994: 161. Second-class status is much more legally problematic in one sense than the status of slavery, with the proviso that the slaves are relentlessly consigned to the status of objects or things. But slave-owning societies, societies in which the institution of slavery is constituted by law, usually experience immense difficulty in maintaining the enslaved group in a status beyond morality and law and therefore beyond dignity. See, e.g., Buckland 1932: 62–6. Consider also the difficulties that our society experiences with maintaining human beings such as children in less than full status, or non-human animals in the status of things, while giving them some legal protection against various kinds of bad treatment because we recognise that they share certain attributes with us human animals, including the capacity to suffer.

such cases is the question of the political ideal that law serves. In his view, judges who endorse positivism will seek out 'plain facts' about legislative intent to avoid imposing their own views on the law.[54]

Because positivists responded to Dworkin both by disowning any such theory of adjudication and by asserting a categorical distinction between a theory of law and a theory of adjudication, legal theory has long appeared to be at an impasse. In addition, Dworkin's positivistic critics followed Hart in claiming that the moral decency of a legal order is contingent on its political history. However, these responses assume exactly the static model of legal order that underpinned Hart's distortion of Radbruch. The law of a legal order is its positive law, as certified by the criteria of legal validity in its most fundamental rules, which leads to the view that Radbruch's position is merely positivism with a minus sign – one subtracts from the positive law of the moment all those laws that are extremely unjust by the standards of a moral position external to the law.

As I have indicated, Radbruch had a dynamic model of legal order in which law is always in a process of becoming, as its officials seek to maintain their 'fidelity to law'[55] where law is understood to have the value structure composed of justice and purposiveness as well as certainty. For such officials, especially judges, the separation thesis is of no help. While judges must understand that their duty is to interpret the law as it is, not as they would like it to be, they must also understand that the law – *Gesetz* – is to be interpreted in a way that accords with justice according to law – *Recht*.

33.5 Conclusion

It is ironic, then, that Radbruch, in his *Legal Philosophy*, commented that 'the past age of legal positivism saw only the positivity and certainty of the law and caused a long standstill in the systematic examination of . . . [the purposiveness], not to mention the justice, of enacted law'.[56] For that comment applies with great force to positivism, as it applies to the theories developed by Hart and his students since 1958, because they maintain the static aspect of their theory of law by expelling anything dynamic, including the pursuit of justice within the law, to an extralegal space where it can

[54] See Dworkin 1986. [55] Fuller 1958. [56] Radbruch 1950: 111.

be considered as if it were a legislative act that strikes out anew, as in their understanding of adjudication as quasi-legislative in nature.[57]

In Bentham and Austin, this expulsion made sense because their command theory of law explained law only as a matter of coercion. Law, one might say, does not have authority but at most legitimacy, which it will possess when and only when it transmits appropriate judgments about utility made outside of law from the apex of the legal hierarchy to the bottom. Judges must, on this view, equate the idea of justice according to law with plain facts about the content of the value judgements that those in power have legislated. It is for this reason that Austin, after having set out the slogan that inspired the separation thesis – 'The existence of law is one thing; its merit or demerit is another' – could use his example of the man condemned to death as an illustration of why natural law thinkers are talking 'stark nonsense'.[58] For, on his theory, law is no more than the commands of an uncommanded commander backed by threats. But it is altogether another thing for Hart, who rejected the command theory, to say of the person objectified in this way that they should regard as authoritative the directive that consigns them to prison and execution.

This is not the only time in *Positivism* that Hart found himself in the grip of the command theory. In part 3, in explaining why a Fullerian theory of adjudication is mistaken, Hart said that a judge in Nazi Germany might have asked in a criminal matter, 'What sentence would both terrorize the public at large and keep the friends and family of the prisoner in suspense so that both hope and fear would cooperate as factors making for subservience?' He noted that the 'prisoner of such a system would be regarded simply as an object to be used in pursuit of these aims'. But, he said, this would 'still be an intelligent and purposive' decision and 'from one point of view the decision would be as it ought to be'.[59]

Hart's point is that a Fullerian theory of adjudication suggests absurdly that the values or purposes implicit in the positive law of a legal order will turn out to be moral, a point that he was to repeat against Dworkin. But this rare example of leakage from one part of *Positivism* to another – from Hart's discussion of the grudge informer case to his earlier treatment of adjudication – in fact exposes his inability to escape from the command theory of law. Consider things from the point of view of the prisoner who

[57] It may not apply to positivism's strange offshoot in 'inclusive' legal positivism.
[58] Austin 1885 vol. I: 214–15. [59] Hart 1983: 70.

has to regard himself as, in Hart's own words, 'an object to be used in pursuit of these aims'. Why, like the condemned man in Austin's example, may the prisoner not draw on the resources of Hart's theory and say that he is the victim of a gunman, not a legal order that purports to exercise authority over him?

Moreover, if one puts to one side the claim about judicial legislation that is properly at home in a command theory of law, one can take both of these problematic examples one step back from the situation of the man already convicted by the judge and ask under what theory the judge should decide to convict him.[60] If judges accept Radbruch's legal theory, or a Fullerian or Dworkinian account of adjudication, or Hart's account of the judicial virtues, they will try to find the interpretative resources within the law to avoid concluding that they have reached the limit situation in which the content of the law is so extremely unjust that its status as law is in doubt. Short of that situation, the law will have a moral quality to it that is at odds with the separation thesis.

Somewhat paradoxically, then, it is the separation thesis that provides the link between positivism as a theory of law and ideological positivism. Ideological positivism is the product of two elements: first, a version of the separation thesis – the claim that the law that governs us is the law with the content it happens to have; second, the claim that law with that content must be understood as authoritative. Moreover, from the perspective of the officials of the legal order, as well as other participants in it including lawyers and those subject to the law, the separation thesis understood as requiring that we view the law as 'normatively inert'[61] is not an option. The law will claim authority over them, and, as Hart's most influential student Joseph Raz argued, it is the case not only that the law necessarily claims authority but also that the claim is necessarily to legitimate authority.[62]

This is a point about practical authority. When judges tell a legal subject what the law obliges the subject to do, they must be understood as asserting not only that they wield authority but also that the authority is legitimate.[63] Hart saw the force of this point. But he worried that Raz's

[60] See Mertens 2002: 202–4. [61] Gardner 2012: 23.

[62] See Raz 1994: 194. I therefore agree with Raz that the theorist's perspective on law presupposes the participant's perspective, but I disagree with him about how to understand that relationship.

[63] See Raz 1983: 146.

account presupposes a 'cognitive account of moral judgement in terms of objective reasons for action'.[64] 'Far better adapted to the legal case', he asserted, is a non-cognitive theory, according to which 'to say that an individual has a legal obligation to act in a certain way is to say that such action may be properly demanded from him according to legal rules or principles regulating such demands for action'.[65] He then confessed that an idea of normatively inert authority is unsatisfactory, but he remained insistent on the separation thesis.[66]

How is such insistence sustainable despite the facts about legal orders that Hart acknowledges in part 5 of *Positivism* and those about the 'minimum content' of natural law in chapter 9 of *The Concept of Law*, and despite the force of Raz's point about legal authority when it is exerted in practice? The explanation is Hart's conviction that the separation thesis sheds valuable light on the morally complex situations faced by legal officials and subjects in practice. That it can survive at all is in turn explained by its being a conceptual claim that floats above the messy contingency of our world as we find it, and so is immune to challenges from these otherwise inconvenient facts.

But we have seen that the separation thesis, far from shedding light, cannot begin to explain how law complicates any moral situation. How, as Fuller and Dworkin asked, can the mere existence of law introduce moral complexity if law is normatively inert?[67] By contrast, Hart's concessions to natural law do illuminate. But he supposes that they are not serious concessions because they apply only to this empirical world and its human inhabitants with the vulnerabilities that we happen to have. But Hart himself does not and cannot keep to the conceptual side of the distinction between the conceptual and the empirical. Most of his arguments for the virtues of the separation thesis take place in our human world, and his conceptual claims are as mysterious as any of the natural law confusions that he had in mind when he allied himself with Bentham's aim 'to pluck the mask of Mystery'[68] from the face of jurisprudence.

[64] Hart 1982: 158–9. [65] Hart 1982: 159–60.

[66] See Hart 1982: 267. In an unpublished work, *The Long Arc of Legality*, I am elaborating an account of legitimate authority that does not rely on realist assumptions about morality and that is close in spirit to Hart's non-cognitivism and his formal account of social morality in chapter 8 of Hart 1994. Others are working to the same end though exploring Hart as an 'expressivist' – Toh 2005. But, in my view, this account of morality is best understood as pragmatist.

[67] See Fuller 1958: 656; Dworkin 1981: 327. [68] Hart 1983: 49.

Consider that in *Positivism*, in support of his appeal to the conceptual, Hart suggests that we could conceive of a world in which we are like giant armoured crabs, so that we would not have the vulnerabilities of us soft-skinned human beings that lead us to make rules prohibiting violence, and so on.[69] But the issue at stake is what is law in our world as we find it, populated by beings like us with the vulnerabilities that we happen to have? We simply don't care about crab-law. Nor does Hart most of the time, for he was deeply concerned with analysing both the benefits and the dangers for individuals who find themselves subject not only to the sheer power of the modern legal state but also to its claim to rule as a matter of authority.

My plea in this chapter is for philosophy of law to return to the task that Radbruch and others set out to accomplish, namely, that of trying to understand how a legal order can vindicate its claim to be an order of legitimate authority, a task that Hart himself well understood, albeit through the distorting lens of the separation thesis. Once that lens is removed, philosophy of law can begin with a general theory of law that facilitates service to that ideal. It can then inquire into the moral resources that are offered by requiring government by law rather than by some other means. And with that theory in place, one will be able to work out the details of the place of the judiciary and other institutions in serving the ideal.

In other words, the place to begin is where Hart ended his main discussion of the truth in natural law in part 5 of *Positivism*. From there, one can work back through part 4 – how the legal order should respond to problems of perceived injustice – to part 3 – the place of the judiciary and the role of interpretation. But it is important to go even further to include the subject matter of part 2 – how an understanding of law as a matter of authority relates to the way in which, in any legal order, fundamental legal principles condition political power so that, as Kelsen once put it, 'might is transformed into legal right'.[70]

But one should stop short of part 1 – insistence on the separation thesis – for the two reasons that my argument here supports. First, it has the perverse effect of turning right into might through the claim that law as such has authority, whatever its content. Second, natural law positions about law's moral quality are not, as Hart charged, naïve. Rather, in their different ways, such positions seek to elaborate the moral resources of

[69] See Hart 1983: 80. [70] Kelsen 1968 vol. 1: 339.

government under law that make it plausible to claim that legal order should be understood not as the gunman situation writ large but as an order that wields legitimate authority.

References

Alexy, R. 2002. *The Argument from Injustice: A Reply to Legal Positivism.* Oxford University Press.

Austin, J. 1885. *Lectures on Jurisprudence or the Philosophy of Positive Law.* The LawBook Exchange LTD.

Buckland, W. W. 1932. *A Text-Book of Roman Law: From Augustus to Justinian.* Cambridge University Press.

Dworkin, R. 1981. *Taking Rights Seriously.* Duckworth.

Dworkin, R. 1986. *Law's Empire.* Fontana.

Dyzenhaus, D. 2008. 'The Case of the Grudge Informer Revisited'. *New York University Law Review* 83: 1000–34.

Dyzenhaus, D. 2010. *Hard Cases in Wicked Legal Systems: Pathologies of Legality.* Oxford University Press.

Fuller, L. L. 1940. *The Law in Quest of Itself.* Beacon Press.

Fuller, L. L. 1956. 'Human Purpose and Natural Law'. *Journal of Philosophy* 53: 697–705.

Fuller, L. L. 1958. 'Positivism and Fidelity to Law: A Reply to Professor Hart'. *Harvard Law Review* 71: 630–72.

Gardner, J. 2012. *Law as a Leap of Faith.* Oxford University Press.

Hart, H. L. A. 1982. *Essays on Bentham: Jurisprudence and Political Theory.* Clarendon Press.

Hart, H. L. A. 1983. 'Positivism and the Separation of Law and Morals'. In H. L. A. Hart. *Essays in Jurisprudence and Philosophy.* Clarendon Press: 49–87.

Hart, H. L. A. 1994. *The Concept of Law.* Clarendon Press.

Hobbes, T. 1997. *Leviathan.* Cambridge University Press.

Kelsen, H. 1968. *Die philosophischen Grundlagen der Naturrechtslehre und des Rechtspositivismus.* In H. Klecatsky, R. Marcic and H. Schambeck (eds.). *Die Wiener rechtstheoretische Schule: Hans Kelsen, Adolf Merkl, Alfred Verdross.* Europa Verlag.

Mertens, T. 2002. 'Radbruch and Hart on Grudge Informer: A Reconsideration'. *Ratio Juris* 15: 186–205.

Nino, C. 1996. *Radical Evil on Trial.* Yale University Press.

Pappe, H. O. 1960. 'On the Validity of Judicial Decisions in the Nazi Era'. *Modern Law Review* 23: 260–74.

Radbruch, G. 1950. *Legal Philosophy.* In E. W. Patterson (ed.). *The Legal Philosophies of Lask, Radbruch, and Dabin.* Harvard University Press: 43–224.

Radbruch, R. 1973. 'Gesetzliches Unrecht und Übergesetzliches Recht'. In G. Radbruch, *Rechtsphilosophie*. K.F. Koehler Verlag: 339–50.
Radbruch, G. 2006. 'Statutory Lawlessness and Supra-Statutory Law'. *Oxford Journal of Legal Studies* 26: 1–11.
Raz, J. 1983. *The Authority of Law: Essays on Law and Morality*. Clarendon Press.
Raz, J. 1994. 'Authority, Law, and Morality'. In J. Raz, *Ethics in the Public Domain: Essays in the Morality of Law and Politics*. Oxford University Press: 194–221.
Toh, K. 2005. 'Hart's Expressivism and His Benthamite Project'. *Legal Theory* 11(2): 75–123.

Index

Lightning Source UK Ltd.
Milton Keynes UK
UKHW050020190421
382143UK00007B/23

9 781108 427678